# Handbook of Black Librarianship

# Handbook of Black Librarianship

Third Edition

*Edited by*
*Andrew P. Jackson, Marva L. DeLoach, and Michele Fenton*

ROWMAN & LITTLEFIELD
*Lanham • Boulder • New York • London*

Published by Rowman & Littlefield
An imprint of The Rowman & Littlefield Publishing Group, Inc.
4501 Forbes Boulevard, Suite 200, Lanham, Maryland 20706
www.rowman.com

86-90 Paul Street, London EC2A 4NE

Selection and editorial matter © 2025 by The Rowman & Littlefield Publishing Group, Inc.
Copyright in individual chapters is held by the respective chapter authors.

*All rights reserved.* No part of this book may be reproduced in any form or by any electronic or mechanical means, including information storage and retrieval systems, without written permission from the publisher, except by a reviewer who may quote passages in a review.

British Library Cataloguing in Publication Information Available

**Library of Congress Cataloging-in-Publication Data**

Names: Jackson, Andrew P., editor. | DeLoach, Marva L., editor. | Fenton, Michele, editor.
Title: Handbook of Black librarianship / edited by Andrew P. Jackson, Marva L. DeLoach, and Michele Fenton.
Description: Third edition. | Lanham : Rowman & Littlefield, 2024. | Includes bibliographical references and index. | Summary: "Almost twenty-five years after the second edition of this classic title was published, this third edition covers black librarianship today"— Provided by publisher.
Identifiers: LCCN 2024008031 (print) | LCCN 2024008032 (ebook) | ISBN 9781538181096 (cloth ; alk. paper) | ISBN 9781538181102 (paperback ; alk. paper) | ISBN 9781538181119 (e-pub)
Subjects: LCSH: African Americans and libraries. | African American librarians. | African Americans--Bibliography. | Libraries--United States--Special collections--African Americans. | LCGFT: Essays.
Classification: LCC Z711.9 .H35 2024 (print) | LCC Z711.9 (ebook) | DDC 020/.896073--dc23/eng/20240329
LC record available at https://lccn.loc.gov/2024008031
LC ebook record available at https://lccn.loc.gov/2024008032

∞™ The paper used in this publication meets the minimum requirements of American National Standard for Information Sciences—Permanence of Paper for Printed Library Materials, ANSI/NISO Z39.48-1992.

**Dr. E. J. Josey, January 20, 1924–July 3, 2009.**

I dedicate this book to my parents, Walter and Bessie L. Jackson Sr., who loved, nurtured, and raised me to be the man I have become. To my older brother, Walter Jr. and sister, Helen, who set examples for me to follow through life. To my triplet brother Anthony Lamar and sister Mabel Olivia, without them I am incomplete, and thanks for sharing our path from birth.

To E. J. Josey, Ginnie Moore, Satia Marshall Orange, Mary and Herb Biblo, Lucille Cole Thomas, Tom Alford Sr., Jessie Carney Smith, and Stanton Biddle, consummate library professionals who believed in me when I doubted and was unsure of myself.

Andrew "Sekou" Jackson

I salute my ancestral parents and grandparents—the Boyd/Wrights and the DeLoaches—my siblings and several mentors, especially E. J. Josey, Clara Stanton Jones, and Esther Blanche Woolls, as well as my patient, loving husband, Manning C. Peterson. Thank you to the staff at my public and community college (Florence Espiritu) libraries also.

This edition of the *Handbook for Black Librarianship* could not have come to fruition without our essayists; thanks to all of you. Amina Jacqueline Josey Turner, E. J.'s daughter, my sister, I acknowledge your graciousness in supporting this project. Special thanks and appreciation to my coeditors Andrew Jackson and Michele Fenton and to the editorial staff at Rowman & Littlefield, Charles Harmon and Erinn Slanina for your masterful guidance and assistance. Lastly, I am indebted to the many unnamed individuals who helped me to become who I am today up through to the coediting of this manuscript.

Graciously,
Marva L. DeLoach

I dedicate this book to my family for encouraging my love of reading and writing—and supporting me in my career as a librarian. To my great-great-great-grandfather, Daniel Artis, for his determination, hard work, and courage.

To E. J. Josey, Lillian Haydon Childress Hall, Effie Lee Morris, Doris Hargrett Clack, Eliza Atkins Gleason, Major Owens, and Hallie Beachem Brooks for paving the way for future generations of librarians. To my colleagues, mentors, professors, and friends for their words of encouragement and pushing me to do my best.

To Andrew Sekou Jackson and Marva DeLoach for this wonderful opportunity to work together in bringing a phenomenal volume such as this into fruition. Many, many thanks!

Michele Fenton

# Contents

**Acknowledgments**—*Andrew P. Jackson (Sekou Molefi Baako)* ... xiii
**Tributes to E. J. Josey** ... xv
    Tribute to Dr. Elonnie J. Josey—*Malikah Lumumba* ... xv
    Tribute to E. J. Josey—*Binnie Tate Wilkin* ... xvii
    My Tribute to E. J. Josey, Activist Librarian: Trailblazer, Colleague, Mentor, and Advocate—*George C. Grant* ... xviii
    Tribute to My Dad—*Amina Turner* ... xix
**Preface: Black Librarianship: A Rich Legacy of Faith and Self-Determination**—*Andrew P. Jackson (Sekou Molefi Baako)* ... xxiii
**Introduction**—*Marva L. DeLoach and Michele Fenton* ... xxix

## PART I. PIONEERS AND LANDMARK EPISODES

### Chapter 1    A Chronology of Events in Black Librarianship ... 3

    1.1    A Chronology of Events in Black Librarianship—*Casper LeRoy Jordan and E. J. Josey; updated by Michele Fenton, Deloice Holliday, and Brenda Johnson-Perkins* ... 3

    1.2    National Conferences of African American Librarians: 1992-Present—*Andrew P. Jackson (Sekou Molefi Baako)* ... 17

    1.3    The BCALA Trailblazer Award and DEMCO/BCALA Award for Excellence in Librarianship—*Michele Fenton* ... 18

### Chapter 2    African American Forerunners in Librarianship ... 20

    2.1    African American Forerunners in Librarianship—*Casper LeRoy Jordan; revised and updated by Michele Fenton* ... 20

    2.2    Dr. Alma E. Dawson: Inspiring a Legacy of Mentorship—*Jacqueline Jones and Melanie Sims* ... 30

    2.3    Hidden Figures in African American Librarianship: Charlemae Hill Rollins, Miriam Matthews, Naomi Willie Pollard Dobson, and Dorothy Burnett Porter Wesley—*Talisha Harrison* ... 33

    2.4    Andre Carl Whisenton—*Vera N. Whisenton* ... 38

    2.5    Black Diasporic Memory Keeper: Arturo Alphonso Schomburg (1874-1938)—*Ana Ndumu and Manuel Mendez* ... 39

## PART II. BLACK LIBRARY/LIBRARIAN ASSOCIATIONS AND COLLABORATIONS IN THE TWENTY-FIRST CENTURY

### Chapter 3    BCALA Leaders, Awards, Affiliates, and Collaborations ... 45

    3.1    Leadership in the Black Caucus of the American Library Association—*Stanton Biddle* ... 45

    3.2a    BCALA Leadership: 1970-2025—*Stanton Biddle* ... 50

| | 3.2b | BCALA Leadership: 1970-2025—*Stanton Biddle* | 61 |
| | 3.3 | Black Library/Librarian Associations and Collaborations in the Twenty-First Century—*Shauntee Burns-Simpson and Nichelle M. Hayes* | 63 |
| | 3.4 | BCALA Affiliates—*Rudolph Clay* | 71 |
| | 3.5 | Black Caucus of the American Library Association Literary Awards: Celebrating Twenty-Nine Years of "Black Resistance"—*Gladys Smiley Bell* | 71 |
| | 3.6 | Librarians and Libraries, Part of Our Foundation—*Wade Hudson and Cheryl Willis-Hudson* | 74 |
| | 3.7 | LiteracyNation: "With Literacy and Justice for All"—*Richard Ashby Jr.* | 76 |

## PART III. VITAL ISSUES

| | | | |
|---|---|---|---|
| **Chapter 4A** | **Issues, Impact, and Values in Black Librarianship** | | 81 |
| | 4.1 | Issues Facing Black Male Librarians in 2023—*Antoine Ajani McDonald* | 81 |
| | 4.2 | A Black Alt-Ac Speaks: Early Career Librarianship Trauma—*Gemmicka Piper* | 86 |
| | 4.3 | Issues, Impact, and Values in Black Librarianship—*Candace Owens* | 91 |
| | 4.4 | Librarian-ish—*Rodney Freeman* | 95 |
| **Chapter 4B** | **Issues in Library and Information Science Education** | | 98 |
| | 4.5 | On the Occasion of the 2018 Graduation Class of SLIS, North Carolina Central University, Durham, North Carolina, Friday, May 11, 2018—*Amina Josey Turner* | 98 |
| | 4.6 | The Beacon Light: North Carolina Central University's School of Library and Information Sciences's Historical Role in Educating Black Librarians and Present Role in Advancing Artificial Intelligence, Biomedical Knowledge, and Digital Equity—*Jamillah Scott-Branch, Vernice Faison, and Danielle Colbert-Lewis* | 99 |
| | 4.7 | HBCUs and LIS Education: A Legacy and Counterstory—*Ana Ndumu, Renate Chancellor, and Tina Rollins* | 105 |
| | 4.8 | As a LIS Instructor, Am I Part of the Problem?—*Jason Alston* | 110 |
| | 4.9 | Historical Chronology of Black LIS Education—*Katie Perry* | 114 |
| | 4.10 | Paving the Way: LIS Education and Black Librarians in Indiana—*Michele Fenton* | 117 |
| **Chapter 4C** | **Issues in Equity, Diversity, Inclusion, and Multiculturalism** | | 125 |
| | 4.11 | Know Your History: Information Organization in House/Ball Culture and the Potential for Librarianship—*Aisha Aminu* | 125 |
| | 4.12 | Reconstitution of Ubuntu Spaces, Leading While an Ujima Culture Keeper—*Roland Barksdale-Hall* | 129 |
| | 4.13 | Fostering Inclusion through Programming and Outreach—*Angiah Davis and Michelle E. Jones* | 134 |
| | 4.14 | How Has Diversity, Equity, and Inclusion Impacted the BIPOC Library Professional?—*Taina K. Evans* | 138 |
| | 4.15 | Ginga Librarianship/Beautiful Librarianship—*Syntychia Kendrick-Samuel* | 142 |
| | 4.16 | If You Don't Understand Me, It's Your Fault: Black Librarians and the Distraction of Equity, Diversity, and Inclusion—*Conrad Pegues* | 145 |
| | 4.17 | Radical Imagination in Libraries: Reimagining Ourselves in Order to Reimagine Our Communities—*Nicole Cooke* | 150 |
| | 4.18 | On Diversity: Proposing an Institutional Commitment to Change and Accountability—*Courtney Shareef* | 154 |
| | 4.19 | In the Weeds: Challenging Performative Allyship amid Widespread Traumatic Events—*Lorin Jackson and Jazmyne Baylor* | 159 |
| | 4.20 | Essay from Assembly Member Jeffrion L. Aubry—*Jeffrion L. Aubry* | 164 |

**Chapter 4D  Issues and Advances in Medical Librarianship**    166

    4.21   Making the Invisible Visible: Amplifying the Contributions of African American Health Sciences Librarians—*Shannon Jones, Kelsa Bartley, and Jamia Williams*    166

    4.22   Up All Night: The First Twenty-Four-Hour Black Health and Healing Summit from Queens Public Library—*Jill Anderson, Tamara Michel, Kim McNeil-Capers, and Janet Umenta*    171

**Chapter 4E  Issues Facing Library Professionals without an MLS/MLIS Degree**    176

    4.23   Who Will Stand on Your Shoulders?—*DJ Bond*    176

    4.24   Support for Library Support Staff—*Robert "C. J." Hall*    180

    4.25   Issues by Library Professionals Without an MLS/MLIS Degree—*Carolyn Lawrence*    183

    4.26   My Contribution to the Library as a Nonlibrarian—*Lisa Soler*    187

## PART IV. SERVICE TO OUR COMMUNITIES

**Chapter 5  Academic Libraries**    191

    5.1   On the Other Side of the Tenure Track: Retention and Promotion of Black Academic Law Librarians—*Renate Chancellor*    191

    5.2   The Accidental Law Librarian—*Melanie E. Sims*    196

    5.3   Getting the Job: Black Librarians in Academic Libraries—*Rashida Scott Blades and Genevia Chamblee-Smith*    198

**Chapter 6  Public Libraries**    204

    6.1   The Importance of Public Library Youth Services in the Community—*Aletta Seales*    204

    6.2   Tribute: My Nontraditional Journey in Librarianship—*Andrew P. Jackson (Sekou Molefi Baako)*    206

    6.3   African American Research Libraries (Public Libraries)—*Andrew P. Jackson (Sekou Molefi Baako)*    210

    6.4   It Takes a Village: Formulating Liaisons between Public Librarians and African American Homeschooling Families—*Raphael Daoud Jackson-Ortiz*    211

    6.5   Leading with Knowledge: Programs and Services in BIPOC Communities and the Importance of Representation (What Progress Has Been Made in Serving the Black Community in over Twenty Years?)—*James Allen Davis Jr. and Leslie Williams*    215

    6.6   Being a Youth Services Librarian—*Tahira Ahmad*    218

    6.7   Land of Endless Dreams & Possibilities!!!!!—*Judi Belle Raines*    219

    6.8   The Great Escape—*C. Atterbury*    222

    6.9   Black Male Librarians: Advocating for Children and Literacy—*Tiffeni Fontno*    225

    6.10   From Badge to Books: A Journey of Community Care and Library Legacy—*Kelly Richards*    235

**Chapter 7  School Libraries**    238

    7.1   The Game Changer: Becoming a School Librarian—*Sandra Michele Echols and Eboni M. Henry*    238

    7.2   The Pivotal Role of Black School Librarians in Promoting Diversity, Equity, and Inclusion in Education vis-à-vis Culturally Responsive Pedagogy—*Miriam Thomas and Chanelle Maynard*    240

**Chapter 8  Special Libraries**    245

    8.1   Counternarratives in Practice—*Jina Duvernay*    245

    8.2   The Blair-Caldwell African American Research Library, Denver, Colorado—*Jameka B. Lewis*    247

    8.3   The Auburn Avenue Research Library on African American Culture and History: A Rich History Leading the Way in the South—*Victor E. Simmons Jr.*    249

| Chapter 9 | **State and Federal Libraries** | 254 |
|---|---|---|
| | 9.1 Twenty Years as County Librarian: A Legacy—*Jos N. Holman* | 254 |
| Chapter 10 | **Collaborations with Museums** | 257 |
| | 10.1 Louis Armstrong as Archivist—*Regina Bain* | 257 |
| Chapter 11 | **Library Trustees** | 261 |
| | 11.1 Experiences as a Library Trustee—*Laura Ellis* | 261 |
| | 11.2 Being a Library Trustee—*Andrew P. Jackson (Sekou Molefi Baako)* | 262 |
| | 11.3 Empowerment, Representation, and Leadership: A Reflection on Joining the QPL Board—*Cloyette Harris-Stoute* | 263 |
| | 11.4 The Importance of the Public Library: A Trustee Perspective—*Earl G. Simons* | 264 |

## PART V. LIBRARY TECHNOLOGY AND BLACK LIBRARIANSHIP

| Chapter 12 | **Open Pedagogy as the Intersection of Digital Skills and Community**—*Willa Liburd Tavernier and Maria E. Hamilton Abegunde* | 269 |
|---|---|---|
| Chapter 13 | **Libraries' Part in Solving Problems of Inclusive Online Education during the Pandemic**—*Ahalya Sudev* | 275 |
| Chapter 14 | **Digital Access and Historically Black College and University Libraries**—*Dawn Kight and Maletta Payne* | 278 |
| Chapter 15 | **How Tech Has Enhanced the Jobs of Library Professionals**—*Kelvin Watson* | 283 |

## PART VI. PEARLS OF WISDOM FROM OUR RETIREES

| Chapter 16 | **BCALA Pearls of Wisdom: Phyllis Green Mack, Retired Librarian, New York Public Library: As Told to S. Michele Echols**—*Sandra Michele Echols and Phyllis Green Mack* | 291 |
|---|---|---|
| Chapter 17 | **Statements from Retirees: Ida D. McGhee, MLS**—*Ida D. McGhee* | 294 |
| Chapter 18 | **Pearls of Wisdom: In Conversation with Marcia Smith-Woodard**—*Michele Fenton and Marcia Smith-Woodard* | 295 |
| Chapter 19 | **Pearls of Wisdom by Joyce C. Wright as Relayed to Marva L. DeLoach**—*Joyce C. Wright and Marva DeLoach* | 297 |
| Chapter 20 | **Stephanie Tolson, Retired Librarian**—*Stephanie Tolson* | 299 |
| Chapter 21 | **The Joy in Retirement**—*Jessie Carney Smith* | 300 |
| Chapter 22 | **My Life's Work in Academic and Public Librarianship**—*Gloria J. Mims* | 301 |
| Chapter 23 | **"When You Become a Librarian . . . "**—*Marshelle Berry* | 302 |
| Chapter 24 | **What Librarianship Has Meant to Me**—*Irene Owens* | 303 |
| Chapter 25 | **Pearls of Wisdom by Linda Jolivet as Relayed to Marva L. DeLoach**—*Marva L. DeLoach and Linda Jolivet* | 304 |
| Chapter 26 | **Customer Service: A Many Splendored Thing**—*Sharon D. Banks* | 305 |

| Chapter 27 | Are You Thinking about . . . Mission? Value? Staff?—*Thomas Alford* | 306 |
| Chapter 28 | **Challenges and Triumphs: Personal Reflection on My Career in the Atlanta Public Library System**—*Carolyn Lowe Garnes* | 307 |
| Chapter 29 | **Reflections, Remembrances, and Ramblings**—*Sandy Bright* | 311 |

## PART VII. GLOBAL ISSUES IN LIBRARIES

| Chapter 30 | **Unlocking Libraries' Potential to Improve the Lives and Prospects of the Members of Our Communities**—*Loida Garcia-Febo* | 315 |
| Chapter 31 | **Brazilian Black Librarianship: Paths, Struggles, and Resistance**—*Franciéle Carneiro Garcês-da-Silva* | 320 |
| Chapter 32 | **Understanding the Journey: Exploring Information Challenges Faced by Migrants in India and Library Interventions**—*Aysha Zakiya A* | 325 |

## PART VIII. BANNED BOOKS AND CENSORSHIP ISSUES

| Chapter 33 | **Racial Colorblind Theory and Book Acquisition**—*Elizabeth Jean Brumfield* | 331 |
| Chapter 34 | **Always Been There: The Cultural Politics of Children's Books and Black Librarians**—*Edith Campbell* | 336 |

## PART IX. BOOKS, PERIODICALS, AND OTHER RESOURCES RECOMMENDED FOR BLACK COLLECTIONS

| Chapter 35 | **Selected Bibliography of Works by Dr. E. J. Josey**—*Andrew P. Jackson (Sekou Molefi Baako)* | 343 |
| Chapter 36 | **Brief Bibliography of Essays and Journal Articles by Dr. E. J. Josey**—*Marva L. DeLoach* | 344 |
| Chapter 37 | **Spring Reading List 2023**—*Carol Gilliam* | 346 |
| Chapter 38 | **Bibliotherapy: African American Youth and Mental Health**—*Mitzi Mack* | 347 |
| Chapter 39 | **Bibliography of Select African and African American Films for Collection Development and Academic Course Instruction**—*Monique Threatt* | 350 |
| Chapter 40 | **Black Heritage Reference Collection: Langston Hughes Community Library and Cultural Center**—*Christine Zarrett* | 354 |
| Chapter 41 | **Selected US Bookstores by State That Are Black-Owned and/or Specialize in Black Books and Other Black Resources**—*Marva L. DeLoach* | 359 |

| Index | 369 |
| About the Contributors | 381 |
| About the Editors | 391 |

# Acknowledgments

Thank you to Charles Harmon and Rowman & Littlefield for believing in this project and the need for a third edition. Charles, thanks for recommending Marva to work on this with me. She is a real jewel.

Special thanks to my coeditors, Dr. Marva L. DeLoach and Michele Fenton, for agreeing to work on this project with me. It has been a real joy working with you both.

Marva, your insight and experience with the second edition has been invaluable.

Michele, we could not have completed this project without your excellent technical advice and skills to put this manuscript together for submission to the publisher.

Thank you to all the contributors for believing in this project and agreeing to have your voices and narratives included in this third edition and being a part of the E. J. Josey Black librarian legacy.

For those who have this *Handbook of Black Librarianship, Third Edition*, in your hands and reading it, I hope you find it as gratifying as we did in producing it.

Lastly, a heartfelt thank you to E. J. Josey for his vision and commitment to Black librarianship and for never taking no for an answer from me or others when we said we could not, and instead replying, "I know, just send me a draft" by such and such a date.

Andrew "Sekou" Jackson

# Tributes to E. J. Josey

## *Tribute to Dr. Elonnie J. Josey*

Malikah Lumumba

Dr. Elonnie Junius Josey (1924–2009): humble elder statesman, renaissance man, leader, professional, educator, activist, brilliant scholar, prolific writer, esteemed and beloved colleague, cherished mentor and friend. These are just a few attributes that anyone of us could select and identify in describing our relationship with Dr. E. J. Josey, also referred to as "Dr. J," or simply "EJ" by those who knew him well or had a special relationship with him. I always called him Dr. Josey, with much respect, holding him in such high esteem. Dr. Josey flashed that wide, warm smile when he saw you, extending a firm handshake or hug—such a classy gentleman. I do not recall Dr. Josey ever speaking ill of anyone, even those adversaries who did not agree with him or were staunch racists. He did not curse them but took the high road, speaking of something positive about them or the hopes thereof.

Dr. E. J. Josey was extremely kind, gracious, helpful, genuinely interested in you personally and professionally, reaching out to assist anyone but especially all librarians and particularly librarians of color. He worked tirelessly to recruit more African Americans into librarianship. Dr. Josey wanted to help you get started in the field, get ahead if you had earned that MLS, to set your goals further on the totem pole and to go beyond, to be all you could be and the very best at it! If you were already at the top, Dr. Josey would encourage you to excel in that role or reach higher for a position of leadership. Or even start your own organization, as he did as the founder of the Black Caucus of the American Library Association (BCALA) in 1970.

Please do not deny yourself the inspiring benefits of researching Dr. Josey's early life, career, participation in professional associations, and the civil rights movement, in addition to noting his distinct honors, awards, and degrees, all too comprehensive to cite here, which is not the scope of this tribute.

Each person has their own individual testimony with Dr. J. Mine began in 1968 when I was a page for the Mount Vernon Public Library (New York) and later the Westchester Library System (New York), attending a conference at which Dr. Josey was the keynote speaker. I was in awe to see an African American male librarian for the very first time and was so impressed with Dr. Josey's eloquent presentation, immaculate attire, cool, dignified stature, and forceful figure before me. I wanted to be like him, and I knew then that I wanted to be a librarian more than ever. He had also indirectly planted the initial seeds of the importance of being a role model. Afterward, I was too shy and in awe to introduce myself.

Years passed and the young aspiring librarian had become one. During my second year after graduating from Columbia University Library School, I received a fellowship to attend the Ethnicity and Librarianship II Institute (1977–1978) at Queens College. Dr. Josey was one of many notables invited to address participants on various selected topics. At the following reception, I initiated a conversation proceeding to share how he had impressed me to become a librarian when I first heard him speak years ago. Before I knew it, Dr. Josey had invited me to submit an article for *The Bookmark*, which he edited as chief of the Bureau of Specialist Library Services, New York State Education Department, Division of Library Development. I had just received a promotion as the Mount Vernon reference librarian to head of the Young Adult

Department. My first published library article, "My Objectives, Principles, and Philosophies as a Young Adult Librarian," was published in the 1978 winter edition under my former name, Barbara Keve Gregory. Dr. Josey gave me confidence to write that article and others. He made suggestions along the way, but any writings' final drafts were unedited. He wanted your words to be in your own voice.

We kept in touch, and he reassured me all the way . . . subsequently working in every department of the Mount Vernon Public Library; then library media specialist Mount Vernon Board of Education Middle Schools; library consultant setting up *Essence* magazine's first library; adjunct professor, Bronx Community College and College of New Rochelle. All along this professional path, Dr. Josey continuously uplifted me to grow and extend myself writing to publish and speak out in response to library issues and especially any cacophony of racist ideas, practices, principles depicted in editorials, magazine articles on pertinent library and general topics whenever I had an opportunity. Dr. Josey taught by his deeds and actions and was a staunch activist in the world's arena of struggle toward liberation, fighting on the front lines for universal human rights to combat racism everywhere.

When Dr. Josey called me to participate in the International Federation of Library Association (IFLA) World Library and Information Congress held in Kenya, I said I could not afford to go. He simply replied, "Charge now and pay later; there will probably not be another opportunity like this once the window closes." He tried unsuccessfully to obtain grant monies for us to participate, but also expressed many times that we African American librarians must pay our own way to attain professional development and experiences.

This was the fiftieth anniversary of IFLA and the first time being held on African soil. Leave it to Dr. Josey's vision to spearhead and organize a contingency of about thirty-five members of the BCALA and other participants to meet and work with the librarians of the Kenya Library Association in Nairobi. What a glorious and unforgettable time we had, professionally stimulating and socially exhilarating while promoting cultural awareness! It was a unique and incredible forum to celebrate this historic IFLA occasion as well as acknowledge and celebrate African librarians of the diaspora, meeting, bonding, and collaborating for the very first time in our "Mama Land!"

How could one ever say no to Dr. E. J. Josey? I could not. So, after much discussion and deliberation, he cheered me on to write "Problems in the Acquisition of and Publishing of African Materials," which I researched extensively and proudly and presented in Kenya at the July 1984 IFLA seminar. I felt so proud of my research and presenting my paper that Dr. Josey, again, had advised and given me the confidence to do! He further invited and encouraged me to write articles about my IFLA experience and who/where to send them to be published in pertinent library literature that was accomplished.

In addition to our professional land-breaking preconference event of presenting papers to our select group, we had meetings, parties, and networking discussions. I had the time of my life staying with a host family that Dr. Josey arranged. It truly was a lifetime dream come true to visit "Home." What a totally edifying and awesome experience it was—all made possible through Dr. E. J. Josey!

Dr. Josey also always motivated librarians to join and become active with the American Library Association (ALA) and BCALA. He promoted me to run for ALA Library Council and confidently confided that I could win as we youth librarians—children, young adult, and library media specialists—supported each other. And I did succeed! When I was elected, Dr. Josey again encouraged me to always speak up and have something to contribute to the cause of liberation. Whenever I heard him speak, Dr. Josey was a straight shooter speaking in a forthright, strong, forceful voice with well-researched fact-filled speeches, always speaking out boldly about and against widespread racism, bias, discrimination, segregation, and just plain ignorance in his life, librarianship, and the world-at-large.

Speaking about ALA, I would be remiss to not highlight an unforgettable time when Dr. Josey was elected president of ALA (1984–1985). It was truly a people's victory as the election process culminated not only as the result of the hard work, determination, and perseverance of a dedicated cadre of many diverse groups, but also the sheer pride and joy that we had finally arrived. We celebrated jubilantly in his presidential suite, which Dr. Josey invited all to! He was ecstatic and shined in his tenure, successfully building coalitions, partnerships, and initiating innovative programs. We finally had real opportunity to sit at these tables, being appointed to key committees on pay equity, information technology, and library access and services to the underserved.

Dr. Josey offered to write a reference if he had recommended you apply for a position, scholarship, special program, etc. or if one asked him for a letter of reference. He did so graciously when I applied and was accepted for a Fulbright Award administered by the US Department of State's Bureau of Educational and Cultural Affairs (ECA). I applied through an ALA component and was thrilled after two interviews in Washington, DC, where I also had to make a presentation to accept a six-month stint to set up the first internet in a school in Zimbabwe. I'm reassured Dr. Josey's letter carried great weight. In addition, he also introduced me to a dear friend of his who resided there. She played a major role in helping our seven-year-old son, who had accompanied me, and myself to successfully navigate my job assignment and living there being immersed in a new culture. This is the kind of full support Dr. Josey rendered to his mentees. The esteemed professional, Dr. Josey was punctual, returned phone calls and emails in a timely manner, and it was a regular treat to receive a letter he had personally written.

But his legacy of mentorship is not just with me, but so many other countless librarians of all hues and nationalities. Dr. Josey advocated for diversity for all people, emboldening folks everywhere to always speak up, speak out, and become active, not just talking about the challenges we face as librarians in our respective workplaces but also as citizens in our communities and of the world. Dr. Josey's view was global, and he wanted you to see and be seen from that view and perspective. He inspired us to write, publish, run for professional and public office, all to make a difference in our lives and the world. Furthermore, to advance in those positions and serve wherever we are, wherever we go!

I clearly and fondly remember ALA conferences where Dr. Josey saw his mentees of all ages and nationalities and invite us to meet him later at a designated time and place (which did not of course conflict with ALA meetings). He would say "spread the word and announce it to others." An eager group excited to be in his presence gathered where he would introduce everyone saying something glowing and about where each one was and what they were doing, inquiring about their next venture, hopes, and dreams. It was a brief and inspiring encounter with which we left empowered. Dr Josey paid for the bill, and we parted with encouraging words from him to grow, succeed, and keep in touch!

Dr. Josey always had an entourage around him, walking so fast one could hardly keep up. The only joy that topped being with his colleagues and mentees at ALA was having his only beautiful daughter, Amina Josey Turner (nee Elaine Jacqueline Josey) accompany him, usually when he was receiving another one of his prestigious and well-deserved awards. The icing on the cake was if one of his beloved six grands accompanied him. Then, Dr. Josey beamed proudly as he spoke of their many accomplishments.

It is no coincidence that Dr. Josey passed July 3, 2009, in Washington, North Carolina, and his homegoing was held simultaneously as the 2009 annual ALA conference was transpiring in Chicago. Surely, Dr. Josey's Spirit was with those thousands of librarians as it will always be with BCALA and ALA proceedings and all of us librarians worldwide. My husband Shaka and I attended the moving homegoing ceremony. We all owe a huge debt to this "Great Gentle Giant." Thank you, Dr. E. J. Josey.

# *Tribute to E. J. Josey*

Binne Tate Wilkin

> We need to foster the recognition among ALA [American Library Association] members that the future of libraries is clearly linked to the welfare of the American people and to reaffirm the inseparable relationship between libraries and the traditional liberties.[1]

These words, written by E. J. Josey, encapsulate his contributions as a librarian, activist, leader, and educator. Inspired by national personalities and responding to changes wrought by civil rights advocacy, Josey dedicated himself to eliminating racial and social barriers. He worked tirelessly to improve information access and to reform biases entrenched in the American Library Association. Understanding the power of organization, E. J. Josey founded the Black Caucus of American Library Association (BCALA) establishing a cultural and professional force formerly nonexistent.

In E. J. Josey's groundbreaking publication, *The Black Librarian in America* published in 1970, voice was given to librarians of color facing continued segregation and professional rejection. This title, followed by several other publications, trumpeted sacrifices and contributions made by African American librarians. Wherever possible, E. J. Josey initiated and activated the inclusion of marginalized professionals on committees, on leaderships councils, and in leading workplace positions.

Those of us mentored by our friend, colleague, and leader, had an inside view of E. J.'s personal wit and charm. He gently guided us in and through the maze of structured organizational privilege revealing deterrents deliberately erected to safeguard positions of a few. My experience with E. J. Josey included bringing my naïve idea, in writing, to the newly formed Black Caucus. Censuring libraries deliberately circumventing integration laws was the focus. He graciously accepted my input and shaped the proposal into a formal resolution. This document became the first resolution from BCALA passed by the ALA council. To follow were many other collaborations with this man with a "calling."

Although E. J. Josey would be pleased with the ALA's recent commitment to diversity, equity, and inclusion, his words from the past have been too long ignored: *I will continue to have an uncompromising opposition to any form of discrimination whether it is racial, gender or age. I will continue to be a great champion of the great cause of diversity.*[2]

With honor, I offer tribute to the quintessential librarian, E. J. Josey.

**NOTES**

1. Josey, E. J. *The Black Librarian in America Revisited.* Scarecrow Press, 1994, p. 355.
2. Ibid., p. 358.

# *My Tribute to E. J. Josey, Activist Librarian: Trailblazer, Colleague, Mentor, and Advocate*

George C. Grant

I first met Dr. E. J. Josey in 1971 at the annual convention of the American Library Association (ALA). There, after learning of the founding of the Black Caucus of the American Library Association (BCALA) in 1970, I found my way through the crowd of African American librarians to offer my expressions of gratitude to him for his initiative and my availability to assist in the organization's achieving its goals. Then, for several years, as I inquired about how I might support the Black Caucus, he suggested activities I might pursue in doing so. And later, much to my surprise, he even invited me to assist him with the coordination of the very successful BCALA Kenya Library Association Conference in Nairobi, Kenya. He honored me!

E. J. was a trailblazer in many regards. His role in the founding of the Black Caucus is legendary, as is his civil rights advocacy throughout his life. For the next forty years that I knew him, he was, in my opinion, the Frederick Douglass, Booker T. Washington, and Martin Luther King in the advancement of Black librarians to the top of the profession and beyond—heights not achieved prior to the 1970s. He organized, spoke, wrote, and fought for opportunities not just for Black librarians but for the underserved in our profession.

To be sure, under E. J.'s leadership, BCALA was organized, and accomplished many things, some that include: (1) sponsoring a successful ALA resolution that called for censure of libraries and/or librarians providing services or materials to racist schools established to circumvent racial integration, (2) supporting Blacks at the University of Maryland Library School, (3) aggressively fighting discrimination in employment and promotion at the Library of Congress, and in libraries everywhere, (4) instituting exchanges of librarians between African and American libraries, (5) beginning to sponsor meetings and programs at all ALA conferences, (6) exposing the racist content and portrayals in the Intellectual Freedom Committee-sponsored film *The Speaker*, (7) sponsoring its first National Conference of African American Librarians in 1992, (8) establishing its E. J. Josey Scholarship Fund in 1990 and annually awarding several scholarships since then, and (9) supporting the successful election of more than six Black librarians, including himself, to president of ALA, to name just a few. He blazed a trail for all of us, and many others!

However, it was almost ten years after he founded BCALA that he pulled me aside and suggested that I could contribute even more profoundly in the role of president of the Black Caucus—one that I had not aspired to, nor even considered. So, with his counsel and support, I ran for and was elected president (1978–1980). Then, for almost forty years, he periodically discussed with me what he perceived to be other opportunities for my development, success, and effectiveness as a library professional, many of which I sought out, but many I did not for lack of time and resources.

But that was just the beginning. For many of us who were not established or recognized for significant past or current achievements, he was always ready to hear, counsel, and support our needs and goals. For example, in 1981 I had made an unwise decision in resigning from a position that I had found untenable because of what I considered to be the illegal professional antics of my supervisor. I found comfort in his wise counsel and subsequent assistance in reestablishing my career and moving on at that time and I sought out that wise counsel for the rest of his life. Would that I had sought that counsel even earlier.

One of the most profound contributions that he made to my professional career was his acceptance of and his advocacy for my own vision for my career. When I declined to submit essays to editions of his landmark books, *Black Librarians in America* and *Handbook of Black Librarianship*, he protested but accepted my decision to pursue other avenues for support of BCALA. He recognized that my library administrative responsibilities, along with my BCALA publishing responsibilities, combined with my book publishing enterprise would have overwhelmed me. So, he directed his comments, his content, and his compliments to me on how to make those type contributions more effective. Then, for twenty years that I edited and published the twenty-eight-page quarterly *Newsletter of the Black Caucus of the ALA*, for the several editions of the *BCALA Membership Directory* that I edited and published, and for my 1992 book, *The Directory of Ethnic Professionals in Librarianship*, he was a constant consultant and contributor.

So, I stayed in my lane, and with his encouragement and his full support. He was, for me, a true advocate!

And, finally, E. J. was as complete a professional role model as one could ever hope or expect to experience. His visions, his inexhaustible commitment to their accomplishment, and his example of "Let's just do it" have and will continue to provide excellent standards for dedication to my own vision with regard to my life, my family, my career, and my legacy.

Thanks, E. J.

# *Tribute to My Dad*

Amina Turner

We tend to think that in order to make change in systems and institutions, a revolution is required, a complete overthrow or overhaul must take place. But those of us who espouse social change, who advocate for a paradigm shift for the common good, who groom new leadership, and who enhance the knowledge base of community members, know that we must actually perform revolutionary acts in evolutionary ways.

That is the legacy of E. J. Josey, my father.

E. J. Josey was one of America's leading thinkers and civil rights activists from the mid-twentiey century and into the early new millennium. Josey was to librarianship what Charles Hamilton Houston was to the law profession. Houston encouraged law students to become *social engineers* to fight racism and discrimination attacking the separate but equal doctrine. E. J. Josey redefined the role of libraries and librarians, challenging the fabric of the American Library Association (ALA), the oldest and largest library association in the world—from within. Later, E. J. Josey was elected president of that same association as the second black and first African American male. A dear and close contemporary, Dr. Vivian D. Hewitt, referred to Josey as the "Jackie Robinson of Librarianship" for his vision and his strategic actions were the catalyst for change that have had a lasting impact during his lifetime, and long after his death upon libraries, librarians, and the ALA.

E. J. Josey was a man of principle who advocated for human rights, for equal access to information, pay equity, intellectual freedom, and social responsibility, all of which are embodied in the noble ideals of equality, justice, and peace. In other words, E. J. Josey forged ahead to conscientiously democratize librarianship, not only in America but throughout the world, the first to include the African diaspora.

If you read the titles or even excerpts of some of Dr. Josey's speeches that span five decades of his library and civil rights career, you hear a fierce leader, a fiery orator, a man of conviction who fought for the voiceless—those marginalized by hate, economics, illiteracy, and their zip code. Equally true, Dr. Josey was a constituency- and coalition-builder, working within the system to bring about change for the benefit of all. He was truly an American patriot who wanted America to be America, and not in name only, but through living ideals and equal opportunities for all.

In his speech entitled "The Right to Information Access" (date unknown),[1] Josey names censorship as one of five barriers to information:

> There are reports of attempts to curtail access to books or other library materials that are 'offensive' to some, and these censorship attempts are at record highs according to the ALA's office for intellectual freedom [OIF]. . . . Reasons for censorship run the gamut of rationales, from racism, sexism, profanity, anti-Christianity and pro-Christianity to simply "inappropriateness." The results are the same: the public is in danger of being deprived of free choice to access to the information it needs from the libraries of the community.[2]

He ended that speech thusly, "It is incumbent upon us all to avoid the creation of another division in society, namely the information rich and the information poor. . . . Access is a better guarantee to our freedom than any constitutional amendment could state, or any administration could promise."[3]

In his ALA presidential inaugural address in 1984, Josey counselled,

> In a time of attack on the basic freedoms and elementary well-being of the most vulnerable sections of the population, professional groups must recognize their stake in the outcome of that attack and their responsibilities. . . . ALA therefore needs to integrate its goals

with the goals of greatest importance to the American people, i.e., the preservation of basic democratic liberties, the enlargement of equal opportunity for women and minorities, and the continuance of earlier national planning to raise the level of education and economic well-being of greater numbers of the population.[4]

And regarding the role of the library, from "The Challenges, Changes and Conflicts Facing American Libraries" (1992): "The point of working for effectiveness in libraries and in library networks and systems, and for collaboration, and for improvement, generally, is the enhancement of human capacity and human wellbeing."[5]

My father was a member of the NAACP since 1960, joining in Savannah, Georgia. He served on the executive board of the Georgia State Conference under the leadership of W. W. Law and was the first state youth advisor of a state-supported college in the South—Savannah State College, now Savannah State University. Both Julian Bond and Carolyn Q. Coleman were some of the active students in the youth chapter. The National NAACP awarded my father for his service with the NAACP youth chapter. Dad was a member of the Savannah branch for twenty years.

In 1962, my dad was invited to the home of the Rev. Dr. Curtis Jackson to have dinner with Dr. Martin Luther King Jr., who was Rev. Jackson's Morehouse classmate. Dad, seated next to Dr. King, was introduced as the director of the library at Savannah State College. Dr. King had heard about the Savannah sit-in movements, and offered congratulations to Dad, and then inquired, "When are the students in Savannah planning to go to the libraries?" At the students' last meeting, sit-ins at the public libraries were planned my dad told Dr. King in response. Later, in the 1980s my father was instrumental with other ALA members in establishing the Coretta Scott King Book Award. The iconic image of Coretta Scott King receiving an award from my dad illuminates the wall in one of our library collections in our home. It speaks to my heart of the sacrifices that they have made for justice.

In a typewritten account that connects his NAACP experience with ALA, Dad stated,

> It was because of my civil rights activities in the 1960's in Georgia, . . . that gave me the strength and the courage to go to ALA and use the tactics that we were taught . . . to confront the racist dragon that was in ALA. I did not separate my civil rights life outside of that profession from my life in the profession. I merged the two, and I think by merging the two it made me stronger and gave me an opportunity to work on behalf of all people in librarianship, because I had learned from the struggle in black communities all across the south.[6]

My NAACP work allowed me to meet a number of civil rights icons who knew my father, such as Julian Bond, Vernon Jordan, Carolyn Q. Coleman, Benjamin Hooks, and Paula Edme Brown, to name a few. My one regret is the time I was planning a trip to Baltimore, Maryland, to attend a regional directors meeting at NAACP headquarters. I was a state executive director of the NC State Conference and not a regional director, but I was always invited to attend a number of these trainings. This particular time I told Dad my schedule, and his response was, "Oh, tell Roy . . ." and I interrupted him, reminding him that Mr. Wilkins had already passed. He paused and said, "Oh yes." Knowing that my dad and Mr. Wilkins knew each other from Dad's work in the Savannah movement in the 1960s, and Dad's contributions to the NAACP scholarship, I should have never stopped his train of thought. What rich pearl did I miss from a man for whom the civil rights movement was not only the backdrop but also the centerpiece of his life?

It is also ironic that I attended a creative writing class at Howard University led by renowned novelist John Oliver Killens. I should have known that Killens's path had crossed my father's, but it was not until going through books in my dad's library that autographs from celebrated authors, poets, and illustrators were discovered: Wole Soyinka, Karl Shapiro, Oliver Tambo, Lani Guinier, Gwendolyn Brooks, Eloise Greenfield, Killens, of course, and many others.

When I think of my father's upbringing, I am humbled. My father grew up in abject poverty and Black in the segregated South. His own father, Willie Josey, a proud man, carried a newspaper under his arm every day after work although he himself was barely literate. His mother, Frances Bailey Josey, graduated from "Normal College"[7] and loved poetry and music. She would sing to her children and encourage the five of them to memorize and recite Bible verses as well as poetry for entertainment. Words and music spoke to my father. Books mattered. His local library in Portsmouth, Virginia, was segregated, but it was not until he served in World War II that Josey was exposed to a desegregated library. I think these experiences in the segregated South and the supports in place in his all-Black public schools and at home, despite the poverty, propelled him to excel in spite of the status quo.

Dad studied the organ at Hampton Institute (Hampton University) with Ernest Hayes after high school and played for various area churches in his hometown. Mr. Hayes was the first Black man to become a member of the Fellow of the American Guild of Organists. A gifted musician himself, E. J. Josey was assigned to the army chaplain in World War II. I remember that he spoke of his deep regret that many of the young infantry men he met had been sent to the front lines. My father knew that he would not see many of them again in life.

As a child, I never fully understood who my father was to the ALA and to librarianship. It was not until I traveled as an adolescent to conferences or award ceremonies with him or witnessed throngs of people—librarians—around him, and heard him speak with vigor about injustices, and our responsibility and obligation to remove barriers, to fight for diversity and inclusion in library leadership and services that I truly appreciated how courageous he was to speak truth to power. I was proud to see my dad in his element leading the charge for justice! A few times, some of my children attended ALA conferences and sessions with my father and engaged in the discussions that took place. Many years ago, I had become a library trustee and two of my children worked in their college libraries.

E. J. Josey was a loving father, a giving grandfather, and was always excited to visit his family in North Carolina just before school opened. He enjoyed school shopping and listening to his grandchildren play Beethoven on the piano, or a newly learned Christmas carol on the violin or flute. He loved European classical music, hymns, Motown, and many popular artists. At the age of four, my father gave me a piano so I could take lessons. I still have that piano and all his grandchildren learned on the very same instrument. His presence was always filled with sharing stories, sometimes singing hymns, and going to some of his favorite restaurants or the latest movie or play.

My father was a consistent financial supporter of many of his beloved social justice organizations: the NAACP, the Urban League, the ACLU, the Southern Poverty Law Center, the Common Cause, as well as his alma maters I. C. Norcom High School, Portsmouth, Virginia; Howard University, Washington, DC; State University of New York at Albany (New York). Years ago, while in Montgomery, Alabama, on NAACP business, I donated in his memory to the Southern Poverty Law Center.

In 2007, the E. J. Josey Foundation for Justice and Peace conducted a number of open-call interviews on E. J. Josey and his work during the ALA Annual Conference in Washington, DC. It was especially moving to meet young practitioners who only knew Dr. Josey through his books and articles and who expressed deep admiration and a sense of awe for my dad. In fact, my best friend from high school was a branch head in North Philadelphia. When the Black Caucus of ALA Conference (BCALA) was held at Winston-Salem State University in Winston-Salem, North Carolina, my friend attended and called Dad a "Rock Star."

During one of my trips to my birthplace—Philadelphia, Pennsylvania—I visited my friend at her branch, the Cecil B. Moore Library. What a pleasant experience to see school-aged children doing homework, some using computers, adults searching for jobs or just reading, and my friend counseling a young man who was trying to decide about school. To add to the excitement, you were greeted by a mural that featured famous African Americans including Cecil B. Moore, but more importantly, some of the faces of the children who frequented the branch were also on the wall. In 2019, my best friend died and at her service they lauded her work in the "likes of E. J. Josey."

In January 2010, my husband and I were invited to receive an award in my dad's honor during the Martin Luther King Jr. holiday at the Economic Opportunity Authority, Savannah-Chatham County, a private nonprofit agency of which my father was the principal founder back in 1964. We were taped on the local TV station and met people who remembered my dad and his days in Savannah.

In September 2014, while standing in the heat at the Library of Congress with LeVar Burton (not planned), waiting to enter for the swearing-in of the librarian of Congress, Dr. Carla Hayden, one young member of the ALA was also in line. As we exchanged names, she referred to me as "library royalty." I did not expect that, but I graciously received the honor due to my father, Dr. E. J. Josey.

In his speech at the National Sankofa Council on the Education Black Children Conference (1998), Dr. Josey stated,

> Equality is not something that may be had by degrees. One is either equal or one is not equal. There are no in-betweens. We as a people may progress towards equality, and we may sometimes mistakenly think that we have reached our goal. But only when every vestige of discrimination and racism is removed not only from the physical aspect of life in America, but also from the hearts and minds of people, then, and only then can we claim to be equal.[8]

I offer my sincere thanks to my "sister" Dr. Marva L. DeLoach, and all the librarians, educators, and other change agents involved with this much needed project—the continuation of the work of one of the most esteemed leaders in civil rights and librarianship, Dr. E. J. Josey. Bring power to his legacy in what you do for libraries and for the profession.

E. J. Josey did the work, so it is up to us to *finish the good fight of faith*!

## NOTES

1. "The Right to Information Access," Speech delivered in Michigan, 1988, p. 9.
2. Ibid., p. 9.
3. Ibid., p. 14.
4. Josey, E. J., "Forging Coalitions for the Public Good," Presidential Inauguration Address, American Library Association, June 27, 1984 (pages are not numbered in the booklet, but quote appears on the fourth page).
5. Josey, E. J., "The Challenges, Changes and Conflicts Facing American Libraries," New Jersey Library Association Annual Conference, Meadowlands Hilton, Secaucus, New Jersey, May 7, 1992, p. 20.
6. Josey, E. J., Unpublished, untitled typewritten autobiographical draft dictated by my father containing his handwritten edits, date unknown, p. 24.
7. "Normal Schools" were established in the United States as preparatory one- to two-year institutions in the 1800s to train men and then women to teach on the elementary school level. Many became the precursors to teachers' colleges. In North Carolina, normal schools launched some of the state's historically black colleges that exist today. (Adapted https://www.ncpedia.org/normal-school and https://www.ncpedia.org/North-Carolina-HBCUs-timeline)
8. Josey, E. J., Speech given at the National Sankofa Council on Educating Black Children Conference, Merrillville, Indiana, April 5, 1998, https://clbc.org/2009/07/speech-by-e-j-josey/.

# Preface

BLACK LIBRARIANSHIP: A RICH LEGACY OF FAITH AND SELF-DETERMINATION

Andrew P. Jackson (Sekou Molefi Baako)

One of the most important legacies of a civilization is the record it leaves behind, archiving its history for research and availability for future generations. Embedded in that history is the representation of its own culture and values, the people and places where history takes place. As Dr. John Henrik Clarke described history in his essay "Image and Mind Control In The African World," *"A people's history tells a people where they have been and what they have been, where they are and what they are. More importantly, a proper understanding of history tells a people where they still must go."*[1] Society's libraries have been, are, and will be the repository of every culture's stories.

The story of that history is imbedded in the term "Black librarianship." It is the history reflecting our heritage, personal stories and struggles, challenges, successes, and issues of librarians and libraries. Black librarianship in and of itself is a rich and often volatile history of struggle that can be identified by the values of the society. One such value is *self-determination*, grounded within another value, *faith*. Together, these values open a window to a tomorrow with a feeling of *hope* by enslaved Black people when hearing the words from President Lincoln's Emancipation Proclamation, *"Henceforth and forever free."*[2] Freedom came with end of the Civil War and ratification of citizenship and *"due process of law"* in the Constitution of the United States of America's Fourteenth Amendment, ratified in 1868.[3] This was the beginning of a new era of struggle for formerly enslaved noncitizens and a test in *equality* as American citizens with an opportunity to experience "Life, Liberty and the Pursuit of Happiness."[4] Formerly enslaved people knew the key to this new life, being free, was education, the need to learn to read, and have access to the knowledge found in books. As Frederick Douglass once said in his speech "The Nature of Slavery," *"Knowledge makes a person unfit for slavery. Knowledge is the pathway from slavery to freedom."*[5]

E. J. Josey stated in his introduction to the first edition of *The Handbook of Black Librarianship*, "Black Americans have a distinguished history in American librarianship . . . and the *Handbook* preserves the heritage of Blacks in librarianship and chronicles current thinking among Afro-American librarians."[6] For hundreds of years the enslaved were forbidden to read, have access to books, and the public library did not welcome them. With some exceptions, slaves were denied access to formal education, books, and the art of reading. The Fourteenth Amendment opened the door to a new chapter in their lives with new possibilities and options.

Knowledge is reflected through progress by African Americans years later as not only readers but as professionals. In the library profession, we must acknowledge a multifaceted legacy by pioneers like Richard T. Greener at the University of South Carolina (1875), Edward C. Williams (1894) at (Case) Western Reserve University's Adelbert College, and Daniel A. P. Murray at the Library of Congress (1880), which opened doors of opportunity at a time when southern Blacks faced severe discrimination and segregation with limited access to education, books, or libraries.

As E. J. Josey stated in his Introduction in the First Edition of *Handbook of Black Librarianship*, "Black Americans have a distinguished history in American librarianship," and "The Handbook, . . . preserves the heritage of Blacks in librarianship and chronicles current thinking among Afro-American librarians."[7] When examining this history, one must acknowledge this multifaceted legacy from pioneers Greener, Williams, and Murray to modern day "firsts": Alma Jacobs, first Black member of the executive board of the American Library Association (1964) and state librarian of Montana (1970); Clara Stanton Jones, first African American director at the Detroit Public Library (1970) and first African American president of the American Library Association (1976); Joseph H. Reason, the first Black president of the Association of College and Research Libraries (1971); Milton S. Byam, first African American director of the Queens Public Library (1974); Lucille C. Thomas, first African American president appointed to the New York State Regents Advisory Council on Libraries

(1973) and the first African American president of the New York Library Association (1977). More recently, Carla Hayden was appointed the first Black woman Librarian of Congress (2016). Today, there are Black library trustees, library president/CEOs, and other administrators, managers, librarians, technical and support staff—all professionals and contributors to the mission of library services.

These librarians share a more basic character trait—principles engrained in people of African ancestry, passed down by our ancestors. This strength to achieve and succeed comes from values to guide our lives by, the belief in oneself from an inner knowledge passed down from generation to generation. As Nelson Mandela wrote in 1990, *"To deny people their human rights is to challenge their very humanity. To impose on them a wretched life of hunger and deprivation is to dehumanize them."*[8]

The winter holiday season concludes with the African American seven-day cultural celebration of Kwanzaa (December 26–January 1), celebrating the seven principles (Nguzo Saba). One principle is recognized each day:

Umoja: Unity
Kujichagulia: Self-Determination
Ujima: Collective Work and Responsibility
Ujamaa: Cooperative Economics
Nia: Purpose
Kuumba: Creativity
Imani: Faith[9]

These principles are based on values engrained in African culture. They have served to help overcome centuries of struggle by people of African ancestry and are at the core of survival and progress for Black librarians.

In the two previous editions of *The Handbook*, one can see how *unity among Black librarians* gave them *a sense of purpose*, to prove their worthiness in a profession riddled with discrimination and racist policies. Grounded in their education and training, Black librarians had a collective mission to enter the profession and prove they were and could be as productive as their counterparts. Against the odds, Black librarians used their creativity to enhance the workplace guided by an unwavering faith in themselves and their mission to succeed. Individual acts of self-determination were faced at the administrative and service levels. Black library professionals overcame obstacles in their efforts to climb the leadership ladder and in their day-to-day roles providing and designing library services to and for communities.

*Collective work* among Black librarians to perform at a high level and provide quality library services in our respective communities is a shared *responsibility*. *Cooperative economics and sufficient funding* are necessary in the ongoing fight for pay and salary equity and for equitable funding of libraries in our communities. Our *purpose*, both as individuals as well as a people, is to succeed and make viable and worthwhile contributions in our chosen fields of librarianship. We make daily expressions of creativity through each person's presentation of themselves and through a wide variety of library programs and services for our customers. These values are incomplete without a strong belief and *faith* (Imani) in ourselves, our mission, and our goals as Black librarians. This reflects the rich history Dr. Josey speaks of in his introduction in the first and second editions of the *Handbook*. This history is also reflected in *The 21st Century Black Librarian: Issues and Challenges* (2012) and the more recent publication of *The Black Librarian in America Reflections, Resistance, and Reawakening* (2022).

More importantly, each edition of the *Handbook* includes the ongoing struggle for full acceptance and recognition of Black librarians and the story of libraries for communities of color across our profession. The preface in *The 21st Century Black Librarian* entitled "The Need for Continued Activism in Black Librarianship" reads,

> The struggle for equality in librarianship is no different from, and, if anything, parallels the struggles for civil and human rights in America. Despite being ignored, dismissed, denied jobs and promotions, discriminated against in the workplace, and denied entry into libraries, hotels, and restaurants, Black men and women librarian ancestors and living elders broke down barriers, kicked in doors, sat in, prayed in, and withstood insults. Black librarians attended conferences and meetings, participated in council sessions and roundtables at ALA annual conferences and mid-winter meetings to move forward an agenda of change and resistance, with or without cooperation of the status quo. . . . Because of those Black librarians of yesterday, black librarians of today, stand tall.[10]

Today, Black librarians are present in every phase of the library profession. From their positions as president and executive director of ALA to president/CEO of public library systems, college and university library directors, and as the librarian of Congress, we stand tall. Although the percentage is small, Black librarians work in public, academic, school, special, and research libraries. Outside the library community, Black librarians also are represented in private industry as well as the publishing industry.

Dr. Josey's published essays and works provide the foundation to understanding the long legacy of struggle by Black librarians. Josey and other colleagues documented this in *The Black Librarian in America* from the 1970s through the last edition published in 2000. The essays examine the growth and progress within our profession while analyzing the similarities of struggle and frustration. In Josey's 1972 book, *What Black Librarians Are Saying*, he wrote in his introduction,

> There is a scarcity of information on Black librarians: views about society in general and about librarianship in particular. Like their fellow Black professionals in other disciplines, they have, for too long, been invisible. Not only have Black librarians been invisible in key lead-

ership positions in the field of librarianship; they have also been scarcely visible in the chronicling of burning issues in the field which affect them as professionals. . . . To paraphrase Professor [Gregory Willis] Hayes, if a history that will include the record of the Black librarian is written, the Black librarian will have to write it.[11]

Since the earlier editions of the Black Librarian series, significant progress has been made in the presence of Black librarians in a wide assortment of positions across our profession. In similar fashion, libraries and library programs and services have improved and expanded in all communities. Dr. James C. Welbourne Jr. in his essay "The Information Potential in the Liberation of Black People" observed that they

> are not as drastic in the 21st Century as they were in the late 20th Century, wrote about imbalance through 20th Century without the presence of Black librarians in the profession as well as in "informationally deprived" inner city communities, where the " . . . information requirements . . . of . . . residents are largely unmet and have resulted in the presence of serious information imbalances. An "information imbalance" is created when the information pool from which a given client pool must draw has been shaped and predetermined by the habits and preferences of so-called professionals, largely drawn from the white American middle class, or else in accordance to the dictates of white racist institutional demands.[12]

Today, communities across our nation are more diverse and multicultural than ever before, represented by multilanguages spoken and multiethnic residents in neighborhoods reflecting the many cultures of the world, all living together. As a result of this world cultural fusion, public, school, and academic library staffing, websites, collections, and programs and services respond to the informational, educational, cultural, and recreational needs of their respective community users. More recently, Carla Hayden wrote in the most recent of the *Black Librarian* series, "The perseverance and contributions of Black librarians will continue to pave the way for the next generations dedicated for service for their communities."[13] ALA past president Julius C. Jefferson Jr. wrote in his afterword to this last edition, "We must center ourselves in the narrative of America's past, present and future and reject the narrative that does not center us. . . . After all, this is the debt we owe our ancestors and the price we pay for our space on earth."[14]

There has been a massive increase in the number of Black librarians since the 1970s. There has also been an incredible increase in diverse and multiethnic library users in public, academic, and school libraries since the mid-1980s. During this same time, there have been invaluable advancements in library technology and an explosion of online information available. Librarians and libraries are on the front line daily, working with students and library customers managing access to accurate information, designing collections, creating programs that respond to the needs of customers, and implementing needed and necessary services. The presence and voice of the Black librarian is invaluable in this effort.

When I reflect on my more than forty years in librarianship that began in 1980, I am thankful for those librarians who guided and nurtured me and are never forgotten. My introduction to the Black Caucus of the American Library Association at the First National Conference of African American Librarians in 1992 exposed me to librarianship on a national level that equally impacted my active participation in the Caucus. On the local and national levels, Karenga's *Nguzo Saba*[15] serve as the window, mirror, and sliding glass door, concepts coined by Rudine Sims Bishop in her narrative on children's literature.[16] We see the world of librarianship as it is and should be through the windows of our homes and communities. Libraries also mirror and reflect the changes and advancements over time to better serve the library customer. At the same time, libraries are the sliding glass doors that allow each person to gain access to multiethnic and multicultural layers of information to see the world as a wonderful place of diversity.

An unforgettable statement from Chimananda Ngozi Adichie's 2009 TED lecture "The Danger of a Single Story" was,

> Stories matter. Many stories matter. Stories have been used to dispossess and to malign, but stories can also be used to empower and to humanize. Stories can break the dignity of a people, but stories can also repair that broken dignity. When we reject the single story, when we realize that there is never a single story about any place, we regain a kind of paradise.[17]

Just as Black history *is* American history, Black librarianship *is* American librarianship. Our voices are important, our stories matter. Our presence at the table is important. Our contributions are an important part of the overall mission of what librarianship is all about and its invaluable contribution to humanity and our future.

Looking at Karenga's seven principles of Kwanzaa connects to those "critical principals for libraries and librarianship" conceived by S. R. Ranganathan (1892–1972): "Books Are for Use; Every Reader His/Her Book; Every Book Its Reader; Save the Time of the Reader; and The Library Must Be a Growing Organism."[18] These laws were updated in 1995 by former ALA president Michael Gorman: "Libraries serve humanity; Respect all forms by which knowledge is communicated; Use technology intelligently to enhance service; Protect free access to knowledge and Honor the past and create the future."

Like Karenga's Nguzo Saba cultural values, Ranganathan's and Gorman's laws serve as values for librarianship. As Rubin states in *Foundations of Library and Information Science Fourth Edition*, "Values are strongly held beliefs that serve to guide our actions . . . we associate them with words like convictions and principals, more than just opinions. Values structure our experiences and provide insight when we must make important decisions."[19]

I close with an excerpt, in remembrance of our Black librarian ancestors, from Bernard J. Keller's poem, "We Are Their Flags and Banners," "We are the product of their struggle, of their stubborn refusal to disappear without a trace. We are the words they could not speak and the thoughts they could not read. We are the dreams they dreamed and hopes they held. We are their legacy, and we are their pride. We are their children." It is our hope that this edition reflects Gorman's fifth law by honoring our past and inspires the future.

## NOTES

1. John Henrik Clarke, *Notes from an African World Revolution Africans at the Crossroads. Image and Mind Control in the African World.* Trenton, NJ: Africa World Press, Inc., 1991.
2. Abraham Lincoln, *A Proclamation by the President of the United States of America.* Washington, DC: War Department Adjutant General's Office, 1863. https://www.archives.gov/exhibits/featured-documents/emancipation-proclamation/transcript.html.
3. *Declaration of Independence and Constitution of the United States of America.* https://www.archives.gov/founding-docs/declaration-transcript.
4. Ibid.
5. Frederick Douglass, *My Bondage and My Freedom.* New York: Miller Orton & Mulligan, 1855.
6. E. J. Josey and Ann Allen Shockley, eds., *Handbook of Black Librarianship.* Littleton, CO: Libraries Unlimited, Inc., 1977, 11.
7. Ibid.
8. Nelson Mandela, *Notes to the Future. Human Rights Are Ingrained.* New York: Atria Books, 2012.
9. Maulana Karenga, *Kwanzaa: A Celebration of Family, Community & Culture* (Los Angeles, CA: University of Sankore Press, 2008).
10. Andrew P. Jackson, "Preface," *The 21st Century Black Librarian in America: Issues and Challenges*, edited by Andrew P. Jackson, Julius C. Jefferson Jr., and Akilah S. Nosakhere (Lanham: Scarecrow, 2012), xviii.
11. E. J. Josey, "Introduction," *What Black Librarians Are Saying*, edited by E. J. Josey (Metuchen, NJ: Scarecrow Press, 1972), 5.
12. James C. Welbourne, "Achieving Black Economic Self-Reliance: The Urban Public Library Strengthens the Economic Base of Its Community," in *The Black Librarian in America Revisited*, edited by E. J. Josey (Metuchen, NJ: Scarecrow Press, 1994), 128-32.
13. Carla D. Hayden, "Foreword," *The Black Librarian in America: Reflections, Resistance, and Reawakening*, edited by Shauntee Burns-Simpson, Nichelle M. Hayes, Ana Ndumu, and Shaundra Walker (Lanham: Rowman & Littlefield, 2022), xii.
14. Julius Jefferson Jr., "Afterword: State of Black Librarianship," *The Black Librarian in America: Reflections, Resistance, and Reawakening*, edited by Shauntee Burns-Simpson, Nichelle M. Hayes, Ana Ndumu, and Shaundra Walker (Lanham: Rowman & Littlefield, 2022), 265.
15. Maulana Karenga, *Kwanzaa: A Celebration of Family, Community & Culture* (Los Angeles, CA: University of Sankore Press, 2008).
16. Rudine Sims Bishop, "Mirrors, Windows and Sliding Glass Doors," *Perspectives: Choosing and Using Books for the Classroom*, 6, no. 3 (1990): ix-xi.
17. Chimananda Ngozi Adichie, "The Danger of a Single Story," *TED*, 2009, https://www.ted.com/talks/chimamanda_ngozi_adichie_the_danger_of_a_single_story?language=en
18. "Future Libraries, Crawford & Gorman," *American Library Association*, 7 December 2006, http://www.ala.org/aboutala/offices/publishing/editions/samplers/futurelibraries, doi: b881f09e-20e5-fca4-a9b5-73212093469.
19. Richard E. Rubin, "Chapter 10: The Values and Ethics of Library and Information Science." In *Foundations of Library and Information Science*, 4th ed. Chicago: ALA Neal-Schuman, an imprint of the American Library Association, 2016.

## BIBLIOGRAPHY

Adichie, Chimananda Ngozi. "The Danger of a Single Story," *TED*, 2009. https://www.ted.com/talks/chimamanda_ngozi_adichie_the_danger_of_a_single_story?language=en.

Bishop, Rudine Sims. "Mirrors, Windows and Sliding Glass Doors," *Perspectives: Choosing and Using Books for the Classroom*, 6, no. 3 (1990): ix-xi.

Clarke, John Henrik. *Notes from an African World Revolution Africans at the Crossroads. Image and Mind Control in the African World.* Trenton, NJ: Africa World Press, Inc., 1991.

*Declaration of Independence and Constitution of the United States of America.* https://www.archives.gov/founding-docs/declaration-transcript.

Douglass, Frederick. *My Bondage and My Freedom The Nature of Slavery.* New York: Miller Orton & Mulligan, 1855.

"Future Libraries, Crawford & Gorman." *American Library Association*, 7 December 2006. http://www.ala.org/aboutala/offices/publishing/editions/samplers/futurelibraries, doi: b881f09e-20e5-fca4-a9b5-73212093469.

Hayden, Carla D. "Foreword," In *The Black Librarian in America: Reflections, Resistance, and Reawakening*, edited by Shauntee Burns-Simpson, Nichelle M. Hayes, Ana Ndumu, and Shaundra Walker. Lanham: Rowman & Littlefield, 2022.

Jackson, Andrew P. "Preface," *The 21st Century Black Librarian in America: Issues and Challenges*, edited by Andrew P. Jackson, Julius C. Jefferson Jr., and Akilah S. Nosakhere. Lanham: Scarecrow, 2012.

Jefferson, Julius. "Afterword: State of Black Librarianship," *The Black Librarian in America: Reflections, Resistance, and Reawakening*, edited by Shauntee Burns-Simpson, Nichelle M. Hayes, Ana Ndumu, and Shaundra Walker. Lanham: Rowman & Littlefield, 2022.

Josey, E. J., and Marva L. DeLoach, eds. *Handbook of Black Librarianship.* 2nd ed. Lanham, MD: The Scarecrow Press, Inc., 2000.

Josey, E. J., and Ann Allen Shockley, eds. *Handbook of Black Librarianship.* Littleton, CO: Libraries Unlimited, Inc., 1977.

Josey, E. J., ed., *What Black Librarians Are Saying*. Metuchen, NJ: The Scarecrow Press, Inc., 1972.

Karenga, Maulana. *Kwanzaa: A Celebration of Family, Community & Culture*. Los Angeles, CA: University of Sankore Press, 2008.

Lincoln, Abraham. *A Proclamation by the President of the United States of America*. Washington: War Dept. Adjutant General's Office, 1863. https://www.archives.gov/exhibits/featured-documents/emancipation-proclamation/transcript.html.

Mandela, Nelson. *Notes to the Future. Human Rights Are Ingrained*. New York: Atria Books, 2012.

Rubin, Richard E. "Chapter 10: The Values and Ethics of Library and Information Science." In *Foundations of Library and Information Science*. 4th ed. Chicago: ALA Neal-Schuman, an imprint of the American Library Association, 2016.

Welbourne, James C. "Achieving Black Economic Self-Reliance: The Urban Public Library Strengthens the Economic Base of Its Community." In *The Black Librarian in America Revisited*, edited by E. J. Josey, 128-132. Metuchen, NJ: Scarecrow Press, 1994.

# Introduction

Marva L. DeLoach and Michele Fenton

It has been over twenty-three years since the second edition of the *Handbook of Black Librarianship* was published. Since then, many advances in libraries and librarianship have taken place with the continued expansion of the internet, the growth of social media, and the rise of artificial intelligence (AI) and ChatGPT. Libraries can now connect with patrons and each other virtually with Zoom and similar platforms and lend ebooks that are downloaded to devices in a matter of minutes. Prospective librarians can complete their entire course online and attend conferences and workshops from home or wherever they may be with just a click of the mouse at a computer or by tapping an app on a mobile device.

In addition to the new innovations in library technology, African Americans are also making tremendous strides in the library profession through leadership and literature. Dr. Carla Hayden, past president of the American Library Association (ALA) and past director of the Enoch Pratt Free Library in Baltimore, Maryland, is the first African American and the first woman to serve as the Librarian of Congress. Tracie Hall is the first African American woman to serve as the executive director of ALA. Two additional volumes have been added to the Black Librarian in America series, *The 21st Century Black Librarian in America: Issues and Challenges* (2012) and *The Black Librarian in America: Reflections, Resistance, and Reawakening* (2022), the latter being the first in the series published by an all-woman editorial team.

Sadly, as mentioned in the previous editions, racism, discrimination, exclusion, inequality, and injustice are still ever-present, fueled by forces within and outside the profession. We see libraries and librarians threatened with loss of funding and jobs because of the political aspirations and hate-filled motivations of persons seeking to ban access to information and ideas that are different from their own and to subjugate, erase, and silence the voices of marginalized communities. The COVID-19 Pandemic exposed the digital divide, as people, especially students, struggled to access needed technology to complete their schoolwork and jobs from home. We have witnessed attacks on and the elimination of diversity, equity, inclusion, justice, and accessibility (DEIJA) initiatives and the dismantling of affirmative action by the United States Supreme Court—all fostered and aided by disgruntled individuals and groups seeking to maintain the status quo through oppression, marginalization, and disenfranchisement. Despite this, librarians, library workers, supporters, and communities are standing together in solidarity to uplift, support, and fight for diversity, equality, equity, access, inclusion, and justice in the library profession, library services, library and information science (LIS) education, and in society as a whole—not just locally but globally; not just for some but for all.

In designing this edition of the *Handbook of Black Librarianship*, we the editors built upon the wisdom and history shared by E. J. Josey, Anne Allen Shockley, and Marva DeLoach in the first and second editions and combined them with those of the new generation of library workers, library supporters, and librarians to produce a reference tool and guide for anyone wanting to explore issues, advances, and contributions of the Black/African diaspora to libraries and librarianship. Arranged into nineteen sections, the third edition of the *Handbook of Black Librarianship* covers issues and topics related to LIS education, health, technology, international libraries, public, school, academic, special, and government libraries, multiculturalism, collaborations between libraries and other institutions, DEIJA, and much more.

Part I, "Pioneers and Landmark Episodes," of the third edition begins with a revised and updated "Chronology of Events in Black Librarianship," first compiled by Dr. E. J. Josey and Casper LeRoy Jordan in the first and second editions. Michele Fenton, Deloice Holliday, and Brenda Johnson-Perkins have added events preceding those of the original timeline, beginning in 1794 and ending in 2023. Next Andrew Sekou Jackson shares the chronology of the National Conference of African American Librarians (NCAAL) followed by the chronology of the BCALA Trailblazer Award and the DEMCO/BCALA Award for Excellence in Librarianship compiled by Michele Fenton. Casper Jordan's "African American Forerunners in Librarianship," which appeared in the two previous editions, is given a much-needed update and revision by Michele Fenton. From Jacqueline Jones and Melanie

Sims, we learn about Dr. Alma E. Dawson, professor emeritus at Louisiana State University and winner of the American Library Association's Equality Award, in their chapter "Alma E. Dawson: Inspiring a Legacy of Mentorship." Talisha Harrison tells the story of four pioneering Black women librarians in "Hidden Figures in African American Librarianship: Charlemae Hill Rollins, Miriam Matthews, Naomi Willie Pollard Dobson, and Dorothy Burnett Porter Wesley." Vera Whisenton shares highlights of the career of her husband Andre Carl Whisenton (1944–2019) in "Andre Carl Whisenton." In "Black Diasporic Memory Keeper: Arturo Alphonso Schomburg (1874–1938)," Dr. Ana Ndumu and Manuel Mendez paint an exquisite portrait of Arturo Alphonso Schomburg, a collector of historical manuscripts and artifacts of the African/Black diaspora and for whom the Schomburg Center for Black Literature and Culture is named.

Part II, "Black Library/Librarian Associations and Collaborations in the Twenty-First Century," examines professional associations for Black library workers and the partnerships between these associations and other organizations. From Dr. Stanton Biddle, we learn of the leaders and officers who served and continue to serve BCALA in "Leadership in the Black Caucus of the American Library Association (BCALA), 1970–2025." Shauntee Burns-Simpson and Nichelle M. Hayes provide a history of the partnerships and collaborations of BCALA with other organizations in "Black Library/Librarian Associations and Collaborations in the Twenty-First Century." Rudolph Clay shares the state, regional, and local affiliates of BCALA in "BCALA Affiliates." From Gladys Smiley Bell's "BCALA (Black Caucus of the American Library Association) Literary Awards: Celebrating Twenty-Nine years of 'Black Resistance,'" we learn of the history of the BCALA Literary Awards and the importance of recognizing and supporting African American authors and literature. In "Librarians and Libraries, Part of Our Foundation," Wade Hudson and Cheryl Willis-Hudson, the power behind JustUs Books, talk about their work with libraries and librarians in publishing books for children that celebrate Black/African American heritage and culture. Closing out this section, past BCALA president Richard Ashby Jr. talks about the importance of literacy initiatives in communities of color in his chapter, "LiteracyNation: 'With Literacy and Justice for All.'"

Part III, "Vital Issues," focuses on issues, impact, and values in Black librarianship. These twenty-six chapters address new areas that were not covered in the first and second editions. In the first section Antoine McDonald speaks on issues facing Black male librarians in "Issues Facing Black Male Librarians in 2023." Gemmicka Piper's "A Black Alt-Ac Speaks: Early Career Librarianship Trauma" speaks on the effects of racism, discrimination, toxic workspaces, and a lack of support on the well-being of Black librarians. Candace Owens's "Issues, Impact, and Values in Black Librarianship" and Rodney Freeman's "Librarian-ish" focus on the obstacles, visible and invisible, faced by Black librarians seeking to grow and advance in the library field.

The next section, "Issues in Library and Information Science Education," Amina Turner shares her address given to the 2018 graduating class of LIS students at North Carolina Central University. We learn of the importance of HBCUs in LIS education in "The Beacon of Light: North Carolina Central University's School of Library and Information Sciences' Historical Role in Educating Black Librarians and Present Role in Advancing Artificial Intelligence, Biomedical Knowledge, Digital Equity" by Jamillah Scott-Branch, Vernice Faison, and Danielle Colbert-Lewis, and in "HBCUs and LIS Education: A Legacy and Counterstory" by Dr. Ana Ndumu, Dr. Renate Chancellor, and Tina Rollins. Dr. Jason Alston speaks on library science education from the instructor's point of view in "As a LIS Instructor, Am I Part of the Problem?" Closing out this section, Katie Perry and Michele Fenton examine the history of educating Black librarians in their essays "Chronology of Black LIS Education" and "Paving the Way: LIS Education and Black Librarians in Indiana."

The third section, "Issues in Equity, Diversity, Inclusion and Multiculturalism," focuses on the benefits, ways, and challenges of promoting equity, diversity, inclusion, and multiculturalism in libraries and the library field. Librarians share their views, experiences, and ideas on this subject in Aisha Aminu's "Know Your History: Information Organization in House/Ball Culture and the Potential for Librarianship," Roland Barksdale-Hall's "Reconstitution of Ubuntu Spaces, Leading While an Ujima Culture Keeper," Angiah Davis and Michelle E. Jones's "Fostering Inclusion through Programming and Outreach," and Taina K. Solano Evans's "How Has Diversity, Equity, and Inclusion Impacted the BIPOC Library Professional?" Additional chapters addressing this topic are Syntychia Kendrick-Samuel's "Ginga Librarianship/Beautiful Librarianship," Conrad Pegues's "If You Don't Understand Me, It's Your Fault: Black Librarians and the Distraction of Equity, Diversity, and Inclusion," Nicole Cooke's "Radical Imagination in Libraries: Reimagining Ourselves in Order to Reimagine Our Communities," Courtney Shareef's "On Diversity: Proposing an Institutional Commitment to Change and Accountability," Lorin Jackson and Jazmyne Baylor's "In the Weeds: Challenging Performative Allyship Amid Widespread Traumatic Events," and Jeffrion L. Aubry's "Essay from Assembly Member Jeffrion L. Aubry."

In the fourth section, "Issues and Advances in Medical Librarianship," Shannon Jones, Kelsa Bartley, and Jamia Williams speak on representation in medical librarianship in "Making the Invisible Visible: Amplifying the Contributions of African American Health Sciences Librarians." In "Up All Night: The First Twenty-Four-Hour Black Health and Healing Summit from Queens Public Library," Jill Anderson, Tamara Michel, Kim McNeil Capers, and Janet Umenta share takeaways from the first Black Health and Healing Summit, a joint event hosted by the Queens Public Library and the Black Caucus of the American Library Association during the pandemic.

In the final section of this chapter, "Issues by Library Professionals without an MLS/MLIS Degree," DJ Bond, Robert Hall, Carolyn Lawrence, and Lisa Soler share their experiences, reflections, and observations on what it is like being a library professional without a library degree and the challenges and successes that come with the role.

Part IV, "Service to Our Communities," examines different types of libraries and the challenges and triumphs of each. This part also focuses on the experiences of those working in these libraries: librarians, directors, trustees, and staff.

Academic libraries are represented by Dr. Renate Chancellor's "On the Other Side of the Tenure Track: Retention and Promotion of Black Academic Law Librarians"; Melanie E. Sims's "The Accidental Law Librarian"; and Rashida Scott Blades and Genevia Chamblee Smith's "Getting the Job: Black Librarian in Academic Libraries." Through their contributions we learn of challenges faced by Black academic librarians in seeking employment, considering and evaluating career choices, and navigating the tenure and promotion process.

Next, public libraries are spotlighted with Aletta Seales's "The Importance of Public Library Youth Services in the Community," and Andrew P. Jackson's two chapters, "My Nontraditional Journey in Librarianship" and "African American Research Libraries (Public Libraries)." Additional pieces on public libraries include "It Takes a Village: Formulating Liaisons between Public Libraries and African American Homeschooling Families" by Raphael Daoud Jackson-Ortiz; "Leading with Knowledge: Programs and Services in BIPOC Communities and the Importance of Representation (What Progress Has Been Made in Serving the Black Community in over Twenty Years?)" by James Allen Davis Jr. and Leslie Williams; "Being a Youth Services Librarian" by Tahira Ahmad; "Land of Endless Dreams & Possibilities!!!!!" by Judi Belle Raines; "The Great Escape" by C. Atterbury; and "Black Male Librarians: Advocating for Children and Literacy" by Tiffeni Fontno. In these chapters on public libraries, the authors touch on the importance of libraries in providing access to materials, services, and programming in meeting the information needs of the communities they serve, and the numerous opportunities for librarians and library workers to engage, share, and connect with patrons. In the final chapter on public libraries, Kelly Richards shares his journey from police officer to library director in "From Badge to Books: A Journey of Community Care and Library Legacy."

For school libraries, we have Sandra Michele Echols and Eboni Henry's "The Game Changer: Becoming a School Librarian" and Miriam Thomas and Chanelle Maynard's "The Pivotal Role of Black School Librarians in Promoting Diversity, Equity, and Inclusion in Education vis-à-vis Culturally Responsive Pedagogy." Both emphasize the importance of school librarians in fostering a love of reading and promoting literacy and critical thinking skills in students, and the necessity for supporting those wanting to pursue a career in school librarianship.

Special libraries are represented by Jina Duvernay's "Counternarratives in Practice," Jameka Lewis's "The Blair-Caldwell African American Research Library, Denver, Colorado," and Victor E. Simmons Jr.'s "The Auburn Avenue Research Library on African American Culture and History: A Rich History Leading the Way in the South." These three chapters emphasize the importance of collecting, documenting, preserving, and providing access to collections representing the cultural heritage of the African/Black diaspora.

For state and federal libraries, past BCALA president Jos N. Holman writes a compelling essay, "Twenty Years as County Librarian: A Legacy," on his experiences as the director of the Tippecanoe County (Indiana) Public Library. For museums, we have Regina Bain's "Louis Armstrong as Archivist," in which Bain shares the history of the Louis Armstrong House Museum and its importance in keeping alive the legacy of Louis Armstrong.

This section concludes with four library trustees sharing their experiences, thoughts, and observations on libraries and library services with "Experiences as a Library Trustee" by Laura Ellis, "Being a Library Trustee" by Andrew P. Jackson, "Empowerment, Representation, and Leadership: A Reflection on Joining the QPL Board" by Cloyette Harris-Stoute, and "The Importance of the Public Library: A Trustee Perspective" by Earl Simons.

Part V, "Library Technology and Black Librarianship," examines the influence of technological advances on communities, education, libraries, and the library profession. Willa Liburd Tavernier and Maria E. Hamilton Abegunde's "Open Pedagogy as the Intersection of Digital Skills and Community" talks about the use of digital tools and technology in enhancing and advancing the learning experiences of users and teaching methods of educators. Ahalya Sudev writes about overcoming the challenges of providing library services to special needs students during the pandemic in "Libraries' Part in Solving Problems of Inclusive Online Education during the Pandemic." Next, Dawn Kight and Maletta Payne talk about the importance of digital repositories in historically Black colleges and universities in "Digital Access and Historically Black College and University Libraries." Finally, Kelvin Watson shares how the Las Vegas-Clark County Library is expanding access to services to underserved communities in "How Tech Has Enhanced the Jobs of Library Professionals."

Part VI, "Pearls of Wisdom from Our Retirees," is filled with advice, wisdom, reflections, and anecdotes from retired librarians and library workers on dealing with racism, advancing in the field, service to communities, and mentoring others. Sharing these pearls are Phyllis Green Mack, Ida D. McGhee, Marcia Smith-Woodard, Joyce C. Wright, Stephanie Tolson, and Jessie Carney Smith. Additional contributors include Gloria J. Mims, Marshelle Berry, Irene Owens, Linda Jolivet, Sharon D. Banks, Thomas Alford, Carolyn Lowe Garnes, and Sandy Bright. Their contributions are testimonies to faith, fortitude, courage, and greatness, and we are grateful to them for lending their voices to uplift, encourage, and inspire librarians and library workers of all generations.

Part VII, "Global Issues in Libraries," focuses on international libraries and the issues, challenges, and triumphs faced by them. Loida Garcia-Febo talks about how libraries can help foster the implementation of the United Nations' 17 Sustainable Development Goals (SDGs) in "Unlocking Libraries' Potential to Improve the Lives and Prospects of the Members of Our Communities." Next, Franciéle Carneiro Garcês-da-Silva shares what it is like being a Black librarian in Brazil in her chapter, "Brazilian Black Librarianship: Paths Struggles, and Resistance." In the final chapter of this section, "Understanding the Journey: Exploring Information Challenges Faced by Migrants in India and Library Interventions," Aysha Zakiya A speaks on the challenges of providing information services to migrants in India during the pandemic and the solutions and lessons learned from this experience.

Part VIII, "Banned Books and Censorship Issues," focuses on the attacks on intellectual freedom and the banning of books, in particular those written by and about Black, Indigenous, and People of Color (BIPOC), LQBTQIA+, and other marginalized communities. We see this subject addressed magnificently in Elizabeth Brumfield's "Racial Colorblind Theory and Book Acquisition" and Edith Campbell's "Always Been There: The Cultural Politics of Children's Books and Black Librarians."

The last section, Part XI, "Books, Periodicals, and Other Resources Recommended for Black Collections," focuses on materials of interest to those wanting to build and enhance their collections of the Black/African Diaspora. In "Selected Bibliography of Works by Dr. E. J. Josey" and a "Brief Bibliography of Essays and Journal Articles by Dr. E. J. Josey," Andrew Sekou Jackson and Marva DeLoach share the contributions of Dr. E. J. Josey to the professional literature. Carol Gilliam shares a beautifully curated list of books on music, health, poetry, and Black history in "Spring Reading List 2023." Next, Mitzi Mack shares resources on bibliotherapy targeted to African American youth in "Bibliotherapy: African American Youth and Mental Health." Monique Threatt explores the Black/African diaspora's contribution to film in "Bibliography of Select African and African American Films for Collection Development and Academic Course Instruction." Next is Christine Zarett's "Black Heritage Reference Collection: Langston Hughes Community Library and Cultural Center," highlighting titles and authors in the library's immense collection of reference materials on Black/African Americans. Concluding this section is Marva DeLoach's "Selected US Bookstores by State That Are Black-Owned and/or Specialize in Black Books and Other Black Resources," an excellent guide for people wanting to purchase Black literature and support Black authors and Black bookstores.

Preceding the nineteen sections are tributes to Dr. Josey and his work by friends, family, and colleagues who knew and collaborated with him—George C. Grant, Binnie Tate Wilkin, Malika Lumumba, and Amina Turner (Elaine Josey Turner). Through their voices we learn of a steadfast, courageous, committed, and unwavering individual who championed for the inclusion, representation, and support of librarians, LIS students, and library workers of the Black/African diaspora in the library field.

In closing, we the editors hope this volume will prove helpful as a vital, valuable, and empowering resource. We extend a hearty, heart-warming thanks to all the authors who contributed to this work. Without them, this project would not have been possible. We are very grateful to Rowman & Littlefield for their support and guidance in making sure this much needed volume came to fruition. We also give thanks to the Black Caucus of the American Library Association and its affiliates for their continued support. Finally, we give many accolades, thanks, gratitude, and honor to Dr. E. J. Josey, Anne Allen Shockley, and Marva DeLoach for paving the way for the *Handbook of Black Librarianship* to be a much revered, honored, sacred, and celebrated work amplifying the voices and contributions of the Black/African diaspora to the world of library and information science!

# Part I
# PIONEERS AND LANDMARK EPISODES

# Chapter 1
# A Chronology of Events in Black Librarianship

# 1.1

## A Chronology of Events in Black Librarianship

Casper LeRoy Jordan and E. J. Josey; Updated by Michele Fenton, Deloice Holliday, and Brenda Johnson-Perkins

| | |
|---|---|
| 1794 | Richard Allen and Absalom Jones, authors of *A Narrative of the Proceedings of the Black People during the Late Awful Calamity in Philadelphia*, become the first African Americans to have their work copyrighted. |
| 1795 | Amos Fortune, a formerly enslaved African American, helped found and establish the Jaffrey Social Library in Jaffrey, New Hampshire. |
| 1808 | *An Enquiry Concerning the Intellectual and Moral Faculties and Literature of Negroes* was published by Henri Greguire. |
| 1816 | A school and library were organized for African Americans in Wilmington, Delaware. |
| 1832 | The Library Company of Philadelphia was founded by African Americans as a literary society. |
| 1842 | The Mt. Pleasant Library opens inside the Mt. Pleasant Church of the Beech Settlement, a community of free African Americans in Rush County, Indiana. |
| 1871 | Daniel Alexander Payne Murray (1852–1925) joined the staff of the Library of Congress as personal assistant to Ainsworth Rand Spofford, Librarian of Congress. |

| | |
|---|---|
| 1875 | Richard T. Greener (1844–1922) functioned as university librarian at the University of South Carolina and reorganized the library and prepared a catalog. Greener was also the first Black person to receive a degree from Harvard University (1870). |
| | Daniel Alexander Payne Murray (1852–1925) was appointed assistant librarian at the Library of Congress. |
| | Edward Christopher Williams (1871–1929) was appointed librarian at Western Reserve University's Adelbert College, Cleveland, Ohio. |
| 1896 | George Washington Forbes (1864–1927) was designated assistant librarian, West End Branch of the Boston Public Library, where he served generations of diverse patrons for over thirty years. |
| | The United States Supreme Court decision *Plessy v. Ferguson* established the "separate but equal" doctrine as a "reasonable" use of state police power and was responsible for segregated library facilities for African Americans. The decision remained in effect until the 1954 *Brown v. Board of Education* decision. |

|  |  |
|---|---|
| 1897 | Alexander Crummel (1819-1898) organized the American Negro Academy to promote literature, science, and art, and to foster higher education. |
| 1900 | A Carnegie library was built at Tuskegee Institute, Alabama. |
| | Daniel Alexander Payne Murray (1852-1925) edited his *Preliminary List of Books and Pamphlets by Negro Authors* for the Negro Exhibit provided for the Paris Exhibition of 1900. |
| | Edward Christopher Williams (1871-1929) graduated from the New York State Library School as the first professionally trained Black librarian. |
| | S. W. Starks (1866-1908) was appointed West Virginia State Librarian and held the position until 1906. |
| 1903 | Charlotte (North Carolina) Public Library created a separate library for African Americans with an independent board of governance, the earliest example of an independent African American library. |
| | Cossitt Library, Memphis, Tennessee, entered into a contract with Lemoyne Institute to provide library service to African Americans. |
| | The General Education Board was established, through the philanthropy of the Rockefellers, to promote education without discrimination, and grew into a great force for progress in African American education and librarianship. |
| 1904 | Carnegie Library buildings were erected at Alabama A&M College, Atlanta University, Benedict College, Talladega College, and Wilberforce University. |
| | Edward Christopher Williams (1871-1929) joined the library school faculty at Western Reserve University. |
| | Rosenberg Library of Galveston, Texas, established a branch for African American patrons. This was the first structure erected to provide public library quarters for exclusive use of the African American population. |
| 1905 | Atlanta University Press published *A Select Bibliography of the Negro American*, compiled by W. E. B. Du Bois. |
| | Carnegie Libraries were built at Cheyney State Teachers College, Johnson C. Smith University, Livingstone College, and Fisk University. |
| | The Hampton Institute Library began special Black collections with the gift of the George Peabody Collection of the Negro. |
| | The Louisville (Kentucky) Free Public Library established the first public library in America exclusively for African Americans. It was operated and administered entirely by African Americans, although supervised by the main library. |
| | Thomas Fountain Blue (1866-1935) joined the staff of Louisville Free Public Library becoming the first African American to head a public library branch. |
| 1906 | A Carnegie Library was erected at Wiley College, Marshall, Texas. |
| | Savannah, Georgia, initiated independent governance for African American branch service, the second instance of this type of action. |
| 1907 | Carnegie Libraries were built at Howard University and Knoxville College. |
| 1908 | The Department of Records and Research was founded by Monroe Nathan Work (1866-1945) at Tuskegee Institute. |
| 1910 | James H. Gregory of Marblehead, Massachusetts, funded a traveling library extension service for southern African Americans. The service was known as the Marblehead Libraries and the extension service for African Americans was administered by Atlanta University. |
| | In the Louisville Free Public Library, an apprentice class for African Americans was organized, the first example of any attempt in the South to provide library training for the prospective African American librarian. The last classes were held in 1928-1929. |
| 1911 | The Negro Society for Historical Research was begun. |
| 1912 | The first edition of *The Negro Yearbook* appeared, edited by Monroe N. Work. Nine editions in all were published (1912-1938). |
| 1913 | William F. Yust attempted, perhaps for the first time, to establish the status of African Americans in the American public library scene with his "What of the Black and Yellow Races?" *ALA Bulletin* 7 (July 1913): 159-67. |

|  |  |
|------|-------|
| 1914 | The Moorland Foundation Collection was formed at Howard University as a gift of Jesse Edward Moorland (1863-1940), a Howard trustee and bibliophile. |
| | The Cherry Street Branch of the Evansville (Indiana) Public Library, a Carnegie Library for African Americans opens for service. It is the sole Carnegie Library for African Americans in the North. |
| 1915 | Lillian Haydon Childress Hall (1889-1958) becomes the first African American awarded a certificate from the Indiana Public Library Commission Summer School for Librarians. |
| 1916 | *A Bibliographical Checklist of American Negro Poets* was published by Arthur Alfonso Schomburg. |
| 1917 | *Negro Education, a Study of the Private and Higher Schools for Colored People in the United States* by Thomas J. Jones was published by the United States Bureau of Higher Education. |
| 1920 | Catherine Allen Latimer (c. 1895-1948) became the first African American professional librarian at the New York Public Library; she was assigned to the 135th Street Branch, which is now the Schomburg Center for Research in Black Culture. |
| 1921 | The American Library Association (ALA) establishes the Work with Negroes Round Table. |
| | Daniel A. P. Murray retired from the Library of Congress after thirty-two years of service. |
| | J. Arthur Jackson was appointed State Librarian of West Virginia. |
| | Thomas Fountain Blue addressed a session of the ALA Conference in Detroit; he is regarded as the first African American to have a place on an ALA program. |
| 1922 | The Paul Laurence Dunbar Branch of the Indianapolis Public Library opens for service. It is the system's first branch to open in an African American neighborhood. Lillian Haydon Childress Hall is the branch's first manager. |
| 1923 | Sadie Petersen Delaney (1889-1959) launched the library at the Tuskegee Veterans Hospital and began her pioneering efforts in the field of bibliotherapy. |
| | Virginia Proctor Powell Florence graduated from the Carnegie Institute of Technology in Pittsburgh, Pennsylvania, becoming the first African American woman librarian to graduate from an accredited library school. |
| 1924 | Belle Da Costa Greene (born Belle Marion Greener) (1879-1950) was appointed director of the Pierpont Morgan Library. |
| 1925 | The Division of Negro Literature, History, and Prints was established at the New York Public Library. |
| | Hampton Institute (Virginia) Library School was established with Florence Rising Curtis as director. |
| 1926 | Negro History Week was inaugurated by Carter G. Woodson and the Association for the Study of African American Life and History (ASALH). |
| | The Schomburg Collection was purchased with funding provided by the Carnegie Corporation at the request of the National Urban League for the New York Public Library. |
| 1927 | The First Negro Library Conference was held at the Hampton Institute, Hampton, Virginia, March 15-17. The conference was chaired by Thomas Fountain Blue and funded by the Carnegie Corporation. |
| | Miriam Matthews (1905-2003) was appointed as the first African American professional librarian in the Los Angeles Public Library system. |
| 1928 | Monroe N. Work compiled the landmark *Bibliography of the Negro in Africa and America*. |
| | *Survey of Negro Colleges and Universities* by Arthur Klein was published by the United States Office of Education. |
| | The American Library Association held its annual conference at the West Baden Springs Hotel in West Baden, Indiana. It is the only ALA conference that was held in Indiana. Several notable African American librarians were in attendance: Reverend Thomas Fountain Blue, Edward C. Williams, Etka Braboy Gaskin, Rachel D. Harris, Lillian Childress Hall, Hallie Beachem Brooks, Elnora McIntyre Roy, Rebecca Bond, and Othella Roberts. |
| 1930 | A conference for African American librarians was held at the Morehouse-Spelman Summer School. It was financed by the Rosenwald Fund. |
| | Louis S. Shores published "Public Library Service to Negroes," *Library Journal* 55 (February 1930): 150-54. |
| | The Second Negro Library Conference was held at Fisk University under the direction of Louis S. Shores, November 20-23. |

|  |  |
|---|---|
| 1932 | Arthur Alphonso Schomburg (1874–1938) was selected curator of the African American research collection, New York Public Library, which was later named for him. |
| | Margaret Reynolds Hunton graduates from the Syracuse University Library Science Program. She is the earliest known African American to graduate from the program. |
| 1933 | The Commission on Interracial Cooperation called a conference on "Education and Race Relations" to discuss the treatment of African Americans in textbooks. |
| 1936 | The American Library Association took a stand against holding segregated conferences. This was prompted by events at the 1936 ALA Annual Conference in Richmond, Virginia, in which African American attendees were denied access to exhibits, dining events, and rooms at the conference hotel because of the state's segregation laws. |
| 1937 | Herbert Isaac Ernest Dhlomo is appointed the first librarian-organizer for the Carnegie Non-European Library Service (Transvaal) in South Africa. |
| 1939 | Hampton Institute Library School closed. |
| 1940 | Eliza Atkins Gleason (1909–2009) was awarded the first PhD in librarianship to an African American. Her University of Chicago dissertation was entitled *The Southern Negro and the Public Library*. |
| 1941 | The Atlanta University School of Library Service opened with Eliza Atkins Gleason as dean. |
| | The North Carolina Central University's School of Library Science was inaugurated with Susan Grey Akers, dean of the Durham school and the library school at Chapel Hill. She held both deanships until 1946. |
| | The Carnegie Corporation and the General Education Board financed a library conference at Atlanta University, heralding the opening of the A.U. School of Library Science. |
| | The Carnegie Corporation made several grants to historically Black colleges and universities (HBCUs) to assist in the upgrading of their library resources. |
| 1942 | The Carnegie Corporation financed the establishment of a field service program to enrich African American school libraries in the South; the program was under the direction of Hallie Beacham Brooks (1907–1985) of Atlanta University. |
| | The establishment of the James Weldon Johnson Collection was announced at Yale University Library as a gift from the noted writer, Carl Van Vechten. |
| 1943 | Arna W. Bontemps (1902–1973) was named the first Black university librarian at Fisk University. Two illustrious white librarians, Louis S. Shores and Carl White, immediately preceded Bontemps. |
| | The E. Azalia Hackley Memorial Collection on Black music, dance, and drama opened in the Detroit Public Library. |
| | Virginia Lacy Jones (1912–1984) was awarded the second PhD in librarianship to an African American; her dissertation was *The Problems of Negro High School Libraries in Selected Southern Cities* (University of Chicago). |
| | *North American Negro Poets: A Bibliographic Checklist of Their Writing* was published by Dorothy B. Porter. |
| 1946 | The Arthur Spingarn Collection of Black Authors was purchased by Howard University to form the Moorland-Spingarn Collection. |
| | The Henry Proctor Collection was purchased by the Atlanta University Library as the nucleus of its Black Collection. |
| 1947 | The Atlanta University School of Library Service held a six-day conference for ninety-seven Black public librarians. |
| 1949 | The Atlanta University School of Library Service initiated a graduate program leading to a master's degree. |
| 1950 | Gwendolyn Brooks received the Pulitzer Prize for Poetry, the first African American to receive the award. |
| | The Ghana Library Authority was established. |
| 1952 | Clarence R. Graham, of the Louisville Free Public Library, became the first public librarian in the South to open the main library to African Americans. |

|  |  |
|---|---|
| 1953 | Augusta Baker (1911–1998) was appointed assistant coordinator of children's services and storytelling specialist, becoming the first African American to hold an administrative position in the New York Public Library. |
| 1954 | The American Library Association approved the idea of a single library association in a state, which led to integrated associations in the South. |
| | In *Brown v. Board of Education*, the US Supreme Court ruled that school segregation was unconstitutional. |
| 1956 | The American Library Association Conference at Miami Beach, Florida, was probably the first completely desegregated association conference held in the South. |
| | Charlemae Rollins (1897–1979) became the first African American to receive the Grolier Foundation Award. |
| 1957 | Alma Jacobs became the first African American elected president of the Pacific Northwest Library Association. |
| | Charlemae Rollins became the first African American elected president of the Children's Services Division of the American Library Association. |
| 1958 | Dorothy B. Porter edited and published *A Catalogue of the African Collection in the Moorland Foundation*. |
| | Effie Lee Morris received the E. P. Dutton-John Macrae Award for advancement of library service to children and young people. |
| 1960 | Alma Jacobs was elected president of the Montana Library Association. |
| | James Jacobs (1930–2023), a graduate of the library science program at the University of California-Berkeley, becomes the first African American librarian at the Berkeley Public Library. |
| | Rice Estes questioned the American Library Association about its position on race and libraries. |
| 1961 | Albert P. Marshall was elected the first African American president of the Missouri Library Association. |
| | Annette Hoage Phinazee (1920–1983) solicited an accounting from the American Library Association at the Cleveland, Ohio, conference as it pertained to race and American libraries. |
| 1963 | *Access to Public Libraries*, a research study prepared for the American Library Association by International Research Associates, Inc., documented racism, both direct and indirect, in library services to African Americans in the United States. |
| | Effie Lee Morris was appointed coordinator of children's services at the San Francisco Public Library. |
| 1964 | Alma Jacobs was elected the first African American member of the Executive Board of the American Library Association. |
| | E. J. Josey presented a resolution at the American Library Association Conference (St. Louis, Missouri) that would prohibit the American Library Association officers and staff members from attending, in their official capacity at American Library Association expense, the meetings of state associations that continued to practice segregation. This resolution led to the integration of the remaining four state associations that refused to extend membership to African American librarians. |
| 1965 | Albert P. Marshall was appointed the first Black member of the American Library Association to chair the nominating committee. |
| | The Atlanta University School of Library Service held a conference on "Materials by and About American Negroes." The school also sponsored a conference on "The Role of the Library in Improving Education in the South." |
| | Dudley Randall, an African American Detroit poet and librarian, founded Broadside Press. |
| | E. J. Josey becomes the first African American librarian member of the Georgia Library Association. |
| 1966 | American Library Association established an ad hoc "Committee on Opportunities for Negro Students in the Library Profession" chaired by Virginia Lacy Jones. |
| | In *Brown v. Louisiana* 383 US 131, the US Supreme Court held that "persons could not be punished for using the library peacefully to protest the illegal segregation of the library itself" (argued in 1963). |
| | *The Negro Handbook* was published by the Johnson Publishing Company, Inc. |

**A Chronology of Events in Black Librarianship**

| | | | |
|---|---|---|---|
| | Helen M. Miller (1940–2023) is hired at the Free Library of Philadelphia. A graduate of Drexel University's library science program, Miller began her career at the library as a children's librarian before moving up through the ranks to become the library's director of public services. | | Howard University Library hosted a conference on Black bibliography, chaired by Dorothy B. Porter. |
| 1967 | The Atlanta University School of Library Service's Conference on "The Georgia Child's Access to Materials Pertaining to American Negroes" was held. | 1970 | E. J. Josey assembled a group of Black librarians to discuss issues and concerns of Black librarians at the 1970 Midwinter Meeting of ALA, which led to the establishment of the Black Caucus of the American Library Association. |
| | The first edition of *The Negro Almanac*, a comprehensive reference work, was published by the Bellwether Publishing Company. | | Alma Jacobs was appointed State Librarian of Montana. |
| | Hannah D. Atkins became the first African American president of the Oklahoma Chapter of the Special Libraries Association, 1967–1968. | | The first Black Caucus of the American Library Association Award was given to Clara S. Jones for Distinguished Service to Librarianship. |
| | Virginia Lacy Jones was the first African American elected president of the Association of American Library Schools. | | *The Black Librarian in America*, edited by E. J. Josey, was published; this was the first book to deal exclusively with Black librarians. |
| 1968 | Milton Byam was appointed chair of the Department of Library Science at St. John's University. | | Burton E. Lamkin was appointed associate commissioner for libraries and educational technology in the United States Office of Education of the Department of Health, Education, and Welfare. |
| | E. J. Josey was appointed chief of the Bureau of Academic and Research Libraries of the New York Education Department. | | Clara S. Jones was appointed director of the Detroit Public Library, the first African American and woman in that position. |
| 1969 | The Committee on Scientific and Technical Information (COSATI) established a Subcommittee on Negro Research Libraries. | | Charlemae Rollins became the first African American woman to win the Constance Lindsay Skinner Award. |
| | The School of Library Media began at Alabama A&M University—the first graduate degree program in library science established for African Americans in Alabama. | | E. J. Josey became the first African American to receive the *Journal of Library History* Award. |
| | A "Conference on the Use of Microphotography and Black Studies" was cosponsored by The Atlanta University School of Library Service, the 3M Corporation, the United Negro College Fund, and the Maude Hill Family Foundation. | | Fisk University Library sponsored the first summer Institute on Black Studies Librarianship, directed by Jessie Carney Smith. |
| | A "Conference for the Evaluation of Materials About Black Americans (CEMBA)" was held at Alabama A&M University at Huntsville. | | The Library of Congress published *The Negro in the United States: A Selected Bibliography*, edited by Dorothy B. Porter. |
| | The Cooperative College Library Center, the first consortium of Black academic libraries, opened in Atlanta, Georgia, with Hillis Davis as director. | 1971 | The Council of the American Library Association adopted a resolution alleging racial discrimination by the Library of Congress in its recruitment, training, and promotion practices. |
| | Hannah D. Atkins became the first African American elected president of the southwestern chapter of the American Association of Law Librarians (1969–1970). | | Effie Lee Morris became the first African American president of the Public Library Association, a division of the American Library Association. |
| | | | Joseph H. Reason was elected the first African American president of the Association of College and Research Libraries (ACRL). |

| | | | | |
|---|---|---|---|---|
| | Rebecca Bingham became the first African American president of the Kentucky Library Association. | | | Charles D. Churchwell was appointed director of Brown University Library. |
| | The United States Office of Education funded the African American Materials Project (AAMP), a six-state library project to identify holdings in Negroana in the southeast. Annette Hoage Phinazee served as the principal investigator. | | | Virginia Lacy Jones became the first African American to receive the Melvil Dewey Medal of the American Library Association. |
| | | | 1975 | Clara S. Jones was elected vice president/president-elect of the American Library Association—the first African American. |
| 1972 | Charlemae Rollins was the first African American granted an honorary membership to the American Library Association. | | | Augusta Baker was the first African American awarded the Clarence Day Award. |
| | E. J. Josey published *What Black Librarians Are Saying*. | | | Louise Giles became both the first African American woman and the first community college librarian to be elected as president of the Association of College and Research Libraries (ACRL). |
| | Fisk University Library sponsored the first conference to be held solely on Black oral history, under the direction of Ann Allen Shockley. | | | |
| | Milton S. Byam was appointed the first African American director of the District of Columbia Public Library. | | | The Alabama A&M School of Library Media's master's program was accredited by the American Library Association. |
| | Dorothy B. Porter received the Black Caucus of ALA Distinguished Achievement Award. | | | The North Carolina Central University's School of Library Science's master's program was accredited by the American Library Association under the deanship of Annette L. Phinazee. |
| | Robert Wedgeworth became the first African American selected as executive director of the American Library Association. | | 1976 | Clara S. Jones became the first African American inaugurated as president of the American Library Association. |
| | Beatrice Bethel Johnson, a graduate of the library science program at Drexel University, became the first African American librarian to work for the School District of Philadelphia. | | | Gwendolyn Brooks, Pulitzer Prize-winning poet read her poem "Other Music," written for the inauguration of Clara S. Jones. |
| 1973 | Lucille C. Thomas became the first African American appointed to the New York State Regents Advisory Council on Libraries. | | | Ella Gaines Yates became the first African American director of the Atlanta (Georgia) Public Library. |
| | Sylvia Lyons Reader was appointed specialist in Afro-American history and culture at the Library of Congress. | | | Jessie Carney Smith was elected the first African American president of Beta Phi Mu, the international library science honor society. |
| 1974 | Ann Allen Shockley and Sue P. Chandler published *Living Black American Authors: A Biographical Directory*. | | | The North Carolina Central University School of Library Science sponsored a colloquium, "Southeastern Black Librarians," to celebrate the school's thirty-fifth anniversary. |
| | E. J. Josey was elected chair of the Association of Cooperative Library Organizations (ACLO). | | | Virginia Lacy Jones was granted an honorary membership by the American Library Association. |
| | Milton S. Byam was appointed the first African American director of the Queens Borough Public Library System. | | | Wallace Van Jackson was the only African American honored with an American Library Association Centennial Award. |
| | Herman L. Totten was selected as the first African American to fill the position of dean at a predominantly white American Library Association-accredited library school program at the University of Oregon. | | 1977 | Lucille C. Thomas became the first African American president of the New York Library Association. |

| | | | |
|---|---|---|---|
| | Alex Haley won the National Book Award and the Pulitzer Prize for *Roots*. | 1982 | Casper L. Jordan was appointed deputy director of the Atlanta Public Library System. |
| | Virginia Lacy Jones received the coveted Joseph Wharton Lippincott Award for distinguished service to librarianship, the first African American so honored. | | Cynthia Jenkins was elected to the New York State Legislature as an assembly member from Queens County. She was formerly a librarian at the Queens Borough Public Library. |
| | The Black Caucus of ALA strongly and vigorously objected to the ALA film, *The Speaker*, for the Black Caucus of ALA felt that it violated the ALA Library Bill of Rights and is an affront to African Americans. | | New York state senator Major R. Owens was the first librarian in the country to be elected to the US House of Representatives. |
| | | 1983 | Clara S. Jones, the first African American president of the American Library Association, was awarded ALA's highest honor, ALA honorary membership, at the 1983 ALA Annual Conference. |
| | *The Handbook of Black Librarianship* is published. Dr. E. J. Josey and Anne Allen Shockley are the editors. | | |
| 1978 | Vivian Davidson Hewitt was the first African American elected president of the Special Libraries Association. | 1984 | E. J. Josey was inaugurated as the second African American president of the American Library Association. |
| | Clara S. Jones was appointed to the National Commission on Library and Information Science by President Jimmy Carter. | | The Black Caucus of the American Library Association cosponsored with the Kenya Library Association a joint preconference of the International Federation of Library Associations and Institutions (IFLA) in Kenya, the first IFLA conference to be held on African soil. |
| 1979 | Rebecca Bingham was the first African American elected president of the American Association of School Librarians (AASL). | | |
| 1980 | Annette Hoage Phinazee, dean of the School of Library Information Sciences, North Carolina Central University, published her book, *The Black Librarian in the Southeast: Reminiscences, Activities, Challenges*. | | Mary F. Lenox was appointed as the first African American dean of the School of Library and Information Sciences at the University of Missouri-Columbia. |
| | E. J. Josey received the ALA Joseph W. Lippincott Award for distinguished service to the profession of librarianship for being a "champion of the rights and needs of minorities and the under-privileged everywhere" . . . his fervent advocacy was a major force in eradicating racial discrimination from many library facilities and services, and from a number of professional organizations. He was the second African American librarian to receive this coveted award. | | Effie Lee Morris received the 1984 Women's National Book Association Award. This award is given biannually to "a living American woman who has made an enduring and unique contribution to the world of books, or through books to society." |
| | | | Howard Dodson was appointed chief of the Schomburg Center for Research in Black Culture. |
| | | | Jessie Carney Smith, University Librarian, Fisk University, became the first African American to receive the ACRL Academic Research Librarian of the Year Award. |
| 1981 | Wendell L. Wray was appointed chief of the Schomburg Center for Research in Black Culture. | | Robert Wedgeworth was the first African American appointed dean of the School of Library Service, Columbia University. |
| | Augusta Baker was awarded the Regina Medal by the Catholic Library Association. She also became a member of the University of South Carolina College of Librarianship faculty as storyteller in residence. | | The Professional Development Committee of the Black Caucus of the American Library Association presented a panel of African American deans of ALA-accredited schools: Lorene Brown, Atlanta University; Benjamin F. Speller, North Carolina Central University; Mary Lenox, University of Missouri; Mohammed M. |
| | Casper L. Jordan received the Black Caucus of the American Library Association Award for Distinguished Service to Librarianship. | | |

| | | | |
|---|---|---|---|
| | Aman, University of Wisconsin-Milwaukee; Miles Jackson, University of Hawaii; and Robert Wedgeworth, Columbia University, who discussed recruitment of minorities to the profession and other critical issues facing African American librarians. | 1989 | Charles W. Brown was elected president of the Public Library Association. |
| | | | Ann Allen Shockley was awarded the Susan Koppelman Award for the best anthology of 1989 for her *Afro-American Women Writers, 1746-1933*. |
| 1986 | Ella Gaines Yates was the first African American appointed Virginia state librarian and Archivist. | | Hiram L. Davis was the first African American to be appointed director of the Michigan State University Libraries. |
| | E. J. Josey was appointed to a tenured professorship at the School of Library and Information Sciences, University of Pittsburgh. | | Elaine P. Adams was appointed assistant commissioner for educational opportunity planning at the Texas Higher Education Coordinating Board. |
| | Monteria Hightower became the first African American appointed state librarian of the state of Missouri. | | Charles D. Churchwell was appointed dean of the School of Library and Information Studies at Clark Atlanta University. |
| | Diane McAfee Hopkins was appointed to the School of Library and Information Sciences (SLIS) faculty, University of Wisconsin-Madison. | | Emily R. Mobley was the first African American appointed dean of libraries, Purdue University. |
| | Barbara Williams Jenkins was the first African American elected president of the South Carolina Library Association. | 1990 | The Black Caucus of ALA had a gala reception in honor of its twentieth anniversary in Chicago at the 1990 Annual Conference of the American Library Association. |
| | Ellen Holly is hired as a librarian at the White Plains (New York) Public Library. Before her career in librarianship, Holly was the first Black soap opera star and appeared in the soap opera *One Life to Live*. Holly also had roles in *School Daze, Guiding Light*, and the television series *In the Heat of the Night*. Holly passed away on December 6, 2023. | | Estelle M. Black was the first African American elected president of the Illinois Library Association. |
| | | 1991 | Dr. Carla Hayden was appointed deputy commissioner and chief librarian of the Chicago Public Library. |
| 1987 | Bertha Cheatham was the first African American appointed editor of *School Library Journal*. | | E. J. Josey was the first African American to receive the ALA Equality Award for outstanding contributions toward promoting equality of all people and between men and women in the library profession and the world at large. |
| | Cynthia Jenkins, a member of the New York State Legislature from the 29th District, was elected the chair of the Subcommittee on Libraries of the New York State Legislature. | | Althea H. Jenkins, library director at the Sarasota/New College Campus, University of South Florida, was appointed executive director of the Association of College and Research Libraries (ACRL). |
| | Casper L. Jordan, deputy director of the Atlanta Fulton County Public Library, was honored by Atlanta University School of Library and Information Studies. | | Herman L. Totten was the first African American to be appointed as a Regents professor at the School of Library and Information Sciences, University of North Texas. |
| | Congressman Major R. Owens received the American Library Association's highest honor, honorary life membership in ALA. | | Elaine P. Adams was appointed president of the northeast campus of Houston Community College, Texas. |
| | Sybil Moses was appointed director of the ALA Office of Library Outreach Services. | | Gregory L. Reese was honored as the 1991 Ohio Librarian of the Year by the Ohio Library Association. |
| 1988 | James F. Williams II was the first African American to be appointed director of libraries at the University of Colorado, Boulder. | | |

**A Chronology of Events in Black Librarianship**

| | | | |
|---|---|---|---|
| | Robert Wedgeworth was the first librarian of African descent to be elected president of the International Federation of Library Associations and Institutions (IFLA). | 1996 | The April 1996 issue of *Ebony Man* profiled seven African American men, all librarians, who were classified as being "among the most powerful Black men in America." |
| 1992 | Effie Lee Morris was honored as the 1992 recipient of the ALA Grolier Foundation Award. | | E. J. Josey was the first African American to be honored with the Pennsylvania Library Association Distinguished Service Award. |
| | The Black Caucus of the ALA held its first national conference in Columbus, Ohio, at the Hyatt Regency, Columbia, September 4-6, 1992. | | Maurice B. Wheeler was the first African American man to be appointed director of the Detroit Public Library. |
| | The Black Caucus of the ALA established its first scholarship fund and named it the E. J. Josey Scholarship Award. | | Billie E. Dancy was the first African American appointed director of the Oakland (California) Public Library. |
| | Robert Wedgeworth was the first African American to be appointed university librarian and professor of library administration at the University of Illinois, Urbana. | 1997 | Robert Wedgeworth, Director of Libraries at the University of Illinois, was awarded the Melvil Dewey Award at the 1997 American Library Association Annual Conference. |
| 1993 | Dr. Carla Hayden, deputy commissioner of the Chicago Public Library was appointed executive director of the Enoch Pratt Free Library, Baltimore. | 1998 | The first cohort of the ALA Spectrum Scholarship Program is selected. |
| | Hardy Franklin was the third African American to be inaugurated as president of the American Library Association. | | President Bill Clinton appointed Rebecca T. Bingham to be a member of the National Commission on Library and Information Science. Bingham was the first African American president of the Kentucky Library Association. |
| 1994 | Lucille C. Thomas, president of the International Association of School Librarianship, was the recipient of the American Association of School Librarians Distinguished Service Award. | | Glenience Robinson was the first African American to be elected president-elect of the Texas Library Association. |
| | Hiram L. Davis, former director of libraries at Michigan State University, was the first African American appointed Deputy Librarian of Congress. | | E. J. Josey, Professor Emeritus of the School of Information Sciences, University of Pittsburgh, was selected to receive the 1998 John Ames Humphrey/OCLC/Forest Press. |
| | E. J. Josey received the first DEMCO/Black Caucus Award for excellence in librarianship. | | Award at the 1998 ALA Annual Conference for significant contributions to international Librarianship. |
| | Charles M. Brown was the first African American to be appointed director of the Hennepin County Library, Minnetonka, Minnesota. | | Edrice G. Ivory was the first African American librarian to be appointed the director of the Shaker Heights Public Library, Shaker Heights, Ohio. |
| 1995 | Charles D. Churchwell was honored by the Council on Library Resources "for his continuing contributions to the Council at many levels of leadership." | 1999 | NCAAL 4 is held in Las Vegas, Nevada. |
| | The Black Caucus of the ALA celebrated its twenty-fifth anniversary at the Harold Washington Center of the Chicago Public Library, June 26, 1995. | | BCALA Connecticut, a BCALA affiliate, is founded at the New Haven Public Library, New Haven, Connecticut. |
| | Sylverna Ford was the first African American to be appointed director of libraries at Mankato State University, Minnesota. | 2000 | *The Handbook of Black Librarianship, 2nd Edition* is published. Dr. E. J. Josey and Dr. Marva DeLoach are the editors. |
| | | | Gladys Smiley-Bell becomes president of BCALA. |

|  |  |
|---|---|
| 2001 | The Indiana Black Librarians Network, a BCALA affiliate, is founded at the Black Culture Center Library at Purdue University in West Lafayette, Indiana. |
| 2002 | NCAAL 5 is held in Fort Lauderdale, Florida. |
| | Bobby Player Sr. becomes president of BCALA. |
| 2003 | Blair-Caldwell African American Research Library opens at the Denver Public Library in Denver, Colorado. |
| | Dr. Carla D. Hayden becomes president of ALA. |
| | Tyrone Cannon is president of the Association of College and Research Libraries (ACRL). |
| | Dr. Lucille Cole Thomas, adjunct professor of library science at Queens College, is awarded Honorary Membership by ALA. Dr. Thomas becomes president of the Brooklyn Public Library's Board of Trustees the same year. |
| 2004 | Andrew P. Jackson (Sekou) is president of BCALA. |
| 2005 | Cornucopia of Rhode Island: A Library Community of Color (CORI) is launched by Dr. Ida McGhee, Dr. Donna Gilton, Denise Dowdell, and Dr. Michael Havener in September 2005 at the University of Rhode Island's University Club. |
| | The African Library Project, a nonprofit organization dedicated to establishing libraries in communities in Sub-Saharan Africa, was established by Chris Bradshaw. |
| | The School of Library and Information Studies at Clark Atlanta University closes. |
| 2006 | The First Joint Conference of Librarians of Color is held in Dallas, Texas. |
| | Wanda K. Brown becomes president of BCALA. |
| 2007 | NCAAL 6 is held in Fort Worth, Texas. |
| | The first cohort of the ALA Emerging Leaders Program was selected. |
| 2008 | The Indiana Librarians Leading in Diversity Fellowship Program (I-LLID) is established at the Indiana University School of Library and Information Sciences (Indiana University Luddy School of Informatics, Computing, and Engineering). Funded by the IMLS Laura Bush 21st Century Librarian Program, I-LLID increased the number of BIPOC librarians in the library profession. |
| | The First National Diversity in Libraries Conference was held in Louisville, Kentucky. |
| | Karolyn S. Thompson becomes president of BCALA. |
| 2009 | Dr. E. J. Josey passes away in Washington, North Carolina. Josey was a cofounder of BCALA and served as its first president. Josey was also a past president of ALA, an author of numerous works on libraries and librarianship, and a professor in the library science program at the University of Pittsburgh. |
| | Effie Lee Morris passes away in San Francisco, California. Morris was the first African American to serve as the president of the Public Library Association (PLA). Morris was also a cofounder of BCALA. |
| | Dr. Eliza Atkins Gleason (1909–2009) died at the age of one hundred in Winston-Salem, North Carolina. Dr. Gleason was the first African American to earn a PhD in library science and was the first dean of the Atlanta University Library School. |
| | The Academic and Cultural Enrichment (ACE) Scholars Program is established at the University of North Carolina Greensboro's Library and Information Studies Department. Funded by the IMLS Laura Bush 21st Century Librarian Program, the ACE Scholars Program increased the number of BIPOC librarians in the library profession. |
| 2010 | NCAAL 7 is held in Birmingham, Alabama. |
| | Jos N. Holman becomes president of BCALA. |
| | BCALA launches Reading is Grand!, a family literacy program focused on grandparents and grandchildren. It is part of the ALA Family Focus Initiative started by ALA president Camila Alire. Karen Lemmons, Tamela Chambers, and Dr. Claudette McLin of the BCALA Services to Children of African Descent Committee serve as the program's administrators. |
| 2011 | The First African Library Summit is held in Muldersdrift, South Africa. |
| | LiteracyNation was established by Richard and Charmaine Ashby. Its mission is to support and promote independent authors and publishers; and to provide access to books uplifting people of color. |
| | *Little Known Black Librarian Facts*, a blog devoted to the history of librarians and libraries in the Black/African Diaspora, is launched by Michele Fenton. |

| | | | | |
|---|---|---|---|---|
| | Yohannes Gebregeorgis, founder of Ethiopia Reads, receives the Honorary Member of the American Library Association Award during the 2011 ALA Annual Conference in New Orleans, Louisiana. Gebregeorgis was also the opening speaker for the conference. | | | BCALA partners with Biblioboard to introduce the Self-e Literary Award. The award recognizes self-published authors of poetry and fiction. |
| 2012 | *The 21st Century Black Librarian in America: Issues and Challenges* is published. | | | Founded by Reverend Father Sylvester A. Nnaso, the Seat of Wisdom Library opens in Abatete, Nigeria, with a grand ceremony on December 31, 2015. |
| | Andrew Sekou Jackson, Akilah Nosakhere, and Julius Jefferson are the editors. | | | Cynthia Hurd, a regional library manager for the Charleston County Public Library, is among several people killed in a massacre on June 17, 2015, at the Emanuel African Methodist Episcopal Church in Charleston, South Carolina. In her memory, the St. Andrews Regional Library was renamed the Cynthia Graham Hurd St. Andrews Regional Library. |
| | Dr. Jerome Offord Jr. becomes president of BCALA. | | | |
| | The Second Joint Conference of Librarians of Color was held in Kansas City, Missouri. | | | |
| 2013 | NCAAL 8 is held in Cincinnati, Ohio. United States representative John Lewis is the closing keynote speaker. | | 2016 | Dr. Carla Hayden becomes the first African American and the first woman appointed as the Librarian of Congress. |
| | African Library and Information Associations and Institutions (AfLIA) is established. | | | Denyvetta Davis becomes president of BCALA. |
| | The Second African Library Summit is held in Pretoria, South Africa, at the University of South Africa. | | | The National Museum of African American History and Culture opens in Washington, DC. |
| | | | 2017 | The Center for Black Literature and Culture opens at the Central Branch of the Indianapolis Public Library in Indianapolis, Indiana. Nichelle M. Hayes is appointed as the center's director. Roland Martin was the speaker at the opening ceremony. |
| | Trevor Dawes becomes president of ACRL. | | | |
| 2014 | Kelvin Watson becomes president of BCALA. | | | |
| | Courtney Young becomes president of ALA. | | | |
| | The Ferguson Municipal Public Library in Ferguson, Missouri, remained opened during protests over the shooting of Michael Brown. The library served as a safe space and temporary school for children and other members of the community. | | | NCAAL 10 is held in Atlanta, Georgia. Reverend Bernice King is the closing keynote speaker. |
| | | | | St. Louis Regional Librarians-BCALA, a BCALA affiliate, was founded. |
| | | | | Metro Atlanta Black Librarians Network, a BCALA affiliate, was founded. |
| | | | 2018 | Richard Ashby becomes president of BCALA. |
| | We Need Diverse Books, an organization dedicated to supporting and promoting diverse books for children, was launched. | | | The Third Joint Conference of Librarians of Color is held in Albuquerque, New Mexico. |
| 2015 | NCAAL 9 is held in St. Louis, Missouri. | | | Colorado Black Library Association was founded. |
| | The Third African Library Summit is held in Accra, Ghana. | | | First Lady Michelle Obama is the opening keynote speaker at the 2018 ALA Annual Conference in New Orleans, Louisiana. |
| | The 2015 World Library and Information Congress (WLIC) is held in Cape Town, South Africa. | | 2019 | Wanda K. Brown becomes president of ALA. |
| | | | | Jason Broughton becomes the first African American appointed as the state librarian of Vermont. |
| | The Pennsylvania Avenue Branch of the Enoch Pratt Free Library remains open during protests over the death of Freddie Gray. The library served as a safe space for patrons and members of the community. | | | |
| | | | | The IDEAL Conference (formerly the National Diversity in Libraries Conference) is held in Columbus, Ohio. Nikole Hannah-Jones, author of *The 1619 Project*, is the closing keynote speaker. |
| | The First AfLIA Conference is held in Accra, Ghana. | | | |

|  |  |
|---|---|
| | The Georgia Library Association's Black Caucus Interest Group, a BCALA affiliate, is founded. |
| | Lonnie G. Bunch III, becomes the first African American to serve as the secretary of the Smithsonian. |
| 2020 | Shauntee Burns-Simpson becomes president of BCALA. |
| | NCAAL 11 originally scheduled to be held in Tulsa, Oklahoma, is postponed due to the COVID-19 Pandemic. |
| | BCALA is awarded a $100,000 grant from the Institution of Museums and Library Services Laura Bush 21st Century Librarian Program. The grant is used to facilitate "Breaking Barriers: The Future of Black Librarianship National Forum," a symposium to educate and support Black/African American LIS students. Dr. Ana Ndumu and Dr. Shaundra Walker are the program administrators. |
| | The BCALA Virtual Summit 2020: Connecting, Cultivating, & Collaboration is held May 15-16, 2020. It is the association's first virtual summit. |
| | Tracie D. Hall becomes the first African American woman to serve as the executive director of ALA. |
| | Julius Jefferson becomes president of ALA. |
| | Jon Cawthorne becomes president of ACRL. |
| | Kathy Carroll becomes president of the AASL. |
| | Dr. Em Claire Knowles receives the 2020 ALA Equality Award. |
| | Pennsylvania Black Librarians' Caucus is inducted as a BCALA affiliate at the 2020 ALA Midwinter Conference in Philadelphia, Pennsylvania. |
| | The Institute of Museums and Library Services National Leadership Grants for Libraries Program awards BCALA $99,934 planning grant to research Black History Month programming in public libraries. Dr. Deborah Robinson and Dr. Grace Jackson-Brown are the project's administrators. |
| | Joan Johnson, a graduate of the University of Washington's library science program, is appointed the city librarian and the director of the Milwaukee Public Library. She is the first African American woman to serve in this role. |
| 2021 | NCAAL 12 is virtual due to the ongoing pandemic. It is the first NCAAL held virtually. |
| | Julius C. Jefferson Jr. appointed chair of the IFLA North American Regional Division. |
| | Rodney Freeman launches the Black Male Archives, a database dedicated to chronicling the achievements and successes of Black men. |
| | On May 16, 2021, BCALA issues a statement to the ALA Council addressing the microaggressions experienced by BIPOC leaders, members, and attendees at council meetings. BCALA requested that the ALA Council reexamine and re-create council meeting policies, codes of conduct, and communication norms through a DEI lens and commit formally to upholding these standards to facilitate a more welcoming and inclusive environment during meetings. |
| | Jason Broughton is appointed as the director of the National Library Service for the Blind and Print Disabled. |
| | iBlackCaucus, a mentoring and support program for Black LIS students, is officially launched by BCALA. |
| | On July 13, 2021, a special meeting was held by the Indiana Library Federation to discuss the investigation into allegations of racism exhibited by officials within its organization toward former Indiana Library Federation president Libre (Latrice) Booker. Booker was the first African American to serve as the organization's president. Members of BCALA, ALA, and the Indiana Black Librarians Network attended the meeting and wore black and had their cameras on to let it be known to the Indiana Library Federation that they stood in solidarity with their colleague Libre (Latrice) Booker. |
| | President Barack Obama is the closing speaker for the 2021 ALA Annual Conference. The conference is virtual due to the ongoing pandemic. It is the second ALA Annual Conference held virtually. |
| 2022 | *The Black Librarian in America: Reflections, Resistance, and Reawakening* is published. Edited by Nichelle M. Hayes, Shauntee Burns-Simpson, Dr. Shaundra Walker, and Dr. Ana Ndumu, it is the first volume in the series to have an all-woman editorial team. |
| | Julius C. Jefferson Jr. is appointed to the National Museums and Library Services Board by President Joseph Biden. |
| | KC Boyd is named School Librarian of the Year by *School Library Journal*. |

| | | |
|---|---|---|
| | Nichelle M. Hayes becomes president of BCALA. | |
| | The Indiana Historical Bureau recognizes the former Paul Laurence Dunbar Branch of the Indianapolis Public Library with a historical marker. Housed inside of Indianapolis Public School No. 26 (John Hope School), it was the first library branch to open in an African American neighborhood. The branch was in operation from 1922 to 1967. | |
| | The Coretta Scott King Book Awards Committee becomes an ALA round table. | |
| | ALA establishes the Satia Marshall Orange Spectrum Scholarship Endowment Fund. | |
| | Vivian Davidson Hewitt, the first African American president of the Special Libraries Association (SLA) dies at 102 in Manhattan, New York. | |
| | *Libraries: Culture, History, and Society*, the peer-reviewed journal of the ALA Library History Round Table (LHRT), publishes a special issue focusing on Black women librarians. Dr. Nicole Cooke, the Augusta Baker Professor of LIS at the University of South Carolina is the guest editor. | |
| | In January 2022, Kelly Richards becomes the first Black president and director of the Free Library of Philadelphia, Philadelphia, Pennsylvania. | |
| 2023 | Kelvin Watson receives the 2023 ALA Medal of Excellence Award. | |

| | |
|---|---|
| Julius C. Jefferson Jr. receives the 2023 Joseph W. Lippincott Award. | |
| Dr. Emily Knox receives the Eli M. Oboler Award from the ALA Intellectual Freedom Round Table. | |
| LiteracyNation becomes an affiliate of ALA. | |
| The Fourth Joint Conference of Librarians of Color is held in St. Pete Beach, Florida. | |
| Tracie D. Hall is listed in *Time* magazine's 2023 TIME100 List of the 100 Most Influential People in the World. | |
| Dr. Ibram X. Kendi, author of *How to Be Anti-Racist*, is the keynote speaker at the Rally to Read held at the Hilton Chicago Hotel during the 2023 ALA Annual Conference. | |
| Dr. Emily Knox, LIS professor and author, testifies before the United States Senate Committee on the Judiciary's hearing, "Book Bans: Examining How Censorship Limits Liberty and Literature." | |
| The International African American Museum opens in Charleston, South Carolina. | |
| Eboni Henry is the DC 2023 School Librarian of the Year. | |
| Richard Ashby Jr. and KC Boyd appear in the anthology *Marvel Super Stories*. Ashby and Boyd are in the story featuring Black Panther, illustrated by Jerry Craft. | |
| Dr. Brandy McNeil is appointed director-at-large of the Public Library Association. | |

# 1.2

## National Conferences of African American Librarians: 1992–Present

Andrew P. Jackson (Sekou Molefi Baako)

NCAAL XII
Culture Keepers XII: Unity in Diversity: Stronger Together in the African Diaspora
July 24–27, 2024, New Orleans, LA
President: Wanda K. Brown
Conference Chairs: Mahasin Ameen and Rhonda Oliver

NCAAL XI
Culture Keepers XI: Sankofa Experience: Inspired by Our Past, Igniting Our Future
July 27–August 1, 2021, A Virtual Conference, Tulsa, OK
President: Shauntee Burns-Simpson
Conference Chairs: Keith B. Jemison and Dr. Tracey J. Hunter-Hayes

NCAAL X
Culture Keepers X: Beyond Library Walls: Innovative Ways to Engage Our Communities
August 9–13, 2017, Atlanta, GA
President: Denyvetta Davis
Conference Chairs: Carolyn Garnes and Dorothy Guthrie

NCAAL IX
Culture Keepers IX: Meet at the Gateway: Reimagining Communities, Technologies, and Libraries
August 4–8, 2015, St. Louis, MO
President: Kelvin Watson
Conference Chairs: Emily Guss and Makiba Foster

NCAAL VIII
Culture Keepers VIII: Challenges of the 21st Century: Empowering People, Changing Lives
August 7–11, 2013, Cincinnati, OH
President: Jerome Offord Jr.
Conference Chairs: Denyvetta Davis and Fannie Mae Cox

NCAAL VII
Culture Keepers VII: Bridging the Divide with Information Access, Activism, and Advocacy
August 4–8, 2010, Birmingham, AL
President: Jos Holman
Conference Chairs: Wanda K. Brown and Roberta Webb

NCAAL VI
Culture Keepers VI: Preserving the Past, Sustaining the Future
August 2–6, 2007, Fort Worth, TX
President: Wanda K. Brown
Conference Chairs: Carolyn F. Norman and Dr. Richard Bradberry

NCAAL V
Culture Keepers V: Access
August 12–15, 2002, Fort Lauderdale, FL
President: Bobby Player
Conference Chairs: Florence Simpkins and Wayne Crocker

NCAAL IV
Culture Keepers IV: Challenges and Opportunities in the New Millennium
July 19–22, 1999, Las Vegas, NV
President: Gregory Reese
Conference Chairs: Florence Simpkins and Wayne Crocker

NCAAL III
Culture Keepers III: Making Global Connections
July 31–Augusts 3, 1997, Winston-Salem, NC
President: Sylvia Sprinkle-Hamlin
Conference Chairs: Gertiana Williams and Emma Pero

NCAAL II
Culture Keepers II: Part I—Unity through Diversity
August 5–7, 1994, Milwaukee, WI
President: Dr. Stanton Biddle
Conference Cochair: Estelle Black

NCAAL I
Culture Keepers I: Enlightening and Empowering Our Communities
September 3–6, 1992, Columbus, OH

President: Alex Boyd
Conference Cochair: Sylvia Sprinkle-Hamlin

**SOURCES**

Black Caucus American Library Association. Past NCALL Conferences, https://www.bcala.org/past-ncaal-conferences.
NCAAL Conference XI, https://www.ncaal.org/ncaal/home.
NCAAL Conference XII, NCAALXII, https://www.ncaal.org/.

# 1.3

## The BCALA Trailblazer Award and DEMCO/BCALA Award for Excellence in Librarianship

Michele Fenton

**BCALA TRAILBLAZER AWARDS**

Established in 1990, the Black Caucus of the American Library Association (BCALA) Trailblazer Award is bestowed every five years upon librarians "whose pioneering contributions have been outstanding and unique, and whose efforts have 'blazed a trail' in the profession."[1]

Recipients of the first BCALA Trailblazer's Award granted at the twentieth anniversary celebration in 1990 were:

- Dr. E. J. Josey
- Dr. Virginia Lacy Jones
- Ms. Clara Stanton Jones
- Dr. Dorothy Burnett Porter Wesley

The recipient of the fifth BCALA Trailblazer Award presented at the BCALA twenty-fifth anniversary celebration in 1995 was:

- Ms. Lucille Cole Thomas

The Recipient of the sixth BCALA Trailblazer Award presented at the thirtieth anniversary celebration in 2000 was:

- Dr. John C. Tyson

The recipient of the seventh BCALA Trailblazer Award presented at the thirty-fifth anniversary celebration in 2005 was:

- Ms. Effie Lee Morris

The recipient of the eighth BCALA Trailblazer Award presented at the fortieth anniversary celebration in 2010 was:

- Mr. Robert Wedgeworth

The recipients of the ninth BCALA Trailblazer Award presented at the forty-fifth anniversary celebration in 2015 were:

- Mr. Thomas Alford
- Ms. Mary Biblo

The recipient of the tenth BCALA Trailblazer Award presented at the fiftieth anniversary celebration in 2021 (the BCALA turned fifty in 2020 but the award was postponed to 2021 due to the COVID-19 pandemic) was:

- Shirley A. Coaston

**DEMCO/BCALA AWARD FOR EXCELLENCE IN LIBRARIANSHIP**

The DEMCO/BCALA Award for Excellence in Librarianship is bestowed annually upon a librarian "who has made significant contributions to promoting the status of African Americans in the library profession. Specific contributions may include, but are not limited to, research and scholarship, recruitment, professional development, planning or implementation of programs, or advocacy (public relations). DEMCO also donates an additional $500.00 each year to assist in funding the E. J. Josey Scholarship Fund."[2] Recipients of the award are given a bronze statuette funded by a grant from DEMCO, Inc.

The following librarians were awarded the DEMCO/BCALA Black Caucus Award for Excellence in Librarianship:

- 1994 recipient: Dr. E. J. Josey, LHD
- 1995 recipient: Dr. Mohammed M. Aman, PhD
- 1996 recipient: Dr. John Tyson, DA
- 1997 recipient: Mr. Samuel F. Morrison
- 1998 recipient: Ms. Rebecca Bingham
- 1999 recipient: Mr. Bobby Player
- 2000 recipient: Ms. Satia Marshall Orange
- 2001 recipient: Dr. Stanton Biddle, DLIS
- 2002 recipient: Ms. JoAnn Mondowney
- 2003 recipient: Ms. Sylvia Sprinkle-Hamlin
- 2004 recipient: Ms. Kathleen Bethel
- 2005 recipient: Ms. Gladys Smiley Bell
- 2006 recipient: Ms. Carla Hayden, PhD
- 2007 recipient: Ms. Sibyl E. Moses, PhD
- 2008 recipient: Mr. John S. Page
- 2009 recipient: Mr. Jerome Offord Jr.
- 2010 recipient: Ms. Irene Owens, PhD
- 2011 recipient: Ms. Pamela Goodes
- 2012 recipient: Mr. Andrew Jackson
- 2013 recipient: Ms. Roberta Webb
- 2014 recipient: Ms. Emily Guss
- 2015 recipient: Ms. Wanda Brown
- 2016 recipient: Dr. Yvonne Chandler
- 2017 recipient: Mr. Kelvin Watson
- 2018 recipient: Ms. Fayrene Muhammad
- 2019 recipient: Mr. Rudolph Clay
- 2020 recipient: Dr. Shaundra Walker
- 2021 recipient: No award given
- 2022 recipient: Tamela Chambers
- 2023 recipient: Shauntee Burns-Simpson

**NOTES**

1. "Trailblazers Award." BCALA, 2019–2023, bcala.org/bcala-awards/trailblazers-award. Accessed August 1, 2023.
2. "DEMCO/BCALA Award for Excellence in Librarianship." BCALA, 2019–2023, bcala.org/bcala-awards/demco-award. Accessed August 8, 2023.

# Chapter 2
# African American Forerunners in Librarianship

## 2.1

*African American Forerunners in Librarianship*

Casper LeRoy Jordan; Revised and Updated by Michele Fenton

If we considered the year 1876 as the formal beginning of American librarianship, African American involvement in the profession is recent. Although the 1890s chronicled the career of Daniel A. P. Murray's achievements at the Library of Congress, and a little later, Edward Christopher Williams, the first professionally trained African American librarian at a time when most American librarians did not possess this training, African Americans in American librarianship were few.

Prior to the establishment of the Hampton Institute Library School in Virginia, professionally trained African American librarians received their education at predominantly White institutions. The Hampton School closed in 1939, and in 1941 the Atlanta University School of Library Service assumed the responsibility of educating most African American librarians until its closing in 2005. Also, let us not forget North Carolina Central University, currently the only historically Black college/university (HBCU) to offer a degree in library science education. With over 130 years of involvement in the field by African Americans, some parameters necessarily were placed on this study. Many "pioneering" librarians are alive, some still working, and others only recently retired. In the previous editions of the *Handbook of Black Librarianship*, the late Casper LeRoy Jordan (1924-2000) focused on librarians who were deceased as of 1960. In this third edition, Michele Fenton updates Jordan's work with the addition of librarians who are deceased as of 2023.

Thus, consideration of the careers of Dr. Carla Hayden, Andrew Sekou Jackson, Dr. Marva DeLoach, Tracie D. Hall, Satia Marshall Orange, Kelvin Watson, Jos N. Holman, Em Claire Knowles, Gladys Smiley Bell, Dr. Stanton Biddle, Robert Wedgeworth, Richard Ashby Jr., Dr. Renate Chancellor, Dr. Jessie Carney Smith, Wanda K. Brown, Julius Jefferson, Binnie Tate Wilkin, Dr. Emily Knox, Nichelle M. Hayes, Dr. Jason Alston, Dr. Tiffeni Fontno, Dr. Grace Jackson-Brown, John Page, Dr. John Cawthorne, Dr. Nicole Cooke, Sybil Moses, KC Boyd, and Rose Dawson to name only a few, must be undertaken at another time.

### ARTHUR ALPHONSO SCHOMBURG (1874-1938)

Arthur Alphonso Schomburg[1] ranks as the foremost bibliophile and collector of books by and about Black people. Schomburg was born in Puerto Rico, was educated there and in the Spanish West Indies, and from an early age had an insatiable curiosity about Negroana. He arrived in New York in 1891, where he read law for five years and served for five years as secretary of Las Dos Antillas, a Cuban/Puerto Rican revolutionary party. He also taught Spanish, worked as a journalist and editor in New York, and finally joined Bankers Trust. He was a member (and, in 1922, president) of the Negro Academy of Washington, DC, was founder and secretary-treasurer for the Negro Society for Historical Research and was an ever-active collector.

Schomburg typified the private collector of this period who had a great interest in amassing sources on the history of Black people. (Libraries at Fisk University, Atlanta University, Howard University, Tuskegee Institute, and Hampton Institute also evidenced their growing assumption of stewardship in conserving the record of the Black past.) Schomburg pursued his interest in helping reclaim the Black heritage by serving as curator of the Negro Collection at Fisk University after his retirement from banking in 1929. He had already received the Harmon Award for his work in Black education in 1926.

Schomburg was a prolific writer and editor. "The Negro Digs Up His Past," was one of his most important essays, was published in *The New Negro* (edited by Alain LeRoi Locke, 1925), and is considered a cornerstone of the Harlem Renaissance. His real passion, however, was collecting—books, pamphlets, manuscripts, documents, letters, photographs, and paintings—anything to do with Black history.

In 1926, the Schomburg Collection was purchased by the New York Public Library (NYPL) with a Carnegie Corporation grant of $10,000, obtained through the efforts of the National Urban League. Schomburg became curator of the collection in 1931, so he actively was able to further his desire that the collection be available for students of Black life. His original collection was housed at the NYPL Harlem Branch on West 135th Street and is the nucleus of the matchless collection that bears his name. Schomburg died in 1938.

## HENRY PROCTOR SLAUGHTER (1871-1958)

Henry Proctor Slaughter[2] was born in Louisville, Kentucky, in 1871. He became fatherless at the age of six and sold newspapers to support his mother and younger sister and brothers. He was educated in the Louisville public schools and graduated as salutatorian of his class. Young Slaughter served an apprenticeship as a printer with the *Louisville Champion* and later became an associate editor. He wrote articles for the local papers and was a contributor to the daily *Louisville Courier-Journal*.

In 1892, Slaughter accepted the foremanship of the printing concerns of *The Lexington Standard* and a year later served as the associate editor. He was ambitious and worked to attend college; in 1894 he went to North Carolina as the manager-foreman of the African Methodist Episcopal Zion Church Publication House at Salisbury. He attended Livingstone College, while he maintained his editorial post at the publishing house.

Slaughter went to Washington, DC, in 1896. He passed, with a high score, the Civil Service examination for compositor in the Government Printing Office, and thus began his long stint with the public printer. In 1899, he received a bachelor of law degree from Howard University and a master's degree in 1900. He was very active in the social, civic, and literary life of the capital and was editor of the *Odd Fellows Journal* from 1910 to 1937.

Henry Slaughter had a consuming passion for books, and built a formidable private library of books, broadsides, documents, autographs, and other memorabilia about African American history. His passion for collecting once caused him to spend the money that his wife had given him to purchase a hat on some rare items he found in a bookstore enroute to the millinery shop. His home was literally crammed with materials on African American life. Slaughter must be included among those outstanding bibliophiles in African American studies—Schomburg and Arthur B. Spingarn.

In 1946, Slaughter sold his collection to Atlanta University (Clark Atlanta University), where it serves as the core for their present Negro Collection, one of the foremost collections in the Southeast documenting the African American experience. Henry P. Slaughter died in 1958 at the age of eighty-seven.

## MONROE NATHAN WORK (1866-1945)

Work[3] was born of slave parentage in Iredell County, North Carolina, in 1866, to Alexander and Elizabeth Work. He grew up in Illinois and Kansas. He first tried his hand as a minister in the African Methodist Church from 1892 to 1893. In 1895 he studied for the ministry at the Chicago Theological Seminary. He realized that he had other aspirations, so he entered the University of Chicago in 1898 for graduate studies in sociology. He received his bachelor's degree in 1902, and in 1903, he was awarded a master of arts in sociology—the first African American man to receive the degree from that institution.

After completing his studies in Chicago, Work then taught for a while at the Georgia Industrial State College in Savannah, Georgia. In 1904, he married Florence F. Hendrickson. Also in 1904, Work published the first of the famous Tuskegee reports on Black lynchings in the United States, and in 1908, he became the founder and director of the Department of Records and Research at Tuskegee Institute in Tuskegee, Alabama. In 1912, Work began to compile an annual encyclopedia, the *Negro Yearbook*, which is still a treasury of facts about life in America. The *Yearbook* went through nine editions (1912-1938) and was the most extensively used book of information on African Americans of its day. The Harmon Award was presented to Work in 1921 in recognition of "scholarly research and educational publicity through the periodicals, compilation, and publication of *The Negro Yearbook*."

In 1921, the Carnegie Corporation made a grant to Tuskegee that enabled Work to begin the compilation of his monumental *Bibliography of the Negro* that, based on comprehensive study, listed titles and authors of books, pamphlets, and serial articles about Black people in Africa and America, and today it stands without a peer in Black bibliography. The compilation took several years, after which Work visited American and European libraries to verify the accuracy of his compilations. The finished tome, revised three times before publication, was finally published in 1928. Work retired in 1938 at the age of seventy-two, after thirty years of service for the Tuskegee Department of Records and Research. Howard University awarded him an honorary doctor of letters degree. At that time, he had collected and organized more than seventy thousand bibliographical citations for a new *Bibliography of European Colonization and the Resulting Conflicts of Peoples, Races, and Culture*. He died at his beloved Tuskegee, May 2, 1945. His passion for truth continues as a blessing to scholars, who are in his debt forever.

## S. W. STARKS (1866-1908)

Little is known about S. W. Starks,[4] an African American man who was West Virginia state librarian from 1901 to 1906. Many holders of the position of state librarian did not have training for the position, but Governor A. B. White appointed Starks to the position in 1901. The state librarian's responsibilities included those of the register of copyrights and chief documents clerk. Starks appointed an assistant, J. Arthur Jackson, also an African American man, as a messenger. In 1917, Jackson became assistance state librarian, and in 1921 he became state librarian—the second African American to hold the position in West Virginia.

Starks was born in Charleston, West Virginia, on March 11, 1866. He was educated in the schools of his hometown and, at the age of sixteen, entered the service of Kanawha and Ohio Railroad as a messenger boy. Later, he became chief telegraph operator. He worked for several railroads and took courses in business at Chicago's Bryant and Stratton Business College. Starks was also active in several Black business ventures in Ohio and West Virginia and was a leader in Black fraternal circles. Politics were of great interest to Starks and took a great deal of his time. In 1900, he was instrumental in West Virginia in efforts to beat back political forces that attempted to institute segregation on public conveyances. Starks died in 1908.

## DANIEL A. P. MURRAY (1852-1925)

Daniel Alexander Payne Murray[5] was born in Baltimore, Maryland, on March 3, 1852, the son of George and Eliza Wilson Murray. He was apparently born of freemen and was educated in Baltimore public schools and at the Unitarian Seminary in his hometown. In 1879, he married Anna Evans of Oberlin, Ohio, and raised seven children.

Murray is a prime example of a librarian of great reputation who was not formally trained as a librarian. However, he made an unusual mark at the Library of Congress during his long tenure there. Murray joined the staff of the Library of Congress in 1871. From 1874 to 1897, he was personal assistant to Aimsworth R. Spofford, Librarian of Congress, and was also an assistant librarian beginning in 1880. In the *1923 Report of the Librarian of Congress*, the then librarian, Herbert Putnam, opined that Murray's "extraordinary record, exceeded in the Library of Congress probably in but a single instance, was remarkable in the almost unbroken continuity and regularity of his attendance."[6] However, regularity of attendance at the Library of Congress was not the only claim to fame of Murray.

Murray was "curator" of a collection of Black books and pamphlets that was the outgrowth of an exhibit of Negroana prepared for the Paris Exposition of 1900; it later was called the "Murray Collection." Murray edited his *Preliminary List of Books and Pamphlets by Negro Authors* for the Exposition—a landmark bibliography of the Black American experience.

In his position at the Library of Congress, Murray fostered an undying interest in Black literature, which led to his editorship of *Murray's Historical and Biographical Encyclopedia of the Colored Race throughout the World* (Washington, DC, 1912). This work was planned to chronicle in six volumes the race's "progress and achievements from the earliest period down to the present time." The *Encyclopedia* promised to its readers "25,000 biographical sketches . . . a bibliography of over 6,000 titles of books and pamphlets . . . a synoptical list of all books of fiction by White authors that deal with the race question, and a list of nearly 5,000 musical compositions by Black composers in every part of the world."[7] This formidable task was to be undertaken with the aid of John E. Bruce, Arthur A. Schomburg, John W. Cromwell, L. M. Henshaw, Bishop J. Albert Johnson, William S. Scarborough, R. R. Wright Jr., and scholars from Africa and the Caribbean area. Twenty years of research went into the project, but it was never completed and published.

Murray was prominent in Washington's social and civic affairs and was also a successful realtor. He was a member of the National Commission to escort Admiral George Dewey to Washington, DC, to receive the accolades of the Washington Civic Centre, Washington Board of Tred, and the Oldest Inhabitants Association. Mr. Murray contributed articles to the *Voice of the Negro* and collaborated in writing *Banneker, the Afro-American Astronomer* (1921).

On December 31, 1922, Murray retired from Library of Congress service at the close of fifty-two years. He died in Washington, DC, three years later, in 1925.

## GEORGE WASHINGTON FORBES (1864-1927)

Another great pioneer Black librarian was George Washington Forbes[8] of Boston, Massachusetts, who was appointed to serve a predominantly Black neighborhood at the West End Branch of the Boston Public Library. However, the color and culture of the area changed, and Forbes soon found himself serving a largely Jewish clientele until his death in 1927.

Forbes was born in Shannon, Mississippi, in 1864, but he left the South at age fourteen to go west. In Ohio, he attended Wilberforce University, he then graduated from Amherst College (Massachusetts) in 1892 and settled in Boston. In Boston, Forbes edited a small, Black weekly newspaper, *The Courant*. Forbes was also a central figure in Black Boston intellectual circles and was a close associate of W. E. B. Du Bois and William Monroe Trotter.

Trotter and Forbes combined forces to establish a radical paper of the day, the *Boston Guardian*. The newspaper was an ardent foe of Booker T. Washington's advocacy of accommodation on the part of Black people, and Forbes wrote highly charged editorials critical of the "Washington Machine" at Tuskegee. The *Boston Guardian* served a very significant role during this period as it provided a platform for progressive Black Americans to express various views. Du Bois described the paper as "bitter, satirical, and personal, but it was well edited."[9]

For several years, Forbes was assistant librarian of the West End Branch of the Boston Public Library, where he joined the staff in 1896 as the only Black member. As librarian for the growing Jewish community, Forbes assisted in the education and encouragement of a generation of immigrant Jews. He was so popular at the branch that users referred to him as "Reference Librarian." Forbes was also greatly responsible for arranging the Theodore Parker Collection in the Boston Public Library.

In addition to his work as librarian, he was also a steady editorial assistant on the *African Methodist Episcopal Church Review* and wrote for the *Springfield Republican* and *Boston Transcript*. Forbes wrote continually on Black history and biography for most his adult life, and at the time of his death, he was just about to publish the *History of the Black Man in the Life the Republic*. Forbes succumbed to influenza, and his funeral was held on March 14, 1927. The West End Branch was closed for services, and children who used the branch presented Forbes's widow with a floral offering and a gift box. The pallbearers were his White associates at the Boston Public Library.

The Jewish Community felt the great loss of Forbes, as did the Black community. *Opportunity* and *Crisis* both carried news of his demise, and *Crisis* reprinted a long eulogy that appeared in *The Jewish Daily Forward*. The final paragraph stated,

> Since his death everybody, especially the children of the West End, misses Mr. Forbes. They feel now like sheep without a shepherd. The joy and happiness that reigned every evening in the children's room is now gone. Though children still come to the Library with their problems, they no longer have Mr. Forbes to assist them. The librarian, too, is in despair because the Library cannot easily find a person to fill his place. Though his death is being mourned by the Negro population that was justly proud of him, still now he is being mourned by the Jewish children of the West End of Boston.[10]

## EDWARD CHRISTOPHER WILLIAMS (1871–1929)

In the annals of American librarianship, Edward Christopher (E. C.) Williams[11] is considered the first professionally trained Black librarian, and according to Eliza A. Gleason, the first Black man to earn his livelihood in the field of librarianship.

Williams was born of a mixed marriage—his father was from a distinguished Black family, and his mother, Mary Kilkary, was Irish—on February 11, 1871. He was educated in the public schools of Cleveland, and in 1892 he graduated from Western Reserve University (Case Western Reserve University). He had been elected to Phi Beta Kappa in his junior year and was valedictorian of his graduating class. Upon graduation, he was appointed assistant librarian of Hatch Library at Western Reserve University, and in 1894 he was appointed librarian of the university's Adelbert College (the undergraduate men's division) in Cleveland, Ohio. In 1900, he graduated from the New York State Library School, having received his certificate after one year's study rather than the normal two. Williams was appointed instructor in library service in the library school of Western Reserve University and still retained his position at Adelbert College.

Western Reserve University was planning a library school, and prior to its establishment, Williams taught an elementary course in national bibliography to a few seniors. He later became an instructor in bibliography and reference work. He then joined the library school faculty in 1904, teaching the courses Public Documents and The Criticism and Selection of Books.

Williams married the eldest daughter of Charles Waddell Chestnutt, the distinguished Black author. Ethel Chestnutt Williams was a graduate of Smith College. They had a son, Charles, who became a lawyer and wrote a biography of his father (which was never published due to the author's sudden death).

Williams devoted a great deal of his time to collection building at Western Reserve University and laid the foundation for the present eminence of the collection there. A charter member of the Ohio Library Association, he served as its secretary in 1904. He was the second vice president of the New York State Library School Association in 1904. He chaired the Constitution Committee of the Ohio Library Association and was chair of its college section. Williams was a member of the American Library Association (ALA) and addressed a session of ALA's College and Reference Section (ACRL) on May 30, 1928, about "Library Needs of Negro Institutions."

After fifteen years at Western Reserve University, E. C. Williams resigned his position in August 1909 to assume the principalship of M Street High School in the nation's capital. M Street High School had a reputation for educating an inordinately large number of students who went on to greater heights after pursuing college work at the elite colleges of the East and New England. Williams brought to the school "the richest and most varied" scholarship of any principal in the school's history. He left M Street High School in June 1916 to become professor of bibliography, director of the library training class, and librarian at Howard University. During his first year, he was also acting instructor in German.

Early in his career at Howard, Williams recognized the pressing need for improved quarters, personnel, and resources if Howard were to realize its goals as the "capstone of Negro education." He set up a library training class in 1917–1918; however, it was not until 1922 that instruction began. In addition to his duties as librarian-instructor, he also served as director of student organization, member of the University-wide Library Committee, associate faculty editor of the *Howard University Record*, and a teacher in the romance languages department.

Williams was an accomplished writer as well and wrote for the student drama group *The Exile*, an Italian classical two-act drama. He wrote two other dramas: *The Sheriff's Children*, an adaptation of his father-in-law's short story, and *The Chasm*, in collaboration with Willis Richardson. He penned a series of articles on the foibles of Black society in Washington, DC, which were published in the *Messenger* from 1925 to 1926.

Williams completed advanced study at Columbia University through a Rosenwald Fellowship in 1929–1930. He had hoped to receive his PhD at the end of his studies, but it was not to be. After a brief illness, Williams died on December 24, 1929.

In the April 1930 issue of *Crisis* it is stated, "But Edward Williams was more than a scientific librarian.... He died a comparatively young man in a career but half-finished, and left the memory of a scientist, a writer, and a loyal and genial friend."[12]

## THOMAS FOUNTAIN BLUE (1866–1935)

When Louisville Free Public Library began service in 1905, there was a plan for ten branch libraries, two of which were designated to give service to African Americans of that Kentucky city. The first branch was opened with a librarian and two assistants—all were Black.

The system soon learned that it took more than mortar, bricks, and books to make a library; it also took trained library personnel to operate an effective library program. An annual library apprentice class was established for those interested in library work, the first example of any attempt in the South to provide library training for the prospective Black librarian. Students from such cities as Houston, Texas, and Memphis, Tennessee, availed themselves of Louisville's project since no other means of training seems to have been available until the inauguration of the Library School at Hampton Institute (Hampton University) in the 1920s.

The guiding light behind these library developments in Louisville was Thomas Fountain Blue.[13] In 1905, Louisville authorities called Blue to head this first branch for African Americans, and for thirty years he worked in the branch. Western Colored Branch was joined by the Eastern Colored Branch in 1914, and Blue was given joint direction. Then in 1920, all work for African Americans was consolidated under the direction of Thomas Blue. Louisville served as the prototype for service to African Americans in the South, and Blue served with the distinction in the vanguard of development of branch library service.

Thomas Blue was the second child of former slaves, Noah and Henri Ann Blue, born near Washington, DC, March 6, 1866. Blue attended Hampton Institute from 1885 to 1888 and received a bachelor of divinity degree from Richmond Theological Seminary in 1898. Although he was primarily educated as a minister, he never held a position as a church pastor. He served as YMCA secretary of the Sixth Virginia Regiment Volunteers in the Spanish-American War. He continued his association with the YMCA after the war, was called to Louisville to head the Colored Branch of the YMCA, and remained as its first regular secretary from 1899 to 1903.

In 1918, Blue was serving temporarily as an educational secretary in the First World War at a camp in Kentucky, where he helped teach thousands of new recruits to read and write. In 1919, he returned to library work. He developed a working arrangement with the schools through library stations and classroom collections, and heavy use of the building was evidenced by the numerous clubs and associations meeting regularly in the branches. Blue served as director of all the African American work in Louisville from 1919 to 1935.

Blue was also active in the American Library Association (ALA). During the Detroit meeting in 1922, he read a paper, "Training Class at the Western Colored Branch," before the "Work with Negroes Round Table" session. It is believed that Blue was the first African American to have a place on the program of ALA. Also, Blue is listed as a delegate to the ALA fiftieth anniversary convention in Atlantic City in 1926. Blue delivered the opening address at the Negro Library Conference of 1927, held at Hampton Institute, speaking on "Arousing Community Interest in the Library." In addition, Blue was one of several African American librarians in attendance at the ALA conference held in 1928 in West Baden, Indiana.

He co-organized the Negro Library Conference of 1930, held at the dedication of the Fisk University Library, and was a prominent speaker at the exercises. He became ill in 1935 and died on November 10, 1935. In recent years, the surviving "Colored Branch" has been placed on the National Register as a landmark, a fitting tribute to the work of Thomas Fountain Blue—a pioneer librarian.

## SUSAN DART BUTLER (1888–1959)

The provision of library services to African Americans in the South was scanty at best up to the early twentieth century, and even the idea of free library service to all persons did not include the Southern African Americans in all instances. As early as 1900, some provisions were made for separate facilities, but still the growth of the number of cities offering segregated library service could be described as sporadic and limited. Since 1920, however, growth has been more consistent. This change in growth and attitude has been due, in part, to individuals and groups having both an interest in library service and a cognizance of the presence of a racial dualism that demanded the leadership of achieving African Americans in the field of library service. The reversal of the trend of not providing service to African Americans can be considered as the result of a combination of efforts on the part of citizens, philanthropic organizations, and librarians. One such committed librarian was Susan Dart Butler of Charleston, South Carolina, who was obsessed from early childhood with the desire to provide library service to Charleston's Black populace.

Susan Dart[14] was born of free parents in Charleston in 1888. Her father, John L. Dart, an ordained Baptist minister, married Julia Pierre, and Susan was the first of five children born to the couple in the parsonage of Morris Street Baptist Church in Charleston. She was educated in the schools of Charleston and Washington, DC, and attended Atlanta University's Normal Department and the McDowell Millinery

School of Boston. She also received some training in library science at Hampton Institute in Virginia in 1932. She married Nathaniel Lowe Butler in 1912, and the young couple moved to Charleston and had one son, Nathaniel Lowe Butler Jr.

After the death of her father and son, Susan turned to civic activities. Her father had erected a building (Dart Hall) years before to provide facilities for educating the young Black children of Charleston. Butler assembled the family library in the building and made the collection available three times a week to the public. A regular story hour was held for youngsters, and the high school used the facility as well. Butler also traveled widely and gained counsel from many library leaders on how to serve her patrons more effectively. The library was maintained at her own expense as she attempted to persuade the Black citizens and the city of Charleston to provide financial support for it. Meanwhile, she motivated women's groups and churches to collect books and raise funds for the project.

The Rosenwald Fund became interested in promoting public library service to African Americans in the South in the 1920s, and in 1925 Butler organized a biracial women's committee to investigate the feasibility of seeking Rosenwald support to start public library service. The Rosenwald interests were so impressed by Butler's work that there was ferment for a five-year plan for the development of the library with Charleston County officials. Rosenwald and the Carnegie Corporation gave funds for the establishment of the Charleston County Free Public Library, and, for one dollar a year, Butler gave use of Dart Hall to the County Library as her contribution to the project.

In 1929, the County Library began service to all citizens. Dart Hall Branch was opened in July 1931, with Butler serving as children's librarian. In 1932, she attended Hampton Institute Library School and returned to Charleston to become librarian of Dart Hall Branch Library. However, Butler's interests went beyond library service to African Americans. Her organizational interests included the Librarians Section of the South Carolina State Teachers' Association, the YMCA, Boy Scouts, Girl Scouts, and the American Red Cross, and she was founder/historian of the South Carolina Federation of Women's Clubs.

At the age of sixty-nine, in May 1957, Susan Dart Butler retired after serving as branch librarian for twenty-six years. She was acclaimed by the library board and citizens for exemplary pioneering spirit that inspired others to work toward similar goals. Susan Dart Butler died in 1959.

## SADIE PETERSON DELANEY (1889-1959)

"What is bibliotherapy?" asked Eleanor Roosevelt in her column, *My Day*. She was writing about an unusual Black librarian, Sadie Peterson Delaney. Bibliotherapy has been defined as "book treatment," the art or science of curing or improving the state of health of the ill and infirm (either physically or mentally) through the skillful selection and reading of appropriate books and use of other media.

Sadie Peterson Delaney[15] was born in Rochester, New York, in 1889, the daughter of James and Julia Johnson. She received her early training at Poughkeepsie High School in New York and at the College of the City of New York. Her first marriage ended in divorce, and she later married Rudicel A. Delaney in 1928. She trained for the library service in the New York Public Library, and in 1919 she was assigned to the 135th Street Branch.

The 135th Street Branch, located in Harlem, was one of the focal points for literary ferment that was later to burst into the Harlem Renaissance. Here, Delaney set a pattern of service that would hold for a lifetime—the consideration and use of books in relation to the practical interest and needs of people. Story hours were started, and special groups for parents and teachers, Boy Scouts, YMCA leaders, social workers, and others brought attention to the library resources and its programs. The first library art exhibits of Black artists' work were held, and a book lovers club caught the interest of the young Countee Cullen, Claude McKay, and Langston Hughes. Delaney placed special emphasis upon building a Negroana Collection at the New York Public Library, and because of this interest she came to know Arthur Schomburg, who later provided the nucleus for the world-famed collection on people of the African/Black diaspora now bearing his name.

While working with various groups and individuals. Delaney became interested in work with the blind; this interest became so great that she learned Braille and Moon Point. In 1923, she was called to organize the hospital library at the Veterans Administration (VA) Hospital at Tuskegee, Alabama. Thus, she began her work at the hospital as a pioneer in bibliotherapy, group therapy for the mentally ill, and organization of work for the blind, all of which would bring her international acclaim.

At Tuskegee, she found very little more than the need and desire for the library service. She said in 1925, "We began work on the wards by carrying books and magazines to the patients in a wire paper carrier,"[16] and the first month's circulation was 275. She started the only VA library in the country, with a literary society and reading classes, and from then on began to create a technique of dealing with hospital patients that has been discussed and imitated throughout the profession in this country and abroad. So marked were Delaney's achievements and her theories that her library was for years a demonstration center for other VA hospitals, as well as the site of internships for library school students.

She was an extremely active member of the ALA and its Hospital Library section, and the library profession as a whole honored her at an ALA testimonial banquet at its convention in 1950. Also, in 1950, Atlanta University, in recognition of her achievement, conferred upon her the doctor of humanities degree, and the citation stated in part that she was a "pioneer in utilizing reading materials in the rehabilitation of delinquent boys and girls, in the rehabilitation and cure of mental patients, and in the development of techniques for teaching the blind to read . . . a great humanitarian." In 1950, she received the

National Urban League Award as Woman of the Year as well, and in September of the same year she was applauded by *Look* magazine. In 1952, she was selected as one of America's outstanding women and given a national award of the National Council of Colored Women's Clubs. The VA also cited Delaney for distinguished contributions to library science and library science education in the United States and abroad. Delaney died in 1959. A scholarship loan fund in her honor was begun at the School of Library Service of Atlanta University.

## RACHEL DAVIS HARRIS (1869-1969)

Rachel Davis Harris[17] was a distinguished children's librarian, a contemporary of Reverend Thomas Fountain Blue, and the first African American female public library director in Kentucky. Harris was born Rachel Davis in 1869 in Louisville, Kentucky, to Jerry and Susan Davis. She married Reverend Everett Harris in 1893, and the couple had a son John Everett Harris three years later.

A former schoolteacher, Harris was a graduate of the library training program founded by Reverend Thomas Fountain Blue at the Western Colored Branch of the Louisville Public Library. In 1914, Harris was appointed manager of the library's Eastern Colored Branch. That same year, Harris was the keynote speaker at the grand opening of the Cherry Street Branch of the Evansville Public Library (Evansville-Vanderburgh County Public Library), a Carnegie library for African Americans in Evansville, Indiana.

Harris and Reverend Blue collaborated with other librarians to organize the First Negro Library Conference, held in 1927 at the Hampton Institute (Hampton University) in Hampton, Virginia. Harris also worked with Blue and other librarians in planning the Second Negro Library Conference, held in 1930 at Fisk University in Nashville, Tennessee. In addition, Harris and Blue were among the group of nine African American librarians attending the 1928 ALA Annual Conference in West Baden, Indiana.

Like Blue, Davis trained librarians at the Western and Eastern Colored Branches. Davis also taught a summer librarian training course at Spelman College that was cosponsored by the Rosenwald Fund and the Southeastern Library Association. When Reverend Blue died in 1935, Harris succeeded him as director of the African American branches of the Louisville Public Library. She directed the two branches for seven years, retiring in 1942. Rachel Davis Harris passed away in 1969 at the age of one hundred years old.

## ETKA BRABOY GASKIN (1885-1972)

Etka Braboy Gaskin[18] was the first African American librarian hired by the Gary (Indiana) Public Library. She was born Etka Braboy on November 13, 1885, in Kokomo, Indiana. Her parents were Joseph Albert Braboy and Alice McCoy Braboy. Gaskin's father was a member of the Kokomo City Council and owned several businesses in the city. In addition, her father served in the 28th Regiment of the United States Colored Troops—Indiana's only African American regiment in the Civil War.

Gaskin was a 1904 graduate of Kokomo High School. She married Edward R. Gaskin in 1911. In 1914, the couple moved to Calgary, Alberta, Canada, and lived there for about four years before returning to the United States and settling in Gary, Indiana. In 1923, Gaskin was hired as an assistant at the Roosevelt Branch of the Gary Public Library. Named for Theodore Roosevelt, the Roosevelt Branch was near 25th and Jackson Streets, not far from where the famous Jackson family (i.e., The Jackson 5) once lived before they left for California.

Gaskin enrolled in and received her librarian's certificate in 1923 from the Indiana Public Library Commission Summer School for Librarians (Indiana State Library Summer School). In 1924, Gaskin was promoted to librarian and moved to the Gary Public Library's Alcott Branch. In 1927, the Gary Public Library opened a branch inside Roosevelt High School and appointed Gaskin as the school's librarian where she remained for the remainder of her career.

Gaskin was a member of the Indiana Library Association (Indiana Library Federation) and the American Library Association. In addition, she was one of nine African American librarians in attendance at the 1928 ALA Annual Conference in West Baden, Indiana.

Etka Braboy Gaskin passed away on October 16, 1972, in Gary, Indiana.

## HALLIE BEACHEM BROOKS (1907-1985)

A renowned library science professor, Hallie Beachem Brooks[19] was born Hallie Mae Beachem in West Baden, Indiana, on October 7, 1907, to Hal and Mary Bowden Beachem. When she was nine years old, Brooks's family moved to Indianapolis. While still a student at Shortridge High School, Brooks applied to and was accepted by the Indiana Public Library Commission Summer School for Librarians (Indiana State Library Summer School). She received her librarian's certificate from the library school in 1924. Brooks worked as a library assistant and then a librarian at the Paul Lawrence Dunbar Branch of the Indianapolis Public Library under the mentorship of Lillian Childress Hall, branch manager and the first African American graduate of the Indiana Public Library Commission Summer School for Librarians. While working at the library, Brooks attended Butler University, a private university in Indianapolis.

In 1930, Brooks left the Indianapolis Public Library to work at the Atlanta University Laboratory School. During the summer months, Brooks would return to Butler University to complete coursework for her bachelor's degree, which she received in 1934. Two years later, she married Victor Brooks.

Brooks furthered her library science education at Columbia University, earning a bachelor of library science degree in 1940. In 1946, at the University of Chicago, she received a master of library science degree. Brooks taught at the Atlanta University School of Library Service from 1942 until her retirement in 1977.

In addition to teaching library science, Brooks directed the Carnegie Field Service Program for Negro School Libraries, chaired the American Library Association's Asian Foundation Grants Committee, wrote several articles for *Phylon*, and presented papers at several library conferences.

Brooks was active in the American Library Association, Georgia Library Association, Association of Library and Information Science Education, the Metropolitan Atlanta Library Association, and the Southeastern Library Association. In addition, Brooks was a member of the Friends of the Atlanta Fulton Public Library's Board of Directors. Brooks passed away in 1985.

**DORIS HARGRETT CLACK (1928–1995)**

A graduate of the library science programs at the University of Michigan and the University of Pittsburgh, Doris Hargrett Clack[20] was a cataloging professor renowned for her extensive knowledge of cataloging and classification of library materials, and her contributions to the creation of the second edition of *Anglo-American Cataloging Rules* (AACR2) and for her dissertation, "An Investigation into the Adequacy of Library of Congress Subject Headings for Resources for Black Studies." Clack was a professor at Florida A&M University and Florida State University and gave lectures on library science in Ghana and Uganda. In addition, she wrote several books on cataloging including *Authority Control: Principles, Applications, and Instructions* and *Black Literature Resources: Analysis and Organization* and edited *The Making of a Code: The Issues Underlying AACR2: Papers Given at the International Conference on AACR2, Held March 11–14, 1979 in Tallahassee, Florida*. In addition, Clack was instrumental in the founding of the Association of College and Research Libraries African American Studies Section (African American Studies Interest Group). Clack passed away on November 22, 1995.

**ELIZA ATKINS GLEASON (1909–2009)**

Eliza Atkins Gleason,[21] the first director of the library science program at Atlanta University (Clark Atlanta University), was the first African American to earn a doctorate in library science and the first African American to serve on the ALA Council.

Gleason was born Eliza Valeria Atkins on December 15, 1909, in Winston-Salem, North Carolina. Her parents were Simon Green Atkins and Oleana Pegram Atkins. Gleason attended college at Fisk University, graduating in 1930. She then went on to study library science, receiving her bachelor in library science in 1931 from the University of Illinois. Gleason also worked at Louisville Municipal College for Negroes (Simmons College) and Talladega College.

Gleason earned two additional degrees in library science, her MLS in 1935 from the University of California-Berkeley and then her PhD at the University of Chicago in 1940. The same year she completed her PhD, Gleason was appointed dean of the Atlanta University Library School. Her dissertation on library services to African Americans in the southern United States was published the following year in 1941 as a book, *The Southern Negro and the Public Library*.

After leaving Atlanta University in 1946, Gleason held positions at Woodrow Wilson Junior College, Northern Illinois University, the Chicago Public Library, the Illinois Institute of Technology, and Chicago Teachers College. Gleason also served on the board of the Chicago Public Library.

Dr. Eliza Atkins Gleason died at the age of one hundred on December 15, 2009. The ALA Library History Round Table's Gleason Award, given every three years for the best book on library history, is named for her.

**VIVIAN DAVIDSON HEWITT (1920–2022)**

Vivian Davidson Hewitt[22] made history when she became the first African American elected as president of the Special Libraries Association in 1978. A native of New Castle, Pennsylvania, Hewitt was born Vivian Ann Davidson on February 17, 1920, to Arthur and Lela Davidson. Hewitt attended public school in New Castle, and after finishing high school, she attended Geneva College in Beaver Falls, Pennsylvania.

After graduating from Geneva College in 1943, Hewitt studied library science at the University of Pittsburgh School of Library and Information Sciences (University of Pittsburgh School of Information Sciences). After receiving her library science degree in 1944, Hewitt worked at the Carnegie Library of Pittsburgh for six years before becoming a library science instructor at the Atlanta University School of Library Service (Clark Atlanta University School of Library and Information Sciences). While in Atlanta, Hewitt met and married John Hewitt in 1949. Hewitt later worked as the head librarian at the Carnegie Endowment for International Peace and at the Rockefeller Foundation Library. In addition, Hewitt spent two years as a researcher at the Crowell-Collier Publishing Company.

Hewitt was a collector of art and established with her husband the Hewitt Art Collection at the Harvey B. Gantt Center for African American Arts and Culture. Hewitt contributed the chapter "Special Libraries, Librarians and the Continuing Education of Black People" for *What Black Librarians Are Saying*, edited and published by Dr. Josey in 1972. Hewitt also wrote about her life and career in her autobiography *The One and Only: Vivian Davidson Hewitt*. Queen Elizabeth II honored Hewitt with the title of Dame in 2016. Vivian Davidson Hewitt lived to the age of 102. She died on May 29, 2022.

**MAJOR R. OWENS (1936–2013)**

A graduate of the Atlanta University Library School and a former librarian at the Brooklyn Public Library, Major R. Owens[23] was the first librarian to serve in the United States Congress. Owens was a US representative for the 11th and 12th congressional districts of New York from 1983 to 2007. He contributed to librarian literature with *The Public Library and Advocacy: Information for Survival: A Commissioned Paper under the Commissioned Papers Project, Teachers College, No. 5* and *The Academic Library and Education for Leadership*. Owens also wrote "The Spector of Racism in an Age of Cultural Diversity: The New Paradigm for African American Librarians" for *The Black Librarian in America Revisited*, edited by Dr. E. J. Josey in 1994, and "The Voice of the Librarian Must Be Heard" for *Educating Black Librarians: Papers from the 50th Anniversary Celebration of the School of Library and Information Science, North Carolina Central University*, edited by Benjamin Speller Jr. in 1991.

Owens introduced legislation in 1993, H.R. 906, that required appointees to the office of the Librarian of Congress to have education and training in library science. Unfortunately, the legislation was never voted on. After leaving Congress, Owens was a scholar-in-residence at the Library of Congress's Kluge Center. Major Owens passed away on October 21, 2013.

## CASPER LEROY JORDAN (1924-2000)

Casper LeRoy Jordan[24] was born on March 5, 1924, in Cleveland, Ohio. He was the son of John and Leola Jordan. Jordan attended Adelbert College (Case Western Reserve University), receiving his bachelor's degree in history in 1947. Jordan furthered his education at the Atlanta University Library School and graduated with an MLS in 1951. He then returned to Ohio, where he served as the chief librarian at Wilberforce University before moving on to the Nioga (New York) Library System ten years later.

In 1968, Jordan became an instructor at the Atlanta University Library School. In 1974, he was university librarian at Atlanta University (Clark Atlanta University) and served in this position for four years before moving on to the Fulton County (Georgia) Public Library where he served as the deputy director until his retirement in 1987.

Jordan was a member of ALA and BCALA and was a life member of the NAACP and the Association for the Study of African American Life and History. Together with E. J. Josey, Jordan compiled "Chronology of Events in Black Librarianship" for the first and second editions of the *Handbook of Black Librarianship*. Jordan also compiled "African American Forerunners in Black Librarianship" for both editions. In addition, Jordan was an editor for *Free Lance* and wrote *A Bibliographical Guide to African American Women Writers*. Jordan passed away on November 22, 2000.

★ ★ ★

As we look back over the nearly 150 years of the Black presence in American librarianship, the record is impressive. Black men and women served in international, national, state, and local libraries, often pioneering in areas of service to all races. Also, they provided access to materials documenting the struggles of Black people in an often hostile society, materials that demonstrate how Black people have surmounted the obstacles placed before them. Despite overwhelming odds, these librarians and bibliophiles attained greatness, and their names are an indelible part of the annals of American librarianship

## NOTES

1. Earl E. Thorpe, *Black Historians, a Critique* (New York: Morrow, 1971), 145-46; Joel A. Rogers, *World's Great Men of Color*, 2 (New York: McMillan, 1972), 449-53; *Who's Who of the Colored Race* (Chicago: Mather, 1915), 237.
2. "A Kentucky Leader," *Colored American*, 10 (1902): 1, 4; Biographical files, Trevor Arnett Library, Atlanta University.
3. Juanita L. Horne, "The Sociological Contributions of Monroe Nathan Work" (master's thesis, Atlanta University, 1975; Jessie Guzman, "Monroe Nathan Work and His Contributions," *Journal of Negro History* (1949): 34; Thorpe, *Black Historians*, 137-39; *Who's Who in Colored America* (New York: Burchel, 1927), 229.
4. Wallace Van Jackson, "Some Pioneer Negro Library Workers," *Library Journal*, no. 64 (1939) 215-17; *Colored American*, 9, no. 2 (1901): 1.
5. *Who's Who of the Colored Race*, 203; Van Jackson, "Some Pioneer Negro Library Workers," 215-17; US Library of Congress, *Report of the Librarian of Congress, 1923* (Washington, DC: Government Printing Office, 1923), 111; *Murray's Historical and Biographical Encyclopedia*. Prospectus (Washington, DC: World's Cyclopedia Company, 1912).
6. US Library of Congress, *Report of the Librarian of Congress, 1923* (Washington, DC: Government Printing Office, 1923), 111.
7. *Murray's Historical and Biographical Encyclopedia*. Prospectus (Washington, DC: World's Cyclopedia Company, 1912).
8. M. Bender, "A People's Tribute," *Opportunity*, no. 5 (1927): 184; Van Jackson, "Some Pioneer Negro Library Workers," 215-17; "George Forbes of Boston," *Crisis*, no. 34 (1927): 151-57; Harold Wade, *Black Men of Amherst* (Amherst, MA: Amherst College Press, 1976), 21-23.
9. W. E. B. Du Bois, *Dusk of Dawn* (New York: Oxford University Press, 2007), 37.
10. "George Forbes of Boston," *Crisis*, no. 34 (1927): 151-57.
11. "Williams," *Crisis*, no. 37 (1930): 138; Van Jackson, "Some Pioneer Negro Library Workers," 215-17; E. J. Josey, "Edward Christopher Williams: A Librarian's Librarian," *Journal of Library History*, 4 (1969): 106-22.
12. "Williams," *Crisis*, no. 37 (1930): 138.
13. Eliza Atkins Gleason, *Southern Negro and the Public Library* (Chicago: University of Chicago Press, 1941), 23; R. D. Harris, "The Advantages of the Colored Branch Libraries," *Southern Workman*, 64 (1915): 389-90; B. W. Bell, "Colored Branches of the Louisville Free Public Library," *ALA Bulletin*, 11 (1917): 170; Lillian T. Wright, "Thomas Fountain Blue, Pioneer Librarian,1866-1935" (master's thesis, Atlanta University, 1955).
14. Ethel Bolden, "Susan Dart Butler: Pioneer Librarian" (master's thesis, Atlanta University, 1959); Virginia L. Jones, "Susan Dart Butler," *Dictionary of American Library Bibliography* (Littleton, CO: Libraries Unlimited, 1977).
15. Morteza D. Sprague, "Dr. Sadie Peterson Delaney, Great Humanitarian," *Service*, 15 (1951): 17-18; Sadie P. Delaney,

"Library Activities in Tuskegee," *Medical Bulletin of the Veterans Administration*, 17 (1940): 163-69; *Who's Who in Colored America*, 48; Clyde H. Cantrell, "Sadie Peterson Delaney: Bibliotherapist and Librarian," *Southeastern Librarian*, 6 (1956): 105-9; Sadie P. Delaney, "U.S. Hospital Library No. 91, Tuskegee Alabama," *Crisis*, 29 (1925): 116-17.

16. Sadie P. Delaney, "U.S. Hospital Library No. 91," 116-17.
17. Mary Mace Spradling, "Black Librarians in Kentucky," in *The Black Librarian in the Southeast: Reminiscences, Activities, Challenges*, edited by Annette L. Phinazee (Durham, NC: NCCU School of Library Science, 1980), 44; Michele T. Fenton, "Stepping Out on Faith: Lillian Haydon Childress Hall, Pioneer Black Librarian." *Indiana Libraries*, 33, no.1 (2014): 6-7; Cheryl Knott Malone, "Quiet Pioneers: Black Women Public Librarians in the Segregated South." *Vitae Scholasticae*, 19, no.1 (2000): 4-8; Reinette Jones, *Library Services to African Americans in Kentucky: From the Reconstruction Era to the 1960s* (Jefferson, NC: McFarland, 2002), 52, 69, 80, 86, 88, 162-63; Rachel D. Harris, "Work with Children at the Colored Branch of the Louisville Free Public Library," *Library Journal*, 35, no. 4 (1910):160-61.
18. "Summer School Students 1923," *Library Occurrent*, 6, no. 1 (1923): 411-12; Berneeze Ward, "Mrs. E. Gaskin Attends Meet," *Annex News*, May 1928, 5; Orpha Maud Peters, *The Gary Public Library, 1907-1944* (Gary, IN: Gary Public Library, 1945), 21, 53; "Roosevelt Branch Library," *Gary Library Bulletin*, 22, no. 3 (1965): 2; Michele T. Fenton, "Stepping Out on Faith," 6; "West Baden, Ind.," *Indianapolis Recorder*, June 9, 1928, 7; Berneeze Ward, "News from the Library Dept.," *Annex News*, October 15, 1927, 3; "1904," in *Sargasso 1905* (Kokomo, IN: Kokomo High School, 1905), 129; "History of the Alcott Branch Library," *Gary Library Bulletin*, 22, no. 5 (1965), 2.
19. Rosalind Miller, "One Georgia Librarian: Hallie Beachem Brooks Remembers, 1930-1977," *Georgia Librarian*, 14, no. 2 (1977), 29-38; "Indianapolis Girls Leave for Positions in the South," *Indianapolis Recorder*, September 9, 1930, 6; Michele T. Fenton, "Stepping Out on Faith," 6-7; "Atlanta U. Professor Heads Asian Study Fund," *Jet*, 27, no. 8 (1964): 20; "Summer School Students Accepted for 1924," *Library Occurrent*, 7, no. 3 (1924): 69.
20. Adeline W. Wilkes, "Doris Hargrett Clack, 1928-1995, Called to Teach," *Cataloging and Classification Quarterly*, 25, 2/3 (1998): 111-25; Joseph H. Reason, "Black Librarians in Florida," in *The Black Librarian in the Southeast: Reminiscences, Activities, Challenges*, edited by Annette L. Phinazee (Durham, NC: NCCU School of Library Science, 1980), 30; Alva T. Stone, "Doris Hargrett Clack, 1928-1995: Educator, Gentle Activist, and Mentor," *Library Resources and Technical Services*, 40, no. 2 (1996): 197-200; Karen Tallman, "Doris Hargrett Clack: Not Subject to Classification," *American Libraries*, 9, no. 8 (1978): 467.
21. Almeta Gould Woodson, "Fifty Years of Service: A Chronological History of the School of Library Service Atlanta University, 1941-1979; the School of Library and Information Studies Atlanta University, 1979-1989; the School of Library and Information Studies, Clark Atlanta University, 1989-1991," *Georgia Librarian*, 28, no. 3 (1991): 71-72, 78; Herman L. Totten, "Southeastern Black Educators," in *The Black Librarian in the Southeast: Reminiscences, Activities, Challenges*, edited by Annette L. Phinazee (Durham, NC: NCCU School of Library Science, 1980), 202; *A Directory of Negro Graduates of Accredited Library Schools, 1900-1936* (Washington, DC: Columbia Civic Library Association, 1937), 6; Alma Dawson, "Celebrating African American Librarians and Librarianship," *Library Trends*, 49, no. 1 (2000): 58; Casper Leroy Jordan and E. J. Josey, "A Chronology of Events in Black Librarianship," in *Handbook of Black Librarianship*, edited E. J. Josey and Marva DeLoach (Lanham, MD: Scarecrow, 2000), 7; "Gleason, Eliza Atkins," *Chicago Tribune*, January 25, 2010, Section 1, 22.
22. Vivian Davidson Hewitt, "A Special Librarian by Design," *Special Libraries*, 62, no. 2 (1971): 71-81; Jordan and Josey, "A Chronology of Events in Black Librarianship," 13; Vivian D. Hewitt and Ann Rothstein-Segan, *The One and Only: Vivian Ann Davidson Hewitt* (San Francisco, CA: Blurb, 2010); George S. Bobinski, *Libraries and Librarianship: Sixty Years of Challenge and Change, 1945-2005* (Lanham, MD: Scarecrow, 2007), 100; Vivian D. Hewitt, "Special Libraries, Librarians and the Continuing Education of Black People," in *What Black Librarians Are Saying*, edited by E. J. Josey (Metuchen, NJ: Scarecrow, 1972), 268-74; Risen, "Vivian Hewitt, 102, Dies; Amassed a Renowned Collection of Black Art," *New York Times*, June 27, 2022, Section D, 8.
23. "New Faces on Capitol Hill," *Ebony*, 38, no, 4 (1983), 38, 40; "Cong. Major Owens Honored in New York," *Jet*, 80, no. 7 (1991): 29; Alma Dawson, "Celebrating African American Librarians and Librarianship," *Library Trends*, 49, no. 1 (2000): 60; Jordan and Josey, "A Chronology of Events in Black Librarianship," 14-15; Major R. Owens, "The Spector of Racism in an Age of Cultural Diversity: The New Paradigm for African American Librarians," in *The Black Librarian in America Revisited*, edited by E. J. Josey (Metuchen, NJ: Scarecrow, 1994), 285-97; "The Voice of the Librarian Must Be Heard," in *Educating Black Librarians: Papers from the 50th Anniversary Celebration of the School of Library and Information Science, North Carolina Central University*, edited by Benjamin Speller Jr (Jefferson, NC: McFarland, 1991), 61-67; *H.R. 906: To Require That the Librarian of Congress Be Appointed among Individuals with Specialized Training or Significant Experience in the Field of Library and Information Science* (Washington, DC: United States Government Printing Office, 1993); "Making a Difference: Our Librarian in Congress," *American Libraries*, 32, no. 6 (2001): 56-59; Joseph P. Fried, "Major Owens, 77, Education Advocate in Congress, Dies," *New York Times*, October 23, 2013: A27; George S. Bobinski, *Libraries and Librarianship*, 100; Donna Urschel, "U.S. Congressman Owens Named Distinguished Visiting Scholar at John W. Kluge Center," *News from the Library of Congress*, December 26, 2006, https://www.loc.gov/item/prn-06-237/.
24. Casper Leroy Jordan, "I Have Paid My Dues," in *The Black Librarian in America*, edited by E. J. Josey (Metuchen, NJ: Scarecrow, 1970), 98-114; "8 New Faculty Members Named at Wilberforce," *Indianapolis Recorder*, October 13, 1951, 9; "About the Contributors," in *Handbook of Black Librarianship*, edited by E. J. Josey and Marva DeLoach, 2nd ed. (Lanham, MD: Scarecrow, 2000), 815; Casper LeRoy Jordan,

*A Bibliographical Guide to Black Women Writers* (Westport, CT: Greenwood, 1993); "Memorial Services: A Celebration of Life for Casper LeRoy Jordan, Saturday, December 2, 2000, 11:00 A.M., Flipper Temple A.M.E. Church," Flipper Temple A.M.E. Church, December 2, 2000, https://dlg.usg.edu/record/aarl_afpc_jordancasperleroy20001202.

---

# 2.2

## *Dr. Alma E. Dawson*

INSPIRING A LEGACY OF MENTORSHIP

Jacqueline Jones and Melanie Sims

---

Alma E. Dawson epitomizes excellence in scholarship, pedagogy, and service as an academic librarian and information science professional. Her level of commitment and passion is evident in her contributions as a professor, researcher, and mentor.

Historically, libraries were not welcoming for many African Americans until the mid-twentieth century. Dawson understood well the struggles of African Americans seeking and finding resources that would have an everlasting impact on their lives, those of their families, and indeed the world in which they lived.

Born in 1943, Dawson was a native of Alexandria, Louisiana. She was the first in her family to attend college and was a 1963 graduate of Grambling State University with a concentration in secondary education. Dawson taught in segregated public schools in the deep south for five years. She understood firsthand the impact of a lack of resources for African American students, which fueled her desire to find ways to make information and resources available.

Having first been inspired by the librarian at her high school, and later by her work as a library associate at Prairie View A&M, Dawson developed an interest in libraries and decided to pursue a master's degree in library science at the University of Michigan. After graduation in 1974, she served as head of serials at Prairie View A&M. Dawson later worked for Louisiana State University (LSU) as the education and library science librarian for fourteen years. She later obtained her PhD in library and information science from Texas Woman's University in 1996. Her dissertation was entitled "The Academic in Intra-Institutional Relationships: Case Studies in Academic Library Finance." Dawson then joined the faculty of the LSU School of Library and Information Science (SLIS).

Serving as the only full-time African American professor in SLIS, Dawson paid careful attention to the needs of minority students in the program. The recruitment and mentoring of library professionals became a passion of Alma Dawson. Early on in her career, she recognized the need for libraries to reflect the communities in which they operate. Recruitment of a diverse population to librarianship continues to be an imperative mission for library and information science programs nationally, and specifically for Louisiana. In March 1990, at the annual conference of the Louisiana Library Association, Alma Dawson, then head of the Library and Information Science Library, LSU Libraries, and Connie Van Fleet, assistant professor, LSU School of Library and Information Sciences, convened a group of academic, school, public, and special librarians to address the challenges of recruiting a diverse population to librarianship in the state. During this meeting, it was decided that an interest group within the Louisiana Library Association (LLA) would provide an organizational structure for member communication and for selected activities. On June 1, 1990, the LLA executive board approved the establishment of the Minority Recruitment and Professional Concerns Interest Group. The purpose of the group was "to facilitate minority recruitment and support of professional activity; to study and spotlight issues of concern to minority librarians; to form a network of minority librarians and those concerned with minority issues."[1] The Interest Group's plan of activities included: "Develop a directory of Louisiana minority librarians in order to facilitate communication; explore avenues for educational support for minority students working toward the MLIS; study career development and professional status of minority librarians in Louisiana and to report the results in the *LLA Bulletin*; organize annual meetings at LLA conferences to formulate strategies and develop plans, including feasibility of a regular newsletter, programming, and recruitment strategies." Dawson and Van Fleet were the first coordinators of this group. In 1993, Dawson began teaching full time for the LSU SLIS program and consequently the partnership between the Minority Recruitment and Professional Concerns Interest Group and the School of Library and Information Science was formed.

Dawson understood the importance of mentoring with respect to advising and training for future library professionals. She involved herself as a mentor based on her belief that the presence or absence of a mentor can ultimately determine success or failure for a new professional. With the support and guidance of a mentor, a recent graduate is more likely to be retained in a new career environment. Mentorship programs can also create potential leadership opportunities that benefit the profession of librarianship as a whole. A trusted and experienced mentor brings influence, respect, and value to the culture of an organization. Dawson so espoused the mentorship concept that she implemented a mentoring program for minority and international students at LSU in 1995. The program was geared toward helping those contemplating a career in librarianship.

The mentorship program included a brunch every fall and spring semester for current and prospective students. Members of the Minority and Professional Concerns Interest Group were invited to attend the program to serve as mentors. The format of the programs would include a keynote speaker, which usually featured a recent or former graduate from the program, tips from students on how to succeed in the program, and a networking period. Notably, each program was carefully planned to give special attention to tone and ambience to create an intimate setting with open dialogue. The program included information professionals from all types of libraries, which left an indelible impression of library culture on new recruits and new librarians. Focus was also given to the varying job responsibilities within libraries such as administration, public services, technical services, and archives. Dawson would pair students with mentors. As the program expanded to other locations around the state through a compressed video delivery system, mentors were asked to attend the special programs in their areas, meet students, and offer mentor support. Students were given literature information on study skills, strategies for job hunting, and interviewing skills.

As one who has firsthand knowledge of Dawson's stalwart commitment to mentoring future librarians, I (Jacqueline Jones) can attest to Dr. Dawson's or "Doc" as many of her students fondly called her, offering countless hours of patience to help students improve their writing skills to complete assigned research papers. Conference attendance training was another career obstacle that she helped me and other new librarians overcome. I am one beneficiary of Dr. Dawson's support; my career success may not have been achieved if not for Dr. Dawson. She took me under her wing and introduced me to professional conference culture. She laid out the etiquette and logistics of conference navigation. Starting with booking airplane tickets to selecting a hotel was merely the beginning. Choosing which conference presentations to attend was another lesson to learn as well as learning to navigate the conference bus transit system with all the connections required to arrive at the selected presentation.

Dr. Dawson's goal of training and mentoring new professionals in order to expand the representation of diversity in libraries goes far beyond Alma Dawson's role as a professor, and it is demonstrated throughout her career. In 1997, Dr. Dawson and Dr. Dana Watson received a grant for over $44,000 from the US Department of Education for a "Multicultural Resources Development Institute." The purpose of the weeklong institute held at LSU was to train sixty school and public librarians on the selection, evaluation, and related services dealing with multicultural literature.

Dawson held a strong belief in African Americans telling our own stories which led to her coauthoring with Connie Van Fleet the book entitled *African American Literature: A Guide to Reading Interests* in 2004. The book was published during a time when there was considerable interest in multicultural or diverse literature. Although at the time there were some advisory and critical sources offering guidance in selecting African American literature, none provided a more comprehensive picture of the work of African American authors. Dawson and Van Fleet wrote the book to serve as a professional tool for librarians to meet the specific needs of African American readers. The book recognized the diverse work of African American authors; it connected African American readers with their literary heritage and future. More importantly, it linked all readers with books about the African American experience. Dawson always stressed the importance of writing and the need to publish. She gave some of her former graduates an opportunity to share in the African American literature book project. She was there once again mentoring and encouraging those writing because for some it was their first major publication, and it was no easy task finding information for some of the genres. The book was a labor of love for Dawson and its contributors.

Dawson's leadership in the partnership of LSU SLIS and the Minority Recruitment and Professional Concerns Interest Group made a positive difference in its quest to recruit a diverse population of information professionals. Minority enrollment in SLIS grew over 10 percent during Dr. Dawson's purview. The Minority Recruitment and Professional Concerns Interest Group provided the mechanism for sustaining a network of practicing professionals for recruitment, professional development, and exploration of issues related to diversity in librarianship. In 2006, the Interest Group was renamed the Diversity Interest Group (DIG) to reflect societal changes and to encourage membership by all members of the Louisiana Library Association.

In 2005, Alma Dawson was honored by the American Library Association as the recipient of the Equality Award, which recognizes contributions for promoting equality in the library profession. The Equality Award jury chair, Mohan Ramaswamy, said, "She [Dr. Dawson] has positively impacted diverse groups of librarians with her contribution to education and research. Dr. Dawson's contributions are not only directed to a wide diverse audience, but also are sustainable." Beth Paskoff, former dean, LSU SLIS said she nominated Dawson because "she has a long and productive record of promoting equality in library and information science. She is quiet and unassuming and has done all of this because it was the right thing to do, not because she expected any recognition."[2]

Dawson realized that in addition to mentorship, students also needed financial assistance. She began investigating what was needed to set up a scholarship for minority students in the LSU SLIS program. In 2007, Dawson, along with several members of the Diversity Interest Group, were able to set up an account at the LSU Foundation for a minority scholarship. Alma Dawson served as general coordinator of the fundraising events for the scholarship. On June 6, 2010, the fundraising goal of $10,000 was reached. The newly endowed scholarship was named in honor of Ollie H. Burns, who was the first African American to earn a degree in library science from Louisiana State University in 1957. Burns was also the first African American appointed to the Ouachita Public Library Board of Control (Trustee). She served two terms as chair of the board. Burns was also the first African American to serve as chair of the Public Libraries Section of the Louisiana Library Association (1986–1987) and received the LLA Modisette Award on March 13, 1991. Burns was an active participant in both professional and civic organizations in many roles. After working for thirty-seven successful years with the Jackson and Ouachita Parishes School Systems, she retired in 1976. Upon her retirement, Burns wrote the proposal for the New Way Center, which has served as a model for other after-school tutorial and study programs throughout the country. She also initiated the first legal aid program in Ouachita Parish and was one of the organizers of the Ouachita Parish's Head Start Program. Ollie Burns passed in February 2004.[3]

Following the establishment of the Ollie Burns scholarship, the recruitment and development of librarians continued to be a major focal point of Dawson's career. This was evident when she was awarded a grant for over $750,000 from the Institute of Museum and Library Services. The Project Recovery Grant enabled thirty graduate students in library and information science to receive scholarships to cover tuition, fees, and a stipend as well as an opportunity to work in academic, public, and school libraries in South Louisiana that experienced staff shortages following Hurricanes Katrina and Rita in 2005. The Project Recovery scholars also received free membership in the Louisiana Library Association and the American Library Association. In addition, the Project Recovery grant covered travel costs to state and national conferences as part of the professional development component of the grant.

Dawson's primary goal has always been to help students develop their skills to be the best librarians that they can be. Her devotion to this goal was clear when she wrote the components to the Project Recovery Grant. After Hurricanes Katrina and Rita, libraries in South Louisiana experienced a tremendous staffing loss because so many people were displaced. Dawson developed three main components to the Project Recovery Grant. The first component was a public relations campaign to recruit and enroll thirty scholars both from in state and out of state. The scholars included students that were enrolled full time and part time. The first cohort of twenty-five Louisiana scholars enrolled in spring 2010 and met the requirements of both the LSU graduate school and LSU SLIS. The five out-of-state scholars enrolled fall 2010. In addition, scholars signed a two-year service agreement to work in libraries impacted by hurricanes Katrina or Rita upon receipt of the MLIS degree. The partners for this collaborative included LSU SLIS, the State Library of Louisiana, the New Orleans Public Library, Jefferson Parish Public School System, Algiers Charter School Association, Calcasieu Parish Public Library System, Terrebonne Parish Public Library System, and New Orleans Recovery School District.[4]

The second component of Project Recovery included an academic program in which students completed core course requirements as well as course work for their specializations in academic, school, or public libraries. Since many students did not have any prior library experience, Dawson created experiential learning opportunities for them to apply classroom theory in practical situations. The experiential learning opportunities were woven into the scholars' program in the form of volunteer assignments, service projects, and field experiences working in partner, supported libraries, or any other library impacted by Katrina or Rita. Dawson said, "It was important to me to make sure that we were connecting what the students were doing in the classroom to everyday experience."[5]

The last component of the Project Recovery Grant centered on professional development, advocacy training, employment issues training, and leadership development training. The Project Recovery Scholars were required to present information on their experiences in the Project Recovery Program. At the 2011 LLA Annual Conference in Lafayette, Louisiana, the scholars presented a program, "SLIS at Work in South Louisiana." This gave scholars the opportunity to plan and present a conference program and to become comfortable with conference presentations. The scholars were also provided advocacy training, an employment training workshop, and a leadership conference during which they were able to plan long-term professional goals. Dawson said, "All these special experiences and events were designed to develop the skills necessary for scholars to become successful twenty-first-century librarians."

The Louisiana Library Association recognized Dawson in 2012 with the Meritorious Service Award. This award is given to publicly recognize an individual who has demonstrated sustained and exemplary leadership and service to further the development, services, and visibility of LLA. She also received the Happy Award in 2012, which is given annually by the LSU Center for Community Engagement, Learning, and Leadership, to ten individuals to recognize excellence in service-learning.

The LSU College of Human Sciences and Education (CHSE) awarded Dawson with the Advocate for Diversity Award in 2013. The CHSE Advocate for Diversity Award recognizes a CHSE faculty or staff member who has made an impact on improving diversity and/or understanding of diverse cultures.

Dawson's career spanned thirty-two years at LSU including fourteen at the LSU Library and eighteen in SLIS. She held the Russell B. Long Fellowship in Library and Information science from 2003 to her retirement in 2014. Dawson was awarded Professor Emeritus status by Louisiana State University in 2015. The Louisiana Library Association bestowed its highest honor to Dawson by awarding her the Essae M. Culver Award in 2019. This award honors a librarian whose professional service and achievements, whose leadership in Louisiana association work, and whose lifetime accomplishments in a field of librarianship within the state merit recognition of particular value to Louisiana librarianship.

Alma Dawson once said, "I think people need to have goals and objectives to move forward. That was what I always tried to do."[6] It is evident from her contributions and leadership that she accomplished her goals while also leaving a legacy of dedication, commitment, and mentorship. She gave unselfishly of herself, never seeking any recognition for the work she was doing for the profession.

**NOTES**

1. Alma Dawson, "Recruitment of Diverse Populations to Librarianship: Documenting the Partnership between the LSU School of Library and Information Science and the LLA Minority Recruitment and Professional Concerns Interest Group." *Louisiana Libraries* 63 (Winter 2001): 5-13.
2. Cheryl Malden, "Alma Dawson receives 2005 Equality Award." March 3, 2005, https://www.ala.org/news/newspressreleases2005/march2005/2005equalityaward. Press release.
3. Alma Dawson, "LLA Diversity Interest Group (Formerly LLA Minority Recruitment and Professional Concerns Interest Group): An Historical Update." *Louisiana Libraries* 74 (Summer 2012): 17-24.
4. Alma Dawson, "From the Guest Editor: Educating the Next Generation of Librarians for South Louisiana Libraries: Project Recovery Scholars Tell Their Stories." *Louisiana Libraries* 75 (Fall 2012): 4-28.
5. Alma Dawson, "From the Guest Editor: Educating the Next Generation of Librarians for South Louisiana Libraries: Project Recovery Scholars Tell Their Stories." *Louisiana Libraries* 75 (Fall 2012): 4.
6. Greg Landgraf, "Blazing Trails: Pioneering African-American Librarians Share Their Stories." *American Libraries Magazine.* January/February 2018, 42.

# 2.3

## *Hidden Figures in African American Librarianship*

CHARLEMAE HILL ROLLINS, MIRIAM MATTHEWS, NAOMI WILLIE POLLARD DOBSON, AND DOROTHY BURNETT PORTER WESLEY

Talisha Harrison

Black history is American history, and that in turn means that the history of Black librarianship is the history of American librarianship. Throughout the history of librarianship, Black people were there, as pioneers, visionaries, risk-takers, hard workers, innovators, organizers, and achievers. This is especially true of Black women.

Despite the many challenges and roadblocks, they carried on and provided service, developed collections and archives for Black people in various communities throughout this country.[1] In addition to their librarian duties, these women also devoted their time and energy to various causes such as civil rights, women's rights, children's rights. They were suffragists and community activists. According to Jessie Carney Smith, these women were "agitators who would not be restricted to the narrow boundaries that male society and white society set for them because of gender and race."[2]

While their activism took different paths, these Black female librarians made a difference in their libraries and in their community. Representation is very important, but to know where one is going, one must know where one comes from.

In looking at Black librarianship, there are many key figures to research that it can be hard to choose whom to discuss. So instead of focusing on those who are well known, this chapter turns the spotlight onto four hidden figures in the history of African American librarianship: Charlemae Hill Rollins, Miriam Matthews, Naomi Willie Pollard Dobson, and Dorothy Burnett Porter Wesley.

## HIDDEN FIGURES IN BLACK LIBRARIANSHIP

### Charlemae Hill Rollins (1897–1979)

The first African American to serve as president of the Children's Services division of the American Library Association[3] and the first African American to receive honorary membership in the American Library Association,[4] Charlemae Hill Rollins was a librarian, storyteller, author, and humanitarian. She gained national prominence for her opposition against racial stereotypes in children's books and used both libraries and her own writings to promote the contributions of Black people.[5] Rollins won many awards for her work and was cited as one of *American Libraries'* one hundred leaders of the twentieth century.[6]

Born in the small farming community of Yazoo City, Mississippi, to a farmer and teacher, Rollins moved at a young age with her family to Oklahoma. There she would listen to the stories told by her grandmother who had been enslaved, while also learning from her experiences. Rollins developed a love of reading thanks to her grandmother, who had collected books for her family to read from her former master who had also fathered her children. Due to racism and segregation, Rollins attended segregated Black schools throughout her educational years all the way to graduation from Western University.[7]

She taught for a while and then married in 1918 and moved with her husband to Chicago where she resided for the remainder of her life. After feeling compelled to enter librarianship, in 1927 Rollins joined the staff of the Chicago Public Library where she was a children's librarian to a multicultural, multiethnic, non-Black population.[8] After receiving professional training at Columbia and the University of Chicago, she was the head of the children's department of the first branch built in a black neighborhood—the George Cleveland Hall Branch. Rollins was very involved in her community as she encouraged class library visits and did community outreach. To highlight the contributions of Black people, Rollins organized book fairs, reading clubs, black history clubs, and held a series of appreciation hours in the library. Rollins was passionate about seeking cultural freedom for Black people so that they would have knowledge, understanding, and appreciation of their culture. She wanted them to break free of stereotypes found in literature about them.[9] Throughout her career as a children's librarian and storyteller, Rollins advocated for books that realistically represented African Americans.[10] Rollins's activism brought her to the national forefront. She gave lectures, reviewed manuscripts on Black themes for publishers and authors, and was appointed to numerous councils and committees on children's literature.[11]

The National Council of Teachers of English (NCTE) commissioned her to compile "a bibliography of criteria created by African Americans to aid librarians and teachers when selecting children's books for their collections."[12] Titled *We Build Together*, the bibliography was first published in 1941 and was followed by two more editions. The final edition in the series was written in 1967, and fellow and notable librarian Augusta Baker helped write it. The bibliography, distributed nationally, was the result of the need and interest of teachers "to be able to share positive depictions of African Americans with their white students."[13]

It was Rollins's goal to provide both teachers and librarians guidance on how to select the best books about African Americans for their libraries. She asserted that African Americans should help create these criteria, and she also anticipated that by exposing white children to these books that depicted African Americans in an accurate and respectful manner, "they will lose some of their feelings of condescension and they will gain in understanding."[14]

While it was always a rule that books chosen by librarians and teachers be chosen for their high quality, some of them depicted African Americans in a stereotypical fashion. To avoid this, Rollins proposed three criteria when selecting African American books: illustrations, language, and theme. In addition to these criteria, she included instructions on how to use books that did not meet the criteria. Rollins "suggested that teachers develop pairings of books: one that incorporated the criteria and one that did not." She suggested that children ought to participate in choosing which book was respectful and which was not and why. To get teachers started with this exercise, Rollins included a list of paired books, based on illustrations and historical stories. She also included "examples of teachers and students who, after completing the exercise, wrote to authors and publishers to urge them to create books that realistically depicted African Americans."[15]

Rollins was also devoted to supporting future librarians. She was a university professor and was actively involved in the American Library Association. She was an avid writer and encouraged others to write. She authored six books for children, including *Christmas Gif'*.[16] As an author, storyteller, librarian, and authority on Black literature, Charlemae Hill Rollins's impact can be felt today.

### Miriam Matthews (1905—2003)

Miriam Matthews was California's first accredited Black librarian. She was a pioneering librarian, historian, and community activist[17] in Los Angeles who played a huge role in promoting research on and access to the history of African Americans in California—specifically her work promoting resources related to African American history and culture during the time in which she lived—the 1930s and 1940s. Matthews was the first

African American librarian to work at the Los Angeles Public Library, and in her role as regional librarian from 1927 to 1960 she supervised twelve branch libraries.[18]

Matthews is also credited with having advanced the celebration of what was then known as Negro History Week—now called Black History Month—in Los Angeles. She was the first to present writers such as Langston Hughes at library programs and prompted interest in African American artists by organizing exhibits at the library, which in the following years became models for other libraries to follow.[19] Matthews was a historian of both African American history and California history. She acquired and personally donated materials that she bought with her own money and collaborated with other researchers. Matthews created collections for and about African Americans and built an extensive image collection of Black Los Angeles that is now housed at the UCLA Library Special Collections along with her papers. Her research efforts have supported the work of many other historians and was also valued by future librarians in the region. Even after her retirement, Matthews continued her work and advocacy.[20]

Matthews was also very active in both the California Library Association (CLA) and the American Library Association (ALA) where she was both a chairperson and a member of both organizations' Intellectual Freedom Committees where she strongly advocated for intellectual freedom and opposing censorship. Matthews wrote an article for ALA's *Library Journal* discussing the CLA's fight against censorship in California. She also worked with other organizations such as the ACLU in the fight against bills that called for the removal of the instruction of certain topics and materials from schools and libraries.[21]

She was also a member of many civic and social organizations in Los Angeles and dedicated many hours to community service. As a member of the California Librarians Black Caucus (CLBC), Matthews was a mentor to many librarians and generously contributed to the organization both personally and financially. She gave several presentations from her historical records and pictures of early African American influences for CLBC-sponsored programs.[22] In 1977, Governor Jerry Brown appointed Matthews to the California Heritage Preservation Commission and the California State Historical Records Advisory Board where she served for seven years. In 1979, she helped secure a permanent archivist and archival program for Los Angeles. At the city's bicentennial celebration in 1981, it was Matthews's proposal that led to the erection of a large monument that honors the city's forty-four founders—all except two were either Black or Indigenous—in El Pueblo de Los Angeles Historical Monument.[23]

According to Matthews, her most important achievements were "leadership in opposing censorship and promoting the cause of intellectual freedom locally and nationally"; second, her research on the history of African Americans in California; and third, her "fight against race prejudice in the Los Angeles Public Library system (and elsewhere)." Matthews believed that her accomplishments made it easier "for those who followed. . . . I greatly appreciate having learned early in life to stand on my own two feet, to form my own opinions, to stick by my principles, and to speak up for what I thought was right."[24]

### Naomi Willie Pollard Dobson (1883-1971)

Educator, librarian, clubwoman, and civic leader, Naomi Pollard Dobson was a pioneer in Black librarianship. In 1905, she became the first Black woman to graduate from Northwestern University and began her teaching career. In 1911, she enrolled in the newly formed Library Training School at the Chicago Public Library along with fourteen other women for an intensive six-month program to work as senior library assistants in the growing library system.[25]

She worked from 1912 to 1915 first as a page and then as a senior assistant children's librarian at the CPL Hebrew Institute Branch. While she did not have an advanced library science degree, Dobson's work experience and training prepared her to become a head librarian at another institution, Wilberforce University, one of the oldest historically Black institutions in the United States. In 1914, she joined its faculty as the instructor of library economy where she taught two courses and oversaw the school's library. She was a perfect fit as she enhanced various aspects of the library by reorganizing the collections by subject area and implementing a new classification system. Dobson also expanded the circulated and reference collections to ten thousand items, which included government documents, magazines, newspapers, and German-language materials.[26]

In her role as the head and instructor of library science, Dobson revived the library's collections and the university community. Under her watch, she was able "to reconstruct how access, use, and support of the curriculum was necessary for the students matriculating at the historic Black institution." While she was only there for two years, Dobson had many accomplishments at the school. She was able to make the Carnegie library on campus central to supporting the educational and instructional needs of the campus community.[27]

After her marriage in 1916, Dobson began the next stage of her life by making immense contributions through her intellectual work. For almost forty years she participated in church and civic duties. Dobson was a member of various club organizations: League of Women Voters, American Association of University Women, the Iowa Federation of Colored Women's Club (where she was elected president in 1931), and as a charter member of the Sioux City NAACP. She gave various talks and speaking engagements and used her position for the rest of her life to focus on service. Naomi Willie Pollard Dobson was a trailblazer for Black librarianship. As Gray states, "Her life offers a view of womanhood and race consciousness that is part of the tradition of Black women's work."[28]

### Dorothy Burnett Porter Wesley (1905–1995)

Known as a human encyclopedia and keeper of the keys to the archives of African American history, Dorothy Porter Wesley was the curator of the Moorland-Spingarn Research Center at Howard University. Porter Wesley first worked as a teacher, and then her passion for books led her to the school library where under the mentorship of the librarian, she entered Columbia University for a summer session in library science.[29] She earned her bachelor's degree in 1928 from Howard University.

In 1930, when she began working at Howard, she started the Moorland-Spingarn Collection. In an interview years later, Porter Wesley described how many items there were in need of organization and how she began that task: "There were boxes of the Jessie Moorland books that had come into the library in 1914, and he had written me a letter saying that he was very unhappy because no one had unpacked his boxes and catalogued the books. There were about three thousand volumes on black history and literature. My problem was to go around in all the corners and find things." She also did not have any staff to help her, just students: "I had to train them and make use of students, so for a long time I was the only person in charge."[30]

Her classification method also challenged the "inherent racism and colonial gatekeeping of knowledge within the Dewey Decimal system."[31] Porter found that every library she consulted for classification guidance relied only on Dewey Decimal, which was highly problematic. Within the system, Black scholarly work was classified either with the number 326-slavery or 325-colonization. It was vital for Porter to develop a classification that did not rely on the stereotypes of Black culture that were rampant in the Dewey Decimal system. To combat this, Porter "classified works within the collection by genre and author in order to highlight the role of black people in all subject areas like art, education, history, medicine, music, and even literature."[32] Her approach celebrated Black self-representation while also combating racist stereotypes and false narratives.

As Porter started to build the collection, she stated that she had to beg publishers and writers: "Then, to build the collection, I had to beg, oh, did I beg! I begged from publishers and writers and when people died, they said that I got there before the body got cold!" She would even go into people's homes and clean up basements and attics, putting anything she could find into the shopping bags that she carried with her.[33]

After becoming the first African American to earn a master's degree in library science from Columbia University in 1932,[34] she returned to Howard to continue to build the college library's collection of resource materials on the African diaspora.[35] As she built the collection, she sought the advice and guidance from historians, book dealers, and bibliophiles among which included Charles Wesley, Arthur Schomburg, and Arthur Spingarn. But the most influential was Dr. Carter G. Woodson, founder of the Association for the Study of Afro-American Life and History (ASLH) and the creator of Negro History Week now known as Black History Month. Not only did Porter Wesley seek guidance from Woodson, but his influence also encouraged her to acquire and preserve primary source materials about the Black experience. In addition, Woodson and Porter Wesley developed a close professional relationship that lasted until Woodson's death in 1953.[36]

By the time of her retirement in 1973, the collection she built had amassed more than two hundred thousand documents, books, photographs, letters, manuscripts, microfilms, and oral history materials. One significant item within the collection is a 1791 letter from Black astronomer Benjamin Banneker to then secretary of state Thomas Jefferson, urging Jefferson to "rethink his position on the inherent inferiority of the Black race." It is vital to underscore the importance of Porter Wesley's contributions to scholarly research. Her work was instrumental in the research efforts of scholars John Hope Franklin, Alain Locke, Sterling Brown, Langston Hughes, Alex Haley, Richard Wright, John Henrik Clarke, and many others.[37]

Porter Wesley was also a noted scholar in her own right. The federal government published her 1936 bibliography of books of Black authors about Black people, and she wrote various articles, books, manuscripts, and bibliographies such as *Early Negro Writings, 1760–1837*; *North American Negro Poets*; *Negro Protest Pamphlets*; and *The Negro in the United States: A Selected Bibliography*. Her bibliographies are influential in bringing attention to the vast scope of publications that document Black history and placing these titles in the hands of scholars.[38] A curator, librarian, scholar, and consultant, she spent two years as a Ford Foundation fellow building the collections of the National Library of Nigeria. Dorothy Porter Wesley was the "national librarian for African Americans"[39] and an enterprising steward of Black culture.

### CONCLUSION

African Americans have a distinguished history in American librarianship. Despite the many challenges facing them, Black librarians have had many achievements and contributions to librarianship. In addition to their library work, Black librarians were also pioneers, visionaries, risk-takers, hard workers, innovators, and organizers.[40] They worked tirelessly to enhance the lives of all Black people as librarians and through their civic, social, and progressive community work as activists, advocates, teachers, etc.

Black women have always been integral to this work. To quote Pollack and Haley: "Black women have always been integral to first literacy movements of the 1800s and later librarianship. It also became clear that literacy, social justice activism, and literacy cultural production have always intersected for middle class, educated Black women. One place where this can be observed is within the profession of librarianship."[41]

While central to the many contributions and achievements in librarianship, many Black women librarians are not as well-known. The purpose of this chapter is to lift the veil and showcase four hidden figures whose contributions are not as well-known to the public: Charlemae Hill Rollins, Miriam Matthews, Naomi Willie Pollard Dobson, and Dorothy Burnett Porter Wesley. As a current student and soon to be graduate of an MLIS program who happens to be a Black woman, learning and researching these four women has inspired me to continue my studies and focus on my career goals in librarianship.

## NOTES

1. Alma Dawson, "Celebrating African-American Librarians and Librarianship," *Library Trends*, 49, no. 1 (2000): 49-87.
2. Jessie Carney Smith, "Black Women, Civil Rights, and Libraries," in *Untold Stories: Civil Rights, Libraries, and Black Librarianship*, ed. John Mark Tucker (Champaign, IL: Publications Office, Graduate School of Library and Information Science, 1998), 141-50.
3. Katisha Smith, "13 Pioneering Black American Librarians You Oughta Know," BOOK RIOT, May 8, 2020, https://bookriot.com/pioneering-black-american-librarians/.
4. Dawson, "Celebrating."
5. Jessie Carney Smith, "Black Women."
6. Dawson, "Celebrating."
7. Jessie Carney Smith, "Black Women."
8. Ibid.
9. Ibid.
10. Cass Mabbott, "The We Need Diverse Books Campaign and Critical Race Theory: Charlemae Rollins and the Call for Diverse Children's Books," *Library Trends*, 65, no. 4 (2017): 508-22, https://doi.org10.1353/lib.2017.0015.
11. Jessie Carney Smith, "Black Women."
12. Mabbott, "We Need Diverse Books."
13. Ibid.
14. Ibid.
15. Ibid.
16. Ibid.
17. Binnie T. Wilkin, *African American Librarians in the Far West: Pioneers and Trailblazers* (Lanham, MD: Scarecrow Press, 2006).
18. Claudia M. Horning, "Trailblazing Black Librarian in the Golden State: The Legacy and Accomplishments of Miriam Matthews, 1905-2003," *Southern California Quarterly*, 104, no. 4 (2022): 407-49.
19. Wilkin, *African American Librarians*.
20. Horning, "Trailblazing Black Librarian."
21. Ibid.
22. Wilkin, *African American Librarians*.
23. Ibid.
24. Horning, "Trailblazing Black Librarian."
25. Laverne Gray, "Naomi Willie Pollard Dobson: A Pioneering Black Librarian," *Libraries: Culture, History, and Society*, 6, no. 1 (2022): 1-20, https://doi.org10.5325/libraries.6.1.0001.
26. Ibid.
27. Ibid.
28. Ibid.
29. Avril Johnson Madison and Dorothy Porter Wesley, "Dorothy Burnett Porter Wesley: Enterprising Steward of Black Culture," *The Public Historian*, 17, no. 1 (1995): 15-40, https://doi.org10.2307/3378349.
30. James V. Hatch, *Interview of Dorothy Porter by James Hatch and Camille Billops* (New York: Hatch Billops Collection, 1991).
31. Katisha Smith, "13 Pioneering Black American Librarians."
32. Ibid.
33. Hatch, *Interview of Dorothy Porter*.
34. Marva Hinton, "From Trailblazers to Today: Greater Representation Serves Young Library Users and the Profession but More Effort Is Needed to Bring In—And Retain—More Black Librarians," *School Library Journal*, 69, no. 2 (2023): 20-24.
35. "Dorothy Burnett Porter Wesley 1905-1995," *The Journal of Blacks in Higher Education*, no. 43 (2004): 1-1, http://www.jstor.org/stable/4133525.
36. Madison and Wesley, "Dorothy Burnett Porter."
37. "Dorothy Burnett Porter Wesley 1905-1995."
38. Madison and Wesley, "Dorothy Burnett Porter."
39. "Dorothy Burnett Porter Wesley 1905-1995."
40. Dawson, "Celebrating."
41. Caitlin M. J. Pollock and Shelley P. Haley, "'When I Enter': Black Women and the Disruption of the White, Heteronormative Narrative of Librarianship," in *Pushing the Margins: Women of Color and Intersectionality in LIS*, ed. Rose L. Chou and Annie Pho (Sacramento: Library Juice Press, 2018), 15-60.

## WORKS CITED

Dawson, Alma. "Celebrating African-American Librarians and Librarianship." *Library Trends*, 49, no. 1 (2000): 49-87.

"Dorothy Burnett Porter Wesley 1905-1995." *The Journal of Blacks in Higher Education*, no. 43 (2004): 1-1. http://www.jstor.org/stable/4133525.

Gray, Laverne. "Naomi Willie Pollard Dobson: A Pioneering Black Librarian." *Libraries: Culture, History, and Society*, 6, no. 1 (2022): 1-20. https://doi.org10.5325/libraries.6.1.0001.

Hatch, James V. *Interview of Dorothy Porter by James Hatch and Camille Billops*. New York: Hatch Billops Collection, 1991.

Hinton, Marva. "From Trailblazers to Today: Greater Representation Serves Young Library Users and the Profession but More Effort Is Needed to Bring In—And Retain—More Black Librarians." *School Library Journal*, 69, no. 2 (2023): 20-24.

Horning, Claudia M. "Trailblazing Black Librarian in the Golden State: The Legacy and Accomplishments of Miriam Matthews, 1905-2003." *Southern California Quarterly*, 104, no. 4 (2022): 407-49.

Mabbott, Cass. "The We Need Diverse Books Campaign and Critical Race Theory: Charlemae Rollins and the Call for Diverse Children's Books." *Library Trends*, 65, no. 4 (2017): 508-22. https://doi.org10.1353/lib.2017.0015.

Madison, Avril Johnson, and Dorothy Porter Wesley. "Dorothy Burnett Porter Wesley: Enterprising Steward of Black Culture." *The Public Historian*, 17, no. 1 (1995): 15-40. https://doi.org10.2307/3378349.

Pollock, Caitlin M. J., and Shelley P. Haley. "'When I Enter': Black Women and the Disruption of the White, Heteronormative Narrative of Librarianship." In *Pushing the Margins: Women of Color and Intersectionality in LIS*, edited by Rose L. Chou and Annie Pho, 15–60. Sacramento: Library Juice Press, 2018.

Smith, Jessie Carney. "Black Women, Civil Rights, and Libraries." In *Untold Stories: Civil Rights, Libraries, and Black Librarianship*, edited by. John Mark Tucker. Champaign, IL: Publications Office, Graduate School of Library and Information Science, 1998.

Smith, Katisha. "13 Pioneering Black American Librarians You Oughta Know." BOOK RIOT, May 8, 2020. https://bookriot.com/pioneering-black-american-librarians/.

Wilkin, Binnie T. *African American Librarians in the Far West: Pioneers and Trailblazers*. Lanham: Scarecrow Press, 2006.

# 2.4

## *Andre Carl Whisenton*

Vera N. Whisenton

In 1976, at the age of thirty-two, Andre Carl Whisenton was named library director of the United States Department of Labor. The library is now called the Wirtz Library, named after Labor Secretary Willard Wirtz in 2000.

A native of Durham, North Carolina, Whisenton was tasked with heading an organization responsible for providing all library services to employees in the Washington, DC, area, ten regions, as well as the public. Whisenton became the first African American to head a federal cabinet-level library.

Whisenton graduated from Morehouse College with a degree in political science and history in 1965 and subsequently earned an MS in library science from the School of Library Science, Atlanta University, in Atlanta, Georgia.

Whisenton began his career as a cataloger and quickly rose to the position of head of cataloging and chief of reference services at the Defense Intelligence Agency (DIA) of the United States Department of Defense. During the latter part of his tenure there, he was named deputy director. While in this position, he researched and developed the Upward Mobility Program for library technicians that was adopted by the DIA and received special recognition. He also assumed an ancillary high security role as an intelligence analyst and was actively involved in sensitive intelligence gathering for the DIA during the Vietnam War.

In 1973, Whisenton took the position as library director with the Naval Sea Systems Command of the defense department in Crystal City, Virginia. He was there for three years before the appointment to the labor library.

When Whisenton assumed the helm of the labor department library, it housed more than five hundred thousand bound volumes of books, periodicals, reports, as well as legal resources, microfilm, microfiche, and cassette items. In addition, it received more than three thousand newspapers, journals, magazines, and other publications. In addition to a newly expanded library, there were several reading rooms and study rooms for special research projects.

Following the role model and strong influence of the late president of Morehouse College, Dr. Benjamin Mays, Whisenton again felt compelled, while library director, to mentor others. To that end, he established the first library internship program at the labor department with several library schools: Catholic University, Atlanta University, and North Carolina Central University. The very successful program was designed to bring minorities and others into the federal government as professional librarians. During the many years of its existence, this program was responsible for filling the void of minorities in federal libraries.

Expanding his responsibilities at the labor department, Whisenton served as an equal employment opportunity (EEO) counselor, investigator and chairman of the department's EEO committee, which led to his selection for the yearlong Senior Executive Development Program. At the culmination of this extensive program, he assumed the role as head of all affirmative action and special emphasis programs and director of the Office of Equal Employment Opportunity at the labor department. In those capacities, his responsibilities broadened to encompass discrimination complaint adjudication for all Department of Labor employees and applicants. To perform those duties, he became certified in mediation and conflict resolution.

When Whisenton left the labor department in 1995, Secretary Robert Reich praised Whisenton for having created "the best special emphasis programs honoring African Americans, women, Hispanics, Asian Americans and individuals with disabilities in the federal government."

Whisenton, coming full circle with his professional training, received the prestigious senior executive appointment at the Library of Congress where he served as director of dispute resolution and equal employment opportunity. He also chaired the Adverse Action and the Mentoring Task Force. In 2000, he was appointed director of human resources initiatives, serving in that capacity until his retirement in 2003.

Significantly, when Whisenton began his tenure at the Library of Congress, a large settlement had just occurred: an $8.5 million cash payment and $1.6 million in legal fees to about two thousand plaintiffs who were employees there. This settlement was the result of a class action lawsuit known as Cook v. Billington, et al. The case originated from a 1975 complaint filed by the Black employees of the Library of Congress who alleged discriminatory practices due to race. The fallout and aftermath of this event were huge challenges for Whisenton, who instituted major library programs designed to enhance the careers of minority employees—*both paraprofessionals as well as professionals.*

Whisenton's early career was greatly influenced by his former cataloging professor, the late Dr. Annette H. Phinazee, who was the first Black person to earn a library degree from Columbia University. She was a mentor to both Whisenton and his wife, Vera, who was named library director of the US Department of Commerce in 1995. It is also noteworthy that Whisenton's late mother, Margret, was a librarian and retired as head of readers' services for the Durham North Carolina Public Library System.

After retirement, Whisenton continued to be an advocate for librarianship as well as community involvement. He mentored many—young and not so young—to pursue their dreams and accomplish goals.

Andre Carl Whisenton and his wife established, after retirement, a residence in Durham, North Carolina, where he was very active until his death in 2019.

# 2.5

## *Black Diasporic Memory Keeper*

ARTURO ALPHONSO SCHOMBURG

Ana Ndumu and Manuel Mendez

When it comes to stewarding knowledge about the Black diaspora, Arturo Schomburg stands out as a tireless champion of African, African American, Afro-Latino, and Afro-Caribbean cultural and scholarly vibrance. Schomburg was provoked to amass as much knowledge of Black life as possible on account of the global, uniform white supremacist ideals that he encountered. Schomburg migrated from Puerto Rico to New York City as a teenager and, given his professional work as a journalist, editor, Spanish instructor,[1] legal assistant, and bank clerk, he rapidly earned a reputation as a polyhistor. Schomburg's civic activities were equally laudable and varied. A consummate intellectual, Schomburg also led societies such as the American Negro Academy and the Freemasons.[2] Few other Black historical figures have demonstrated such a profound level of commitment to Black recordkeeping.

In this chapter, we chronicle how Schomburg approached his curatorial and bibliographic work as life-giving sustenance. Indeed, our African ancestors have expressed that our carers and keepers of memories—that is, our *griots*—function very much the same as blood to the body.[3] Schomburg himself asked, "What of it if the darker races are getting consciousness, isn't the world large enough for the people of all bloods to dwell therein?"[4] In thinking of how the metaphor of blood denotes how Black knowledge injects vitality into the collective body, we organize this chapter along the theme of harm, healing, and flow to characterize Arturo Schomburg's remarkable story.

### SCAR: SCHOMBURG'S EARLY LIFE

Arturo Schomburg was born to parents of Puerto Rican and Danish West Indies heritage in 1874. His quest for Black records was prompted when a "fifth-grade teacher remarked that 'Black people had no history, no heroes, no great moments."[5] This moment, this wound provoked—though it did not define—Schomburg, who became obsessed with showing evidence of global Black lived experience beyond enslavement. Even as a boy, he was affixed with Black humanity. He took inspiration from radical teachers like Jose Julian Acosta and activist-artists like Salvador Brau.[6] Schomburg recounted the tensions he faced with white youth as part of a youth club. His interest in bibliophiles was set in motion through his observance that white and mestizo youth had "more pride in the achievements of their white ancestors."[7] A quest toward combating white supremacy "to gather the material, in multiple languages and from across the diaspora"[8] matured in Schomburg's early teenage years.

Soon after, at seventeen years of age, he migrated to New York and was deeply influenced by the Cuban and Puerto Rican liberation movements. His activist work within the Las Dos Antillas revolutionary party afforded Schomburg a grounding in a global Black perspective. His eagerness to disseminate "evidence"[9] of global African historical documentation grew into a lifestyle—indeed, not simply a hobby. Like his Harlem contemporaries, Schomburg rejected the notion that Blacks had solely been "thingified and become walking dead, floating in the western hemisphere, regarded as people with no history."[10] Promise, not perversity, is the lens from which Schomburg viewed our people.

**REPAIR: SCHOMBURG'S INFORMATION PRACTICES**

Schomburg's efforts to repair these wounds set him on a path to challenge old tropes that historically suggested African history has no value. Indeed, the late bell hooks described this curatorial mandate as a "struggle of memory against forgetting"[11] and perhaps a defiant attempt at racial healing after forced migration, chattel slavery, and state-sanctioned racial segregation. Schomburg's "racial vindication"[12] resisted through Afrocentric documentation and artifacts, white canonical methods. White supremacist ignorance could only be combated with proudly Black evidence, Schomburg posited. He accomplished this feat without formal training. While white institutions, namely Columbia University's school of library science, routinely denied inclusion to Blacks, Schomburg made way for unrestricted access to people of all types. Scholars seldom emphasize Schomburg's insistence on granting Blacks unfettered access regardless of social status. While some Black intellectual elites maintained a professional and social distance from the working class and underserved African Americans and Black diasporic immigrants, Schomburg, like his close colleague Carter G. Woodson,[13] adamantly promoted equality in learning.

Schomburg was known to generously loan material to schools, libraries, and conferences.[14] He is celebrated in the children's book *Schomburg: The Man Who Built a Library* as a detective who hunted for clues and found facts affirming the role of African descent in building nations and shaping cultures.[15] His travels to carefully collect Black-centered material would take him from Cuba to Spain.[16] Schomburg designed publishing pamphlets, newsletters, and essays for the National Association for the Advancement of Colored People's *Crisis*, the National Urban League's *Opportunity*, and the Universal Negro Improvement Association's *Negro World*. Yet he welcomed invitations from smaller organizations such as the American Negro Academy, the Negro Actors Guild of America, and the Committee of One Hundred for Negro Workers.[17] As a public scholar, Schomburg was equally excited to present before elementary school children as well as the ivory tower. Schomburg's memory-keeping strategies demonstrate that healing from anti-Black racism cannot be left to the white status quo. To this, Schomburg asserted, "History must restore what slavery took away, for it is the social damage of slavery that the present generation must repair and offset."[18]

**CIRCULATION: ARTURO SCHOMBURG'S LEGACY TODAY**

Schomburg has stimulated new generations of librarians, bibliophiles, archivists, and curators. His collection was eventually purchased for $10,000 from the New York Public Library, and the Harlem branch that became a safe haven for Schomburg and so many other African American thinkers now bears his name: Schomburg Center for Research in Black Culture. In keeping with Schomburg's widespread outreach, the center offers seminars, forums, and workshops along with the renowned Schomburg Center Literary Festival. It boasts one of the most comprehensive collections of Black artists' work in a research center, including paintings, sculptures, works on paper and textiles, and material culture, as well as more than five hundred thousand items from nineteenth- and twentieth-century Black artists, political figures, actors, musicians, athletes, and social activists. The manuscripts, archives, and rare books collections along with the photographs, moving images, and recorded sounds divisions offer Black chronicles from all over the world. And true to Schomburg's mission of public good, since 1986 the Scholars in Residence program has supported long-term research projects that benefit from the center's collections and resources.

Even after the New York Public Library acquired his enormous catalog of material, Schomburg collaborated with libraries, including Fisk University, in curating, exhibiting, and displaying important ephemera for whoever wanted access. We must acknowledge Schomburg as a multilingual and transnational thinker whose influence started and spanned beyond the United States. His presence in the Harlem Renaissance and legacy in African American history represents what Nancy Mirabal calls "Afro-diasporic revolutionary" thought that continues to inspire Black brilliance.

**NOTES**

1. V. K. Valdés, *Diasporic Blackness: The Life and Times of Arturo Alfonso Schomburg* (Albany: SUNY Press, 2017); E. D. V. Sin-

nette, *Arthur Alfonso Schomburg, Black Bibliophile & Collector: A Biography* (New York: New York Public Library, 1989).
2. E. J. Josey and Marva DeLoach, editors, *The Handbook of Black Librarianship*, 2nd ed. (Lanham: Scarecrow, 2000), 5-6, 20-21; Sinnette, *Schomburg*, 8, 10, 33, 38-39, 41-42.
3. Trevor H. J. Marchand, "Review of *'It's In Our Blood': Mali's Griots and Musical Enskilment*, by Lucy Durán, Michele Banal, and Lassana Diabaté," *Africa: Journal of the International African Institute*, 85, no. 2 (2015): 356-64, http://www.jstor.org/stable/24525743; Greg Carr, "Dr. Greg Carr Discusses His Black Curriculum," *YouTube*, November 18, 2019, https://www.youtube.com/watch?v=vljpZao8RUs.
4. Valdés, *Diasporic Blackness*, 55.
5. Sinette, *Schomburg*, 3.
6. Valdés, *Diasporic Blackness*, 45-50.
7. Floyd J. Calvin, "Race Colleges Need Chair in Negro History," *Pittsburgh Courier*, March 5, 1927: 3; A. A. Schomburg, *The Negro Digs Up His Past,* Schomburg Center for Research in Black Culture, Manuscripts, Archives and Rare Books Division, The New York Public Library (March 1925). https://digitalcollections.nypl.org/items/61304dd0-ea1f-0138-4343-0242ac110004.
8. Laura E. Helton and Rafia Zafar, "Arturo Alfonso Schomburg in the Twenty-first Century: An Introduction," *African American Review* 54, no. 1 (2021): 1-18. doi:10.1353/afa.2021.0000.
9. Schomburg, *The Negro*, 670.
10. Frank B. Wilderson, *Red, White & Black: Cinema and the Structure of U.S. Antagonisms* (Durham: Duke University Press, 2010); Aimé Césaire, Robin D. G. Kelley, and Joan Pinkham, *Discourse on Colonialism* (New York: Monthly Review Press, 2000); Lorenzo Veracini, *Settler Colonialism: A Theoretical Overview* (Houndmills Basingstoke: Palgrave Macmillan, 2010).
11. bell hooks, 81.
12. Valdés, *Diasporic Blackness*, 17.
13. Jarvis R. Givens, *Fugitive Pedagogy: Carter G. Woodson and the Art of Black Teaching* (Cambridge, MA: Harvard University Press, 2021), 64-65, 216.
14. Sinette, *Schomburg*, 10, 38-42.
15. Weatherford, C. B. *Schomburg: The man who built a library* (Candlewick Press, 2020).
16. Valdés, *Diasporic Blackness*, 66-68.
17. Helton and Zafar, "Arturo Alfonso Schomburg"; Nancy Raquel Mirabal, "Schomburg, Futurity, and the Precarious Archives of Self" *Small Axe*, 24, no. 1 (2020): 111-19, https://doi.org/10.1215/07990537-8190650; Valdés, *Diasporic Blackness*, 79.
18. Schomburg, *The Negro*.

*Part II*

# BLACK LIBRARY/LIBRARIAN ASSOCIATIONS AND COLLABORATIONS IN THE TWENTY-FIRST CENTURY

# Chapter 3

# BCALA Leaders, Awards, Affiliates, and Collaborations

## 3.1

*Leadership in the Black Caucus of the American Library Association*

Stanton F. Biddle

Since its founding in 1970, over 275 people have been elected to positions of leadership in the Black Caucus of the American Library Association. Using a number of sources, we have compiled a list of those individuals, the positions they held, and their dates of service. These positions included the founders (1970), members of the original Steering Committee (1970-1975) and later executive board (1976-2022) that served as the governing body of the organization. The officers have been the chairs, presidents, vice president/president elects, secretary/treasurers, secretaries, and treasurers. Also, twelve individuals have served as editors of the *BCALA Newsletter* (1972-2012) and later the *BCALA News* (2013-2022).

The list of individuals, positions, and dates of service has been compiled from the minutes of the meetings of the executive board and membership, the membership directories issued between 1973-2006, issues of the *BCALA Newsletter* and *BCALA News*, copies of official BCALA letterhead stationery, and souvenir journals from the National Conferences of African American Librarians. A copy of the full database with sources has been submitted to the BCALA secretary and to the chair of the BCALA history committee.

### LEADERSHIP IN THE BLACK CAUCUS OF THE AMERICAN LIBRARY ASSOCIATION

#### Founders, 1970

Josey, E. J.
Alford, Thomas
Bolton, Willis
Copeland, Emily
Jackson, Audrey N.
Jones, Virginia Lacy
Morris, Effie Lee
Robinson, Carrie
Spencer, Edith Prunty
Welbourne, James
Wilkins, Binnie Tate

#### Chairs, 1970-1990

| | |
|---|---|
| Josey, E. J. | 1970-1971 |
| Cunningham, William D. | 1971-1973 |
| Wright, James R. | 1973-1974 |
| Robinson, Harry, Jr. | 1974-1976 |
| Williams, Avery | 1976-1978 |
| Grant, George C. | 1978-1980 |
| Madden, Doreitha R. | 1980-1982 |
| Wright, Robert | 1982-1984 |
| Jenkins, Barbara Williams | 1984-1986 |
| DeLoach, Marva | 1986-1988 |
| Fisher, Edith Maureen | 1988-1990 |

#### Presidents, 1990-2022

| | |
|---|---|
| Tyson, John C. | 1990-1992 |
| Boyd, D. Alex | 1992-1994 |
| Biddle, Stanton F. | 1994-1996 |
| Sprinkle-Hamlin, Sylvia | 1996-1998 |
| Reese, Gregory | 1998-2000 |
| Bell, Gladys Smiley | 2000-2002 |
| Player, Bobby, Sr. | 2002-2004 |

| | |
|---|---|
| Jackson, Andrew P. | 2004-2006 |
| Brown, Wanda K. | 2006-2008 |
| Thompson, Karolyn S. | 2008-2010 |
| Holman, Jos N. | 2010-2012 |
| Offord, Jerome, Jr. | 2012-2014 |
| Watson, Kelvin | 2014-2016 |
| Davis, Denyvetta | 2016-2018 |
| Ashby, Richard E., Jr. | 2018-2020 |
| Burns-Simpson, Shauntee | 2020-2022 |
| Hayes, Nichelle M. | 2022-2024 |

**Chairs Elect, 1971-1990**

| | |
|---|---|
| Wright, James R. | 1971-1972 |
| Robinson, Harry, Jr. | 1973-1974 |
| Williams, Avery | 1974-1976 |
| Grant, George C. | 1976-1978 |
| Madden, Doreitha R. | 1978-1980 |
| Wright, Robert | 1980-1982 |
| Jenkins, Barbara Williams | 1982-1984 |
| DeLoach, Marva | 1984-1986 |
| Fisher, Edith Maureen | 1986-1988 |
| Tyson, John C. | 1988-1990 |

**Vice Presidents, 1990-2022**

| | |
|---|---|
| Boyd, D. Alex | 1990-1992 |
| Biddle, Stanton F. | 1992-1994 |
| Sprinkle-Hamlin, Sylvia | 1994-1996 |
| Reese, Gregory | 1996-1998 |
| Bell, Gladys Smiley | 1998-2000 |
| Player, Bobby, Sr. | 2000-2002 |
| Jackson, Andrew P. "Sekou" | 2002-2004 |
| Brown, Wanda K. | 2004-2006 |
| Thompson, Karolyn S. | 2006-2008 |
| Holman, Jos N. | 2008-2010 |
| Offord, Jerome, Jr. | 2010-2012 |
| Watson, Kelvin | 2012-2014 |
| Davis, Denyvetta | 2014-2016 |
| Ashby, Richard E., Jr. | 2016-2018 |
| Burns-Simpson, Shauntee | 2018-2020 |
| Hayes, Nichelle M. | 2020-2022 |
| Love, Tatanisha "Tiki" | 2022-2022 |
| Alston, Jason K. | 2022-2024 |

**Secretary/Treasurers, 1970-1976**

| | |
|---|---|
| Spencer, Edith Prunty | 1970-1971 |
| Giles, Louise | 1972-1974 |
| Wilson, Louis C. | 1974-1976 |

**Secretaries, 1976-2022**

| | |
|---|---|
| Madden, Doreitha R. | 1976-1978 |
| Haith, Dorothy | 1978-1982 |
| Griffin, Richard | 1982-1986 |
| Smith-Epps, E. Paulette | 1986-1990 |
| Trammell, Phyllis | 1990-1992 |
| Williams, Barbara | 1992-1994 |
| Knowles, Em Claire | 1994-1996 |
| Thompson, Karolyn S. | 1996-2002 |
| Norman, Carolyn | 2002-2004 |
| Revels, Ira | 2004-2006 |
| Lang, Jennifer | 2006-2008 |
| Curry, Eboni R. (Njoki) | 2008-2010 |
| Cobb, Jannie | 2010-2012 |
| Covington, Diane | 2012-2014 |
| Keeton, kYmberly | 2014-2015 |
| Covington, Diane | 2015-2016 |
| McCurtis, Kirby | 2016-2018 |
| Garcia, Elisa | 2018-2020 |
| Johnson-Perkins, Brenda | 2020-2022 |
| Fenton, Michele | 2022-2024 |

**Assistant Secretaries, 2020-2023**

| | |
|---|---|
| Fenton, Michele | 2020-2022 |
| Dunsen-White, Naomi | 2022-2023 |
| Brooks, Taylor | 2023-2024 |

**Treasurers, 1976-2022**

| | |
|---|---|
| Jenkins, Barbara Williams | 1976-1982 |
| Haith, Dorothy | 1982-1988 |
| Biblo, Mary | 1988-1992 |
| Brown, Wanda K. | 1992-1996 |
| Player, Bobby, Sr. | 1996-1998 |
| Mondowney, JoAnne G. | 1998-2002 |
| Biddle, Stanton F. | 2002-2012 |
| Ford, Annie Marie | 2012-2016 |
| Brown, Wanda K. | 2016-2018 |
| McKnight, Cherese | 2018-2020 |
| McNeil, Brandy | 2020-2022 |
| Brown, Wanda K. | 2022-2024 |

**BCALA Newsletter/BCALA News Editors 1972-2022**

| | |
|---|---|
| English, Jeanne E. | 1972 |
| Shockley, Ann Allen | 1972-1974 |
| Baker, Michael E. | 1974-1975 |
| Jordan, Casper LeRoy | 1975-1978 |
| Reid, Edna F. | 1979-1983 |
| Grant, George C. | 1983-2000 |
| Lowe, Greta | 2000-2002 |
| Barksdale-Hall, Roland | 2002-2007 |
| Harris, S. D. | 2007-2010 |
| Foster, Makiba | 2010-2013 |
| Alston, Jason | 2013-2017 |
| Hayes, Nichelle M. | 2020- |

## Steering Committee Members, 1971–1975

### 1971–1973

Adams, Elaine
Coleman, Barbara
Ford, Robert
Grant, George C.
Guilford, Benjamin
Jackson, Ada
Josey, E. J.
Millender, Dolly
Randall, Ann
Sumbi, Joyce
Wilkins, Binnie Tate
Williams, Joslyn
Wright, Robert

### 1973–1975

Aman, Mohammed
Axam, John
Biblo, Mary
Biddle, Stanton F.
Brown, Richard E.
Cole, Joan E.
Cunningham, Thelma
Gaymon, Nicholas
Grant, George C.
Harris, Jewel H.
Hooker, Cathy Lenix
Irving, Ophelia
Jordan, Casper LeRoy
Josey, E. J.
Joyce, Donald
Morris, Effie Lee
Partridge, James
Perry, Pennie
Phinazee, Annette L.
Primm, Gloria
Rier, Nadine S.
Robinson, Harry, Jr.
Spradling, Mary Mace
Thomas, Lucille
Totton, Herman
Williams, Avery
Wilson, Louis C.

## Executive Board Members, 1976–2025

### 1976–1978

Biblo, Mary
Biddle, Stanton F.
Brown, Gloria Primm
Brown, Richard E.
Cole, Joan E.
Harris, Jewel H.
Jordan, Casper LeRoy
Morris, Effie Lee
Mothershed, S. W.
Phinazee, Annette L.
Rier, Nadine S.
Smith, Jessie Cottman
Spradling, Mary Mace
Taylor, Carole R.

### 1978–1980

Biblo, Mary
Dillon, Irma
Gaymon, Nicholas
Harris, Jewel H.
Hightower, Monteria
Hooker, Cathy Lenix
Jackson, Adele
Jackson, Audrey
Packwood, Cyril
Partridge, James
Randall, Ann
Rudd, Amanda
Smith, Alice
Smith, Gloria
Wilson, Louis C.

### 1980–1981

Beal, Billy
Griffin, Richard
Hightower, Monteria
Jackson, Adele M.
Randall, Ann
Smith, Gloria
Williams, Helen

### 1980–1982

Battle, Thomas
Biddle, Stanton F.
Brown, Florence
Crayton, James
DeLoach, Marva
Grant, George C.
Partridge, James
Rudd, Amanda
Wilson, Louis C.

### 1981–1983

Clack, Doris H.
Guydon, Janet
Morrison, Samuel F.
Perry, Pennie
Searcy, David
Smith, Alice
Williams, Helen

### 1982–1984

Conley, Binford
Curtis, Jean T.
Packwood, Cyril
Randall, Ann
Royster, Vivian
Thomas, Lucille
Tyson, John C.
Wilson, Patricia A.

### 1983–1985

Bingham, Rebecca
Boyd, D. Alex
Cash-Menzies, Pam
Curry, Anna
Lenox, Mary
Simms, Oscar
Venable, Andrew, Jr.

### 1984–1986

Crayton, James
Fisher, Edith Maureen
Freeman-Smith, Patricia
Guss, Emily
Harris, Jewel H.
Kemp, Emma
Madden, Doreitha R.
McCoy, Cheryl

### 1985–1987

Brown, Lorene B.
Hopkins, Diane McAfee
Passmore, William A.
Rhodes, Leila G.
Speller, Benjamin F., Jr.
Tate, Thelma
Wilkins, Binne Tate

### 1986–1988

Biblo, Mary
Broady, Jessie
Collins, Margaret
Francois, Honore
Grant, George C.
Knowles, Em Claire
Randall, Ann
Searcy, David

### 1987–1989

Axam, John
Jones, Barbara
Miles, Fiolina B.
Morrison, Samuel F.
Patterson, Grace
Player, Bobby, Sr.
Tyson, John C.

*1988-1990*

Chisholm, Clarence
Grant, George C.
Henderson, Carolyn J.
Hughes, M. Elaine
Knowles, Em Claire
Leonard, Gloria J.
Tyler, Audrey Q.
Venable, Andrew, Jr.

*1989-1991*

Axam, John
Biddle, Stanton F.
Boyd, D. Alex
Jones, Barbara
Jones-Trent, Bernice
Miller, Robert
Player, Bobby, Sr.

*1990-1992*

Brooks, Violette
Butler, Elizabeth Ann
Grant, George C.
Hughes, M. Elaine
Leonard, Gloria J.
Robinson, Gleniece
Searcy, David
Williams, Barbara A.

*1991-1993*

Chisholm, Clarence
Holman, Jos
Jones, Rita
Knowles, Em Claire
Sanders, Lou Helen
Smith-Epps, E. Paulette
Unaeze, Felix Eme

*1992-1994*

Bradberry, Richard
Cash-Menzies, Pam
Crenshaw, Wanda L.
Hixon, Cecil
Jelks, Joyce E.
Kyles, Rubye Childs
Reese, Gregory

*1993-1995*

Brown, Charles
Hughes, M. Elaine
Hunter-Hayes, Tracey
Johnson-Cooper, Glendora
Kelker, Patricia
Turner, Marcellus
Weir, Birdie

*1994-1996*

Bethel, Kathleen
Ford, Sylverna
Hawkins, Ernestine
Johnson-Houston, Debbie
Joynes, Roy L.
Melton, Vivian
Player, Bobby, Sr.
Williams, Barbara A.

*1995-1997*

Bell, Gladys Smiley
Brown, Malore I.
Cawthorne, Jon E.
Hughes, M. Elaine
Neely, Teresa Y.
Plair, Norman V.
Walker, Michael C.

*1996-1998*

Abif, Khafre K.
Ballard, R. Rochelle
Beal, Billy C.
Cochran, Myrtis
Ford, Sylverna V.
Mosley, Madison M., Jr.
Orange, Satia Marshall
Williams, Barbara A.

*1997-1998*

Bell, Gladys Smiley
Bethel, Kathleen E.
Neely, Teresa Y.
Player, Jewel Armstrong
Richards, Kelly C.
Toliver, Virginia Dowsing
Walker, Michael C.

*1998-2000*

Grant, George C.
Hawkins, Ernestine L.
Holmes, Gerald V.
Kelker, Patricia
Mack, Phyllis Green
Morrison, Samuel F.
Perry, Emma Bradford
Zulu, Itibari M.

*1998-1999*

Jackson, Andrew P. "Sekou"*

*1999-2001*

Abif, Khafre K.
Biddle, Stanton F.
Brown, Florence Simkins
Crocker, Wayne M.
Garnes, Carolyn Lowe
Jackson, Andrew P. "Sekou"
Walker, Michael C.

*2000-2002*

Avery, Gail W.
Brasley, Eric
Brown, Wanda
Johnson, Shirley E.
Knowles, Em Claire
Lee, Rodney Jackson
Lumumba, Malikah Dada
Mack, Phyllis Green

*2001-2003*

Allen, Cassandra
Jackson, Andrew P. "Sekou"
Lowe, Greta
McGinn, Jane Moore
Moses, Sibyl E.
Page, John
Player, Jewel Armstrong

*2002-2004*

Barksdale-Hall, Roland
Hamlin, Sylvia Sprinkle
Hardin, Willie
Jones, Rita
Kelker, Patricia
Leonard, Gloria J.
Lumumba, Malikah Dada
Mondowney, JoAnne G.

*2003-2004*

Revels, Ira*

*2003-2005*

Dawson, Rose Timmons
Fontno, Tiffeni J.
Holman, Jos N.
Thompson, Karolyn S.
Westbrooks, Lainey
Williams, Karen Y.

*2004-2005*

Stokes, Hellena Olivia*

*2004-2006*

Ballard, Rochelle
Epps, Sharon K.
Guss, Emily
Lawson, Rhea Brown
Lemmons, Karen L.
Moses, Sibyl E.
Robinson, LeRoy
Webb, Roberta V.

*2005-2006*

Lang, Jennifer*

*2005-2007*

Dawes, Trevor A.
Grant, George C.
Hawkins, Ernestine L.
Holman, Jos N.
Lang, Jennifer
Thompson, Karolyn S.
Westbrooks, Lainey

*2006-2007*

LaFleur, LeRoy*

*2006-2008*

Davis, Denyvetta
Epps, Sharon K.
Harris, S.D.
Holmes, Gerald V.
Offord, Jerome, Jr.
Sprinkle-Hamlin, Sylvia
Watson, Kelvin
Weil, Teri B.

*2007-2009*

Abdullah, Talia
Bordeaux, Vivian
Boyd, Lisa
Cobb, Jannie
Covington, Diane
Jefferson, Julius, Jr.
Jordan, Alys
Washington, Dorothy

*2008-2010*

Bell, Gladys Smiley
Davis, Denyvetta
Gray, LaVerne
Harris, S. D.
Holmes, Gerald V.
Norman, Carolyn
Watson, Kelvin
White, Joel

*2009-2011*

Bordeaux, Vivian
Covington, Diane
Ford, Annie Marie
Grant, D. L.
Jackson, Andrew P. "Sekou"
Robinson, LeRoy

*2010-2012*

Alston, Jason K.
Bell, Gladys Smiley
Guss, Emily
Guthrie, Dorothy
Hayes, Ailene
Sprinkle-Hamlin, Sylvia
Watson, Kelvin
Webb, Roberta V.

*2011-2013*

Black, Bettye
Covington, Diane
Ford, Annie Marie
Grant, D. L.
Jackson, Andrew P. "Sekou"
Shell, Lambert
Stokes, Eboni

*2012-2013*

Brumfield, Elizabeth*
Nurse, Carol*

*2012-2014*

Alston, Jason K.
Bell, Gladys Smiley
Biddle, Stanton F.
Curry, Eboni R. (Njoki)
Keeton, kYmberly
Knowles, Em Claire
Mosley, Derek
Nosakhere, Akilah

*2013-2015*

Ashby, Richard E., Jr.
Black, Bettye
Brumfield, Elizabeth
Clay, Rudolph
Guss, Emily
Jackson, Andrew P. "Sekou"
Nurse, Carol

*2014-2016*

Bordeaux, Vivian
Brown, Wanda K.
Duck, Tiffany A.
Fenton, Michele
Foster, Makiba
Lemmons, Karen L.
McCurtis, Kirby
Tomlinson, Monya

*2015-2016*

Ashby, Richard E., Jr.*

*2015-2017*

Brumfield, Elizabeth
Curry, Eboni R. (Njoki)
Hart, Brian
Jackson, Andrew P. "Sekou"
Johnson, Sammie
McNeil-Capers, Kim

*2016-2017*

Cox, Fannie M.*

Stokes, Eboni

*2016-2018*

Alston, Jason K.
Bordeaux, Vivian
Clay, Rudolph
Holman, Jos N.
Kuykendall, Bradley
Lemmons, Karen
Luster, Dominique
Muhammad, Fayrene

*2017-2019*

Burns-Simpson, Shauntee
Cox, Fannie M.
Fontono, Tiffeni
Hart, Brian
Landrum, Cyndee Sturgis
McNeill-Capers, Kim
Moore, Jerrod

*2018-2020*

Brumfield, Elizabeth
Carter, Valerie
Dickerson, Pricilla
DuVernay, Jina
Hayes, Nichelle
Love, Tatanisha "Tiki"
Peeples, Donald
Simmons, Jasmine

*2019-2021*

Booker, Latrice "Libre"
Bordeaux, Vivian
Clay, Rudolph
Davis, James
Munson, Tashia
Ndumu, Ana
Ward, Regina Renee

*2020-2022*

Boyd, K. C.
Brown, Dolores
Carter, Valerie
Fouche, Taryn
Mosley, Derek
Muhammad, Fayrene
Orange, Satia Marshall
Simpson, Shamika

*2021-2023*

Carter, Tiffani
Gleason, Yolanda
Lyles, Denise
Ndumu, Ana
Overbey, Tracey
Scott, Tracey
Tingling, Jessica

*2022-2024*

Chambers, Tamela
Clay, Rudolph
Darden, Lakeshia
Etienne, Leslie
Fouche, Taryn
Johnson, Laura
Johnson-Perkins, Brenda
Olaniyi, Olanike

*2023-2025*

Bell, Gladys Smiley
Cox, Fannie
Fontno, Tiffeni
Hayes, Andrea
Hunter, Kimberly
Tingling, Jessica
Torres, Michael

*Filled vacancy in preceding class, usually because a board member has been elected to an office.

# 3.2a

## *BCALA Leadership: 1970–2025*

Stanton F. Biddle

| Name | Office | Term |
|---|---|---|
| Abdullah, Talia | Executive Board | 2007–2009 |
| Abif, Khafre K. | Executive Board | 1996–2001 |
| Adams, Elaine | Steering Committee | 1971–1975 |

| Name | Office | Term |
|---|---|---|
| Alford, Thomas | Founding Member | 1970 |
| Allen, Cassandra | Executive Board | 2001–2003 |
| Alston, Jason K. | Executive Board | 2010–2018 |

| Name | Office | Term |
|---|---|---|
| Alston, Jason K. | Vice President | 2022-2024 |
| Aman, Mohammed | Steering Committee | 1973-1975 |
| Ashby, Richard E., Jr. | Executive Board | 2013-2016 |
| Ashby, Richard E., Jr. | Vice President | 2016-2018 |
| Ashby, Richard E., Jr. | President | 2018-2020 |
| Ashby, Richard E., Jr. | Past President | 2020-2022 |
| Avery, Gail W. | Executive Board | 2000-2002 |
| Axam, John | Steering Committee | 1973-1975 |
| Axam, John | Executive Board | 1987-1991 |
| Baker, Michael E. | Editor-Newsletter | 1974-1975 |
| Ballard, Rochelle | Executive Board | 1996-1998 |
| Ballard, Rochelle | Executive Board | 2004-2006 |
| Barksdale-Hall, Roland | Executive Board | 2002-2004 |
| Barksdale-Hall, Roland | Editor-Newsletter | 2002-2005 |
| Battle, Thomas | Executive Board | 1980-1982 |
| Beal, Billy C. | Executive Board | 1980-1981 |
| Beal, Billy C. | Executive Board | 1996-1998 |
| Bell, Gladys Smiley | Executive Board | 1995-1998 |
| Bell, Gladys Smiley | Vice President | 1998-2000 |
| Bell, Gladys Smiley | President | 2000-2002 |
| Bell, Gladys Smiley | Past President | 2002-2004 |
| Bell, Gladys Smiley | Executive Board | 2008-2014 |

| Name | Office | Term |
|---|---|---|
| Bell, Gladys Smiley | Executive Board | 2023-2025 |
| Bethel, Kathleen E. | Executive Board | 1994-1999 |
| Biblo, Mary | Steering Committee | 1973-1975 |
| Biblo, Mary | Executive Board | 1976-1980 |
| Biblo, Mary | Executive Board | 1986-1988 |
| Biblo, Mary | Treasurer | 1988-1992 |
| Biddle, Stanton F. | Steering Committee | 1973-1975 |
| Biddle, Stanton F. | Executive Board | 1976-1978 |
| Biddle, Stanton F. | Executive Board | 1980-1982 |
| Biddle, Stanton F. | Executive Board | 1989-1991 |
| Biddle, Stanton F. | Vice President | 1992-1994 |
| Biddle, Stanton F. | President | 1994-1996 |
| Biddle, Stanton F. | Past President | 1996-1998 |
| Biddle, Stanton F. | Executive Board | 1999-2001 |
| Biddle, Stanton F. | Treasurer | 2002-2012 |
| Biddle, Stanton F. | Executive Board | 2012-2014 |
| Bingham, Rebecca | Executive Board | 1983-1985 |
| Black, Bettye | Executive Board | 2011-2015 |
| Bolton, Willis | Founding Member | 1970 |
| Booker, Latrice "Libre'" | Executive Board | 2019-2021 |
| Bordeaux, Vivian | Executive Board | 2007-2011 |
| Bordeaux, Vivian | Executive Board | 2014-2018 |

| Name | Office | Term |
|---|---|---|
| Bordeaux, Vivian | Executive Board | 2019-2021 |
| Boyd, D. Alex | Executive Board | 1983-1985 |
| Boyd, D. Alex | Executive Board | 1989-1991 |
| Boyd, D. Alex | Vice President | 1990-1992 |
| Boyd, D. Alex | President | 1992-1994 |
| Boyd, D. Alex | Past President | 1994-1996 |
| Boyd, K. C. | Executive Board | 2020-2022 |
| Boyd, Lisa | Executive Board | 2007-2009 |
| Bradberry, Richard | Executive Board | 1992-1994 |
| Brasley, Eric | Executive Board | 2000-2002 |
| Broady, Jessie | Executive Board | 1986-1988 |
| Brooks, Taylor | Asst. Secretary | 2023-2024 |
| Brooks, Violette | Executive Board | 1990-1992 |
| Brown, Charles | Executive Board | 1993-1995 |
| Brown, Dolores | Executive Board | 2020-2022 |
| Brown, Florence Simkins | Executive Board | 1980-1982 |
| Brown, Florence Simkins | Executive Board | 1999-2001 |
| Brown, Gloria Primm | Executive Board | 1976-1978 |
| Brown, Lorene B. | Executive Board | 1985-1987 |
| Brown, Malore I. | Executive Board | 1995-1997 |
| Brown, Richard E. | Steering Committee | 1973-1975 |
| Brown, Richard E. | Executive Board | 1976-1978 |

| Name | Office | Term |
|---|---|---|
| Brown, Wanda K. | Treasurer | 1992-1996 |
| Brown, Wanda K. | Executive Board | 2000-2002 |
| Brown, Wanda K. | Vice President | 2004-2006 |
| Brown, Wanda K. | President | 2006-2008 |
| Brown, Wanda K. | Past President | 2008-2010 |
| Brown, Wanda K. | Executive Board | 2014-2016 |
| Brown, Wanda K. | Treasurer | 2016-2018 |
| Brown, Wanda K. | Treasurer | 2022-2024 |
| Brumfield, Elizabeth | Executive Board | 2012-2020 |
| Burns-Simpson, Shauntee | Executive Board | 2017-2019 |
| Burns-Simpson, Shauntee | Vice President | 2018-2020 |
| Burns-Simpson, Shauntee | President | 2020-2022 |
| Burns-Simpson, Shauntee | Past President | 2022-2024 |
| Butler, Elizabeth Ann | Executive Board | 1990-1992 |
| Carter, Tiffani | Executive Board | 2021-2023 |
| Carter, Valerie | Executive Board | 2018-2022 |
| Cash-Menzies, Pam | Executive Board | 1983-1985 |
| Cash-Menzies, Pam | Executive Board | 1992-1994 |
| Cawthorne, Jon E. | Executive Board | 1995-1997 |
| Chambers, Tamela | Executive Board | 2022-2024 |
| Chisholm, Clarence | Executive Board | 1988-1993 |
| Clack, Doris H. | Executive Board | 1981-1983 |

| Name | Office | Term |
|---|---|---|
| Clay, Rudolph | Executive Board | 2013-2024 |
| Cobb, Jannie | Executive Board | 2007-2009 |
| Cobb, Jannie | Secretary | 2010-2012 |
| Cochran, Myrtis | Executive Board | 1996-1998 |
| Cole, Joan E. | Steering Committee | 1973-1975 |
| Cole, Joan E. | Executive Board | 1976-1978 |
| Coleman, Barbara | Steering Committee | 1971-1973 |
| Collins, Margaret | Executive Board | 1986-1988 |
| Conley, Binford | Executive Board | 1982-1984 |
| Copeland, Emily | Founding Member | 1970 |
| Covington, Diane | Executive Board | 2007-2009 |
| Covington, Diane | Executive Board | 2009-2013 |
| Covington, Diane | Secretary | 2012-2016 |
| Cox, Fannie M. | Executive Board | 2016-2019 |
| Cox, Fannie M. | Executive Board | 2023-2025 |
| Crayton, James | Executive Board | 1980-1986 |
| Crenshaw, Wanda L. | Executive Board | 1992-1994 |
| Crocker, Wayne M. | Executive Board | 1999-2001 |
| Cunningham, Thelma | Steering Committee | 1973-1975 |
| Cunningham, William D. | Chair | 1971-1973 |
| Curry, Anna | Executive Board | 1983-1985 |
| Curry, Eboni R. (Njoki) | Secretary | 2009-2010 |

| Name | Office | Term |
|---|---|---|
| Curry, Eboni R. (Njoki) | Executive Board | 2012-2017 |
| Curtis, Jean T. | Executive Board | 1982-1984 |
| Darden, Lakeshia | Executive Board | 2022-2024 |
| Davis, Denyvetta | Executive Board | 2006-2010 |
| Davis, Denyvetta | Vice President | 2014-2016 |
| Davis, Denyvetta | President | 2016-2018 |
| Davis, Denyvetta | Past President | 2018-2020 |
| Davis, James | Executive Board | 2019-2021 |
| Dawes, Trevor A. | Executive Board | 2005-2007 |
| Dawson, Rose Timmons | Executive Board | 2003-2005 |
| DeLoach, Marva | Executive Board | 1980-1982 |
| DeLoach, Marva | Vice Chair | 1984-1986 |
| DeLoach, Marva | Chair | 1986-1988 |
| DeLoach, Marva | Past Chair | 1988-1990 |
| Dickerson, Pricilla | Executive Board | 2018-2020 |
| Dillon, Irma | Executive Board | 1978-1980 |
| Duck, Tiffany A. | Executive Board | 2014-2016 |
| Dunsen-White, Naomi | Assist. Secretary | 2022-2023 |
| DuVernay, Jina | Executive Board | 2018-2020 |
| English, Jeanne E. | Editor-Newsletter | 1972 |
| Epps, Sharon K. | Executive Board | 2004-2008 |
| Etienne, Leslie | Executive Board | 2022-2024 |

| Name | Office | Term |
|---|---|---|
| Fenton, Michele | Executive Board | 2014-2016 |
| Fenton, Michele | Assist. Secretary | 2020-2022 |
| Fenton, Michele | Secretary | 2022-2024 |
| Fisher, Edith Maureen | Executive Board | 1984-1986 |
| Fisher, Edith Maureen | Vice Chair | 1986-1988 |
| Fisher, Edith Maureen | Chair | 1988-1990 |
| Fisher, Edith Maureen | Past President | 1990-1992 |
| Fontno, Tiffeni J. | Executive Board | 2003-2005 |
| Fontno, Tiffeni J. | Executive Board | 2017-2019 |
| Fontno, Tiffeni J. | Executive Board | 2023-2025 |
| Ford, Annie Marie | Executive Board | 2009-2013 |
| Ford, Annie Marie | Treasurer | 2012-2016 |
| Ford, Robert | Steering Committee | 1971-1973 |
| Ford, Sylverna V. | Executive Board | 1994-1998 |
| Foster, Makiba | Executive Board | 2014-2016 |
| Fouche, Taryn | Executive Board | 2020-2024 |
| Francois, Honore | Executive Board | 1986-1988 |
| Freeman-Smith, Patricia | Executive Board | 1984-1986 |
| Garcia, Elisa | Secretary | 2018-2020 |
| Garnes, Carolyn Lowe | Executive Board | 1999-2001 |
| Gaymon, Nicholas | Steering Committee | 1973-1975 |
| Gaymon, Nicholas | Executive Board | 1978-1980 |
| Giles, Louise | Secretary-Treasurer | 1972-1974 |
| Gleason, Yolanda | Executive Board | 2021-2023 |
| Grant, D. L. | Executive Board | 2009-2013 |
| Grant, George C. | Steering Committee | 1971-1976 |
| Grant, George C. | Vice Chair | 1976-1978 |
| Grant, George C. | Chair | 1978-1980 |
| Grant, George C. | Executive Board | 1980-1982 |
| Grant, George C. | Editor-Newsletter | 1983-2000 |
| Grant, George C. | Executive Board | 1986-1992 |
| Grant, George C. | Executive Board | 1998-2000 |
| Grant, George C. | Executive Board | 2005-2007 |
| Gray, LaVerne | Executive Board | 2008-2010 |
| Griffin, Richard | Executive Board | 1980-1981 |
| Griffin, Richard | Secretary | 1982-1986 |
| Guilford, Benjamin | Steering Committee | 1971-1973 |
| Guss, Emily | Executive Board | 1984-1986 |
| Guss, Emily | Executive Board | 2004-2006 |
| Guss, Emily | Executive Board | 2010-2015 |
| Guthrie, Dorothy | Executive Board | 2010-2012 |
| Guydon, Janet | Executive Board | 1981-1983 |
| Haith, Dorothy | Secretary | 1978-1982 |
| Haith, Dorothy | Treasurer | 1982-1988 |

| Name | Office | Term |
|---|---|---|
| Hardin, Willie | Executive Board | 2002–2004 |
| Harris, Jewel H. | Steering Committee | 1973–1975 |
| Harris, Jewel H. | Executive Board | 1976–1980 |
| Harris, Jewel H. | Executive Board | 1984–1986 |
| Harris, S. D. | Executive Board | 2006–2010 |
| Harris, S. D. | Editor-Newsletter | 2007–2010 |
| Hart, Brian | Executive Board | 2015–2019 |
| Hawkins, Ernestine L. | Executive Board | 1994–2000 |
| Hawkins, Ernestine L. | Executive Board | 2005–2007 |
| Hayes, Ailene | Executive Board | 2010–2012 |
| Hayes, Andrea | Executive Board | 2023–2025 |
| Hayes, Nichelle M. | Executive Board | 2018–2020 |
| Hayes, Nichelle M. | Vice President | 2020–2022 |
| Hayes, Nichelle M. | President | 2022–2024 |
| Henderson, Carolyn J. | Executive Board | 1988–1990 |
| Hightower, Monteria | Executive Board | 1978–1981 |
| Hixon, Cecil | Executive Board | 1992–1994 |
| Holman, Jos N. | Executive Board | 1991–1993 |
| Holman, Jos N. | Executive Board | 2003–2007 |
| Holman, Jos N. | Vice President | 2008–2010 |
| Holman, Jos N. | President | 2010–2012 |
| Holman, Jos N. | Past President | 2012–2014 |

| Name | Office | Term |
|---|---|---|
| Holman, Jos N. | Executive Board | 2016–2018 |
| Holmes, Gerald V. | Executive Board | 1998–2000 |
| Holmes, Gerald V. | Executive Board | 2006–2010 |
| Hooker, Cathy Lenix | Steering Committee | 1973–1975 |
| Hooker, Cathy Lenix | Executive Board | 1978–1980 |
| Hopkins, Diane McAfee | Executive Board | 1985–1987 |
| Hughes, M. Elaine | Executive Board | 1988–1997 |
| Hunter, Kimberly | Executive Board | 2023–2025 |
| Hunter-Hayes, Tracey | Executive Board | 1993–1995 |
| Irving, Ophelia | Steering Committee | 1973–1975 |
| Jackson, Ada | Steering Committee | 1971–1973 |
| Jackson, Adele M. | Executive Board | 1978–1981 |
| Jackson, Andrew P. "Sekou" | Executive Board | 1998–2003 |
| Jackson, Andrew P. "Sekou" | Vice President | 2002–2004 |
| Jackson, Andrew P. "Sekou" | President | 2004–2006 |
| Jackson, Andrew P. "Sekou" | Past President | 2006–2008 |
| Jackson, Andrew P. "Sekou" | Executive Board | 2009–2017 |
| Jackson, Audrey N. | Founding Member | 1970 |
| Jackson, Audrey N. | Executive Board | 1978–1980 |
| Jefferson, Julius, Jr. | Executive Board | 2007–2009 |
| Jelks, Joyce E. | Executive Board | 1992–1994 |
| Jenkins, Barbara Williams | Treasurer | 1976–1982 |

**BCALA Leadership: 1970–2025**

| Name | Office | Term |
|---|---|---|
| Jenkins, Barbara Williams | Vice Chair | 1982–1984 |
| Jenkins, Barbara Williams | Chair | 1984–1986 |
| Jenkins, Barbara Williams | Past Chair | 1986–1988 |
| Johnson, Laura | Executive Board | 2022–2024 |
| Johnson, Sammie | Executive Board | 2015–2017 |
| Johnson, Shirley E. | Executive Board | 2000–2002 |
| Johnson-Cooper, Glendora | Executive Board | 1993–1995 |
| Johnson-Houston, Debbie | Executive Board | 1994–1996 |
| Johnson-Perkins, Brenda | Secretary | 2020–2022 |
| Johnson-Perkins, Brenda | Executive Board | 2022–2024 |
| Jones, Barbara | Executive Board | 1987–1991 |
| Jones, Rita | Executive Board | 1991–1993 |
| Jones, Rita | Executive Board | 2002–2004 |
| Jones, Virginia Lacy | Founding Member | 1970 |
| Jones-Trent, Bernice | Executive Board | 1989–1991 |
| Jordan, Alys | Executive Board | 2007–2009 |
| Jordan, Casper LeRoy | Steering Committee | 1973–1975 |
| Jordan, Casper LeRoy | Editor-Newsletter | 1975–1978 |
| Jordan, Casper LeRoy | Executive Board | 1976–1978 |
| Josey, E. J. | Founder | 1970 |
| Josey, E. J. | Chair | 1970–1971 |
| Josey, E. J. | Steering Committee | 1971–1976 |

| Name | Office | Term |
|---|---|---|
| Joyce, Donald | Steering Committee | 1973–1975 |
| Joynes, Roy L. | Executive Board | 1994–1996 |
| Keeton, kYmberly | Executive Board | 2012–2014 |
| Kelker, Patricia | Executive Board | 1993–1995 |
| Kelker, Patricia | Executive Board | 1998–2000 |
| Kelker, Patricia | Executive Board | 2002–2004 |
| Kemp, Emma | Executive Board | 1984–1986 |
| Knowles, Em Claire | Executive Board | 1986–1993 |
| Knowles, Em Claire | Secretary | 1994–1996 |
| Knowles, Em Claire | Executive Board | 2000–2002 |
| Knowles, Em Claire | Executive Board | 2012–2014 |
| Kuykendall, Bradley | Executive Board | 2016–2018 |
| Kyles, Rubye Childs | Executive Board | 1992–1994 |
| LaFleur, LeRoy | Executive Board | 2006–2007 |
| Landrum, Cyndee Sturgis | Executive Board | 2017–2019 |
| Lang, Jennifer | Executive Board | 2005–2006 |
| Lang, Jennifer | Secretary | 2006–2008 |
| Lawson, Rhea Brown | Executive Board | 2004–2006 |
| Lee, Rodney Jackson | Executive Board | 2000–2002 |
| Lemmons, Karen L. | Executive Board | 2004–2006 |
| Lemmons, Karen L. | Executive Board | 2014–2018 |
| Lenox, Mary | Executive Board | 1983–1985 |

| Name | Office | Term |
|---|---|---|
| Leonard, Gloria J. | Executive Board | 1988-1992 |
| Leonard, Gloria J. | Executive Board | 2002-2004 |
| Love, Tatanisha "Tiki" | Executive Board | 2018-2020 |
| Love, Tatanisha "Tiki" | Vice President | 2022-2024 |
| Lowe, Greta | Editor-Newsletter | 2000-2002 |
| Lowe, Greta | Executive Board | 2001-2003 |
| Lumumba, Malikah Dada | Executive Board | 2000-2004 |
| Luster, Dominique | Executive Board | 2016-2018 |
| Lyles, Denise | Executive Board | 2021-2023 |
| Mack, Phyllis Green | Executive Board | 1998-2002 |
| Madden, Doreitha R. | Secretary | 1976-1978 |
| Madden, Doreitha R. | Vice Chair | 1978-1980 |
| Madden, Doreitha R. | Chair | 1980-1982 |
| Madden, Doreitha R. | Executive Board | 1984-1986 |
| McCoy, Cheryl | Executive Board | 1984-1986 |
| McCurtis, Kirby | Executive Board | 2014-2016 |
| McCurtis, Kirby | Secretary | 2016-2018 |
| McGinn, Jane Moore | Executive Board | 2001-2003 |
| McKnight, Cherese | Treasurer | 2018-2020 |
| McNeil, Brandy | Treasurer | 2020-2022 |
| McNeil-Capers, Kim | Executive Board | 2015-2019 |
| Melton, Vivian | Executive Board | 1994-1996 |

| Name | Office | Term |
|---|---|---|
| Miles, Fiolina B. | Executive Board | 1987-1989 |
| Millender, Dolly | Steering Committee | 1971-1973 |
| Miller, Robert | Executive Board | 1989-1991 |
| Mondowney, JoAnne G. | Treasurer | 1998-2002 |
| Mondowney, JoAnne G. | Executive Board | 2002-2004 |
| Moore, Jerrod | Executive Board | 2017-2019 |
| Morris, Effie Lee | Founding Member | 1970 |
| Morris, Effie Lee | Steering Committee | 1973-1975 |
| Morris, Effie Lee | Executive Board | 1976-1978 |
| Morrison, Samuel F. | Executive Board | 1981-1983 |
| Morrison, Samuel F. | Executive Board | 1987-1989 |
| Morrison, Samuel F. | Executive Board | 1998-2000 |
| Moses, Sibyl E. | Executive Board | 2001-2006 |
| Mosley, Derek | Executive Board | 2012-2014 |
| Mosley, Derek | Executive Board | 2020-2022 |
| Mosley, Madison M., Jr. | Executive Board | 1996-1998 |
| Mothershed, S. W. | Executive Board | 1976-1978 |
| Muhammad, Fayrene | Executive Board | 2016-2018 |
| Muhammad, Fayrene | Executive Board | 2020-2022 |
| Munson, Tashia | Executive Board | 2019-2021 |
| Ndumu, Ana | Executive Board | 2019-2023 |
| Neely, Teresa Y. | Executive Board | 1995-1999 |

| Name | Office | Term |
|------|--------|------|
| Norman, Carolyn | Secretary | 2002–2004 |
| Norman, Carolyn | Executive Board | 2008–2010 |
| Nosakhere, Akilah | Executive Board | 2012–2014 |
| Nurse, Carol | Executive Board | 2012–2015 |
| Offord, Jerome, Jr. | Executive Board | 2006–2008 |
| Offord, Jerome, Jr. | Vice President | 2010–2012 |
| Offord, Jerome, Jr. | President | 2012–2014 |
| Offord, Jerome, Jr. | Past President | 2014–2016 |
| Olaniti, Olanike | Executive Board | 2022–2024 |
| Orange, Satia Marshall | Executive Board | 1996–1998 |
| Orange, Satia Marshall | Executive Board | 2020–2022 |
| Overbey, Tracey | Executive Board | 2021–2023 |
| Packwood, Cyril | Executive Board | 1978–1980 |
| Packwood, Cyril | Executive Board | 1982–1984 |
| Page, John | Executive Board | 2001–2003 |
| Partridge, James | Steering Committee | 1973–1975 |
| Partridge, James | Executive Board | 1978–1980 |
| Partridge, James | Executive Board | 1980–1982 |
| Passmore, William A. | Executive Board | 1985–1987 |
| Patterson, Grace | Executive Board | 1987–1989 |
| Peeples, Donald | Executive Board | 2018–2020 |
| Perry, Emma Bradford | Executive Board | 1998–2000 |
| Perry, Pennie | Steering Committee | 1973–1975 |
| Perry, Pennie | Executive Board | 1981–1983 |
| Phinazee, Annette L. | Steering Committee | 1973–1975 |
| Phinazee, Annette L. | Executive Board | 1976–1978 |
| Plair, Norman V. | Executive Board | 1995–1997 |
| Player, Bobby, Sr. | Executive Board | 1987–1991 |
| Player, Bobby, Sr. | Executive Board | 1989–1991 |
| Player, Bobby, Sr. | Treasurer | 1996–1998 |
| Player, Bobby, Sr. | Vice President | 2000–2002 |
| Player, Bobby, Sr. | President | 2002–2004 |
| Player, Bobby, Sr. | Past President | 2004–2006 |
| Player, Jewel Armstrong | Executive Board | 1997–1999 |
| Player, Jewel Armstrong | Executive Board | 2001–2003 |
| Primm, Gloria | Steering Committee | 1973–1975 |
| Randall, Ann | Steering Committee | 1971–1973 |
| Randall, Ann | Executive Board | 1978–1984 |
| Randall, Ann | Executive Board | 1986–1988 |
| Reese, Gregory L. | Executive Board | 1992–1994 |
| Reese, Gregory L. | Vice President | 1996–1998 |
| Reese, Gregory L. | President | 1998–2000 |
| Reese, Gregory L. | Past President | 2000–2002 |
| Reid, Edna F. | Editor–Newsletter | 1979–1983 |

| Name | Office | Term |
|---|---|---|
| Revels, Ira | Executive Board | 2003-2004 |
| Revels, Ira | Secretary | 2004-2006 |
| Rhodes, Leila G. | Executive Board | 1985-1987 |
| Richards, Kelly C. | Executive Board | 1997-1999 |
| Rier, Nadine S. | Steering Committee | 1973-1975 |
| Rier, Nadine S. | Executive Board | 1976-1978 |
| Robinson, Carrie | Founding Member | 1970 |
| Robinson, Gleniece | Executive Board | 1990-1992 |
| Robinson, Harry, Jr. | Vice Chair | 1973-1974 |
| Robinson, Harry, Jr. | Steering Committee | 1973-1975 |
| Robinson, Harry, Jr. | Chair | 1974-1976 |
| Robinson, LeRoy | Executive Board | 2004-2006 |
| Robinson, LeRoy | Executive Board | 2009-2011 |
| Royster, Vivian | Executive Board | 1982-1984 |
| Rudd, Amanda | Executive Board | 1978-1982 |
| Sanders, Lou Helen | Executive Board | 1991-1993 |
| Scott, Tracey | Executive Board | 2021-2023 |
| Searcy, David | Executive Board | 1981-1983 |
| Searcy, David | Executive Board | 1986-1988 |
| Searcy, David | Executive Board | 1990-1992 |
| Shell, Lambert | Executive Board | 2011-2013 |
| Shockley, Ann Allen | Editor-Newsletter | 1972-1974 |
| Simmons, Jasmine | Executive Board | 2018-2020 |
| Simms, Oscar | Executive Board | 1983-1985 |
| Simpson, Shamika | Executive Board | 2020-2022 |
| Smith, Alice | Executive Board | 1978-1980 |
| Smith, Alice | Executive Board | 1981-1983 |
| Smith, Gloria | Executive Board | 1978-1981 |
| Smith, Jessie Cottman | Executive Board | 1976-1978 |
| Smith-Epps, E. Paulette | Secretary | 1986-1990 |
| Smith-Epps, E. Paulette | Executive Board | 1991-1993 |
| Speller, Benjamin F., Jr. | Executive Board | 1985-1987 |
| Spencer, Edith Prunty | Founding Member | 1970 |
| Spencer, Edith Prunty | Secretary-Treasurer | 1970-1971 |
| Spradling, Mary Mace | Steering Committee | 1973-1975 |
| Spradling, Mary Mace | Executive Board | 1976-1978 |
| Sprinkle-Hamlin, Sylvia Y. | Vice President | 1994-1996 |
| Sprinkle-Hamlin, Sylvia Y. | President | 1996-1998 |
| Sprinkle-Hamlin, Sylvia Y. | Past President | 1998-2000 |
| Sprinkle-Hamlin, Sylvia Y. | Executive Board | 2002-2004 |
| Sprinkle-Hamlin, Sylvia Y. | Executive Board | 2006-2008 |
| Sprinkle-Hamlin, Sylvia Y. | Executive Board | 2010-2012 |
| Stokes, Eboni | Executive Board | 2009-2013 |
| Stokes, Hellena Olivia | Executive Board | 2004-2005 |

| Name | Office | Term |
|---|---|---|
| Sumbi, Joyce | Steering Committee | 1971–1973 |
| Tate, Thelma | Executive Board | 1985–1987 |
| Taylor, Carole R. | Executive Board | 1976–1978 |
| Thomas, Lucille C. | Steering Committee | 1973–1975 |
| Thomas, Lucille C. | Executive Board | 1982–1984 |
| Thompson, Karolyn S. | Secretary | 1996–2002 |
| Thompson, Karolyn S. | Executive Board | 2003–2007 |
| Thompson, Karolyn S. | Vice President | 2006–2008 |
| Thompson, Karolyn S. | President | 2008–2010 |
| Thompson, Karolyn S. | Past President | 2010–2012 |
| Tingling, Jessica | Executive Board | 2021–2025 |
| Toliver, Virginia Dowsing | Executive Board | 1997–1999 |
| Tomlinson, Monya | Executive Board | 2014–2016 |
| Torres, Michael | Executive Board | 2023–2025 |
| Totton, Herman | Steering Committee | 1973–1975 |
| Trammell, Phyllis | Secretary | 1990–1992 |
| Turner, Marcellus | Executive Board | 1993–1995 |
| Tyler, Audrey Q. | Executive Board | 1988–1990 |
| Tyson, John C. | Executive Board | 1982–1984 |
| Tyson, John C. | Executive Board | 1987–1989 |
| Tyson, John C. | Vice Chair | 1988–1990 |
| Tyson, John C. | President | 1990–1992 |
| Tyson, John C. | Past President | 1992–1994 |
| Unaeze, Felix Eme | Executive Board | 1991–1993 |
| Venable, Andrew, Jr. | Executive Board | 1983–1990 |
| Walker, Michael C. | Executive Board | 1995–2001 |
| Ward, Regina Renee | Executive Board | 2019–2021 |
| Washington, Dorothy | Executive Board | 2007–2009 |
| Watson, Kelvin | Executive Board | 2006–2012 |
| Watson, Kelvin | Vice President | 2012–2014 |
| Watson, Kelvin | President | 2014–2016 |
| Watson, Kelvin | Past President | 2016–2018 |
| Webb, Roberta V. | Executive Board | 2004–2006 |
| Webb, Roberta V. | Executive Board | 2010–2012 |
| Weil, Teri B. | Executive Board | 2006–2008 |
| Weir, Birdie | Executive Board | 1993–1995 |
| Welbourne, James | Founding Member | 1970 |
| Westbrooks, Lainey | Executive Board | 2003–2007 |
| White, Joel | Executive Board | 2008–2010 |
| Wilkins, Binne Tate | Founding Member | 1970 |
| Wilkins, Binne Tate | Steering Committee | 1971–1973 |
| Wilkins, Binne Tate | Executive Board | 1985–1987 |
| Williams, Avery | Steering Committee | 1973–1975 |
| Williams, Avery | Vice Chair | 1974–1976 |

| Name | Office | Term |
|---|---|---|
| Williams, Avery | Chair | 1976–1978 |
| Williams, Barbara A. | Executive Board | 1990–1992 |
| Williams, Barbara A. | Secretary | 1992–1994 |
| Williams, Barbara A. | Executive Board | 1994–1998 |
| Williams, Helen | Executive Board | 1980–1983 |
| Williams, Joslyn | Steering Committee | 1971–1973 |
| Williams, Karen Y. | Executive Board | 2003–2005 |
| Wilson, Louis C. | Steering Committee | 1973–1975 |
| Wilson, Louis C. | Secretary-Treasurer | 1974–1976 |

| Name | Office | Term |
|---|---|---|
| Wilson, Louis C. | Executive Board | 1978–1982 |
| Wilson, Patricia A. | Executive Board | 1982–1984 |
| Wright, James R. | Vice Chair | 1971–1972 |
| Wright, James R. | Chair | 1973–1974 |
| Wright, Robert | Steering Committee | 1971–1973 |
| Wright, Robert | Vice Chair | 1980–1982 |
| Wright, Robert | Chair | 1982–1984 |
| Wright, Robert | Past Chair | 1984–1986 |
| Zulu, Itibari M. | Executive Board | 1998–2000 |

# 3.2b

## *BCALA Leadership: 1970–2025*

Stanton F. Biddle

Founders, Officers, Steering Committee Members, Executive Board Members, and Editors of the *BCALA Newsletter* and *BCALA News*

Abdullah, Talia
Abif, Khafre K.
Adams, Elaine
Alford, Thomas
Allen, Cassandra
Alston, Jason K.
Aman, Mohammed
Ashby, Richard E., Jr.
Avery, Gail W.
Axam, John
Baker, Michael E.

Ballard, Rochelle
Barksdale-Hall, Roland
Battle, Thomas
Beal, Billy C.
Bell, Gladys Smiley
Bethel, Kathleen E.
Biblo, Mary
Biddle, Stanton F.
Bingham, Rebecca
Black, Bettye
Bolton, Willis

Booker, Latrice "Libre'"
Bordeaux, Vivian
Boyd, D. Alex
Boyd, K. C.
Boyd, Lisa
Bradberry, Richard
Brasley, Eric
Broady, Jessie
Brooks, Taylor
Brooks, Violette
Brown, Charles

Brown, Dolores
Brown, Florence Simkins
Brown, Gloria Primm
Brown, Lorene B.
Brown, Malore I.
Brown, Richard E.
Brown, Wanda K.
Brumfield, Elizabeth
Burns-Simpson, Shauntee
Butler, Elizabeth Ann
Carter, Tiffani

Carter, Valerie
Cash-Menzies, Pam
Cawthorne, Jon E.
Chambers, Tamela
Chisholm, Clarence
Clack, Doris H.
Clay, Rudolph
Cobb, Jannie
Cochran, Myrtis
Cole, Joan E.
Coleman, Barbara
Collins, Margaret
Conley, Binford
Copeland, Emily
Covington, Diane
Cox, Fannie M.
Crayton, James
Crenshaw, Wanda L.
Crocker, Wayne M.
Cunningham, Thelma
Cunningham, William D.
Curry, Anna
Curry, Eboni R. (Njoki)
Curtis, Jean T.
Darden, Lakeshia
Davis, Denyvetta
Davis, James
Dawes, Trevor A.
Dawson, Rose Timmons
DeLoach, Marva
Dickerson, Pricilla
Dillon, Irma
Duck, Tiffany A.
Dunsen-White, Naomi
DuVernay, Jina
English, Jeanne E.
Epps, Sharon K.
Etienne, Leslie
Fenton, Michele
Fisher, Edith Maureen
Fontno, Tiffeni J.
Ford, Annie Marie
Ford, Robert
Ford, Sylverna V.
Foster, Makiba
Fouche, Taryn
Francois, Honore
Freeman-Smith, Patricia
Garcia, Elisa
Garnes, Carolyn Lowe
Gaymon, Nicholas
Giles, Louise
Gleason, Yolanda
Grant, D. L.
Grant, George C.

Gray, LaVerne
Griffin, Richard
Guilford, Benjamin
Guss, Emily
Guthrie, Dorothy
Guydon, Janet
Haith, Dorothy
Hardin, Willie
Harris, Jewel H.
Harris, S. D.
Hart, Brian
Hawkins, Ernestine L.
Hayes, Allene
Hayes, Andrea
Hayes, Nichelle M.
Henderson, Carolyn J.
Hightower, Monteria
Hixon, Cecil
Holman, Jos N.
Holmes, Gerald V.
Hooker, Cathy Lenix
Hopkins, Diane McAfee
Hughes, M. Elaine
Hunter, Kimberly
Hunter-Hayes, Tracey
Irving, Ophelia
Jackson, Ada
Jackson, Adele M.
Jackson, Adele M.
Jackson, Andrew P. "Sekou"
Jackson, Audrey N.
Jefferson, Julius, Jr.
Jelks, Joyce E.
Jenkins, Barbara Williams
Johnson, Laura
Johnson, Sammie
Johnson, Shirley E.
Johnson-Cooper, Glendora
Johnson-Houston, Debbie
Johnson-Perkins, Brenda
Jones, Barbara
Jones, Rita
Jones, Virginia Lacy
Jones-Trent, Bernice
Jordan, Alys
Jordan, Casper LeRoy
Josey, E. J.
Joyce, Donald
Joynes, Roy L.
Keeton, kYmberly
Kelker, Patricia
Kemp, Emma
Knowles, Em Claire
Kuykendall, Bradley

Kyles, Rubye Childs
LaFleur, LeRoy
Landrum, Cyndee Sturgis
Lang, Jennifer
Lawson, Rhea Brown
Lee, Rodney Jackson
Lemmons, Karen L.
Lenox, Mary
Leonard, Gloria J.
Love, Tatanisha "Tiki"
Lowe, Greta
Lumumba, Malikah Dada
Luster, Dominique
Lyles, Denise
Mack, Phyllis Green
Madden, Doreitha R.
McCoy, Cheryl
McCurtis, Kirby
McGinn, Jane Moore
McKnight, Cherese
McNeil, Brandy
McNeil-Capers, Kim
Melton, Vivian
Miles, Fiolina B.
Millender, Dolly
Miller, Robert
Mondowney, JoAnne G.
Moore, Jerrod
Morris, Effie Lee
Morrison, Samuel F.
Moses, Sibyl E.
Mosley, Derek
Mosley, Madison M., Jr.
Mothershed, S. W.
Muhammad, Fayrene J.
Munson, Tashia
Ndumu, Ana
Neely, Teresa Y.
Norman, Carolyn
Nosakhere, Akilah
Nurse, Carol
Olaniti, Olanike
Orange, Sãtia Marshall
Overbey, Tracey
Packwood, Cyril
Page, John
Partridge, James
Passmore, William A.
Patterson, Grace
Peeples, Donald
Perry, Emma Bradford
Perry, Pennie
Phinazee, Annette L.
Plair, Norman V.
Player, Bobby, Sr.

Player, Jewel Armstrong
Randall, Ann
Reese, Gregory L.
Reid, Edna F.
Revels, Ira
Rhodes, Leila G.
Richards, Kelly C.
Rier, Nadine S.
Robinson, Carrie
Robinson, Gleniece
Robinson, Harry, Jr.
Robinson, LeRoy
Royster, Vivian
Rudd, Amanda
Sanders, Lou Helen
Scott, Tracey
Searcy, David
Shell, Lambert
Shockley, Ann Allen
Simmons, Jasmine
Simms, Oscar
Simpson, Shamika
Smith, Alice
Smith, Gloria
Smith, Jessie Cottman
Smith-Epps, E. Paulette
Speller, Benjamin F., Jr.
Spencer, Edith Prunty
Spradling, Mary Mace
Sprinkle-Hamlin, Sylvia Y.
Stokes, Eboni
Stokes, Hellena Olivia
Sumbi, Joyce
Tate, Thelma
Taylor, Carole R.
Thomas, Lucille C.
Thompson, Karolyn S.
Tingling, Jessica
Torres, Michael
Toliver, Virginia Dowsing
Tomlinson, Monya
Totton, Herman
Trammell, Phyllis
Turner, Marcellus
Tyler, Audrey Q.
Tyson, John C.
Unaeze, Felix Eme
Venable, Andrew, Jr.
Walker, Michael C.
Ward, Regina Renee
Washington, Dorothy
Watson, Kelvin
Webb, Roberta V.
Weil, Teri B.
Weir, Birdie

Welbourne, James
Westbrooks, Lainey
White, Joel
Wilkins, Binne Tate
Williams, Avery
Williams, Barbara A.
Williams, Helen
Williams, Joslyn
Williams, Karen Y.
Wilson, Louis C.
Wilson, Patricia A.
Wright, James R.
Wright, Robert
Zulu, Itibari M.

# 3.3

## Black Library/Librarian Associations and Collaborations in the Twenty-First Century

Shauntee Burns-Simpson and Nichelle M. Hayes

The Black Caucus American Library Association serves as an advocate for the development, promotion, and improvement of library services and resources to the nation's Black community and provides leadership for the recruitment and professional development of Black librarians and library workers.

—Black Caucus of the
American Library Association[1]

The mission of the Black Caucus of the American Library Association (BCALA), as mentioned in the quote above, has remained the same for over fifty-plus years, however, strategy for implementation has been altered over time. With information-gathering and services going from analog to digital, the work of BCALA and collaboration has grown to fit the needs of the members. The 1970s to 2020 all play a pivotal role in society.

As early as the 1930s, Black librarians would gather in hotel rooms at American Library Association (ALA) conferences and discuss the inequities within the profession. Under the suggestion of Effie Lee Morris, Black librarians met at the 1968 (Kansas City, Missouri) annual conference to discuss their concerns about not having a voice in the ALA. At a meeting in 1969, it was decided by several Black librarians that ALA was not serving the needs of Black Library professionals, and the Black Caucus of the American Library Association (BCALA) was formed to address concerns. The following year, E. J. Josey, a member of the ALA Nominating Committee, wanted to find qualified Black candidates and socially responsible white candidates to run for council in the 1971 election.

Josey sent out letters inviting all African American librarians to attend the 1970 mid-winter meeting to discuss a candidate they would support.[2]

The goals of BCALA[3] include:

To call to the attention of the ALA the need to respond positively on behalf of Black members of the Association.

To review the records and evaluate the positions of candidates for the various offices within ALA.

To monitor the activities of the Divisions, Round Tables and Committees of the ALA, to make sure they are meeting the needs of the Black librarian.

To serve as a clearinghouse for Black librarians in promoting wider participation by Black librarians at all levels of the profession and Association.

To support and promote efforts to achieve meaningful communication and equitable representation in state associations and on the governing and advisory boards of libraries at the state and local levels.

To facilitate library service which will meet the information needs of Black people.

To encourage the development of authoritative information resources about Black people and the dissemination of this information to the larger community.

| Josey, E. J. | Chair | 1970–1971 |
|---|---|---|
| Cunningham, William D. | Chair | 1971–1973 |
| Wright, James R. | Chair | 1973–1974 |
| Robinson, Harry, Jr. | Chair | 1974–1976 |

| Williams, Avery | Chair | 1976-1978 |
|---|---|---|
| Grant, George C. | Chair | 1978-1980 |
| Madden, Doreitha R. | Chair | 1980-1982 |
| Wright, Robert | Chair | 1982-1984 |
| Jenkins, Barbara Williams | Chair | 1984-1986 |
| DeLoach, Marva | Chair | 1986-1988 |
| Fisher, Edith Maureen | Chair | 1988-1990 |
| Tyson, John C. | President | 1990-1992 |
| Boyd, D. Alex | President | 1992-1994 |
| Biddle, Stanton F. | President | 1994-1996 |
| Hamlin, Sylvia Sprinkle | President | 1996-1998 |
| Reese, Gregory | President | 1998-2000 |
| Bell, Gladys Smiley | President | 2000-2002 |
| Player, Bobby, Sr. | President | 2002-2004 |
| Jackson, Andrew P. | President | 2004-2006 |
| Brown, Wanda K. | President | 2006-2008 |
| Thompson, Karolyn S. | President | 2008-2010 |
| Holman, Jos N. | President | 2010-2012 |
| Offord, Jerome, Jr. | President | 2012-2014 |
| Watson, Kelvin | President | 2014-2016 |
| Davis, Denyvetta | President | 2016-2018 |
| Ashby, Richard E. | President | 2018-2020 |
| Burns-Simpson, Shauntee | President | 2020-2022 |
| Hayes, Nichelle M. | President | 2022-2024 |

**PRESIDENTS TO DATE (FROM 1970 TO 1990 CHAIR WAS USED IN LIEU OF PRESIDENT)[4]**

E. J. Josey (1924-2009):[5] cofounder of BCALA, past ALA president (1984-1985), and actively involved in the civil rights movement. Josey was also an author, professor, mentor, and advocate. Josey's scholarship and vision continue to guide librarians. His mentorship transcended the library profession.

Effie Lee Morris (1921-2009):[6] cofounder of BCALA. A children's librarian, educator, and activist who pioneered public library services for minorities and the visually impaired. She was the first African American president of the Public Library Association and was elected to honorary membership in the American Library Association, this is the organization's highest honor given to a living member of the association.

Albert Prince Marshall (aka AP Marshall):[7] cofounder of BCALA. He was a librarian and educator, and similar to E. J. Josey participated in the civil rights movement. Mr. Marshall was a director of library services at Eastern Michigan University (EMU) and went on to serve as EMU's dean of academic services. He was the first African American to serve as chair of the nominating committee for ALA president and is listed as one of the four most prominent librarians who stood to oppose racial segregation in the library profession (ALA Council resolution to honor those who fought segregation).

Shauntee Burns-Simpson became president and Nichelle M. Hayes became vice president during a virtual ceremony in June 2020,[9] at the height of the COVID-19 outbreak. This unprecedented time provided no framework on how BCALA should move forward as an organization. The caucus pivoted by hosting webinars for professional development and having Zoom meetings to keep members informed. During Burns-Simpson and Hayes's tenure, BCALA quadrupled programming and tripled membership with many new members being recruited from library schools. Along with recruitment this was a pivotal time for collaboration.

**INSTITUTE OF MUSEUMS AND LIBRARY SERVICES**

In 2020, BCALA received a $100,000 grant from the Institution of Museums and Library Services (IMLS) Laura Bush 21st Century Librarian Program. The grant is used to facilitate "Breaking Barriers: The Future of Black Librarianship National Forum," a symposium to educate and support Black/African American library information science (LIS) students: https://breakingbarriers.bcala.org/.[10] Dr. Ana Ndumu and Dr. Shaundra Walker were the program administrators. The IMLS funding allowed LIS students and professionals to convene in order to learn and increase BCALA's outreach to emerging librarians. In the overall assessing and strategic planning for BCALA, there was a need for student-centered community building, culturally relevant marketing, and mentorship. This work supports the future leaders in the library profession. BCALA has a long history of leaders in the field, and it will continue to support members in their leadership goals.

IMLS also awarded BCALA a $99,934 planning grant to research Black History Month (BHM) programming in public libraries. Dr. Deborah Robinson and Dr. Grace Jackson-Brown were the administrators of the project. The planning grant assembled stakeholders from across the country in this work. At the end of the project, a comprehensive literature review was created, along with a taxonomy of BHM programming, and a draft framework for the next IMLS project on the national research study and BHM toolkit for beginners.[11]

**BLACK LIBRARIANS (@*BLACKLIBRARIANS* INSTAGRAM)**

Shannon Bland, founder of the social media account Black Librarians[12] stated, "We began a collaboration for the inaugural virtual commencement for LIS students of color. Since that event we have continued to work together on a host of programs including BCALA's 'Plant a Book, Grow a Reader' program."

## PENGUIN RANDOM HOUSE

Penguin Random House sponsored and donated books in support of BCALA's "Plant a Book, Grow a Reader." This event was a virtual "baby shower" designed to promote the importance of literacy and literature to children and young adults of the Black/African diaspora and celebrate the president's pregnancy (the 2020 election included many firsts including the first time BCALA had a pregnant president who gave birth while in office). All participants were able to give the name of a school or early literacy center where their books would be shipped.[13]

## NETFLIX

The Netflix partnership with the Black Caucus of the American Library Association occurred in cooperation with the Association for Library Service to Children. *Bookmarks: Celebrating Black Voices* is a live-action collection of twelve five-minute episodes featuring prominent Black celebrities and artists reading children's books from Black authors that highlight the Black experience. This partnership encompassed booklists, webinars, resources, etc.[14]

## LIBRARIES

The New York Public Library and the Black Caucus of the American Library Association partnered on meditative programming for library staff on race relations. The two-part program series offered a safe space for BIPOC staff to reflect on race in America. Part 1, *Fortitude: Brave Conversations and Mediation*, covered the impact of race trauma, race-related stress, and how racism impacts the health of Black, Indigenous, and People of Color. The twelve weekly conversations and healing sessions were facilitated by Dr. Janet Taylor, whose work focuses on BIPOC mental health and stress management, and Robert Brace, who is known as the "mind, body-soul connector." Part 2, *Patience: ALA/Kellogg Foundation Racial Healing Circle*, is a small and private dialogue for staff to talk openly about race. For eight weeks these discussions were scheduled for twice a week to provide participants the opportunity to work through ways of past wrongdoings and think of possible solutions that will provide a positive impact.[15]

Prince George County Library and the Black Caucus of the American Library Association partnered on a series of author programs that really touched reader's interests:[16]

Bassey Ikpi, *I'm Telling You the Truth But I'm Lying*
    *New York Times* Bestseller, collection of essays, Nigerian-American author, mental health focus

Michele Harper, *The Beauty in Breaking: A Memoir*
    *New York Times* Bestseller, memoir of being a Black female doctor in contemporary America

Calvin Baker, *A More Perfect Reunion: Race Integration, and the Future of America*
    Author is a Hurston-Wright Award finalist

Eddie S. Glaude Jr., *Begin Again: James Baldwin's America and Its Urgent Lessons for Our Own*

The Queens Public Library, National Library of Medicine, and the Black Caucus American Library Association partnered on a groundbreaking event, "*The Black Health and Healing Virtual Summit.*" This twenty-four-hour program provided participants with virtual panels, informative lectures, and interactive workshops.

Nichelle M. Hayes, vice president (2018–2020) of BCALA, explained why this event was necessary: "Health and healing are critical to everyone but especially for the Black community due to racism and discrepancies in health care. The stress of racism also has an impact on the Black community. Self-empowerment and support are key."[17]

The event featured top experts in the fields of medicine and science, as well as notable entertainers, musicians, and athletes. Presenters delved into a plethora of health and wellness issues faced by the Black community. Shauntee Burns-Simpson, president of the Black Caucus American Library Association (2018–2020) shared that "2020 has been a challenging time, especially for Black and Brown communities. This summit will offer resources that can help educate, transform, and activate healthier practices for the mind, body, and soul."[18] Some of the many topics covered include mental health, parenting, health equity, contemporary civil rights, racism, and COVID-19.

Keynote speaker, Dr. Kizzmekia S. Corbett, PhD, is one of the leading scientists at the forefront of coronavirus vaccine development. Dr. Corbett discussed the COVID-19 vaccine in the context of medical mistrust and historical abuses and more, such as health equity. "The COVID-19 pandemic has not only disproportionately affected Black Americans with respect to infection and death rates, but it has also brought into sharp focus the inequities and disparities in the U.S. healthcare system," said Queens Public Library president and CEO Dennis M. Walcott.[19]

Additional keynote speakers were Patrick "Blake" Leeper, eight-time Paralympic Games medalist and world and American record holder; Dr. M. Jocelyn Elders, the fifteenth US surgeon general; beatboxing legend Doug E. Fresh, joined by hip-hop pioneer DJ Ralph McDaniels and Dr. Olajide Williams. They hosted "Friday Night Live: Building Health Equity through the Transformative Power of Music."

The overall theme of the event was broken into four categories:

*Health Education*, where we focus on common health issues with individuals in our Black/Brown communities

*Health Connections for Mind and Body*, participants learned how to connect with their medical community

*Activating Your Health through Transformative Practices*, participants learn how to practice self-care

*Networking*, attendees engaged and interacted with other participants and speakers in the virtual networking hall[20]

## CELEBRATING FIFTY YEARS!

In 2020, BCALA turned fifty years old, and we celebrated in a multitude of ways. We first created a new logo to commemorate the occasion. With the updated logo, we worked with ALA to have a multitude of items sold with the new logo in the ALA store. BCALA members received a 15 percent discount.

The November/December 2020 edition of *American Libraries* magazine featured the Black Caucus of the American Library Association celebrating fifty years and looking ahead to the next fifty of Black librarianship. Members highlighted in the article were Andrew P. Jackson (Sekou Molefi Baako), Stanton F. Biddle, Dolores Brown, James Allen Davis Jr., Jermaine Dennis, Rhonda Evans, Makiba Foster, Em Claire Knowles, Victor Simmons, Shaundra Walker, Renate L. Chancellor, Nichelle M. Hayes, and Shauntee Burns-Simpson.[21]

The featured title for BCALA's full page ad in *USA Today's* special Race in America edition was *Building insights. Breaking boundaries.* This article promoted the caucus to the larger world outside of the library profession. We were able to promote NCAAL (National Conference for African American Librarians), the Career Center, our resources, and scholarships. The print and digital ad was seen by millions and connected us with organizations committed to racial equity.[22]

*The Black Librarian in America: Reflections, Resistance, and Reawakening* was published on February 18, 2022, by Rowman & Littlefield. Its four-person editing team includes Shauntee Burns-Simpson, Nichelle M. Hayes, Dr. Ana Nduma, and Dr. Shaundra Walker. This was the first time in the life of the organization that BCALA had an all-female editorial team for one of its publications. All members of BCALA received a 30 percent discount for the book.[23]

## THE NATIONAL CONFERENCE OF AFRICAN AMERICAN LIBRARIANS

The 11th National Conference of African American Librarians, "Culture Keepers XI the Sankofa Experience: Inspired by Our Past, Igniting Our Future," was originally scheduled for August 2020, but due to the ongoing COVID-19 pandemic the conference was rescheduled for July 28–August 1, 2021, virtually. This was the first time the conference was held in a virtual space with the host city being Tulsa, Oklahoma, in commemoration of the Tulsa race massacre of 1921. This conference also celebrated BCALA's fiftieth anniversary, and thanks to the following sponsorships (see list below), everyone who attended was able to learn, laugh, and grow in community with one another:[24]

- Abrams
- The American Library Association
- Baker & Taylor
- Believe in Reading
- Center for Black Literature & Culture at the Indianapolis Public Library
- Clemson University
- Communico
- FE Technologies
- Findaway
- Gale
- Ingram
- Midwest Tape
- Netflix
- NoveList
- Omnigraphics
- Overdrive
- Phame Marketing
- Prince George's County Memorial Library System
- Roosevelt Public Library
- Simon & Schuster
- Tech Logic
- University of South Florida

*School Library Journal* (*SLJ*) collaborated with BCALA on NCAAL XI's Preconference, "Build a Racially Equitable Collection" on July 27, 2021. This all-day event engaged participants with how-to workshops where they gained practical ideas for "waking up" their book collections to reflect a diversity of voices, as well as learning how to engage with their community and build curriculum and programs that leverage BCALA's award-winning book list and 2021 finalists.

The learning outcome goals of this event were

- integrate curriculum that celebrates and honors the diversity of the Black experience and cultural traditions;
- create innovative, inclusive programs for your library relevant to the Black experience and to your unique community;
- bring to life the triumphs of well- and lesser known African American voices through books;
- support educators and families with resources and teaching aids; and
- provide outreach to parents, administrators, and the community.

*SLJ* is the premiere publication for librarians and information specialists who work with children and teens. A source of quality journalism and reviews for seventy years, *SLJ* produces award-winning features and news coverage on literacy, best practices, technology, education policy, and other issues of interest to the school library and greater educator community. *SLJ* evaluates a broad range of resources, from books and digital content to databases, in six thousand-plus reviews published annually.[25]

## LONG-STANDING COLLABORATIONS/SCHOLARSHIPS

### DEMCO

Beginning in 1994, an annual award of $500 and an engraved bronze statuette made possible by a grant from DEMCO, Inc. of Madison, Wisconsin, is presented to the librarian who has made significant contributions to promoting the status of African Americans in the library profession. DEMCO also donates an additional $500 each year to assist in funding the E. J. Josey Scholarship Fund.

DEMCO was founded in 1905 as the Library Department of the Democrat Printing Company to help make librarians' lives easier. Today, DEMCO's mission is to serve both libraries and the broader education community to foster lifelong learning. And, as the roles of schools and libraries continue to evolve and expand, they are committed to evolving their services and product selection to meet the needs of all patrons.

See the list of the notable librarians, to date, who have been honored by this award.[26]

|  |  |
|---|---|
| 1994 Recipient: | Dr. E. J. Josey, LHD |
| 1995 Recipient: | Dr. Mohammed M. Aman, PhD |
| 1996 Recipient: | Dr. John Tyson, DA |
| 1997 Recipient: | Mr. Samuel F. Morrison |
| 1998 Recipient: | Ms. Rebecca Bingham |
| 1999 Recipient: | Mr. Bobby Player |
| 2000 Recipient: | Ms. Satia Marshall Orange |
| 2001 Recipient: | Dr. Stanton Biddle, D.IS |
| 2002 Recipient: | Ms. JoAnn Mondowney |
| 2003 Recipient: | Ms. Sylvia Sprinkle-Hamlin |
| 2004 Recipient: | Ms. Kathleen Bethel |
| 2005 Recipient: | Ms. Gladys Smiley Bell |
| 2006 Recipient: | Ms. Carla Hayden, PhD |
| 2007 Recipient: | Ms. Sibyl E. Moses, PhD |
| 2008 Recipient: | Mr. John S. Page |
| 2009 Recipient: | Mr. Jerome Offord Jr. |
| 2010 Recipient: | Ms. Irene Owens, PhD |
| 2011 Recipient: | Ms. Pamela Goodes |
| 2012 Recipient: | Mr. Andrew Jackson |
| 2013 Recipient: | Ms. Roberta Webb |
| 2014 Recipient: | Ms. Emily Guss |
| 2015 Recipient: | Ms. Wanda K. Brown |
| 2016 Recipient: | Dr. Yvonne Chandler |
| 2017 Recipient: | Mr. Kelvin Watson |
| 2018 Recipient: | Ms. Fayrene Muhammad |
| 2019 Recipient: | Mr. Rudolph Clay |
| 2020 Recipient: | Dr. Shaundra Walker |
| 2021 Recipient: | No award given |
| 2022 Recipient: | Tamela Chambers |
| 2023 Recipient: | Shauntee Burns-Simpson |

In 2010, BCALA launched the "Reading Is Grand!" family literacy program focused on grandparents and grandchildren. It is part of the ALA Family Focus Initiative started by ALA president Camila Alire. Karen Lemmons, Tamela Chambers, and Dr. Claudette McLin of the BCALA Services to Children of African Descent Committee served as the program's administrators.[27]

In 2015, Biblioboard and BCALA formed a partnership to introduce the Self-e Literary Award, which recognizes self-published authors of poetry and fiction.[28]

### Baker & Taylor

Since 2019, during the presidency of Richard E. Ashby (twenty-sixth president from 2018–2020), Baker & Taylor has sponsored the BCALA Support Staff Award. Ashby was integral in reaching out to Baker & Taylor requesting and securing their sponsorship for the award. Professor John Page served as the Award Committee chair during this time. This award recognizes dedicated and outstanding performance by a library support staff member. During the inaugural year, an award of $1,000 and a commemorative plaque was awarded during the BCALA membership meeting at the 2019 ALA Annual Conference in Washington, DC.

The following individuals were awarded the Baker & Taylor/BCALA Support Staff Award during its inaugural year:

2019—Gail Littleton (Virginia Commonwealth University)
2019—Renee Robertson Tecco (Public Library of Cincinnati/Hamilton County)

Gail Littleton is the coordinator of acquisitions accounting at Virginia Commonwealth University (VCU) in Richmond, Virginia, and is a forty-year professional of VCU libraries. Her nomination was submitted by Amanda Echterling, head of licensing and acquisitions at the university. Her nomination described her as follows:

> She is an excellent manager of her staff, supervising, training and advocating for them. She is the departmental expert in the fiscal procedures of the university. She is the go-to resource for errors in eVA requisitions. She also worked with vendors and university procurement to get the VCU voluntarily into compliance. Ms. Littleton continues to prove she is an essential, detailed, strategic and forward-thinking leader of VCU Libraries.

Renée Robertson Tecco serves as senior library services assistant in the Youth Services Department at the main branch of the public library of Cincinnati and Hamilton County. She has worked at the library system for twenty-five years and was a founding staff member of TeenSpot in 2008. Her nominator described her as "dedicated to the lives and emotional wellbeing [sic] of teen and tween library patrons in Cincinnati." In the early days of TeenSpot, she led efforts to contact high school teachers to create summer reading lists. More recent accomplishments include her leadership in helping teens and tweens create a podcast called *Brain Pizza* and her advocacy for the library systems creation of a Mock

Coretta Scott King Awards event to accompany their Mock Caldecott, Newbery, and Printz events. Ms. Tecco consistently creates engaging independent programming and is currently working to revive a Cincinnati-area chapter of BCALA.

The mission of Baker & Taylor is to support libraries in their efforts to serve their communities. Founded in 1828, Baker & Taylor has proudly served as a trusted partner for public and academic libraries for nearly two centuries, helping libraries improve community outcomes through literacy and learning.[29]

In 2023, Black Caucus was one of several major sponsors for the Indiana Library Federation's 2023 Annual Conference. Also, the Indiana Library Federation, the Indiana Black Librarians Network, and BCALA have joined together to fund the Lauren Freeman Excellence in Librarianship Award.[30]

**RESOURCES**

The Community, Connecting, Cultivating, & Constructing Conversations through Literacy is a social justice reading list in collaboration with the Association for Library Service to Children. This pre-K–eighth grade list was created to help dismantle racial capitalism and white supremacy in all of its forms. Some titles may include mature content. Parents, caregivers, and educators are encouraged to discuss these topics/experiences with their children: see https://www.bcala.org/booklists/community-connecting-cultivating-constructing-conversations-through-literacy.[31]

Black Lives Matter, Black Literature Matters is a reading list in collaboration with the Graphic Novels & Comics Round Table. This list is for all ages that's centered on Black creators, Black stories, and Black histories. The goal of the list is not to be a prescriptive spectrum of all the subject or format content out there in the landscape of Black stories or comics. Rather this is another step toward building collections and conversations that spark hope, demand justice, address erasure, and agitate for learning using both sides of the brain through pictures and words: see https://www.bcala.org/wp-content/uploads/2020/10/BCALA-x-GNCRT_-Black-Lives-Matter-final.pdf.[32]

**BANNED BOOKS**

The last several years have seen a dramatic increase in the number of book challenges across the United States. According to ALA, the push to censor books and materials is occurring in public, school, and academic libraries. Between January 1 and August 31, 2023, ALA's Office for Intellectual Freedom reported 695 attempts to censor library materials and services and documented challenges to 1,915 unique titles.

The number of unique titles challenged has increased by 20 percent from the same reporting period in 2022, the year in which the highest number of book challenges occurred since ALA began compiling this data more than twenty years ago. Most of the challenges were to books written by or about a person of color or a member of the LGBTQIA+ community.[33]

BCALA, along with affiliate Indiana Black Librarians Network, partnered with Delta Sigma Theta Sorority Inc. Indianapolis Alumnae Chapter to bring awareness to the importance of literacy and the rise of book bans. On September 30, 2023, BCALA and Delta Sigma Theta Sorority Inc. Indianapolis Alumnae Chapter had an amazingly impactful MIDS event called "Seeing Black In REaD" focusing on African American literacy and banned book awareness. The event brought together local authors, reading specialists, educators, Black Librarian organizations, and book clubs as well as a Banned book reading from *The Color Purple* by Alice Walker and *The 1619 Project* by Nikole Hannah Jones.

A book giveaway of over $500 worth of books by African American authors was held for adults and young readers. Information was provided by reading specialists that proved useful for students, parents, and teachers. The importance of literature was center stage alongside the banned books displayed with poetry and author readings.

The event as a whole was a truly amazing and informative experience. There were powerful personal testimonies of the featured soror authors (members of Delta Sigma Theta Sorority Inc.), India Johnson, and Carmen Glen. They shared what inspires them to write and create as well as bits of their stories. Audience members remarked that it was empowering to see these women follow their dreams and passions to write and create soul-stirring pieces of literature. Many people were thankful to have access to a varied assortment of books.

Ms. Tasha Jones, spoken word poet and teacher, gave an impassioned speech about African Americans' need to become more involved as a community regarding what is going on within our schools and to take action in regard to our Black voices being silenced and our history erased or whitewashed. Ms. Jones then gave a wonderful presentation of her amazing poem "Pyramids to Plantations, to Projects, to Penitentiaries," which visibly stirred many emotions within the audience members. It was truly a remarkable piece of work and to watch Ms. Jones in action was truly a treat.

There was an awesome performance by actress and singer Vickie Daniel, as she brought Madam C. J. Walker and her story to life in living color. She reenacted her backstory as well as her rise to wealth and prominence in the still very racist and sexist society that America is still growing from. Through Madam C. J. Walker, Daniel was able to make us reflect and go back in time with her through song, humor, and a history lesson on how hard it was as a Black woman in this country. It was a triumphant story and a blessing to learn and experience it. The overall message throughout the event was that Black stories cannot be silenced, and we have the power as a community to make great changes for the better since the fight for improving the literacy rates still remains.[34]

**NOTES**

1. "About BCALA," BCALA, https://www.bcala.org/about-bcala.
2. E. J. Josey, "Black Caucus of the American Library Association," in *Handbook of Black Librarianship*, edited by E. J. Josey and Anne Allen Shockley (Littleton, CO: Libraries Unlimited, 1977), 67–69.
3. "About BCALA."
4. Stanton F. Biddle, *BCALA Executive Files*.
5. Renate Chancellor, *E. J.: Transformational Leader of the Modern Library Profession* (Lanham, MD: Rowman & Littlefield, 2020).
6. Josey, "Black Caucus of the American Library Association," 67–68.
7. Ibid., 67.
8. Biddle, *BCALA Executive Files*.
9. Ibid.
10. "Breaking Barriers," BCALA, https://breakingbarriers.bcala.org/.
11. "Black History Month," BCALA, https://blackhistorymonth.bcala.org/.
12. "@Black Librarians," Instagram, https://www.blacklibrarians.com/.
13. "Bringing Books to Kids in Need: The Invaluable Role of Our Warehouses," Penguin Random House, https://global.penguinrandomhouse.com/announcements/bringing-books-to-kids-in-need-the-invaluable-role-of-our-warehouses/.
14. "ALSC, BCALA leadership to join national Netflix conversation on race, identity, and social justice in children's literature," American Library Association, September 17, 2020, https://www.ala.org/news/press-releases/2020/09/alsc-bcala-leadership-join-national-netflix-conversation-race-identity-and.
15. "The New York Public Library and BCALA Partner on Meditative Programming for Library Staff on Race Relations," BCALA News & Press Releases, July 28, 2020, https://www.bcala.org/the-new-york-public-library-and-bcala-partner-on-meditative-programming-for-library-staff-on-race-relations.
16. Shauntee Burns-Simpson, "The First Six Months," *BCALA Newsletter*, 46, 2 (2020): 2, https://www.bcala.org/wp-content/uploads/2020/12/BCALA-Newsletter-December-2020.pdf.
17. BCALA, "Press Release: The Black Health and Healing Summit," BCALA News & Press Releases, January 15, 2021, https://www.bcala.org/the-black-health-and-healing-virtual-summit.
18. Ibid.
19. Ibid
20. "The Black Health and Healing Summit," BCALA News & Press Releases, January 15, 2021, https://www.bcala.org/the-black-health-and-healing-virtual-summit; "Black Health and Healing 24 Hour Virtual Summit," Urban Libraries Council, 2021, https://www.urbanlibraries.org/innovations/black-health-and-healing-24-hour-virtual-summit; BCALA, "Press Release: The Black Health and Healing Summit."
21. Alison Marcotte, "Black Caucus of ALA Celebrates 50 Years," *American Libraries*, November 22, 2020, https://americanlibrariesmagazine.org/2020/11/02/black-caucus-of-the-ala-celebrates-50-years/.
22. Shauntee Burns-Simpson, "President's Note: Congratulations Black Caucus!" *BCALA Newsletter*, 47, 1 (2021): 12, https://www.bcala.org/wp-content/uploads/2021/11/BCALA-2021-Newsletter-Web-spreads.pdf.
23. "The Black Librarian in America Book," BCALA, https://www.bcala.org/orderbook; April M. Hathcock, "Book Reviews: The Black Librarian in America: Reflections, Resistance, and Reawakening," *College and Research Libraries*, 83, no. 6 (2022):1039, https://crl.acrl.org/index.php/crl/article/view/25688/33607; "The Black Librarian in America: Reflections, Resistance, and Reawakening," Rowman & Littlefield, 2022, https://rowman.com/ISBN/9781538152676/The-Black-Librarian-in-America-Reflections-Resistance-and-Reawakening.
24. "Past NCAAL Conferences," BCALA, https://www.bcala.org/past-ncaal-conferences; Michele Fenton, "ALA Black Caucus of ALA Holds 11th National Conference of African American Librarians," *International Leads*, 46, no. 3 (2021): 11, https://www.ala.org/rt/sites/ala.org.rt/files/content/intlleads/leadsarchive/202109.pdf.
25. Kathy Ishizuka, "SLJ and BCALA Offer One-Day Workshop on Diverse Collections," *School Library Journal*, June 29, 2021, https://www.slj.com/story/slj-and-bcala-offer-one-day-workshop-on-diverse-collections.
26. "DEMCO/Black Caucus of the American Library Association Award for Excellence in Librarianship," BCALA, https://www.bcala.org/bcala-awards/demco-award.
27. "BCALA Launches Reading Is Grand! Celebrating Grand-Families @yourlibrary," American Library Association, May 24, 2010, https://www.ala.org/news/press-releases/2010/05/bcala-launches-reading-grand-celebrating-grand-families-your-library.
28. Henrietta Verma, "BCALA, Biblioboard Launch Self-Publishing Award," *Library Journal*, August 12, 2015, https://www.libraryjournal.com/story/bcala-biblioboard-launch-self-publishing-award.
29. "Baker and Taylor Support Staff Award," BCALA, https://www.bcala.org/bcala-awards/baker-taylor-support-staff-award; "Baker & Taylor Announces Sponsorship of BCALA Support Staff Award," Baker & Taylor, February 21, 2019, https://www.baker-taylor.com/article.cfm?topic=baker++taylor+announces+sponsorship+of+bcala+support+award&nid=26.
30. "Meet the 2023 ILF Annual Conference Sponsors." *Focus Newsletter*, October 27, 2023, https://inlf.memberclicks.net/focus-newsletter.
31. Community, Connecting, Cultivating, & Constructing Conversations through Literacy, BCALA, https://www.bcala.org/booklists/community-connecting-cultivating-constructing-conversations-through-literacy.
32. BCALA and the ALA Graphic Novels and Comics Round Table (GNCRT), "BCALA x GNCRT: Black Lives Matter: Black Literature Matters Reading List," BCALA, https://www.bcala.org/wp-content/uploads/2020/10/BCALA-x-GNCRT_-Black-Lives-Matter-final.pdf.
33. "Book Ban Data," American Library Association, March 20, 2023, https://www.ala.org/advocacy/bbooks/book-ban-data.

34. "Midwest Impact Day of Service: Seeing Black in REaD," Indianapolis Alumnae Chapter of Delta Sigma Theta, Inc., 2023, https://www.indydeltas.org/midwest-impact-day-of-service.html.

**WORKS CITED**

"About BCALA." BCALA. https://www.bcala.org/about-bcala.

"ALSC, BCALA leadership to join national Netflix conversation on race, identity, and social justice in children's literature." American Library Association, September 17, 2020. https://www.ala.org/news/press-releases/2020/09/alsc-bcala-leadership-join-national-netflix-conversation-race-identity-and.

"@Black Librarians." Instagram. https://www.blacklibrarians.com/.

"Baker & Taylor Announces Sponsorship of BCALA Support Staff Award." *Baker & Taylor*, February 21, 2019. https://www.baker-taylor.com/article.cfm?topic=baker++taylor+announces+sponsorship+of+bcala+support+award&nid=26.

"Baker and Taylor Support Staff Award." BCALA, https://www.bcala.org/bcala-awards/baker-taylor-support-staff-award.

BCALA and the ALA Graphic Novels and Comics Round Table (GNCRT). "BCALA x GNCRT: Black Lives Matter: Black Literature Matters Reading List." BCALA, https://www.bcala.org/wp-content/uploads/2020/10/BCALA-x-GNCRT_-Black-Lives-Matter-final.pdf.

"BCALA Launches Reading Is Grand! Celebrating Grand-Families @yourlibrary." American Library Association, May 24, 2010. https://www.ala.org/news/press-releases/2010/05/bcala-launches-reading-grand-celebrating-grand-families-your-library.

Biddle, Stanton F. *BCALA Executive Files*.

"Black History Month." BCALA. https://blackhistorymonth.bcala.org/.

"Book Ban Data." American Library Association, March 20, 2023. https://www.ala.org/advocacy/bbooks/book-ban-data.

"Breaking Barriers." BCALA. https://breakingbarriers.bcala.org/.

"Bringing Books to Kids in Need: The Invaluable Role of Our Warehouses." Penguin Random House. https://global.penguinrandomhouse.com/announcements/bringing-books-to-kids-in-need-the-invaluable-role-of-our-warehouses/.

Burns-Simpson, Shauntee. "President's Note: Congratulations Black Caucus!" *BCALA Newsletter*, 47, 1 (2021): 12. https://www.bcala.org/wp-content/uploads/2021/11/BCALA-2021-Newsletter-Web-spreads.pdf.

———. "The First Six Months." *BCALA Newsletter*, 46, 2 (2020):2. https://www.bcala.org/wp-content/uploads/2020/12/BCALA-Newsletter-December-2020.pdf.

Community, Connecting, Cultivating, & Constructing Conversations through Literacy. BCALA, https://www.bcala.org/booklists/community-connecting-cultivating-constructing-conversations-through-literacy.

"DEMCO/Black Caucus of the American Library Association Award for Excellence in Librarianship." BCALA, https://www.bcala.org/bcala-awards/demco-award.

Fenton, Michele. "ALA Black Caucus of ALA Holds 11th National Conference of African American Librarians." *International Leads*, 46, no. 3 (2021): 11. https://www.ala.org/rt/sites/ala.org.rt/files/content/intlleads/leadsarchive/202109.pdf.

Hathcock, April M. "Book Reviews: The Black Librarian in America: Reflections, Resistance, and Reawakening." *College and Research Libraries*, 83, no. 6 (2022):1039. https://crl.acrl.org/index.php/crl/article/view/25688/33607.

Ishizuka, Kathy. "SLJ and BCALA Offer One-Day Workshop on Diverse Collections." *School Library Journal*, June 29, 2021. https://www.slj.com/story/slj-and-bcala-offer-one-day-workshop-on-diverse-collections.

Josey, E. J. "Black Caucus of the American Library Association." In *Handbook of Black Librarianship*, edited by E. J. Josey and Anne Allen Shockley, 67-69. Littleton CO: Libraries Unlimited, 1977.

Marcotte, Alison. "Black Caucus of ALA Celebrates 50 Years." *American Libraries*, November 22, 2020. https://americanlibrariesmagazine.org/2020/11/02/black-caucus-of-the-ala-celebrates-50-years/.

"Meet the 2023 ILF Annual Conference Sponsors." *Focus Newsletter*, October 27, 2023. https://inlf.memberclicks.net/focus-newsletter.

"Midwest Impact Day of Service: Seeing Black in REaD." Indianapolis Alumnae Chapter of Delta Sigma Theta, Inc., 2023. https://www.indydeltas.org/midwest-impact-day-of-service.html.

"Past NCAAL Conferences." BCALA, https://www.bcala.org/past-ncaal-conferences.

"The Black Health and Healing Summit." BCALA News & Press Releases, January 15, 2021. https://www.bcala.org/the-black-health-and-healing-virtual-summit.

"The Black Health and Healing 24 Hour Virtual Summit." Urban Libraries Council, 2021. https://www.urbanlibraries.org/innovations/black-health-and-healing-24-hour-virtual-summit.

"The Black Librarian in America Book," BCALA, https://www.bcala.org/orderbook."The Black Librarian in America: Reflections, Resistance, and Reawakening." Rowman & Littlefield, 2022, https://rowman.com/ISBN/9781538152676/The-Black-Librarian-in-America-Reflections-Resistance-and-Reawakening.

"The New York Public Library and BCALA Partner on Meditative Programming for Library Staff on Race Relations." BCALA News & Press Releases, July 28, 2020. https://www.bcala.org/the-new-york-public-library-and-bcala-partner-on-meditative-programming-for-library-staff-on-race-relations.

Verma, Henrietta. "BCALA, Biblioboard Launch Self-Publishing Award." *Library Journal*, August 12, 2015. https://www.libraryjournal.com/story/bcala-biblioboard-launch-self-publishing-award.

# 3.4

## BCALA Affiliates

Rudolph Clay

California Librarians Black Caucus
Chicago Chapter of BCALA
Colorado Black Librarians Association
Connecticut Affiliate—BCALA
Georgia Library Association—Black Caucus
Indiana Black Librarians Network
Maryland Library Association Black Caucus

Missouri Chapter—BCALA
New York Black Librarians Caucus
Pennsylvania Black Librarians' Caucus
South Carolina Black Librarians Caucus
St. Louis Regional Black Librarians
Tennessee Network of Black Library Employees
Virginia Library Association Librarians of Color

# 3.5

## Black Caucus of the American Library Association Literary Awards

CELEBRATING TWENTY-NINE YEARS OF "BLACK RESISTANCE"

Gladys Smiley Bell

For almost thirty years, the Black Caucus of the American Library Association, Inc. (BCALA) Literary Awards has been encouraging "new" and "old" voices by promoting an award opportunity for African American writers that never existed before. BCALA engages emerging and established authors, poets, and audiences through readings, publications, book signings, and other worthwhile opportunities. The BCALA Literary Awards were founded by Dr. Alex Boyd and Mr. Cecil Hixon to acknowledge outstanding achievement in the presentation of the cultural, historical, and sociopolitical aspects of the Black diaspora. Dr. Brenda Mitchell-Powell and Cecil Hixon established the awards criteria, guidelines, and procedures. The first awards were presented at the Second National Conference of African American Librarians in Milwaukee, Wisconsin, in August 1994.

In 2016, BCALA and the BiblioBoard platform of BiblioLabs, LLC, a Charleston, South Carolina, library technology firm, launched the 2016 Self-Publishing eBook Award. Following the model of the current BCALA Literary Awards, the new award honors the best self-published e-books in fiction and poetry by an African American author in the United States. The first awards were dedicated to Cynthia Hurd, a librarian whose life was tragically cut short in the Mother Emanuel AME Church attack in Charleston, South Carolina, in 2015. Hurd was a beloved public servant and dedicated librarian at Charleston County Public Library for over thirty-one years. Dudley Gregorie, Charleston City councilman, and a trustee of Mother Emanuel AME, believes this to be an outstanding tribute to Hurd. "Cynthia [Hurd] was a cherished member of our church and our community. Her exceptional work in service of the library and local community and her tremendous spirit are more than deserving of an award in her honor, especially an award of such significance."[1]

The BCALA 2016 Self-Publishing eBook Award marked the first award from an American Library Association affiliate to acknowledge literary excellence in self-published digital content. In addition, the BCALA Self-Publishing Literary Award was presented by BCALA for digital content, as well as recognizing self-published work. The award represents an exciting new opportunity to recognize African American authors and books in a digital format.

## BLACK LITERATURE AS BLACK RESISTANCE

The 2023 Black History Month theme was "Black Resistance." It explored how "African Americans have resisted historic and ongoing oppression, in all forms, especially the racial terrorism of lynching, racial pogroms and police killings."[2] African American authors and readers celebrate Black resistance every day by writing and/or reading literature that encourages the expression of freedom, justice, and equality.

About four hundred years ago it was illegal to teach kidnapped enslaved Black people to read or write. But our ancestors resisted. Despite the illegal nature of reading and writing at that time, our ancestors resisted. They resisted and risked their lives because they understood literacy was a weapon to fight enslavement and other atrocities as well as defied the norm that they may have faced over the decades. And we continue to resist today.

In 1994, BCALA announced the first winners for the BCALA Literary Awards at the ALA Annual Midwinter meeting in Los Angeles, California. The awards recognized excellence in adult literature by African American authors published in 1993. From that time, three winners stand out as works of definitive resistance.

### *Free Enterprise* by Michelle Cliff

In 1858, two Black women meet at a restaurant and begin to plot a revolution. Mary Ellen Pleasant owns a string of hotels in San Francisco that secretly double as havens for runaway slaves. Her comrade, Annie, is a young Jamaican who has given up her life of privilege to fight for the abolitionist cause. Together, they join John Brown's doomed enterprise and narrowly escape with their lives. With mesmerizing skill, Cliff weaves a multitude of voices into a gripping, poignant story of the struggle for liberation that began not long after the first slaves landed on America's shores.

Early resistance writings were against slavery. Both a moral manifesto and a prescription for emancipation, freedom enterprise helped kidnapped enslaved Blacks translate the philosophy of free enterprise into action and resistance.

### *A Lesson Before Dying* by Ernest J. Gaines

Set in a small Cajun community in the late 1940s, *A Lesson Before Dying* is an enormously moving novel of one man condemned to die for a crime he did not commit and a young man who visits him in his cell. In the end, the two men forge a bond as they both come to understand the simple heroism of resisting—and defying—the expected.

*A Lesson Before Dying* offers instructions that resist the notion that life is not worth living. It teaches readers to be brave and to value their lives even at the time of death.

### *W. E. B. Du Bois: Biography of a Race, 1868-1919* by David Levering Lewis

William Edward Burghardt Du Bois, the premier architect of the civil rights movement in the United States, was a towering and controversial personality, a fiercely proud individual blessed with the language of the poet and the impatience of the agitator. This monumental biography (eight years of research and writing) treats the early and middle phases of a long and intense career: a crucial fifty-year period that demonstrates how Du Bois changed forever the way Americans think about themselves.

W. E. B. Du Bois had an extraordinarily long and distinguished career that shaped critical thinking about race. He resisted the Negro as a repulsive savage with a vision of an educated, elite "Talented Tenth."

In 2023, BCALA awarded twelve books of resistance. Books about telling the truth; books about what one sacrifices to win freedom "by any means necessary"; books about movements, protests, and change; biographies about African Americans who resisted; and poetry that expresses the anger, resistance, and hope of the African American experience. These awards were announced by BCALA Literary Awards at the ALA LibLearnX: The Library Learning Experience (LLX) in New Orleans, Louisiana. The awards recognized excellence in adult literature (fiction, nonfiction, and poetry) by African American authors published in 2022.

Four of these modern-day works of resistance stand out.

### *Take My Hand: A Novel* by Dolen Perkins-Valdez

*Take My Hand* illustrates the truth of young Black women and girls victimized by medical misinformation and experimentation. Sisters Erica and India are prescribed birth control, leading to a series of escalating and irreversible interventions into their young lives. Delivered from the present-day perspective of their childhood nurse, Civil Townsend quests to finish what she started in an Alabama family planning clinic in 1973. Perkins-Valdez's intricately crafted tale of tragedy and redemption weaves back and forth in time and is inspired by true events.

There is a history of exclusionary or exploitive treatment of African Americans within medical institutions. It is important to educate ourselves on the inequities and disparities in maternal mortality and morbidity and resistance.

### *Yonder: A Novel* by Jabari Asim

*Yonder* is a gut-wrenching, fast-paced novel about slavery, love, and what an enslaved person is willing to sacrifice for freedom. The story follows several characters from the same plantation through their journey on the Underground Railroad to "yonder." This novel is filled with African spirituality and its power to sustain those who suffered the most. The magical realism seeped throughout helps to create such power in the depth of the story. *Yonder* is a work that breaks your heart and builds it back up again. Of course, the enslaved African Americans resisted the constraints under deplorable conditions and were willing to sacrifice their all for love, friendships, and freedom.

### *The Tuskegee Student Uprising: A History* by Brian Jones

*The Tuskegee Student Uprising* brings together research and interviews with former students, professors, and administrators. Brian Jones provides an in-depth account of one of the most dynamic student movements in United States history. The writing takes the reader through Tuskegee students' process of transformation and intellectual awakening as they stepped off campus to make unique contributions to southern movements for democracy and civil rights in the 1960s. Accounts of violence and injustice galvanized students and others for radical change in their communities. *The Tuskegee Student Uprising* is a little-known historical fact.

### *His Name Is George Floyd: One Man's Life and the Struggle for Racial Justice* by Robert Samuels and Toluse Olorunnipa

*His Name Is George Floyd* is a multigenerational story that explores the effects of systemic racism on George Floyd's family, dating back three generations. This is a thoughtful examination of Floyd's strengths and weaknesses to invite the reader to begin to understand the composite factors that led Floyd to his heartrending end. Samuels and Olorunnipa humanize Floyd through this holistic illustration of his life.

Startling in its intensity and the unrelenting attack on George Floyd, police brutality alarmed and inspired African Americans to resist and speak out across the United States. The resistance hastened the Black Lives Matter movement, and others across the nation, and in the world. Say his name.

### *Claim Ticket for Stolen People* by Quintin Collins

In the variety of poems, in various poetic formats, Collins "hands out" claim tickets for anger, resistance, and hope while he presents scenarios for stolen people (Africans who became enslaved), and to claim what is rightfully theirs. The poems take us through the Black existence, starting with a sonogram and through all the trials and tribulations encountered in one's life journey. This collection of poems leads one on a voyage from being stolen to claiming and reclaiming our *ukweli* (Swahili for truth). It emphasizes the resistance in combatting injustices and expressing indignity about the plight of African American people.

> "Once you learn how to read, you will be forever free."
>
> —Frederick Douglass

I conclude by stating that BCALA is committed to challenging those who want to ban books, prohibit, or erase and downplay the diverse African American experience and history. BCALA reinforces the publishing and writing of the stories, telling the truth, whether it be pictorial or poetic by recognizing and honoring our Black brothers and sisters who write. We have an unwavering commitment to supporting "intellectual freedom" and the "right to read."

### NOTES

1. Tom Gilson, "ATF Newsflash: Cynthia Hurd Honored with Literary Award," Charleston Hub, February 25, 2016, https://www.charleston-hub.com/2016/02/atg-newsflash-cynthia-hurd-honored-with-literary-award/
2. Zebulon Miletsky, "We Are Running to the Fight! ASALH Brings Its Conference to Jacksonville, Florida with Annual Theme: 'Black Resistance,'" ASALH: Association for the Study of African American Life and History, August 1, 2023, https://asalh.org/document/we-are-running-to-the-fight/

### BIBLIOGRAPHY

Gilson, Tom. "ATF Newsflash: Cynthia Hurd Honored with Literary Award," Charleston Hub, February 25, 2016. https://www.charleston-hub.com/2016/02/atg-newsflash-cynthia-hurd-honored-with-literary-award/

Miletsky, Zebulon. "We Are Running to the Fight! ASALH Brings Its Conference to Jacksonville, Florida with Annual Theme: 'Black Resistance,'" ASALH: Association for the Study of African American Life and History, August 1, 2023. https://asalh.org/document/we-are-running-to-the-fight/

# 3.6

## Librarians and Libraries, Part of Our Foundation

Wade Hudson and Cheryl Willis Hudson

**THE BEGINNING**

**Cheryl Willis Hudson**

When I was growing up in Mansfield, Louisiana, there was no public library that I could frequent. Jim Crow laws that mandated "separate but equal facilities" made sure of that. Of course, there was very little that Black people were relegated to that was equal. The best always went to White people. Sometimes, as in the case of a library, there wasn't anything to even be unequal.

It was in the library at All-Black Desoto High School in Mansfield, Louisiana, where I found another home amid the books there. I could learn, dream, and escape to faraway places in my imagination. I wondered what it was like for youngsters my age growing up in Japan, Sweden, England, Germany, and in countries in Africa. I found the answers in the geography section. I shared the adventures of Hawkeye in James Fenimore Cooper's *Last of the Mohicans* and sailed with Captain Ahab in his pursuit of the great white whale in Herman Melville's *Moby Dick*.

As in most aspects of life where White people had control, the books in our library were carefully approved by the all-White school board. So, they almost always maintained and promoted a worldview with Western culture the epicenter. Most of the books, like those in our school library, were traditional classics, and those about history, science, space exploration, math, and literature, all written by White authors. Our school librarian, Mrs. Jacobs, augmented this offering with biographies about a few important Black people such as Booker T. Washington, again, written by White authors. I would not be exposed to Black history, culture, and literature until I left my small hometown to attend Southern University, an HBCU (historically black colleges and universities).

But Mrs. Jacobs, the school librarian at Desoto, loved books. She loved her students even more. And she recognized the importance of learning. She always had a ready recommendation for my thirst to learn so quickly.

"Slow down and enjoy," she would sometimes say. The books in that library, although there were few about my own history, and culture, opened my eyes to a different world and different possibilities. And I embraced them despite the limitations with which Jim Crow sought to define me. Libraries and librarians have always been special to me.

**Wade Hudson**

When I was growing up, the public library in Portsmouth, Virginia, where I lived, was still segregated and off-limits to "Negroes." The Portsmouth Colored Community Library, on the other hand, was a warm and welcoming, two-room building staffed by Mrs. Bertha Edwards, who was a family friend and a wonderful librarian. That was the place Black people had access to and where they could borrow books. It had been established in 1945, after more than twenty years of petitioning the city for a library for its Black citizens. The land on which it was built was paid for by donations from individual Black citizens, Black churches, and Black businesses. Black people comprised one-third of the total population of the City of Portsmouth, but the Colored Community Library's operating budget was $4,000 per year compared to the $22,000 that was budgeted for the "White" library. It was clearly separate but *not* equal.

The Colored Library was a real community endeavor. Many of the books were bought and donated by members of the Black community. Taxes from all Portsmouth's citizens, however, paid for books, staff, and facilities at the "White" library. If you wanted a contemporary or reference title not available in the Colored Community Library, a messenger was sent on their bicycle with a note and a basket to make the request and pick up the desired book to be checked out. Talk about being put on a long waiting list!

On December 17, 1959, Dr. Hugo Owens and Dr. James Holley, two leading Black citizens in Portsmouth, filed a lawsuit against the city demanding that it open the doors of the city library to all citizens. They won the lawsuit, and in 1963 the Portsmouth Public Library was officially integrated. The Colored Community Library was merged with it, and the old Court Street Post Office building was renovated and became the new Portsmouth Public Library. Mrs. Edwards was assigned to the reference desk. It was then that I applied for a library card and began to frequent the once segregated Portsmouth Library as often as I could, usually with my buddy,

Linda Bailey. Together we roamed the stacks for books on science, mathematics, and literature. Linda and I were nerds, and we loved exploring the shelves for new ideas for projects for our school science, math, and culture clubs. Mrs. Edwards consistently recommended new titles and embraced us as regular library patrons. She was an outstanding reference librarian. And if we couldn't find enough material in Portsmouth, we'd hop the tunnel bus for a fare of ten cents to visit the Norfolk Public Library, across the river, also now open to patrons who were Black and White.

My love of libraries comes from the fond memories and spirit of the loving, inspiring, knowledgeable, and always helpful librarian Mrs. Bertha Edwards and the welcoming atmosphere of the Portsmouth Colored Community Library.

**Cheryl Willis Hudson**

*Our Book Publishing Journey*

When we started our publishing efforts nearly thirty-five years ago, we didn't know much about trade book publishing. We had a general understanding of how a book publishing company should operate but had no real experience managing one. What we did know, in a most profound way, was that there needed to be books available for young readers that drew from Black history, culture, and experiences. And that was more than enough to inspire us to take a leap of faith and publish these books ourselves. As so many of our ancestors had done, we saw a need and dared to address it.

Social media had not become as prominent as it is now. The plethora of information currently available was quite miniscule at that time. So, we had to learn by doing.

What we did know, however, was how important libraries could be in our effort to get our books to our intended customers. Like churches, especially in Black communities, libraries have often been the life blood of the neighborhoods where they are located. Not only are they the places where great books can be found, for many members of their communities they are sources of information, meeting venues, and often comfortable places of refuge.

Author signings and engagements at libraries were not common during this time, and those by Black book creators were indeed rare, almost as rare as those in retail bookstores. Early on we saw libraries as relevant to our marketing efforts and full of potential because of our past experiences.

Our publishing efforts began in 1987 with two titles, the *AFRO-BETS ABC Book* and *AFRO-BETS 123 Book*. They featured six Black youngsters called the AFRO-BETS Kids who twisted and bent their bodies to make the letters of the alphabet and the numbers one through ten. Also that year, we released the AFRO-BETS rap song that taught the letters of the alphabet through music. We further branded this concept by creating and offering the AFRO-BETS Kids T-shirts. That year, with our two books and other products in tow, we journeyed to Portsmouth, Virginia, and the Portsmouth Public Library. Our earlier effort to sell our books had focused on several direct mail campaigns. Both had been successful, and we had sold almost five thousand copies of the *AFRO-BETS ABC Book* through these and other grassroots channels. The book event in Portsmouth, sponsored by the local chapter of the Alpha Kappa Alpha sorority, drew well over a hundred youngsters, their parents, and educators and became an annual event. The reception our books received inspired us to connect with national distributors, wholesalers, and bookstores, especially those that were Black-owned. In September, we held a book party at the East Orange Public Library in New Jersey.

The year 1998 was seminal for us. We published our third title, *AFRO-BETS Book of Black Heroes from A to Z*, a title that spotlights forty-nine historical and contemporary Black achievers and innovators. It was among the first titles for young people to present biographies of a wide variety of Black people who had made important contributions to our world. Later that year we established Just Us Books, Inc. as an independent publishing corporation.

With three titles on our list we decided to attend our first major conference, the American Library Association convention. In June, we headed to New Orleans, Louisiana, with our daughter Katura, aged twelve, and son Stephan, almost six. We didn't know what to expect. We were filled with apprehension and expectation.

Our first presence at ALA was at a six-foot-long table set up in the New Orleans Convention Center's small press section. It was draped with a handmade quilt that spelled out AFRO-BETS.

We welcomed hundreds of librarians and educators to our table with a trifold brochure, some photocopied fliers describing our new titles, and three stacks of books featuring the AFRO-BETS Kids: Langston, 'Tura, 'Stef, Glo, Nandi, and Robo.

We sold all our inventory and had an opportunity to talk to librarians from all over the United States about our vision and our books for young people. That year, we established an annual book event at the East Orange Public Library. With the support and encouragement of the children's librarian Lois Miles and her associates, the event drew a large audience from the surrounding communities each year.

When the Daniel A. P. Murray Association requested that we offer a book event at the Library of Congress, we could scarcely believe it. Members of the association felt that we were carrying on the legacy of Murray, who, in 1871, became the second African American to work at the Library of Congress. Ten years later, he was named assistant librarian, a position he held for forty-one years. He also compiled a valuable collection of books and pamphlets authored by *African Americans* prior to 1900.

For the Daniel A. P. Murray Association to see us connected with such an awesome legacy was humbling. A second event at the Library of Congress the following year included Veronica Freeman Ellis, author of *First Book about Africa*, the fourth title published by Just Us Books. It was illustrated by the veteran artist George Ford.

In 1990, an invitation to participate in a conference sponsored by the Cooperative Children's Book Center (CCBC) at the University of Wisconsin and a subsequent publication that followed, *The Multicolored Mirror*, were important markers for Just Us Books. Invited by librarians Ginny Moore Kruse and Kathleen Horning, the conference featured writers, artists, scholars, and editors such as Walter Dean Myers, Tom Feelings, and Rudine Sims Bishop. The CCBC has consistently recognized Just Us Books for helping to increase the quantity and quality of Black interest titles in the canon of American children's literature.

During our earlier years of operation, we made presentations at libraries in cities such as Arlington, Virginia; Boston, Massachusetts; Stamford, Connecticut; Brooklyn, New York; Queens, New York; Columbus, Ohio; Newark, New Jersey; Hackensack, New Jersey; Broward County, Florida; Washington, DC; White Plains, New York; Madison, Wisconsin; and the Schomburg Center in Harlem, New York. We continued to attend the ALA Convention, making sure we attended the annual meeting of the Black Caucus of the American Library Association. And we became friends with so many supportive librarians from all parts of the country. Many helped to champion our publishing efforts, sharing valuable information and resources.

Just Us Books has created a legacy as a publisher of books for children and young adults that focus on Black history, culture, and experiences. Along with other independent presses, we have helped to blaze trails, open doors, and break down barriers in the book publishing industry. We have increased Black representation in children's book publishing and offered our voices, resources, and commitment to diversity, inclusion, and equity in the industry. But we know how essential those hometown librarians, Mrs. Jacobs and Mrs. Edwards, were to our journey. Our love of reading and joy in creating and sharing books were nurtured by these dedicated librarians and in those library spaces that racism often rendered not quite adequate. We stand on the shoulders of those pioneers in literature and publishing who came before: Phillis Wheatly, the African Methodist Episcopal publishing enterprise, John Russwurm and Samuel Cornish, William Wells Brown, Frances Ellen Harper, Paul Lawrence Dunbar, Langston Hughes, Richard Wright, Gwendolyn Brooks, John H. Johnson, Haki Madhubuti, and so many others who fought to tell our stories and claim our humanity. Yes, we stand on their shoulders, but Mrs. Jacobs and Mrs. Edwards, and librarians like them, gave us a huge lift.

---

# 3.7

## *LiteracyNation*

"WITH LITERACY AND JUSTICE FOR ALL"

Richard Ashby Jr.

### OUR HISTORY

The inspiring journey of LiteracyNation began in February 2010 when Richard Ashby was looking for a way to promote literacy as supervisor at the Wyandanch Public Library in Wyandanch, New York. He discussed the idea with his wife Charmaine. Richard told her about a dream he had about having an organization that promoted literacy. They took it upon themselves to address the critical need for literacy promotion. Their shared passion for books and education led them to establish LiteracyNation, Inc., with a profound mission to spread the love for reading and make literacy accessible to all individuals, regardless of their background or circumstances.

In 2011, the dreams of Richard and Charmaine came to fruition as LiteracyNation, Inc. was officially founded. The organization's journey started with humble beginnings but quickly gained momentum and garnered unwavering support from the community. His brother Dennis created the first logo. The current logo is very similar to the original.

Early on, the couple obtained a coveted 501(c) (3) nonprofit status, laying the foundation for the organization's long-term impact. To establish their first library, Richard and Charmaine received the use of a building on 39th and Mount Vernon Avenue in Philadelphia's Mantua section. Through dedication and hard work, Richard personally built a library that had twelve rooms and an impressive collection of five thousand books. These books were sourced from The Book Thing in Baltimore, Maryland, and First Book, providing a diverse range of reading materials to the community.

The library soon gained popularity, and Richard's passion for literacy education led him to attend classes at the Philadelphia Free Library, where he obtained certification as a reading tutor. Empowered with these skills, Richard was able to assist others in developing their reading abilities, instilling a love for literature in the hearts of many.

However, the journey was not without its challenges. The safety of the neighborhood surrounding the library became a concern. After arriving to work one morning, a bullet hole was found in the door, just missing Richard's chair. In response, Charmaine urged Richard to close the library due to safety risks. Instead of giving up, Richard produced an innovative solution: he transformed the library into a sidewalk initiative. Charmaine said, "Now you will be known as 'The Sidewalk Librarian.'" Thousands of new books were given away through this unique approach, spreading the joy of reading to schools, churches, daycares, and book festivals across the country.

As Richard's influence in the library community grew, he took on significant leadership roles, including serving as the president of the New York Black Librarians Caucus and the Black Caucus of the American Library Association. In 2014, these positions allowed him to take the position of director of the Yeadon Public Library in Yeadon, Pennsylvania. Richard continues to advocate for diversity in literature, amplifying diverse voices, and pushing for inclusivity within the literary world.

In 2019, Richard left his position at the Yeadon Public Library to become the director of the Sto-Rox Public Library in McKees Rocks, Pennsylvania. There, he continued his efforts to promote literacy by vetting independent authors' books and ensuring proper cataloging in OCLC WorldCat with the Allegheny Library System. Richard was unhappy with some of the cataloging of the independent author books. For example, the book *All Black Errythang*, by Chanel Miller was cataloged as "All Black Everything." Richard spoke with the cataloger. HE WAS TOLD THERE IS NO SUCH WORD AS "Errythang." The cataloger refused to correct the title. This was frustrating and disappointing to Richard and the author, nevertheless Richard managed to get over 1,600 independent books cataloged into the Alleghany Library System.

The year 2022 marked another significant milestone as Richard assumed the position of director at the Sharon Hill Public Library. His passion for supporting independent authors remained unwavering, and he continued to expand Sharon Hill's collection with a diverse selection of books by independent authors as he did in the Sto-Rox Public Library.

While working at Sharon Hill, Richard had to figure out a way to enhance the cataloging process and take ownership of the cataloged independent author's books. LiteracyNation purchased a subscription to the OCLC WorldCat system in 2023. Richard recognized the importance of accurate representation in cataloging and formed a group of skilled catalogers known as "Indiec@ts" to meticulously catalog independent books themselves. This effort aimed to ensure that diverse authors' works received the recognition they deserved and were accessible to readers worldwide.

During the COVID-19 pandemic, LiteracyNation adapted to the new normal by harnessing the power of social media. The LiteracyNation Library was launched on the emerging app, Clubhouse, where Richard gathered a community of independent authors to address the need for diverse books. Richard's influence in the library community grew significantly.

With their growing success and impact, LiteracyNation, Inc. earned recognition as a Candid-approved organization (formerly Guidestar) and achieved Gold Seal of Transparency. The organization's commitment to supporting diverse authors, libraries, and community organizations garnered support from various corporations and organizations, further expanding their reach and services.

In October 2022, LiteracyNation set out to become an affiliate of the American Library Association. In January 2023, LiteracyNation, Inc., was officially recognized as an Affiliate of the American Library Association, thereby solidifying its ability to better support its members with information and resources needed to achieve goals and maintain standards of literary professionalism.

The collaborative spirit of LiteracyNation led to partnerships with esteemed organizations such as the Black Caucus of the American Library Association, the Ethnic and Multicultural Information Exchange Round Table, the Freedom to Read Foundation, the Joint Council of Librarians of Color, the Coretta Scott King Book Award Round Table, and NOVELIST. Together, they championed the cause of literacy and embraced the freedom to read, promoting diverse voices and perspectives in the literary landscape.

The Right to Read-a-Thon emerged as one of LiteracyNation's most impactful fund-raisers. Beyond financial support, this event served as a platform to raise awareness about the significance of literacy rights. All funds raised during the Right to Read-a-Thon were dedicated to the LeRoy C. Merritt Humanitarian Fund. Established in 1970 in memory of Dr. LeRoy C. Merritt, the fund provided support, medical care, and welfare to librarians facing discrimination based on gender, sexual orientation, race, color, creed, religion, age, disability, or national origin.

Throughout its remarkable journey, LiteracyNation remained steadfast in its commitment to the tagline, "With literacy and justice for all." It continued to foster a passion for reading, champion the right to access diverse literature, and advocate for equal opportunities for individuals to engage with books.

LiteracyNation's dedication to embracing diversity in literature and promoting inclusivity has remained unwavering. Through its collaboration with esteemed organizations, it has enriched its programs and initiatives, furthering its mission of breaking down barriers to literacy and fostering a sense of belonging within the literary community.

As LiteracyNation, Inc. looks to the future, its vision is of a world where knowledge is accessible to all, and prejudice is challenged through the power of reading. It stands as a beacon of hope, spreading the message that every person, regardless of their background, has the right to read and explore the wonders of the written word.

With each step it takes, LiteracyNation brings us closer to a world where literacy and justice truly prevail for all, empowering minds through reading and fostering a brighter future for generations to come.

The impact of LiteracyNation's efforts goes far beyond the books they distribute. They have nurtured a community of lifelong learners and advocates for literacy and social justice. Through their outreach programs, workshops, and collaborations, LiteracyNation has become a driving force in promoting reading as a tool for personal growth, empathy, and understanding.

Humbly Submitted

"With Literacy and Justice for All"

# Part III
# VITAL ISSUES

# Chapter 4A

# Issues, Impact, and Values in Black Librarianship

## 4.1

*Issues Facing Black Male Librarians in 2023*

Antoine Ajani McDonald

**CURRENT STATE OF BLACK MALE LIBRARIANS**

In 2008, National Public Radio published an article titled "'Endangered Species': Black Male Librarian." It stated that "of the roughly 110,000 credentialed librarians in the United States, only about 600 are Black men.[1] In 2018, the numbers increased, slightly; 14,250 of the estimated 190,000 credentialed librarians in the United States identified as Black or African American according to the United States Bureau of Labor Statistics—this figure includes both men and women. In 2022, the Bureau of Labor Statistics' latest figures from the year 2021 estimated there were 127,790 librarians working nationally.[2]

I have yet to find a recent librarian-specific demographic breakdown that can accurately, or at least approximately, estimate the current number of credentialed librarians in the United States, male and female, who identify as Black or African American. In the past, the American Library Association conducted a diversity count, which is a comprehensive study of gender, race, and age in the library profession. It sought to identify the percentage of racial and ethnic minorities working as credentialed librarians in the nation's public, academic, and school library systems. Although the study was originally conducted in 2006, released in 2007, and updated in 2012, using 2009–2010 American Community Survey analyses,[3] there has not been any update in the decade since—this is the current state of Black male librarianship.

Given this current state for our Black men, me included, it is not hard to identify issues. However, it is hard to identify the most pertinent among the many. It becomes even harder trying to find viable, long-term solutions. Based on my nine years of experience as a Black man in the world of librarianship, the biggest issue that resonates with me is representation. This discussion will explore and explain two areas where the issue of representation has and in some ways continues to run rampant. The two issues I have encountered and worked to address the most are the representation of Black male librarians and Black men in general within librarianship and the lack of representation for Black male librarians and Black men in general, in the historical record. Both issues are not new to the profession, and they both have a long, complicated, and interconnected history. Exploring this history not only sheds light on, but it can also explain the current state of Black male librarianship and hopefully provide the tools to navigate the challenges we currently face. Numbers aside, the issues surrounding Black male librarians and Black men in general within librarianship is obvious and apparent, and at some point, every Black male librarian and Black man in general will be subjected to one if not all these issues in some form or fashion. My intention is to not only use my experience to identify issues facing Black male librarians today but to also interpret and explain the impact of those issues on both the library and the community. I also intend to highlight how the values held by Black male librarians have and continue to prove themselves vital in the fight to combat the issues we face.

**ISSUES FACING BLACK MALE LIBRARIANS TODAY**

Quick history lesson: libraries have been around since the beginning of advanced civilizations: ancient Egypt, Greece, and even the world's oldest known library, founded sometime in the seventh century BC in Nineveh, or modern-day Iraq.[4] Librarianship became a formal profession during the late 1800s. As a corresponding professional organization, the American Library Association was founded in 1876.[5] Despite its early beginnings, the world of librarianship would go on for some time before the first Black professional staff began entering the library in formal capacities. The first Black librarian, Edward Christopher Williams, born in 1871, is regarded as the first professionally trained Black librarian in the United States.[6] Williams worked as an assistant librarian, and eventually went on to become a university librarian in 1898. He joined the American Library Association and earned his master's degree in library science from the New York State Library School in Albany, New York, in 1899.[7] Catherine Allen Latimer was the New York Public Library's first African American librarian.[8] Latimer was instrumental in forming the library's Division of Negro History, Literature and Prints.[9] In 1901, Samuel W. Starks became the first African American in the United States to serve as a state librarian.[10] Each of these early pioneers were trailblazers of their time, achieving unheard of milestones in their pursuit for equality in education, in opportunities, and in representation.

When you look around libraries today, although there has been much progress, you still tend to see predominantly white faces looking back at you both as a library patron and as a library professional. The question often echoed is why are there so few Black librarians? The question has a multifaceted answer. For there to be more Black librarians, there first must be higher enrollment rates into library science programs, both bachelors and masters' programs need to see an increased number of Black applicants, particularly Black men. To see increased enrollment rates, first there needs to be increased interest in the profession. Here lies the problem. Circling back to the 2008 statistic for Black male librarians: 0.5 percent—that was the number ingrained into my mind as a graduate student.

As I navigated through graduate school, 0.5 percent was routinely mentioned from those who looked like me as well as those who did not. From that moment on I accepted that number as a reality that would never change—a decade later, it has not. Today, librarians between the ages of twenty and thirty make up 4 percent of the national workforce. Librarians that identify as Black or African American make up 6.0 percent of the national workforce.[11] Combine those figures and you will find me, an anomaly—a Black male librarian under thirty. When I would look around and wonder why I did not see more Black men in the library spaces around me, I thought back to my undergraduate studies where my professional interest in libraries began. I could not think of any other students who were interested in working in a library or yet aspiring to become a librarian professionally, not even myself.

In 2011, my sophomore year on campus at The Lincoln University of Pennsylvania, the nation's first degree-granting historically black college and university (HBCU), the Langston Hughes Memorial Library underwent a multimillion-dollar renovation and received a new library director. During that time, I was looking for employment on campus and turned my sights to the new library and reached out to the newly appointed library director, who turned out to be a Black man. Fast forward one year, I never successfully gained employment, but I did find a mentor in the new library director. After connecting with Mr. Roseboro and learning about the world of librarianship and law librarianship, my interests quickly grew. I applied for and was accepted into the North Carolina Central School of Library and Information Sciences. This is a testament to the power of connections, to the power of seeing a familiar face in a professional environment, and the impact each of these interactions has the potential to create. If my library director were not a Black man, I still likely would not have become employed; moreover, the opportunity to make a connection and the opportunity to plant the seed, would not have occurred. This is an experience Black male librarians across the nation can share; this is the power, the impact, and the value of representation. A Black man serving as the library director at an HBCU inspired a Black male student to become a librarian. Highlighting the impact of this connection further displays the importance of ensuring that libraries' patron demographics are reflected and represented in their staffing demographics.

Aside from being mentored by a Black male librarian, in what ways are Black youth, particularly men, being drawn into the field of librarianship? The short and simple answer is, they are not. Black youth are not being drawn toward the field of librarianship. Not only is this reflected in the values held by the youth, but you can also see it reflected in the availability of library science programs offered at HBCUs. The Lincoln University of Missouri offers a bachelor's degree program in library science, and North Carolina Central University School of Library and Information Sciences offers a master's degree program in library science. Still, there are only a handful of library science degree programs offered at HBCUs. Sadly, this is the case for scholars seeking either a bachelor's or a master's. How does this change? How can we ensure there will be library science programs offered at HBCUs in the future? This is the part of the conversation where you begin to hear about the word "retention" and its potential to retain librarians of color, not just Black men.

Retention is the ability to keep or continue having something, but as we know from our brief history lesson, the library has never *truly* had, or had the ability to keep, librarians of color, especially Black male librarians. Although there are considerable steps that can be taken to intensify the library's commitment to retaining Black men as librarians, retention is just part of the issue. For example, library systems should look for opportunities to employ Black male librarians in neighborhoods where they have connections with the local community as well as for opportunities to promote Black male librarians to leadership positions in both upper-level and management-level staffing roles. Library systems should also look for opportunities to highlight Black male librarians to the larger community by highlighting achievements and proving an interest in their professional endeavors.

One of the most important steps library systems can take to intensify their commitment to retaining Black men as librarians is to demonstrate continuous and genuine support: support in providing equal financial compensation, professional development, continuing education resources, and daily emotional and environmental support. Among the suggested steps, support is what ties them all together. These are examples of how library systems can commit to retaining Black men as librarians. Not only do they serve as examples, but they serve as concepts that can be replicated and repeated profession-wide aiding in the retention of Black men in varying roles. Black men can be found among all library professionals: support staff, technical staff, librarians, degreed and nondegreed library professionals, library administration, trustees, volunteers, friends of the library, retirees, and patrons—their stories deserve to be told.

As I mentioned before, for Black men to be retained in the profession, they first must enter the field. The only way to ensure an increase in admissions to library science programs is by first increasing the interest in librarianship and creating the demand for librarians within the community. I have committed myself to addressing this need with the creation of the Total Wellness, Academic & Advocacy Network. I founded my literacy-based limited liability company in 2020 during the COVID-19 pandemic to increase and improve literacy rates and promote librarianship, both in the field and in the profession among Black and brown youth ages thirteen to nineteen. My goal is to *"Make Reading Cool Again,"* and my vision toward that path is to develop, increase, and improve literacy skills through reflective reading and writing exercises, develop and practice public speaking skills in a supportive environment, cultivate a love for reading, and inspire youth to enter the field of librarianship. I intend to challenge the commonly held notion among our youth that reading is boring and to combat the societal obstacles that derail youth from aspiring toward a career path such as librarianship. I have been able to collaborate with community organizations such as fraternities and sororities, charter school systems and libraries to meet youth where they are before attempting to teach and inform. Libraries and library systems should *want* to be in on this action.

Serving as a platform to boost the values of their Black male librarians and their impact, libraries are uniquely situated in the community to do so because they inheritably foster the connection of resources. Library systems, library directors, and librarians themselves can and will benefit from looking for opportunities to collaborate with community and grassroots organizations that have demonstrated a commitment to the betterment of the lives of Black men. This is just one way libraries can commit to improving how Black men are represented in their systems and retain Black men across the board, from undergraduate and graduate programs to library staff and patrons. The examples and suggestions outlined are salient to fostering *and maintaining* a sense of undisputed belonging for our Black men.

## REPRESENTATION IN THE HISTORICAL RECORD

Like their predecessors, Black male librarians of today often find themselves in spaces where there are few others who look like them, thus the sole responsibility of representation falls onto their shoulders. That sense of responsibility, unofficially bestowed upon the sole person of color in the room, can manifest itself in many different iterations. For example, Black male librarians can be misrepresented or typecast into one singular representation that does not represent that gambit of our existence. Underrepresentation or no representation trumps them all. As I previously mentioned, there was an extended period in history where Black men were not represented in the historical account of how the field of librarianship developed over time. With the librarianship field being heavily centered around data documentation, data omission in historic and modern documentation becomes especially glaring.

Take Samuel W. Starks, for instance, the first Black state librarian, leader of his fraternal order and founder of the West Virginia newspaper the *Advocate*, which ran from 1901 to 1913.[12] For those researching the life of this early prominent Black figure, there are few articles covering his life up until his sudden death. In terms of a historical record, for this instance, the Library of Congress's Name Authority File, or the LCNAF record, is a compilation of authority records for personal, corporate, and family names maintained by the Library of Congress.[13] This collection of authorized data and controlled vocabulary highlights how seemingly unintentional classification errors can circumvent researchers in their pursuit of information. According to Jeannette Schollaert's article, "Phantom Records: A Two-Part Series on Searchability and Records in Chronicling America, Part 2," she explains how in her work with title essays she came across Samuel W. Starks's name with the LCNAF record that included a notation from the old catalog. Schollaert then wondered, *"What does it mean for a reference to be in the 'old catalog;? Does this mean that Starks's record was 'retired' at some point, for some unclear reason? If so, how then can we 'revive' Starks's record so that his name becomes part of the linked data connecting the Advocate* (the newspaper he founded) *to other resources about him online?"*[14] This is a prime example highlighting how systemic variables can contribute to the issue of underrepresentation for Black male librarians. Starks's record was being overlooked in the historical record due to how his *record* was being classified in the Library of Congress's search system. Schollaert was fortunate enough to find a simple explanation for this occurrence and was also fortunate enough to witness its simple solution. The old catalog note was the result of outdated catalog records that were not fully verified when transitioning from a print to digital record and therefore not included in the Library of Congress's updated catalog, as is the case for millions of other names as well. How many of those millions of other names are Black male librarians? Due to Schollaert's inquisitiveness, researchers accessing records on any given name can now rest assured they are being shown the full scope of results from both the old catalog records and from the updated catalog without potentially overlooking valuable information. Black male librarians of the past deserve for their stories, achievements, and contributions to the field to be easily discoverable and accessible.

That is also the case for today's Black male librarians. When I first began working as a librarian in my public library system in 2017, I was one of only five or six Black librarians. In 2023, I am now one of only three or four Black librarians. Among them, I am the only male. It did not take long for me to inquire about those who may have come before me. In my search for past Black male librarians who served in the same public system as myself, I came across the name of a man who was still living and serving in the community as a pastor. I was honored with the opportunity to meet Reverend James R. Wright. After several in-depth, informational, and humorous discussions, I learned Mr. Wright was responsible for one of the largest oral history projects conducted in our local public library system—the Phyllis Wheatley Oral History project. The oral recordings produced by this effort are still being used, advertised as educational resources, and currently being incorporated into the curriculum for local K–12 students. This information was new to me, and if I did not seek it out, I may have never known. This is the impact of underrepresentation and no representation at all. In the past, representations of Black men in the historical records of institutions such as libraries has been inadequate. Often, our contributions and even our existence were completely omitted, or sparsely documented only from the perspective of others. Those times have not completely ended. There are still many gaps in the historical record, but we are now in a time where there is a major push against the status quo. Black special collections librarians and Black archivists have unique challenges when interacting with dated materials that contain language and/or imagery that is harmful, offensive, or vestiges of white supremacist and/or racist thought as they navigate potentially conflicting personal feelings versus professional obligations. Another instance with the potential to create this dichotomy within and among Black male librarians lies within the library's collections. Whether the collection is print or digital, all libraries—public, academic, specialized, etc.—have and continue to struggle with diversity.

Diversity in services and programming offered to patrons diversity in staffing, particularly senior and management-level staff. However, diversity in collection materials is one area where representation plays a key role. I have been responsible for collection development in several capacities with varying scopes and varying budget sizes. In many of those cases I noticed that prior to my purchase decisions, there existed a disproportionate amount of print materials that covered topics such as slavery, the slave trade, the transatlantic slave system, Jim Crow, and civil rights. Repeatedly seen were the same themes of slavery or the same familiar names: Martin Luther King and Frederick Douglass. Why was this the only way I was seeing myself represented? Most public libraries are situated in areas where the majority demographic is low-income people of color, many of which are men. Why are *they* only seeing themselves represented in this way? This is also the impact of underrepresentation and no representation at all.

I currently serve as project manager for the Documenting, Preserving and Improving Access to Local Black Collections project for the Local History and Genealogy Division at the Central Public Library of Rochester & Monroe County. In this role I have been tasked with facilitating the establishment of a permanent and sustainable community curated Archive of Black History & Culture. Some of the primary goals of the archive include identifying existing collections that document local Black history and compiling a comprehensive guide to those collections to aid researchers, identifying relevant materials that are not currently in the public realm and making a plan to preserve and provide public access to them in the future, establishing a community advisory board of at least ten community members chosen to represent diverse and intersecting constituencies within Rochester's Black communities, identifying and connecting with community stakeholders and encouraging their participation in project efforts.

This project also seeks to identify themes, organizations, and individuals significant to Rochester's Black history and culture both past and present, identify and assess community needs and desires through a process of surveys and/or focus group meetings, develop a mission and vision statement and draft a three- to five-year strategic and collection policy for the new archive.

As we work to complete each of our outlined goals, we find ourselves one step closer to our overarching goal of repairing the historical record by collecting, preserving, and sharing resources that document the history of Rochester's Black residents—past, present, and future—to ensure that the historical stories we tell about the Greater Rochester community—and the resources that allow us to tell them—better reflect all residents' experiences and contributions.[15]

Through this service I have witnessed firsthand the progress and change being implemented into library systems and the values incorporated into the framework of the library's structure because of efforts by Black male librarians. It is not just librarians doing this work. Our approach to the Archive of Black History & Culture demonstrated our belief that it is important for us to seek representation from varying spectrums of the Black community. Both our internal and external boards were comprised with a variation of library professionals such as support staff, technical staff, librarians, degreed and non-degreed library professionals, library administration, trustees, volunteers, friends of the library, and retirees who are Black, Indigenous peoples of color who can best speak to the needs and desires of people like themselves. Too often in the past, white people have dictated the terms of representation within historical institutions and the collections they hold. This has resulted in skewed narratives that reinforce white supremacist viewpoints, whether inadvertently or intentionally. Black male librarians are often subjected to the manifestations of said skewed narratives.

One way we looked at addressing the discrepancies that continuously appeared in historical narratives is by including disclaimers in our special collections finding aids. Finding aids are meant to provide patrons with a glimpse into a collection, but we wanted to take it a step further and provide patrons with a disclaimer whenever they are interacting with a material that contains harmful and/or offensive langue or white supremacist language and/or thought. The disclaimer provides patrons with explanations for materials that contain period-specific terminology and/or imagery. Again, this is a concept that be replicated and duplicated across library systems. This effort can aid in addressing materials already collected, but in terms of materials that will be collected in the future, Black librarians like me are ensuring that our values are not only heard but reflected in the policies and procedures that will guide future decision-making. To ensure the dignity of future decision-making remains intact, the Archive of Black History Culture's Community Advisory Board is bringing about a change to the historical record by revising and revamping the library's documented guidelines.

As mentioned, we are updating and drafting mission and vision statements as well as collection policies and revisiting requirements for accessing materials. We're taking the necessary steps to develop, and most importantly, implement said changes into the fabric of the library's structure to ensure our changes are not overridden five to ten years down the line. Without a personal stake or long-term commitment, failure is inevitable. Library systems and the people who staff them, not just the Black ones, must be fully on board for there to be sustainability. Representation is not just a one-off act of inclusion. Addressing the varying issues regarding the representation of Black male librarians and Black men in general within libraries and in the historical and modern record will take intentional decision-making and it will take time. Therefore, our work starts now if we want our kids and their kids to have access to resources that are truly reflective of the accurate accounts of history. We must lay the foundation today. The @BlackMaleLibrarian on Instagram is an example of how we can continue to lay that groundwork.

In conclusion, the Black male librarians of today face the same issues that challenged our predecessors. Today, the difference is the tools we have in our tool kit to fight back. The issues of representation are all being met with force this time around. The @BlackMaleLibrarian on Instagram is a cohort uniting Black male librarians across the nation for community mentorship and to promote the librarianship profession to Black youth. This interactive online engagement tool has created a platform to amplify the voices of Black male librarians. A community-centered cohort is needed; a centralized resource dedicated primary to the betterment of the lives of Black men, which will create sustainable change within the profession. This will drum up more interest in the profession,

increase admission rates into library science programs, and aid in increasing the retention rates for Black male librarians and other Black male staff in varying roles with the profession. These are the kinds of initiatives library systems should be looking for to support and collaborate with. Showing solidarity among community-led organizations working toward the same goals allows libraries to demonstrate their commitment and invested interest to the cause. It is a proven fact—one is more likely to succeed when one is supported and encouraged by the community around them. I have explained why it is imperative for the library to be truly invested in the fight for improved representation for Black male librarians and Black men in general within the field. I hope I have demonstrated how librarians can be stewards in the pursuit to foster change in the profession by ensuring that their values reflect the values of *all* its constituents, including those of our Black male librarians.

**NOTES**

1. "'Endangered Species': Black Male Librarian," National Public Radio, June 27, 2008, http://www.npr.org/templates/story/story.php?storyId=91955374.
2. Bureau of Labor Statistics, https://www.bls.gov/.
3. "Diversity Counts, American Library Association, March 29, 2007, https://www.ala.org/aboutala/offices/diversity/diversitycounts/divcounts.
4. Evan Andrews, "8 Legendary Ancient Libraries," History.com, November 17, 2016, https://www.history.com/news/8-impressive-ancient-libraries#:~:text=The%20world%27s%20oldest%20known%20library,organized%20according%20to%20subject%20matter.
5. Dennis Thomson, *A History of the American Library Association, 1876-1972* (Chicago: American Library Association, 1978).
6. "Black Leaders in Library History," *Fordham Library News*, February 22, 2021, https://librarynews.blog.fordham.edu/2021/02/22/leaders-in-library-history/.
7. Ibid.
8. Ibid.
9. Ibid.
10. "Samuel W. Starks," Biographies of Prominent Blacks in West Virginia, 2021, https://archive.wvculture.org/history/archives/blacks/blackbio.html.
11. "PLA Surveys and Data," American Library Association, June 21, 2021, https://www.ala.org/pla/sites/ala.org.pla/files/content/data/PLA_Staff_Survey_Report_2022.pdf.
12. "Samuel W. Starks."
13. "National Archives Catalog—Authority Sources," National Archives, August 15, 2016, https://www.archives.gov/research/catalog/lcdrg/elements.
14. Jeannette Schollaert, "Phantom Records: A Two-Part Series on Searchability and Records in Chronicling America, Part 2," National Endowment for the Humanities, August 31, 2021, https://www.neh.gov/blog/phantom-records-two-part-series-searchability-and-records-chronicling-america-part-2.
15. "Archive of Black History and Culture," Rochester Public Library (New York), 2023, https://roccitylibrary.org/archive-of-black-history-culture/.

## WORKS CITED

Andrews, Evan. "8 Legendary Ancient Libraries," History.com, November 17, 2016, https://www.history.com/news/8-impressive-ancient-libraries#:~:text=The%20world%27s%20oldest%20known%20library,organized%20according%20to%20subject%20matter.

"Archive of Black History and Culture." Rochester Public Library (New York), 2023. https://roccitylibrary.org/archive-of-black-history-culture/.

"Black Leaders in Library History." *Fordham Library News*, February 22, 2021. https://librarynews.blog.fordham.edu/2021/02/22/leaders-in-library-history/.

Bureau of Labor Statistics. https://www.bls.gov/.

"Diversity Counts." American Library Association, March 29, 2007. https://www.ala.org/aboutala/offices/diversity/diversitycounts/divcounts.

"'Endangered Species': Black Male Librarian." National Public Radio, June 27, 2008. http://www.npr.org/templates/story/story.php?storyId=91955374.

"National Archives Catalog—Authority Sources." National Archives, August 15, 2016. https://www.archives.gov/research/catalog/lcdrg/elements.

"PLA Surveys and Data." American Library Association, June 21, 2021. https://www.ala.org/pla/sites/ala.org.pla/files/content/data/PLA_Staff_Survey_Report_2022.pdf.

"Samuel W. Starks." Biographies of Prominent Blacks in West Virginia, 2021. https://archive.wvculture.org/history/archives/blacks/blackbio.html.

Schollaert, Jeannette. "Phantom Records: A Two-Part Series on Searchability and Records in Chronicling America, Part 2." National Endowment for the Humanities, August 31, 2021. https://www.neh.gov/blog/phantom-records-two-part-series-searchability-and-records-chronicling-america-part-2.

Thomas, Dennis. *A History of the American Library Association, 1876–1972*. Chicago: American Library Association, 1978.

# 4.2

## *A Black Alt-Ac Speaks*

EARLY CAREER LIBRARIANSHIP TRAUMA

Gemmicka Piper

According to the Department for Professional Employees AFL-CIO Fact Sheet (2021), librarian employment in "colleges, universities, and professional schools" accounts for almost 15 percent of the library and information science field.[1] The US Bureau of Labor estimates that African Americans account for 4.3 percent of total librarian and media collection specialists, and 6.3 percent of archivists, curators, and museum technicians.[2] These two statistics are further noteworthy given that the most recent internal ACRL Membership Survey (2018) suggested that of the librarians surveyed (10.52% of all registered ARL librarians) only 4 percent identified as African American.[3] Lastly, the ALA Demographic Study (2017) revealed that while 25 percent of librarians held multiple master's-level degrees, only 4.5 percent of those surveyed held PhDs.[4] As such, non-white, doctoral degree holders employed as subject specialist in an academic library are an almost mythical presence. Yet they are still out there. I should know. I am one of these mythical unicorns. I graduated in 2015 from the University of Iowa with a PhD in English followed by an MLIS with dual certificates in POROI (Projects On Rhetoric's Of Inquiry) and public digital humanities. Entering librarianship as an under thirty, Black Alt-Ac (alternative academic), and cis-gendered woman, gives me a perspective that I have not seen represented at all in any scholarship related to BIPOC librarians. Finally, I am ready to tell my story of librarianship. In no particular order the path of librarianship has been riddled with intergenerational trauma, microaggression, misogynoir, and social anxiety from surviving extremely toxic work environments.

### NO FORMAL LIS MENTORING

Within librarianship, "Mentoring programs provide a much-needed connection between the individual librarian and the library community he or she inhabits. When expressing dissatisfaction, many minority librarians made the distinction between their environment and the librarian profession as a whole."[5] When actually fostered, the mentor-mentee relationship can be source of both vulnerability and intimacy. I was already in a doctoral program where I was blessed to experience a strong and close mentoring bond with another Black woman.[6] However, as a student in SLIS (School of Library and Information Sciences) I never received formal mentoring. Rather, I was constantly reminded that "librarianship is a small discipline defined by civility, and collaboration." The then director of my SLIS program discussed how great it was to have librarians who advocate, bragged about being a DEI friendly culture, and then doubled down that I was "rude," "loud," and "a bull in a China shop." "Rude" because I would directly head to scheduled appointments with the program coordinator rather than entertain the secretary out front. "Loud" because I called him out for the nepotistic hiring of his to teach computing foundations yet could never figure out how to turn on the machine nor navigate the required Zoom. In the next breath, he then offered to personally "mentor" me. For obvious reasons, I declined.

Unsurprisingly, the program had lost five faculty (a few BIPOC members) the same semester I had finally decided to enter the program.[7] One of those who left was the person I directly would have been mentored by as we both had shared interests in race and technology. This was another BIPOC individual who had been recruiting me to take their course for a while. The only nonwhite student in my cohort, I was never informed of BCALA, the Josey Award, or the Spectrum Scholars Program.[8] For context, the Black Caucus of the American Library Association was founded "to provide for black activist librarians a united front to address the issues of Black librarianship and ensure that black people would receive first-class access to library services and resources."[9] Dr. Betty J. Turock founded the Spectrum Scholars Program in 2003 as "a program designed to recruit and fund members of underrepresented minority populations to graduate programs in library and information science."[10] The one thing I had been informed of was residencies, especially for early career librarians. Residencies were framed as a chance to both gain professional experience and to form close mentoring bonds that would later help individuals find their space within the pantheon of ALA.

## CAN I GET A REFUND? THE "F--" RESIDENCY EXPERIENCE

In 2016, I applied for and eventually accepted the Visiting Assistant Librarian/Resident for Miami University, in Oxford, Ohio. Sylvia Hu and Demetria Patrick's article, "Our Experience as Minority Residents,"[11] and the residency program they experienced at Miami University was vastly different from mine. Afterall, at the core a residency program "generally offer[s] a newly-graduated librarian a multitude of varied experiences, usually by rotating them through various departments within the library."[12] As an additional point, "Residencies are often hampered by miscommunication and lack of organization. This causes real harm to the new resident and the current employees by creating a tense, sometimes even hostile, work environment."[13] Recruited by a BIPOC librarian, for a library lead by another BIPOC-identified person, very naively I went into the residency trusting that I would be taken care of and finally professionally mentored.

During the in-person interview I mentioned firstly that I am a nondriver and secondly I prefer housing near my work area. The librarians at the institution, most of whom had been there almost two decades, assured me of there being direct bus routes between Oxford and Hamilton. Hamilton was the next town over, maybe a thirty-minute bus ride. Upon acceptance of the offer for employment, I secured housing in Hamilton since there were zero openings in Oxford. I informed the department head of securing housing in my price range in Hamilton. Days later, she called me back and informed me that the housing in Hamilton would not work. In her words, the bus system was not reliable enough for a daily work schedule. Additionally, it was imperative that I be on site by the first week of October. She demanded I get my deposit back and secure housing in town immediately. Needless to say, I was deliberately misled regarding the availability of housing in Oxford and then pressured to arrive early. As a result, the first week of my residency I spent homeless in a completely unfamiliar city. Adding insult to injury, the predicted "wave" of instruction ended up being eleven cotaught sections. No administrative acknowledgment was ever made of the situation they created.

Apparently, there was something set up between my then direct supervisor and the library dean. While the library did foot the bill for a stay in a campus bed and breakfast, and a weekend in an on-campus hotel, the library dean explicitly framed their assistance as a "favor."[14] Being a "favor" and not their responsibility, they automatically deducted the taxation for my hotel fees for the first several months of my employment. I noticed my paycheck being shorted and approached it directly as a breach of contract. Instantly combative, the library dean immediately started explaining how I should be "grateful" they helped me out. Then informed me that this was something set up with the previous department head, that I don't recall being notified of prior to that moment. I was expected to secure accommodation by the end of the first week. The instruction rush lasted a week, but the resultant work-related trauma from being in an extremely dysfunctional work environment, continues to negatively impact me.

As an added layer of complexity to this situation, the instructional librarian unit I was hired into and the entire administrative team I had encountered were part of a large cycle of toxic leadership feedback loop. The dysfunction I was seeing in the administrative team extended to all units within the library. Alma Ortega cites toxic leadership as "egregious actions taken against some or all of the members, even among peers, of the organization a leader heads."[15] In my second week I moved into the only available place, which cost a significant portion of my monthly check in base rent and utilities. Between a persistent cough, a freezing room, and unpacking, I didn't get much sleep. The following day, I attended my first department meeting. Afterword, the department chair, the same BIPOC woman who recruited me in our one-on-one let me know that my behavior during the departmental meeting was unbecoming. I was "too quiet" and needed to "work harder" to show my engagement.

This was the first of many glimpses into the danger of toxic leadership. Toxic leadership includes "humiliation, bullying, ridicule, belittling, telling employees publicly or privately that they are not part of the organization, ignoring, shunning, overworking, among many other forms of emotional and psychological abuse."[16] Immediately after that, telling a colleague "She is not going to make it here" when speaking to another colleague. The "she" referred to was me. Being that the fishbowl setup of the office suite amplified sound, and they were speaking in the office right next to mine, I might as well have been in the room with them as they gossiped about me. After this event, I directly reached out to her regarding her thoughts on how this experience was going. Smiling, she tossed the question back to me. When I answered not well, she assured me I was doing fine. A lot of destructive shenanigans happened after she left, enough that I could write a novel. I kept an active list that I compiled into a document that I submitted in lieu of doing an exit interview.

**SHOW AND TELL: WHEN LEADERSHIP IS OUT OF POCKET**

There is a persistent emphasis within the LIS literature of assuming a White leader-Black subordinate when discussing power dynamics. What happens when there is both an intraracial and intergenerational dynamic? Put simply, my positionality presented a potential disruption to the already contentious cultural ecosystem. As the only PhD holder within the building, I possessed "subject expertise, in-depth knowledge of the research and writing process, practical understanding of graduate education and university-level teaching, and a connection to the faculty born of common experience."[17] This made for some expressed fear among my colleagues regarding my potential. Additionally, the first four-to-five months of the residency I was the only one not already associated with the institution. The other resident, a white female, was employed up from within the organization. Following her departure, a white female librarian took over responsibility for supervising the residents. When faced with my frustration at her lack of mentorship or any active guidance, she explained to me that she "couldn't" mentor me. However, this particular supervisor had no issue mentoring nor even inserting my co-resident into our conversations whenever I shared ideas with her for campus engagement activities.[18] She said, "It's because of the interest alignment." Eventually another outside resident, a white male pursuing his PhD, arrived in the Spring semester. There was a deep empathy with that person, but also a bit of a contrast in how navigated the environment.

New to the field, but with advanced research and instruction skills, there was an added layer where, being the only Black person on staff, they immediately assumed I had an "immediate in" with the library dean. Requests related to budget increases and information were some of the highlight points of which my colleagues would ask for me to *specifically* convey to the dean. They assumed I would get a favorable answer because of our shared existences as black individuals. The reality was, I might be Black, but I was also a woman. A strange mix of race, power, and gender often clashed in the dynamic of our interactions. Sometimes speaking through the blatant misogynoir of the 1960s, other times speaking like an administrator, and aside from that just extremely petty, I never understood him, but he constantly made me very uncomfortable. For example, I had the occasion for him to have gone to a lunch as part of introducing me to the former Black Studies chair. He introduced me as: "A sista, educated with a degree . . . you know we had swoop her up." This moment expressly highlights how the top administrative team saw me. Shortly after the lunch incident, I recall another one in which he pointed and came running toward me from the main foyer staircase, stating, "See, I told you I had a Black librarian on staff." There was showing me off to another Black male dean, in a separate and higher administrative unit. He introduced this person, along with another Black female who served as part of the EEOC team. The EEOC representative and the library dean were close friends, and the campus climate of Miami University remained very much "boy's club." I later found out that many prior female librarians had submitted harassment claims against the dean for similar misogynistic behavior, which had fallen on deaf ears. The Black Alt-Ac position, the almost mystical being, was reduced to an object to use in a power play among the boys' cross-campus leadership. Nicole Cooke summarizes this experience beautifully:

> Minority faculty members can be hired as tokens, and are certainly treated as such, particularly when they are the "only one" or one of few people of color in a school, department, or unit; they routinely experience microaggressions and repetitive injuries (in some cases they have been physically touched or aggressed upon); they face denials of abuse and mistreatment and are labeled as angry and/or overly sensitive, or are accused of playing the "race card"; they are sometimes implicitly and explicitly retaliated against.[19]

Where should I have begun to get help? To *whom* would I have even reported this? Miami University had no ombudsperson. I couldn't trust the EEOC as their representative had a close friendship with my dean. There was a small sister circle formed after I had been enduring the situation for a year. My library dean had even attended the preceding presentation before the women circle meeting. The leader recommended I go talk to a different Black male dean about the issues I experienced. The person she referred me to was the same Black male dean whom my dean pointed me out to in the previous incident. I no longer cared about staying. Wasn't even sure about remaining a librarian. I spoke with him in detail about my experiences since coming to Miami University. I had even assembled a full three-page letter covering a slew of details, dates, people that were standing around, and on which occasions multiple incidents had happened. An older gentleman, he simply smiled blankly as I finished, almost in tears, reading off these events. He then asked, "Are you positive that you won't be able to stay? Miami is bleeding its Black people. We can only change the situation by staying." Any sense of personal safety, financial security, and emotional wellness that I needed was secondary to his mission of retaining Black employees at Miami University.

The power and the connection of the library dean on this campus was clear. Always one for action, my rage steadily built up. This residency was a desperation move after not immediately landing a position postgraduation. The cost of moving, relying on my credit card for necessities, being forced to rent at nearly double the rent rate, then being forced to abruptly move again when my housing complex was sold placed me into financial hardship. Anywhere from two-thirds to three-quarters of my paycheck was spent on living expenses. The persistent coughing since starting the position went untreated. My first doctor's visit was in the summer of 2017. I went in for an annual exam and was diagnosed with hypothyroidism. Increasingly withdrawn and silent in meetings, my body was constantly tremoring. I was nervous, paranoid, and had no one to help me navigate this situation. I had sympathizers outside of my unit, but ultimately, I knew they were just as powerless.[20]

## SERVICE AND NATIONAL BLACK ORGANIZATIONS

I sought to become more involved with national service and activities geared toward minorities or African American/Black-identified librarians in response to the situation. I desperately needed someone to guide me, to give me some wisdom. I prayed to be recruited somewhere else. I had applied and received a grant to attend and present at NCAAL X.[21] I remember going intentionally to BCALA meetings to seek out a space to speak about this situation and to get guidance in terms of career navigation. However, BCALA ended up having way more public than academic librarians as well as having librarians generationally closer to retirement than just starting out in the profession. Generationally speaking, these were the librarians who were definitely used to suffering in silence. I am in the camp of "women who have shared stories of interpersonal violence to a public audience, giving voice to silence can be seen as part of a developmental progression from trauma 'victim' to 'survivor' and/or 'advocate.'"[22] I own my power and agency through naming and speaking the story of what happened to and against me in librarianship. My situation is work-related trauma, but there is a definite language overlap between domestic abuse and sexual violence survivors in the public responses to call out what hurts you. When you dare to openly name professional spaces those rhetorically protected under the guise of civility.

My second BCALA meeting had Black academic librarians in attendance. The silencing and subtle chastising began. A well-meaning older Black librarian quickly reminded me that "not everyone at this meeting is a friend" and that I should keep these experiences to myself. Sort of like, "Be silent. You shouldn't have worn those clothes." Or "You know how his temper is; provoking him—what were you thinking?" For a profession steeped in the feminine, how easily academic librarians slip into demanding the repression of work trauma. The hyperbole here is not that far off from when a woman names the source of her wounds. In Black spaces, this is doubly so when the oppressor is a Black male: "Making transparent the intersection of racism, sexism, and a variety of other factors that impact Black women in particular is dependent largely on Black Women reporting their experiences, possibly risking their privacy, career success, and reputations."[23] At the time, I swallowed it all back down. It gagged against my internal rage and dissatisfaction. I knew it would come up again, words vomiting out of my mouth spewing my despair. I lost interest in trying to engage in Black librarian spaces and stopped trying to foster my interest in publishing.

A few months later and I attended an event hosted by AASLIG.[24] During a presentation there were many suggestions for navigating racial microaggressions. But when I revealed my situation in its entirety . . . no guidance came forth on dealing with this level of toxicity and misogynoir. Maintaining silence and civility will not save you. It will not magically fix what is wrong in your work environment. Ignoring, shunning—I became equally as toxic toward my colleagues. I spent almost two years stuck in this position. I finally made the decision to share publicly. Randomly, a former Black female college friend reached out to me. She placed me in contact with her mom, a public librarian, who served as a source of guidance as I navigated departing from the residency. Eventually, I landed my current tenure track position in December 2017. I immediately started my new role in January 2018. No time for self-care. No psychological counseling. Just walked into a new position with lingering negativity still clinging to me, and a very unhealthy amount of internal pressure to prove myself. Professionally, I have gone on to accomplish a lot. So much so, I have had colleagues constantly express that I make it look easy. They assume that having a PhD means I have somehow never experienced any lows within this profession. I despise the concept of "resiliency."

Proper mentorship from the jump, open discussion of toxicity in librarianship, and frank preparedness for navigating dysfunctional workplaces, with intentional focus on properly identifying and applying for the right job and environment, would have shortened my stay, if not allow me to avoid it completely. As much as I loathed my SLIS program, I maintained a fairly good relationship with most of the library practitioners within the institution. This was good, as I ended up reaching back out to the then library HR director at my alma mater. I informed them of what I was going through and how culturally "normalized" dysfunction and toxicity was by my colleagues.

Seeing someone equally as shocked at what I experienced finally validated for me that nothing about my first librarianship position was normal. It is not normal, it will not get better. If you encounter any of what I did, leave as soon and as you are able. Sticking around only hurts you more.

**NOTES**

1. "Library Professionals: Facts and Figures: 2021 Fact Sheet," https://www.bls.gov/cps/cpsaat11.htm.
2. US Bureau of Labor Statistics, "Employed Persons by Detailed Occupation, Sex, Race, and Hispanic or Latino Ethnicity," *Labor Force Statistics from the Current Population Survey, 2022*, 25 January 2023, https://www.bls.gov/cps/aa2022/cpsaat11.htm. A note related to the national stats presented, IPEDS Annual Survey draws upon the code from the US Bureau of Labor. This code lumps together librarians along with media specialist, the data collected is also not cross tabbed by gender and race.
3. Association of College and Research Libraries, "ACRL Membership Survey, 2018." Benchmark: Library Metrics and Trends (Chicago: Association of College and Research Libraries, 2021). https://www.ala.org/acrl/proftools/benchmark. Accessed 02/22/2023. This data was sourced directly from ACRL Benchmark.
4. Kathy Rosa and Kelsey Henke, *ALA Demographic Study* (Chicago: ALA Office for Research and Statistics, 2017), 1–3.
5. Ava Iuliano, Melody Royster, Margeaux Johnson, Anne Larrivee, and Lori Driver, "Reaching Out to Minority Librarians: Overcoming Diversity Challenges through Mentorship," *ACRL 16th National Conference*, 2013, https://alair.ala.org/handle/11213/18125
6. Lori D. Patton and Shaun Harper, "Mentoring Relationships among African American Women in Graduate and Professional Schools," *New Directions for Student Services*, 2003, no. 104 (2003): 67–78.
7. I was influenced to consider library information science as a profession. Until this moment I didn't really have a set goal for postdoctoral life. I knew that the professoriate track, specifically the stress of teaching, was causing social anxiety.
8. Nicole Cooke, "The Spectrum Doctoral Fellowship Program: Enhancing the LIS Professoriate," *InterActions: UCLA Journal of Education and Information Studies*, 10, no. 1 (2014): 6. https://doi.org/10.5070/D4101018980.
9. Julius Jefferson Jr., "Searching for Spring," in *The 21st-Century Black Librarian in America: Issues and Challenges*, edited by Andrew P. Jackson, Akilah Nosakhere, and Julius Jefferson Jr. (Lanham, MD: Scarecrow, 2012), 257–61.
10. Cooke, "The Spectrum," 6.
11. Sylvia S. Hu and Demetria E. Patrick, "Our Experience as Minority Residents: Benefits, Drawbacks, and Suggestions," *College & Research Libraries News*, 67, no. 5 (2006): 297–300.
12. Jason K. Alston, "Interns or Professionals?: A Common Misnomer Applied to Diversity Resident Librarians Can Potentially Degrade and Divide," in *Where Are All the Librarians of Color*, edited by Rebecca Hankins, Miguel Juarez, and Loriene Roy (Sacramento, CA: Library Juice Press, 2015), 72.
13. LaTesha Velez et al., "Mapping the Residency Program Landscape," *Journal of Academic Librarianship*, 47, no. 5 (2021): 2. https://doi.org/10.1016/j.acalib.2021.102389.
14. As an aside, if I had received proper mentorship from SLIS, I probably would not have been as shocked. Having been on the professoriate track, I was told to expect most institutions to cover moving expenses. I had also assumed that all librarians were tenure track faculty members. Meaning they would have research support. I learned very quickly none of this was true.
15. Alma Ortega, *Academic Libraries and Toxic Leadership* (Cambridge: Chandos, an imprint of Elsevier, 2017), 6. *ProQuest Ebook Central*, http://ebookcentral.proquest.com/lib/iupui-ebooks/detail.action?docID=4798445
16. Ortega, *Academic Libraries*, 7.
17. Todd Gilman and Thea Lindquist, "Academic/Research Librarians with Subject Doctorates: Experiences and Perceptions, 1965–2006," *Portal*, 10, no. 4 (2010): 399–412.
18. While I do not begrudge my fellow resident, I will say that I did speak openly to both my then supervisor and her about the very obvious favoritism and difference in treatment between the two of us. This person just routinely insisted, uncritically, that because she had also experienced her fair share of hardship in the office culture that she was not "favored." This led to some mild gaslighting.
19. Nicole A. Cooke and Joe O. Sánchez. "Getting It on the Record: Faculty of Color in Library and Information Science," *Journal of Education for Library and Information Science*, 60, no. 3 (2019): 171.
20. I want to acknowledge the archivist and special collections and technical services units for providing a personal space after realizing how inadequate my residency experiences with the instruction unit were.
21. "Past NCAAL Conferences," *BCALA*, 2024, https://www.bcala.org/past-ncaal-conferences. The 10th National Conference of African American Librarians (NCAAL) was held in Atlanta, Georgia.
22. Brenna C. Delker, Rowan Salton, and Kate McLean, "Giving Voice to Silence: Empowerment and Disempowerment in the Developmental Shift from Trauma 'Victim' to 'Survivor-Advocate,'" *Journal of Trauma and Dissociation*, 21, no. 2 (2019): 243.
23. Candice P. Baldwin and Monica D. Griffin, "Challenges of Race and Gender for Black Women in the Academy," in *Disrupting the Culture of Silence*, edited by Kristine De Welde and Andi Stepnick (Sterling, VA: Sylus, 2015), 66.
24. African American Subject Librarian Interest Group.

**WORKS CITED**

Association of College and Research Libraries. "ACRL Membership Survey, 2018." *Benchmark: Library Metrics and Trends* (Chicago: Association of College and Research Libraries, 2021). https://www.ala.org/acrl/proftools/benchmark.

Alston, Jason K. "Interns or Professionals? A Common Misnomer Applied to Diversity Resident Librarians Can Potentially Degrade and Divide." In *Where Are All the Librarians of Color*, edited by Rebecca Hankins, Miguel Juarez, and Loriene Roy. Sacramento: Library Juice Press, 2015.

Baldwin, Candice P., and Monica D. Griffin. "Challenges of Race and Gender for Black Women in the Academy." In *Disrupting the Culture of Silence: Confronting Gender Inequality and Making Change in Higher Education*. Sterling, VA: Stylus, 2015.

Cooke, Nicole A. "The Spectrum Doctoral Fellowship Program: Enhancing the LIS Professoriate." *InterActions: UCLA Journal of Education and Information Studies*, 10, no. 1, 2014. https://doi.org/10.5070/D4101018980.

Cooke, Nicole A., and Joe O. Sánchez. "Getting It on the Record: Faculty of Color in Library and Information Science." *Journal of Education for Library and Information Science*, 60, no. 3 (2019): 169-81. utpjournals.press (Atypon), https://doi.org/10.3138/jelis.60.3.01.

Delker, Brianna C., Rowan Salton, and Kate C. McLean. "Giving Voice to Silence: Empowerment and Disempowerment in the Developmental Shift from Trauma 'Victim' to 'Survivor-Advocate.'" *Journal of Trauma & Dissociation*, 21, no. 2 (2020): 242-263.

Gilman, Todd, and Thea Lindquist. "Academic/Research Librarians with Subject Doctorates: Experiences and Perceptions, 1965-2006." *Portal: Libraries and the Academy*, 10, no. 4 (2010): 399-412.

Hu, Sylvia S., and Demetria E. Patrick. "Our Experience as Minority Residents: Benefits, Drawbacks, and Suggestions." *College & Research Libraries News*, 67, no. 5 (2006): 297-300.

Iuliano, Ava, Melody Royster, Margeaux Johnson, Anne Larrivee, and Lori Driver. "Reaching Out to Minority Librarians: Overcoming Diversity Challenges through Mentorship," *ACRL 16th National Conference*. https://alair.ala.org/handle/11213/18125.

Jefferson, Julius C., Jr. "Searching for Spring." In *The 21st-Century Black Librarian in America: Issues and Challenges*, edited by Andrew P. Jackson, Akilah Nosakhere, and Julius Jefferson Jr. Lanham: Scarecrow, 2012.

Ortega, Alma. *Academic Libraries and Toxic Leadership*. Cambridge: Elsevier Science & Technology, 2017. *ProQuest Ebook Central*. http://ebookcentral.proquest.com/lib/iupui-ebooks/detail.action?docID=4798445.

"Past NCAAL Conferences." *BCALA*, 2024. https://www.bcala.org/past-ncaal-conferences.

Patton, Lori D., and Shaun R. Harper. "Mentoring Relationships among African American Women in Graduate and Professional Schools." *New Directions for Student Services*, 2003, no. 104 (2003): 67-78.

Rosa, Kathy, and Kelsey Henke. *ALA Demographic Study*. Chicago: ALA Office for Research and Statistics, 2017.

US Bureau of Labor Statistics. "Employed Persons by Detailed Occupation, Sex, Race, and Hispanic or Latino Ethnicity." *Labor Force Statistics from the Current Population Survey*, 2022, 25 January 2023. https://www.bls.gov/cps/aa2022/cpsaat11.htm.

Velez, LaTesha, Jason Alston, Nataly Blas, Kathy Bradshaw, Orolando Duffus, Denelle Eads, Gerald, Holmes, and Olivia Patterson. "Mapping the Residency Program Landscape." *Journal of Academic Librarianship*, 47, no. 5 (2021): https://doi.org/10.1016/j.acalib.2021.102389.

---

# 4.3

## Issues, Impact, and Values in Black Librarianship

Candace Owens

John Lewis marks history and civil rights with his inspirational quote, "We must never be afraid to make some noise and get in good trouble, necessary trouble, and help redeem the soul of America."[1] The soul of America is reflected in the libraries and archives of our communities. The issue is that libraries and archives have not always reflected all the souls of America and this negligence has considerably impacted the profession and its professionals. It has been with great prejudice, pain, and noise that African Americans and the Indigenous souls of America have begun to be valued, respected, served, protected, and represented accordingly.

African Americans have fought a fight that seemed to have no end or recognition from the battlefields on foreign lands to the battlefields on their homelands.[2] With a novice perspective of libraries and archives of America, one may be inclined to think they were designed and opened for all, but this was not the case. Library representatives and their leading association in America, the American Library Association (ALA), was negligent and apprehensive in accepting African Americans into their establishments and/or the profession.[3] For example, in March 1899, when presented with a concern about a session on public library services to Black people, ALA president William Coolidge Lane was cautious and wrote ALA officials that "the question of . . . the Negro in relation to Libraries, we will leave untouched all together."[4] Over two decades later, in 1925, "the Carnegie Corporation announced it would follow an ALA recommendation to fund a library school in Virginia's Hampton Institute to train Black librarians for the colored branches of city library systems across the country."[5] However, the racial discrimination of location and proportion of resources allocated to Deep South public libraries were disturbing and a shortcoming according to the ideals of librarianship.[6] While seeming progressive in supporting a position of "separate but equal," Wiegand presents the ongoing issues of discrimination and unjust behaviors toward African Americans within librarianship and community activism. The decline in ALA's membership and the formation of Black library associations were fueled by issues on segregation reported in ALA's publications.[7] In June 1939, ALA amended its Library Bill of Rights in theory but not in practice. "Despite a growing number of protests against segregation in southern society in the 1950s, however, the library press largely overlooked Jim Crow public library practices."[8] As a result, library and information science professionals and paraprofessionals began to fight against separation, segregation, and unequal library services. For example, Bay State librarian editor John Berry III asserted his position in the matter to ALA stating, "We violently oppose any award to strengthen institutions which maintain a system of service that in any way separates one citizen from another."[9] Wiegand points out that southern public libraries offer platforms for racial reconciliation but do not empathize with the African American experience or commemorate their direct connection to the integration of public libraries in the South.[10] ALA's philosophy had been visible but unresourceful and in some form disrespectful to African Americans and the African American experience in public libraries, especially in the South. The many protesters that risked their lives to exercise their civil rights in their establishments are unrecognized and forgotten.[11] Wiegand effortlessly educates the audience on the biased foundation of ALA and the events leading to a less biased and discriminating condition of ALA and its members. With a considerable number of ALA's members failing to acknowledge issues, impacts, and the value of African Americans during the integration of public libraries, Wiegand poses the question, "Any ideas?" Wiegand encourages ALA to start the process by encouraging libraries to recognize them in a commendation to their courage to be posted on the wall next to copies of a Library Bill of Rights that provided them no support in the 1960s.[12] African American or Black Librarians must be held accountable and responsible for the research, encouragement, information, and engagement of staff members and community members regarding the legacy of African Americans and BIPOC in libraries and librarianship. Furthermore, any ideas on how to encourage, enforce even MLIS/MLS instructors to prepare and present reading materials and discussions on the African American and BIPOC experience in librarianship should be embraced and executed.

Cynthia Greenlee, a historian of African American experience and law, authored an online piece titled "On the Battle to Desegregate the National Libraries: When the Public Library Wasn't So Public" on Literary Hub. Greenlee provides an historical account of Violet Wallach and her involvement with the racial exclusion of the back-door entrance experience for Black people seeking to enter Navesink Library in 1944, a story like many that were told mostly through letters and bureaucratic memos. As a library or information science professional and community member, Wallach was willing to fight and address the appalling discrimination and irrational condition of African Americans entering a back door when they were risking their lives fighting for a county that did not see them as equal or worthy to enter through the front door of their public institutions.

Library and information science professionals and paraprofessionals, archivists (and curators) have a monumental opportunity to reshape and redeem America by examining, comprehending, and acknowledging that there are active racism, social injustices, and discrimination in these professions and/or in the training of their professionals; then asking themselves, "If or how am I perpetuating or prolonging such errors and how can I address the issue'" before informing, engaging, and interacting with community (and staff) members. Lastly, a library or information science professional or paraprofessional must speak up and out on the noted errors and create a transparent space for professional development and involve the workforce, workflow, and public or private users accordingly; not only toward African Americans but toward many other people, especially a variety of people of color now grouped as BIPOC (Black, Indigenous, and People of Color) in collaborating organizations or institutions. The Transform Libraries Campaign and Outreach have impacted the library and information science profession recently with accountable and valuable methods and tools in reaching and involving communities far and near while evolving libraries. Furthermore, library (and community) members, professionals, and paraprofessionals are in a position to collect library materials and items appropriately and justly regarding the community they surround and the populations they serve; inform and engage citizens of all ages, ethnicities, or nationalities; and create a holistic space to receive and give community values and resources.

As of 2023, the Academy of Certified Archivists has expanded the knowledge and skills necessary for archival work in preparing and presenting an addition to the role of delineation statement for professional archivists, which reflects the commonly accepted responsibilities of a professional archivist. In theory, "Cultural Competency" was added to address the issue of diversity, equity, and inclusion. In practice, Cultural Competency could create further issues in the profession in defining culture (cultural) and creating gaps in archival work while attempting to achieve and reflect the term and related skills in its entirety (e.g., conservation, description, accessibility, and disposition). However, it is outlined by tasks, knowledge, and application in the role delineation statement and follows the "Professional, Ethics, and Legal Responsibilities," which is practical. In Cultural Competency, task 7 states, "A professional archivist promotes cooperative acquisition and disposition strategies respecting any cultural protocols," which is imperative to "include." Furthermore, a knowledge and application statement regarding Cultural Competency states that "a professional archivist must be knowledgeable of the evolution, nature, and variety of recordkeeping systems and practice as they apply to diverse cultures." The archival profession acknowledges that there are issues in archival work of the past and present that have impacted the field and its workers legally and morally. The archival profession has also challenged aspiring, novice, and leading archivists to remain informed and engaged information professionals. The addition of Cultural Competency attempts to value the cultural differences and various backgrounds of the populations and audiences archives should and can impact.

Library and information specialists and scholars have documented that the Library of Congress subject headings and the Dewey decimal system are considerably search engines; and in theory and practice have supported and fueled insults of misrepresentation with their negligence or prolongation of critical changes that challenge their foundations and operations. Traditional library and information science organization systems (e.g., subject cataloging and classification) are an important part of understanding the landscape of how information science has inherited and continues biased practices in current systems designs, especially on the web.[13] Classification systems have some boundaries and limits, as they are often defined in whole by what is included and what is excluded.[14] In addition to this awareness, as library and information professionals and paraprofessionals, we must understand that search engines function as a type of personal record and as records of communities, albeit unstable ones.[15] Search engines, like other databases of information, are equally bounded, limited to providing only information based on what is indexed within the network.[16] Dr. Noble reiterates that "library science scholars know that bibliographic and naming controls are central to making knowledge discoverable, however, the issue lies in identifying and understanding who the audience is and naming and organizing information in ways that can be discovered by the public."[17] Dr. Noble demonstrates that we need public search engine alternatives united with public interest journalism and librarianship to ensure that the public has access to the highest-quality information available.[18] The future of information culture refers to Google as a monopoly of information and presents evidence as to why public policy is important to conclusively ensure that the public reclaim its institutions and strive to develop and sustain a multiracial democracy.[19]

Dr. Ruha Benjamin's *Race after Technology* outlines and defines the issues with emerging technologies that often target, presume, and dangerously affect those who are racially marked.[20] Furthermore, Dr. Benjamin elaborates on the term "New Jim Code" and the development of a new racial caste system, labeled as "criminals," by the US carceral system.[21] Dr. Benjamin demonstrates the term "New Jim Code" as "the employment of new technologies that reflect and reproduce existing inequities but are promoted and perceived as more objective or progressive than the discriminatory systems of a previous era."[22] Dr. Benjamin points out that tech fixes often hide, speed up, and even deepen discrimination, while appearing neutral and benevolent when compared to racism of a previous era.[23] Technical fixes masquerade as moral behavior disguised to prevent or eliminate human bias. However, they are designed by humans with histories of biases that have the potential to intensify discrimination.[24] *Race after Technology* is offered as a field guide in which Benjamin educates and informs her readers on how proposed technology advances are detrimental to our civil rights in a digital world and reinforces racism[25]—for example, tailored marketing, dragging viral hashtags and memes, crime prediction software, and digital divide.[26] In conclusion, Dr. Benjamin develops a framework she terms as "race critical code studies" to impact how technologies are produced, who has access, and how race and racism influence those with access.[27]

In recent years, the American Library Association, Library of Congress, and comparative organizations and systems that employ library and information science and its professionals have acknowledged their negligence, apprehensions, and difficulties in respecting, serving, or representing ethnicities or nationalities other than their founding and or initial members or representatives. As a result, libraries or information organizations and archival institutions have begun to examine the imbalance or unjust representation of individuals who have been coined or referred to as BIPOC, which represents and concerns Black, Indigenous, and People of Color. Library and information science administrations, professionals, and paraprofessionals are organizing to present and facilitate historical changes in these professions to redeem the soul of America through restorative library culture, reparative description, and decolonizing the catalog.

Restorative justice is a means to a communal end. Restorative libraries are approaching communities holistically to address and repair any harm that has been done repeatedly (in some instances) to individuals, populations, and communities. Every voice matters and every case involves all persons affected by the harm (e.g., the person offended or harmed, the person responsible for the offense, and the community that was impacted by the offense).[28] Restorative library culture practices identify ways to strengthen relationships between individuals and the communities they belong to.[29] Restorative library culture allows an individual to interface with the community in a positive and productive way. RLC holds all community members accountable for their actions and explores alternatives to restoring the many broken souls of America. Restorative justice includes Community Court, which are alternatives to mitigating criminal offenses in the community versus the criminal justice system and partnering with social services to better serve the community and individuals.[30] Restorative library culture and practices have begun to facilitate wellness in our communities, challenge individuals to be accountable in all areas of life and professions, and create an environment that is reflective of traditional and Indigenous cultures.

The Social Networks and Archival Context (SNAC), a free online resource that helps users find archival materials from cultural heritage institutions around the world, its project team, and the indigenous advisory board presented a SNAC edit-a-thon during Indigenous People's Day.[31] Archival materials' records including description are deficient in their representation of Indigenous people, thus increasing misrepresentation and or underrepresented records. SNAC's project team explored and employed and Indigenous advisory board for reparative description to facilitate discovery and sharing, create fuller records, develop recommendation protocols, and build community capacity.[32] The Indigenous advisory board consisted of Indigenous library and archives practitioners and academics.[33] SNAC intends to further its work in establishing an Indigenous Description Group under the umbrella of SNAC's Editorial and Standards Working Group.[34] Most importantly, an Indigenous SNAC editorial guide was developed and utilized during the edit-a-thon. The goal of the project team and advisory board is to publish the guide with open access to help assist archivists with archival cataloging and description of Indigenous materials.[35] It is crucial that Black, Indigenous, and People of Color remain attentive and responsive to advocacies and events related and regarding representation and description in America to effectively influence the future of libraries and archival work.

Decolonizing the catalog was initially a webinar provided by ALA's Reference and User Services Association that explored and argued that with the rise of social injustices, critical conversations about library work, and antiracist description practices related to African American materials and anti-Black racism are necessary and inevitable. Elizabeth Hobart demonstrates challenges users face when searching titles related to racism and antiracism, how usable and findable the material is, and her research method and analysis involving this topic to further support cataloging and discovery.[36] Staci Ross argues that the Library of Congress subject headings are not as reflective of inclusive languages as they should be in serving a diverse population. Ross works with the African American Subject Funnel Project, a part of the Subject Authority Cooperative Program that advocates for more inclusive terminology in LCSH.[37] Michelle Cronquist is a cataloger at the University of North Carolina at Chapel Hill and explains the difficulties in transforming an old nineteenth-century vocabulary with interconnected terms and the project proposals prepared and presented to the Library of Congress that were rejected while others are considered (e.g., the concept of leasing enslaved labor, the preference of enslaved instead of slave).[38] Kelly Farrell works for the Triangle Research Libraries Network, a consortium of four university library systems in North Carolina and supplements the argument with solutions on promoting inclusive languages in information professionals' own perspective and local institutions. Research, proposals, challenges, restorative work ethics, and workflow collaboration related to cataloging are unavoidable to eliminate racial discrimination, digital segregation, and oppression.

We must never forget the leaders and activists who protested, marched, fought, lost, and won on behalf of the liberties in libraries. There has been an increased effort on library and information science officials to acknowledge underrepresented populations and underdeveloped archival works. However, we must never cease to educate, inform, and hold ourselves accountable in the journey to a restorative library culture. With empathy and passion, leaders and community members are capable and willing to organize and execute good and necessary trouble for the soul(s) of America. While technologies are emerging, library and information professionals and archivists are reshaping and transforming library and information science, their professions, and society to handle the drastic and inevitable shift in information and resources. Outreach and advocacy are vital parts of the holistic approach necessary to reshape and transform the library and information science profession. However, if we are not aware, attentive, and active in these theories, then we are not fulfilling our role as information professionals to develop them with effective practices.

**NOTES**

1. Malik Miah, "John Lewis: 'Never Be Afraid to Get in Good Trouble, Necessary Trouble,'" *GreenLeft*, no. 1274, July 26, 2020, https://www.greenleft.org.au/content/john-lewis-never-be-afraid-get-good-trouble-necessary-trouble.
2. Cynthia R. Greenlee, "On the Battle to Desegregate the Nation's Libraries: When the Public Library Wasn't So Public," *Literary Hub*, July 5, 2016, 3. https://lithub.com/on-the-battle-to-desegregate-the-nations-libraries/.
3. Wayne Wiegand, "'Any ideas'? The American Library Association and the Desegregation of Public Libraries in the American South," *Libraries: Culture, History, and Society*, 1, no. 1 (2017): 1–22, https://doi.org/10.5325/libraries.1.1.0001.
4. Ibid., 2.
5. Ibid.
6. Ibid., 14.
7. Ibid., 3.
8. Ibid., 4.
9. Ibid., 12.
10. Ibid., 16.
11. Ibid., 15.
12. Ibid., 18.
13. Safiya U. Noble, *Algorithms of Oppression: How Search Engines Reinforce Racism* (New York: New York University Press, 2018), 137.
14. Ibid., 140.
15. Ibid., 116.
16. Ibid., 141.
17. Ibid., 144.
18. Ibid., 152.

19. Ibid.
20. Ruha Benjamin, *Race after Technology: Abolitionist Tools for the New Jim Code* (Cambridge, UK: Polity Press, 2020), 2.
21. Ibid., 9.
22. Ibid., 5.
23. Ibid., 8.
24. Ibid., 10.
25. Ibid., 36.
26. Ibid.
27. Ibid., 34.
28. Stephen Jackson and Tatiana Swancy, "Creating a Restorative Library Culture," *WebJunction,* March 22, 2023, slide 7, https://www.webjunction.org/content/dam/WebJunction/Documents/webJunction/2023-03/slides-restorative-library-culture.pdf.
29. Ibid., slide 8.
30. Ibid., slide 20; Kirsti MacPherson, "Courting Libraries: Partnerships Bring Social Services and Restorative Justice to Communities," *American Libraries,* 50, no. 6 (2019): 16–17.
31. Lydia Curliss et al., "Reparative Description, Indigenous Partners, and the SNAC edit-a-thon," *Archival Outlook* (March/April 2022): 4–5, 19.
32. Ibid.
33. Ibid., 4.
34. Ibid., 19.
35. Ibid.
36. Elizabeth Hobart et al., "Decolonizing the Catalog: RUSA Webinar Explores Avenues for Antiracist Description," *American Libraries,* 52, nos. 11–12 (2021): 39.
37. Ibid., 40.
38. Ibid., 41.

## WORKS CITED

Benjamin, Ruha. *Race after Technology: Abolitionist Tools for the New Jim Code.* Cambridge, UK: Polity Press, 2020.

Curliss, Lydia et al. "Reparative Description, Indigenous Partners, and the SNAC edit-a-thon." *Archival Outlook* (March/April 2022): 4–5, 19.

Greenlee, Cynthia R. "On the Battle to Desegregate the Nation's Libraries: When the Public Library Wasn't So Public." *Literary Hub,* July 5, 2016. https://lithub.com/on-the-battle-to-desegregate-the-nations-libraries/.

Hobart, Elizabeth et al. "Decolonizing the Catalog: RUSA Webinar Explores Avenues for Antiracist Description." *American Libraries,* 52, nos. 11–12 (2021): 38–41.

Jackson, Stephen, and Tatiana Swancy. "Creating a Restorative Library Culture." *WebJunction,* March 22, 2023. https://www.webjunction.org/content/dam/WebJunction/Documents/webJunction/2023-03/slides-restorative-library-culture.pdf.

MacPherson, Kirsti. "Courting Libraries: Partnerships Bring Social Services and Restorative Justice to Communities." *American Libraries,* 50, no. 6 (2019): 16–17.

Miah, Malik. "John Lewis: 'Never Be Afraid to Get in Good Trouble, Necessary Trouble.'" *GreenLeft,* no. 1274. July 26, 2020. https://www.greenleft.org.au/content/john-lewis-never-be-afraid-get-good-trouble-necessary-trouble.

Noble, Safiya U. *Algorithms of Oppression: How Search Engines Reinforce Racism.* New York: New York University Press, 2018.

Wiegand, Wayne. "'Any ideas'? The American Library Association and the Desegregation of Public Libraries in the American South." *Libraries: Culture, History, and Society,* 1, no. 1 (2017): 1–22. https://doi.org/10.5325/libraries.1.1.0001.

# 4.4

# *Librarian-ish*

Rodney Freeman

Librarians are more than just the titles and boxes that, at times, the general public and sometimes we put ourselves in. I had a dream that a snake bit me. No, it was not a snake. It was a python. I had a dream that a python attacked me. In dreams, creatures and symbols have meanings and sometimes mean something totally different from the initial assumption. What I understand from our family traditions and beliefs is from a book of dreams that rested on my grandma's nightstand. I remember my grandma looking up every dream, and she would rejoice when she had dreams with red birds in them. She was adamant that red birds brought her good luck and money. My grandma would describe her dreams fully and then explain what they meant. She was not the only one in the family who was an avid dream researcher. My grandma's sister and mom also participated in this family tradition. To this day, I love seeing a red bird cross my path, and it makes me think of my grandma and her dream book. So, my dream goes like this: I was riding my bike in a park on a greenway trail with another person I could only see from the back. They were riding in front of me, but I felt something familiar about this person, like someone I used to know. As I am looking forward, I see this person with an orange hoodie riding alongside me and speeding up to get in front of me. I notice we are coming up on an underpass, a pitch-black tunnel. Oh yeah, Chance The Rapper was also riding on a bike beside us, and both Chance The Rapper and my friend passed me by while riding. Up ahead I saw a snake slowly slithering in slow motion and lunging for my friend, but it missed. I stopped and looked while Chance The Rapper tried to ride past, it struck twice, but he fought it off, and then the python, slowly quivering, rose so that it was towering over me, showing its fangs and biting me repeatedly until I wake up, and that is the dream. Jumping back to reality, I glanced at my phone's clock, which flashed 3:14 a.m.

I did a full body check, looking over my chest and arms where I felt the python sink his teeth into me in the dream and making sure it wasn't real, asking myself questions: What the hell was that about and was that a snake or a python and why did it bite me and why the hell was Chance The Rapper in my dream? Of course, I did not have my grandma's handy book of dreams by my bed, but I did have my cell phone. Looking for answers, I did an internet search for what it means to be bitten by a snake or python, and with so many search results and so much information at my fingertips, I had to figure out the correct meaning for this dream. I guess that's how these times are different because my grandma's handbook of dreams was definitive. But searching the internet provides so much information to choose from and sort through that you have to be the one that selects the meaning. I am not a dream expert, so I select the meaning closest to the dream: "A warning signal from your unconscious mind for urgent action to be taken regarding a key situation you are avoiding, neglecting, or disregarding." So that makes me think of everything in my life that I could be neglecting or disregarding. Is it my family, my kids, my job, my business, or my relationship? No, it can't be. Maybe it's something that I am not thinking about. Yeah, maybe it is that distant friend of the family that I am avoiding or something I can't imagine. I see it. An email notification on my phone chimes saying, "Hi Rodney, just checking in to see how you are coming with the essay about your journey as a librarian." Then it hits me. Is this what I have been avoiding and neglecting? Have I not shared my story as a librarian, from being demoted to starting my business, and to why I started using my skills as a librarian to create a database that captures the numerous positive stories about Black people? So maybe it is time to tell why it is so important for Black people to tell their story and tell it the way they see it. An old African proverb goes, "Until the lion learns how to write, every story will glorify the hunter." We are the lions, and we must learn how to write, tell our story, and most importantly, make sure our kids know our story. So let me give you a glimpse into my story.

This pivotal part of my tale started as my managerial career in librarianship was ending. It started at a point in time when I was blind. Maybe that's not the right word; let's say I was unaware and did not know my worth. I was working at a library in Chicago and was brought into an office and told that I would be demoted, not because of my performance but because they wanted to go in a different direction. Not fired, but what they call "reclassified." I was being demoted when just a year prior, I was promoted to assistant commissioner for the downtown library in Chicago. I came to understand that not everyone is the "right fit" for certain positions and titles—that is, you don't conform to us, and you are not supposed to use the role to actually accomplish work—you are a token. Plus, we are having to do too much work to make you fit in. I was not surprised I did not fit in with the administration team and everything they thought they wanted me for. I was the antitoken. I spoke up on issues I believed were wrong and called out people when they were wrong, so I did not neatly fit into a box of their ideas of me. Being told I was being demoted left me questioning who I was and how I messed up this job so badly when I was being praised for my work just a year ago. For a short second, my mind shifted to library science school, thinking that they never mentioned to me or my other classmates of color that politics and racism play a significant role in this profession and can make or break someone's career. These invisible obstacles have toyed with Black librarians and people of color for a long time. Some of our fellow white librarians feel that because a few people of color are becoming administrators, managers, and supervisors, we are taking these positions away from other, well-qualified, more deserving people of noncolor. I would answer yes we are because we are just as qualified as they are and sometimes have more experience coming into the job. After internalizing the situation and a bit of self-reflection, I decided to take back my narrative. I told myself I couldn't just be a librarian, I needed to be more. Before that slight dip in my story, I only wanted to be a library director for the rest of my life. I didn't imagine being or doing anything else, but this experience changed me and made me find myself and who I wanted to become. It was that trauma that ripped off the blinders and made me self-aware.

Aware that I am more than just one thing and that we, as librarians, are also more than just that. It made me question myself, and I came back with answers and more questions. Yes, I am a librarian and work in the profession I fell in love with many years ago, but I am also a Black man, an educated father, and a nerd. Sometimes I can be very social, and sometimes I do not want to talk. How can I reveal to people that many Black librarians are going through similar situations, some even more severe than what I went through? At the same time, show them and us that we are essential to this information profession. One of the conclusions I left my ordeal with is that some of our white counterparts do not know. So, let us build something they can see and find stories that will show them that there are so many more positive stories than the negative ones that are prevalent in mainstream media about Black men and women. I will use the skill set I learned as a librarian and cataloguer to fight against false narratives and stereotypes, calling out lies like the current Florida state curriculum that implies slavery benefited the enslaved. Let us create a platform online where anyone can find these positive stories about us, and the best part of this skillful activism is that we will use the librarian skills to fight against those outlandish narratives. To combat these false images, we will start by posting positive stories on social media because that is where most people get their news, and then we are going to build a database and integrate new technologies that will allow us to attract people to want to use and learn from the content. Let us not make this homework but something fun for everyone to learn Black history. Let us not stop there. Let us uncover all types of stories and bring them to the public. What more can we do?

The point of this chapter is that we librarians are more than just our jobs. We have skills that can be used in many ways that can sustain and help preserve our culture. We continue to be told that we are only one thing. Unfortunately, if you believe that, then that one thing is all you will ever be. However, if you believe you are much more than a title, or a position, you will be surprised at how much more you can become. I believe that Black librarians are much more than we get credit for. We are the ones to make sure books about us and other marginalized communities and little-known histories are captured and archived and that all stories are told and celebrated. We ensure that all people have the ability to find the information that they are looking for. Without Black librarians, finding various stories from varied perspectives and communities would be much more challenging.

I never wanted to become a librarian. I say that because I never considered what it meant to be a librarian or what it means to be a Black librarian and why it matters that we exist in today's society. I identify as a Black man in an overwhelmingly white profession. A profession whose sole importance is ensuring that all citizens of the United States of America have access to information. However, our profession did not always practice what they preached. There are many historical accounts of segregated libraries and libraries for "colored" people that did not provide the same access to information that they had for "white" libraries. So being a librarian, especially a Black librarian, is so important. Because in this world, the only way to truly pursue happiness is if you have the information and knowledge you need to obtain your dreams. So no, I do not identify as just a librarian but something more—a Black man, a creative (I did not know that until I was almost forty) nerd, a comic book historian, a South Side Chicagoan. Because you see, I cannot just identify myself as one thing. I believe when we want to tell our true story, we want the ability to tell the story as we see it, and I did what my heart and God put me on this planet for.

Dreams are funny and often have dual purposes. The more I think about that crazy dream of being bitten by the python and Chance The Rapper riding his bike by my side, maybe that dream was there to push me to write these intended words of encouragement to my fellow librarians, and specifically to Black librarians that we are more than what they say we are, that we are more, and we can do more. We are the torchbearers, the light-bringers. We are the ones that help people because we know that one of the main things that people need and are looking for is information.

# Chapter 4B
# Issues in Library and Information Science Education

## 4.5

## *On the Occasion of the 2018 Graduation Class of SLIS, North Carolina Central University, Durham, North Carolina, Friday, May 11, 2018*

Amina Josey Turner

**REMARKS DELIVERED BY AMINA JOSEY TURNER**

Congratulations Graduates and Good Afternoon.

To Dr. Jon Gant, dean of SLIS; Dr. Ismail Abdullahi, faculty, graduates and friends.

Thank you, Dr. Gant, for extending the invitation to me and to my husband to join in this historic occasion . . . the graduation of the School of Library and Information Sciences' class of 2018 of North Carolina Central University.

This day is historic personally for me because it brings back memories of my father's relationship with North Carolina Central University. I remember my father receiving the Honorary Doctorate of Humanities from North Carolina Central in 1991 presented at St. Joseph's AME Church. My six children, who were school aged then, were with me along with my father's only sister, Melba from Houston. In Dr. Abdullahi's book, *E. J. Josey an Activist Librarian*, Dr. Benjamin Speller referred to E. J. Josey as a true friend of North Carolina Central University citing his several decades of service in an advisory role to the School of Library and Information Sciences.

My father stopped in Fountain, North Carolina, to visit me and the children on his way to NCCU to deliver his papers to the School of Library and Information Sciences back in the 1990s. A more recent memory is captured in a photograph. I was state executive director for NC NAACP at the time when my husband brought Dad on campus to visit Dr. Irene Owens, Dr. Ismail Abdullahi, and Dr. Floyd Hardy along with Dr. George Grant. Dad was in a wheelchair then and we believe that was ten or eleven years ago. I also remember representing my father at the retirement celebration for Dr. Hardy.

Another tidbit of family history: my son had work-study here in the library when Dr. George Grant was the SLIS dean.

But of course, today is an historic occasion for you and for the world because NCCU has deployed highly trained, energetic, tech-savvy professional purveyors of information. Yes, I used a military term because I believe that we are in a state of war: war against disinformation, war against misinformation, war against inequity and poverty, and war against ignorance and racism. I referred to the world because you are not limited to one zip code. You have to see the entire globe as your zip code because of the reach of technology—an integral part of library information science today.

E. J. Josey was a man of principle and vision who advocated for human rights, for equal access to information, pay equity, academic freedom, social responsibility all of which are embodied in the noble ideals of equality, justice, and peace. In other words, E. J. Josey forged ahead to conscientiously democratize librarianship, not only in America but throughout the world. On behalf of the memory of E. J. Josey, God speed to you as we all do our part to win the war!

# 4.6

## *The Beacon Light*

NORTH CAROLINA CENTRAL UNIVERSITY'S SCHOOL OF LIBRARY AND INFORMATION SCIENCES'S HISTORICAL ROLE IN EDUCATING BLACK LIBRARIANS AND PRESENT ROLE IN ADVANCING ARTIFICIAL INTELLIGENCE, BIOMEDICAL KNOWLEDGE, AND DIGITAL EQUITY

Jamillah Scott-Branch, Vernice Faison, and Danielle Colbert-Lewis

North Carolina Central University (NCCU) School of Library and Information Sciences (SLIS) has a distinguished and impressive history characterized by ingenuity and innovation. On April 9, 2023, NCCU SLIS celebrated its eighty-third anniversary. This significant milestone represents the tireless efforts of administrators and support staff at SLIS, both past and present, accomplished and distinguished faculty members, and thousands of SLIS graduates who have contributed significantly to the field of librarianship. The School of Library and Information Sciences at North Carolina Central University has played a significant role in educating Black librarians. The pioneering civil rights activist and library leader E. J. Josey (1924-2009), cofounder of the Black Caucus of the American Library Association (BCALA) and past president of the American Library Association, stated that "NCCU SLIS has stood as a beacon light and served as an intellectual oasis in an environment that was hostile to African Americans who aspired to become librarians."[1] NCCU SLIS preserves and makes accessible the E. J. Josey papers and the history of BCALA n the SLIS archives.[2] Throughout its history, NCCU SLIS has always welcomed a diverse and global student body to prepare them for library and information science careers. This work continues today, providing NCCU SLIS students with valuable opportunities for gaining a competitive edge and real-world work experience. NCCU SLIS award-winning faculty members remain dedicated to addressing issues of diversity, equity, and inclusion and have made meaningful strides in advancing innovation through grant initiatives that promote artificial intelligence and equity research, digital skills development, and mobilizing computable biomedical knowledge. This chapter provides a detailed historical account of NCCU SLIS's past and highlights current initiatives and achievements that offer a modern perspective on the significant efforts undertaken by the last remaining HBCU (Historically Black Colleges and Universities) accredited by the American Library Association to offer the master of library science degree.

## FOUNDING OF THE NCCU AND THE SCHOOL OF LIBRARY AND INFORMATION SCIENCES

North Carolina Central University, located in Durham, North Carolina, was founded as a private institution by Dr. James Edward Shepard in 1910. The school at its inception was named the National Religious Training School and Chautauqua for the Colored Race. In the course of its history, the school's name has changed five times. It finally adopted its current name, North Carolina Central University, in 1969.[3] In 1923, the National Training School, currently North Carolina Central University (NCCU) received funding from the North Carolina General Assembly and was renamed the Durham State Normal School and became the first state-supported liberal arts college for Black students in the nation under the leadership of Dr. Shepard.[4] Dr. James E. Shepard served as president of the school from its founding until his death on October 6, 1947.

According to Crumpton, "In Spring 1934, Dr. Shepard stated that it was important for Black teachers to have knowledge about Library Science."[5] During this time, African Americans were not permitted to attend white schools, and states operated under the separate but equal doctrine. This doctrine "gave constitutional sanction to laws designed to achieve racial segregation by means of separate and equal public facilities and services for African Americans and whites."[6] However, the facilities that were designated for African Americans did not possess the same resources and were of lower quality. There were only a few institutions that provided education and training in librarianship for African Americans. NCCU was one of these institutions, and it was the third library school in the country to be located at an African American university, according to Stevenson.[7] In the summer of 1934, "the first library science courses at North Carolina College for Negroes (NCCN) were taught by the university librarian, Parepa Watson Jackson, and assistant librarian, Marjorie Shepard, daughter of President Shepard."[8] The library courses were taught in the law school basement. In 1938, "Eloise Ward Phelps became the school's first full-time library science teacher."[9] The North Carolina College for Negroes was in the early stages of developing a library science program that would become one of the few higher education institutions responsible for educating and training a significant number of African Americans in the librarianship profession and preparing students for leadership positions in libraries.

In 1939, the supervisor for the North Carolina State Department of Public Instruction, Mary Peacock Douglas, came to NCCN and "organized a program for school librarians—this formed the nucleus of the School of Library Science."[10] The library science program at NCCN continued its development and the North Carolina General Assembly in the 1939 Session Law Chapter 65, Action 2 states the following authorization:

> WHEREAS the number of Negroes in North Carolina who de-sire graduate and professional courses is increasing; and WHEREAS, it is the duty of the State of North Carolina to provide for such needs: Now, therefore, The General Assembly of North Carolina do enact: The Board of Trustees of the North Carolina College for Negroes is authorized and empowered to establish Departments of Law, Pharmacy, and Library Science at the above-named institution whenever there are applicants desirous of such courses. That said Board of Trustees of the North Carolina College for Negroes may add other professional courses from time to time as the need for the same is shown, and the funds of the State will justify.[11]

In 1941, approximately two years later, the library science program at NCCN became a professional school of library science. The University of North Carolina dean of library science, Dr. Susan Gray Akers, served as the first dean of NCCN's newly developed School of Library Science program. She served in this position part time working one day a week on the NCCN campus. Akers held this position until her death in 1946.[12] According to SLIS,

> Three programs were offered during the first two years of operation of the School of Library Science. The professional program for the Bachelor of Library Science (BLS) degree was established for persons holding a baccalaureate degree at the time of entrance, and undergraduate majors and minors were offered through the College of Arts and Science. The undergraduate major was discontinued in 1943 and in 1953 the School awarded its final BLS degree.[13]

Daniel E. Moore became the dean of the library school in 1949 and remained in that position until 1963. Under his leadership, the school sponsored events such as its annual Book Bazaar during Book Week to market the library science program. This event brought together teachers, parents with young children, future students, staff across campus, and community members from throughout the region to learn about the library school. Furthermore, the library school incorporated annual trips to places such as the Library of Congress, the Smithsonian Institution, Folger Shakespeare Library, the Supreme Court Building, the National Archives, Howard University, the Time Magazine Archives, and the Life Magazine Archives to enhance student knowledge and exposure to the various types of libraries.[14]

North Carolina Central University, like many Black institutions of higher learning, was hampered by a "budget which was very small in proportion to what was needed. The school needed funds to buy books, fill in gaps in periodicals, hire ample staff, and operate sufficiently."[15] In spite of all these financial difficulties, 1950 was a time of significant "growth and enrollment more than doubled in 1950 to one hundred and ten students from forty-eight students in 1940 and from 28 students in 1930."[16]

In 1946, Miss Dorothy Williams was appointed the first full-time dean of the library science program. Her tenure was for one year and she was succeeded by Benjamin F. Smith, and he served as dean for two years (1947-1949).[17] The library science program directed its efforts toward gaining accreditation from the American Library Association. At the conclusion of summer school in 1947, "Miss Evelyn Pope and Mrs. Ann Johnson worked to make a listing of items needed by the library school before inviting the American Library Association for an accreditation visit. That same year Dr. Shepard was preparing to contact Miss Anita Miller Hostetter from the American Library Association for this purpose."[18] Miss Hostetter was never contacted due to the unforeseen death of Dr. Shepard, college president. In the 1950s, the library science program continued to flourish. The school implemented the library of science master's degree program in 1950 and the first recipient of the MLS degree was in 1951. The School of Library Science relocated to the third floor of the James E. Shepard Memorial Library, previously housed in the administration building.[19] It is still located on the third floor of James E. Shepard Memorial Library. The School of Library Science program served and educated students from the entire southern region. In the summer of 1955, the student body was comprised of individuals including eighty-three students from North Carolina, eleven students from South Carolina, six students from Virginia, three students from Georgia, two students from Florida, and one student from New Jersey.[20] Upon the death of Dr. Daniel Moore, Ms. Evelyn Pope, a faculty member since 1945, succeeded him as acting dean of the School of Library Science and served in that position from 1963 to 1970.[21]

The North Carolina College at Durham's name was changed to the North Carolina Central University by the North Carolina General Assembly in 1969, and later in 1970, Dr. Annette Lewis Phinazee became the dean of the North Carolina Central University School of Library Science. She was the first faculty member of the School of Library Science to hold a doctoral degree. In the same year, "Phinazee was given the charge by Dr. Albert Whiting, president of North Carolina Central

University, to prepare the school for accreditation by 1975 or the school would be closed."[22] This was a great challenge with a budget of only $96,937, just two other faculty members, a small student body of twenty-one students (four full-time students), and a small collection of four thousand volumes.[23]

In the 1970s. the library science program received needed funds from private organizations such as a $44,000 grant from the United States Office of Education to implement an Institute for Public Librarians; a $20,000 grant from the Xero Corporation to start an Early Childhood Library Specialist Program; $53,265 from the United States Office of Education for the African American Materials Project; and $150,000 from the Andrew Mellon Foundation that was distributed in increments of $50,000 for three years. The school's budget increased during the duration of 1970 through 1975 from $96,930 to $321,734. These monies were essential and allowed the faculty size to increase from three to nine; allowed the addition of a librarian and support staffs; and collection size increased from four thousand volumes to twenty-five thousand volumes.[24]

The library science program was accredited by the American Library Association in the spring of 1975. In the midst of this achievement, the department received numerous congratulations and well wishes from individuals throughout the country for this major accomplishment. Other accomplishments and highlights in the 1970s included the establishment of the NCCU SLS Alumni Association in 1971; the publishing of two books, *Black American Writers, 1773–1949* and *Newspapers and Periodicals by and about Black People: Southeastern Library Holdings* with a grant from the US Office of Education; establishment of the Beta Xi Chapter of Beta Phi Mu in 1976; the election of Dr. Phinazee as vice president/president-elect of the North Carolina Library Association in 1973; expansion of public library courses in 1974; Dr. Kenneth Shearer's appointment as editor of *Public Libraries* in 1978; the establishment of the William Tucker Collection, a collection of children's works by African American authors and illustrators; establishment of the first NCCU alumni dinner at the ALA conference in 1976; the establishment of late afternoon, evening, and Saturday morning classes; Dr. Benjamin Speller's appointment as assistant dean in 1973; Dr Phinazee's appointment to the Public Librarian Certification Commission in 1978; and Dr. Phinazee serving as a North Carolina delegate to the 1979 White House Conference on Libraries and Information Science.[25]

The major accomplishments and highlights of the School of Library Science program in the 1980s included the name of the school changing to the NCCU School of Library and Information Sciences; Dr. Mohamed H. Zehery, former faculty member 1974–1975, inviting Dr. Phinazee, Dr. Speller, Dr. Shearer, and Dr. Morien to conduct a workshop in the Persian Gulf for librarians and information specialists; the school establishing the first computer laboratory in a library school in North Carolina in 1980; *The Black Librarian in the Southeast: Reminiscence, Activities, Challenges* being published; and in 1982 Dr. Robert Ballard taking on the role of editor for *Sci-Tech News*.[26]

On July 25, 1983, Dr. Phinazee was surprised with a luncheon in her honor for her years of outstanding service and the many contributions she made to librarianship and educating African Americans. Over three hundred people attended, including faculty, staff, alumni, NCCU officials, and representatives from all across the nation from different library organizations. The event was held at the Governor's Inn in Research Triangle Park.[27] On September 17, 1983, Dr. Aletha Annette Lewis Hoage Phinazee died after serving as dean of the School of Library Science since 1970. Dr. Benjamin Speller served as acting dean and became dean of the School of Library Science in 1986.[28]

The major accomplishments and highlights of the School of Library Science program in the 1990s included the school establishing an interdisciplinary program in information science leading to the master of information science (MIS) degree, establishing a joint master's degree with the School of Business.[29]

Accomplishments and highlights of the School of Library Science program in the 2000s included establishing the first digital class and digital collection by the students in that class in 2007. Also, the School of Library and Information Sciences hosted the first digital conference entitled "Digital Libraries: Continuing the Vision of Dr. James E. Shepard" at NCCU on April 27, 2007.[30]

The deans of the School of Library and Information Sciences are as follows:

- Susan Grey Akers, 1941–1946
- Dorothy Williams, 1946–1947
- Benjamin F. Smith, 1947–1949
- Daniel Eric Moore, 1949–1963
- Evelyn B. Pope, 1963–1970
- Annette Phinazee, 1970–1983
- Benjamin F. Speller, 1983–2003
- Robert Ballard, 2003–2005 (acting dean)
- Irene Owens, 2005–2015
- Jon P. Gant, 2015–Present

## NCCU SLIS CURRENT RESEARCH PROJECT AND INITIATIVES

The library and information sciences graduate programs have expanded thanks to the valuable contributions of NCCU SLIS faculty and administrators working to secure external funding. Since 2020, SLIS has been awarded over $3 million in grant funding to support program offerings and implement innovative projects. The National Science Foundation awarded Siobahn Day Grady, PhD, an assistant professor at NCCU SLIS, a $190,000 grant in 2020 to improve the functionality of self-driving cars.[31]

In 2020, NCCU SLIS established the Laboratory for Artificial Intelligence and Equity Research (LAIER).[32] LAIER is an interdisciplinary learning space at SLIS that provides graduate researchers with the opportunity to explore topics such as machine learning, human-computer interaction, and other special topics in artificial intelligence. Under the leadership of Dr. Grady, the laboratory also focuses on diversity and inclusion and looks at how technology can be accessible to more people. Among the many benefits of this grant is that it contributes to safety and efficiency in the transportation sector, as well as demonstrating SLIS faculty members' cutting-edge research and technical expertise.

In 2021, Deborah Swain, PhD, a full professor at NCCU SLIS, was awarded a $94,695 Institute of Museum and Library Services (IMLS) grant to create a pilot course and online learning materials in support of mobilizing computable biomedical knowledge. This initiative aims to enable librarians and information professionals to build and maintain repositories and databases. This course addressed the need for information professionals to stay current with advancements in technology, information, and knowledge management. Research and practice can be brought closer together through the availability of computational information. Training through the pilot course demonstrated how "electronic journals offer 'dynamic knowledge' that readers can immediately validate."[33] Through this project, LIS professionals learned how to design better archives and repositories to increase access to information and create sustainable open educational resources.[34]

Providing opportunities for growth and graduating students with marketable skills is a top priority for NCCU SLIS. To help facilitate the process of digital skills development, SLIS has partnered with IBM Skills Academy to provide learners a multiyear opportunity to upskill and learn marketable technical skills and earn IBM industry-recognized digital badges. Topics covered in the IBM Quantum Education initiative include artificial intelligence, cybersecurity, blockchain technology, data science, the Internet of Things, cloud computing, design thinking, and quantum computing. This partnership was announced in September 2020 with IBM providing guest lectures, curriculum content, software and faculty training. Moreover, both faculty and students can receive badges and learn relevant skills.[35] Furthermore, in 2022, NCCU SLIS also partnered with Princeton University Library to offer two-year fellowships for library and information science graduates. This fellowship provides SLIS graduates new to the profession with valuable opportunities to gain practical experience and learn from experienced library professionals. This partnership is significant because it provides NCCU SLIS graduates with access to resources and expertise from a leading research institution.[36]

Additionally in 2022, NCCU was awarded a $2,996,134 grant from the National Telecommunications and Information Administration's Connecting Minority Communities Program to support the Digital Equity Leadership Program (DELP).[37] This program aims to address the lack of broadband access, connectivity, adoption, and equity in the university and surrounding communities. This initiative is led by NCCU SLIS faculty and leadership within the NCCU information technology department. In addition to addressing an issue that affects many communities, the program highlights the role that information professionals can play in promoting and advocating for digital equity.[38]

Throughout its eighty-three-year history, the North Carolina Central University School of Library and Information Science has played a crucial role in empowering African American students to succeed in librarianship and a variety of other fields. While originally established as one of the few institutions accessible to African Americans, the school has since diversified its student body, attracting students from a range of backgrounds and cultures. SLIS remains a leader in producing exceptional information professionals thanks to its outstanding faculty and commitment to innovation and advocacy. As NCCU's School of Library and Information Sciences continues to educate and inspire a new generation of professionals, its legacy as a pillar of library and information science education remains as strong as ever.

## NCCU SLIS TIMELINE OF RECENT ACHIEVEMENTS (2020–PRESENT)[39]

- 2020: Siobahn Day Grady, PhD, assistant professor at NCCU School of Library and Information Sciences was awarded a $190,000 grant from the National Science Foundation to help improve the function of self-driving cars.
- 2020: NCCU SLIS established The Laboratory for Artificial Intelligence and Equity Research (LAIER) led by Siobahn Day Grady, PhD, assistant professor, library and information science.
- 2020: NCCU SLIS partners with IBM Skills Academy, a comprehensive, skills-oriented training and badging program designed to empower students and help them gain skills needed to excel in today's high demand job market. Training areas include artificial intelligence, cybersecurity, blockchain technology, data science, Internet of Things, cloud computing, design thinking, and quantum computing.
- 2021: Alexandra Chassanoff, PhD, assistant professor at the NCCU School of Library and Information Sciences was awarded the 2021 Preservation Publication Award, presented by the Society of American Archivists for the handbook *OSSArcFlow: Guide to Documenting Born-Digital Archival Workflows* that she and Colin Post developed.
- 2021: Deborah Swain, PhD, professor at the NCCU School of Library and Information Sciences awarded an IMLS grant for $94,695 to develop a pilot course and deliver online learning materials to enable librarians and information professionals to build and maintain repositories and databases for mobilizing computable biomedical knowledge.
- 2022: NCCU is awarded a $2,996,134 grant from the Department of Commerce's National Telecommunications and Information Administration's Connecting Minority Communities Program. This grant supports NCCU's Digital Equity Leadership Program (DELP), which aims

- to address the lack of broadband access, connectivity, adoption, and equity at the university and surrounding anchor communities. This initiative is led by the NCCU SLIS faculty and leadership within NCCU's information technology department.
- 2022: Jon Gant, PhD, dean of the NCCU School of Library Sciences, was appointed to the Federal Communication Commission's Communication Equity and Diversity Council.
- 2022: Maya Hamer and Christopher Lawson, NCCU SLIS graduate students, were selected as University Innovation Fellows at Stanford University.
- 2022: NCCU School of Library and Information Sciences partners with the Princeton University Library, offering opportunities for library and information science graduates to earn valuable knowledge during a comprehensive two-year fellowship.
- 2022: NCCU SLIS students are hired to work in partnership with Getty Images and NCCU's James E. Shepard Memorial Library to digitize and preserve the NCCU photographic collection.

Degree programs and collaborations include:

- NC Central University School of Law, MLS/JD, MIS/JD
- NC Central University School of Education Technology, MA/MIS
- NC Central University School of Business, MBA/MIS
- NC Central University Department of Public Administration, MPA/MIS
- Quality Matters (QM) Training for instructors, courses are mostly online at SLIS. The MIS degree program at SLIS is all online.
- Dean Gant is a member of the North Carolina Public Librarian Certification Commission. The commission sets minimum standards for public librarians to assure the best public library service to all North Carolinians.

**NOTES**

1. Kathryn C. Stevenson, "Annette Lewis Phinazee and the North Carolina Central University School of Library and Information Sciences, 1970–1983," in *Educating Black Librarians. Papers from the 50th Anniversary Celebration of the School of Library and Information Sciences, North Carolina Central University*, edited by Benjamin F. Speller Jr. (Jefferson, NC: McFarland & Company, 1991), 120.
2. "Archives," Black Caucus of the American Library Association, accessed October 26, 2022, https://www.bcala.org/ejjoseyarchives.
3. "Our Heritage," North Carolina Central University, accessed April 6, 2023, https://www.nccu.edu/we-are-nc-central/our-heritage#:~:text=In%201923%2C%20the%20North%20Carolina,arts%20college%20for%20black%20students.
4. Kathryn C. Stevenson and Benjamin F. Speller Jr., "An Historical Chronology of the North Carolina Central University School of Library and Information Sciences," in *Educating Black Librarians. Papers from the 50th Anniversary Celebration of the School of Library and Information Sciences, North Carolina Central University*, edited by Benjamin F. Speller Jr. (Jefferson, NC: McFarland & Company, 1991), 143.
5. K. Crumpton, "The Development of the North Carolina Central University School of Library Science," North Carolina Central University (1976), 3.
6. "Separate But Equal," Cornell Law School, accessed April 6, 2023, https://www.law.cornell.edu/wex/separate_but_equal#:~:text=Implementation%20of%20the%20%E2%80%9Cseparate%20but,for%20African%20Americans%20and%20whites.
7. Stevenson, "Annette Lewis Phinazee," 119.
8. Stevenson and Speller, "An Historical Chronology," 143.
9. Ibid.
10. Crumpton, "Development," 1.
11. General Assembly of North Carolina, "1963/65 Session Laws, Ch. 65, Sec. 2," On the Books, https://onthebooks.lib.unc.edu/law/1963-65-session-laws-ch-65-sec-2/.
12. Rosemary Ruhig Dumont, "The Educating of Black Librarians: An Historical Perspective," *Journal of Education for Library and Information Science*, 26, no. 4 (1986): 233–49, https://www.jstor.org/stable/40323272.
13. "About SLIS," About SLIS, North Carolina Central University, https://www.nccu.edu/slis/about-slis.
14. Crumpton, "Development," 5.
15. Ibid., 4.
16. Ibid.
17. Stevenson and Speller, "An Historical Chronology," 144.
18. Crumpton, "Development," 3.
19. Stevenson and Speller, "An Historical Chronology," 144.
20. Crumpton, "Development," 4.
21. "North Carolina Central University's School of Library and Information Sciences Host Digital Conference," Targeted News Service, April 20, 2007, ProQuest, http://nclive.org/cgi-bin/nclsm?url=http://search.proquest.com/wire-feeds/north-carolina-central-universitys-school-library/docview/468245333/se-2.
22. Stevenson, "Annette Lewis Phinazee," 126.
23. Ibid.
24. Crumpton, "Development," 5–6.
25. Stevenson, "Annette Lewis Phinazee," 128–32.
26. Stevenson and Speller, "An Historical Chronology," 148–49.
27. "About," North Carolina Central University School of Library & Information Science Digital Library, North Carolina Central University School of Library & Information Sciences, https://www.nccuslis.org/digitallibrary/about.html.
28. Stevenson and Speller, "An Historical Chronology," 148.
29. Andre' Vann, "Soaring of the Legacy: A Concise History of North Carolina Central University 1910–2010," NCCU NC DOCKS (North Carolina Digital Online Collection of Knowledge and Scholarship), 2021, 31, https://libres.uncg.edu/ir/nccu/clist.aspx?id=25607.
30. "North Carolina Central University's School of Library and Information Sciences Host Digital Conference," Targeted News Service, April 20, 2007. ProQuest.

31. Renee Elder, "Information Systems Professor to Research Self-Driving Cars," North Carolina Central University, May 19, 2020, https://www.nccu.edu/news/information-systems-professor-research-self-driving-cars.
32. "The Laboratory for Artificial Intelligence and Equity Research (LAIER)," North Carolina Central University, https://www.nccu.edu/slis/laboratory-artificial-intelligence-and-equity-research-laier.
33. "MCBK Recruitment," MCBK Recruitment, North Carolina Central University, https://www.nccu.edu/mcbk-home/mcbk-recruitment.
34. Ibid.
35. "NCCU SLIS Partners with IBM Skills Academy," North Carolina Central University School of Library and Information Sciences, North Carolina Central University, 2020, https://www.nccu.edu/slis/nccu-slis-partners-ibm-skills-academy.
36. Princeton University, "Princeton University Library/North Carolina Central University Early Career Fellowship Program," Princeton University, February 24, 2022, https://inclusive.princeton.edu/news/princeton-university-librarynorth-carolina-central-university-early-career-fellowship-program.
37. National Telecommunications and Information Administration, "Biden-Harris Administration Announces $10.6 Million in Internet for All Grants to Five Minority-Serving Colleges and Universities," October 5, 2022, https://www.ntia.gov/press-release/2022/biden-harris-administration-announces-106-million-internet-all-grants-five.
38. "Digital Equity Leadership Program (DELP)," North Carolina Central University School of Library and Information Science, North Carolina Central University, 2022, https://www.nccu.edu/school-of-library-and-information-sciences/digital-equity-leadership-program.
39. "About SLIS."

**WORKS CITED**

"About." North Carolina Central University School of Library & Information Sciences Digital Library, North Carolina Central University School of Library & Information Sciences. https://www.nccuslis.org/digitallibrary/about.html.

"About SLIS." North Carolina Central University School of Library and Information Sciences, North Carolina Central University. https://www.nccu.edu/slis/about-slis.

"Archives." Black Caucus of the American Library Association, October 26, 2022. https://www.bcala.org/ejjoseyarchives.

Crumpton, K. "The Development of the North Carolina Central University School of Library Science." North Carolina Central University, 1976.

"Digital Equity Leadership Program (DELP)." North Carolina Central University School of Library and Information Sciences, North Carolina Central University, 2022. https://www.nccu.edu/school-of-library-and-information-sciences/digital-equity-leadership-program.

Dumont, Rosemary Ruhig. "The Educating of Black Librarians: An Historical Perspective." *Journal of Education for Library and Information Science*, 26, no. 4 (1986): 233–49. https://www.jstor.org/stable/40323272.

Elder, Renee. "Information Systems Professor to Research Self-Driving Cars." North Carolina Central University, May 19, 2020. https://www.nccu.edu/news/information-systems-professor-research-self-driving-cars.

General Assembly of North Carolina. "1963/65 Session Laws, Ch. 65, Sec. 2." On the Books. https://onthebooks.lib.unc.edu/law/1963-65-session-laws-ch-65-sec-2/.

Institute of Museum and Library Services. https://imls.gov/grants/awarded/re-250159-ols-21.

"The Laboratory for Artificial Intelligence and Equity Research (LAIER)." North Carolina Central University. https://www.nccu.edu/slis/laboratory-artificial-intelligence-and-equity-research-laier.

"MCBK Recruitment." MCBK Recruitment. North Carolina Central University. https://www.nccu.edu/mcbk-home/mcbk-recruitment.

National Issues Forums Institute. "Jon Gant." National Issues Forums. https://www.nifi.org/en/directors/jon-gant.

National Telecommunications and Information Administration. "Biden-Harris Administration Announces $10.6 Million in Internet for All Grants to Five Minority-Serving Colleges and Universities." October 5, 2022. https://www.ntia.gov/press-release/2022/biden-harris-administration-announces-106-million-internet-all-grants-five.

"NCCU SLIS Partners with IBM Skills Academy." North Carolina Central University School of Library and Information Sciences, North Carolina Central University, 2020. https://www.nccu.edu/slis/nccu-slis-partners-ibm-skills-academy.

North Carolina Central University: A History of Units and Programs from 1910–2010. North Carolina Central University, 2010.

"North Carolina Central University's School of Library and Information Sciences Host Digital Conference." Targeted News Service, April 20, 2007. ProQuest, http://nclive.org/cgi-bin/nclsm?url=http://search.proquest.com/wire-feeds/north-carolina-central-universitys-school-library/docview/468245333/se-2.

"Our Heritage." North Carolina Central University. https://www.nccu.edu/we-are-nc-central/our-heritage#:~:text=In%201923%2C%20the%20North%20Carolina,arts%20college%20for%20black%20students.

Princeton University. "Princeton University Library/North Carolina Central University Early Career Fellowship Program." Princeton University, February 24, 2022. https://inclusive.princeton.edu/news/princeton-university-librarynorth-carolina-central-university-early-career-fellowship-program.

"Separate But Equal." Cornell Law School. https://www.law.cornell.edu/wex/separate_but_equal#:~:text=Implementation%20of%20the%20%E2%80%9Cseparate%20but,for%20African%20Americans%20and%20whites.

Society of American Archivists. "Preservation Publication Award: Alexandra Chassanoff and Colin Post." Society of American Archivists. https://www2.archivists.org/2021-Preservation-Publication-Award-Alexandra-Chassanoff-and-Colin-Post.

Speller, Benjamin F., Jr. *Educating Black Librarians. Papers from the 50th Anniversary Celebration of the School of Library and Information Sciences, North Carolina Central University.* Jefferson, NC: McFarland & Company, 1991.

Stevenson, Kathryn C. "Annette Lewis Phinazee and the North Carolina Central University School of Library and Information Sciences, 1970-1983." In *Educating Black Librarians. Papers from the 50th Anniversary Celebration of the School of Library and Information Sciences, North Carolina Central University*, edited by Benjamin F. Speller Jr. Jefferson, NC: McFarland & Company, 1991.

Stevenson, Kathryn C., and Benjamin F. Speller Jr. "An Historical Chronology of the North Carolina Central University School of Library and Information Sciences." In *Educating Black Librarians. Papers from the 50th Anniversary Celebration of the School of Library and Information Sciences, North Carolina Central University*, edited by Benjamin F. Speller Jr. Jefferson, NC: McFarland & Company, 1991.

Vann, Andre'."Soaring of the Legacy: A Concise History of North Carolina Central University 1910-2010. NC Docks Digital Online Collection of Knowledge and Scholarship." NCCU NC DOCKS (North Carolina Digital Online Collection of Knowledge and Scholarship). https://libres.uncg.edu/ir/nccu/clist.aspx?id=25607.

Wills, L. D. "NCCU Students Join Prestigious University Innovation Fellows Program." North Carolina Central University. July 20, 2022. https://www.nccu.edu/news/nccu-students-join-prestigious-university-innovation-fellows-program.

# 4.7

## HBCUs and LIS Education

A LEGACY AND COUNTERSTORY

Ana Ndumu, Renate Chancellor, and Tina Rollins

The 2000 edition of the *Handbook of Black Librarianship* captured the then state of higher education specifically in relation to historically Black campuses. Affirmative action, perceptions of Historically Black Colleges and Universities' (henceforth HBCU) inferiority and irrelevance, along with technological and financial solvency were top of mind. E. J. Josey aptly noted that "an excellent library is central to the intellectual life of a Black college, and the future of the Black college may very well depend on the quality of the library."[1]

Certainly, HBCUs were robustly covered in previous iterations of the *Handbook of Black Librarianship*, as they are in this volume. However, there has not yet been a dedicated chapter on the contributions of these campuses toward library and information science education itself. Stated differently, as Josey and DeLoach aptly note, HBCU librarians are instrumental in achieving their campus missions. Yet what of would-be, current, and emerging influences in the other direction, that is, what HBCUs did, could have, continue, and are sure to bring to the library professions? Our aim in this chapter is to first chronicle the history of LIS education at HBCU campuses, the ways in which these efforts were vehemently subjugated by white racialized LIS powers that be, and how HBCU librarians continue to interrupt and advance mainstream LIS professionalization. The remarkable efforts of HBCU library faculty and thinkers, like the (counter)stories of HBCUs librarians, deserve to be told.

### HISTORIC SUPPRESSION

Black librarian training and development traces back to African Americans' renegade literacy and educational tactics that existed long before the first school of library economy at Columbia University came to be in 1887.[2] By the time that Melville Dewey and his contemporaries matured both the American Library Association and the Columbia program, Black information scientists such as Ida B. Wells, Arturo Schomburg, Carter G. Woodson—none of which held library credentials—were well on their way to profound information management and Black cultural recordkeeping. Further, dozens of African American institutions of higher learning, eventually recognized as HBCUs in 1964, had by this point been established, several with reading rooms and acting librarians.[3] Simply put, Black efforts to create libraries of all types—and, crucially, worldwide—existed well before the makings of what is now known as library and information science. Edward Christopher Williams, the first professionally trained Black librarian and first to pursue a doctorate at Columbia University, along with Dorothy Porter Wesley, the first librarian to graduate from Columbia's library school, succeeded in spite of, not because of, white library professionalization. Black librarianship defies US librarianship's origin story.

One might consider Columbia University a microcosm of the field's views toward Black people who were barred from this and other early library schools. We look to examples such as Syracuse University's 1943 assertion that "the attitude toward the admission of negroes [sic] at Syracuse has not changed" as well as the University of Pittsburgh's unequivocal denial of Black enrollment: "On the admission of Black students to Carnegie Library School, I will have to ask you to not list this school as one that admits Black people. There has been a longstanding trustee policy against it."[4] Ironically, Dr. Josey would eventually avail his professorship at the University of Pittsburgh[5] to create a powerful pipeline of African American PhDs in library and information sciences, including Dr. Ismail Abdullahi, who trained as many as 1,500 librarians as a Clark Atlanta University and North Carolina Central University LIS professor, along with Dr. Carla Hayden, the first woman and African American librarian of Congress.

Once we ascertain how oppressive race-making or racial stratification in the United States has undermined Black intellectual aspirations,[6] efforts to thwart HBCU *and* African American involvement in LIS become apparent.[7] This strategic icing out is such that early twentieth-century white library leaders called for a separate, far-away library school for Black people in Hampton, Virginia, which we discuss further in this chapter. The same anti-Black racist divide would see that there were separate, neighboring Black and white library schools in Atlanta (Clark Atlanta University and Emory University) and Durham (North Carolina Central University and University of North Carolina at Chapel Hill). Given the LIS field's divisive tactics, African Americans' endeavors to create their own LIS programs upend the LIS status quo. Early and present-day HBCU-centered library pedagogy and professionalization must be spotlighted, and we do so in this chapter.

## HISTORIC DEVELOPMENT

### Hampton University (1925–1949)

Hampton University's past and present display a commitment to promoting the education and advancement of people of color within the library and information science (LIS) field. The Hampton Library School was founded in September 1925 by a grant from the Carnegie Corporation. The first and only library school for Black people to issue a bachelor's degree in library science, the program earned accreditation from the Board of Education for Librarianship of the American Library Association. Beginning as a junior undergraduate school, the entrance requirement was raised to three years of approved college work in 1929, and to graduation from a standard four year college in 1934.[8] The library school program lasted until 1939 when it was sadly cut due to lack of funding.

Hampton played a major role in providing a space to advance the state of Black librarianship. In 1927, the Carnegie Corporation financed a conference of librarians at what was then Hampton Institute. Thomas Fountain Blue, head of the Louisville Free Libraries Colored Branches was the conference founder.[9] The mantle of convening Black librarians continues. Through generous grants from the Institute of Museum and Library Services (IMLS) in 2017 and 2020, Hampton University's William R. and Norma B. Harvey Library continues to be on the forefront of initiatives to bring attention to the lack of diversity regarding people of color in the LIS field. The 2017 IMLS grant funded a national forum that brought attendees from across the country to discuss the persistent lack of diversity in the field. The 2020 IMLS award funds a project that pairs EDI consultants with library organizations to help create, implement, and assess recruitment and retention initiatives.

### North Carolina Central University (1939–Present)

The School of Library and Information Sciences (SLIS) at North Carolina Central University (NCCU) is the sole remaining HBCU library and information science (LIS) program. It was authorized by the state legislature in 1939 when the charter of the then North Carolina College for Negroes was amended to allow for the establishment of graduate and professional programs at the college, thus furthering the goal of educating Black librarians in the state of North Carolina.[10]

During the first two years of the program, the bachelor of library science degree was offered to undergraduate majors and minors in the College of Arts and Sciences. SLIS was formed as a professional school in 1942.[11] It became the first state-funded library school in the nation at a HBCU.[12] Although the undergraduate major was discontinued in 1943, the master of library science (MLS) program was developed seven years later in 1950 with the first MLS awarded in 1951.[13] The program has been continuously accredited by the American Library Association since 1975. Similar to many library science programs in the 1980s, the name of the school was changed to the School of Library and Information Sciences in 1984.

SLIS has been led by a number of trailblazing deans: Susan Gray Ackers (1941–1946), Dorothy Williams Collins (1946–1947), Benjamin Smith (1947–1948), Daniel Moore (1949–1963), Evelyn Pope (1963–1979), Annette Phinazee (1970–1983), Benjamin Speller (1983–2003), Irene Owens (2005–2016), and the most recent dean, Jon Gant (2016–2024). From 1970 to 1995, E. J. Josey played a prominent advisory role in the school. He mentored faculty and guided them in their research, he worked closely with deans to recruit students, and he often mentored students he helped recruit.[14] For eighty-four years, North Carolina Central has successfully educated librarians for the state of North Carolina. Through strong leadership and advisory from leading Black librarians, NCCU remains the sole HBCU LIS program.

### Clark Atlanta University (1941-2005)

The School of Library Services in Atlanta, Georgia, opened in September 1941, just two years after the closing of the Hampton University library science program.[15] The closure of the Hampton program created a pipeline of sixty-three applicants and twenty-four students who enrolled in the inaugural class. Students were Black undergraduates from four neighboring HBCUs in the predominantly Black Atlanta region and from HBCUs from other parts of Georgia, as well as Florida, Kentucky, Louisiana, Massachusetts, North Carolina, Tennessee, Texas, and Virginia.[16]

The school had three overarching goals: 1) to provide one year of training that would prepare students to work in a variety of library settings; 2) serving library patrons in the South (particularly due to racist Jim Crow laws in the Deep South); and 3) offer a curriculum that emphasized the core techniques and tenets of librarianship, such as situating every library as a democratizing place where everyone is welcome regardless of race, gender, and socioeconomic status.[17] The library science program was also invigorated by the civil rights movement that prompted activism and mobilizing efforts between Birmingham, Alabama, and Atlanta, Georgia.[18]

The school was accredited by the American Library Association Board of Education for Librarianship in 1943 and was led by two pioneering women deans: Eliza Gleason (1941-1945), the first African American to earn a doctorate in library sciences, and Virginia Lacy Jones (1945-1981), the second African American to earn a doctorate in library science who served as the school's second dean.[19] In 1989, Atlanta University merged with neighboring Clark University to form Clark Atlanta University. Although both universities were a part of a consortium of five HBCUs in Atlanta, Atlanta University exclusively offered graduate education with one of its programs being the School of Library Studies.[20]

The Clark Atlanta University School of Library and Information Studies closed in 2005 under much controversy. And, while there are still many questions around the reason for the closure, administrators attributed the university's financial challenges as the main factors. In 2017, a reception was held at the National Conference for African American Librarians to commemorate the historic Clark Atlanta University School of Library and Information Studies. The event included former deans Lorene Brown and Anita O'Neal and featured testimonies from Clark Atlanta University SLIS faculty and alumni, along with proclamations from national leaders such as the late John Lewis, Georgia's longtime US congressional representative.[21]

### University of the District of Columbia (1971-1979)

As the only public university and one of two HBCUs in the nation's capital, the University of the District of Columbia (UDC) is the product of a 1977 consolidation of three universities: Federal City College, Washington Technical Institute, and D.C. Teacher's College. The UDC Department of Media, Information and Learning Systems was established during the transition. Developed to be an affordable alternative to strict admissions policies at the Catholic University's library science program, the only other library science program in Washington, DC, the mission of the UDC library science program was to produce culturally conscious community-oriented librarians. The program administrators believed it was "virtually impossible for many minority members to enroll" at Catholic University.[22] They further stated "the need for Black people—especially Black men—in the media science professions."[23]

The library science program, designed for students seeking a master's of media services, was centered around the organization and dissemination of print and electronic resources. The first classes were offered in 1971. The core curriculum consisted of ten courses that included: Media Bibliographic Organization and Description; Building Media Collections; Multimedia Technology Techniques;[24] Research and Evaluative Techniques, among others. Electives included six courses: Theory of Media Cataloging and Classification; Systems Analysis; Seminar on the Computer & Media Resources Centers; Data Processing & the Media Center; Media for Children; and Multimedia Technology Techniques. In March 1977, the UDC library school submitted a self-study for accreditation review. Unfortunately, the director of the library science program became ill and progress on accreditation halted. The American Library Association external review board denied accreditation and the school closed in 1979.

### Alabama A&M University (1969-1982)

Alabama A&M University's School of Library Media program was, from the onset, innovative and transformative. The university had robust degree offerings, including a dozen graduate programs. The university regularly partnered with predominantly white institutions, and such was the case with the School of Library Media, which collaborated with Auburn and Purdue Universities.

As one of the largest of HBCUs in the state, Alabama A&M was poised to sustain an interdisciplinary library science department. It received substantial funding from both the state—indeed, it was the first state-sanctioned library media program—and the Kellogg Foundation.[25] The program emphasized hands-on multimedia training and community-based programming such as library-centered drug prevention outreach. In fact, the program established the Institute for Training in Librarianship for Drug Education, a project made possible through the Department of Education's Title II-B grants.

Headed by Dr. Marbury, the program included core courses such as Library and Media Centers, Advanced Reference Materials and Bibliography, and Introduction to Information Science. The program received accreditation in 1975 and eventually closed in 1982.[26]

## HBCUS AND BLACK-CENTERED LIS EDUCATION TODAY

Today, the US public has improved its recognition and understanding of HBCUs' contributions to many fields. First, HBCUs have captured significant mainstream media attention, what with influential television shows such as *A Different World* and, more recently, popular documentaries such as *Tell Them You Are Rising* along with chart-topping albums such as Beyoncé's *Homecoming*. Moreover, HBCUs are collectively lauded for having produced leaders who are shaping the highest ranks of US institutions—for example, Vice President Kamala Harris who is a Howard University graduate. There is room, however, for the LIS field to glean from and build upon the successes of HBCUs, especially the realized and unrealized promise of the historical HBCU-based library schools. In fact, library leaders strategically and systemically denied accreditation to these programs, as we write about elsewhere,[27] and the degradation of HBCU-based library schools is part and parcel of the underestimation of the Black intellect in general.

It is for this reason that Black librarians persevere in the tradition of eschewing established channels by carving flows of our own. Although North Carolina Central University remains the only HBCU-based LIS program,[28] HBCU librarians have initiated robust efforts to recruit, support, and celebrate emerging librarians. Traditional, mainstream library organizations are also recognizing the value of HBCUs in strengthening library professionalization. For example, in 2023, the American Library Association established the Building Library Capacity Funds grants program for HBCUs and other minority-serving institutions.[29] Notwithstanding, as the past has so poignantly proven, fostering a fervent network of new Black/African American librarians cannot be left to the American Library Association nor LIS programs. It is for this reason that Black-centered associations are leading in the area of librarian professionalization and training.

## HBCU LIBRARY ALLIANCE

In 2002, just as talks of closing the Clark Atlanta University SLIS surfaced, one hundred library directors and deans from 103 HBCU institutions convened to ideate how they could collectively increase their institutions' capacities and build a strong network of library workers. This initial meeting culminated in the HBCU Library Alliance. In 2003, the group established bylaws, a website, and secured a planning project grant through the Andrew W. Mellon Foundation.[30] Two years later, the HBCULA held its first Leadership Institute to build pathways for new HBCU library directors. This rapid momentum set the course for strong but sustained development. Twenty years later, the HBCU Library Alliance has recruited new librarians to the profession through innovative programs such as the HBCULA-Cornell University Library Digitization (HBCU-CUL) initiative aimed at preserving HBCUs' rich historical collections while providing digital curation experience for HBCU undergraduate students.[31] The HBCULA's interinstitutional collaboration eventually expanded in 2016 to LIS education through Project IDOL, an initiative in partnership with Wayne State University that helped produce a cohort of new Black librarians. In the same thread of molding new professionals, the HBCU-LA and Council on Library and Information Resources' (CLIR) Digital Library Federation (DLF) reunited in 2019 to establish the Authenticity Project to stimulate racial diversity and collaboration among the digital library workforce. The HBCU Library Alliance continues to attract a vibrant, new professional community by redefining professional development beyond the parameters of a formal master's in library and information science programs.

## BLACK CAUCUS OF THE AMERICAN LIBRARY ASSOCIATION

In 2019, the Black Caucus of the American Library Association (BCALA) received a grant from the Institute of Museum and Library Services (IMLS) to establish a national, virtual MLIS student organization to support Black/African American emerging library professionals. In keeping with BCALA's mission and in celebration of its fiftieth anniversary, the project's aim rested on deepening Black librarian professionalization through racial realism and cultural immersion. iBlackCaucus, as it is now known, drew from a combination of an HBCU-inspired framework for Black student success,[32] the critical racial theoretical premise of counterstorytelling,[33] and BCALA data on Black MLIS student realities.[34] The goal was to eschew the largely solitary and individual nature of distance MLIS-education by building a network of Black/African American LIS graduate students across the fifty-three US ALA-accredited programs. iBlackCaucus provides access to mentorship, study groups, scholarship opportunities and clinics, a speaker series, and practical training. Most importantly, iBlackCaucus includes free customizable tools for HBCU student recruitment along with a self-paced minicourse, Black Librarian History.

## ONWARD AND UPWARD

LIS education is better—indeed, richer—on account of the historic HBCU educational praxis and lived experiences of HBCU librarians. Long before the Hampton Institute was founded and the "HBCU" moniker became ingrained in US higher education, Black librarians defied white standards of knowledge work, including librarianship. Although all but one HBCU-based library schools and/or LIS programs closed, the spirit of Black agency in LIS education persists.

## NOTES

1. Floyd C. Hardy and Renee F. Stiff, "The Future of the Black College Library," in *Handbook of Black Librarianship*, 2nd ed., edited by E. J. Josey and Marva DeLoach (Lanham, MD: Scarecrow, 2000), 387.

2. Francis L. Miksa, "The Columbia School of Library Economy, 1887-1888," *Libraries and Culture,* 23, no. 3 (1988): 249-80.
3. Aisha M. Johnson-Jones, *The African American Struggle for Library Equality: The Untold Story of the Julius Rosenwald Fund Library Program* (Lanham, MD: Rowman & Littlefield, 2019).
4. Lorna Peterson, "Alternative Perspectives in Library and Information Science: Issues of Race," *Journal of Education for Library and Information Science,* 37, no. 2 (1996): 168, https://doi.org/10.2307/40324271.
5. Renate Chancellor, *E. J. Josey: Transformational leader in the Modern Library Profession* (Lanham, MD: Rowman & Littlefield, 2020).
6. Jarvis R. Givens, *Fugitive Pedagogy: Carter G. Woodson and the Art of Black Teaching* (Cambridge, MA: Harvard University Press, 2021), https://doi.org/10.2307/j.ctv1h9dg3p.
7. Ana Ndumu and Renate Chancellor, "Dumont, 35 Years Later: HBCUs, LIS Education, and Institutional Discrimination," *Journal of Education for Library and Information Science,* 62, no. 2 (2021): 162-81, doi: 10.3138/jelis.2019-0076.
8. S. I. Smith, "The Passing of the Hampton Library School," *The Journal of Negro Education* 9, no. 1 (1940): 51-58, https://doi.org/10.2307/2292881.
9. Casper LeRoy Jordan and E. J. Josey, "Chronology of Events in Black Librarianship," in *Handbook of Black Librarianship,* 2nd ed., edited by E. J. Josey and Marva DeLoach (Lanham, MD: Scarecrow, 2000), 6.
10. "About NCCU SLIS," North Carolina Central University, accessed April 23, 2023, https://www.nccu.edu/slis/about-slis.
11. Ibid.
12. Ibid.
13. Ibid.
14. Chancellor, *E. J. Josey*.
15. Almeta G. Woodson, "Fifty Years of Service: A Chronological History of the School of Library Service Atlanta University, 1941-1979," *The Georgian Librarian,* 28, no. 3 (1991): 71-79.
16. Ibid.
17. Ibid.
18. Ndumu and Chancellor, "Dumont, 35 Years Later."
19. Alma Dawson, "Celebrating African American Librarians and Librarianship," *Library Trends*, 49, no. 1 (2000), 49-87.
20. Ndumu and Chancellor, "Dumont, 35 Years Later."
21. Ibid.
22. Ibid., 166.
23. Ibid.
24. Ibid.
25. Ibid.
26. Ibid.
27. Ibid.
28. In 2020, Chicago State University, a predominantly Black institution, received ALA accreditation for its MLIS program.
29. "Building Library Capacity Grants," *American Library Association*, April 12, 2023, http://www.ala.org/aboutala/Building-Library-Capacity-Grants.
30. Carolyn Hart et al., "The HBCU Library Alliance: Developing Leadership," *Virginia Libraries*, 53, no. 4 (2007): 16-20; Ana Ndumu and Shaundra Walker, "Adapting an HBCU-inspired Framework for Black Student Success in US LIS Education," *Education for Information*, 37, no. 2 (2021): 219-29; Loretta O'Brien Parham and Janice R. Franklin, "Preserving a Historic Legacy: The HBCU Library Alliance," *Against the Grain*, 16, no. 1 (2004): 5.
31. Joshua Lynch, "The HBCU-CUL Initiative: A Case Study of the Digitization of Archives of the Black Experience," *Fire!!!*, 3, no. 2 (2017): 37-65.
32. Ndumu and Walker, "Adapting an HBCU-inspired Framework," 219-29.
33. Richard Delgado and Jean Stefancic, eds., *Critical Race Theory: The Cutting Edge*, 3rd ed. (Philadelphia, PA: Temple University Press, 2000).
34. Ana Ndumu, Shaundra Walker, Shauntee Burns-Simpson, Nichelle M. Hayes, and Tiffany Mack, "Space, Story, and Solidarity: Designing a Black MLIS Student Organization amidst Crisis and Tumult," *Education for Information*, 38, no. 4 (2022): 367-88.

**WORKS CITED**

"About NCCU SLIS." North Carolina Central University. Accessed April 23, 2023. https://www.nccu.edu/slis/about-slis.

Chancellor, Renate. *E. J. Josey: Transformational Leader in the Modern Library Profession*. Lanham, MD: Rowman & Littlefield, 2020.

Dawson, Alma. "Celebrating African American Librarians and Librarianship." *Library Trends*, 49, no. 1 (2000), 49-87.

Delgado, Richard, and Jean Stefancic, eds. *Critical Race Theory: The Cutting Edge,* 3rd ed. Philadelphia, PA: Temple University Press, 2000.

Freeman, Sharon Ferguson. *Creating Access to HBCU Library Alliance Archives: Needs, Capacity, and Technical Planning. A Focus Group Study*. Alexandria, VA: Council on Library and Information Resources, 2022.

Givens, Jarvis R. *Fugitive Pedagogy: Carter G. Woodson and the Art of Black Teaching*. Harvard University Press, 2021. https://doi.org/10.2307/j.ctv1h9dg3p.

Hardy, Floyd C., and Renee F. Stiff. "The Future of the Black College Library." In *Handbook of Black Librarianship*, 2nd ed., edited by E. J. Josey and Marva DeLoach, 387. Lanham, MD: Scarecrow, 2000.

Hart, Carolyn, Lillian Lewis, Elizabeth McClenney, V. Tessa Perry, Iyanna Sims, and Adrienne Webber. "The HBCU Library Alliance: Developing Leadership." *Virginia Libraries*, 53, no. 4 (2007): 16-20.

Johnson-Jones, Aisha M. *The African American Struggle for Library Equality: The Untold Story of the Julius Rosenwald Fund Library Program*. Lanham, MD: Rowman & Littlefield, 2019.

Jordan, Casper LeRoy, and E. J. Josey. "Chronology of Events in Black Librarianship." In *Handbook of Black Librarianship*, 2nd ed., edited by E. J. Josey and Marva DeLoach. Lanham, MD: Scarecrow, 2000.

Lynch, Joshua. "The HBCU-CUL Initiative: A Case Study of the Digitization of Archives of the Black Experience." *Fire!!!*, 3, no. 2 (2017): 37-65.

Miksa, Francis L. "The Columbia School of Library Economy, 1887-1888." *Libraries and Culture*, 23, no. 3 (1988): 249-80.

Ndumu, Ana, and Renate Chancellor. "Dumont, 35 Years Later: HBCUs, LIS Education, and Institutional Discrimination." *Journal of Education for Library and Information Science*, 62, no. 2 (2021): 162-81. doi: 10.3138/jelis.2019-0076.

Ndumu, Ana, and Shaundra Walker. "Adapting an HBCU-inspired Framework for Black Student Success in US LIS Education." *Education for Information*, 37, no. 2 (2021): 219-29.

Ndumu, Ana, Shaundra Walker, Shauntee Burns-Simpson, Nichelle M. Hayes, and Tiffany Mack. "Space, Story, and Solidarity: Designing a Black MLIS Student Organization amidst Crisis and Tumult." *Education for Information*, 38, no. 4 (2022): 367-88.

Parham, Loretta O'Brien, and Janice R. Franklin. "Preserving a Historic Legacy: The HBCU Library Alliance." *Against the Grain*, 16, no. 1 (2004): 5.

Peterson, Lorna. "Alternative Perspectives in Library and Information Science: Issues of Race." *Journal of Education for Library and Information Science* 37, no. 2 (1996): 163-74. https://doi.org/10.2307/40324271.

Smith, S. L. "The Passing of the Hampton Library School." *The Journal of Negro Education*, 9, no. 1 (1940): 51-58. https://doi.org/10.2307/2292881.

Woodson, Almeta G. "Fifty Years of Service: A Chronological History of the School of Library Service Atlanta University, 1941-1979." *The Georgian Librarian*, 28, no. 3 (1991): 71-79.

# 4.8

## As a LIS Instructor, Am I Part of the Problem?

Jason Alston

At this point, it is no secret that the field of librarianship is not as diverse—in terms of race and ethnicity—as it should be and has failed to attract professional librarians of color, especially Black librarians with professional rank. If numbers published by Zippia in September 2022 are accurate, 6.4 percent of librarians practicing in the United States are Black.[1] This represents a severe underrepresentation, as—per the 2020 Census—13.7 percent of the US population identifies as non-Hispanic Black or African American.[2] Ideally, the professional librarianship ranks would also be roughly 13 percent Black and would reflect the US Black population at large; instead, professional librarianship is about half as Black as the US Black population at large.

To add further to existing injury, these numbers have been rather static. Professional librarianship in the United States was roughly 5.1 percent Black in 2009-2010.[3] In 2000, Black librarians represented 4.8 percent of the professional librarian workforce in the United States, and—interestingly enough—in 1990, Black librarians represented 6.2 percent of the professional librarian workforce, meaning representation slightly declined at the turn of the century.[4] Black men are especially underrepresented in professional librarianship in the United States; in 2008, it was estimated that only 0.5 percent of professional librarians in the United States were Black[5]; no recent literature suggests that there has been a significant change to this figure. So, when comparing 1990 figures to 2022 figures, Black professional librarianship in the United States has only grown by 0.2 percentage points over a thirty-two-year period. This underrepresentation has persisted despite the field implementing numerous remedying strategies such as scholarships to library science programs for students of color, diversity residency programs, internships tailored specifically to Black potential librarians, mentoring programs, and the continued presence of ethnic caucuses and a Joint Council of Librarians of Color.

It is not known why US librarianship has such a hard time recruiting and retaining Black librarians. People have posed numerous reasons over the years. One common suggestion is that Black students who have the potential to succeed in fields requiring a graduate degree likely gravitate to more lucrative fields. Another common suggestion is that Black Americans may not be aware of opportunities for employment in librarianship or that they do not know how much library jobs might pay. Observers have also posited that the dearth of undergraduate library science programs contributes to the underrepresentation, as well as there being only one accredited graduate library science program at an HBCU in the entire nation. Concerning retention specifically, there is a frequently-stated concern that libraries are toxic and racist workplaces that Black practitioners do not enjoy working in.

I have some beliefs of my own regarding what factors into the difficulty of recruiting Black librarians, many of which you will not often hear uttered publicly. For starters, I believe that most Black librarians who have gained widespread name recognition and become leaders within this field arrived there because of their ability to impress white liberals; I have been around these librarians enough at this point to know that they do not have the ability to impress most Black people or to convince them to consider librarianship. I also personally implicate the overemphasis on "BIPOC" recruitment as a detriment to recruitment of Black librarians; we have allowed this field to create a binary of "white versus BIPOC" for diversity research purposes, and because Black people have so little in common with other nonwhite populations outside of not being white, important nuance gets lost (strategies to recruit Asian Americans into the field will not necessarily work for recruiting Black people into the field, for instance). I also suspect that there are a lot of Black library workers with library technician or paraprofessional rank who are capable of doing the work of professional librarians but who employers—especially white ones—assume are not capable of earning master's degrees or doing professional library work; these workers are never encouraged to go to library school and become professional librarians. And finally, I think a lot of white employers are prone to hiring Black librarians who make them comfortable, versus Black librarians who are best suited to serve Black library users; with this said, most Black Americans are not friends with mostly white people, did not go to school mostly with white people, and do not mostly marry white people, but if you look at who gets hired as a Black librarian, you would likely think otherwise (these are the Black people who have high proximity to whiteness and therefore are comfortable hires for white library employers).

**THE HURDLE OF MLIS REQUIREMENT**

Also implicated in the lack of racial and ethnic diversity within US professional librarianship is the MLIS requirement itself. Though this criticism seems sparse within the professional literature, the rumblings within librarian circles have endured for years. And they make a lot of sense. The MLIS degree requires money, and Black people tend to have less money to invest in education. The MLIS degree requires time, and Black people often have additional tasks and obligations in life that limit the amount of time they have to devote to school. The MLIS degree requires the patience to endure library school curricula that are largely unrelatable to Black students. The MLIS degree often requires the emotional labor of having to be the representative "Black voice" in the majority-white spaces that are LIS classrooms. The MLIS degree requires a lot out of prospective Black students but does not offer them anything similar to a guarantee that they will land a professional job in return.

It should come as no surprise that so few Black people have MLIS degrees and so few Black people have any interest in getting an MLIS degree. It is no secret that Black Americans tend to be risk-averse when it comes to monetary investment, especially in playing the stock market.[6] I doubt that this risk aversion toward monetary investment spills over into investing in undergraduate education. But for graduate school, I am certain that reluctance to invest in graduate school and incur more student loan debt deters many Black Americans from pursuing graduate degrees, though admittedly, the literature does not support (or refute) this belief. It is known, however, that a higher percentage of Black American student loan borrowers owe more in student loan debt currently than they did originally. Per data published in 2021, 75 percent of Black student loan borrowers owed more on their loans in 2019 than they originally owed, compared with 60 percent of Hispanics, 50 percent of whites, and 48 percent of Asians.[7] When Black Americans are struggling so hard to escape crushing student loan debt, convincing them to invest in another graduate degree for a moderately paying job like librarianship is likely a tough sell.

And if so few Black people are inclined to go to library school and get an MLIS degree, it is not unreasonable for people to conclude that the MLIS degree might be one of the very barriers preventing Black people from joining the ranks of professional librarianship. As long as this is the case, rumblings in librarian circles that the best way to bring more Black people into professional librarianship is to get rid of the MLIS degree requirement will continue.[8]

**DOES THIS MEAN I AM PART OF THE PROBLEM?**

If some practitioners are arriving at the question of "Is the MLIS degree a barrier in bringing more Black people into the ranks of professional librarianship?" this means the question I need to ask is, "Am I part of the problem?" As of this writing, and hopefully until I retire, I am a full-time instructor for an ALA-accredited library science program. This means I make my living preparing people for careers in librarianship. This means that I teach for a graduate school program that people have to pay actual money to enroll in. And this may mean, that despite my belief that I am fair to and genuinely concerned for the well-being of all my students, that I aid in the gatekeeping of intellectually-qualified Black people out of librarianship by working within the system that grants degrees as a way of "proving" that someone is capable of being a professional librarian. So, am I wrong to teach in a library science degree program if I am truly concerned about the ethnic and racial diversity within this field? And if so, do I need to leave the teaching ranks and return to being a full-time practitioner in order to align my values with my source of income?

I grappled with this question for a long time, but thankfully, this is librarianship. And if there is one thing I would say about librarianship, it is that if you do not like how people are thinking at a particular moment in time, just give it a minute. Eventually, you will find at least a small group of people who have moved on from that line of thinking. In March 2023, while I was casually viewing Twitter, I came across a tweet that presented the dilemma in terms I had not considered. Nimisha Bhat, an editor for *The Librarian Parlor*, offered the following pearls of wisdom:

> I get that it might seem radical when a white person says we should make the MLIS optional for hiring library workers, but I don't think I would even be considered

over a white guy with a history PhD if that were the case–it "allows" POC to be seen as "equals."[9]

Bhat's tweet was met with over two hundred likes and a lot of BIPOC librarians weighing in to agree. In addition to agreeing with Bhat that removing the MLIS requirement would result in white PhDs being hired over people of color for librarian and archival jobs, librarians responding to this tweet also suggested that having the MLIS requirement lends credibility to librarianship and archiving as fields that need specific skill sets, and not just careers that people with PhDs could just default into without formal training and a grounding in LIS theory. These sentiments afforded me a great deal of relief, as they signified that there is at least a debate to be had regarding whether my teaching for an MLIS program is "feeding the beast" if you will, or rather, contributing to a system that prevents librarianship from recruiting more Black practitioners.

I will hope that if librarians of color want there to be library science programs and MLIS degree requirements, that they will also want instructors of color teaching in these programs. The reasons for this are hopefully self-apparent. Having instructors of color in MLIS programs would demonstrate that this type of mobility is possible and that professor jobs in our field are not reserved for some small group of elite whites. Instructors of color can also advise the rest of the LIS faculty on best approaches for teaching, caring for, and otherwise addressing students of color. Instructors of color are able to serve as mentors to students of color, advising them before they even hit the job market on how to navigate professional librarianship, as well as how to navigate the MLIS program itself (as these tend to have few students of color, with those few students of color having to endure being spokespeople for their race or dealing with insensitive perspectives on race from white classmates constantly). BIPOC LIS instructors are crucial for building bridges with other university faculty; particularly, faculty of color in other disciplines and all faculty within various ethnic studies departments may appreciate and build natural bonds with BIPOC LIS professors. Also, lest we forget, there need to be BIPOC professors in place to do all the necessary LIS research and serve on all those committees.

**WHY I FEEL I BELONG AS A LIS INSTRUCTOR**

Due to quoting non-Black people of color in the previous section, I had to use the term "BIPOC" while explaining why it benefits LIS to have nonwhite people teaching in library science programs. Now, however, I would like to bring it back to Blackness. Specifically, I would like to talk about the underrepresentation of Black professors among the ranks of American LIS educators. In 1980, prior to my birth, Black people comprised roughly 12 percent of the total US population but represented 5.5 percent of American library science faculty. In 2021, as I was coming to terms with being in my very late thirties, the US population was 13 percent Black, but Black people made up 4 percent of LIS faculty in the United States. Over a forty-year period wherein this nation and its academic institutions were especially conscious of the need for recognizing diversity and hearing from diverse voices, representation of Black Americans within the teaching ranks of my field actually slightly declined. I believe this suggests that no matter how conscious of racial and ethnic diversity our academic institutions and national climate are, there are persistent limits in how diverse our teaching departments in LIS are likely to be. It is hard enough to get Black people to consider careers in librarianship, as we explored earlier in this chapter. Extracting individuals to earn PhDs and become LIS professors out of the already small pool of Black librarians is not exactly impossible, but it is extremely difficult and probably not something that many already-overcommitted people in our field can devote time to.

I have been a full-time LIS professor since 2018. Since my hire, I have dedicated time to doing things that I am uniquely positioned to do as one of only about fifty Black LIS full-time teaching faculty nationwide.[10] I have recruited students into the Black Caucus of the American Library Association, as well as our field's other ethnic caucuses. I have found mentors for my students of color and helped them appreciate the importance of mentoring for new professionals of color in our field. I have taken two Black students on as mentees myself. I have written countless letters of recommendation for students of color for jobs, scholarships, fellowships, and admission into additional graduate degree programs; letters highlighting content and attributes that my white colleagues I believe would not have thought to mention. I have shared coping strategies with my students of color on how to navigate librarianship and given them reading suggestions. I have done career counseling and guidance for several students of color. I have infused my courses with content intended to recognize concerns of Black and other patrons and library workers of color. And I have incorporated Pan-African readings and multimedia into several of my courses, especially the one I created for my program titled Cultural Heritage.

Though I hate that I am centering whiteness here, I also wish to note in this section that I have served as the first ever Black teacher for dozens of white midwestern students. Yes, even at the graduate school level, I have had plenty of students who have never had a Black teacher before. But I have seen that my students generally need this experience. Many students from the Midwest grow up in very monochromatic environments where they do not learn how to effectively communicate with people who are ethnically or culturally different from them. Particularly, not knowing how to communicate effectively with Black people means also not knowing how to work for Black supervisors and bosses, and I have found that many of my white students from the Midwest are prone to saying things that a white subordinate just should not say to a Black person in authority. Also, students who are not used to how Black people communicate may overreact to "typical"

Black communication, thinking for instance, that Black people are angry or otherwise emotional when we are not. In teaching evaluations, my own midwestern students often apply terms like "aggressive," "abrasive," and "defensive" to me, as well as saying they do not feel comfortable asking me questions (these were concerns that my southern-based students never had of me when I adjuncted, but the South is home to way more Black people than the Midwest). In response to all of this, I begin my classes each semester by saying explicitly that I am Black, and I recognize that I am the first Black teacher a lot of my students have had. I then go on to tell them to consider whether or not their interpretations of me are really based on my behavior and demeanor as an individual, or if racial bias may play into whatever discomfort they may feel toward me as their first Black teacher or first Black male teacher. This approach has been effective, as my teaching evaluations have improved since I started doing this. Additionally, I have seen respect from my students of the position I am in, and I think this ultimately prepares them to better work for Black supervisors/bosses and better serve communities with significantly-Black populations; many white midwestern students who grow up in homogenous white communities still wind up working in metropolitan areas where Black people and other people of color may be present and may be serving as library supervisors and administrators. Having Black LIS professors does not just help students of color, it indeed helps white students as well.

## SO, I AM STAYING PUT

I am open to having discussions about whether or not there should be an MLIS requirement for professional librarianship and whether or not the MLIS hinders efforts to make librarianship more racially and ethnically diverse. And I can be persuaded by good arguments. If the evidence and arguments eventually do suggest that the best way to diversify librarianship is to remove the MLIS requirement, I will leave the teaching ranks and advocate for the abolishment of the MLIS and graduate library science programs. But we are not there yet. As long as there are strong arguments made that the MLIS does not harm efforts to recruit Black librarians and other librarians of color, I will continue to teach and try to do the things that I am better suited than white LIS instructors to do. As long as the MLIS is a requirement for becoming a librarian in most cases, it is best that we have Black faculty in teaching roles so that we maintain a seat at the table and can speak up for Black library school students, Black library workers, and Black library users. And if I ever get to the point where I am not doing these things, call me out and call for my resignation. I want to be of special service to Black people in whatever professional roles I occupy, and if I am no longer of special service to my race as an instructor, I will be compelled to reevaluate my career choices.

## NOTES

1. "Librarian Demographics and Statistics in the US," *Zippia*, September 2022, https://www.zippia.com/librarian-jobs/demographics/.

    Zippia provides an occupational overview of librarianship that includes demographic information.

2. "Quickfacts: United States," *United States Census Bureau*, 2022, https://census.gov/quickfacts/fact/table/US/PST045222.

    Includes 2022 estimates and updates on the 2020 Census.

3. Ibid.

4. Thomas Godfrey and Stephen J. Tordella, *Librarians, Library Technicians and Assistants: Diversity Profile 2000 and 1990, Library Employees Living in Same-Sex Partner Households, First Look from the American Community Survey,* Decision Demographics, 2006.

    Source contains figures for 1990 and 2000 on an assortment of demographic data.

5. "Endangered Species: Black Male Librarian," NPR, June 27, 2008, https://www.npr.org/templates/story/story.php?storyId=91955374#:~:text=Of%20the%20roughly%20110%2C000%20credentialed,0.5%20percent%20of%20all%20librarians.

6. Yun Li, "Black Americans' Lack of Participation in the Stock Market Likely to Widen Post-Pandemic Wealth Gap," CNBC, February 2, 2022, https://www.cnbc.com/2022/02/02/black-americans-lack-of-participation-in-the-stock-market-likely-to-widen-post-pandemic-wealth-gap.html.

7. Andre M. Perry, Marshall Steinbaum, and Carl Romer, "Student Loans, the Wealth Divide, and Why We Need Full Student Debt Cancellation," Brookings Institute, June 23, 2021, https://www.brookings.edu/articles/student-loans-the-racial-wealth-divide-and-why-we-need-full-student-debt-cancellation/.

8. Caroline H. Weigle, "The MLIS: Gatekeeper or Necessary Credential," Hack Library School, December 22, 2020, https://hacklibschool.wordpress.com/2020/12/22/the-mlis-gatekeeper-or-necessary-credential/.

9. @mishiebhat, "I get that it might seem radical when a white person says we should make the MLIS optional for hiring library workers, but I don't think I would even be considered over a white guy with a history PhD if that were the case–it 'allows' POC to be seen as 'equals.'" *Twitter*, March 27, 2023, https://twitter.com/mishiebhat/status/1640371858041356289.

10. "2020 Statistical Report: Trends and Key Indicators in Library and Information Science Education," ALISE, 2020, https://ali.memberclicks.net/assets/documents/statistical_reports/2020/ALISE%202020%20Statistical%20Report%20Summary%20Final_Revised%2020210106.pdf.

## WORKS CITED

"2020 Statistical Report: Trends and Key Indicators in Library and Information Science Education." ALISE, 2020. https://

ali.memberclicks.net/assets/documents/statistical_reports/2020/ALISE%202020%20Statistical%20Report%20Summary%20Final_Revised%2020210106.pdf.

@mishiebhat. "I get that it might seem radical when a white person says we should make the MLIS optional for hiring library workers, but I don't think I would even be considered over a white guy with a history PhD if that were the case–it 'allows' POC to be seen as 'equals.'" *Twitter*, March 27, 2023. https://twitter.com/mishiebhat/status/1640371858041356289.

"Endangered Species: Black Male Librarian." NPR, June 27, 2008. https://www.npr.org/templates/story/story.php?storyId=91955374#:~:text=Of%20the%20roughly%20110%2C000%20credentialed,0.5%20percent%20of%20all%20librarians.

Godfrey, Thomas, and Stephen J. Tordella. *Librarians, Library Technicians and Assistants: Diversity Profile 2000 and 1990, Library Employees Living in Same-Sex Partner Households, First Look from the American Community Survey.* Decision Demographics, 2006.

"Librarian Demographics and Statistics in the US." *Zippia*, September 2022. https://www.zippia.com/librarian-jobs/demographics/.

Li, Yun. "Black Americans' Lack of Participation in the Stock Market Likely to Widen Post-Pandemic Wealth Gap." CNBC, February 2, 2022. https://www.cnbc.com/2022/02/02/black-americans-lack-of-participation-in-the-stock-market-likely-to-widen-post-pandemic-wealth-gap.html.

Perry, Andre M., Marshall Steinbaum, and Carl Romer. "Student Loans, the Wealth Divide, and Why We Need Full Student Debt Cancellation." Brookings Institute, June 23, 2021. https://www.brookings.edu/articles/student-loans-the-racial-wealth-divide-and-why-we-need-full-student-debt-cancellation/.

"Quickfacts: United States." *United States Census Bureau*, 2022. https://census.gov/quickfacts/fact/table/US/PST045222.

Weigle, Caroline H. "The MLIS: Gatekeeper or Necessary Credential." Hack Library School, December 22, 2020. https://hacklibschool.wordpress.com/2020/12/22/the-mlis-gatekeeper-or-necessary-credential/.

# 4.9

## Historical Chronology of Black LIS Education

Katie Perry

In 2006, the American Library Association (ALA) published a study compiled by Denise Davis and Tracie Hall titled *Diversity Counts,* which explored diversity in the library profession. The study used census estimates from 2000 to acknowledge that only 5 percent of credentialed librarians identified as Black. This was a drop from the 1990 census, which estimated that 9 percent of professional librarians were Black.[1] Despite diversity and inclusion efforts in the profession, as of 2023, there has continued to be very little growth and retention in the field when it comes to Black librarians. Current statistics show that in the nearly twenty years since *Diversity Counts* was published, Black librarianship remains low, with just over 6 percent of librarians identifying as Black despite accounting for about 13 percent of all people living in the United States.[2]

To truly be of service to Black prospective students and aid in the creation of programming geared toward recruiting and retaining Black students to the library and information profession, we must first understand the successes and downfalls of the education services that came before us. It has then been this researcher's task to understand the evolution of Black LIS education and to gain insight into the successes and failures of LIS educational programs found at historically Black colleges and universities (HBCUs), as well as diversity programs that have aimed to increase the representation of Black students in library schools. The scope of this study has focused on the historical chronology of Black LIS education. The study was compiled between February 2023 and July 2023. It consisted of gathering information from archives, previous publications, and scholarly literature to aid in understanding the evolution of Black LIS education in America.

### THE DEVELOPMENT OF BLACK LIS EDUCATION

The research found that professional librarianship in the United States started forming around 1890, but it was not until 1920 that Black librarians were first included in census information. Edward Christopher Williams was the first African American to enroll in the New York Library School in 1899. He graduated in 1900, becoming the first professionally trained Black librarian in the United States. The research would show us that he was an outlier. Although a few northern institutions would occasionally accept Black students into their programs, there is evidence that this was not a common practice. Written documents from the directors of Pratt University and the University of Michigan reveal a practice of nonadmittance for the Black population,[3] stating that Black students would not be able to meet academic standards and their simple presence would be a "distinct embarrassment."[4]

The first evidence of organized training for Black librarians occurred in 1912. It was directed by Thomas Fountain Blue, who had been designated as department head of the Colored Branch Library of Louisville, Kentucky, upon its opening in 1905. Blue organized and provided library apprentice training at the Eastern Colored Branch from 1912 to 1931, with nine women successfully completing the program in the first year. In 1925, the Hampton Institute Library School was established with funding from the General Education Board (GEB). The program accepted teachers into the program who wanted to become librarians. The first director for the program was a white woman named Florence Rising Curtis, who said that library schools for Blacks needed to be "quite different." She minimized the focus to elementary librarianship, discounting the intellect of African Americans.[5] At the time, it was the first and only school to offer a bachelor's degree in library science to Black Americans and was accredited by the ALA. The school closed in 1939, and in its fourteen years, it graduated 183 Black librarians. Cited reasons for the school's closure were loss of financial support and the retirement of Curtis.[6]

The Negro Teacher-Librarian Training Program (NTLTP) consisted of summer sessions held on four campuses (Atlanta University, Fisk University, Hampton University, and Prairie View State College) that trained 279 teacher-librarians from 1936 to 1939. The program's mission was to improve conditions of Black public schools and consisted of a twelve-credit-hour program funded by the GEB. Florence Rising Curtis, the director of the Hampton Institute, coordinated the program and used an all-white staff except in the case of Prairie View. Prairie View is located in Texas, and Texas had laws that forbade white teachers from teaching Black students. Virginia Lacy Jones, a graduate of the Hampton Institute, was chosen for instruction at this campus.[7]

In 1940, Eliza Atkins Gleason became the first African American to graduate with a PhD in library science from the University of Chicago. A year later, in 1941, the Atlanta University School of Library Studies, later known as Clark Atlanta University, was established. Gleason became the school's first dean, and she helped create and establish the program. The program was accredited by the ALA in 1943, retroactively to 1941, and would go on to graduate more Black librarians than any other program. The year 1941 also saw North Carolina College for Negroes (North Carolina Central University) School of Library Science establish a professional library school, although its program would not be accredited until 1975. Clark Atlanta School of Library and Information Science (CAU SLIS) remains the longest-lasting accredited library program at an HBCU despite its controversial closure announced in 2003. Both NCCU and CAU established master's programs for library science in 1950, over twenty years after the University of Chicago established its Graduate Library School.

Diversity efforts in LIS education first became apparent in the 1960s, most likely as a response to the *Brown v. Board of Education* decision that declared segregation in schools unconstitutional. In February 1966, ALA formed an ad hoc committee that called on "opportunities for Negro students in the library profession" to offer suggestions on steps that could be taken by ALA to "identify promising new Negro undergraduates who might, once identified, be effectively counseled and aided towards entering library school and securing positions in the library profession." The progress report in 1967 admitted past barriers that kept Black students unaware of the opportunities in the profession. Other objectives included securing financial assistance and scholarships for interested Black students and reviewing "choice positions in the library profession available to Negroes."[8]

It could be argued that the 1970s was the best decade for Black LIS education as two southern HBCUs were well established, and two more would offer programs throughout the decade. In 1969, Alabama A&M University School of Library Media opened, with accreditation occurring in 1975. The school had a social justice orientation and organized the Institute for Training in Librarianship for Drug Education in 1971, emphasizing drug prevention programs. The school would close by 1982. The University of the District of Columbia established a media, information, and learning systems program in 1975 as an affordable option for Black minorities to receive a library degree. However, the school was never accredited and closed in 1979. The beginning of this decade also saw diversity efforts outside of HBCUs by the University of Illinois. With funding from the Carnegie Corporation and the US Department of Education, the Graduate School of Library Science recruited thirty minority students into its program, creating a class that had more students of color than the program has seen before or since.[9]

Much has been published on the 2005 closure of Clark Atlanta University, School of Library and Information Studies. The ALA, faculty, and students all protested its closure when announced. It took away the only library school in the state of Georgia and affected the whole region. It was the first HBCU library program to have a Black dean and administration, which may have contributed to its success.

The program also provided built-in mentorship and internship opportunities, both of which are important in the recruitment and retention of Black librarians. Today, only one HBCU hosts a school of library and information sciences, and that can be found at North Carolina Central University. It is recommended to explore further the correlation in the drop of Black librarians to the closure of CAU SLIS and to compare enrollment to NCCU.

**LOOKING BACK, LOOKING FORWARD**

The research revealed that historically, HBCU programs for library education have been geared toward recruiting teachers to work as teacher-librarians or offering an alternative to working as a teacher. This is made evident by the admission process of Hampton Institute, which only accepted applications from teachers, and the organization and establishment of the Negro Teacher-Librarian Training Program, as well as the short-lived UDC program. Modern recruitment efforts are focused on something other than cherry-picking from other employment sectors. Instead, recruitment efforts are organizational, as seen in ALA's Spectrum Initiative, which acknowledges the need for a more diverse workforce in this field and provides scholarships, training programs, and mentoring opportunities. Likewise, LIS schools have been employing similar efforts by providing scholarships and creating more inclusive curriculums.[10] Still, data show that Black librarianship remains low.

More than one study suggests that individual librarians are the most critical factor in attracting students to librarianship.[11] The challenge, then, in recruitment could be underrepresentation itself. Being that Black librarians are continually underrepresented in the workforce, it is possible that a cycle has been created where fewer Black individuals pursue librarianship because they have never been shown that it is a viable career option, as seen by example. If students saw more diverse librarians in leadership roles, it may inspire more Black individuals to pursue careers in librarianship, leading to increased diversity in the profession. The problem seems cyclical but is a reminder that librarians as individuals do have an impact on the future of their profession. Interactions with patrons and students can encourage recruitment.

**COMPLEX DEMOGRAPHICS**

While researching this topic, it was noted that the definition of what is considered Black in America has changed with time. If one asks this author if she is Black, she will answer yes. However, if given a form to fill out regarding her racial makeup and there is an option for two or more races, that is the box that will be marked. It was not until relatively recently in our history that this option for mixed-race individuals was available. The Census Bureau created this option for the first time in 2000, and other organizations followed suit. So, when discussing the data behind Black librarianship, it is important to note that the multiracial population is growing three times as fast as the population as a whole. This is especially important when one considers that nearly 70 percent of mixed-race Americans with a Black background remain more closely aligned with the Black community than any other and would likely identify as Black in social situations.[12] With this newer option to categorize racial demographics, it may appear that there was a drop in Black librarianship when in fact there may have just been a change in self-reporting race when given a multiracial option. It is recommended that further study be done on this topic, and this idea in no way suggests that Black librarianship is not in desperate need of recruitment or that librarianship does not remain overwhelmingly white. The only suggestion is that the drastic drop in Black librarianship that seemed to occur between 1990 and 2000 may not be so drastic.

**CONCLUSION**

This history of Black library education and HBCU library programs is a testament to the resilience and trailblazing efforts of African Americans in the field of library science. With determination and resilience, Black librarians pursued knowledge and professional development in this area. Oftentimes, programs and opportunities were made available by the organization and drive of single individuals, as seen through Thomas Fountain Blue's example of creating the first apprentice programs. Systemic racism and discriminatory practices challenged Black Americans to access equal education opportunities. Despite this, we have built institutions that allowed us to thrive and slowly increase the diversity in our profession with unique perspectives, experiences, and expertise. However, it is essential to acknowledge that the journey toward full representation and equity in LIS education will be ongoing. Continued efforts are necessary to address disparities, create more accessible pathways to education, and support Black students in pursuing careers in library and information science.

**NOTES**

1. Denise Davis and Tracie Hall, *Diversity Counts*, ALA.org, 2006, https://www.ala.org/ala/ors/diversitycounts/DiversityCounts_11_20_06.pdf.
2. US Census Bureau, "U.S. Census Bureau QuickFacts: United States," Census Bureau QuickFacts, https://www.census.gov/quickfacts/fact/table/US/PST045221.
3. Anthony Cocciolo, "Complicit Exclusion: Education for Black Librarianship in the Jim Crow North, 1890-1940." thinkingprojects.org, July 2016, https://www.thinkingprojects.org/Complict_Exclusion_forweb.pdf. Accessed 2 May 2023.
4. Nicole Cooke, "The GSLS Carnegie Scholars: Guests in Someone Else's House," *Libraries: Culture, History, and Society*, 1, no. 1 (2017): 46, https://doi.org/10.5325/libraries.1.1.0046.
5. Ana Ndumu and Renate Chancellor, "DuMont, 35 Years Later: HBCUs, LIS Education, and Institutional Discrimination," *Journal of Education for Library and Information Science*, 62, no. 2 (2021): 162-81, https://doi.org/10.3138/jelis.2019-0076.
6. Robert Sidney Martin and Orvin Lee Shiflett, "Hampton, Fisk, and Atlanta: The Foundations, the American Library Association, and Library Education for Blacks, 1925-1941," *Libraries & Culture*, 31, no. 2 (1996): 299-325.
7. Prairie View A&M, "Negro Teacher-Librarian Training Program (1936-1939)-Library." Library, November 4, 2021, https://www.pvamu.edu/library/about-the-library/history-of-the-library-at-prairie-view/negro-teacher-librarian-training-program-1936-1939.

8. "ALA AD HOC Committee on Opportunities for Negro Students in the Library Profession Report," Atlanta University Center, June 27, 1967, https://radar.auctr.edu/islandora/object/auc.115%3A0019.
9. Cooke, "The GSLS Carnegie Scholars," 46.
10. Kyung-Sun Kim and Sei-Ching Joanna Sin, "Increasing Ethnic Diversity in LIS: Strategies Suggested by Librarians of Color," *The Library Quarterly: Information, Community, Policy*, 78, no. 2 (2008): 153–77, https://doi.org/10.1086/528887.
11. Barbara I. Dewey, "Selection of Librarianship as a Career: Implications for Recruitment," *Journal of Education for Library and Information Science*, 26, no. 1 (1985): 16–24, https://doi.org/10.2307/40323180.
12. Kim Parker et al., "Multiracial in America: Proud, Diverse and Growing in Numbers." Pew Research Center, June 2015, https://www.pewresearch.org/social-trends/wp-content/uploads/sites/3/2015/06/2015-06-11_multiracial-in-america_final-updated.pdf.

**WORKS CITED**

"ALA AD HOC Committee on Opportunities for Negro Students in the Library Profession Report." Atlanta University Center, June 27, 1967. https://radar.auctr.edu/islandora/object/auc.115%3A0019.

Cocciolo, Anthony. "Complicit Exclusion: Education for Black Librarianship in the Jim Crow North, 1890-1940." thinkingprojects.org, July 2016. https://www.thinkingprojects.org/Complict_Exclusion_forweb.pdf.

Cooke, Nicole. "The GSLS Carnegie Scholars: Guests in Someone Else's House." *Libraries: Culture, History, and Society*, 1, no. 1 (2017): 46. https://doi.org/10.5325/libraries.1.1.0046.

Davis, Denise, and Tracie Hall. *Diversity Counts*. ALA.org, 2006. https://www.ala.org/ala/ors/diversitycounts/DiversityCounts_11_20_06.pdf.

Dewey, Barbara I. "Selection of Librarianship as a Career: Implications for Recruitment." *Journal of Education for Library and Information Science*, 26, no. 1 (1985): 16–24. https://doi.org/10.2307/40323180.

Kim, Kyung-Sun, and Sei-Ching Joanna Sin. "Increasing Ethnic Diversity in LIS: Strategies Suggested by Librarians of Color." *The Library Quarterly: Information, Community, Policy*, 78, no. 2 (2008): 153–77. https://doi.org/10.1086/528887.

Martin, Robert Sidney, and Orvin Lee Shiflett. "Hampton, Fisk, and Atlanta: The Foundations, the American Library Association, and Library Education for Blacks, 1925-1941." *Libraries & Culture*, 31, no. 2 (1996): 299–325.

Ndumu, Ana, and Renate Chancellor. "DuMont, 35 Years Later: HBCUs, LIS Education, and Institutional Discrimination." *Journal of Education for Library and Information Science*, 62, no. 2 (2021): 162–81. https://doi.org/10.3138/jelis.2019-0076.

Parker, Kim, Rich Morin, Juliana Menasce Horowitz, Mark Hugo Lopez, and Molly Rohal. "Multiracial in America: Proud, Diverse and Growing in Numbers." Pew Research Center, June 2015. https://www.pewresearch.org/social-trends/wp-content/uploads/sites/3/2015/06/2015-06-11_multiracial-in-america_final-updated.pdf.

Prairie View A&M. "Negro Teacher-Librarian Training Program (1936-1939)-Library." Library, November 4, 2021. https://www.pvamu.edu/library/about-the-library/history-of-the-library-at-prairie-view/negro-teacher-librarian-training-program-1936-1939.

US Census Bureau. "U.S. Census Bureau QuickFacts: United States." Census Bureau QuickFacts. 2022. https://www.census.gov/quickfacts/fact/table/US/PST045221.

# 4.10

## *Paving the Way*

LIS EDUCATION AND BLACK LIBRARIANS IN INDIANA

Michele Fenton

In May 2010, history was made as the first cohort of the Indiana Librarians Leading in Diversity (I-LLID) Fellowship Program graduated from the Indiana University School of Library and Information Science. A joint effort of the library school and the Indiana State Library, I-LLID recruited and educated students from underrepresented populations as a means of increasing the number of librarians of color in Indiana and bringing diversity to the profession. The program would graduate three more cohorts, the last graduating in 2011. Of the thirty-one students recruited, twenty-three were African American.[1]

The effort put into making I-LLID successful is commendable. However, what efforts were made in Indiana's past to recruit and educate librarians of color, specifically African American librarians? What educational options and opportunities were available for African Americans in Indiana wanting to pursue librarianship as a career? What roles did the American Library Association, the Rosenwald Fund, the Carnegie Corporation, and the federal government play in fostering the training and education of African American librarians? What challenges did the library science programs and the students face?

## INDIANA PUBLIC LIBRARY COMMISSION SUMMER SCHOOL FOR LIBRARIANS

The services provided by public libraries in Indiana were seen as a public good; however, there were few librarians with formal training or education in library science to run them. According to an article in *Library Occurrent*, as of 1899, out of all the librarians practicing in the state, there was only one with formal training. If the citizens of Indiana were to truly experience the benefits of library services, then trained library staff were needed.[2]

In 1899, by order of the Indiana General Assembly, the Indiana Public Library Commission was formed. It was charged with establishing and overseeing library services across the state and training librarians to run them. Jacob Piatt Dunn, a historian, attorney, and author was appointed by Governor James A. Mount as the commission's first president. Prior to serving on the commission, Dunn served as the state librarian of Indiana. In addition, Dunn served as the recording secretary for the Indiana Historical Society. Other appointees to the commission were Elizabeth Claypool Earl of the Indiana Union of Literary Clubs and Joseph Rawlins Voris of Citizens National Bank. W. E. Henry, state librarian of Indiana, served as the secretary.[3]

Although the Indiana General Assembly approved funds to hire librarians for the state's public libraries, the Indiana Public Library Commission recognized that the salaries generated from those funds discouraged persons with a more solid library education from coming to Indiana:

> Librarians do not get much for their services, the commission finds. Only ten librarians in the State get $600 to $1,000 annually. Seventeen receive from $300 to $600, and twenty-eight receive compensation from $75 to $300.[4]

Knowing this, the Indiana Public Library Commission concluded that establishing a library school offering a curriculum with just the basics seemed more fitting for Indiana's situation, and so made plans to establish an annual six-week summer course for the training of librarians. The program, however, came with a caveat:

> This summer course should not be considered by any student or by the people of the state as sufficient training for librarianship. It provides the minimum essentials only. It is hoped that an increasing number of those who attend this summer school will add college work and other library training to the elementary instruction given here.[5]

On October 31, 1901, the Indiana Public Library Commission Summer School for Librarians began its first class. Students were trained in the practical aspects of librarianship and participated in field trips to various libraries. Upon successful completion of the course, students were awarded a diploma and certified to work as librarians. The first class graduated with thirteen students.[6]

In 1915, the school accepted and graduated its first African American student, Lillian Sunshine Haydon Childress Hall. Hall was employed as an apprentice at the Cherry Street Branch of the Evansville Public Library (Evansville-Vanderburgh County Public Library). Hall's acceptance into the program made her one of a small number of African Americans granted admission into library schools established by White institutions during this period. In 1900, Edward Christopher Williams became the first African American to receive a formal education in librarianship, upon graduating from the New York State Library School (Columbia University Library School).[7]

Whether the Indiana Public Library Commission Summer School for Librarians prohibited the acceptance of African Americans into the school before Hall's admission is not known. What is known is that the school continued to accept and award librarian certificates to African Americans students after Hall graduated:

Lillian Haydon Childress Hall, 1915 graduate: Evansville Public Library, Indianapolis Public Library
Nannie Mae Glover, 1916 graduate: Evansville Public Library
Milie Lewis, 1917 graduate: Evansville Public Library
Sara Etta Robinson Proctor, 1921 graduate: Evansville Public Library
Etka F. Braboy Gaskin, 1923 graduate: Gary Public Library
Anna Stubbins, 1923 graduate: Evansville Public Library
Hallie Mae Beachem Brooks, 1924 graduate: Indianapolis Public Library
Octavene Beachem Ferguson, 1925 graduate: place of employment unknown
Georgia L. Lewis, 1926 graduate: Indianapolis Public Library
Othella B. Roberts, 1926 graduate: Evansville Public Library
Wyetta Diggs Gilmore, 1931 graduate: Indianapolis Public Library
Thelma Rochelle, 1945 graduate: Evansville Public Library
Leanna Moore, 1947 graduate: Indianapolis Public Library

In 1925, the Public Library Commission, per order of the Indiana General Assembly, was absorbed into the Indiana State Library and became the library's Extension Division (Library Development Office). The summer school then became known as the Indiana State Library School. It received accreditation as a summer library school in 1926 from the American

Library Association Board of Education for Librarianship. In 1934, the Indiana State Library received its own building and became the permanent home of the summer school (the library was previously housed in the lower level of the Indiana Statehouse—the state capital building of Indiana).[8]

## INDIANA UNIVERSITY SCHOOL OF LIBRARY AND INFORMATION SCIENCE

After forty-six years of educating librarians through its annual summer school, the priorities and focus of the Indiana State Library shifted. In 1947, the Indiana State Library began a series of discussions with Indiana University about the possibility of the university offering the summer course. The university agreed, and the Indiana State Library gave its final class in the summer of 1947. Leanna Moore was the state library's summer school's last African American graduate. In 1948, Indiana University began offering the summer course as a nine-credit-hour class. The course was eventually absorbed into the Library Science Division of the University Graduate School, which was established in 1949. The master of arts (MA) was the degree offered. The American Library Association had instituted changes in library education requiring the master's degree as the entry point into the profession. Florabelle Williams Wilson, the first African American director of an academic library in Indiana, received her MA in 1961. In 1966, Indiana University added doctoral degrees.

When Indiana University began offering doctoral degrees, the Library Science Division became the School of Library Science. Also, the master of arts was changed to the master of library science (MLS). The first African American to receive an MLS degree from the library school was Nancy Ann Saine Amos in 1966. Ms. Amos worked for the Morrison-Reeves Library in Richmond, Indiana, then later served as branch manager of the Northeast Branch of the Louisville Free Public Library. In 1972, Dorothy May Haith became the first African American to receive a doctorate in library science from the library school.[9]

## WESTERN COLORED BRANCH OF THE LOUISVILLE PUBLIC LIBRARY TRAINING PROGRAM

While some of Indiana's early African American librarians were trained within Indiana, others received their training elsewhere. In 1912, the Western Colored Branch of the Louisville Public Library in Louisville, Kentucky, established a library training program. It is the earliest known training program for African Americans library workers in the United States. Rev. Thomas Fountain Blue, head of the Colored Libraries of the Louisville Free Public Library, instituted the program. At the time the program was established, there were no schools in the South that would accept African Americans. Although not a formal training program, Blue's program provided students with the basics of library service. Students were mostly from the South, however one Indiana resident participated in the program: Fannie C. Porter, 1914—Evansville Public Library.

After completing the program, Porter was appointed manager of the Cherry Street Branch of the Evansville Public Library before resigning in the spring of 1915 after getting married. Why Porter was sent to Kentucky for training instead of the Indiana Public Library Commission Summer School for Librarians is not known nor has any documentation been found.[10]

When the ALA Work with Negroes Round Table met in Detroit, Michigan, during the 1922 ALA Annual Conference, Blue presented a paper on the training program, "Training Class at the Western Colored Branch." In his paper, Blue discussed the necessity and merits of the program and its success in providing trained library staff for not just the Colored Libraries of the Louisville Free Public Library but for other libraries providing services to African Americans.

The library training program at the Western Colored Branch of the Louisville Public Library was in operation for seventeen years. The program ended in 1929.[11]

## HAMPTON INSTITUTE LIBRARY SCHOOL

In 1925, the Hampton Institute of Virginia (Hampton University) established the first formal library school for training African American librarians. Funded with a grant from the Carnegie Corporation and accredited by the Board of Education for Librarianship of the American Library Association, the Hampton Institute Library School was the first library school in the South to accept African American students and the first library school at a historically Black college or university (HBCU). The establishing of the program was supported by the Julius Rosenwald Fund, the General Education Board, and the American Library Association.

Florence Rising Curtis was chosen as the school's director. A graduate of the New York State Library School, Curtis had previously served as the associate director of the Drexel Institute (Drexel University) and was an instructor at the University of Illinois Library School. In addition, she had occasionally taught courses at the Indiana Public Library Commission Summer School for Librarians. Notable lecturers at the school included Rev. Thomas Fountain Blue and Edward C. Williams. Students who successfully completed the program were awarded the bachelor of library science (BLS) degree.[12]

Unfortunately, funding for the school was discontinued, and in 1939 the school closed.[13] Luckily, some of Hampton's graduates made their way to Indiana and settled into positions in the cities of Indianapolis; Richmond; West Lafayette; and Evansville. Hampton graduates in Indiana included:

Minnie B. Slade Bishop, 1939 graduate: Evansville Public Library
Judith F. Davis, 1937 graduate: Evansville Public Library
Ruth McCoy Harry, 1938 graduate: Indianapolis Public Library

Edna Howard, 1937 graduate: Indianapolis Public Library
Carrie Coleman Robinson, 1930 graduate: Purdue University (Visiting Professor)
Martha Roney Leathers, 1935 graduate: Evansville Public Library
Effie Stroud, 1933 graduate: Indianapolis Public Library
Julia Wrenn Partner, 1927 graduate: Townsend Community Center of Richmond, Indiana

Some of these librarians took positions as branch managers and others as assistant/junior librarians—some even became professors.[14]

## THE ATLANTA UNIVERSITY SCHOOL OF LIBRARY SERVICE

After the Hampton Institute Library School ceased operation, hope was around the corner. The Carnegie Corporation and Atlanta University funded the creation of the Atlanta University School of Library Service. Housed in the university's Trevor Arnett Library, the School of Library Service opened for service in the fall of 1941 with a class of twenty-six students. Dr. Eliza Atkins Gleason, the first African American to earn a PhD in library science, was the school's dean. Instructors at the school included Dr. Virginia Lacy Jones, Wallace Van Jackson, Hallie Beachem Brooks, Annie L. McPheeters, Annette Hoage Phinazee, Vivian Davidson Hewitt, and numerous others. The school also had guest lecturers, among them Effie Lee Morris and S. R. Ranganathan.

Graduates of the Atlanta University School of Library Service were awarded the bachelor of library science (BLS) degree. Beginning in the 1949–1950 school year, the Atlanta University School of Library Service added the master of library science (MLS) degree. Eventually, as did other library science programs, the Atlanta University School of Library Service did away with the BLS degree following the recommendations made by ALA in 1951 regarding librarian education.[15]

Some early Indiana librarians who attended the Atlanta University School of Library Service were:

Betsie Lou Baxter Collins, 1945 graduate: Indianapolis Public Library
Daisy J. Dillard, 1945 graduate: Gary Public Library
Martha Louise Harry, 1947 graduate: Indiana State Library
Delorez A. Hunter, 1948 graduate: Gary Public Schools
Lillian Davis Owens, 1947 graduate: Crispus Attucks High School, Indianapolis, Indiana

There were other librarians in Indiana that graduated from the Atlanta Library School after the ones mentioned above, but for the purpose of this chapter the focus is on those who graduated in the early years of the program.[16]

The Atlanta University School of Library Service became the School of Library and Information Studies in 1979. Ten years later, due to the merger of Atlanta University and Clark College, the school's name was changed to the Clark Atlanta University School of Library and Information Studies.[17]

In the early 2000s, the university experienced budgetary problems. As a solution, a decision was made to cut some programs. Unfortunately, the library school was one of the programs eliminated. The Clark Atlanta University School of Library and Information Studies closed in 2005.[18]

## FELLOWSHIP PROGRAMS

In 1973, the United States Office of Education (United States Department of Education), under Title II-B of the Higher Education Act of 1965, awarded a grant of $150,000 to Indiana University to administer a program for training minority librarians. The program, Institute of Education for Librarianship in Urban Community Colleges, was one year in length and was held on the university's Bloomington campus. There were eighteen students in the program, thirteen of whom were African American. Each student successfully completed the program and upon graduation was awarded an MLS degree. Although some of the graduates did leave the state, a few did stay in Indiana accepting positions at Indiana University, the Gary Public Library, the Indianapolis Public Library, the Indiana Historical Society, and DePauw University. One graduate, Wilma Gibbs Moore, was the senior archivist for African American history at the Indiana Historical Society for thirty years. After her passing in 2018, a library science scholarship for underrepresented students, the Wilma Gibbs Moore Graduate Endowed Scholarship, was created in her honor by the Indiana University Luddy School of Informatics, Computing, and Engineering (formerly the Indiana University School of Library and Information Science).[19]

In 2008, the Indiana State Library and Indiana University came together to start the Indiana Librarians Leading in Diversity (I-LLID) Fellowship Program, an initiative to recruit and educate librarians from underrepresented populations. The fellowship program was made possible through a $1 million grant from the Institute of Museum and Library Services (IMLS) and was directed by Marcia Smith Woodard of the Indiana State Library's Library Development Office. A total of thirty-one students were selected for the program, twenty-three of whom were African American. Students had the option of earning their MLS from the Bloomington campus or the Indianapolis campus. After graduation, the I-LLID fellows were required to work in Indiana for two years. Presentations about the I-LLID Fellowship Program were given at the 2009 Indiana Library Federation (ILF) Conference, and in 2010, at the 7th National Conference of African American Librarians (NCAAL). In the spring of 2010, the program's first nine students graduated. The last cohort of students graduated in the summer of 2011.[20]

Several graduates of the I-LLID Fellowship Program became leaders in the library field. Nichelle M. Hayes served as president of the Black Caucus of the American Library Association (BCALA) and as the president of the Indiana Black

Librarians Network (IBLN), an affiliate of BCALA. Rodney Freeman created the Black Male Archives, a database of the history and achievements of African American men, and wrote a children's book, *Little Rodney the Librarian*. Another graduate, Willie Miller, is a 2016 Library Journal Mover and Shaker.[21]

**LOOKING BACK AND LOOKING FORWARD**

It has been over a hundred years since the first African American graduated from an Indiana library school, and since that time much success has been achieved, both at the state and national level. Hallie Beachem Brooks became a library professor at the Atlanta Library School, Dr. Joyce Taylor Manual at Indiana University, two scholarship initiatives were started, three librarians from Indiana have served as BCALA presidents, four have received BCALA awards, three librarians have served on the ALA Council, one librarian has served as Special Library Association president and another as president of the Indiana Library Federation, several have received Indiana Library Association/Indiana Library Federation Awards, several have written books, and some have started blogs. Others have served as library directors and deans in Indiana and other states.[22]

As we enter the midpoint of the second decade of the twenty-first century, it is hoped and expected that Indiana's African American librarians will continue to advance the profession, leaving a legacy to be built upon by future generations.

**NOTES**

1. Michele Fenton and Deloice Holliday, "We Need Some Color in Here: Educating and Recruiting Minority Librarians in Indiana," in *The 21st Century Black Librarian in America: Issues and Challenges*, edited by Andrew P. Jackson, Julius C. Jefferson Jr., and Akilah S. Nosakhere (Lanham, MD: Scarecrow Press, 2012), 144–45; Rodney Freeman, "A Snapshot of Indiana Librarians Leading in Diversity Fellowship Participants after the Program Has Concluded," *Indiana Libraries*, 33, no. 1 (2014): 12–15; Marcia Smith-Woodard, "The Importance of Achieving Diversity in Libraries," *Indiana Libraries*, 31, no. 1 (2012): 50–53.
2. Hazel B. Warren, "The Indiana Public Library Commission," *Library Occurrent*, 10, no. 1 (1931): 34.
3. Nick Sacco, "Creating the Public Library Commission of Indiana," *The Public Library Commission of Indiana: Public Libraries in the Hoosier State, 1899-1925*, Summer 2013, https://www.publiclibrarycommissionofindiana.wordpress.com/the-public-library-commission-of-indiana/creating-the-public-library-commission-of-indiana/; Warren, "Indiana Public Library Commission," 31–35.
4. "Needs of State Library," *Indianapolis Journal*, December 10, 1902, 7.
5. "Summer Course in Library Service, State Library, June 14–July 31, 1937," *Library Occurrent*, 12, no. 5 (1937): 125–27.
6. "Summer School for Librarians, 1914," *Library Occurrent*, 3, no. 10 (1914): 170; "Summer School," *Library Occurrent*, 3, no. 12 (1914): 195; Warren, "Indiana Public Library Commission," 32.
7. Michele Fenton, "Stepping Out on Faith: Lillian Haydon Childress Hall, Pioneer Black Librarian," *Indiana Libraries*, 33, no. 1 (2014): 5–11; Rebecca D. Hunt, "African American Leaders in the Library Profession: Little Known History," *Black History Bulletin*, 76, no. 1 (2013): 16; E. J. Josey, "Edward Christopher Williams: Librarian's Librarian," *Negro History Bulletin*, 33, no. 3 (1970): 70-77; Dorothy B. Porter, "Phylon Profile, XIV: Edward Christopher Williams," *Phylon (1940-1956)*, 8, no. 4 (1947): 315–21; Warren, "Indiana Public Library Commission," 32.
8. Warren, "Indiana Public Library Commission," 34–35; "Summer School 1915," *Library Occurrent*, 4, no. 4 (1915): 51; "Summer School," *Library Occurrent*, 4, no. 7 (1916): 119–20; "Summer School," *Library Occurrent*, 5, no. 1 (1918): 16–18; "Summer School Students 1921," *Library Occurrent*, 6, no. 3 (1921): 112; "Summer School Students for 1923," *Library Occurrent*, 6, no. 11 (1923): 411–12; "Summer School Students Accepted for 1924," *Library Occurrent*, 7, no. 3 (1924): 69; "Summer School Students Accepted for 1925," *Library Occurrent*, 7, no. 7 (1924): 318; "1926 Summer School Students," *Library Occurrent*, 7, no. 12 (1926): 318; "Summer School 1931," *Library Occurrent*, 10, no. 4 (1931): 185; "1945 Summer School," *Library Occurrent*, 15, no. 2 (1945): 1, 393; "I.S.L. Summer Course in Library Service," *Library Occurrent*, 15, no. 10 (1947): 645.
9. "Summer Training Course," *Library Occurrent*, 15, no. 9 (1947): 615; "Indiana University Library Training Program," *Library Occurrent*, 15, no. 9 (1947): 609–10; "Summer School Held," *Library Occurrent*, 16, no. 3 (1948): 81; "Summer Training," *Library Occurrent*, 16, no. 9 (1950): 278; Susan A. Stussy, "Profile of an Indiana Career in Libraries: Florabelle Wilson," *Indiana Libraries*, 6, no. 2 (1986): 34–39; Handsel G. Ingram, "Black Librarians with Earned and Honorary Doctorates," in *Handbook of Black Librarianship*, 2nd ed., edited by E. J. Josey and Marva L. DeLoach (Lanham, MD: Scarecrow, 2000), 192; Herman L Totten, "Southeastern Black Library Educators," *The Black Librarian in the Southeast: Reminiscences, Activities, Challenges*, ed. Annette L Phinazee (Durham, NC: NCCU School of Library Science, 1980), 202–4; Michele Fenton, "Re: Ask a Librarian Question," Received by: Reference Department, Herman B. Wells Library, Indiana University-Bloomington, April 7, 2010.
10. Rosemary Ruhig Dumont, "The Educating of Black Librarians: An Historical Perspective," *Journal of Education for Library and Information Science*, 26, no. 4 (1986): 234–35; Maurice Wheeler and Debbie Johnson-Houston, "A Brief History of Library Service to African Americans," *American Libraries*, 35, no. 2 (2004): 42–45; "Personals," *Library Occurrent*, 3, no. 12 (1914): 204; Michele Fenton, "Way Down Yonder at the Cherry Street Branch: A Short History of Evansville's Negro Library," *Indiana Libraries*, 30, no. 2 (2011): 37–38; Reinette Jones, *Library Services to African Americans in Kentucky: From Reconstruction Era to the 1960s* (Jefferson, NC: McFarland, 2006), 53–55.
11. "Mr. T. F. Blue on American Library Association Program," *Louisville Leader*, July 8, 1922, 1; Thomas F. Blue, "Work with the Negro Round Table," *The Southern Workman*, 51,

no. 9 (1922): 437-38; "American Librarians Confer on Work among Negroes," *The New York Age*, July 15, 1922, 8; James Weldon Johnson, "Segregation in Public Libraries," *The New York Age*, September 30, 1922, 4; Cheryl Knott Malone, "Louisville Free Public Library's Racially Segregated Branches, 1905-35," *The Register of the Kentucky Historical Society*, 93, no. 2 (1995): 173-74.

12. Florence Rising Curtis, "Librarianship as a Field for Negroes," *Journal of Negro Education*, 4, no. 1 (1935): 94-98; Robert Sidney Martin and Orvin Lee Shiflett, "Hampton, Fisk, and Atlanta: The Foundations, the American Library Association, and Library Education for Blacks, 1925-1941," *Libraries & Culture*, 31, no. 2 (1996): 299-25; Louis Shores, "Library Service and the Negro," *Journal of Negro Education*, 1, no. ¾ (1932): 376; Wallace Van Jackson, "Negro Library Workers," *Library Quarterly: Information, Community, Policy*, 10, no. 1 (1940): 95-108; Sarah C. N. Bogle, "Training for Negro Librarians," *Bulletin of the American Library Association*, 25, no. 4 (1931): 133; Ana Ndumu and Renate Chancellor, "DuMont, 35 Years Later: HBCUs, LIS Education, and Institutional Discrimination," *Journal of Education for Library and Information Science*, 62, no. 2 (2021): 169; *Accredited Library and Information Studies Masters Programs from 1925 through the Present*, American Library Association, https://www.ala.org/educationcareers/accreditedprograms/directory/historicallist; O. Lee. Shiflett, "The American Library Association's Quest for a Black Library School," *Journal of Education for Library and Information Science*, 35, no. 1 (1994): 68-71.

13. S. L. Smith, "The Passing of the Hampton Library School," *The Journal of Negro Education*, 9, no. 1 (1940): 51-58; Anita M. Hostetter, "A Library School for Negroes," *ALA Bulletin*, 13, no. 4 (1939): 247; *A Directory of Negro Graduates of Accredited Library Schools, 1900-1936* (Washington, DC: Columbia Civic Library Association, 1937), 18; Lucy B. Campbell, "Hampton Institute Library School," in *Handbook of Black Librarianship*, 2nd ed., ed. E. J. Josey and Marva L. DeLoach (Lanham, MD: Scarecrow, 2000), 46; "News Notes," *Library Occurrent*, 13, no. 3 (1939): 87; Mary Mace Spradling, "Black Librarians in Kentucky," in *The Black Librarian in the Southeast: Reminiscences, Activities, Challenges*, ed. Annette L Phinazee (Durham, NC: NCCU School of Library Science, 1980), 43; "News Notes," *Library Occurrent*, 14, no. 8 (1943): 223; "Explains Library Methods," *Indianapolis Recorder*, March 29, 1941, 9; Jones, *Library Services to African Americans in Kentucky*, 83, 163.

14. Jordan and Josey, "A Chronology of Events in Black Librarianship," 6; Florence Rising Curtis, "Colored Librarians in Conference," *Library Journal*, 52, no. 8 (1927): 408; "Personals," *Library Occurrent*, vol. 8, no. 2 (1927), 66; David M. Battles, *The History of Public Library Access for African Americans in the South, or Leaving Behind the Plow* (Lanham, MD: Scarecrow, 2009), 60; Jones, *Library Service to African Americans in Kentucky*, 54; "Prominent Woman Returns," *Indianapolis Recorder*, April 2, 1927, 5.

15. Ndumu and Chancellor, "DuMont," 166-67; Boyd Keith Swigger, *The MLS Project: An Assessment after Sixty Years* (Lanham, MD: Scarecrow Press, 2010); Shiflett, "American Library Association's Quest," 68; Martin and Shiflett, "Hampton, Fisk, and Atlanta," 299-325.

16. "Alumni News," *Atlanta University Bulletin*, Series 3, no. 52 (1945): 16-17; George Grant, *The Directory of Ethnic Professionals in LIS* (Winter Park, FL: Four-G Publishers, 1991), 106; "Receives Appointment (Photo)," *Indianapolis Recorder*, September 6, 1947, 5; *Crispus Attucks High School Yearbook, 1962* (Indianapolis, IN: Crispus Attucks High School, 1962).

17. Almeta Gould Woodson, "Fifty Years of Service: A Chronological History of the School of Library Service Atlanta University, 1941-1979; the School of Library and Information Studies Atlanta University, 1979-1989; the School of Library and Information Studies, Clark Atlanta University, 1989-1991," *Georgia Librarian*, 28, no. 3 (1991): 76, 78.

18. John N. Berry, "Not Just Another Library School: Tragedy at Clark Atlanta's School of Library and Information Studies," *Library Journal*, 128, no. 19 (2003): 8; Ndumu and Chancellor, "DuMont," 167-68; Norman Oder, "Clark Atlanta University to Close 62-Year-Old LIS School," *Library Journal*, 128, no. 19 (2003): 16.

19. Charles Hale, *Narrative Evaluation Report of USOE Title II-B Institute Education for Librarianship on Urban Community Colleges* (Bloomington: Graduate Library School, Indiana University, 1974); Charles Hale and Shirley Edsall, "The Education of Community College Librarians," *Journal of Education for Librarianship*, 16, no. 2 (1975): 75-85; Johannah Pollert, "Untold Stories: Wilma Gibbs Unearths the Hidden History of Blacks in Indiana," *Indianapolis Woman*, 10, no. 2 (2003): 36-41; Celeste Williams, "Indiana's History Is Her Career Passion: Archivist Ensures Hoosiers Have Works That Teach Them about Their Past," *Indianapolis Star*, February 15, 2001, 1, 11; Wilma Gibbs Moore Graduate Endowed Scholarship. Indiana University Luddy School of Informatics, Computing and Engineering, 2023, https://luddy.iupui.edu/alumni-partners/moore-scholarship.html.

20. Fenton and Holliday, "We Need Some Color in Here," 143-46; Freeman, "Snapshot," 12; Smith-Woodard, "Importance of Achieving Diversity in Libraries," 51.

21. "Willie Miller: Movers & Shakers 2016—Innovators." *Library Journal*, March 17, 2016, https://www.libraryjournal.com/story/willie-miller-movers-shakers-2016-innovators; Rodney E. Freeman, *Little Rodney the Librarian* (Charlotte, NC: Preservation Media LLC, 2022); "Unique Historical Database, The Black Male Archives, Chronicles the Success of Black Men," Black Enterprise, March 15, 2022, https://www.blackenterprise.com/unique-historical-database-the-black-male-archives-chronicles-the-success-of-black-men/; "IndyPL's Hayes and Indiana State Library's Fenton Appointed as BCALA Officers," *Wednesday Word: The Latest in Indiana Library News*, May 27, 2020, https://content.govdelivery.com/accounts/INLIBRARY/bulletins/28c933d.

22. Joyce G. Taylor, "The Smile That Hooked Me for Life," *Indiana Libraries*, 22, no. 2 (2003): 8-10; *A Tribute to Hallie Beachem Brooks for 47 Years of Service at Atlanta University, May 13, 1977, Atlanta Hilton*. Atlanta: Robert W. Woodruff Library, Atlanta University Center, 1977, radar.auctr.edu/islandora/object/auc.115%3A0012; BCALA.

## WORKS CITED

"1926 Summer School Students," *Library Occurrent*, 7, no. 12 (1926): 318.

"1945 Summer School," *Library Occurrent*, 15, no. 2 (1945): 1, 393.

*A Directory of Negro Graduates of Accredited Library Schools, 1900-1936*, 18, Washington, DC: Columbia Civic Library Association, 1937.

*A Tribute to Hallie Beachem Brooks for 47 Years of Service at Atlanta University, May 13, 1977, Atlanta Hilton*. Atlanta: Robert W. Woodruff Library, Atlanta University Center, 1977. radar.auctr.edu/islandora/object/auc.115%3A0012; BCALA.

*Accredited Library and Information Studies Masters Programs from 1925 through the Present*. American Library Association. https://www.ala.org/educationcareers/accreditedprograms/directory/historicallist.

"Alumni News." *Atlanta University Bulletin*, Series 3, no. 52 (1945): 16-17.

"American Librarians Confer on Work among Negroes." *The New York Age*, July 15, 1922, 8.

Battles, David M. *The History of Public Library Access for African Americans in the South or Leaving Behind the Plow*. Lanham, MD: Scarecrow, 2009.

Berry, John N. "Not Just Another Library School: Tragedy at Clark Atlanta's School of Library and Information Studies." *Library Journal*, 128, no. 19 (2003): 8.

Blue, Thomas, F. "Work with the Negro Round Table." *The Southern Workman*, 51, no. 9 (1922): 437-38.

Bogle, Sarah C. N. "Training for Negro Librarians." *Bulletin of the American Library Association*, 25, no. 4 (1931): 133.

Campbell, Lucy B. "Hampton Institute Library School." In *Handbook of Black Librarianship*, 2nd ed., edited by E. J. Josey and Marva L. DeLoach, 46. Lanham, MD: Scarecrow, 2000.

*Crispus Attucks High School Yearbook, 1962*. Indianapolis: Crispus Attucks High School, 1962.

Curtis, Florence Rising. "Colored Librarians in Conference." *Library Journal*, 52, no. 8 (1927): 408.

———. "Librarianship as a Field for Negroes." *Journal of Negro Education*, 4, no. 1 (1935): 94-98.

Dumont, Rosemary Ruhig. "The Educating of Black Librarians: An Historical Perspective." *Journal of Education for Library and Information Science*, 26, no. 4 (1986): 234-35.

"Explains Library Methods." *Indianapolis Recorder*, March 29, 1941, 9.

Fenton, Michele. "Re: Ask a Librarian Question." Received by: Reference Department, Herman B. Wells Library, Indiana University-Bloomington, April 7, 2010.

———. "Stepping Out on Faith: Lillian Haydon Childress Hall, Pioneer Black Librarian." *Indiana Libraries*, 33, no. 1 (2014): 5-11.

———. "Way Down Yonder at the Cherry Street Branch: A Short History of Evansville's Negro Library." *Indiana Libraries*, 30, no. 2 (2011): 37-38.

Fenton, Michele, and Deloice Holliday. "We Need Some Color in Here: Educating and Recruiting Minority Librarians in Indiana." In *The 21st Century Black Librarian in America: Issues and Challenges*, edited by Andrew P. Jackson, Julius C. Jefferson Jr., and Akilah S. Nosakhere, 144-45, Lanham, MD: Scarecrow Press, 2012.

Freeman, Rodney. "A Snapshot of Indiana Librarians Leading in Diversity Fellowship Participants after the Program Has Concluded." *Indiana Libraries*, 33, no. 1 (2014): 12-15.

———. *Little Rodney the Librarian*. Charlotte, NC: Preservation Media LLC, 2022.

Grant, George. *The Directory of Ethnic Professionals in LIS*. Winter Park, FL: Four-G Publishers, 1991.

Hale, Charles. *Narrative Evaluation Report of USOE Title II-B Institute Education for Librarianship on Urban Community Colleges*. Bloomington: Graduate Library School, Indiana University, 1974.

Hale, Charles, and Shirley Edsall. "The Education of Community College Librarians." *Journal of Education for Librarianship*, 16, no. 2 (1975): 75-85.

Hostetter, Anita M. "A Library School for Negroes." *ALA Bulletin*, 13, no. 4 (1939): 247.

Hunt, Rebecca D. "African American Leaders in the Library Profession: Little Known History." *Black History Bulletin*, 76, no. 1 (2013): 16.

"Indiana University Library Training Program." *Library Occurrent*, 15, no. 9 (1947): 609-10.

"IndyPL's Hayes and Indiana State Library's Fenton Appointed as BCALA Officers." *Wednesday Word: The Latest in Indiana Library News*, May 27, 2020. https://content.govdelivery.com/accounts/INLIBRARY/bulletins/28c933d.

Ingram, Handsel G. "Black Librarians with Earned and Honorary Doctorates." In *Handbook of Black Librarianship*, 2nd ed., edited by E. J. Josey and Marva L. DeLoach, 192. Lanham, MD: Scarecrow, 2000.

"I.S.L. Summer Course in Library Service." *Library Occurrent*, 15, no. 10 (1947): 645.

Johnson, James Weldon. "Segregation in Public Libraries." *The New York Age*, September 30, 1922, 4.

Jones, Reinette. *Library Services to African Americans in Kentucky: From Reconstruction Era to the 1960s*, 53-55. Jefferson, NC: McFarland, 2006.

Josey, E. J. "Edward Christopher Williams: Librarian's Librarian." *Negro History Bulletin*, 33, no. 3 (1970): 70-77.

Malone, Cheryl Knott. "Louisville Free Public Library's Racially Segregated Branches, 1905-35." *The Register of the Kentucky Historical Society*, 93, no. 2 (1995): 173-74.

Martin, Robert Sidney, and Orvin Lee Shiflett. "Hampton, Fisk, and Atlanta: The Foundations, the American Library Association, and Library Education for Blacks, 1925-1941." *Libraries & Culture*, 31, no. 2 (1996): 299-325.

"Mr. T. F. Blue on American Library Association Program." *Louisville Leader*, July 8, 1922, 1.

"Needs of State Library." *Indianapolis Journal*, December 10, 1902, 7.

Ndumu, Ana, and Renate Chancellor. "DuMont, 35 Years Later: HBCUs, LIS Education, and Institutional Discrimination." *Journal of Education for Library and Information Science*, 62, no. 2 (2021): 166-69.

"News Notes." *Library Occurrent*, 13, no. 3 (1939): 87.

"News Notes." *Library Occurrent*, 14, no. 8 (1943): 223.

Oder, Norman. "Clark Atlanta University to Close 62-Year-Old LIS School." *Library Journal*, 128, no. 19 (2003): 16.

"Personals." *Library Occurrent*, 3, no. 12 (1914): 204.

"Personals." *Library Occurrent*, 8, no. 2 (1927): 66

Pollert, Johannah. "Untold Stories: Wilma Gibbs Unearths the Hidden History of Blacks in Indiana." *Indianapolis Woman*, 10, no. 2 (2003): 36-41.

Porter, Dorothy B. "Phylon Profile, XIV: Edward Christopher Williams." *Phylon (1940-1956)*, 8, no. 4 (1947): 315-21.

"Prominent Woman Returns." *Indianapolis Recorder*, April 2, 1927, 5.

"Receives Appointment (Photo)." *Indianapolis Recorder*, September 6, 1947, 5.

Sacco, Nick Sacco. "Creating the Public Library Commission of Indiana." *The Public Library Commission of Indiana: Public Libraries in the Hoosier State, 1899-1925*, Summer 2013. https://www.publiclibrarycommissionofindiana.wordpress.com/the-public-library-commission-of-indiana/creating-the-public-library-commission-of-indiana.

Shiflett, O. Lee. "The American Library Association's Quest for a Black Library School." *Journal of Education for Library and Information Science*, 35, no. 1 (1994): 68-71.

Shores, Louis. "Library Service and the Negro." *Journal of Negro Education*, 1, no. ¾ (1932): 376.

Smith, S. L. "The Passing of the Hampton Library School." *The Journal of Negro Education*, 9, no. 1 (1940): 51-58.

Smith-Woodard, Marcia. "The Importance of Achieving Diversity in Libraries." *Indiana Libraries*, 31, no. 1 (2012): 50-53.

Spradling, Mary Mace. "Black Librarians in Kentucky." In *The Black Librarian in the Southeast: Reminiscences, Activities, Challenges*, edited by Annette L Phinazee, 43. Durham, NC: NCCU School of Library Science, 1980.

Stussy, Susan A. "Profile of an Indiana Career in Libraries: Florabelle Wilson." *Indiana Libraries*, 6, no. 2 (1986): 34-39.

"Summer Course in Library Service, State Library, June 14-July 31, 1937." *Library Occurrent*, 12, no. 5 (1937): 125-27.

"Summer School." *Library Occurrent*, 3, no. 12 (1914): 195.

"Summer School." *Library Occurrent*, 4, no. 7 (1916): 119-20.

"Summer School." *Library Occurrent*, 5, no. 1 (1918): 16-18.

"Summer School for Librarians, 1914." *Library Occurrent*, 3, no. 10 (1914): 170.

"Summer School Held." *Library Occurrent*, 16, no. 3 (1948): 81.

"Summer School 1915." *Library Occurrent*, 4, no. 4 (1915): 51.

"Summer School 1931." *Library Occurrent*, 10, no. 4 (1931): 185.

"Summer School Students for 1923." *Library Occurrent*, 6, no. 11 (1923): 411-12.

"Summer School Students 1921." *Library Occurrent*, 6, no. 3 (1921): 112.

"Summer School Students Accepted for 1924." *Library Occurrent*, 7, no. 3 (1924): 69.

"Summer School Students Accepted for 1925." *Library Occurrent*, 7, no. 7 (1924): 318.

"Summer Training. " *Library Occurrent*, 16, no. 9 (1950): 278.

"Summer Training Course." *Library Occurrent*, 15, no. 9 (1947): 615.

Swigger, Boyd Keith. *The MLS Project: An Assessment after Sixty Years*. Lanham, MD: Scarecrow Press, 2010.

Taylor, Joyce G. "The Smile That Hooked Me for Life." *Indiana Libraries*, 22, no. 2 (2003): 8-10.

Totten, Herman L. "Southeastern Black Library Educators." *The Black Librarian in the Southeast: Reminiscences, Activities, Challenges*, edited by Annette L Phinazee, 202-04. Durham, NC: NCCU School of Library Science, 1980.

"Unique Historical Database, The Black Male Archives, Chronicles the Success of Black Men." *Black Enterprise*, March 15, 2022. https://www.blackenterprise.com/unique-historical-database-the-black-male-archives-chronicles-the-success-of-black-men/.

Van Jackson, Wallace. "Negro Library Workers." *Library Quarterly: Information, Community, Policy*, 10, no. 1 (1940): 95-108.

Warren, Hazel B. "The Indiana Public Library Commission." *Library Occurrent*, 10, no. 1 (1931): 32-35.

Wheeler, Maurice, and Debbie Johnson-Houston. "A Brief History of Library Service to African Americans." *American Libraries*, 35, no. 2 (2004): 42-45.

Williams, Celeste. "Indiana's History Is Her Career Passion: Archivist Ensures Hoosiers Have Works That Teach Them about Their Past." *Indianapolis Star*, February 15, 2001, 1, 11.

"Willie Miller: Movers & Shakers 2016—Innovators." *Library Journal*, March 17, 2016. https://www.libraryjournal.com/story/willie-miller-movers-shakers-2016-innovators.

Wilma Gibbs Moore Graduate Endowed Scholarship. Indiana University Luddy School of Informatics, Computing and Engineering, 2023. https://luddy.iupui.edu/alumni-partners/moore-scholarship.html.

Woodson, Almeta Gould. "Fifty Years of Service: A Chronological History of the School of Library Service Atlanta University, 1941-1979; the School of Library and Information Studies Atlanta University, 1979-1989; the School of Library and Information Studies, Clark Atlanta University, 1989-1991." *Georgia Librarian*, 28, no. 3 (1991): 76, 78.

# Chapter 4C
# Issues in Equity, Diversity, Inclusion, and Multiculturalism

## 4.11

*Know Your History*

INFORMATION ORGANIZATION IN HOUSE/BALL CULTURE AND THE POTENTIAL FOR LIBRARIANSHIP

Aisha Aminu

Most librarianship is done within formalized institutions, whether public, private, or academic. The information and resources in these institutions are often guarded, requiring registration or membership fees from patrons in exchange for access and denying access from nonpatrons altogether. As a result, many marginalized and racialized communities that experience systemic oppression from the intersecting systems of white supremacist cisheteropatriarchy are often denied access from the valuable information in our institutions. Librarians committed to information equity should be willing to look outside institutions and work with organizers and activists from these communities that often have their own established systems and hierarchies of information. One such community is the queer ballroom community. Contemporary ballroom culture is a decentralized network of Black and brown queer people, which although originally started in New York City, can now be found in different pockets around the world. In ballroom, community members use performance to create an alternative kinship structure that critiques and revises dominant white cisheteropatriarchal ideals and practices.[1] Ballroom culture has two prominent dimensions: houses and balls. Houses are familial structures that are socially rather than biologically created. Although in some cases houses serve as homes where members live and congregate, by and large, houses are social configurations that serve as sources of support for the diverse membership of the ballroom community.[2] Houseparents provide guidance and life skills for their children of various ages, races/ethnicities (usually BIPOC), genders, and sexualities. Another important role of houses is to organize and compete in ball events. Members of houses produce and participate in these competitive and celebratory performance events on an international scale.

The ball is the central means through which members of the community affirm, celebrate, and constructively critique their fellow members.[3] Within the ball environment, the key information roles are clearly defined and can be classified.

**COMMENTATOR**

Equal parts emcee, director, and historian, the commentator plays an integral part in ensuring the success of a ball so integral that larger functions often have two commentators with one serving in a more supportive role. Commentators must be in harmony with themselves and other players in the ball situation. The commentator is responsible for presiding over the ball's proceedings, pumping up the audience, maintaining the flow and energy of the ball, and so on. A good commentator makes the difference between an okay ball and an "ovah" ball. Most of the commentator's directing is done through moving through the ball space, speaking, and chanting on the microphone. A chant is a freestyle usually done over a ballroom track (that usually features minimal lyrics and the signature Ha crash to allow for the commentator's voice to ring clear and direct the ball's proceedings). The chant is instrumental to how information is communicated at a ball, helping to direct the chaotic ball energy and keep everyone on the same page. The commentator's chant helps the walkers during their performance by keeping them on beat and enabling them to show off their performance and their effects.[4]

**WALKERS**

Walkers are the ball competitors. They walk the categories at a ball in their "effect," which is their interpretation of what the category calls for. Walkers are often members of a ballroom "house"—an alternative family structure within the ballroom subculture, often named after fashion houses, which provides members with support within and outside of balls—or they walk as "007s" or independent walkers without a house. The walker's role in a ball is to "get their 10s" from the judges by demonstrating their mastery of the basic elements of their category and an understanding of what the category calls for and to battle and shade their opponent(s) for the grand prize (GP).

**JUDGES PANEL**

Judges are prominent members of the community, often walkers or former walkers themselves, who have proven themselves to be experts by consistently walking and winning in their category. Judges are responsible for giving 10 or chopping walkers and for picking battle winners.

**AUDIENCE**

The audience usually consists of ballroom community members who are not walking and admirers adjacent to and outside of the community. Members of the same house are often seen together (sometimes in uniform) chanting in support of a house member that is walking the ball. They also help walkers prepare their effects and productions for their respective categories. While entirely theatrical, balls forgo the pretense of fourth-wall realism and instead require active participation from the audience. Do not go to a ball if you are not ready to scream and/or clap.

**DJ**

The music is the heartbeat of the ball. The DJ controls the music, which is often a fusion of house, funk, disco, samples, and the signature Ha crash.[5] The DJ must be able to stay in sync with the commentator(s), walkers, and the audience for the duration of the ball.

**LSS (OR LISS)**

Traditionally done at the beginning of the ball before the categories, the commentator calls out Legends, Icons, Stars, and Statements, one by one, who are considered notable in the community, affirming the social practices of the community.

The LSS is a key information landmark of a ball, as it allows the community to recognize other members within the ballroom scene for their consistent wins and moments that they have created on the runway for their category. For a successful LSS, the commentator must be able to call out members knowing what categories they walk, how they walk their categories—for example, soft and cunt versus dramatics for vogue—what prizes they've won and where, what house the members are currently in, and in some cases who their rivals are if the members are "stormed" during their LSS. MCs must also be able to give a chant that suits each member and their performance style and draws out a sickening performance and allows those called out to show their talents. The LSS also functions to get the audience excited for the main categories.

Competitors "walk" against one another on behalf of their respective houses to be judged by the panel of community leaders who themselves have walked and won their categories many times over. Usually, walkers are first called to "get their 10s" by embodying what the category calls for to the audience and the judges. The commentator calls for "anybody walking" and begins a countdown and one by one walkers strut out, aiming to get "10s across the board" from the panel. Judges either give their 10 or a chop; if at least one judge chops a walker, they are disqualified and do not advance to battles (sometimes a two-chop rule is implemented for beginner categories). Walkers then battle in pairs (or sometimes in threes), trying to win the vote of the judges, often while throwing shade at their opponents until one walker emerges as the GP winner. Most mainstream balls often have prize money attached to GP. This all happens while the audience screams chants affiliated with a walker's house if they have one.[6] Even for the seasoned ballgoer, balls can be dizzying and overwhelming, overloaded with beautiful costume effects, dazzling theatricality, and intoxicating sounds. For the uninitiated, the proceedings of the ball can be confusing especially as the rituals of a ball and the meanings behind them are never made explicit. The unique experience of witnessing a ball can be hard to capture or put into mere words; a ball can feel like a spiritual endeavour, a ritual, and a sporting event all at once. A ball is the quintessential "black queer space" as defined by Marlon Bailey as organizing one often requires the "place-making practices that Black LGBT people undertake to affirm and support their non-normative sexual identities, embodiment, and community values and practices."[7] This carving out of Black queer space is often necessary as Black queer people often find themselves outside of the margins of systems of white supremacist cisheteropatriarchy and are systematically excluded from and oppressed within more normative spaces because of their intersecting identities.

**CATEGORIES**

Categories can be defined as performance classifications that structure a ball. The requirements of a category usually go hand in hand with the theme of a ball and are given beforehand so walkers can prepare their "effect," which is their interpretation of the category. Typical categories found at a ball include virgin vogue/runway, face, runway, realness, body, sex siren, and performance. Categories are often divided into subcategories based on loose gender classifications found in ballroom that include:

Male Figure (MF)
Butch Queens (BQ): gay/bi cisgender men
Butches: masculine presenting lesbians and women of all sexual orientations
Trans men: transmasculine or transgender men
Female Figure (FF)
Femme Queens (FQ): transgender women at various stages of their transitions
Butch Queens up in Drag: gay men who perform in drag but do not take hormones and do not live as women)
Women: feminine-presenting cisgender women of all sexual orientations
Open To All (OTA)

To battle in a category, contestants must first "get their 10s" by showing the basic elements of their category for the judges' approval or they are chopped and are disqualified from moving on to battles.

During the categories, the commentator is responsible for communicating to the contestants, panel, and audience simultaneously and for directing the flow of the walkers. They communicate everything from what the category calls for, where walkers should stand, if they got their 10 or got chopped, who just won a battle and will be advancing, who wins in their individual subcategories, and who wins GP. They do all this while chanting and assisting the walkers during their performance by keeping them on beat. They also are responsible to keep the energy of the room up as the ball progresses, sometimes having to instruct the audience if their energy does not match the energy of the walkers.

The runway is the central fixture of the ball where all the proceedings take place. It is where recognition and affirmation are given and where partakers engage in competition and critique with one another. It usually features a long stretch of space with the audience positioned on either side with the judges' panel positioned at the end and the commentator on the side. As the focal point of the event, the runway is instrumental in giving the ball its sense of Black queer space; the runway makes explicit the relationship between the information channels and highlights the continuous exchange of information between them. On the runway, the commentator is usually found between the judges and the participants, and functions as an intermediary for the exchange of energies and information that occurs over the course of the ball.[8] The runway also functions as a microcosm of the larger ballroom scene; the physical and social dynamics that play out on the runway are hierarchical but fluid, and they often reinforce the "social organization of Ballroom culture that is widely accepted by its members."[9] The runway helps give the ball a sense of space, thereby fostering community and belonging for the often marginalized members of ballroom.

Outside of the community, ballroom is more popular than it has ever been. Although the origins of the scene can be found as far back as the Harlem Renaissance, ballroom was first thrust into the mainstream spotlight in the 1990s through the eyes of Jennifer Livingston in *Paris is Burning*, and later, Madonna's "Vogue."[10] Though both have garnered criticism over time, they helped cement the world of ballroom as a cultural touchstone for many queer youths around the world. The advent of the internet and social media platforms like Facebook, YouTube, and Instagram have helped to propel the scene internationally with sizable communities in countries like Canada, Japan, and the UK, with houses like Ninja and Miyake Mugler having house chapters all over the world, allowing for queer youths to engage in ballroom on a global scale.[11] In today's world, ballroom exists in the mainstream through prominent works like Beyoncé's *Renaissance* album, the TV shows *Pose* and *Legendary*, and through social media outlets like TikTok where ballroom tracks now go viral and users post videos of themselves voguing to various degrees of proficiency. However, this popularity within the wider white supremacist capitalist cisheteropatriarchal structure complicates the sociopolitical context of the ballroom scene. In some ways, members of the community are still often racialized working-class queer people who live in vulnerable and precarious situations.[12] In other ways, the scene is more commercialized with some houses functioning as talent management and production companies.[12] However, the kinship and alternative family structure that houses provide still plays a prominent role in the community. Houses encourage a sense of belonging among members, which is reinforced through the competitive ritual of the balls, where walkers take pride in representing and honoring the house they belong to.[13] Houses also often provide members with financial support, accommodation, and job opportunities. As voguing and ballroom have become more popular, as a result more centralized, some houses have been able to cement their place in the mainstream market. More localized houses that are not able to enter the mainstream (or that refuse to for many reasons, capitalist exploitation being one of them) risk falling into social and cultural irrelevancy.

Ballroom is not a utopia; in a scene made up of marginalized and racialized queer people from all walks of life, conflict is inevitable. Beyond interpersonal conflict, the scene is also plagued with the fallout of adhering to and enforcing the European and white supremacist beauty standards it attempts to satirize and subvert. As a result, instances of colorism, fatphobia, ableism, and transphobia entangled with desirability politics are prevalent in the scene and can often manifest hierarchically with the most marginalized, and least desirable, in wider society once again finding themselves at the bottom. The increased popularity of ballroom in the mainstream, and the aspirations of members to capitalize on that attention, means that the scene must contend with the commodition and fetishization of the market economy and how that creates a more normative version of the subculture. Within balls, this tension can be found in categories like Face where the requirements include clear skin, perfect white teeth, facial symmetry, and angular facial structures or Labels where walkers have to come out decked in expensive pieces from prominent fashion houses or Realness where walkers are required to "pass as real" and embody racially-coded archetypes of masculinity and femininity (e.g., the subcategories of "thug/banjee realness" and "prettyboy/prettygirl realness"). Additionally, while the gender system found in ballroom is more expansive than that found in wider society and fluid in some ways, it is rigid in many others with an adherence to the gender binary and the idea of sexual dimorphism. As a result, nonbinary and gender nonconforming members can find themselves caught in the intersections of the gender system as they are forced to choose or walk categories that may not align with their gender identities. Additionally, within the scene the most power and resources are concentrated within the house structures with 007s or independents often having trouble finding practice space, putting together effects, and making an overall statement at balls. Finding a house is also harder for members who do not walk balls, as many houses often require some form of talent and performance ability as a prerequisite for membership.

Documentation and oral history are an important facet of ballroom culture. Ballroom is filled with its historians, archivists, and librarians. In many ways these roles are fluid and shared among community members, for example, "know your history" is a popular refrain you might hear in the scene. Entities like Ballroom Throwbacks Television (Brtbtv) on YouTube, Ballvoyeurs, and *TENz* magazine on Instagram are just a few entirely dedicated to documenting and circulating videos from balls on social media. The contributions of exceptional members in the scene are also documented through the titles of Legend, Icon, Star, and Statement and the ritual of the LSS. These titles denote the amount of time a member has spent in the scene and are given to the member by their peers or elders at significant balls. Awards Balls are also a mainstay in the scene, with the Dorian Corey Awards ball where notable members are inducted into the hall of fame being the most prominent. The oral traditions of ballroom, while in line with other Black diasporic oral documentations, can often clash with the writing-oriented knowledge synthesis methods of the larger white supremacist cisheteropatriarchal information systems. There is a great potential for librarianship with groups like the ballroom community, which are often greatly marginalized through epistemic injustice and under our current system of surveillance capitalism. However, librarians must be sensitive to the possible power relationships with these communities, the communities' sociocultural dynamics and how they might align or clash with those of mainstream society, and the dangers of traditional anthropological and ethnographic practices. Librarians, if not part of these communities themselves, must also be committed to a participatory relationship that empowers the community members, adds sizable and demonstrable value to these communities, and minimizes harm.

## NOTES

1. Marlon M. Bailey, "Gender/Racial Realness: Theorizing the Gender System in Ballroom Culture," *Feminist Studies*, 37, no. 2 (2011): 365–86. https://doi.org/10.1353/fem.2011.0016.
2. Ibid.
3. Marlon M. Bailey, "Engendering Space: Ballroom Culture and the Spatial Practice of Possibility in Detroit," *Gender, Place & Culture*, 21, no. 4 (2013): 489–507. https://doi.org/10.1080/0966369x.2013.786688.
4. Ibid.
5. PBS LearningMedia, "Ballroom: The Sound of NYC's Underground Vogue Scene | Sound Field." PBS LearningMedia, https://www.pbslearningmedia.org/resource/ballroom-nycs-underground-vogue-scene-video/sound-field/.
6. Bailey, "Engendering Space."
7. Ibid.
8. Ibid.
9. Ibid.
10. Constantine Chatzipapatheodoridis, "Strike a Pose, Forever: The Legacy of Vogue and Its Re-Contextualization in Contemporary Camp Performances," *European Journal of American Studies*, 11, no. 11-3 (Jan. 2017). https://doi.org/10.4000/ejas.11771.
11. Bailey, "Engendering Space."
12. Chatzipapatheodoridis, "Strike a Pose."
13. Ibid.

## WORKS CITED

Bailey, Marlon M. "Engendering Space: Ballroom Culture and the Spatial Practice of Possibility in Detroit." *Gender, Place & Culture*, 21, no. 4 (2013): 489–507. https://doi.org/10.1080/0966369x.2013.786688.

———. "Gender/Racial Realness: Theorizing the Gender System in Ballroom Culture." *Feminist Studies*, 37, no. 2 (2011): 365–86. https://doi.org/10.1353/fem.2011.0016.

Chatzipapatheodoridis, Constantine. "Strike a Pose, Forever: The Legacy of Vogue and Its Re-Contextualization in Contemporary Camp Performances." *European Journal of American Studies*, 11, no. 11-3 (Jan. 2017). https://doi.org/10.4000/ejas.11771.

PBS LearningMedia. "Ballroom: The Sound of NYC's Underground Vogue Scene | Sound Field." PBS LearningMedia. www.pbslearningmedia.org/resource/ballroom-nycs-underground-vogue-scene-video/sound-field/.

# 4.12

## Reconstitution of Ubuntu Spaces, Leading While an Ujima Culture Keeper

Roland Barksdale-Hall

Black Sugar

Dew drops of Kalinago past
Cane on my sinewy strapped back,
    Cleanse my fester, your refined rum.
Freedom songs, Uhuru comes,

Emancipation night watch,
Heated ancestral memories I wash
First distilled black cane sugar
    I rise berry black sweet rum.

—Roland Barksdale Hall

Shiraz Durrani migrated from Kenya, taught at London Metropolitan University, and identified two components to Black librarianship: "services to the Black community" through partnership and "work environment."[1] *Ubuntu*, a Xhosa term, affirms the meaning of shared existence and humanity. Tutu expounds on the human relations aspect: "Ubuntu recognizes that human beings need each other for survival and well-being. A person is a person only through other persons, we say. We must care for one another in order to thrive."[2] John Clarke, a historian, posited that critical to achieving our "responsibility" for "restoration of humanity to the world" was a possession of a "liberation" mind-set and passion for *uhuru*.[3] Uhuru and *ujima*, both Kiswahili words, respectively mean "freedom" and "collective work and responsibility." An ujima culture keeper includes the following: pursue personal freedom; promote appreciation of culture; partner with antiracists, community, and agencies with responsibility to speak, act; and meet the needs of Black people and marginalized communities.

In the first edition of *The Handbook of Black Librarianship* Professor Wendell Wray identified limited financial resource allocations, structural barriers, and the "role of politics."[4] He advocated for "resourcefulness," "collaboration," and "use of volunteers" to ensure services in the Black community. The contradiction of libraries being "radical institutions" that are free and designed with "space that demands nothing from you to enter and nothing for you to stay" and serve as icons of culture while also being "places of objectification, racism"[5] is further exacerbated by the disruptions caused by the pandemic and has contributed to greater challenges in meeting the needs of marginalized communities and belies the hunger for Ubuntu spaces. As an ujima culture keeper, I found a passion for uhuru, drive to lead, faith, support of colleagues, and the resolve to meet people's needs and make a difference. This chapter discusses reconstitution of Ubuntu spaces, moments in time on a leadership path while an ujima culture keeper, the role of the Black Caucus of the American Library Association (BCALA) and the National Conference of African American Librarians in leadership development, the Progressive African Librarian and Information Activists' Group (PALIAct), and success strategies. Over several decades I asked, "How can Ubuntu spaces be incorporated on the path to liberation?"

## RECONSTITUTION OF UBUNTU SPACES

Mathabane and Lief and Thompson[6] examine ubuntu for "racial healing in America" to partnership for development of a restorative learning-rich "people-focused" center in South Africa. My vision of ubuntu spaces in libraries was Sankofa restorative work with parallels that took on theoretical and practical applications framed in the context of a global community. Sankofa, one of the Adinkra symbols from the Akan culture in West Africa, means to go back and fetch what is lost. Adinkra symbols represent significant African icons; form part of a vast knowledge system of ideas, wisdom, and euphemisms; and offer much to reconstitution of ubuntu space.

Black health has been and continues to be a significant issue in global communities. Broadnax discussed biomedical librarianship; identified the Edwin Smith papyrus, the "oldest medical book," as a product of ancient Egypt; and provided an overview of the Association of Health Information and Libraries in Africa.[7] In the emerging role of the BCALA, Alston has noted "collective concerns," including "erasing the educational gap between Black and white students, addressing crime and poverty in Black-majority communities, addressing higher rates of obesity, diabetes, heart disease, cancer, and HIV/AIDS and other issues."[8] At the Sixth National Conference of African American Librarians (NCAAL) I presented on timely health issues pertinent to the Black community and celebrated the release of Sankofa publications. I received a free copy of the book *Medical Apartheid* and presented on the health and wellness trek at Culture Keepers VI NCAAL in Fort Wealth, Texas.[9]

Dr. E. J. Josey, a BCALA cofounder, gave me an autographed copy of his Sankofa reading, *What Black Librarians Are Saying*, on a visit to his home in Pittsburgh, Pennsylvania. The book instantly became one of my treasures, has appreciated in value over time, and been a source in my exploration of how Black librarians got here. In *What Black Librarians Are Saying* James Welbourne[10] identified an "information imbalance" and addressed a need for "information re-education" and "black liberational" initiatives with inclusion of "historical precedents in African culture for the design and conduct of cultural and social systems." Here was someone I knew and respected. When I worked as the African American specialist at the CLP Homewood Branch, I reported to Mr. Welbourne. He became a trusted mentor. His essay's position as the second chapter in the book in part II, titled "Black Communities and Informational Needs," belies significance. In E .J. Josey's book, published over a half century ago, I found the essays to be topics of interest which resonated and related to present times. I benefited from networking opportunities through participation in BCALA.

At the turn of the twenty-first century, I embraced the role of a culture keeper due in part to pioneer library leaders. I say *asante sana*, Kiswahili for thank you, to Dr. E. J. Josey, Effie Lee Morris, and the other sage elders in founding BCALA, sharing ancestral wisdom and setting me on an ujima culture keeper leadership trek. In 1984, Dr. Josey led a delegation of forty to the IFLA conference held in Nairobi, Kenya, when I was in library school at the University of Pittsburgh. Effie Lee Morris, a cofounder of BCALA, was one of the first to contribute to the Black Library Pioneers Oral History Project, conducted along with librarian and colleague Jocelyn Poole. The struggle of Bongiwe Nkabinde from political prisoner to Johannesburg public library manager was published to provide a global vantage point.

## MOMENTS IN TIME—1990s

Durrani noted that librarians have comfortably hidden behind "neutrality" and exhibited a lack of social responsibility. When I served as CLP African American specialist, I displayed social responsibility, questioned social practices, and wrote "Violence saves a life," an on-point commentary on the irony of the former Pennsylvania governor, receiving a transplant from a Black victim of violence, appearing in the "Sunday Perspectives" of the June 27, 1993, issue of *The Pittsburgh Post-Gazette*. Upon reading the piece, one of the African American CLP administrators responded, "You got plenty of guts more than me."

I spearheaded an ujima book donation project for Kwanzaa, made a direct appeal for books about African American historical figures, and distributed them to youth in the community. Black business and civic leaders respected my work, recognized an intrinsic value in literacy, and donated funds for the book purchase. When I was head librarian at Penn State Shenango, in Farrell, Pennsylvania, I provided leadership in planning and spatial utilization for the Penn State Shenango Library. Yet I experienced harassment.

My trek was a highly spirited one, retracing my ancestor's journey from freedom through the doors of return, the last stop in West Africa prior to embarking on slave ships. I visited the Kwame Nkrumah Memorial in Accra, W. E. B Du Bois Centre, George Padmore Library, and donated a copy of my book *People in Search of Opportunity*. I felt a spirit of oppression outside the Cape Coast dungeon, decided to walk up the hill to shops. I moseyed into a cluttered shop, picked up a walking stick and noticed the carved handle with the Sankofa bird, "Go back and fetch what is lost"; the midsection, Gye Ame, "God is everywhere"; and bottom inscribed with "Black Survive." The proprietor told me, "It's one of a kind." I thought, "I've heard that before." Though I felt a deep calling and a message for me, I, too, felt God wanted me to speak out.

## MOMENTS IN TIME—2000s

I chose to rise in personal freedom, cofounded an African-focused cultural arts group, JAH Kente International, in Washington, DC. A year later, I experienced an attack on my home while my wife and children were present. I placed an ad offering a reward in the newspaper. In 2005, I served as editor of the BCALA Newsletter. I provided "renewed interest and support" for development of the Progressive African Librarian and Information Activists' Group (PALIAct). I joined other "committed" supporters, including Del R. Hornbuckle and Alfred Kagan, to promote progressive African library workers.[11]

Progressive African Librarian and Information Activists' Group (PALIAct) supports "the principles of social justice, equality, equity, human welfare and the development of cultural and social democracy" and using your influence to bring attention to "issues of social responsibility on the agenda" or whatever other platform exists.[12] PALIAct proposed an "activist agenda," pushed for recognition of the rights of African people not only in "theory" but in "practice," and supported "pilot projects" in countries to "develop ideas and practices" of "people-oriented information services"[13]

PALIAct principle supports leadership development for Black library workers, advances "investigating and organizing" efforts for a more democratic workplace," and "resistance to the managerialism of the of the present time."

Second, PALIAct principle is marginalized communities deserve "equal access to information services" and "inclusiveness of information services."

Third, PALIAct principles encourage "organizing in partnerships with other activists in cultural and educational fields."

Fourth, PALIAct principles include "supporting the collection, organization, preservation and dissemination of the documents of people's struggles in all forms and languages."

Fifth, PALIAct principles emphasize collections need to address the needs of people. Building collections comprised of "alternative materials representing a wide range of progressive viewpoints from within Africa and overseas, which are often excluded from traditional libraries" is critical.

Last, PALIAct principles oppose "corporate globalization" and "prioritizes human value and need over profits."[14]

The first issue of *Information Equality, Africa*—formerly known as *PALIAct Ideas and Action*—changed its name due in part to "growth," "development," and ongoing "development" in *Information Equality, Africa*'s inaugural issue. The fifty-five-page black-and-white issue, available online and in print, included reports from the Kenya Centre and Naivashia (Kenya) Centre, correspondences, queries, review of electronic resources, training opportunities, and PALIAct news. The "Information Serving People: Experience & Ideas Section" included reviews and shared ideas from China, India, Nigeria, Angola, Zimbabwe, South Africa, Mexico, Vietnam, Namibia, Uganda, and Egypt.

The documentation section included minutes from "Millenium Development Goals and Health Information Provision in Africa" from the Association for Health Information and Libraries. Of special import to a postpandemic world, goals included "by 2015, every person worldwide will have access to an informed healthcare provider" and development of an African index medicus (AIM). Broadnax discussed the progress of AIM and recognized it as an example of a successful African collaborative, "breaking the traditional Western model."[15]

Durrani contributed an article about PALIAct and responded to a "searching question" about the Quality Leaders Project (QLP) at London Metropolitan University. I posed, "Does QLP deliver an 'ideal information world'?" John Gabriel, Department of Applied Social Sciences, London Metropolitan University, provides a series "working paper on social exclusion." Two pieces, "The Role of the Library in the WSF Process" and "Librarians to Extend the World Social Forum" by Mikal Book and "Internet AND Intention" (abstract) by Toni Samek filled out the article section. I contributed the final two articles, "Developing Critical Thinkers for Today and Tomorrow" and an overview of a conference paper, "Politics of Information, Knowledge, and Transformation in Africa and Its Diaspora" from the inaugural Dubois-Nkrumah-Dunham conference of the African Studies Department at the University of Pittsburgh, held March 31–April XX, 2006. The issue included coverage from *The Journal of Pan African Studies*. Three pages of *mashairi*, the Kiswahili word for "poetical," rounded out the *Information Equality, Africa* issue.

## MOMENTS IN TIME—2010s

I served as the director of the Quinby Street Resource Center, when I developed an innovative six-session life and empowerment program for people living in poverty with life skills, health literacy, and financial literacy components. *Farrell* showed the "multidimensional humanity" in ethnic mutual support groups and was noted for "capturing Farrell's ethnic heritage."[16] I received the 2015 BCALA Award at the Ninth National Conference of African American Librarians in St. Louis, Missouri.

## MOMENTS IN TIME—2020s

In 2021, I completed my service as chairman of JAH Kente International with twenty-one years of service and was named chairman emeritus. As branch manager at the Farrell Library, I developed and implemented the Purpose of the Day (POD), which is a monthly democratic team meeting where staff listens to one another and shares ideas. The Muddiest Moment, a staple on the agenda, offers a time to share the most challenging occurrence. I implemented the Muddiest Moment, empowered library workers, and facilitated open discussion about challenges faced in libraries.

Leading while an ujima culture keeper, I developed human relations and deep connections in the community to combat the resistance. I solicited a private donation of seven new computers with gaming keyboards when three of the public computers were broken. I was rewarded in seeing the surprised faces of our youth. Over sixty youth attended a private showing of the African-themed movie *Wakanda Forever* through a partnership between the Farrell Library, Farrell Recreation Commission, the local unit of the NAACP, the Urban League, Alpha Kappa Alpha sorority, and Subivu. Program offerings included two educational and cultural modules in the library Farrell: STEM pyramid making and mask making. *Wakanda Forever* library scholars received a free copy of book *Black Panther: Rise Together* with a positive message about the significance of community and respect of elders.

## CONCLUSION

Today's challenges should not be viewed as insurmountable to social progress, though the persistence of an underdevelopment or lack of acknowledgment by library boards of Black staff for senior library positions, lack of equity in resource allocations to libraries serving Black people and other marginalized communities present challenges.

How might Black librarians make ubuntu spaces in times of stagnation? You can choose to persevere, focus on mutual humanity, and operate in personal freedom.

You can partner to identify funding streams to meet your community's needs. Resourcefulness and innovation continue to be required, though the rewards far outweigh the costs.

You can choose to learn, establish global connections, and extend the radius of trust to library workers, partners, and community. PALIAct emphasizes cooperation with neighbors and partners. Goleman identifies "sensing others' development needs," "bolstering abilities," as part of competencies in emotional intelligence.[17] "Empowering Black staff and communities to be part of the real decision-making process in a structured, organized way, and creating more friendly working conditions for Black staff can result in improving Black communities.[18]

You can participate in the International Federation of Libraries and Institutions (IFLA), join the Black Caucus of the American Library Association, serve on a committee, and commiserate with liberation-minded folks.

You can provide innovations in services, invite "the rhythms and vibrations" in our libraries. The POD meeting is a source of innovation. I partnered with government, civic, and sorority leaders in the "*Wakanda Forever* Project" in welcoming an African presence. Wray noted, "Nothing is more depressing than to find a library in the Black community which does not reflect the life of the community."[19]

You can perform a community study, meet the people, and look for the "multidimensionality of human reality" in ubuntu spaces. "For a community to be of relevance in this respect, it has to either be a community that has been part of a person's life in the past already or it has to be a community that is the process of being created because its members are strengthening their relations in their daily lives."[20] Parallels in historical precedents in a community context offer analogues for framing reconstitution of ubuntu space. My published study of Farrell's Twin City Elks Lodge showed a unifying presence in the African American community, provided a context for common community understanding, reinforced memories, and resulted in *Farrell*.

You can offer ubuntu spaces for sharing ideas, community forums, and book talks. I hosted community forums; developed the program "Sharing Reflections, Uncovering Hidden Figures," where people from the community shared their stories of resistance to oppression; and held a book talk on the graphic history *Man on a Mission: James Meredith and the Battle of Ole Miss* with an audio appearance from civil rights activist James Meredith.[21]

You can speak out against racism. I am an antiracist. I interviewed for a feature about celebrating Kwanzaa in our community for several decades, addressed unjust policing practices, identified inequities in education, and celebrated the resilience of Black people. Though we seek common ground in the reconstitution of ubuntu spaces, truth-telling is part of the reconciliation process.

You can contribute to blogs, podcasts, teach a course, and write for publication. I align with antiracists, appeared on the Oregon Library Association Equity Diversity Inclusion Antiracism podcast, and wrote a guest blog, "Making Ubuntu Spaces, Addressing Inequalities and Peopling the Commons" for *Librarian with Spines*. I taught a literature course in the Africana Studies program at Youngstown State University and challenged stereotypes and myths about Black inferiority through a study of Sankofa readings. I later authored *Leadership under Fire: Advancing Progress, Communicating, Teaching and Setting Communities at Liberty*.[22]

You can build a diverse collection and challenge censorship. Library workers can ill afford to remain neutral and be silent in the face of censorship and inequities in our society. Building a diverse collection through innovative programming, inclusion, and collaboration produces results. At the end of the second community forum, I gave the community a six-month progress report. Forum presenters included a youth leader as a panelist and solicited feedback. Though building diverse collections remains a challenge on a limited budget, the Farrell library strives to maintain a set aside Black Studies Collection and collect materials of all local authors. The NAACP has purchased several books for Black Studies Collection. The library collection includes *Africa Is Not a Country*, *Afro Atlantic Histories*, and other books have been added that challenge myths through memorial donations.[23]

You can advance STEM and health literacy in Black communities. Libraries serving Blacks and other marginalized communities require hotspots and up-to-date computers and experience with science, technology, engineering, and mathematics (STEM).

You can promote affirmation of humanity and make ubuntu spaces in libraries. I initiated the Farrell Library Caught in The Act Award to honor youth for acts of friendship, kindness, and doing the right thing. Yes, you too can make ubuntu spaces and be caught in the act in creating a better world. Let's rise together.

## NOTES

1. Shiraz Durrani, *Information and Liberation: Writings on the Politics of Information and Liberation* (Duluth, MN: Library Juice Press, 2008).
2. Desmond Tutu and Mpho Tutu, *Made for Goodness: And Why This Makes All The Difference* (New York: Harper, 2010), 15.
3. John H. Clarke, *My Life in Search of Africa* (Chicago: Third World Press, 1999), 34-35.
4. Wendell Wray, "Library Services to Black Americans," in *Handbook of Black librarianship*, edited by E. J. Josey and Anne Allen Shockley (Littleton, CO: Libraries Unlimited, 1977), 90-93.
5. Amanda Oliver, *Overdue: Reckoning with Public Libraries* (Chicago, IL: Chicago Review Press, 2022), 12.
6. Jacob Lief and Andrea Thompson, *I Am Because You Are: How the Spirit of Ubuntu Inspired an Unlikely Friendship and Transformed a Community* (New York: Rodale, 2015); Mark Mathabane, *The Lessons of Ubuntu: How an African Philosophy Can Inspire Racial Healing in America* (New York: Skyhouse, 2018).
7. Lavonda Broadnax, "The Association of Health Information and Libraries in Africa," in *Handbook of Black Librarianship, 2nd ed.*, edited by E. J. Josey and Marva DeLoach (Lanham, MD: Scarecrow, 2000), 739.
8. Jason Alston, "The Importance of Librarian Ethnic Caucuses and the Slander of Self-Segregation," in *Librarians with Spines: Information Agitators in an Age of Stagnation*, edited by Max Macias and Yago S. Curar (Los Angeles: Hinchas Press, 2017), 45-58.
9. Harriett A. Washington, *Medical Apartheid: The Dark History of Medical Experimentation on Black Americans from Colonial Times to the Present* (New York: Doubleday, 2006).

10. James C. Welbourne, "The Information Potential in the Liberation of Black People," in *What Black Librarians Are Saying*, edited E. J. Josey (Metuchen, NJ: Scarecrow Press, 1972), 50-59.
11. Durrani, *Information and Liberation*, 295; Jocelyn Poole, "From Political Prisoner to Johannesburg Public Library Manager: An Interview with Bongiwe Nkabinde," *Journal of Pan African Studies*, 3, no. 1 (2009): 2-8.
12. Durrani, *Information and Liberation*, 206-7.
13. Ibid., 206.
14. Ibid., 207.
15. Broadnax, "Association of Health Information," 745.
16. Roland Barksdale-Hall, *Leadership under Fire: Advancing Progress, Communicating, Teaching and Setting Communities at Liberty* (Phoenix, AZ: Amber Books, 2016); US Census, "Farrell City, Mercer County, PA," Census Reporter, https://censusreporter.org/profiles/06000US4208525360-farrell-city-mercer-county-pa/.
17. Daniel Goleman, *Working with Emotional Intelligence* (New York: Bantam Books, 2000), 27.
18. Durrani, *Information and Liberation*, 87.
19. Wray, "Library Services to Black Americans," 91-93.
20. Niels Weidtmann, "The Philosophy of Ubuntu and the Notion of a Vital Force," in *Ubuntu and the Reconstitution of Community*, edited by James Ogude (Bloomington: Indiana University Press, 2019), 110-12.
21. Aram Goudsouzian, *Man on a Mission: James Meredith and the Battle of Ole Miss* (Fayetteville: University of Arkansas Press, 2022).
22. Barksdale-Hall, *Leadership under Fire*.
23. Dipo Faloyin, *Africa Is Not a Country: Breaking Stereotypes of Modern Africa* (London: Harvill Secker, 2022).

**SOURCES**

Adams, S. "New Photo Book Captures Farrell's Ethnic Heritage." *Life & times*, July 2012, 3.

Alston, Jason. "The Importance of Librarian Ethnic Caucuses and the Slander of Self-Segregation." In *Librarians with Spines: Information Agitators in an Age of Stagnation*, edited by Max Macias and Yago S. Curar, 45-58. Los Angeles: Hinchas Press, 2017.

Barksdale-Hall, Roland. *Leadership under Fire: Advancing Progress, Communicating, Teaching and Setting Communities at Liberty*. Phoenix, AZ: Amber Books, 2016.

Broadnax, Lavonda. "The Association of Health Information and Libraries in Africa." In *Handbook of Black Librarianship*, 2nd ed., edited by E. J. Josey and Marva DeLoach, 739-53. Lanham, MD: Scarecrow, 2000.

Clarke, John H. *My Life in Search of Africa*. Chicago: Third World Press, 1999.

Durrani, Shiraz. *Information and Liberation: Writings on the Politics of Information and Liberation*. Duluth, MN: Library Juice Press, 2008.

Faloyin, Dipo. *Africa Is Not a Country: Breaking Stereotypes of Modern Africa*. London: Harvill Secker, 2022.

Goleman, Daniel. *Working with Emotional Intelligence*. New York: Bantam Books, 2000.

Goudsouzian, Aram. *Man on a Mission: James Meredith and the Battle of Ole Miss*. Fayetteville: University of Arkansas Press, 2022.

Hammer, Joshua. *The Bad-Ass Librarians of Timbuktu: And Their Race to Save the World's Most Precious Manuscripts*. New York: Simon and Schuster, 2016.

Lief, Jacob, and Andrea Thompson. *I Am Because You Are: How the Spirit of Ubuntu Inspired an Unlikely Friendship and Transformed a Community*. New York: Rodale, 2015.

Mathabane, Mark. *The Lessons of Ubuntu: How an African Philosophy Can Inspire Racial Healing in America*. New York: Skyhouse, 2018.

Oliver, Amanda. *Overdue: Reckoning with Public Libraries*. Chicago: Chicago Review Press, 2022.

Poole, Jocelyn. "From Political Prisoner to Johannesburg Public Library Manager: An Interview with Bongiwe Nkabinde." *Journal of Pan African Studies*, 3, no. 1 (2009): 2-8.

Tutu, Desmond, and Mpho Tutu. *Made for Goodness: And Why This Makes All the Difference*. New York: Harper, 2010.

US Census. "Farrell City, Mercer County, PA." Census Reporter, https://censusreporter.org/profiles/06000US4208525360-farrell-city-mercer-county-pa/.

Washington, Harriett A. *Medical Apartheid: The Dark History of Medical Experimentation on Black Americans from Colonial Times to the Present*. New York: Doubleday, 2006.

Weidtmann, Niels. "The Philosophy of Ubuntu and the Notion of a Vital Force." In *Ubuntu and the Reconstitution of Community*, edited by James Ogude. Bloomington: Indiana University Press, 2019.

Welbourne, James C. "The Information Potential in the Liberation of Black People." In *What Black Librarians Are Saying*, edited E. J. Josey, 50-59. Metuchen, NJ: Scarecrow Press, 1972.

Wray, Wendell. "Library Services to Black Americans." In *Handbook of Black Librarianship*, edited by E. J. Josey and Anne Allen Shockley, 90-93. Littleton, CO: Libraries Unlimited, 1977.

# 4.13

## Fostering Inclusion through Programming and Outreach

Angiah L. Davis and Michelle E. Jones

The academic library is a safe place for students on a college campus where everyone should feel welcome. It is an inclusive place that offers diverse programming and opportunities for students, faculty, and staff. During the summer of 2020, the world experienced a global pandemic and civic unrest. Millions of people are experiencing the trauma of living through COVID-19. The nation was forced to watch the murders of Ahmaud Arbery, George Floyd, Breonna Taylor, and others. Libraries responded by creating and sharing resources on social justice, providing virtual programming to expand their reach, and offering a safe space to relieve stress, just to name a few.

On campus, academic librarians are in unique positions and must support their learning communities in several ways. One of them is to help educate and shape the college campus by fostering inclusion through programming and outreach. As a result of this, the academic library may be viewed as a collaborative partner with campus entities for all students. For example, the library may be asked to participate in or conduct a new or transfer student orientation.

This chapter will share opportunities for library programming and outreach initiatives that have been successful in medium and small academic libraries, Columbus State University, and Gordon State College located in the state of Georgia. By fostering inclusion through programming, this chapter also aims to encourage social integration and retention for all students.

### AN AFRICAN AMERICAN READ-IN

Gordon State College (GSC) is located in Barnesville, Georgia. The town is approximately fifty miles south of Atlanta, Georgia. It is rural with a student FTE (full time equivalent) of 3,231 at the time of this writing. The demographics of students are: 53 percent White; 37 percent Black or African American; 5 percent Hispanic or Latino; and 1 percent Asian. The college offers twenty-seven degrees and has a 20-to-1 student-to-professor ratio. In this chapter, we will consider GSC a small college library.

Columbus State University (CSU) is located in Columbus, Georgia. The city is located one hundred miles southwest of Atlanta, Georgia. The student enrollment is approximately 8,300. The demographics of students are: 46.7 percent White; 38.9 percent Black or African American; 6.7 percent Hispanic or Latino; and 2.6 percent Asian. There are forty-five undergraduate degree programs and more than thirty-five graduate degree programs with a student faculty ratio of 15 to 1. CSU is considered a medium university library.

During Black History Month, the CSU library found that one way to foster inclusion is through programming. One day in February, the library hosted an African American read-in. The National African American Read-In is a national event sponsored by the National Council of Teachers of English (NCTE).[1] Each year thousands of people participate in various read-in events worldwide. The purpose of this event is to bring awareness as well as celebrate and promote various African American writers, specifically during Black History Month.

To assist with planning the program, we researched the 2021 theme for Black History Month. This information was found on the Association for the Study of African American Life and History (ASALH) website.[2] According to ASALH, the 2021 theme was "Black Family: Representation, Identity, and Diversity." Students, faculty, and staff were invited to read works that were significant to them in under ten minutes. Participants also explained the rationale for their choice. The reflective activity allowed the audience to learn more about the reader so that the audience was able to have a greater understanding of each participant. This event aligned with both the strategic plans of the institution and the library, and it may be duplicated to support all cultures or celebrations as well (e.g., National Hispanic Heritage Month, Rainbow Book Month, etc.). A read-in program is adaptable in a number of ways. At GSC, a partnership with the English Department was conducive to planning and promoting the program. Library displays and subject guides can supplement read-in programs, and the programs can be effective in-person or virtually. Also note that there were no associated costs for this program. In fact, the library is considered to be a "type of community" or "safe space" because of the services and programming provided to fit the needs of the students.[3]

CSU held a virtual program during February 2021. Panelists from various sectors of the community were invited to talk about a short documentary on minority leadership. A moderator asked questions of the panelists and invited audience members to do the same. Students, faculty, and staff were given access to the documentary for viewing prior to the event. Since the event was recorded, those unable to attend the initial event have the option of watching it at a more convenient time. Social media was the primary avenue for advertising this event. Holding the event virtually allowed speakers from outside the university to participate more readily with fewer travel and schedule conflicts.

## NATIONAL POETRY NIGHT EVENT

Just as the African American read-in event promoted literacy and inclusion, another similar event encouraged social integration and retention for all students that was held at GSC: National Poetry Night. April is National Poetry Month. This event may be held any time during the year, however. Many students appreciate poetry and spoken words, and librarians should encourage the celebration of it. Everyone can probably remember a poem they have read. In order to plan such an event, the coordinators should choose a theme. If this proves to be a difficult task, the library can opt for an open night of sharing. Giving the audience random words to create a poem with and/or have the audience read original poems can add an unexpected twist to the poetry program. People enjoy expressing themselves, and these words can unite people. Words can inspire, motivate, and provoke emotion. In the age of the global pandemic and civil unrest, students want their voices heard.

During poetry night, or events similar to it, students and faculty let their guards down and share their vulnerability. Poetry night develops public speaking and artistry. It allows students to perform their art and express themselves while allowing others to enjoy the work. This type of event may also counter stress and give students the opportunity to network on campus. Many students need to be pushed out of their comfort zone, so poetry night cultivates leadership and builds confidence. Plus, students learn about other perspectives that are not their own. Faculty can support students by encouraging them to participate in various campus events like this one. Librarians can help students find poetry resources available in the library or online. Again, recording the event and taking photos is very beneficial. Student leaders can be contacted for assistance. They can lead the program and/or provide input from a student's perspective, which will also make the event more inclusive.

We have found that when students connect with peers and faculty, they have a vested interest in developing and enhancing their learning environment, which gives them ownership of the college experience and encouraging retention. Oliveira states that "students are more inclined to return to the university influenced by their level of social interaction with peers and faculty outside the classroom."[4]

## NEW STUDENT/TRANSFER STUDENT ORIENTATION

It is essential that the library has a role in new student orientation. It does not have to be large, but the information should be available to all students. Simple and low-cost ways to participate in orientation may be to provide a link or QR (quick response) code to library information, include a page about the library in the student planner, or create a new student orientation video. In-person activities can be very effective. Many of us are doing more with less, so the virtual indirect participation in orientation is acceptable.

Everyone desires acceptance and acknowledgment. This can be fulfilled for students by personalizing an orientation. Transfer students may resonate more with such an offering. At GSC, an electronic subject guide provides access to the library's information, thereby providing participation in the transfer student orientation. Additionally, students received a personalized tour of the library and had a question-and-answer session with their assigned librarian. In all, customized experiences for students contribute to the idea of social integration and inclusion.

## NEW FACULTY ORIENTATION

The CSU library's participation in new faculty orientation familiarizes faculty members with tools to assist student matriculation, which helps students become academically successful. New faculty are filtered through the Faculty Center for the Enhancement of Teaching and Learning. Through this process they begin their journey with the university as a cohort. The cohort model creates unity among the faculty members, providing an avenue that fosters relationships. An array of faculty development options are available for new faculty participation within a given year. As a whole, the options form the New Faculty Seminar Series. Faculty members are expected to attend a certain number of events from a menu of options listed as a new faculty seminar series.

One of the options is the orientation to library services. Librarians may offer individual or small group sessions with new faculty in their liaison areas. The Faculty Center can coordinate the sessions if librarians prefer this method. Such a meeting provides context for new faculty members regarding helpful library resources. Librarians may provide a suite of topics to discuss or customize the session depending on the faculty members' preferences. When faculty members effectively use library resources in class, students gain skills through high-level research projects and are prepped for advanced degrees. Students benefit from faculty members who value the library and the work librarians provide. Yamaguchi asserts that faculty endorsement of the library may lead to increased student use of the library and higher academic achievement.[5] It has been my experience that these same faculty members are more likely to request librarians provide bibliographic instruction sessions for their classes as well as have an embedded presence in online courses.

## FAIRS FOR FACULTY, STAFF, AND STUDENTS

In order to foster a presence throughout the campus, CSU's library participates in the annual Faculty/Staff Resource Fair. This event has been coordinated with the director of the Faculty Center for the Enhancement of Teaching and Learning. Various other entities within the university, such as campus police, computer services, and the bookstore have also participated. The purpose of the event is to relay available campus services to the campus community. Attendees have the opportunity to speak with representatives from each participating department in order to gain knowledge about helpful tools and resources. These items can help employees successfully complete their job duties. In this way, faculty and staff will be better equipped to assist students.

In addition, there is a similar fair exclusively held for students. Some of the same campus departments participate in both; however, groups that are more student-focused tend to be a part of this one. During the student-centered event, the library is able to make a more direct impact with students since there is one-on-one contact. Students are able to identify their liaison librarian and learn how to access relevant resources. Students respond well to the mini-lesson on helpful databases and other online items. It is also a time for students to ask that one question they may have always wondered about but were too afraid to ask. Making a face-to-face connection with a subject librarian eases the library anxiety that some students have, and learning about librarian assistance and varied online resources usually proves to be intriguing to students.

## INCLUSION IN INFORMATION LITERACY

Librarians at CSU formerly taught an undergraduate credit-bearing general information literacy course. Library statistics verified that students who took the course were more likely to graduate on time (four years or less) and had better grades than those who had not taken it. Due to a revamp of the general education core curriculum, the course as it once existed is no more. In order to continue to reach students and help them achieve proper research skills, some librarians have availed themselves of the opportunity to teach a modified version of the course under a new umbrella of perspectives courses. These courses have themes and seek to address problem-solving related to the subject matter.

Each academic year faculty have an opportunity to submit a course proposal. Several librarians have taught the course centered around various subjects with the primary objective of providing information literacy. At my institution students have found the classes to be interesting due to the applicable course titles. In many ways librarians appreciate the flexibility to adjust the course content and credit hours.

One way to improve the current course proposal process is to utilize an opportunity to coordinate coteaching with another faculty member in a different discipline. In this way the course could also have the potential to be multi-disciplinary. Such a designation creates a greater likelihood to reach even more students. The student increase could stem from a larger number of students in each discipline or a higher level of interest piqued by various faculty members. Thereby, retention, progression, and graduation are increased through course delivery.

## OUTREACH

Outreach can happen in a number of ways these days. It can be direct or indirect and have an impact on students and faculty. For example, GSC's library was able to conduct outreach by participating in monthly county meetings, and library staff learned information about the county that can help support students and their families. While the campus is able to provide most of the services that students need, it is also helpful for the library to serve as a referral center for local information as needed. In turn, the GSC library is also able to share information and network with potential collaborators who are also interested in fostering inclusion through programming and outreach.

Collaborating with the advising arm of the university is an outreach activity embarked upon by the library. Since this department often assists students who are having difficulties with academics, including those needing tutoring services, the instruction team creates short instructional videos. These library-related videos are five minutes or less and center on teaching or highlighting how to complete an important task. Though the library produces them, they are shared with the advising department so that students who need them the most will have access.

The videos are hosted on the CSU library's YouTube channel. The idea is to share information via video instead of posting items buried within the library's website where students might not realize they are available. If the videos are not on the home page of the library's website, it is not likely students will find them.

There is room for improvement regarding outreach. The advising department can send a link to the students as needed after appointments have revealed knowledge deficiencies concerning available assistance. Students can utilize the videos by accessing them as many times as needed. Additionally, the students have the ability to pause and resume the recording for any confusing content. If there is no video on a frequently asked resource, one can quickly be created. Students may feel hesitant about requesting videos. As such, advising staff could suggest contacting the librarians for one-on-one consultations about online services. Additionally, advising staff can direct students to current tutorials or request new videos for the students based on student questions.

Since the pandemic, physical wellness has become a hot topic. As an outreach activity, the GSC library came up with an idea to create wellness packs for students. These packs were for all students who were interested in having one.

Wellness packs included a mask, hand sanitizer, inspirational button, snack, and a bookmark with library and counseling center information. These items were donated by staff. However, it may be possible to enlist grants, local organizations, or student life partners for collaboration.

**TELL THE STORY**

Be sure to assess your library program or event. Assessment tells your library's story. It tells the who, what, when, where, how, and whys. Assessment provides tangible and measurable data on predetermined goal effectiveness. While your library is doing great work, if there is no data to support that work or story, it may be left on the shelf. Think of assessment as a SWOT analysis (your library's strengths, weaknesses, opportunities, and threats). There are many ways to conduct an assessment: a quiz, a reflection paper, survey, etc.—just be sure to record the responses. We have found that surveys work best for events because they are quick, and participants can complete them on their mobile device. Some assessment questions are:

- How did you hear about the event?
- What did you like most about the event?
- What did you like least about the event?
- Would you attend the event again?
- Other comments.

After you have acquired the data, make sure to keep track by year so that you are able to accurately tell the history of your library. Decide in the beginning whether you want to use the fiscal year or the calendar year. This is also important to make annual comparisons for improvement as well as successes. Setting up an assessment plan can be time-consuming, however, it is worth it. Your hard work needs to be documented in both numbers and words. Remember, nobody can tell your library's story better than its staff. Take a stand to own your library's story.

**CONCLUSION: LITTLE THINGS MATTER**

Academic libraries have always found innovative ways to meet the changing needs of students. The mission of the academic library is to support the teaching and learning needs of the institution. As librarians and library advocates, we believe that libraries should create a welcoming environment on our campuses. We recognize the changing needs of students and lend the library as a supportive arm to assist with these needs.

We work to remove barriers to information and provide inclusive programming that helps achieve it. This chapter has shared some of the many ways to create and foster these types of environments through programming and outreach.

The college campus depends on the library for many things. While the academic library can create and present opportunities for library programming and outreach initiatives to encourage social integration and retention, libraries should also be willing to partner with other campus departments to foster inclusion through programming and outreach. If there is an event on campus, libraries should reach out to the campus leaders to find ways to be involved or be of assistance. Regular interaction with the library staff helps create a sense of community on campus. If there is one thing that the library should be known for, it is the fact that the library is an inclusive place for the basics, such as the wellness packs and bigger endeavors like diverse programming and resources. Finally, connection helps build courage while simultaneously providing support to help students thrive both in college and life.

**NOTES**

1. National Council of Teachers of English (NCTE), https://ncte.org/get-involved/african-american-read-in/.
2. The Association for the Study of African American Life and History (ASALH), https://asalh.org/about-us/our-history/.
3. Jennifer Mayer et al., "Undergraduate Student Success and Library Use: A Multimethod Approach." *College & Research Libraries*, 81, no. 3 (2020): 378-98.
4. Silas M. Oliveira, "The Academic Library's Role in Student Retention: A Review of the Literature." *Library Review*, 66, no. 4 (2017): 310-29.
5. Masami Yamaguchi, "Demonstrating Academic Library Impact to Faculty: A Case Study." *Digital Library Perspectives*, 34, no. 2 (2018): 137-50.

**WORKS CITED**

Mayer, Jennifer, Rachel Dineen, Angela Rockwell, and Jane Blodgett. "Undergraduate Student Success and Library Use: A Multimethod Approach." *College & Research Libraries*, 81, no. 3 (2020): 378-98.

Oliveira, Silas M. "The Academic Library's Role in Student Retention: A Review of the Literature." *Library Review*, 66, no. 4 (2017): 310-29.

Yamaguchi, Masami. "Demonstrating Academic Library Impact to Faculty: A Case Study." *Digital Library Perspectives*, 34, no. 2 (2018): 137-50.

# 4.14

## How Has Diversity, Equity, and Inclusion Impacted the BIPOC Library Professional?

Taina K. Evans

In the aftermath of George Floyd's murder by Minneapolis police officers on May 25, 2020, protests across the country initiated a nationwide discussion, not only about racist policing, but racist and discriminatory practices in all aspects of our lives. Employees at organizations across the country, including corporations, sports teams, universities, and museums, started to look internally at their processes and practices, and public libraries were no exception.[1] Library directors and boards largely agree that their libraries must be diverse, equitable, and inclusive (DEI) places to work, serve, enroll, visit, attend, heal, learn, pray, or play. It was, however, this organizational change that challenged public libraries attempting to implement meaningful policies and practices, as both insiders and researchers grappled with the concept of, and the path to, DEI.

The purpose of this chapter is to explore the importance of diversity in libraries for Black, indigenous, and people of color (BIPOC) staff, and to examine the barriers that exist to achieving greater representation within organizations. By doing so, we can better understand the ways in which libraries can become more inclusive institutions and better serve the needs of all members of the community.

### DIVERSITY TO THE BIPOC PROFESSIONAL

The American Library Association (ALA) states that diversity promotes equal access to information for all persons and recognizes the ongoing need to increase awareness of and responsiveness to the diversity of the communities we serve. As defined, libraries can and should play a crucial role in empowering diverse populations for full participation in a democratic society.[2] As such, it is important that libraries reflect the diversity of the communities they serve, both in terms of their collections and their staff. However, historically, libraries have been predominantly staffed by white individuals, particularly in leadership and decision-making roles. This has created a lack of representation for BIPOC individuals within the library profession and has led to challenges and barriers for BIPOC staff in terms of recruitment, retention, and advancement.[3]

The Department for Professional Employees found that in 2020, "just over 83 percent of librarians identified as white" and that as of 2018, "31.5 percent of the library workforce" was over the age of fifty-five, versus only 19.6 percent of the total United States workforce.[4] According to the ALA's 2020 Diversity Counts report, the library profession still has a long way to go when it comes to BIPOC staff representation. Despite BIPOC individuals making up 40 percent of the US population, only 13.9 percent of credentialed librarians identify as BIPOC. Additionally, the report found that BIPOC staff members in libraries are more likely to experience microaggressions, discrimination, and lack of support from colleagues and management. The lack of BIPOC staff representation in libraries has significant implications, including the burden of representation, lack of career advancement opportunities, and challenges related to microaggressions and discrimination in the workplace.[5]

In recent years, to address the lack of diversity in the library profession and to provide more opportunities for BIPOC individuals, organizations such as ALA have launched initiatives to recruit and retain more diverse staff, and to push for more inclusive hiring practices and professional development opportunities for BIPOC staff members. Wingfield hints that, even though diversity and inclusion policies are now commonplace, many organizations still fail to devote resources toward the types of initiatives that improve the numbers of underrepresented workers. She concludes, instead, that the organizations rely on Black professionals to find, recruit, and support Black employees, and otherwise make organizational spaces more amenable to Black customers and clients.[6]

Creating inclusive and equitable workplaces requires a commitment to ongoing education and training, intentional efforts to create an inclusive work environment, and implementing equitable hiring and promotion practices.[7] While progress has been made in recent years to address these issues and increase diversity in libraries, the current state of diversity in the profession is still far from ideal.

## INCLUSION AND EQUITY TO THE BIPOC LIBRARY PROFESSIONAL

ALA states that to be inclusive, our association, profession, and society must recognize the inherent worth and dignity of every member of the community; involve and empower all members to participate and contribute; promote and sustain a sense of belonging; and value and practice respect for the talents, beliefs, backgrounds, and ways of living of all members.[8] Equity recognizes that some groups were, and are, disadvantaged in accessing educational and employment opportunities, and are, therefore, underrepresented or marginalized in many organizations and institutions. Equity, therefore, means increasing diversity by ameliorating conditions of disadvantaged groups.[9] Even with this shared framework, this definition has not helped to give a voice to BIPOC library professionals who have not felt supported or valued with their professional contributions. Even after the civil rights movement of the 1960s, libraries remained largely inaccessible to BIPOC communities.

Additionally, BIPOC staff members who were able to secure positions in libraries often faced discrimination and marginalization within the profession. They were often given fewer desirable roles and were not given the same opportunities for professional development and advancement as their white colleagues. Many libraries continued to discriminate against BIPOC patrons, denying them access to materials or limiting their access to certain sections of the library. This discrimination was often reflected in the lack of diversity among library staff, as libraries continued to hire predominantly white individuals. Intentionally or unintentionally, through the general hierarchical practices within library systems, BIPOC staff are underrepresented in library staff at all levels, particularly in leadership positions, resembling systematic racism while hindering accountability.

In articulating a path for transformation and change, libraries must counter systemic biases within the work environment and the world. In noninclusive spaces, BIPOC professionals encounter the psychological and exhaustive practice of censoring and watering down views, thoughts, and personalities to avoid being viewed differently. Behaviors include avoiding stereotypes such as the idea that Black librarians are lazy, nappy hair is unprofessional, or feeling forced to downplay their interests, to align with the shared interests of the dominant group. It is the unwritten necessity to accept jokes or negative comments from white colleagues, and to adapt to their ignorance in order to maintain workplace peace. Ultimately, these patterns leave Black workers coping with burnout, alienation, and often stalled at middle levels with limited opportunities for advancement and mobility.[10]

On the other hand, employers that promote inclusion offer the space within the workforce to allow BIPOC staff to be their true selves. Of course, all of this is complex and nuanced, but BIPOC staff brings exponential cultural capital, and their involvement is as crucial as the experience of others bring. Finding the appropriate balance involves retaining a diverse workforce and welcoming opportunities for multiple perspectives and innovation. At the same time, an inclusive workspace alleviates the feeling of burden within the process of the BIPOC staff trying to fit in with a homogenous group. When employees can be themselves at work, they are no longer distracted by keeping up the dominant professional façade. They can focus on work and ultimately be more productive.

## EQUITY TO THE BIPOC PROFESSIONAL

Below are a few key takeaways from chapter 2 of *The Practice of Adaptive Leadership*.[11]

Suppose you take it upon yourself to regularly point out the gap between the company's stated value of transparency and the reality that most people in the organization tightly control the flow of information. You are not likely to be rewarded or greeted with applause for identifying this disconnect, particularly by those who benefit from controlling information. Clearly, the system as a whole has decided to live with the gap between the espoused value and the current reality, the value-in-practice. Closing that gap would be more painful to the dominant coalition than living with it. The importance of this idea lies in the impact it has on the techniques for trying to address the problem.[12] As the BIPOC community struggles to deal with a difficult issue, it is a leadership act to help keep open interpretations that are adaptive, systemic, and conflictual rather than technical, individual, and benign. It is important to push against the default interpretations, which are often deeply ingrained.

When BIPOC staff are engaged with others in trying to name and frame an equitable issue, it is important to hold on to multiple interpretations rather than gravitate toward the first one that gains broad acceptance or meets the need to just do something. Test several interpretations simultaneously.

When you realize that what you see as dysfunctional works for others in the system, you begin focusing on how to mobilize and sustain people through the period of risk that often comes with adaptive change, rather than trying to convince them of the rightness of your cause.[13] Equity issues in the workplace call attention to tough questions and the library's sense of responsibility beyond the job description. Diagnosis is an art, not a science. But it is an essential skill in the effective exercise of DEI leadership on difficult civil challenges where equity and progress have been inconsequential or nonexistent.

## DEI INITIATED BY BIPOC LIBRARIANS

Libraries can make systematic changes in their work culture, collections, or programs by developing strategies to assess DEI. As a case study, we can review how two organizations plan a path forward collectively in fostering a culture of diversity, ones that were creative and produced resilient places to work: Brooklyn Public Library (BPL) and the Free Library of Philadelphia.

Allegations of racial inequity at the Free Library of Philadelphia have recently attracted national spotlight, but the problem has been simmering for a while. The situation burst into view late June, when Black staffers published an open letter calling on the library to address various staffing and protocol inequities linked to the coronavirus pandemic and the Movement for Black Lives.[14] The Concerned Black Workers of the Free Library of Philadelphia (CBWFLP) penned "An Open Letter from Concerned Black Workers at the Free Library of Philadelphia," requesting that the Free Library board, which is 58 percent Black, remove director Reardon.[15] The open letter also demanded the following:

- a commitment to protecting Black lives on staff
- a formal and transparent investigation of Black staff's concerns regarding the person to which they physically report
- a plan, developed with Black staff, to provide library services that take into account Black people's increased COVID-19 infection and mortality rates
- support and accommodations for Black staff whose library work makes them susceptible to racial violence
- providing Black staff opportunities to work from home, a luxury already afforded to the white staff
- the demand that staff with librarian degrees who work in management, executive, and specialty positions be redeployed to cover the shortages in staff due to COVID-19 and the layoff of seasonal employees, most of whom are Black

At BPL during the Race Real Talk Forums, Evans and co-authors documented five weeks of virtual organizational-wide listening sessions entitled Real Talk: Race, Truth and Transformation.[16] Moderated by outside facilitators, staff bravely shared personal, often painful experiences, and identified the many ways BPL has failed to live up to its values when it comes to diversity, equity, and inclusion.[17] To make the changes necessary to live up to the organizational ideals and stand against racist practices and behaviors in the workplace, as well as in Brooklyn's communities, the collective made the following recommendations:[18]

- Make an organization-wide commitment to racial justice going forward. There were calls for structural and procedural changes in the institution that will ensure a long-term commitment to racial justice, such as a vocal stance against injustice, asking about how people might handle scenarios involving racism in the interview process, and training at all levels.
- Create a diversity audit of all staff by title, as well as the board of trustees, and publish to the organization. To prioritize diversity initiatives going forward, staff should know where the biggest discrepancies are.
- Invest in recruiting, hiring, retaining, and promoting qualified BIPOC candidates and staff across the institution. This consists of an immediate and comprehensive salary equity review to ensure competitiveness and equity for all positions.
- Establish a diversity council with authority to create policies and equity assessment with a dedicated budget.
- Require an annual antiracism training for all staff, volunteers, and trustees to normalize an antiracist workplace. Ensure all staff know the various procedures for reporting violations of professional conduct (in person and anonymously), operationalizing, and advance antiracist work and include accountability measures within annual performance evaluations.
- BPL could better serve frontline staff by providing resources, legitimacy, and visibility to the Community Justice Action Committee and social work programs that work alongside Public Safety.
- Reestablish a BPL trainee program that includes diversifying the profession and offering ongoing mentorship, leadership development, and tuition support.

In both examples, library staff identified the need for organizational changes regarding diversity, equity, and inclusion and setting up internal goals to be community-centered while fully integrating these concepts within their missions and strategic priorities. The Free Library of Philadelphia has since taken a step toward inclusivity by hiring a new chief diversity and inclusion officer, one who acknowledged that continued adjustments are needed in order to navigate the Free Library's path forward as it relates to addressing inequity within the organization, and the promise to include many more voices in further conversations, workshops, and trainings that will address systemic racism and white supremacy on a deeper level.[19] BPL established a Diversity, Equity & Inclusion Council in September 2020 that continues to engage a variety of staff to assess relevant data, set goals, measure results, and hold the institution accountable. Informed by the findings and recommendations of an additional task force team, the Council reevaluated policies and practices related to recruitment and hiring to ensure the organization was representative at every level, including leadership. It also continues to develop BPL's diversity, equity, and inclusion training so that employees receive training in areas such as implicit bias, microaggressions, and active bystander-ship.

**WHY DIVERSITY, EQUITY AND INCLUSION MATTERS**

In conclusion, the importance of diversity in libraries for BIPOC staff cannot be overstated. While progress has been made in recent years, there are still significant challenges and issues that must be addressed in order to create truly inclusive and equitable workplaces. From historical challenges and biases to current issues around holding institutions accountable, it is clear that libraries must take active steps to improve the current state of diversity, equity, and inclusivity in the profession. Josh Chan's article entitled "Beyond Tokenism: The Importance of Staff Diversity in Libraries" points out the benefits and positive implications for developing library collections, services, and programs.[20] Staff diversity also has positive implications for retention, which is an important benefit for any organization.

Instead of expecting assimilation, libraries should look upon librarians of color and their unique backgrounds as advantages, not impediments to the profession. And librarians of color need to feel that their unique cultural backgrounds are respected at the workplace.[21]

In April 2021, ALA's Committee on Diversity developed the DEI scorecard, an evaluative tool that centers accountability and transparency in determining organizational effectiveness in diversity, equity, and inclusion in the recruitment, hiring, retention, and promotion of people of color.[22] No matter the score, the value of diversity is intrinsic on the visibility of BIPOC staff.

There is reason for hope, as we have seen BIPOC librarians and support staff add an incredible benefit to the profession and to the institutions. They're not just working in the community but are truly of the community. Identified through the examination of best practices and strategies for promoting diversity, there are concrete steps that libraries can take to create more inclusive and equitable workplaces for BIPOC staff. Ultimately, by embracing diversity and creating inclusive environments for all staff, libraries can better understand and serve the diverse needs of their patrons and become truly integral and valuable institutions in our communities.

BIPOC professionals, you are valued! Keep up the good work!

**NOTES**

1. Christina Pavlou, "What Is Diversity?" *Recruiting Resources: How to Recruit and Hire Better*, 8 July 2022, resources.workable.com/hr-terms/diversity-definition.
2. "B.3 Diversity (Old Number 60)," *American Library Association*, 4 August 2010, www.ala.org/aboutala/governance/policymanual/updatedpolicymanual/section2/3diversity (Document ID: 5914dd45-6914-0c64-5192-88a6784af423). Accessed March 18, 2023.
3. Anne Ford, "Underrepresented, Underemployed," *American Libraries Magazine*, 1 Nov. 2018, americanlibrariesmagazine.org/2018/11/01/underrepresented-underemployed.
4. "Library Professionals: Facts, Figures, and Union Membership—Department for Professional Employees, AFL-CIO," *Department for Professional Employees, AFL-CIO*, 10 June 2021, www.dpeaflcio.org/factsheets/library-professionals-facts-and-figures.
5. "Diversity Counts: A Snapshot of Diversity in the Library Profession," *American Library Association*, 2020, www.ala.org/aboutala/sites/ala.org.aboutala/files/content/diversity/diversitycounts/diversitycountssnapshot.pdf.
6. Adia H. Wingfield, "Race, Repression and the Future of New Labor Activism," *Work and Occupations*, 50, no. 3 (2023): 351-58.
7. "Diversity Counts: A Snapshot of Diversity in the Library Profession."
8. From the B.3 Diversity (Old Number 60) policy manual with the ALA.
9. "Equity, Diversity, Inclusion: An Interpretation of the Library Bill of Rights," *American Library Association*, 5 July 2017, www.ala.org/advocacy/intfreedom/librarybill/interpretations/EDI.
10. Wingfield, "Race," 351-58.
11. Ronald Heifetz, Alexander Grashow, and Marty Linsky, *The Practice of Adaptive Leadership* (Boston: Harvard Business Review Press, 2009).
12. Ibid.
13. Ibid.
14. Jones, Layla, "Why Free Library Workers Are Calling for Their Director to Resign." *Billy Penn at WHYY*, 12 July 2020, billypenn.com/2020/07/28/free-library-board-mostly-silent-as-workers-demand-involvement-in-selecting-new-leader/.
15. CBWFLP. "An Open Letter from Concerned Black Workers at the Free Library of Philadelphia," June 25, 2022, *Google Drive* file; Mensah M. Dean, "Library Board Gets Input from Workers—Board Chair Thanked Black Employees for 'Bravery' in Citing Workplace Discrimination," *Philadelphia Inquirer*, 29 July 2020, p. B4. Newsbank.com.
16. Taina Evans, David Giles, Nick Higgins, Eva Raison, and Maya Wagoner, "The Real Talk Forums: Report Back on the Summer 2020 Systemwide Conversations on Race, Truth and Transformation," July 2021.
17. Ibid.
18. Ibid.
19. Jeroslyn JoVonn, "Free Library Workers Upset over Diversity Training That Called White Privilege a 'Myth,'" *Black Enterprise*, 25 Mar. 2021, www.blackenterpreise.com/free-library-workers-upset-over-diversity-traiving-that-called-white-privilege-a-myth.
20. Josh Chan, "Beyond Tokenism: The Importance of Staff Diversity in Libraries-BCLA Perspectives," *BCLA Perspectives*, 30 Nov. 2020, bclaconnect.ca/perspectives/2020/11/30/beyond-tokenism-the-importance-of-staff-diversity-in-libraries.
21. Ibid.
22. "Diversity, Equity, and Inclusion (DEI) Scorecard for Library and Information Organizations," *American Library Association | Awards, publishing, and conferences: ALA membership advocates to ensure access to information for all*, Apr. 2021, www.ala.org/aboutala/sites/ala.org.aboutala/files/content/2021%20EQUITY%20SCORECARD%20FOR%20LIBRARY%20AND%20INFORMATION%20ORGANIZATIONS.pdf.

**WORKS CITED**

"B.3 Diversity (Old Number 60)," *American Library Association*, August 4, 2010, www.ala.org/aboutala/governance/policymanual/updatedpolicymanual/section2/3diversity (Document ID: 5914dd45-6914-0c64-5192-88a6784af423). Accessed March 18, 2023.

*Black Lives Matter: Equity, Inclusion, and Antiracism at Brooklyn Public Library.* Brooklyn Public Library, June 19, 2020, www.bklynlibrary.org/black-lives-matter.

*Black Lives Matter: Equity, Inclusion, and Antiracism at Brooklyn Public Library.* Brooklyn Public Library, 19 June 2020, www.bklynlibrary.org/black-lives-matter

CBWFLP. "An Open Letter from Concerned Black Workers at the Free Library of Philadelphia," June 25, 2022, *Google Drive* file.

Chan, Josh. "Beyond Tokenism: The Importance of Staff Diversity in Libraries–BCLA Perspectives." *BCLA Perspectives*, November 30, 2020, bclaconnect.ca/perspectives/2020/11/30/beyond-tokenism-the-importance-of-staff-diversity-in-libraries.

Dean, Mensah M. "Library Board Gets Input from Workers—Board Chair Thanked Black Employees for 'Bravery' in Citing Workplace Discrimination." *Philadelphia Inquirer*, July 29, 2020, p. B4. *Newsbank.com*.

"Diversity Counts: A Snapshot of Diversity in the Library Profession." American Library Association, 2020, www.ala.org/aboutala/sites/ala.org.aboutala/files/content/diversity/diversitycounts/diversitycountssnapshot.pdf.

"Diversity, Equity, and Inclusion (DEI) Scorecard for Library and Information Organizations." *American Library Association | Awards, publishing, and conferences: ALA membership advocates to ensure access to information for all*, April 2021, www.ala.org/aboutala/sites/ala.org.aboutala/files/content/2021%20EQUITY%20SCORECARD%20FOR%20LIBRARY%20AND%20INFORMATION%20ORGANIZATIONS.pdf.

"Equity, Diversity, Inclusion: An Interpretation of the Library Bill of Rights," American Library Association, 5 July 2017, www.ala.org/advocacy/intfreedom/librarybill/interpretations/EDI.

"Library Professionals: Facts, Figures, and Union Membership—Department for Professional Employees, AFL-CIO." Department for Professional Employees, AFL-CIO, 10 June 2021, www.dpeaflcio.org/factsheets/library-professionals-facts-and-figures.

Evans Taina, David Giles, Nick Higgins, Eva Raison, and Maya Wagoner. "The Real Talk Forums: Report Back on the Summer 2020 Systemwide Conversations on Race, Truth and Transformation," July 2021.

Ford, Anne. "Underrepresented, Underemployed." *American Libraries Magazine*, November 1, 2018, americanlibrariesmagazine.org/2018/11/01/underrepresented-underemployed.

Heifetz, Ronald, Alexander Grashow, and Marty Linsky. *The Practice of Adaptive Leadership*. Boston: Harvard Business Review Press, 2009.

Jones, Layla. "Why Free Library Workers Are Calling for Their Director to Resign." *Billy Penn at WHYY*, July 12, 2020, billypenn.com/2020/07/28/free-library-board-mostly-silent-as-workers-demand-involvement-in-selecting-new-leader/.

JoVonn, Jeroslyn. "Free Library Workers Upset over Diversity Training That Called White Privilege a 'Myth.'" *Black Enterprise*, March 25, 2021, https://www.blackenterprise.com/free-library-workers-upset-over-diversity-training-that-called-white-privilege-a-myth/.

"Library Professionals: Facts, Figures, and Union Membership—Department for Professional Employees, AFL-CIO." *Department for Professional Employees, AFL-CIO*, 10 June 2021, www.dpeaflcio.org/factsheets/library-professionals-facts-and-figures.

Pavlou, Christina. "What Is Diversity?" *Recruiting Resources: How to Recruit and Hire Better*. July 8, 2022. resources.workable.com/hr-terms/diversity-definition.

"The Practice of Adaptive Leadership: Tools and Tactics for Changing Your Organization and the World by Ronald Heifetz, Alexander Grashow, and Marty Linsky." *Personnel Psychology*, vol. 63, no. 1, 2010, pp. 255–58.

Wingfield, Adia H. "Race, Repression and the Future of New Labor Activism." *Work and Occupations*, vol. 50, no. 3, 2023, pp. 351–58, https://doi.org/10.1177/07308884231162962.

# 4.15

## *Ginga Librarianship/Beautiful Librarianship*

Syntychia Kendrick-Samuel

When the iconic soccer legend Edson Arantes do Nascimento, Pele, died in 2022, the world mourned, and his home nation of Brazil despaired over the loss of their hero. While watching news reports about his death and then subsequent documentaries and biographical films about his life, the term "ginga" kept being mentioned. It described the traditional Brazilian style of soccer that he and his teammates brought to the world stage when they defeated the favorite, Sweden, in the 1958 World Cup championship.

What is Ginga? *New York Latin Culture Magazine* said that the "concept comes from capoeira, the Afro-Brazilian martial art dance. It basically means African spirit."[1] For

Brazilians, ginga is swagger, it is beautiful, something innate in most Brazilians, especially those born of the African diaspora. In 1958, the European style of soccer was dominant and that's the style that the Brazilian coaches wanted Pele and his teammates to emulate. Long story short, they chose what they knew and that was ginga, the "beautiful game," and they won. As *New York Latin Culture Magazine* put it, "The moral of the story is to be true to yourself. You can't be anybody else but you."[2]

How does this relate to librarianship? Each librarian has their own potential for ginga, their own potential to bring beauty to whatever form of librarianship that they specialize in, whether it be engagement, outreach, programs, collection development, etc. For Black librarians, this is especially true. Who we are as Black people makes us unique in an overwhelmingly white profession. Many of us may at times feel unseen or unheard in our places of work. Perhaps we work in communities that prefer ideals and demographics that were more prevalent in precivil rights America. In spite of these obstacles, we can still shine. We do not have to whitewash ourselves to quietly survive until retirement or climb the career ladder. We can tap into our ginga, our cultural swagger, to produce beautiful librarianship in many ways. This chapter will discuss this concept through programming and community engagement.

**PROGRAMMING/COMMUNITY ENGAGEMENT**

In 2019, *School Library Journal* published an article I wrote entitled, "Free Summer Meals and Diverse Storytimes Are a Winning Combination at This Library."[3] The article was about how me, my staff, and my community basically tapped into our ginga to transform a struggling summer meal program into a vibrant program that celebrated the diverse cultures and, yes, even the unapologetic blackness, of our community. My team and I offered programs that brought daycare centers and caregivers into the library to enjoy programs that reflected them. Then we were able to get them to stay to enjoy a healthy meal by creating an inviting atmosphere in our meeting room.

They knew that they were welcome. My support staff, clerks, a library aid, and a custodian set up the room with toys, played music (everything from Luther Vandross to Marc Anthony) over the sound system, and provided a low-key craft. It was truly beautiful. I remember a grandmother who would bring her eight grandchildren. She would chat with other caregivers while the children ate and played. The ginga in this situation is that we built on the basic rules of the lunch program; but we made it an event of laidback fun.

Some of the rules included that the kids had to eat at the library. They could not take extra unless the food came from the "share table" or "leftover table." The free lunch program filled a need in the community. When it comes to food, rules are necessary, especially if we didn't want children getting sick because we broke a rule and did not properly store the meals. We abided by the rules, but we wanted the two hours of free lunches to feel like a family gathering of good times.

The children played while the adults relaxed and talked to one another. Once I spotted a pregnant mother taking a bite from her child's sandwich. A rule was broken (parents cannot eat their children's lunches), but I continued serving lunches. The way I viewed it was that two kids were getting sustenance that day, the child just had not made it to the outside world yet. As the summer progressed, more people began showing up, they told their friends and relatives. This became a summer of beautiful librarianship, all the players (library staff and patrons) came to together and believed in what we were doing, and it benefited our spirits and our community. What is the takeaway? Offer your community a quality experience that is safe and yet preserves the dignity of the participants. That experience looks different depending on the library. Regardless of how it looks, persist in making it a beautiful experience.

**PASSION PROJECTS**

I have written extensively about my almost twenty years of advocacy for teens during my time as a teen librarian. My record during that time is full of ginga moments; empowering and celebrating teens of color is my professional passion. Now that I am an administrator (since 2021), I have been forced to find new ways to allow the beauty of librarianship to manifest. Again, each person's ginga is unique. For me I have always known that I cannot just be an administrator focused on the day-to-day operations of the library. I had to have passion projects that were relevant to the community I serve, a community of color and oftentimes marginalized people.

As an assistant director, I no longer managed a department with a program budget. If I had a passion project, I would have to find funding. My pipeline to funding was through winning a grant. Grant writing is something that every librarian can do, it is a rewarding experience to write, win, and implement a grant. Doing such makes the librarian something of a project manager (looks great on a resume). The community I work in has a growing and vocal Haitian population. Over the years I have gotten to know many of the Haitian residents, and I've watched their population grow. As the first "Black free nation" of the Western Hemisphere, Haiti has undergone hardship since its formation. Political machinations, natural disasters, and the cultural demonizing of its people by the outside world have not been able to quash the fiery spirits of its people. I wanted to do something to let our Haitian patrons know that they are seen by us at the library. They are admired and respected because of their resilience and ability to overcome adversity without giving into despair. This desire to recognize such an inspiring people inspired me to write a grant that funded The Haitian Resilience Project. The final project resulted in a permanent mural created with community input by a Haitian artist, Frenal Mezilas. The mural is on display in the library's lobby. In addition, the grant funded dance rehearsals led by Haitian dancer/choreographer Jessica St. Ulysses, who over three months worked with a group of dancers who named themselves the Uniondale Library Dancers to present a show that celebrated Haitian culture and history.

Is this the type of project found at every library like a cupcake program or defensive driving? Many would agree, no, it is not. The Haitian community and others embraced this project and made their own play to ensure success. The reverends/pastors/priests in the area encouraged their congregants at their Kreyol church services that they should go to the library for the program after services. A local Haitian bakery supplied food, the grant paid for most of it, but the owner donated a free dish of a meat-filled pastry dish. The library and community were making harmonious plays for a successful program. What was the final score?

A New York State senator sat in the library auditorium filled with his constituents for the presentation of both the mural and the dance. Sounds of appreciation were heard when the mural was unveiled with the clapping of hands in time with the rhythm of the djembe drum and the applause as the young dancer triumphantly blew the conk horn (Haitian symbolism) at the end of a dance. Instead of calling it a success, call it ginga manifesting itself, which is the beauty of librarianship happening. Even though I am not Haitian, as an African American, as a Black librarian, something within spurs me to create opportunities like this that allow my brothers and sisters of the diaspora to shine. Programs like this probably would not happen if I allowed myself to become bland or whitewashed in how I engage in my professional activities.

**ONE FOR THE ROAD**

As stated previously, empowering teens was and is one of my professional passions. The teenage years are tough for many, and for youth of color they have unique challenges that stem from structural and institutional racism. I am no longer the head of Teen Services, so I don't have that day-to-day interaction with them, yet I do have the garden and the ability to instruct in basic gardening. During the pandemic, our library director and trustees gave permission for two garden beds to be built on the strip of green on the south side of the building. The Children's Department oversees one of the garden beds, and the other bed is used for the instruction of teens in the basic principles of gardening.

During the growing season I have been able to schedule one to two days per week to teach our teen volunteers how to garden during one-hour sessions. We try to keep everything organic, and the teens work the soil, grow the plants, and harvest the fruitage of their labor. They know how to tell when a specific fruit or vegetable is ripe. They have also learned the history of certain plants, such as okra. Casually while they harvested okra, we discussed how the enslaved Africans brought okra seeds with them on the Middle Passage. They also learned about different cultures. Teens from Ecuador harvest Jamaican sorrel pods (Roselle Hibiscus) and made the popular West Indian drink for their family. My style of librarianship includes gardening and teaching young people how to grow their own food. It is a beautiful thing.

We have also created a seed library. Many other libraries have done this, but we are new to this game, and we have put our own spin on it here at UPL. As assistant director, I manage the seed library, but nothing would happen without the help of the staff. They help repackage the seeds, promote the library, and assist in keeping track of the inventory. This year we received massive amounts of seed donations from reputable companies. Initially, some of the clerks weren't happy about repackaging seeds, but eventually they saw the beauty of us working together on this project. When that happened, it was obvious. Clerks started printing fancy labels for the repackaged seeds and they shared how their view of the project changed. They saw that their work was being acknowledged by myself and other staff, and they also saw the good that the free seeds would do in the community. The hours that they worked on it became a relaxing time for them. This changed viewpoint was ginga in action. We were all working together for a common goal for the greater good.

**PASSING THE BALL**

Pele did not win those three World Cups by himself. It was a team sport. Each of his teammates exhibited their own ginga skills as they won games. The same is true of ginga librarianship. Some of the experiences already related has touched on the teamwork involved in creating impactful programs and meaningful community engagement. One of the best examples of how passing the ball to another member of your team can lead to ginga librarianship is Uniondale Public Library's Umoja Book Club. The popular Freeport Memorial Library Soul with Heart book club inspired this relatively new book club. The Freeport book club was centered around works of literature written by authors who are Black or African American. I wanted to bring something like this to Uniondale, and it resulted in the creation of the Umoja Book Club. My right-hand person was Ms. Aisha Cooper, who at the time was a librarian trainee. I could "pass her the ball" or give her the responsibility of helping me to grow this book club because she is a talented staff member who grew up both in the library and the community we serve. She always brings excellence. I gave her the freedom to create the publicity for the club, flyers, social media posts, and a club member newsletter. Under the direction of our librarian discussion leaders, she curates the book selections. She puts a lot of time and effort into finding books that fit the spirit of what Umoja is about. It was her idea to include monthly raffles as a way to entice people to attend and stay for the discussion. Lastly, her biggest strength, or ginga power play, is her ability to connect with the patrons. She reminds them to pick up their books and to block out time for the monthly discussion. What is the result? The book club is almost two years old, and we have a steady following of participants. Club members have shared personal stories about themselves or their families and their slice of the Black experience. Umoja is a safe place and patrons know this. The club was my idea, but I had the sense to allow Ms. Cooper to play a larger role and add her own zest to make this book club more than just another library book club, which in turn benefited our community.

## THE TAKEAWAY

In short, the point of this chapter is to encourage Black librarians to be themselves, to bring the beauty of their experiences, culture, and uniqueness to the table. There is no need to emulate something that is not you. Pele and his Brazilian soccer team won three World Cups because they were themselves. Being yourself is a powerful tool, and YOU are the best person to do it right. You will benefit, your library will benefit, and it will keep you in tune with your community. Remember, ginga truly works when the librarian, library staff, and the community are working together in harmony, which brings about beautiful results. Be yourself, find your professional passion and let it manifest. If you are new to this profession, it may take time to get your ginga working, but give it time. Start small. Maybe it is the design of a flyer, perhaps you want to use images of people of color. Does your collection need more diversifying, or can you offer a program about Black history outside of the month of February? Go for it and allow ginga librarianship to enter your career mind-set and be your own fabulous self!

## NOTES

1. Editors, "Pele Made Soccer the Beautiful Game with His Ginga Style," *New York Latin Culture Magazine*, December 25, 2022, https://www.newyorklatinculture.com/pele-made-soccer-the-beautiful-game-with-his-ginga-style/.
2. Ibid.
3. Syntychia Kendrick-Samuel, "Free Summer Meals and Diverse Storytimes Are a Winning Combination at This Library," *School Library Journal*, December 6, 2019, https://www.slj.com/story/Free-Summer-Meals-and-Diverse-Storytimes-are-a Winning-Combination-at-Library.

## WORKS CITED

Editors. "Pele Made Soccer the Beautiful Game with His Ginga Style." *New York Latin Culture Magazine*, December 25, 2022. https://www.newyorklatinculture.com/pele-made-soccer-the-beautiful-game-with-his-ginga-style/.

Kendrick-Samuel, Syntychia. "Free Summer Meals and Diverse Storytimes Are a Winning Combination at This Library." *School Library Journal*, December 6, 2019. https://www.slj.com/story/Free-Summer-Meals-and-Diverse-Storytimes-are-a Winning-Combination-at-Library.

---

# 4.16

## *If You Don't Understand Me, It's Your Fault*

BLACK LIBRARIANS AND THE DISTRACTION OF EQUITY, DIVERSITY, AND INCLUSION

Conrad Pegues

If you don't understand me, it's your fault.

—Earth, Wind & Fire[1]

The very serious function of racism is a distraction. It keeps you from doing your work. It keeps you explaining over and over again, your reason for being.

—Toni Morrison[2]

To address issues of historical inequities in the workplace for Black people, there have been efforts like affirmative action and now equity, diversity, and enclusion (EDI). Previous to these programs to position Black people in the labor force, Black labor was "free" in enslavement and so intricate to the workings of America that the country would not have existed without it. That labor and its pool of laborers were never paid but received egregious treatment from which Black people have yet to recover, economically or psychologically before or after the Civil War. Labor policies like affirmative action were instituted to correct the historical injustices that continue to this day, but they have diminished in power over time with legal and political resistance.

Affirmative action was the concerted effort to support Black integration into positions of labor they would not have accessed waiting on the compassion of White America. Affirmative action has a lengthy and spotty history beginning with the American Association for Access, Equity and Inclusion. President John F. Kennedy established the Committee on Equal Employment Opportunity in 1961 requiring federal contractors to take "affirmative action to ensure that applicants are treated equally without regard to race, color, religion, sex, or national origin."[3] Affirmative action would morph over the years under Presidents Lyndon B. Johnson, Richard Nixon, Jimmy Carter, and others. By 1979, the Supreme Court would uphold some affirmative action efforts as long as they did not "violate the rights of white employees."[4] By 1995, federal and state legal actions would begin to slowly erode consideration of race for employment, contractors, or education, which has continued to this day.[5] Although affirmative action was originally a response to segregation and racism aimed at Blacks, white women, other minorities, and those with physical challenges would see court action to expand the meaning of affirmative action beyond the interpretation of race.

Initially called diversity, equity, and inclusion (DEI), it shadowed affirmative action as it came out of the fight for racial equality with John F. Kennedy's executive order. DEI programs had roots in the fight for fair employment:

> The field of DEI in Corporate America has its roots in the 1960s, beginning as a result of the anti-discrimination legislation of that decade—the Equal Pay Act of 1963, Title VII of the Civil Rights Act of 1964, and the Age Discrimination in Employment Act of 1967.[6]

Other areas of discrimination were framed with racial discrimination eventually getting more space in the discussion of race and in some respects eclipse race over time. In efforts to make working spaces diverse that had been historically framed by segregation, discrimination, and prejudice, other identifiers for legal protection were added including but not limited to gender, sexual orientation, ethnicity, age, race (i.e., other minority groups), etc. With a growing list of the disenfranchised, racial disparities have become less of a public issue as other "rights" gained political ground.

Over time, EDI issues have become conflated with issues of other ethnic and racially identified groups in the label of BIPOC (Black, Indigenous, and People of Color) lumping together multiple disenfranchised groups together, which diminishes their power and voice but allows white supremacy to maintain dominance while creating a cacophony of protests that make BIPOC groups out to be one voice when they have distinct histories and complaints to be addressed.

Libraries have been no different struggling with diversifying their workforce for the sake of employees and those they serve but not always successful. Colleen Foy states, "Diversity, equity and inclusion (DEI) efforts have been unsuccessful over the years in libraries."[7] The lack of success of DEI programs over the years has more to do with the competition for limited spaces and monies provided for "diverse candidates" in a world that no longer unapologetically posts "whites only" signs. What remains in policy and politics includes continued racist hiring practices, gerrymandering, gentrification, and police brutality. There is the illusion that race is less an issue and Black people are either considered to be whining or practicing so-called reverse racism.

The DEI movement came out of the civil rights movement of Black people opposing segregation and social resistance to viable employment in traditionally white spaces. DEI has since changed to EDI as some companies feel "equity" is more important than "diversity" and diversity comes with "baggage" as "no one knows what diversity entails."[8] Equity puts white people at ease that they will not be cheated out of job opportunities. Equity means anyone can speak about ethnic, racial, and gender identities diminishing the importance of lived experience (i.e., a white person is wholly qualified to explain the Black experience in America).

EDI programs place Black people in competition with other groups when the racism that created the problems has gone nowhere and morphed into more complex racist strategies. Black people, and in particular Black librarians, are left in a quandary of limited opportunity within white-dominated library spaces. Some 83 percent of librarians identify as white, which reflects the need for overhauling a systematic structure in favor of white people.[9] It must be noted that the phrasing "identifying as white" is problematic as identification can be a matter of choosing to identify with another group outside of experience. Philosopher Olefemi O. Taiwo highlights the original concept of identity politics taken from the Combahee River Collective centering identity in the oppression and needs of the communities where a person is born and reared.[10] Identity politics (listed in EDI policies) will be the next level of threat to Black librarians expanding their presence through EDI programs as race takes a backseat to created identities or identities with more political clout at the time. Since white supremacy will concede no more power than it needs, BIPOC groups and others are forced to jockey for position and power with other disenfranchised groups.

Affirmative action is contested in the courts as racist by white people and other ethnic/racial groups. Identities can be contested on "feelings" not history and experience.

In the 2009–2012 American Library Association (ALA) survey 104,392 librarians claimed white as their identity; 6,160 librarians identified as African American (563 males; 5,597 females).[11] In a 2017 ALA demographic study, 4.4 percent of ALA member respondents identified as Black or African American.[12]

The seed of disempowerment of affirmative action programs is included in the section that outlined EDI in the original documents of the 1960s. The political anxiety and social unrest of the civil rights movement gave the country a sense that Black people might choose armed conflict over the nonviolence preached by Dr. King. Affirmative action was one means to distill Black anxiety with American social policy. Over time affirmative action has been whittled down to a paper tiger policy. Sometimes, whites hired Black people for their skin color and not for qualifications to do the job. This fomented a backlash from whites that viable jobs were being handed over to Black people. When Black people were qualified, there was still white resentment. Further, affirmative action led to a quota system where a small number of Black people would be hired, which would not change white supremacist dynamics in the workplace and still bred white resentment.

Libraries were no different to hire more Black people, but the resistance was just as much in the library system as anywhere else in the American workforce. The American Library Association was no leader to effect change even before affirmative action. The ALA's Library Bill of Rights adopted a policy in 1939 stating a "person's right to use a library should not be denied or abridged because of origin, age, background, or views."[13] It is no accident "race" is not a consideration of this abridged policy.

The ALA practiced racism by segregating Black librarians at conventions and did not decry the denial of membership in southern library associations. In 1964, the Mississippi branch of ALA withdrew from the larger ALA system because it did not want Black members, which library pioneer E. J. Josey challenged.[14] It would be decades before libraries ceased segregating library systems with libraries built specifically for Black people to keep them out of white libraries.

E. J. Josey was often on the front lines to oppose racist ALA practices and policies which would eventually lead to the formation of the Black Caucus of the American Library Association in the 1970s. The ALA had no intention of granting full access to Black librarians until it was forced to do so, which was a battle waged over decades. The ALA was not moved by moral outrage but Black outrage and Black librarian pushback against policies that would not have been changed otherwise. Black people forced the issue. Any "allies" came after the fact.

Now there are EDI efforts to change the landscape of libraries by informing employers and employees of racist policies and practices and how they discriminated against historically disenfranchised groups. Presently, Black librarians have been crowded out of making claims of discrimination by other groups. John F. Kennedy established the Committee on Equal Employment Opportunity with Executive Order 10925 in 1961, which instructed federal contractors to ensure "applicants are treated equally without regard to race, color, religion, sex, or national origin."[15] Race is included with the executive order in response to the civil rights movement against racial segregation in America. The other groups, which rightfully are due protections as well, were not the impetus of the executive order. The civil rights movement's fight against racism was!

EDI programs are a part of professional development with Black librarians. Black librarians do bear some responsibility for representation and their voice in the library profession rendering unto Caesar time and feedback for antiracist workspaces. What Black librarians must understand is that they have been put in a position of explaining their experience to people who may not care and have no interest in changing the machinery of white supremacy in the library field. Why would people want to change things from which they benefit both socially and economically? All too often in EDI training, Black librarians are given lip service, sympathy, tears, outrage born of ignorance, and stunned disbelief at what many of us have experienced. None of these will change an environment that is not overwhelmingly committed to such changes as to protect, promote, and enhance the representation of groups who have been historically disenfranchised around skin color. EDI programs in libraries are for white librarians and staff, not Black librarians who already understand the machinery that is white supremacy.

EDI must be about self-empowerment. Black librarians must commit to information literacy programs within Black communities that are suffering from a lack of knowledge in a social media–driven world that has grown increasingly complex.

Recently, I received several phone calls from family and friends asking me what was critical race theory? It is not enough to tell someone to go look it up on the internet as information literacy librarians know it is not unusual to have online websites that are not vetted. Black neighborhoods are concerned with life issues such as work, paying bills, and raising children, which are more real to them than the political firestorms of the day. While CRT was a political football, voting rights were being erased with gerrymandering, which more readily impacts Black life than a graduate level law class (CRT) being disseminated within primary education. EDI must educate in Black neighborhoods in or out of the library as anti-Black legislation and violence gains momentum across the country.

The Earth, Wind & Fire quote at the beginning of this chapter[16] speaks to the perpetual explaining of Black life and librarian experience to white people. How long must we explain ourselves? Black people have constantly challenged segregationist policies to go to the library. In some places Black library branches were built to mitigate against the angst of Black people who wanted library access without fear. Some libraries like the Carnegie Library in Albany, Georgia, closed altogether in 1962 rather than give Black patrons access.[17]

EDI must become an issue within our own communities as we become aware of our own diversity and inclusivity issues with sexism, same gender loving librarians and patrons, trans-people, neurodiverse, gender conflicts, and those facing physical challenges both in and out of the library.

EDI must look at the mental toll on Black librarians working in hostile environments, especially those with "microaggressions," which may have a more lethal and long-term effect than calling someone out of their name. Being told that "you don't smile enough," "you don't participate in the office gatherings," "you walked through here like you have an attitude," or using policy to reinforce racist behaviors that undermine library managers, comments on hiring too many Blacks, or the insistence that race isn't the only diversity issue with librarians when race is brought up and can leave a Black librarian questioning their sanity.

All these issues affect a person's mental health, and it behooves EDI programs to be about supporting Black librarians as they encounter microaggressions. Sometimes just having someone to vent to can relieve the pressure of not being understood or feeling like the only Black person in the room or workplace. Outreach to one another is necessary to avoid burnout and keep Black librarians in the library field.

EDI programming must include supportive management styles. Too often I have witnessed Black librarians be cruel to other Black librarians under the aegis of "this is the way I am," "this is my style," "I am the manager," and any other deflective hindering an evolution to better managerial skills. Sometimes it is to prove to white management that the Black librarian is no threat to the status quo.

Black people were subject to chattel slavery like no other group in America. The list of the aggrieved in America is almost endless and each group has similarities and distinct differences that have to be faced to heal, but you cannot lot all people together under BIPOC. It is insulting to the living and the dead.

The machinery that is white supremacy historically resets itself to undermine the efforts of racial progress. Lawsuits against affirmative action have been legion since its inception.[18] EDI efforts are seeing a backlash especially from white men who feel they are losing opportunities to minorities.[19]

If there is any doubt as to the depth of racial resentment by white people, look no further than the so-called January 6, 2021, insurrection on Capitol Hill to overthrow the government. Sociologist Dr. Robert Pape says that almost half of the overwhelming white insurrectionists were CEOs, white collar workers, business owners, middle managers, military professionals, and police officers representing millions of Americans who fear Black and Hispanic people are taking jobs and opportunities from white people.[20] Basically, this hails back to white supremacists' resets in history to roll back the gains of Black people in America with Jim Crow laws, separate but equal laws, the Great Migration of Blacks from the South due to racial violence, the brutality against the civil rights movement, and now court rulings that no longer see race as an issue in Black lives.

Black librarians have an opportunity that may very well take precedence over EDI programs in libraries alone. EDI has to be refocused on Black people to inform and rectify false information in our communities that set us against one another. EDI information literacy efforts have to focus on race as the machinery of white supremacy to set white people against Black people sociopolitically and legally.

EDI programs are a distraction to the long history of Black resistance in the United States. It is time that Black librarians change the game by being less reactive to the changing laws and more reactive to the needs of Black people to resist by any means necessary the consistent reversal of gains against white supremacy in the United States. There is no need for continual explanation of our plight in the United States to gain place and power. As noted with the second quote at the beginning of the chapter from Toni Morrison:

> The very serious function of racism is a distraction. It keeps you from doing your work. It keeps you explaining over and over again your reason for being.[21]

White people must educate themselves. Black librarians must take on the task of information literacy toward our own people as a matter of self-preservation in a racist system that will not be satisfied until we are no longer here to challenge it.

## NOTES

1. Earth, Wind & Fire, "Runnin'," track 9 on *All 'N All*, Columbia Records, 1977, compact disc.
2. Toni Morrison, "A Humanist View," Portland State University's Oregon Public Speakers Collection, May 30, 1975, https://www.mackenzian.com/wp-content/uploads/2014/07/Transcript_PortlandState_TMorrison.pdf.
3. "Affirmative Action Policies throughout History," American Association for Access, Equity and Diversity, 2023, https://www.aaaed.org/aaaed/History_of_Affirmative_Action.asp.
4. Ibid.
5. Ibid.
6. Stacey Williams, "Evolution of Diversity in the Workplace," Linkedin, February 24, 2020, https://www.linkedin.com/pulse/evolution-diversity-workplace-stacey-williams/.
7. Colleen Foy, "Successful Applications of Diversity, Equity, and Inclusion Programming in Various Professional Settings: Strategies to Increase DEI in Libraries," *Journal of Library Administration*, 2021, https://libres.uncg.edu/ir/uncg/f/C_Foy_Successful_2021.pdf.
8. DeEtta Jones and Associates, "EDI vs DEI: 4 Reasons to Lead with Equity," *DeEtta Jones: Next Generation Global Achievement*, 2022, https://blog.deettajones.com/edi-vs-dei-4-reasons-to-lead-with-equity.
9. Foy, "Successful."
10. Zak Cheney Rice, "What's Wrong with Identity Politics? Philosopher Olefemi O. Taiwo's New Book Reclaims the Concept from Elite Power Brokers," *New York Magazine*, May 11, 2022, https://nymag.com/intelligencer/article/olufemi-taiwo-identity-politics-elite-capture.html.
11. "Diversity Counts 2012 Table," American Library Association, 2012, https://www.ala.org/aboutala/sites/ala.org.aboutala/files/content/diversity/diversitycounts/diversitycountstables2012.pdf.
12. Kathy Rosa and Kelsey Henke, "2017 ALA Demographic Study," American Library Association, Office of Research and

Statistics, 2017, https://www.ala.org/tools/sites/ala.org.tools/files/content/Draft%20of%20Member%20Demographics%20Survey%2001-11-2017.pdf.
13. Renate Chancellor, "E. J. Josey: Transformational Leader," *Library Journal*, 145, no. 2 (2020): 18-21, https://www.libraryjournal.com/story/E-J-Josey-Transformational-Leader-excerpt.
14. Ibid.
15. American Association for Access, Equity and Diversity, "Affirmative Action Policies throughout History."
16. Earth, Wind & Fire, "Runnin'."
17. Anne Ford, "'I Always Will Refuse': Civil Rights Protests in Public Libraries," *American Libraries Magazine*, June 1, 2017, https://americanlibrariesmagazine.org/2017/06/01/i-always-will-refuse-civil-rights-library-sit-in/.
18. American Association for Access, Equity and Diversity, "Affirmative Action Policies throughout History."
19. Denise Hamilton, "The Diversity Backlash Is Underway. Here's How to Resist It," World Economic Forum, October 11, 2022, https://www.weforum.org/agenda/2022/10/the-diversity-backlash-here-s-how-to-resist-it/.
20. Evan Garcia, "Who Stormed the US Capitol? New Report Digs into Demographics of Those Arrested," WTTW, April 7 2021, https://news.wttw.com/2021/04/07/who-stormed-us-capitol-new-report-digs-demographics-those-arrested.
21. Toni Morrison, "A Humanist View."

**WORKS CITED**

"Affirmative Action Policies throughout History." American Association for Access, Equity and Diversity, 2023. https://www.aaaed.org/aaaed/History_of_Affirmative_Action.asp.

Beavers, Danielle. "Diversity, Equity and Inclusion Framework: Reclaiming Diversity, Equity, and Inclusion for Racial Justice." The Greenlighting Institute, March 2018. https://greenlining.org/wp-content/uploads/2018/05/Racial-Equity-Framework.pdf.

Chancellor, Renate. "E. J. Josey: Transformational Leader." *Library Journal*, 145, no. 2 (2020): 18–21. https://www.libraryjournal.com/story/E-J-Josey-Transformational-Leader-excerpt.

DeEtta Jones and Associates. "EDI vs DEI: 4 Reasons to Lead with Equity." *DeEtta Jones: Next Generation Global Achievement*, 2022. https://blog.deettajones.com/edi-vs-dei-4-reasons-to-lead-with-equity.

"Diversity Counts 2012 Table." American Library Association, 2012. https://www.ala.org/aboutala/sites/ala.org.aboutala/files/content/diversity/diversitycounts/diversitycountstables2012.pdf.

Earth, Wind & Fire. "Runnin'." Track 9 on *All 'N All*. Columbia Records, 1977, compact disc.

Ford, Anne. "'I Always Will Refuse': Civil Rights Protests in Public Libraries." *American Libraries Magazine*, June 1, 2017. https://americanlibrariesmagazine.org/2017/06/01/i-always-will-refuse-civil-rights-library-sit-in/.

Foy, Colleen. "Successful Applications of Diversity, Equity, and Inclusion Programming in Various Professional Settings: Strategies to Increase DEI in Libraries." *Journal of Library Administration*, 2021. https://libres.uncg.edu/ir/uncg/f/C_Foy_Successful_2021.pdf.

Garcia, Evan. "Who Stormed the US Capitol? New Report Digs into Demographics of Those Arrested." WTTW, April 7, 2021. https://news.wttw.com/2021/04/07/who-stormed-us-capitol-new-report-digs-demographics-those-arrested.

Hamilton, Denise. "The Diversity Backlash Is Underway. Here's How to Resist It." World Economic Forum, October 11, 2022. https://www.weforum.org/agenda/2022/10/the-diversity-backlash-here-s-how-to-resist-it/.

Morrison, Toni. "A Humanist View." Portland State University's Oregon Public Speakers Collection, May 30, 1975. https://www.mackenzian.com/wp-content/uploads/2014/07/Transcript_PortlandState_TMorrison.pdf.

Rice, Zak Cheney. "What's Wrong with Identity Politics? Philosopher Olefemi O. Taiwo's New Book Reclaims the Concept from Elite Power Brokers." *New York Magazine*, May 11, 2022. https://nymag.com/intelligencer/article/olufemi-taiwo-identity-politics-elite-capture.html.

Rosa, Kathy, and Kelsey Henke. "2017 ALA Demographic Study." American Library Association, Office of Research and Statistics, 2017. https://www.ala.org/tools/sites/ala.org.tools/files/content/Draft%20of%20Member%20Demographics%20Survey%2001-11-2017.pdf.

Williams, Stacey. "Evolution of Diversity in the Workplace." Linkedin, February 24, 2020. https://www.linkedin.com/pulse/evolution-diversity-workplace-stacey-williams/.

# 4.17

## Radical Imagination in Libraries

REIMAGINING OURSELVES IN ORDER TO REIMAGINE OUR COMMUNITIES

Nicole Cooke

> A more critical dismantling of the structures of oppression within the library can help libraries better partner with communities who are creatively working beyond boundaries. In adopting a radical and experimental lens that seeks to change the world rather than simply maintain it, librarianship can engage more fully with the world that could be, rather than the world that is.
>
> —Jennie Rose Halperin, "The Library Commons: An Imagination and an Invocation," In the Library with the Lead Pipe[1]

Let's begin with an analogy.

Imagine the front of the most beautiful library building you have ever seen. It has amazing etched glass doors; has a big, bright sign; and is surrounded by flowers. It looks inviting, it looks like a place you would want to visit. You might also want to browse and borrow from the collection or partake in one of their programs. If we are to consider this more carefully, compare this attractive building to what their diversity initiatives look like. What do their policies look like? Are they as welcoming, as inclusive, and as warm and inviting as the building portrays? Or do they portend that the building is a decrepit, dark, uninviting, and perhaps even dangerous space? A place where you would absolutely not want to be. The building is not welcoming, inviting, or safe. If we continue with the analogy, this space is not inclusive, nor is it meant for everyone in the community. This is a gap between idealism and reality; this is a gap between what our outside looks like versus what our inside looks like. Taking the analogy a step further, a library can have all the right policies, it could have all the right words in the vision and mission statements, but if it doesn't *enact* those policies or that vision, then the space is dark and unsafe. The space is inequitable and represents the difference between "talking the talk" and "walking the walk."

When we think of radically imagining/reimagining library and information science (LIS) and its organizations, we want to reimagine our profession in such a way that our outside façades will always reflect and match our inside environments. We no longer have the luxury of having organizations that have visible gaps in their services and in their culture. This is a disservice to the communities being served (or not served), and it is a disservice to the library professionals that keep our organizations running. Equity should begin at home, and in-house. Much of the EDI literature and professional development initiatives in our profession focus on libraries and their collections and services, however, they also need to focus more on the *people* that comprise our libraries.

The previous analogy can stand for racism, sexism, xenophobia, ableism, or any of the "isms" of our society that are also embedded into our libraries and organizations. We still have racial profiling, tone policing, people being criticized for their accents, people being accused of playing the race card, people who say, "I don't see color," all in the library! These are harder to talk about and are things that make it difficult to hold people accountable, and these are the things that keep us from eliminating that gap between what we espouse versus what we do. These are the things that keep us from walking the walk and not just talking the talk, and thereby perpetuating the status quo and the systemic barriers and inequities that bombard our society. If we cannot name these issues, we cannot address them, much less fix them. We need to radically imagine and proclaim that we will no longer be complacent with the status quo; we must be willing and able to recognize, identify, name the mechanisms of systemic injustice, and ultimately think and dream bigger.

> Radical imagination requires us to think of the impossible, dream big, and think of a future where inequities do not exist, oppression does not exist, and people have the agency and autonomy to live fulfilling lives.[2]

And before we can do that with our communities, we must first make sure our own homes are in order and ensure that the library's organizational culture is not relying on the status quo and "this is the way it's always been." If our own homes are not in order, then we are positioning ourselves as complicit and hypocritical to the community.

## RADICAL IMAGINATION[3]

When we have radical imagination (RI) we are dreaming bigger and manifesting the best and brightest possible outcomes, experiences, and resources for society, communities, systems, and individuals. Scholars Harper and Jenkins describe radical imagination as "imagining what could be and how our current social order, policies, and practices prevent the liberation of marginalized and oppressed groups and the betterment of higher education as an institution,"[4] and at its core it is a reawakening process."[5] RI is a way to create new ideas, and it's also a way to devise solutions and alternatives that will hopefully relieve situations and correct oppression, barriers, and other challenges. With this dual purpose in mind, Indigenous scholars Duarte and Belarde-Lewis caution that we should be determined to focus on the good "rather than focusing on the marginalization, we choose to imagine; in order to imagine, we must not allow the trauma of past harms to cloud our future vision."[6]

What does it mean to be radical? According to Dr. Angela Davis, radical simply means grasping things at the root.[7] It means being critical in our thinking and asking questions. Instead of accepting the status quo and accepting responses of "this is just how things are," how can things be made better? How can we ask questions that will improve a situation or a scenario? How can we engage in services we have never tried that might provide increased equity for our diverse communities? Instead of being complacent and being comfortable, being radical means getting uncomfortable and doing some hard work. We all have privileges and advantages, and we cannot solely rely on our privileges. We must recognize not only our disadvantages but the disadvantages of others, and we must think about how we can reconcile those disadvantages. Being radical is asking questions and being proactive, engaging in social justice, engaging in action to make things more equitable for everyone.

## WE NEED TO RADICALLY IMAGINE A BETTER PROFESSION

> Kelley teaches us that imagining freedom, dignity, democracy, inclusion, and respect before they have been directly experienced is a radical act of the imagination.[8]

Prison abolitionist, educator, and librarian Mariame Kaba is widely quoted for her mantra "Let this radicalize you rather than lead you to despair."[9] Instead of being overwhelmed, how can we be radical and radically imagine the future of LIS? How can we use our radicalism to work together and to get through the various parts of the storm? One thing to keep in mind is that small changes matter. Small actions matter. Incremental change matters. It all adds up for the better and for the common good. There are consequences for not being radical, not asking critical questions, and not engaging in small actions. Many of these are consistent problems in LIS. The examples that follow are recent and ongoing and prevent LIS from successfully getting our own house in order, which subsequently prevents us from unhypocritically doing equity and social justice work in our communities. A radically imagined future of LIS eliminates the following problems.

### Microaggressions

Microaggressions are comments or even physical gestures aimed at people that are different. They are typically directed toward marginalized, stereotyped, and minoritized people or communities. Whether it is someone who is racially or ethnically different, someone from the LGBTQ community, someone experiencing developmental or intellectual delays, etc., these are comments that are based on implicit biases and based on explicit biases, assumptions, and prejudices.

### LGBTQ+ Communities and Censorship

In June 2022, LGBTQIA+ Pride Month, Prince George's County Memorial Library System in Maryland was targeted by vandals because of their programming and displays. One of the libraries had their front doors labeled with the word "groomer," spraypainted in neon paint (Peet 2022). The term "groomer" suggests that the vandal thinks that the library staff is promoting pornography, pedophilia, and other crimes against children, namely "turning them gay" (NPR 2022). What is particularly disturbing about this event is that the vandal is a school librarian. Again, we have much work to do within the profession. We do indeed have this type of behavior and this type of thinking in the profession.

### Book Challenges

As of the writing of this chapter in 2023, the United States is experiencing an acute and divisive rash in book challenges and bans, the likes of which the profession has not seen since the McCarthy Era.[10] Protesters want certain books, materials, programs, and information removed from libraries because they say that these publications are promoting pedophilia, pornography, and other heinous crimes against children. Library workers are being censored and prevented from doing their jobs, library workers are losing their jobs and receiving death threats, and libraries are being closed and losing their funding all because people disagree with information that should be available to *all*. They do not want their rights infringed upon, but they are happy to do it to others. They are upholding the status quo of racism, xenophobia, and homophobia at the expense of the safety and the humanity of others who will be deprived of this information. This is but one example of what happens when people are not radical, ask critical questions, and do not make their voices heard—a small and hateful minority who take over all who disagree with them.

## RADICAL IMAGINATION ENABLES HUMANITY AND ACTION

> I am fully human when I recognize your humanity.
>
> —Dr. Tutaleni Asino[11]

Among the goals we should have as a profession is recognizing, valuing, and celebrating everyone's humanity. When microaggressions, book challenges, and other inequities remain, the humanity of others is not being recognized. How can the humanity of others be emphasized and prioritized? And how do we normalize the idea that the humanity of others is just as important as our humanity, that the humanity of others who are different is equally important.

Inviting people to become radical and share in radical imagining are ways to break through passivity and encourage more people to care and get involved.

## BECOMING AND STAYING RADICAL

Today's fugitive librarians are free to transgress institutional conventions, operating outside the demands placed on (or imposed by) state-supported and commercial institutions.[12]

How do we become and stay radical? I argue that it requires a proactive and ongoing mixture of radical imagination, critical self-reflection, radical empathy, cultural competence, and cultural humility.

## CRITICAL SELF-REFLECTION

Critical self-reflection is asking ourselves better, harder, and more probing questions, thinking about our stances and viewpoints, think about our organization's stance, and considering what we can do to align the two. Critical self-reflection is something that we are always engaged in and not a one-time event or process.

## CULTURAL COMPETENCE AND CULTURAL HUMILITY

Cultural competence[13] and cultural humility comprise part of the internal work that we do before we attempt equity and social justice work on behalf of others. Cultural humility is part of the critical self-reflection process and says, along with intellectual humility, "I know I don't know everything, and I know that there's more that I can learn, and there's more that I can do to improve things for everyone and to move toward equity."[14]

Cultural competence occurs and builds as you gain cultural awareness and knowledge of groups, people, and cultures that are different from you. This information requires constant maintenance and improvement. Once you reach a level of cultural competence, this new knowledge should be used to improve your collections, services, and practice as an information professional. This is a process of moving from information to action.

Cultural humility and cultural competence are dovetail topics that work very much together. You must have some level of cultural humility before you can say that you want to become culturally competent. When you maintain or achieve some level of cultural competence, you realize there is still more to learn (which is another level of cultural humility). They work together to create an ongoing cycle of reflection and improvement.

Becoming radical and developing cultural competence and cultural humility is partially about improving ourselves and becoming better humans, but it is also largely about our patrons and feeling welcome and included in our institutions.[15] We work to bring our whole and authentic selves to the organization so that our patrons can bring their whole selves to the environment we have created for them.

### Radical Empathy

Radical empathy also brings us right back to critical self-reflection and the importance of bringing our whole selves to the library. Radical empathy challenges us to be vulnerable and is therefore related to cultural humility. We must be vulnerable and admit that we do not know everything, that we are not perfect, and that our organizations can always be better. Radical empathy also challenges us to be grounded in who we are as people, with complex and nuanced identities, characteristics, privileges, and disadvantages. We must know who we are before we can attempt to understand our community and *their* nuances and complex needs.

Givens provides six tenets of radical empathy:[16]

1. willingness to be vulnerable
2. becoming grounded in who you are
3. opening yourself to the experiences of others
4. practicing empathy
5. taking action
6. creating change and building trust

And Ventura lists seven archetypes of applied empathy:[17]

1. Be Present: Inhabit the here and now.
2. Question: Interrogate assumed truths.
3. Host: Anticipate the needs of others.
4. Experiment: Test and learn at all costs.
5. Listen: Develop the ability to observe and absorb.
6. Dare: Be confident and fearless.

All the tenets and archetypes are about self-reflection and action, and that is what the goal is when we discuss social justice: action, whether physical or verbal, implicit or explicit, the actions that we undertake to work toward equity for everyone. While we engage in this work of critical self-reflection and radical empathy as individuals, we do also need collectively to address systemic inequities in our organizations and in our communities. We cannot fight systemic inequities and barriers without a like-minded team.

**RADICAL REFLECTION AND PLANNING**

Circling back to Mariame Kaba, who gave us the earlier quote about being radical instead of being overwhelmed, she also encourages us to engage in radical thinking and planning. She suggests that we ask ourselves:[18]

- What resources exist so I can better educate myself?

    Doing this work is not about re-creating the wheel. So much work has been done and there is excellent work and information at our fingertips. We should take advantage of the hard work of others. She says to try and find information that is by and for impacted people and that centers their lived experiences. Instead of asking people to educate you individually, read their work—they have already told us, we just need to pay attention.

- Who is already doing the work around this particular injustice?

    Whatever topic you are interested in, there are already people doing the work. How do we join them? How do we help them *build* on the work that has already been done?

- Do I have the capacity to offer concrete support?

    When doing this work, you will have varying levels of capacity, and that is perfectly normal. How much can you give to others on a given day and still be effective and remain healthy? You also must think about the capacity of those working with you and those that you're asking to support you. As this is a collective effort, we need to be cognizant that everyone is not always in the same place.

- How can I be constructive?

    How can I come up with solutions? How can I come up with those necessary critical questions that I need to continually ask? This work is definitely a marathon and not a sprint.

If you are not angry, you are either a stone, or you are too sick to be angry. You should be angry. You must not be bitter. Bitterness is like cancer. It eats upon the host. It does not do anything to the object of its displeasure. So, use that anger, yes. You write it. You paint it. You dance it. You march it. You vote it. You do everything about it. You talk it. Never stop talking it.[19]

I challenge you to never stop talking about it, reading about it, learning about it, and reflecting on it. Be ready and stay ready.

**NOTES**

1. Jordan Harper and Henry Jenkins, "Confronting Horror, Embracing Fantasy: A Conversation about Lovecraft Country and Radical Imagination in Higher Education." *Policy Futures in Education*, 20, no. 1 (2022): 76.
2. Ibid., 75.
3. TK
4. Ibid., 75.
5. Ibid., 76.
6. Marisa Elena Duarte and Miranda Belarde-Lewis. "Imagining: Creating Spaces for Indigenous Ontologies." *Cataloging & Classification Quarterly*, vol. 53, no. 5-6 (2015), 678–79, https://doi.org/10.1080/01639374.2015.1018396.
7. Angela Davis, *Women, Culture & Politics* (New York: Random House, 1989), 14.
8. Harper and Jenkins, "Confronting Horror," 77.
9. @haymarketbooks (Mariame Kaba). "Let this radicalize you rather than lead you to despair." Twitter, November 29, 2021, 11:30 am, twitter.com/haymarketbooks/status/1461778819761725444?s=20.
10. Adriane Herrick Juarez, "103. Dealing with Book Banning with Tracie D. Hall," *Library Leadership Podcast,* April 28, 2022, libraryleadershippodcast.com/103-dealing-with-book-banning-with-tracie-d-hall/.
11. Dr. Tutaleni Asino, personal communication, July 13, 2022.
12. Shannon Mattern. "Fugitive Libraries." *Places Journal*, no. 2019, https://doi.org/10.22269/191022.
13. Nicole A. Cooke, *Information Services to Diverse Populations: Developing Culturally Competent Library Professionals* (Libraries Unlimited Incorporated, 2016), chapter 2.
14. Melanie Tervalon and Jann Murray-Garcia, "Cultural Humility versus Cultural Competence: A Critical Distinction in Defining Physician Training Outcomes in Multicultural Education," *Journal of Health Care for The Poor and Underserved*, 9, no. 2 (1998): 117–25.
15. Nicole A. Cooke, "Leading with Love and Hospitality: Applying a Radical Pedagogy to LIS," *Information and Learning Sciences*, 120, no. 1-2 (2019): 119–32.
16. Terri Givens, *Radical Empathy: Finding a Path to Bridging Racial Divides* (Policy Press, 2021).
17. Michael Ventura, *Applied Empathy: The New Language of Leadership* (Hachette UK, 2019).
18. @prisonculture (Mariame Kaba). "Questions I regularly ask myself when I'm outraged about injustice." Twitter, May 26, 2018, 9:28 am, twitter.com/prisonculture/status/1000413472356696065.
19. "Iconoclast: Dave Chappelle + Maya Angelou," *Iconoclast: Dave Chappelle + Maya Angelou [Full Episode]*, Sundance Channel, November 30, 2006, youtube.com/watch?v=okc6COsgzoE. Accessed March 21, 2023.

**WORKS CITED**

Ahmed, Sara. *On Being Included: Racism and Diversity in Institutional Life*. Durham, NC: Duke University Press, 2012.

Block, Melissa. "Accusations of 'Grooming' Are the Latest Political Attack–with Homophobic Origins." NPR, May 11, 2022, npr.org/2022/05/11/1096623939/accusations-grooming-political-attack-homophobic-origins.

Caswell, Michelle, and Marika Cifor. "Neither a Beginning nor an End: Applying an Ethics of Care to Digital Archival Collections." *The Routledge International Handbook of New Digital Practices in*

Galleries, Libraries, Archives, Museums and Heritage Sites. New York: Routledge, 2019, 159-68.

Cooke, Nicole A. "Leading with Love and Hospitality: Applying a Radical Pedagogy to LIS." *Information and Learning Sciences*, vol. 120, no. 1-2 (2019): 119-32.

Cooke, Nicole A. *Information Services to Diverse Populations: Developing Culturally Competent Library Professionals*. Libraries Unlimited Incorporated, 2016, chapter 2.

Davis, Angela Y. *Women, Culture & Politics*. New York: Random House, 1989, p. 14.

Duarte, Marisa Elena, and Miranda Belarde-Lewis. "Imagining: Creating Spaces for Indigenous Ontologies." *Cataloging & Classification Quarterly*, vol. 53, no. 5-6 (2015): 677-702, https://doi.org/10.1080/01639374.2015.1018396.

Gilliland, Anne et al. "JLSC Board Editorial 2019." *Journal of Librarianship and Scholarly Communication*, vol. 7, no. 1 (2019), https://doi.org/10.7710/2162-3309.2334.

Givens, Terri. *Radical Empathy: Finding a Path to Bridging Racial Divides*. Bristol, UK: Policy Press, 2021.

Halperin, Jennie Rose. "The Library Commons: An Imagination and an Invocation." *In the Library with the Lead Pipe*, 2020, https://www.inthelibrarywiththeleadpipe.org/2020/the-library-commons/.

Harper, Jordan, and Henry Jenkins. "Confronting Horror, Embracing Fantasy: A Conversation About Lovecraft Country and Radical Imagination in Higher Education." *Policy Futures in Education*, vol. 20, no. 1 (2022): 73-85.

@haymarketbooks (Mariame Kaba). "Let this radicalize you rather than lead you to despair." Twitter, 29 November 2021, 11:30 am, twitter.com/haymarketbooks/status/1461778819761725444?s=20.

"Iconoclast: Dave Chappelle + Maya Angelou." *Iconoclast: Dave Chappelle + Maya Angelou [Full Episode]*. Sundance Channel, November 30, 2006, youtube.com/watch?v=okc6COsgzoE. Accessed 21 Mar. 2023.

Juarez, Adriane Herrick. "103. Dealing with Book Banning with Tracie D. Hall." *Library Leadership Podcast*, April 28, 2022, libraryleadershippodcast.com/103-dealing-with-book-banning-with-tracie-d-hall/.

Mattern, Shannon. "Fugitive Libraries." *Places Journal*, no. 2019, https://doi.org/10.22269/191022.

Peet, Lisa. "Prince George's County Memorial Library System Targeted by Anti-LGBTQIA+ Vandalism." Library Journal, Media Source Incorporated, June 17, 2022, libraryjournal.com/story/prince-georges-county-memorial-library-system-targeted-by-anti-lgbtqia-vandalism.

@prisonculture (Mariame Kaba). "Questions I regularly ask myself when I'm outraged about injustice." Twitter, 26 May 2018, 9:28 am, twitter.com/prisonculture/status/1000413472356696065.

Tervalon, Melanie, and Jann Murray-Garcia. "Cultural Humility Versus Cultural Competence: A Critical Distinction in Defining Physician Training Outcomes in Multicultural Education." *Journal Of Health Care for The Poor and Underserved*, vol. 9, no. 2 (1998): 117-125.

Ventura, Michael. *Applied Empathy: The New Language of Leadership*. Hachette UK, 2019.

# 4.18

## On Diversity

PROPOSING AN INSTITUTIONAL COMMITMENT TO CHANGE AND ACCOUNTABILITY

Courtney Shareef

In the second edition of *Handbook of Black Librarianship*, E. J. Josey reported that, in 1999, African Americans represented just 6.5 percent of the total number of librarians, according to data provided by the Bureau of Labor Statistics. This suggested that "African American librarians have not made much progress since the publication of the first edition of this book in 1977."[1]

Unfortunately, that appears to still be the case today. The statistics show very little increase in Black librarianship since the 1977 publication. In fact, the data shows a decrease in Black librarianship since Josey's 1999 reporting. And much of the second edition's discussion on diversity in librarianship remains applicable today. Maurice B. Wheeler, for example, described an increase in reports of reverse discrimination as the country debated the validity of and need for policies that established or maintained diversity.[2] Simmona E. Simmons-Hodo referenced Clifford Adelman, longtime researcher of higher education, who described the diversity rhetoric of the 1990s as having "been pounded and bleached into nothing."[3] Teresa Y. Neely opined that, while Black librarianship of the time thrived, "it is not by any means where it could be, or should be in a profession that, every chance it gets, trumpets its liberal attitudes on freedom of speech, freedom from censorship, and, more recently, support for diversity efforts."[4] She warned that such slow progress presented a bleak future for Black librarianship.

We are now living that future.

In the almost fifty years since the publication of the *Handbook*'s first edition, very little progress has been made in the recruiting, hiring, retaining, and promoting of librarians of color. If significant change is to occur, it will require institutional commitments to change and accountability that necessitate the leveraging of professional opportunities and resources and radical restructuring of professional organizations. Only then will the field of library and information science achieve its goal of being diverse, equitable, and inclusive.

## *THIS* FUTURE OF BLACK LIBRARIANSHIP

Despite the assessments and recommendations of librarians and scholars in the *Handbook*'s second edition and even with decades of initiatives intended to address disparities within the profession, the American Library Association's (ALA) most recent demographic survey from 2017 reported African American library and information professionals as only 4.4 percent.[5] Part of this decline may be attributed to today's more nuanced categorization (e.g., the addition of an "Other" category and a distinction between race and ethnicity). But even with this, white representation has remained consistent. Though Josey's 1999 data did not state the percentage of White librarians or professionals, a 1997 article examining race within the profession published in *Library Journal* reported whites as having represented 87.7 percent in 1991; the 2017 ALA demographic survey reported 86.7 percent.[6]

It has been almost fifty years since the *Handbook*'s first edition was published. Policies have been devised and initiatives launched with the goal of ensuring parity. In 2007, Teresa Neely and Lorna Peterson emphasized that the strategy for recruitment should be extended beyond simply increasing the numbers in librarianship to match US demographics to focus "strategically on increasing diversity in order to serve the diverse communities libraries serve."[7] Yet the library and information science profession has continued to make little impact to diversity within its ranks. Such a persisting disparity that seemingly defies all efforts is indicative of the profession having yet to make a sincere commitment to the principles of diversity, equity, and inclusion it has long offered lip service.

Now is an ideal time to begin that commitment. As in the 1990s, the nation again discusses diversity (now with equity and inclusion) with fervor. The Supreme Court's recent decision to overturn *Roe v. Wade* signaled that what were once considered civil rights are in fact privileges that can be revoked at any time with enough lobbying. Knowing this makes states' attempts to stifle efforts toward diversity, equity, and inclusion of greater national concern. The possibility of today's legislation undoing even more hard-won civil rights accomplishments hangs before us.

Some of the more public battles are regarding diversity, equity, and inclusion in public and higher education. Florida House Bill 999 may be the most notorious. In its initial iteration, the bill sought to remove from Florida's public colleges and universities "any major or minor in Critical Race Theory, Gender Studies, or Intersectionality, or any derivative major or minor of these belief systems"[8] and prohibited institutions from expending funds that intend to "promote, support, or maintain programs or campus activities that . . . espouse diversity, equity, and inclusion."[9] But Florida is not alone. *The Chronicle of Higher Education* has created an online tracker that monitors which states propose and pass legislation that bans diversity, equity, and inclusion initiatives on higher education campuses. At the time of this writing, there have been thirty-three bills introduced in nineteen states. Three have received final legislative approval: Texas House Bill 1, North Dakota Senate Bill 2247, and a Kansas budget bill.[10] The thirty-three bills typically seek to prohibit the funding of DEI offices, initiatives, or staff on campus; the mandating of DEI training; identity-based preferences; and/or the requirement of diversity statements from students or employees for hiring, promotion, or admission.[11]

The situation is even more dire when you consider similar challenges to diversity, equity, and inclusion among resources available within K–12 and public libraries. In 2022, ALA's Office for Intellectual Freedom reported a record 1,269 book and resource challenges—the highest ever in its twenty-year history.[12]

## OVERVIEW OF DEI EFFORTS

In their course on the history of libraries, Annette Lamb and Larry Johnson explain how the social responsibility of the library and information science profession may reside in the work of individual librarians or in that of institutions like ALA.[13] Founded in 1876, ALA is the oldest and largest library association in the world. Its 2019 annual report, the most recent available, recorded its membership as being "more than 58,000 members, including librarians, library workers, library trustees and other interested people from every state and many nations."[14] Its history and vast professional reach have distinguished ALA as the professional organization best equipped to establish and maintain strategic initiatives within the organization. Though the terminology has shifted over the years, ALA has historically discussed diversity, equity, and inclusion within the profession with varying degrees of success.

In 1921, for example, ALA established its first roundtable specifically intended to encourage library patron diversity and equitable access. As its Equal Access timeline explains, "[The Work with Negroes Round Table] began to examine the state of equitable access to library materials for African

Americans" and was intended to promote patron diversity. Unfortunately, the roundtable could not reach a consensus between librarians of the North and librarians of the South on the administration of library services to Negroes in the South. The heated meeting resulted in ALA permanently disbanding the Work with Negroes Roundtable after just two years.[15]

In 1967, ALA established the Office of Intellectual Freedom (OIF) with the purpose of "implementing ALA policies concerning the concept of intellectual freedom as embodied in the *Library Bill of Rights*, the Association's basic policy on free access to libraries and library materials."[16] In recent years, predominant challenges are for books and resources by and about people of color and other diverse populations. OIF has increasingly collaborated with other offices, such as the Office for Diversity, Literacy, and Outreach Services and its Office for Library Advocacy.[17]

According to Brewer, many academic and research libraries in the 1980s began to focus on recruiting minority librarians, and most often did so through residency programs.[18] Now known as the Pauline A. Young Residency Program, the University of Delaware's residency program is believed to be the first of its kind and has existed since at least 1984.[19] In 1998, the ALA Council established five Key Action Areas as its guiding principles: Diversity, Equity of Access, Education and Continuous Learning, Intellectual Freedom, and 21st Century Literacy.[20] That same year, it also founded the Spectrum Scholarship Program, which by 2018 had funded 1,063 master's degree scholarships and eighteen doctoral fellows.[21] In 2006, ALA launched its "Emerging Leaders" program, a national professional development program that provides an annual cohort of early- and mid-career librarians opportunities to gain leadership skills and experience. In 2017, the Association for College and Research Libraries (ACRL), the largest division within ALA, established its Diversity Alliance. In addition to attempting to standardize and synthesize the diversity residency experience among academic and research libraries, the Alliance also provides principles for diversity, equity, and inclusion to which every library and information organization interested in joining the Alliance must commit. Unfortunately, only nineteen colleges and universities are currently participating in the Alliance. The greatest participation ever reported was in 2021 with fifty-eight institutional members.

These examples are by no means exhaustive of the conversations within the profession regarding diversity, equity, and inclusion broadly, and the hiring and recruiting of people of color specifically. But as Wheeler suggested, "Nothing short of a rebellion will cause libraries, associations, and individuals to step forward and act upon the affirmative action and diversity rhetoric of the past."[22] Wheeler posited that progress could be attained through a multipronged approach occurring simultaneously from a variety of directions. His solution highlighted the individual, organizational, and institutional levels.

## VIEWING INSTITUTIONAL COMMITMENT AS AN ASSOCIATION-WIDE RESPONSE

In 1990, ACRL's Task Force on Recruitment of Underrepresented Minorities reported three reasons for the patterns of low recruitment and retention of underrepresented groups: "Lack of institutional commitment to change and accountability, personal and institutional racism, and barriers to advancement and retention."[23] As James LaRue and Eleanor Diaz explained, "Issues related to free speech and universal access affect the entire profession and require an Association-wide response."[24] Likewise, the broad issues of diversity, equity, and inclusion and specific issue of recruitment and retention of librarians of color necessitate an Association-wide response. As much was stated in the 2007 white paper produced by the ACRL Board of Directors Diversity Task Force. The paper's primary recommendation in addressing recruitment was to develop "a profession-wide concerted effort [that] will eliminate duplication and channel all efforts through one resource."[25] As already expressed, ALA's historic accomplishments make it best suited to develop such a profession-wide, concerted effort. The ACRL's Diversity Alliance is already now attempting to channel strategies to evaluate and improve disparate diversity residency experiences. The Spectrum Scholars and Emerging Leaders programs represent additional attempts by the Association to break down barriers to advancement and retention.

But the meatier issues surrounding an institutional commitment to change and accountability and against racism have relied primarily on rhetoric. This may be most recently evidenced in 2015, when the ALA Council adopted a new three- to five-year strategic plan that did not initially include equity, diversity, and inclusion as a strategic direction. This would be added in 2017.[26]

ALA already has at its disposal the institutional knowledge, literature research, white papers, assessments and evaluations, frameworks, and more that could transform the profession if properly aligned. Article 3, Section 2 of ALA's bylaws asserts that any person, library, or organization interested in library service and librarianship shall be eligible for membership, which is determined by completing an application and paying dues.[27] Consider how much progress could be achieved if the entire Association considered itself to be an alliance of libraries that sincerely infused the ideals of diversity, equity, and inclusion across all divisions, sections, groups, and programs. Only once the Association as a whole—not just the designated offices, sections, subcommittees, and groups of interested librarians—is committed to ensuring change and holding its members accountable will there be change.

One example of what such an institutional commitment could look like would be if the ALA developed and mandated that the deans and directors of each member institution regularly completed a standardized assessment of its own diversity, equity, and inclusion efforts. This is an expansion of the Diversity Alliance's requirement for the leaders of its member institutions to annually recommit to the principles established by the Alliance. This assessment should also require supplemental materials that substantiate the score—from a library's published strategic plan to data on its recruitment, hiring, retention, and promotion efforts.

In 2021, ALA's Committee on Diversity developed an optional Equity, Diversity, and Inclusion Scorecard for "library and information organizations to evaluate their efforts in advancing diversity, equity, and inclusion."[28] This scorecard, which assesses an institution's effectiveness in 1) embedding DEI within the culture and climate; 2) providing timely trainings and educational opportunities on the topics of racism and equitable workplaces; 3) recruiting, hiring, retaining, and promoting candidates of color; 4) prioritizing diversity, equity, and inclusion within the budget; and 5) establishing plans to track and procedures to monitor data on its DEI goals and objectives, could be further developed and used as the framework for the proposed standardized assessment.

Currently, the scorecard's rubric ranges from 0 (insufficient in all areas) to 15 (excellent in all areas). Library and information organizations with scores within a specific range of insufficiency predetermined by the ALA Council should be placed on probation. While their librarians and staff may remain members of ALA, its divisions, and sections and may still attend conferences and programs, members from these institutions would not be able to hold a leadership position, serve on a committee, present at conferences, be published ALA's scholarly publications, or otherwise promoted on ALA's platforms until their institution's DEI scorecard improved. With their professional development stymied in this way, it is anticipated that librarians and staff at insufficiently progressive institutions will exert pressure upon leadership to enact changes to allow their continued participation.

### AN ESTABLISHED PRECEDENT

This proposal for an institutional commitment to change and accountability with regard to diversity, equity, and inclusion within the profession comes with the Black Caucus of ALA's (BCALA) own history in mind. BCALA's first resolution, submitted in 1970, was for censure and sanctions against libraries and librarians that provided service to private schools then emerging as a countermeasure to the Supreme Court's ruling for public school desegregation. Until this resolution, those librarians and libraries faced no repercussions by ALA, despite the association being "cognizant of the social responsibilities of libraries serving the people of the United States and . . . opposed to racism in any and all of its forms."[29] As she presented both the resolution and a statement of concern before the council during that conference, Effie Lee Morris described the library and information science profession's hesitancy in responding to the racism and socioeconomic issues faced by Black and other minorities. Though the resolution in opposition of supporting racist institutions passed successfully, it was only after much debate and because, Josey suspected, councilmember Hugh Atkinson requested ALA's first roll call vote.[30] The publicly identifiable voting method held council members accountable for their response. Likewise, this contemporary proposal seeks to censure and hold accountable the libraries uninterested in an authentic commitment to diversity, equity, and inclusion.

### THE FUTURE OF BLACK LIBRARIANSHIP, REVISITED

This chapter proposes just one example of what a sincere institutional commitment to diversity, equity, and inclusion in all areas might look like. It acknowledges that implementing such a proposal would require a restructuring of ALA. This proposal also comes with a recommendation for further research, including an additional accountability framework that may exist within ALA or other professional organizations.

But the time is ripe for the exploration and implementation of a radically new approach.

In 1997, Brewer determined "librarianship in general, and academic librarianship in particular, continues to be a predominantly white, female profession."[31] In 2000, Neely concluded her chapter in the *Handbook's* second edition by saying, "At the rate of recruitment and retention in this field, we will all have passed on before we can even imagine parity."[32] Despite the scholarship of so many, demographics for the library and information science profession remain such that in 2021, Velez et al. could still accurately assert "it is well known that librarianship is a predominantly White, particularly White female, profession."[33]

Many people committed to this work, including Josey and Morris, have passed without experiencing the hoped-for parity. For those of us who remain, we must make it our mission to ensure the issues that allow persisting issues of disparity within the profession do not prevail. Because of its reach and impact, this chapter proposes an approach that is specific to ALA. But committing to change and accountability, eradicating racism, and defeating barriers to advancement and retention can and should be addressed at every level of the profession—individual, organizational, and institutional.

Only once this is achieved will Black librarianship thrive, which means more than achieving a demographic figure that is on par with census data. It means spurring the profession so that it is best positioned to consider and meet the needs of all its patrons. It means establishing a legacy of progressiveness in honor of all of those who have passed on. It means demonstrating a commitment to all those who will come after.

### NOTES

1. E. J. Josey, "Statistical Facts Pertaining to Black Librarians and Libraries," in *Handbook of Black Librarianship*, 2nd ed., edited by E. J. Josey and Marva L. DeLoach (Lanham, MD: Scarecrow Press, 2000), 207.
2. Maurice B. Wheeler, "Averting a Crisis: Developing African American Librarians as Leader," in *Handbook of Black*

*Librarianship*, 2nd ed., edited by E. J. Josey and Marva L. DeLoach (Lanham, MD: Scarecrow Press, 2000), 169.
3. Simmona E. Simmons-Hodo, "The Language of Diversity: What Is It?" in *Handbook of Black Librarianship*, 2nd ed., edited by E. J. Josey and Marva L. DeLoach (Lanham, MD: Scarecrow Press, 2000), 144.
4. Teresa Y. Neely, "Effects of Diversity on Black Librarianship: Is Diversity Divergent?" in *Handbook of Black Librarianship*, 2nd ed., edited by E. J. Josey and Marva L. DeLoach (Lanham, MD: Scarecrow Press, 2000), 130.
5. Kathy Rosa and Kelsey Henke, "2017 ALA Demographic Study," ALA Office for Research and Statistics, 2017, https://www.ala.org/tools/sites/ala.org.tools/files/content/Draft%20of%20Member%20Demographics%20Survey%2001-11-2017.pdf.
6. Ibid.; Evan St. Lifer and Corinne O. Nelson, "Unequal Opportunities: Race Does Matter," *Library Journal*, 122 (1997): 42-46.
7. Teresa Y. Neely and Lorna Peterson, "Achieving Racial and Ethnic Diversity among Academic and Research Librarians: The Recruitment, Retention, and Advancement of Librarians of Color," White Paper, Association of College and Research Libraries, July 2007, 5, https://www.ala.org/acrl/sites/ala.org.acrl/files/content/publications/whitepapers/ACRL_AchievingRacial.pdf.
8. Alex Andrade, "HB 999: Postsecondary Education Institutions," HB 999, February 21, 2023, https://www.flsenate.gov/Session/Bill/2023/999/BillText/c2/PDF.
9. Ibid., 14.
10. Adrienne Lu et al., "DEI Legislation Tracker," *The Chronicle of Higher Education*, May 2023, https://www.chronicle.com/article/here-are-the-states-where-lawmakers-are-seeking-to-ban-colleges-dei-efforts.
11. Ibid.
12. "Censorship by the Numbers," *Advocacy, Legislation & Issues*, April 20, 2023, https://www.ala.org/advocacy/bbooks/by-the-numbers.
13. Annette Lamb and Larry Johnson, "Lesson 10—Contemporary Libraries: 1950s-2000s," *The History of Libraries* (Eduscapes.com, 2020), 20, https://eduscapes.com/wp/the-history-of-libraries/.
14. *Finding the Library at Your Place: American Library Association 2019 Impact Report*, American Library Association, 2019, https://www.ala.org/aboutala/sites/ala.org.aboutala/files/content/2019-ALA-Impact-Report-ac.pdf.
15. "Equal Access—About ALA," American Library Association, Dynamically Generated Page, 1996-2023, https://www.ala.org/aboutala/equal_access.
16. "Office for Intellectual Freedom." American Library Association, June 9, 2008, https://www.ala.org/aboutala/offices/oif.
17. James LaRue and Eleanor Diaz, "50 Years of Intellectual Freedom," *American Libraries Magazine*, November 1, 2017, https://americanlibrariesmagazine.org/2017/11/01/50-years-office-intellectual-freedom/.
18. Julie Brewer, "Post-Master's Residency Programs: Enhancing the Development of New Professionals and Minority Recruitment in Academic and Research Libraries," *College & Research Libraries*, 58, no. 6 (1997): 529, https://doi.org/10.5860/crl.58.6.528.
19. LaTesha Velez et al., "Mapping the Residency Program Landscape," *The Journal of Academic Librarianship*, 47, no. 5 (2021): 2, https://doi.org/10.1016/j.acalib.2021.102389.
20. "Equal Access—About ALA."
21. "Reflections on Spectrum's Beginnings," *Advocacy, Legislation & Issues*, January 3, 2018, https://www.ala.org/advocacy/spectrum/beginningsreflection.
22. Wheeler, "Averting a Crisis," 171.
23. Janice Y. Kung et al., "Diversity Initiatives to Recruit and Retain Academic Librarians: A Systematic Review," *College & Research Libraries*, 81, no. 1 (2020): 88, https://doi.org/10.5860/crl.81.1.96; Janice Beaudlin et al., "Recruiting the Underrepresented to Academic Libraries," *College and Research Libraries News*, 51, no. 11 (1990): 1018, https://doi.org/10.5860/crln.51.11.1016.
24. LaRue and Diaz, "50 Years of Intellectual Freedom."
25. Neely and Peterson, "Achieving Racial and Ethnic Diversity," 6.
26. "About ALA," About ALA, https://www.ala.org/aboutala/.
27. ALA Council, "Bylaws of the American Library Association," ALA Bylaws, November 24, 2010, https://www.ala.org/aboutala/governance/constitution/bylaws.
28. Amber Hayes, "ALA's Committee on Diversity Announces Diversity, Equity, and Inclusion (DEI) Scorecard for Library and Information Organizations," News and Press Center, July 7, 2021, https://www.ala.org/news/member-news/2021/07/alas-committee-diversity-announces-diversity-equity-and-inclusion-dei-scorecard.
29. E. J. Josey, "Black Caucus of the American Library Association: The Early Years," in *Handbook of Black Librarianship*, 2nd ed., edited by E. J. Josey and Marva DeLoach (Lanham, MD: Scarecrow Press, 2000), 86.
30. Ibid.
31. Brewer, "Post-Master's Residency Programs," 529.
32. Neely, "Effects of Diversity," 140.
33. Velez, "Mapping," 4.

**WORKS CITED**

"About ALA." About ALA. https://www.ala.org/aboutala/. Accessed May 1, 2023.

ALA Council. "Bylaws of the American Library Association." ALA Bylaws, November 24, 2010. https://www.ala.org/aboutala/governance/constitution/bylaws.

Andrade, Alex. "HB 999: Postsecondary Education Institutions." HB 999. February 21, 2023. https://www.flsenate.gov/Session/Bill/2023/999/BillText/c2/PDF.

Beaudlin, Janice, Em Claire Knowles, Edith Maureen Fisher, and Ichiko Morita. "Recruiting the Underrepresented to Academic Libraries." *College and Research Libraries News*, 51, no. 11(1990): 1016-29. https://doi.org/10.5860/crln.51.11.1016.

Brewer, Julie. "Post-Master's Residency Programs: Enhancing the Development of New Professionals and Minority Recruitment in Academic and Research Libraries." *College & Research Libraries*, 58, no. 6 (1997): 528-37. https://doi.org/10.5860/crl.58.6.528.

"Censorship by the Numbers." *Advocacy, Legislation & Issues*, April 20, 2023. https://www.ala.org/advocacy/bbooks/by-the-numbers.

"Equal Access—About ALA." American Library Association, Dynamically Generated Page. https://www.ala.org/aboutala/equal_access. Accessed May 5, 2023.

*Finding the Library at Your Place: American Library Association 2019 Impact Report.* American Library Association, 2019. https://www.ala.org/aboutala/sites/ala.org.aboutala/files/content/2019-ALA-Impact-Report-ac.pdf.

Hayes, Amber. "ALA's Committee on Diversity Announces Diversity, Equity, and Inclusion (DEI) Scorecard for Library and Information Organizations." News and Press Center, July 7, 2021. https://www.ala.org/news/member-news/2021/07/alas-committee-diversity-announces-diversity-equity-and-inclusion-dei-scorecard.

Josey, E. J. "Black Caucus of the American Library Association: The Early Years." In *Handbook of Black Librarianship*, 2nd ed., edited by E. J. Josey and Marva L. DeLoach, 83–97. Lanham, MD: Scarecrow Press, 2000.

———. "Statistical Facts Pertaining to Black Librarians and Libraries." In *Handbook of Black Librarianship*, 2nd ed., edited by E. J. Josey and Marva L. DeLoach, 207–9. Lanham, MD: Scarecrow Press, 2000.

Kung, Janice Y., K-Lee Fraser, and Dee Winn. "Diversity Initiatives to Recruit and Retain Academic Librarians: A Systematic Review." *College & Research Libraries*, 81, no. 1 (2020): 96–108. https://doi.org/10.5860/crl.81.1.96.

Lamb, Annette, and Larry Johnson. "Lesson 10—Contemporary Libraries: 1950s–2000s." *The History of Libraries*. e-Book, Eduscapes.com, 2020, 1–69. https://eduscapes.com/wp/the-history-of-libraries/.

LaRue, James, and Eleanor Diaz. "50 Years of Intellectual Freedom." *American Libraries Magazine*, November 1, 2017. https://americanlibrariesmagazine.org/2017/11/01/50-years-office-intellectual-freedom/.

Lu, Adrienne, et al. "DEI Legislation Tracker." *The Chronicle of Higher Education*, May 2023. https://www.chronicle.com/article/here-are-the-states-where-lawmakers-are-seeking-to-ban-colleges-dei-efforts.

Neely, Teresa Y. "Effects of Diversity on Black Librarianship: Is Diversity Divergent?" In *Handbook of Black Librarianship*, 2nd ed., edited by E. J. Josey and Marva L. DeLoach, 129–42. Lanham, MD: Scarecrow Press, 2000.

Neely, Teresa Y., and Lorna Peterson. "Achieving Racial and Ethnic Diversity among Academic and Research Librarians: The Recruitment, Retention, and Advancement of Librarians of Color." Association of College and Research Libraries, July 2007. https://www.ala.org/acrl/sites/ala.org.acrl/files/content/publications/whitepapers/ACRL_AchievingRacial.pdf.

"Office for Intellectual Freedom." American Library Association, June 9, 2008. https://www.ala.org/aboutala/offices/oif.

"Reflections on Spectrum's Beginnings." Advocacy, Legislation & Issues, January 3, 2018. https://www.ala.org/advocacy/spectrum/beginningsreflection.

Rosa, Kathy, and Kelsey Henke. "2017 ALA Demographic Study." American Library Association, January 2017. http://www.ala.org/tools/research/initiatives/membershipsurveys.

Simmons-Hodo, Simmona E. "The Language of Diversity: What Is It?" In *Handbook of Black Librarianship*, 2nd ed., edited by E. J. Josey and Marva L. DeLoach, 143–47. Lanham, MD: Scarecrow Press, 2000.

St. Lifer, Evan, and Corinne O. Nelson. "Unequal Opportunities: Race Does Matter." *Library Journal*, 122 (1997): 42–46.

Velez, LaTesha, Jason Alston, Nataly Blas, Kathy Bradshaw, Orolando Duffus, Dennelle Eads, Gerald Holmes, and Olivia Patterson. "Mapping the Residency Program Landscape." *The Journal of Academic Librarianship*, 47, no. 5 (2021): 102389. https://doi.org/10.1016/j.acalib.2021.102389.

Wheeler, Maurice B. "Averting a Crisis: Developing African American Librarians as Leaders." In *Handbook of Black Librarianship*, 2nd ed., edited by E. J. Josey and Marva L. DeLoach, 169–18. Lanham, MD: Scarecrow Press, 2000.

---

# 4.19

## *In the Weeds*

CHALLENGING PERFORMATIVE ALLYSHIP AMID WIDESPREAD TRAUMATIC EVENTS

Lorin Jackson and Jazmyne Baylor

Performative allyship is an issue that grows out of widespread traumatic events in our social climate. Traumatic events impact everyone and seem to be increasing by the day. As they become more normalized and rooted in our experiences, they influence the ways we exist and work in the world. For Black librarians, trauma is a familiar experience, entrenched in our historical memory, so how do we continue to exist in the library profession alongside growing performative allyship that threatens our ability to work and to live? What is at stake with performative allyship in impacting the well-being of Black librarians? In this chapter, we examine the specific challenges and concerns for Black library workers and the related dangers of performative allyship toward marginalized library workers amid widespread traumatic events. The chapter will conclude with a call to action about confronting performativity and provide recommendations for making the library safer and more inclusive.

Beyond current high rates of traumatic events and gun violence, anti-Black hate crimes account for the highest number of hate crimes in this country, according to a 2022 *Time* magazine article by Janell Ross:

> As the country publicly declared itself to be in the midst of a racial reckoning, it turns out Black Americans were being hunted and hurt at a level unmatched since 2008—the year that saw the election of the first Black president and an attendant, hate-fueled backlash. In 2020, the most recent year for which the FBI has gathered and reported nationwide hate crime data, 2,871 Black Americans became victims of hate crimes. The number represents nearly 35% of all hate crime reported to the FBI that year. What's more, systems for reporting hate crime have long been flawed and limited in ways known to researchers, suggesting that 2020's already high numbers fail to capture the full picture.[1]

As Ross states, we do not have accurate statistics regarding how much danger Black people in this country face due to continually rising traumatic events of anti-Black violence. The Federal Bureau of Investigation (FBI) released statistics that provide strong evidence of anti-Black crime's prevalence in the United States; even though "Black Americans made up 13.4% of the US population in 2020 yet 35% of all hate crime victims. The same disparity has persisted over the years."[2] In addition to high rates of traumatic events, rising gun violence, and violence against Black people, since 2020 everyone experiences the trauma of living in a global pandemic with COVID-19. So, the question becomes: *What do we do with all this trauma?*

## STUDYING TRAUMA AND ITS IMPACT ON LIBRARY WORKERS

Recent scholarship shows increases in the research about trauma and its impact on workers. While there have been discussions about trauma in the workplace, most of the scholarly literature focuses on the experiences of health-care workers, social workers, and first responders.[3] When researchers discuss librarians' traumatic experiences in the workplace, the perspective tends to focus on the experiences of public library workers. The research also skews toward generalizing about librarians overall without calling attention to the experiences of different kinds of library workers.[4] So, how do traumatic events impact Black library workers, specifically? What may be unique about how Black librarians experience trauma that needs further examination?

In addition to scholarly literature ignoring how trauma impacts different groups differently, institutional leadership often does not acknowledge trauma within and around libraries. Over the last decade, only selectively have traumatic events been amplified. With recent statistics on the prevalence of traumatic events, there are, unfortunately, numerous opportunities for library institutions and their leadership to "show" what they perceive as solidarity without being *in solidarity*. This could be because the trauma of those in leadership has not been processed, so the impact continues to live in their bodies and psyches. Resmaa Menakem thoughtfully explains how trauma is primarily a bodily experience in *My Grandmother's Hands: Racialized Trauma and the Pathway to Mending Our Hearts and Bodies*: "Trauma is a wordless story our body tells itself about what is safe and what is a threat. Our rational brain can't stop it from occurring, and it can't talk our body out of it."[5] Furthermore, for library leaders, refusing to process trauma impacts their inability to serve authentically and support others experiencing trauma.

Performativity then becomes a stand-in to catalyzing substantial change in the library profession, especially for Black librarians. Suppose we do not confront our own traumatic experiences and process them. We will then continue to allow displays of solidarity and trauma instead of moving through trauma and creating opportunities for healing. Instead of establishing thoughtful ways to care wholistically for library workers and, notably, Black library workers, performativity works to maintain the status quo in libraries or "business as usual" without getting *into the weeds* of how to help others. Institutional leadership performs solidarity without confronting the layers of complication that strain our profession and push Black library workers to abandon the profession altogether.

## UNIQUE CONCERNS FOR BLACK LIBRARIANS

In 2005, Dr. Joy DeGruy coined the term "Post Traumatic Slave Syndrome" (PTTS) to describe the enduring impacts of the legacy of chattel slavery on Black people and the world. DeGruy defines PTSS as a

> theory that explains the etiology of many of the adaptive survival behaviors in African American communities throughout the United States and the Diaspora. It is a condition that exists because of multigenerational oppression of Africans and their descendants resulting from centuries of chattel slavery—a form of slavery which was predicated on the belief that African Americans were inherently/genetically inferior to whites.[6]

DeGruy goes on to explain that institutionalized and systemic racism continues to manifest in the lives of modern Black Americans. Library luminary and scholar April Hathcock takes DeGruy's research a step further by analyzing the library profession as a plantation in her 2019 blog post, "Librarianship as Plantation." In this post, Hathcock lays out how the plantation hierarchy and gatekeeping protocols of the plantation mimic the experience of library workers today. She presents a compelling analogy that corroborates the unique relationship between library work and Black people at this time in history.[7] Coupling the enduring impacts and legacy of chattel slavery with the manifestations of trauma against Black Americans, we live with this trauma daily as Black library workers. When another traumatic event occurs, we are brutally reminded and transported back to the reality of our continued epistemicide and systemic oppression.[8] How are we to deal with this as library workers? What is being broken and reopened within us each time an event like this occurs?

We have many problems regarding how Black library workers can continue to live and thrive in libraries. More librarians are leaving the profession at high rates. While recruitment and retention in libraries for librarians of color have been a problem, with mounting incidents of trauma experienced by Black library workers and users alike, something must give. One of the ways that library workers can mitigate the growing impacts of trauma on the community is by avoiding worsening what is happening by becoming more aware of performative allyship and addressing it at the root as another form of oppression.

**THE NUANCES OF PERFORMATIVE ALLYSHIP**

On May 25, 2020, George Floyd was murdered by Derek Chauvin, a Minneapolis police officer. The next day, protests against police brutality and racism sparked across the globe. Businesses and institutions—including libraries—made public announcements denouncing the actions of officers and supporting the Black Lives Matter movement. The statements were those of solidarity, and some organizations followed up by providing a call to action, naming white supremacy, donating funds to communities and organizations doing the work, and more. Library administration across the country made statements condemning police brutality and providing library resources on antiracist materials. The Black Caucus of the American Library Association (BCALA) released a statement on May 28, 2020, that encouraged members to act against injustices and provided a list of methods for members to engage in.[9] Despite the overwhelming number of declarations of solidarity that appeared online, many organizations and individuals failed to follow through with action beyond a statement. Public statements of solidarity and support means nothing if there is no action that confronts white supremacy, police brutality, and capitalism. It is merely nothing but a performance.

Peter Kalina defines performative allyship as "the actions that are enacted in front of an audience with the goal to gain popularity and respect."[10] It is quite easy to get caught up in performative allyship, because it is a "safe" way to engage in social justice work without any of the risk or consequences that come along with it—particularly for those not vulnerable to institutional discrimination. The conservative nature of institutions makes it difficult for libraries and library workers to engage in social justice work without it conflicting with other organizational priorities.[11] Despite this, many of us continue to center our work around social justice issues. To continue to fight against injustices while experiencing racial trauma (in-person or vicariously) is a heavy burden to carry. To experience trauma while our peers and place of employment try to remain neutral or do the bare minimum to address systemic and institutional racism adds to that burden. Adding #BlackLivesMatter to social media profiles, acknowledging our trauma behind closed doors, creating statements of solidarity, or remaining silent are all empty gestures if no one names or acts against the problems—white supremacy and neoliberal capitalism.[12]

Capitalism is rarely named when discussing performative allyship, but it is often a driving factor of why people engage in performative actions—mostly because we often fail to understand the political and economic ideology of (neo)liberal capitalism and how it influences our institutions. Sidney and Beatrice Webb define capitalism as

> the particular stage in the development of industry and legal institutions in which the bulk of the workers find themselves divorced from the ownership of the instruments of production in such a way as to pass into the position of wage-earners, whose subsistence, security and personal freedom seem dependent on the will of a relatively small proportion of the nation.[13]

Capitalism relies on the exploitation of workers and comes to dominate all our important institutions, including libraries. Most libraries' funding is in the hands of stakeholders, such as the government, donors, board members, and other entities that provide financial support. This reality makes it difficult for us to act against injustices and puts us in the position of choosing between speaking out or remaining silent. This is not an excuse for inaction, but a note on how capitalism impacts our lives. Despite libraries being not-for-profit entities, we operate under a for-profit model. Libraries management practices, marketing structure, the issuing of fines, and competing against other departments (i.e., school and police) for funding are all examples of a for-profit organization. Libraries are not invisible to the impacts of neoliberal capitalism and to acknowledge this is the first step in acting against this harmful and dangerous system.

White supremacy and capitalism are related, and it is difficult to talk about one without addressing the other. To dismantle white supremacy, we must address capitalism. Scholar Frances Lee Ansley defined white supremacy as a

> political, economic and cultural system in which whites overwhelmingly control power and material resources, conscious and unconscious ideas of white superiority and entitlement are widespread, and relations of white dominance and non-white subordination are daily reenacted across a broad array of institutions and social settings.[14]

Historically, the concept of whiteness was constructed to justify the dehumanization of Black and Indigenous people while procuring power to white people. Brand strategist Cara Nguyen states that "the use and abuse of nonwhite communities to propel white institutions into further economic, social, and political gain is attributable to the reality that all social forces exist in a direct relationship to white supremacy."[15] The system of white supremacy is ingrained in our lives and within the profession, and we cannot ignore this fact. The library and information science professions are overwhelmingly white, and the link between white supremacy and (neo)liberal capitalism means that a lot of efforts of white allies are inherently compromised and fail to address fundamental problems stemming from capitalism. In part, this has to do with the comfortable distance that white liberals have from Black/brown communities, but when that distance is perceived to be shortened, this often resorts to racist norms.[16]

As Black individuals existing during a time where we are constantly exposed to anti-Black violence and tragedies, we do not have the capacity to engage with performative allyship. Our coworkers claim that they stand in solidarity, but only share this sentiment behind closed doors. Our places of employment release statements of solidarity for Black Lives, but fail to support Black workers by providing opportunities for advancement within the field, hiring more Black workers, paying adequate salaries, listening to concerns, and investing in Black workers.[17] According to the US Bureau of Labor Statistics, Black library workers are less than 5 percent of the library profession, which means that we—as Black library workers—need each other to show up as a community to sustain ourselves personally and professionally.[18] We spend a significant amount of our time at work, and this does not include the physical, emotional, and mental labor that we engage in off the clock, especially when tragedy impacts our lives and our communities. We need each other more than ever to get through the trauma that we will inevitably be exposed to and to start calling out performative allies.

## CALL TO ACTION

Library leaders must acknowledge the importance of admitting that trauma occurs and then take steps to address their individual trauma and the trauma of the people using and working in the library. This requires library management to be willing to address their personal trauma in a vulnerable way to create space and opportunity for others to address their trauma. Acknowledging and addressing trauma can assist with laying the foundation for interrupting performativity. Here, we present a call to action that will assist in challenging performative allyship amid widespread traumatic events.

First, we propose that we continue to call out neutrality. Maintaining the idea that libraries are neutral is doing more harm than good, especially within the current political and social climate. Assistant professor and librarian Candise Branum discussed the political nature of libraries by stating, "Though libraries claim a space of neutrality, one of the major responsibilities of libraries is to fill information deficiencies and bring knowledge to the masses, which is inherently political; in this way, the idea of neutrality de-politicizes the very political nature of librarianship."[19] Branum goes on to discuss how libraries should not ask systematically oppressed groups to adopt a neutral lens, because it asks us to ignore our "community history, struggles and identity."[20] Libraries have never been neutral, and history has shown us that. During Jim Crow, public libraries across the country implemented policies that prevented Black residents from accessing facilities and those who allowed access provided unequitable services and resources. Today, library workers are actively taking a stance against prejudices by providing programs, services, and resources to those who are targeted by harmful bills and laws. To continuously push the idea that libraries are neutral is dangerous and insensitive because it creates a narrative that libraries are impartial to occurrences that are taking place around us.

Next, we call for the naming of neoliberal capitalism and white supremacy in libraries. Many people understand capitalism as a driving force for what is wrong today, but shy away from socialism/communism because of how slandered the terms are in popular culture and even academia. Socialism and communism are presented as enemies of capitalism. Many Black activists that we celebrate fought for a socialist future such as W. E. B. Du Bois, Fred Hampton, Kwame Ture, Langston Hughes, Lorraine Hansberry, and Ella Baker. We must continue to educate ourselves on the dangers of capitalism and how it works with white supremacy to keep marginalized communities in oppressed positions. There is a way to an alternative and better future if we choose to fight for it.

Our final proposal is for libraries to conduct reading groups about *My Grandmother's Hands* by Resmaa Menakem. We strongly encourage libraries to call on social workers and trauma therapists to facilitate workplace trauma-informed training to process better and provide for the communities they serve. We encourage colleagues to solicit feedback and ideas from library workers and users about how the library could help them with their trauma. Focus groups with community members where gift cards and transit fare are provided are a great way, regardless of the type of library in which you work, to connect and rebuild after traumatic experiences. You can also employ community advocates from users in the library to facilitate these groups after training CAs to enhance the safety and security of the folks who attend.

## CONCLUSION

This chapter does not discuss Black library workers' experiences with trauma and performative allyship at length but is the beginning of further work needed to get into the weeds. We encourage you to take what you have read here and continue to dig deeper. With white supremacy and capitalism as the foundation of the soil of this country, we will inevitably be exposed to trauma. With knowledge, we can continue to combat these systems and start the process of truly healing.

**NOTES**

1. Janell Ross, "Anti-Black Violence Has Long Been the Most Common American Hate Crime—And We Still Don't Know the Full Extent," *Time*, May 19, 2022.
2. Ibid.
3. Agata Benfante et al., "Traumatic Stress in Healthcare Workers during COVID-19 Pandemic: A Review of the Immediate Impact," *Frontiers in Psychology*, 1 (2020), https://doi.org/https://doi.org/10.3389/fpsyg.2020.569935.
4. Leah T. Dudak et al., "You Can't Self-Care Your Way Out of a Broken System: The 2022 Urban Libraries Trauma Forum," *Public Library Quarterly*, 42, no. 6 (2023): 650-64, https://doi.org/10.1080/01616846.2022.2148826.
5. Resmaa Menakem, *My Grandmother's Hands: Racialized Trauma and the Pathway to Mending Our Hearts and Bodies*. London: Penguin Books, 2021.
6. "Post Traumatic Slave Syndrome," Dr. Joy DeGruy, https://www.joydegruy.com/post-traumatic-slave-syndrome.
7. April Hathcock, "Librarianship as Plantation," At the Intersection, April 6, 2019, https://aprilhathcock.wordpress.com/2019/04/06/librarianship-as-plantation/.
8. Beth Patin et al., "Interrupting Epistemicide: A Practical Framework for Naming, Identifying, and Ending Epistemic Injustice in the Information Professions." *Journal of the Association for Information Science and Technology*, 72, no. 10 (2021): 1-13, https://doi.org/10.1002/asi.24479.
9. Black Caucus of the American Library Association, "Statement Condemning Increased Violence and Racism towards Black Americans and People of Color," Black Caucus American Library Association, June 1, 2020, https://www.bcala.org/statement-condemning-increased-violence-and-racism-towards-black-americans-and-people-of-color.
10. Peter Kalina, "Performative Allyship." *Technium Social Sciences Journal*, 11 (2020): 478-81, DOI.org (Crossref), https://doi.org/10.47577/tssj.v11i1.1518.
11. Amelia N. Gibson et al., "Libraries on the Frontlines: Neutrality and Social Justice," *Equality, Diversity and Inclusion: An International Journal*, 36, no. 8 (2017): 751-66, DOI.org (Crossref), https://doi.org/10.1108/EDI-11-2016-0100.
12. Kelsey Blair, "Empty Gestures: Performative Utterances and Allyship," *Journal of Dramatic Theory and Criticism*, 35, no. 2 (2021): 53-73, DOI.org (Crossref), https://doi.org/10.1353/dtc.2021.0005; John Buschman, "The Library in the Life of the Public: Implications of a Neoliberal Age," *The Library Quarterly (Chicago)*, 87, no. 1 (2017): 55-70.
13. Sidney Webb and Beatrice Webb, *The Decay of Capitalist Civilization*. New York: Harcourt, Brace and Company, 1923.
14. Frances Ansley, "Stirring the Ashes: Race Class and the Future of Civil Rights Scholarship." *Cornell Law Review*, 74, no. 6 (1989): 993-1077, https://scholarship.law.cornell.edu/clr/vol74/iss6/1.
15. Cara Nguyen, "The Relationship between White Supremacy and Capitalism: A Socioeconomic Study on Embeddedness in the Market and Society," *SUURJ: Seattle University Undergraduate Research Journal*, 4, no. 1 (2020), https://scholarworks.seattleu.edu/suurj/vol4/iss1/6.
16. Eduardo Bonilla-Silva, "Rethinking Racism: Toward a Structural Interpretation," *American Sociological Review*, 62, no. 3 (1997): 465-80.
17. Karen Yuan, "Black Employees Say 'Performative Allyship' Is an Unchecked Problem in the Office," *Fortune*, 2020, https://fortune.com/2020/06/19/performative-allyship-working-while-black-white-allies-corporate-diversity-racism/.
18. US Bureau of Labor Statistics, "Labor Force Statistics from the Current Population Survey," 2023, https://www.bls.gov/cps/cpsaat11.htm.
19. Candise Branum, "The Myth of Library Neutrality," *Humanities Commons*, 2008, https://hcommons.org/deposits/item/hc:18389/.
20. Ibid., 7.

**WORKS CITED**

Ansley, Frances. "Stirring the Ashes: Race Class and the Future of Civil Rights Scholarship." *Cornell Law Review*, 74, no. 6 (1989): 993-1077. https://scholarship.law.cornell.edu/clr/vol74/iss6/1.

Benfante, Agata, Marialaura Di Tella, Annunziata Romeo, and Lorys Castelli. "Traumatic Stress in Healthcare Workers during COVID-19 Pandemic: A Review of the Immediate Impact." *Frontiers in Psychology*, 1 (2020). https://doi.org/https://doi.org/10.3389/fpsyg.2020.569935.

Black Caucus of the American Library Association. "Statement Condemning Increased Violence and Racism towards Black Americans and People of Color." Black Caucus American Library Association, June 1, 2020, https://www.bcala.org/statement-condemning-increased-violence-and-racism-towards-black-americans-and-people-of-color.

Blair, Kelsey. "Empty Gestures: Performative Utterances and Allyship." *Journal of Dramatic Theory and Criticism*, 35, no. 2 (2021): 53-73. DOI.org (Crossref), https://doi.org/10.1353/dtc.2021.0005.

Bonilla-Silva, Eduardo "Rethinking Racism: Toward a Structural Interpretation." *American Sociological Review*, 62, no. 3 (1997): 465-80.

Branum, Candise. "The Myth of Library Neutrality." *Humanities Commons*, 2008. https://hcommons.org/deposits/item/hc:18389/.

Buschman, John. "The Library in the Life of the Public: Implications of a Neoliberal Age." *The Library Quarterly* (Chicago), 87, no. 1 (2017): 55-70.

Dudak, Leah T., L. Comito, and C. Zabriskie. "You Can't Self-Care Your Way Out of a Broken System: The 2022 Urban Libraries Trauma Forum." *Public Library Quarterly*, 42, no. 6 (2023): 650-64.

Gibson, Amelia N., Renate Chancellor, Nicole Cooke, Sarah Park Dahlen, Shari A. Lee, and Yasmeen Shorish. "Libraries on the Frontlines: Neutrality and Social Justice." *Equality, Diversity and Inclusion: An International Journal*, 36, no. 8 (2017): 751-66. DOI.org (Crossref), https://doi.org/10.1108/EDI-11-2016-0100.

Hathcock, April. "Librarianship as Plantation." At the Intersection, April 6, 2019. https://aprilhathcock.wordpress.com/2019/04/06/librarianship-as-plantation/.

Kalina, Peter. "Performative Allyship." *Technium Social Sciences Journal*, 11 (2020): 478-81. DOI.org (Crossref), https://doi.org/10.47577/tssj.v11i1.1518.

Menakem, Resmaa. *My Grandmother's Hands: Racialized Trauma and the Pathway to Mending Our Hearts and Bodies*. London: Penguin Books, 2021.

Nguyen, Cara. "The Relationship between White Supremacy and Capitalism: A Socioeconomic Study on Embeddedness in the Market and Society." *SUURJ: Seattle University Undergraduate Research Journal*, 4, no. 1 (2020). https://scholarworks.seattleu.edu/suurj/vol4/iss1/6.

Patin, Beth, Melinda Sebastian, Jieun Yeon, Danielle Bertolini, and Alexandra Grimm. "Interrupting Epistemicide: A Practical Framework for Naming, Identifying, and Ending Epistemic Injustice in the Information Professions." *Journal of the Association for Information Science and Technology*, 72, no. 10 (2021): 1–13. https://doi.org/10.1002/asi.24479.

"Post Traumatic Slave Syndrome." Dr. Joy DeGruy. https://www.joydegruy.com/post-traumatic-slave-syndrome.

Ross, Janell. "Anti-Black Violence Has Long Been the Most Common American Hate Crime—And We Still Don't Know the Full Extent." *Time*, May 19, 2022.

US Bureau of Labor Statistics. "Labor Force Statistics from the Current Population Survey." 2023. https://www.bls.gov/cps/cpsaat11.htm.

Webb, Sidney, and Beatrice Webb. *The Decay of Capitalist Civilization*. New York: Harcourt, Brace and Company, 1923.

Yuan, Karen. "Black Employees Say 'Performative Allyship' Is an Unchecked Problem in the Office." *Fortune*, 2020. https://fortune.com/2020/06/19/performative-allyship-working-while-black-white-allies-corporate-diversity-racism.

---

# 4.20

## *Essay from Assembly Member Jeffrion L. Aubry*

Jeffrion L. Aubry

My library experience began in the "shush" era of seen but not heard. Reading was a solitary undertaking with any discussion to be held at a later time. Noise disturbed concentration. It was a distraction. Sit still and be quiet. Rarely a scene of cultural or literary diversity for people of color. From the 1950s to the 1960s the nation stirred with emergent forces of dissent—dissenters with voices from the underground challenging the status quo.

Freedom, justice, equality for all, literature, artists, writers, painters, and culture brought enlightenment to the masses. In 1969, the Corona Langston Hughes Community Library and Cultural Center was born, spawned by the swirling waters of change. It was community controlled and culturally focused to serve the people who had been excluded and deprived but always striving, relentless. The library was nestled in a community that had become home to Malcolm X, Louis Armstrong, Dizzy Gillespie, Ella Fitzgerald, Jimmy Heath, Helen Marshall, Judge Bill Booth, Willie Mays, Solitaire Fernandez, Andrew (Sekou) Jackson, Grace Lawrence, Attorney General Eric Holder, Harry Belafonte, Tommie Agee, Ed Charles, Jackie Robinson, Tuskegee Airman Col. Harry Stewart Jr., Denise Peas, Eric B., and many others. Its first home was a two-story building that was formerly a Woolworths at 102nd Street and Northern Boulevard, a vestige of the generations before and hope for generations to come.

The Langston Hughes Library was born in a community where the act of organizing was in its DNA. Churches and organizations by the score, Corona Congregation, First Baptist, Mt. Horeb, the Black Panthers, Mosques, Elmcor Youth and Adult Activities, the Civic Association, Corona East Elmhurst Community Corporation, the Church of Resurrection, created a network of entities seeking empowerment, survival, and a better future for their members and the community as a whole, whether they knew it or not.

My introduction to The Langston Hughes Community Library and Cultural Center came as I returned to Corona East Elmhurst from New Mexico where I had attended college and worked at the New Mexico state prison as a teacher. Almost immediately I began volunteering with Elmcor, ultimately working there. I was asked to start a school for the clients of Elmcor as they dealt with their challenges of addiction. My students were mostly Black and Brown with disrupted educational experiences. The Langston Hughes Community Library and Cultural Center was a natural resource for them and their teachers. It was both relevant to their life experiences because of the collection of books, authors, and poets that represented the students' race and culture and presented them with a welcoming atmosphere that was culturally affirming. Many had never had positive library experiences. Langston Hughes made their journey back to the world of education easier and more accessible. The lectures, music, and art offered the community at-large experiences and insights into African history in both the Americas and the world.

In 1986, I left Elmcor to work in the office of the borough president of Queens, Claire Shulman. Helen Marshall was the state assemblywoman for the community, the first director of Langston Hughes, and a lifelong advocate. Together, they conceived of a new home for the Langston Hughes Library just blocks away at a former lumberyard between 100th and 101st Streets. Langston Hughes's exclusion from the traditional library system had ended and the era of themed community libraries was ushered into existence. "Shush" was mobilized as local culture and art. Library vibrancy was gaining acceptance. The Langston Hughes Community Library and Cultural Center became the model and political forces embraced this community-centered focus. I continued to support its efforts after I entered the New York State Assembly in 1992.

I served as the chair of the New York State Black, Puerto Rican, Hispanic, and Asian Legislative Caucus and in that position was able to increase funding for the Langston Hughes Library. The Library Action Committee represented the communities interested in the Langston Hughes Library. While the State of New York supported libraries generally, the dollars flowed through the Queens Public Library and were subject to their board of directors. Because of the creation of the Langston Hughes Library a special budget was established and sustained. The designation has survived over the years. The Langston Hughes Community Library and Cultural Center and the Schomburg Center for Research in Black Culture are the only two libraries that share this distinction.

**Essay from Assembly Member Jeffrion L. Aubry**

# Chapter 4D
# Issues and Advances in Medical Librarianship

## 4.21

*Making the Invisible Visible*

AMPLIFYING THE CONTRIBUTIONS OF AFRICAN AMERICAN HEALTH SCIENCES LIBRARIANS

Shannon Jones, Kelsa Bartley, and Jamia Williams

Founded in 1898, the Medical Library Association (MLA) is the leading professional organization for librarians working in health and biosciences environments. The history of African American librarians' involvement in MLA is not well documented, despite having served on many national committees, in its caucus communities, and in regional chapters. There was a time when African American librarians were excluded from the MLA's decision-making tables, serving on committees, and being nominated or awarded some of the organization's highest awards. In the retelling of MLA's history, neither their names nor contributions have been sufficiently highlighted. To this end, this chapter highlights several African American librarians who have made an indelible mark on medical/health sciences librarianship. The terms "medical librarian" and "health sciences librarian" are used interchangeably in our profession. For this chapter, we will use "health sciences librarian" to describe health information professionals who work in various health and biosciences environments. The purpose of this chapter is to discuss the creation of the African American Medical Librarians Alliance (AAMLA) Caucus, amplify notable African American medical/health sciences librarians, and describe current caucus initiatives to support members' wellness and well-being.

AAMLA is a personal identity caucus in MLA, a nationally recognized, volunteer-based library organization that represents the interests of medical librarians across the United States and Canada. Founded by African American librarians in the predominantly white, female spaces of health sciences librarianship (Pionke, 504), AAMLA initially originated from social gatherings and meetings during MLA annual conferences in the 1980s and 1990s. The group's initial aims were to build connections, create opportunities, and facilitate collaboration and networking within the profession. In the early years, many African American health sciences librarian pioneers were among a few, or they stood alone as the only, African Americans at their libraries. Hence, meetings at the conferences offered tangible spaces for in-person professional and personal mentoring, to learn about the profession from one another, and quite often the chance to vent about the unique challenges and struggles that come with being minority librarians at majority-white libraries and institutions. After years of gathering socially, AAMLA members at the time needed to become more strategic in engaging and navigating within MLA. AAMLA founders understood that they needed to become a formal group within MLA to become more visible and progressive and, more importantly, to provide representation and recognition for the contributions, interests, and voices of African American health sciences librarians within the association and librarianship.

Founders Sandra Franklin, Rosalind Lett, and Sandra Martin proposed the creation of the African American Medical Librarians Group (now AAMLA) because they wanted African American librarians to have a stronger voice in MLA. AAMLA became an official MLA Special Interest Group (SIG) in 2000 at the annual meeting in Vancouver, Canada. At that time, it was the second identity-based SIG to be formed, following the Lesbian, Gay, and Bisexual Special Interest Group (SIG), which was formed in 1994. AAMLA's initial goals included becoming more involved in MLA activities, especially those related to the organization's governance, goals, and initiatives.

Since 2000, AAMLA member advocacy has centered on increasing the presence of African American librarians in MLA through establishing and accessing leadership and service opportunities. In addition, members cultivated opportunities for outreach and networking among information professionals at all levels through onsite programming at the annual conference. Lastly, members pushed for recruiting and retaining minority librarians in the profession.

AAMLA members wanted to become more engaged and active with other MLA groups (now caucuses) to create and collaborate on annual conference programming, to track the history of engagement and contributions to MLA, to increase communication and networking for AAMLA members, and to provide mentoring opportunities, especially for new African American librarians. Part of the group's purpose statement emphasizes the importance of embracing cultural diversity in the profession as a whole and the impact doing so can have on healthcare overall:

> AAMLA stands committed to bringing the challenges and issues of minority librarians and information professionals to the forefront. Our role is to help all health sciences librarians and other information professionals understand and appreciate the dynamics of cultural diversity, as well as recognize and address the need for cultural competence and humility in healthcare environments.

## AFRICAN AMERICAN LIBRARIANS IN HEALTH SCIENCES LIBRARIANSHIP

In this section we amplify the contributions of early African American health sciences librarian pioneers who paved the way for current African American librarian activity in MLA. The journey to an increased presence of African American librarians within the MLA community has not been without its challenges. In her review of race and librarianship, Lipscomb (2004) found that MLA lagged other professional library associations regarding integration. First, MLA leaders and members' personal beliefs slowed the association's integration efforts (Lipscomb, 299). Second, in the 1930s membership in MLA was limited to institutional members. It did not include any libraries serving historically Black colleges and universities (HBCUs) until the 1939–1940 membership year when the executive committee voted to approve Howard University Medical Department and Meharry Medical College membership after repeated attempts by those institutions to join (Lipscomb, 300). Among the most notable opponents of integration was Mary Louise Marshall, the longest serving president of MLA. When it was time for the executive committee to vote on whether to approve Howard and Meharry's institutional membership, Marshall abstained from voting and explained her abstention by saying,

> As a scientific body, there is, of course, no reason for the exclusion of negro library members. On the other hand, one of the principal advantages of our Association—I might even say its greatest advantage, has been the opportunity which has been offered for close acquaintance with others in our field, and the amalgamation of our whole group.... With my head I know this is a wrong attitude, and with my heart I regret it from the bottom of my heart, but I truly believe a serious social problem will be created for our meetings if negro librarians come to our meetings and become a part of our group. (Marshall, 1939, as cited in Lipscomb, 2004, 300)

Marshall's abstention opened the door for approval of Howard and Meharry's membership in MLA. Mr. Alderson Fry, the librarian for Meharry Medical College and Ms. Josephine G. Morton, chief medical librarian at Howard University School of Medicine for both institutions, began attending MLA's annual meeting in 1940 and 1941, respectively. Because this chapter focuses on African American medical/health sciences librarians, Mr. Fry's contribution as a librarian for Meharry Medical College will not be discussed due to his racial identity as white.

### JOSEPHINE G. MORTON

In 1940, Mrs. Josephine G. Morton, chief medical librarian for the Howard University School of Medicine, became the first African American librarian to attend an MLA conference ("Attendance at the Forty-Second Annual Meeting," 1940). For nearly twenty-five years, Mrs. Morton served Howard University and was instrumental in developing its medical library. The Medical Library Association awarded her one of the first medical librarian certificates (Anonymous 1953, 100). At the time of her death in 1952, Mrs. Morton served on MLA's Criteria for Medical School Libraries Committee.

### ARLEE MAY

In June 1979, Arlee May became the first African American librarian elected to the MLA board of directors. In addition to her national service, Ms. May was an influencer in two MLA chapters: the North Atlantic Health Sciences Libraries (NAHSL) and the New York/New Jersey (NY/NJ) (now the Liberty Chapter). She served as NAHSL chapter chair from 1976 to 1977 and on the executive committee for the NY/NJ chapter (Levine and Nesbit, 1997). During her career, she held positions at the National Library of Medicine's New England Regional Medical Library Service (NERMLS), which at the time was based at Harvard University's Countway Library of Medicine and the State University of New York (SUNY) Stony Brook Health Sciences Library.

### GWENDOLYN CRUZAT

Since 1967, MLA has chosen an individual to share their unique perspective on the history or philosophy of medical librarianship, honoring Janet Doe, former librarian of the New York Academy of Medicine, historical scholar, and past MLA president ("Janet Doe Lectureship"). On June 2, 1979, at the Seventy-Ninth Annual Meeting of the MLA, Dr. Gwendolyn S. Cruzat presented "Medical Librarianship: A Systems Perspective" ("Janet Doe Lectureship"). Since 1979, one other African American librarian has delivered the Janet Does lecture. A long-time MLA member, Dr. Cruzat held multiple leadership roles in MLA. She served as chair of the Medical Library Education Section (1977–1978), the Honors and Awards Committee (1982–1983), the Library Research Section (now Research Caucus) (1983–1984), and the Janet Doe Lectureship Committee (1982–1983). Dr. Cruzat held positions at Fisk University, Detroit's Harper Hospital Library, and Wayne State University. From 1979 to 1993, she served on the University of Michigan's School of Information faculty, where she is credited with developing a concentration in health sciences librarianship. A nod to her influence in health sciences librarianship, in 1993, MLA recognized Dr. Cruzat as a Fellow of the association and as one of MLA's Notable 100 in 1998 (Shedlock, 2015).

**MADELYN V. TAYLOR**

Madelyn V. Taylor played an instrumental role in reorganizing and restructuring MLA to allow its regional chapters to become an integral part of the association. Ms. Taylor served on the board of directors from 1983 to 1986. She wrote the first procedure manual for the MLA's Chapter Council (Henderson, 2014), a version still used today. In addition to our national service, Ms. Taylor was a leader in the MLA's New York–New Jersey Chapter (now the Liberty Chapter), where she served as chapter chair from 1979 to 1980. Ms. Taylor held positions at the University of Medicine and Dentistry of New Jersey–Newark, Columbia University's Harlem Hospital Library, New York's Physicians News Services and Medical Tribune, and Jewish Chronic Diseases Hospital. In 1994, Ms. Taylor became the second African American librarian recognized as an MLA fellow.

Although much work is still needed to document African American librarian presence and contributions to medical/health sciences librarianship, the pioneers mentioned above paved the way for them to follow in their footsteps. In 2016, the MLA membership elected its first African American president, Beverly Murphy (MLA, 2018); the second, Shannon Jones, was elected in 2021 (MLA, 2021). Six African American librarians are fellows of the Association: Dr. Gwendolyn Cruzat (1993), Madelyn V. Taylor (1994), Beverly Murphy (2015), Sandra Franklin (2017), Brenda Faye Green (2017), and Shannon D. Jones (2022) ("MLA Fellows Awardees," 2022). Fellows "are members elected by the Board of Directors for sustained and outstanding contributions to health sciences librarianship and the advancement of the purposes of MLA" ("Fellows and Honorary Members," para 1). Following Dr. Cruzat, Sandra Franklin became the second African American librarian to deliver the prestigious Janet Doe Lecture in 2021 ("Janet Doe Lectureship," para 7). Ms. Franklin presented "Diversity That Defines Us: The View through a Crystal Lens" during the 2021 MLA virtual conference. In January 2023, the MLA board voted to rename two scholarships to recognize two African American librarians: Dr. Gwendolyn Cruzat and Ms. Beverly Murphy. The first recipients of the Gwendolyn S. Cruzat MLA Scholarship and the Beverly Murphy MLA Scholarship for Underrepresented Students were announced in February 2023. This section aims to illustrate how African American medical/health sciences librarians have contributed to the MLA. In the next section, we provide an overview of the initiatives spearheaded by current African American medical/health sciences librarians within MLA.

**RADICAL SELF-CARE AND WELLNESS**

bell hooks wrote about self-recovery, and that choosing wellness is a way to resist and also a political act (7). Wellness as health sciences librarians is vital; we frequently provide information about this topic for others and their research or programming. Therefore, AAMLA has been able to provide wellness initiatives by helping African American health sciences librarians professionally and personally. This has happened in three ways: First, through the formation of the Virtual Engagement Committee (VEC), which created programming that helped professional well-being. Second, the Radical Self-Care and Wellness series helped with personal well-being. Third, AAMLA's weekly Chat and Chew continues to help professionally and personally. As African American health sciences librarians, we must center our own well-being meaningfully and genuinely, so that we can continue supporting others.

One of the essential tenets of librarianship is professional development. AAMLA created the VEC to provide a forum where African American health sciences librarians could present their research and scholarship, which is important for those on the promotion and tenure track. VEC provides free virtual programming, also for those on the tenure track, but for librarians who do not have the institutional funding to afford professional development. Lastly, attending VEC events is helpful to many African American health science librarians who work in places where they are the only African American person working in their library. Hathcock states, "Being a non-white librarian playing at whiteness is an isolating and lonely practice, so it is essential that new librarians from diverse backgrounds get the support they need and have safe spaces to go amid this work." This sense of community is essential for growth and development.

As health sciences librarians, we provide health information to students, faculty, clinicians, and community members, which can inform their research endeavors or personal health and well-being. The stress of systematic racism in medicine and within higher education can take a toll on many of us. As a result, VEC's inspiration was The BIPOC in LIS Mental Health

Summits created by Davis-Kendrick et al., and the AAMLA caucus wanted to continue the conversation around self-care and wellness. Working and existing in the predominantly white spaces of libraries and librarianship can be physically and mentally exhausting for African American librarians. African American librarians were experiencing the impact of stress from ongoing systematic racism against the backdrop of the COVID-19 pandemic. The stress from this global pandemic disproportionately impacted communities of color in the United States. Librarians from these communities would likely know people affected by COVID-19 (Centers for Disease Control and Prevention, 2020).

The double pandemic of systematic racism and COVID-19 is best addressed deliberately. As such, members of the AAMLA caucus created a webinar series titled "Radical Self-Care and Wellness for Information Professionals." Thanks to funding from the then Southeastern Atlantic Region (now Region 2) of the Network of the National Library of Medicine (NNLM), AAMLA was able to host this series. As caucus members started to plan the series, they centered planning around Audre Lorde's assertion, "Caring for myself is not self-indulgence; it is self-preservation, and that is an act of political warfare" (Lorde, 131). The series aimed to help combat barriers often faced by communities of color, including disparities in access to mental health and wellness resources and stigma against receiving care. The importance of having wellness and radical self-care/therapy resources readily available to African American, Indigenous, and People of Color (BIPOC) helps mitigate these added stressors' impact. By providing a virtual wellness series, the AAMLA caucus wanted to help reduce the barriers mentioned above, and support information professionals' health and well-being. The series started with hosting weekly sessions from January 2021 until March 2021. The series had speakers like Amanda M. Leftwich, Twanna Hodge, Rayna Smaller, Deya Patterson, Kaetrena Davis-Kendrick, Dr. Carenado Davis, Tristan R. Ebron, Carl Leak, Dr. Tamara Tucker-Ibarisha, Dr. Othelia Pryor, Dianne Bondy, Dr. Kari L. Jordan, Dr. Kari L. Jordan, Dr. Natasha Lecque Gourdine, Dr. Alice Freeman, and Dr. Eboni Butler. The series taught attendees about yoga, mindfulness practices, nutrition, fitness, rest, mental health awareness, and more. In addition, the webinar recordings are still available for viewing on the AAMLA website.

In March 2020, an AAMLA leader suggested a virtual weekly check-in to allow us to provide care, comfort, and camaraderie to one another as the caucus navigated events around us. These weekly virtual check-ins became known as "Chat and Chew." Motivational Educational Entertainment (MEE) Productions defines a "Chat and Chew" as a small group information session focused on engaging and activating people in a safe space to hear about, air concerns, and share potential solutions. Membership is open to people who are not African American. However, "Chat and Chew" is only for those that identify as African American. Having room for communal care is essential and necessary. García Peña stated,

> Women of color have been taking care of one another for centuries. It is through our communal care that we have managed to survive the atrocities of slavery, colonialism, capitalism, and migration. It is through our reliance on one another that our histories—despite being erased and silenced from official archives—continue to emerge and be re-membered to sustain us.

This initiative was the focus of a 2022 chapter, "Virtual Chat and Chew: Radical Self-Care for BIPOC Information Professionals," in the book *Leadership Wellness and Mental Health Concerns in Higher Education*, edited by Cynthia J. Alexander and Amy Tureen. Our chapter gave extensive details about the origins of "Chat and Chew" and how we were able to support African American health sciences librarians. This tradition is still occurring. Even though the world is trying to go back to prepandemic days, there are some things that we should still hold on to, and that is uplifting and supporting each other as much as possible. Being part of a community is essential to begin to thrive in our lives.

**THE LEGACY CONTINUES**

Today, the AAMLA caucus is an active caucus community within MLA and has made great strides in building upon the founders' goals. Since the group's formation, African American librarians have become much more visible in MLA. In 2016, MLA members elected the first African American MLA president, Beverly Murphy, and in 2021 elected the second, Dr. Shannon D. Jones. Both are active AAMLA members, who along with other members in strategic positions, have been instrumental in creating and highlighting opportunities for African American health sciences librarians to thrive within the association and in the profession. AAMLA members serve on the MLA board and nominating committees; lead diversity, equity, and inclusion initiatives and activities; lead and plan entire MLA annual conference meetings, and use their considerable expertise and experiences in almost every aspect of MLA. Increased visibility has translated into more opportunities for African American librarians to shine outside the association through advanced career, professional development, service, and scholarship opportunities.

The caucus continues to be committed to community engagement and creating professionally and psychologically safe spaces for new and experienced African American health sciences librarians. The focus on safety and well-being heightened during the COVID-19 pandemic and the disturbing incidents of police violence in the summer of 2020. The caucus sponsored a series of well-attended initiatives to help librarians deal with the traumatic events' physical and mental health challenges while continuing to offer programming for professional development and career growth. Wellness became one of MLA President Jones's central initiatives during her term. She has extended the librarian health and wellness theme beyond AAMLA and begun integrating it into the health sciences library community. The Be Well MLA campaign has allowed many librarians to share their health and wellness practices and activities and collaborate, connect, and participate with others while pursuing a healthier postpandemic work-life balance. The campaign is just one example of how the wellness of African American health sciences librarians and the AAMLA caucus has influenced and impacted the health and wellness of the entire profession. Lastly, "We are, just now, thinking about the people that work in libraries . . .not just the buildings" (Kendrick, 2020). African American health sciences librarians must continue to do self-care and collective care in order to thrive personally and professionally. AAMLA will continue to do this work, and we are proud of the strides that we have made.

**WORKS CITED**

African American Librarians Alliance Caucus. "About AAMLA." N.d. https://sites.google.com/view/aamla-mla/about-aamla

African American Librarians Alliance Caucus. "Radical Wellness and Self-Care." Spring 2021. https://sites.google.com/view/aamla-mla/events-meetings/prior-events/spring-2021/radical-self-care-wellness.

"Attendance at the Forty-Second Annual Meeting." *Bulletin of the Medical Library Association,* 29, no. 1 (1940): 54-56.

Centers for Disease Control and Prevention [CDC] (2020). Health equity considerations and racial and ethnic minority groups. https://www.cdc.gov/coronavirus/2019-ncov/community/health-equity/race-ethnicity.html?CDC_AA_refVal=https%3A%2F%2Fwww.cdc.gov%2Fcoronavirus%2F2019-ncov%2Fneed-extra-precautions%2Fracial-ethnic-minorities.html.

Davis Kendrick, Kaetrena. Interview. Conducted by Amanda M. Leftwich, Jamia Williams, and Jamillah Gabriel. *LibVoices*, Spotify for Podcasters, May 10, 2020. https://podcasters.spotify.com/pod/show/libvoices/episodes/Episode-3-Kaetrena-Davis-Kendrick-on-The-Authentic-Self-at-Work-ebmo1n.

Davis Kendrick, Kaetrena, Amanda M. Leftwich, and Twanna Hodge. "Providing Care and Community in Times of Crisis: The BIPOC in LIS Mental Health Summit." *College & Research Libraries News (C&RL News)*, 82, no. 8 (2021). https://crln.acrl.org/index.php/crlnews/article/view/25125/32964.

García-Peña, Lorgia. *Community as Rebellion: A Syllabus for Surviving Academia as a Woman of Color.* Chicago: Haymarket Books, 2022.

Hathcock, April. "White Librarianship in Blackface: Diversity Initiatives In LIS." *In the Library with a Lead Pipe*, October 7, 2015. https://www.inthelibrarywiththeleadpipe.org/2015/lis-diversity/.

Henderson, Cynthia. 2014. *Taylor, Madeline V. (AHIP, FMLA).* Medical Library Association.

hooks, bell. *Sisters of the Yam: Black Women and Self-Recovery.* New York: Routledge, 2015.

Kendrick, Kaetrena Davis, and Ione T. Damasco. "Low Morale in Ethnic and Racial Minority Academic Librarians: An Experiential Study." *Library Trends*, 68, no. 2 (2019): 174-212. doi:10.1353/lib.2019.0036.

Levine, Marion H., and Kathryn W. Nesbit. 1997. "Arlee May, 1940-1996." *Bulletin of the Medical Library Association* 85, no. 1: 73-74.

Lipscomb, Carolyn E. "Race and Librarianship: Part II." *Journal of the Medical Library Association*, 93, no. 3 (2005): 308-10.

Lipscomb, Carolyn E. "Race and Librarianship: Part I." *Journal of the Medical Library Association*, 92, no. 3 (2004): 299-301.

Lorde, Audre. *A Burst of Light: Essays.* Ithaca, NY: Firebrand Books, 1988.

"Moving beyond Survival Mode: Important Community Conversations." Motivational Educational Entertainment. https://www.meeproductions.com/chat-chew/.

Medical Library Association. "African American Medical Librarians Alliance Caucus Purpose Statement." https://www.mlanet.org/page/caucus-aamla.

"Mrs. Josephine Morton." *Bulletin of the Medical Library Association*, 41, no. 1 (1953): 100.

"News Items." *Bulletin of the Medical Library Association*, 58, no. 4 (1970): 610-22.

Pionke, J. J. "Medical Library Association Diversity and Inclusion Task Force 2019 Survey Report." *Journal of the Medical Library Association*, 108, no. 3 (2020): 503-12. https://doi.org/10.5195/jmla.2020.948.

"Proceedings, Seventy-ninth Annual Meeting Medical Library Association, Inc. Honolulu, Hawaii June 2-9, 1979." *Bulletin of the Medical Library Association,* 68, no. 1 (1980): 93-189.

Shedlock, James. "Cruzat, Gwendolyn S. (Ph.D., AHIP, FMLA)." Medical Library Association, September 9, 2015. https://www.mlanet.org/blog/cruzat,-gwendolyn-s.-(phd,-ahip,-fmla).

# 4.22

## *Up All Night*

THE FIRST TWENTY-FOUR-HOUR BLACK HEALTH AND HEALING SUMMIT FROM QUEENS PUBLIC LIBRARY

Jill Anderson, Tamara Michel, Kim McNeil Capers, and Janet Umenta

In late 2020, Queens Public Library was still destabilized from the COVID-19 pandemic and shutdown. The library was also hyperaware of the recent and ongoing news about violence against and disparate health outcomes among Black Americans. We wanted to bring something meaningful, fun, and innovative to the Black community. We created the all-virtual twenty-four-hour Black Health and Healing Summit. The summit, which occurred in February 2021, gave a national audience for these topics and reached thousands of participants. We wanted the event to be fun because we knew so many communities were experiencing such collective trauma. We also wanted it to feel culturally relevant and responsive to community needs and interests. Libraries are trusted institutions, and we wanted to employ that trust to provide health and self-care information. The summit was also an opportunity for collaboration. The library collaborated with many health, professional, and medical organizations.

## BACKGROUND

In the winter of 2020, Black health and Black health disparities were at the forefront of many minds at Queens Public Library. Queens Public Library, located in New York City, was deeply experiencing the effects of COVID-19 and the accompanying shutdown. Additionally, Black health and Black health disparities were topics with relevance beyond COVID-19.

Here are some examples of the context surrounding the library's discussions around Black health. As pointed out by Assari, across almost all domains, Black Americans experience worse health compared to White Americans.[1] These health disparities are lifelong: starting in utero and extending through older adulthood.[2] These health disparities include greater infant mortality rate and greater incidence of chronic diseases.[3] Additionally, as pointed out by Alsan et al., Black men have the lowest life expectancy of any major demographic in the United States.[4]

Alsan et al. cited some possible reasons for this disparity, including lack of health insurance and lower socioeconomic status.[5] However, research shows insurance and socioeconomic status alone do not explain the health-care gaps. For example, Alsan et al. notes that one study showed that African American men are six percentage points less likely to visit the doctor and eight percentage points less likely to report receipt of the flu shot and that insurance and education do not fully explain these gaps.[6] Another possible cause cited by Alsan et al. to explain these gaps is structural racism. Assari's research supported Alsan: the current American social structure causes advantages like economic resources and psychological assets to generate larger health gains for White Americans than they do for Black Americans.[7] Additionally, there is a historical legacy involving the exploitation and persecution of and discrimination against Black people and communities. This history includes using slaves for involuntary medical experimentation, the infamous Tuskegee syphilis study, and forced sterilization initiatives.[8] This historical legacy has affected generations of Black people, including their health.[9] This historical legacy is a direct contributor to the phenomenon of Black health disparities, but it also is one of the causes of another phenomenon that is itself a probable cause for these disparities: a lack of trust in the health-care system. As stated by Rusoja and Thomas, "Decades of torment have led to generalized mistrust of the health-care system among many in the Black community."[10] This mistrust has consequences. Some research suggests that Black people are reluctant to engage in clinical trials and might refuse suggested treatment.[11]

## PURPOSES BEHIND THE SUMMIT

With this background in mind, the library wanted to create a compelling, innovative program that would focus on Black health. The concept we finally created was our "Black Health and Healing Virtual Summit." Here were some different purposes and goals we had for the summit.

## CENTER BLACK COMMUNITIES

We never wanted to forget that this program was for Black people and Black communities. We wanted to center Black communities fully. We did this by courting presenters that were accessible and representative. We also curated our topics to be those that were of interest to Black people, including COVID-19, mental health, chronic illnesses, insomnia, and self-care. A focus on self-care was especially important; we wanted Summit participants to experience self-care and to learn new ways to practice self-care.

Additionally, we wanted to keep Black, representative health-care professionals visible. We were hoping to steer participants and other stakeholders toward careers in healthcare by modeling representative presenters. Black people, Black men especially, are underrepresented as physicians, comprising about 12 percent of the male population, but only 3 percent of male doctors.[12] This trend hasn't necessarily gotten better over time. One study showed that the number of Black male medical students remained constant from 1978 to 2015.[13] Encouraging Black people into the medical field might have a direct impact on nationwide Black health. For example, Alsan et al. discovered that Black patients are more likely to talk with their assigned doctor about health issues if their doctor is Black, especially if the health issue involves an invasive exam.[14] Another study found that nearly 65 percent of Black respondents and 70 percent of White respondents reported that a doctor of their own race would understand their concerns best.[15]

### PROVIDE CRITICAL HEALTH INFORMATION

It was important to us to bring in top medical experts. Libraries are trusted institutions, and it is our top priority to maintain and honor our customers' trust. Related, summit organizers agreed it was of critical importance to demonstrate that there are representative top medical experts. As mentioned above, there is less trust in the medical system among Black communities. For example, studies demonstrate that Black men score higher on medical mistrust than other groups.[16] We wanted this event to provide an antidote to community mistrust, not to feed into it.

Additionally, we wanted participants to gain the tools to monitor their own healthcare. We wanted to inform participants of reliable resources and accurate tools, such as Medline Plus. Similarly, we also wanted to shed light on some of the weaknesses found in medical research that does not focus on Black people. For example, "Genomic research on African ancestry groups lags behind studies of European ancestry groups, despite evidence that more multiethnic research is needed."[17] The summit provided relevant education and encouraged our participants to take part in medical research, through the All of Us Research Program as a way to increase health equity as it pertains to racial disparities in medical research.

We had a few other purposes for the summit:

- Creating both a local and a national reach. We wanted participants from diverse geographic areas to engage, connect with, or serve in the health community.
- Maintain the fun. We knew our message wouldn't be as powerful if we forgot about fun or enjoyment.
- Strengthen the relationship between the library and the Black Caucus of the American Library Association (BCALA).

### THE SUMMIT

After months of planning, the twenty-four-hour Black Health and Healing Summit began on February 21, 2021, at 8:00 a.m. It was partially funded by a $49,500 grant from the National Network of Libraries of Medicine (NNLM) and the All of Us Research Program. Very early on in the planning stages, we also discovered we would need more funding to create the immersive and compelling event that we wanted. In the end, we found other funding sources and spent a total of $96,988 on the event, not including library staff time. We were able to use some of that funding to provide honoraria to speakers to ensure we included top-tier presenters in our sessions.

The summit provided health information centering Black and African American communities of all ages in Queens and beyond. We were able to include top medical experts, entertainers, and advocates. We also included a focus on deaf and hard-of-hearing people. We were able to present hourly workshops that were both accessible and representative. The top-three most-viewed sessions were Barbershop Talk, which emphasized the unique role barber shops play in promoting health literacy and health interventions to Black men; the Careers in Healthcare Panel; and the Diabetes Health Equity Now session. The sessions attracted people of all ages, from youth to age eighty-nine. Unsurprisingly, a large portion of our participants identified as Black. Seventy percent of participants identified as Black. The summit brought participants from throughout the United States (and a few international participants), but a large portion of our participants were from New York: about 36 percent.

The summit provided many opportunities for learning lessons to apply to future programs. For example, we recommended to realistically plan for scale from the very start. If you are interested in providing a multihour national event such as this one, think realistically about the scale and your capacity right from the beginning. One specific lesson about capacity and scale that we learned is that you might need to look outside your organization. Our consultants were critical partners. We used a tech consultant to help design the website and virtual presence and a marketing consultant to assist with the look. However, when using consultants and when providing innovative or unusual programs, be sure to keep your organization's policies in mind. Our use of virtual conference platforms created data collection and patron privacy challenges. We needed to ensure that patron privacy was protected, even as we utilized responsive technology. Another lesson related to capacity and scale is that you should incorporate your legal and procurement processes as soon as possible, to make sure all departments are aligned. Another lesson we derived from this experience is that it never hurts to ask for what you need; there might be a lot of passion and interest about your topic into which you can tap. Relatedly, we confirmed that there is tremendous demand and appreciation for Black health and healing programming. However, we also learned that overnight programming garners significantly lower attendance, even if people express an interest in the topic.

**COLLABORATION ASPECTS**

We were able to create or deepen many collaborations as a result of the summit, including our partnerships with BCALA and with NNLM. In the weeks leading up to the summit, we were meeting with BCALA at least weekly. We also created relationships with some of the presenters. These relationships allowed us to work with those partners in future library programs and events. This work supported a culture shift within the library. Our presenters included other libraries, universities, medical associations, health-related nonprofits, library associations, local Black organizations, government departments, local health entities, and a website that focuses on Black authors. The medical associations that were involved included the American Diabetes Association, the Vaccine Research Center of the National Institute of Allergy and Infectious Diseases at the National Institutes of Health, and Johns Hopkins School of Medicine.

**SUCCESSES**

We took time to reflect on the successes we were proud of at the Summit. Something we were very proud of was the inclusion of Dr. Kizzmekia S. Corbett, PhD. Dr. Corbett, one of the leading scientists at the forefront of coronavirus vaccine development, discussed the COVID-19 vaccine in the context of medical mistrust and historical abuses. Dr. Corbett's session was the fourth most-viewed session. We were pleased to bring in a Black scientist who was so instrumental to the creation of a COVID-19 vaccine. A related success was an increase in participants' trust levels in the COVID-19 vaccine specifically. In an exit survey of participants, 62.5 percent of respondents stated that the summit increased their trust in the COVID-19 vaccine. Only 6.2 percent of respondents stated the summit DID NOT increase their trust in the vaccine. The other 31.2 percent of respondents answered "Not Sure" to the question.

Similarly, we discovered from postevent surveys that participants felt called to make immediate health changes after their participation in the summit. We were very excited by this result because we were hoping summit sessions would create immediate results. Here are some things that participants stated they were going to make immediate changes on as a result of their participation in the summit:

- Get the vaccine
- Always research and get the facts
- Allow myself self-care to reduce anxiety rather than push it to the side
- Not just rely on social media but rather discuss with my doctor and research the best course of options
- Sleep better
- Access mental health therapy
- Move
- Pay more attention to spiritual health
- Get a checkup
- Get a blood test
- Eat better
- Share health information with friends and family

Two of these listed results were especially exciting to us: the many participants who responded to the postsummit survey with a drive to get the COVID-19 vaccine and the many respondents who mentioned the summit as a wakeup call for their own mental health. Taking steps to improve their mental health was a predominant theme that emerged from survey results. We were excited by this because a focus on mental health was a major goal of the summit.

Another success for us was that we exceeded the participant attendance goals that we had set for ourselves. Before the summit occurred, we had proposed to reach a) five hundred participants; b) one hundred participants through pre-event programming; and c) seventy-five participants through postevent programming. After the summit, our data showed that we had actually reached: a) 2,574 summit registrants; b) 7,906 live event sessions; c) 371 session replays as of one month after the event; d) 99,192 views of our session with entertainer and activist Amanda Seales; e) 990 participants reached through pre-event programming; and f) 1,101 participants reached through postevent programming. We also were pleased with the number of library staff who attended the event and the positive feedback we received. We were glad that library staff found the content compelling as well. As mentioned previously, the summit was reflective of the library's culture shift, including being responsive to staff concerns around race.

A final success we want to mention was our use of the summit and its planning to showcase Black professionals. From the beginning, we wanted to involve Black professionals in the event. When we were selecting consultants and staff, we were mindful of showcasing Black professionals and their work and talent. We also wanted to create opportunities specifically for Black librarians, as moderators, high-ranking representatives of various national organizations, and panelists. In addition to seeing representative faces, this was also one way that we could ensure that the event *felt* representative, amplified the voices and work we wanted to project, and be fully centered on Black communities. Of course, a major focus of the event was showcasing Black health and medical professionals. For example, we hosted a Careers in Healthcare panel, and two Racism Is a Public Health Issue: Young Health Professionals' Perspectives panels. Existing research demonstrates why keeping Black medical professionals in the forefront is important. For example, one study demonstrated that consulting with a Black doctor increased interest in preventative measures among Black men, more than consulting with a non-Black doctor.[18] The Alsan et al. study suggested that it was the communication between the Black patients and Black doctors that provided for the increased interest.[19] Alsan et al. believed that the Black physicians' counseling and rapport with patients could increase trust by correcting false beliefs and increasing demand for medical intervention.[20] Our postsummit survey questions about the vaccine support this finding. Similarly, Prather et al. asserted that correcting the lack of Black public health professionals would be significant in improving the distribution of high-quality healthcare.[21] In the same study, Prather et al. noted that patient/provider relationships are a factor in patient satisfaction, medication adherence, and high-quality health services.[22]

## BLACK PROFESSIONALS IN LIBRARIANSHIP AND THE MEDICAL FIELD IN THE PAST TWENTY YEARS

Over the last several decades, the number of Black physicians and the number of Black librarians has not increased significantly. For example, the number of Black medical school graduates sat at 6 percent for most of the 2010s, which is a disproportionately lower share than of the number of Black people in the population.[23] Similarly, in 2018, only 6.8 percent of librarians identified as Black or African American.[24] As of 2012, 7.1 percent of librarians were Black and 87 percent of librarians were White, which has been the average since 2013.[25]

The Black Health and Healing Summit was an effort to ameliorate these low numbers and is part of larger efforts to correct them. For example, the American Library Association—the national organization for library professionals—identified diversity, equity, and inclusion as some of their core values in the 2010s.[26] In 2020, the executive director of the association, Tracie Hall, noted the importance of librarians and library staff of color feeling supported and included in decision-making processes.[27] Hall pointed out the Association's Spectrum Scholarship program, which began in 1998 and has since helped more than 1,300 people of color achieve librarianship schooling.[28] Hall was the first Black woman to be appointed the executive director of the association, which serves fifty-six thousand members.[29] The Black Health and Healing Summit was a unique way to address the issues in Black librarianship and Black health.

## NOTES

1. Shervin Assari, "Health Disparities Due to Diminished Return among Black Americans: Public Policy Solutions," *Social Issues and Policy Review*, 12, no. 1 (2018): 112–45, https://deepblue.lib.umich.edu/bitstream/handle/2027.42/141210/sipr12042.pdf?sequence=2.
2. Ibid.
3. Ibid.
4. Marcella Alsan, Owen Garrick, and Grant Graziani, "Does Diversity Matter for Health? Experimental Evidence from Oakland." NBER Working Paper Series, no. 24787, June 2018, revised August 2019, 1–54. https://www.nber.org/papers/w24787.
5. Ibid., 1.
6. Ibid., 1–2.
7. Ibid., 113.
8. E. A. Rusoja and B. A. Thomas, "The COVID-19 Pandemic, Black Mistrust, and a Path Forward," *EClinicalMedicine*, 35 (2021): 1–2, https://doi.org/10.1016/j.eclinm.2021.100868.
9. Ibid.
10. Ibid., 1.
11. Cynthia Prather, Taleria R. Fuller, William L. Jeffries, Khiya J. Marshall, A. Vyann Howell, Angela Belyue-Umole, and Winifred King. "Racism, African American Women, and Their Sexual and Reproductive Health: A Review of Historical and Contemporary Evidence and Implications for Health Equity," *Health Equity*, 2, no. 1 (2018): 249–59, https://www.liebertpub.com/doi/10.1089%2Fheq.2017.0045.
12. Alsan, Garrick, and Graziani, "Does Diversity Matter," 8.
13. Ibid.
14. Ibid., 5.
15. Ibid., 21.
16. Ibid., 2.
17. Bridget Goosby, Jacob Cheadle, and Colter Mitchell. "Stress-Related Biosocial Mechanisms of Discrimination and African American Health Inequities," *Annual Review of Sociology*, 44 (2018): 319–40. http://www.researchgate.net/profile/Bridget-Goosby/publication/325183758_Stress-Related_Biosocial_Mechanisms_of_Discrimination_and_African_American_Health_Inequities/links/5b619255458515c4b2573e87/Stress-Related-Biosocial-Mechanisms-of-Discrimination-and-African-American-Health-Inequities.pdf.
18. Alsan, Garrick, and Graziani, "Does Diversity Matter," 15.
19. Ibid., 18.
20. Ibid., 29.
21. Prather, "Racism."
22. Ibid.
23. Alsan, Garrick, and Graziani, "Does Diversity Matter," 27.
24. Maya Pottiger, "Why Aren't There More Black Librarians?" Charles County Public Library, February 11, 2022, https://ccplonline.org/news-press/why-arent-there-more-black-librarians/; ALA. "Libraries Respond: Black Lives Matter," https://www.ala.org/advocacy/diversity/librariesrespond/black-lives-matter.
25. Natalia Contreras, "'Must Reflect the Communities We Serve': The Critical Role That Black Librarians Play, *Indianapolis Star*, August 12, 2021, https://www.indystar.com/story/news/local/indianapolis/2021/08/12/indianapolis-library-black-librarians-play-critical-role-community/8091776002/.
26. Ibid.
27. Pottiger, "Why."
28. Contreras, "'Must Reflect.'"
29. Ibid.

## WORKS CITED

ALA. "Libraries Respond: Black Lives Matter." https://www.ala.org/advocacy/diversity/librariesrespond/black-lives-matter.

Alsan, Marcella, et al. "Does Diversity Matter for Health? Experimental Evidence from Oakland." NBER Working Paper Series, no. 24787, June 2018, revised August 2019, pp. 1–54. www.nber.org/system/files/working_papers/w24787/w24787.pdf. Accessed March 29, 2023.

Assari, Shervin. "Health Disparities Due to Diminished Return among Black Americans: Public Policy Solutions." *Social Issues and Policy Review*, 12, no. 1 (2018): 112–45. https://deepblue.lib.umich.edu/bitstream/handle/2027.42/141210/sipr12042.pdf?sequence=2.

Contreras, Natalia. "'Must Reflect the Communities We Serve': The Critical Role That Black Librarians Play." *Indianapolis Star*, August 12, 2021. https://www.indystar.com/story/news/local/indianapolis/2021/08/12/indianapolis-library-black-librarians-play-critical-role-community/8091776002/.

Goosby, Bridget, Jacob Cheadle, and Colter Mitchell. "Stress-Related Biosocial Mechanisms of Discrimination and African American Health Inequities." *Annual Review of Sociology*, 44 (2018): 319–40. http://www.researchgate.net/profile/Bridget-Goosby/publication/325183758_Stress-Related_Biosocial_Mechanisms_of_Discrimination_and_African_American_Health_Inequities/links/5b619255458515c4b2573e87/Stress-Related-Biosocial-Mechanisms-of-Discrimination-and-African-American-Health-Inequities.pdf.

Pottiger, Maya. "Why Aren't There More Black Librarians?" Charles County Public Library. February 11, 2022. https://ccplonline.org/news-press/why-arent-there-more-black-librarians/.

Prather, Cynthia, Taleria R. Fuller, William L. Jeffries, Khiya J. Marshall, A. Vyann Howell, Angela Belyue-Umole, and Winifred King. "Racism, African American Women, and Their Sexual and Reproductive Health: A Review of Historical and Contemporary Evidence and Implications for Health Equity." *Health Equity*, 2, no. 1 (2018): 249–59. https://www.liebertpub.com/doi/10.1089%2Fheq.2017.0045.

Rusoja, E. A., and B. A. Thomas. "The COVID-19 Pandemic, Black Mistrust, and a Path Forward." *EClinicalMedicine*, 35 (2021): 1–2. https://doi.org/10.1016/j.eclinm.2021.100868.

# Chapter 4E
# Issues Facing Library Professionals without an MLS/MLIS Degree

## 4.23

*Who Will Stand on Your Shoulders?*

DJ Bond

Everyone's journey into library employment is different, but what unites us all is that we all need help in our careers. My journey into libraries as a professional might be different than most as someone who does not have an MLS, but from what I know, we all need some help getting into the field and growing in our roles.

If you can, imagine yourself standing on a rope net reaching upward for a hanging rope to pull yourself onto a high platform. You cannot reach for it and it is too high to jump for. Somehow, someone underneath the rope net is able to use their body to lift you higher, but it is still not enough. You need multiples of people to lift all at the same time to finally propel you upward fast enough to where you can jump and grab the rope. From there, you have to climb to reach the platform you have set your goal for.

But how are you going to get enough people willing to do that?

What this rope net represents is the effort it takes to lift you to your goal. The goal in this circumstance is working in libraries, regardless of your background or degree. It takes inertia to start something in motion, as we know from physics, but how does that work with people? In order to propel you forward, there has to be enough people willing to help you launch. The people in your life who choose to put you on their shoulders can help you make it to the next platform.

The problem is that often these launching pads are not equal. For some, all they need is one person with the right connections, influence, or privilege to push in order to make it to the next step; while others, specifically those who belong to marginalized communities, may need more. This is never fair, but it is real. That makes it even more important for you to help those who also need their nets lifted. It is not enough to just arrive at where you are going, but you also have to empower those who need your help to get where they want to go.

The goal of this chapter is to talk about how we get through library doors and the people that can help us.

**WHOSE SHOULDERS DO YOU STAND ON?**

I stood in Barnes & Noble in fall of 2020 looking for books, for several reasons, on job searching. I had found myself a part of the early days of the Great Resignation in which I had quit my terrible tech job that I had been trying to leave since the year before, because it had grown increasingly worse during the pandemic. I now found myself unemployed, which was starting to give me flashback anxiety of graduating from college both times, once with a bachelors in English and again with an MBA, where I was unable to secure a job before graduation. I had jobs on campus while in school, which really only worked so long as you were going to school. A few months after graduation from undergrad, I took a job recruiting for a staffing firm, while after my MBA I managed to turn my volunteer work at my local library into a part-time job doing social media and marketing. I did this until I could get full-time employment at the tech company I had just quit.

I ended up picking up two books, both of which I learned something important from. The first was *The 2-Hour Job Search: Using Technology to Get the Right Job FASTER* by Steve Dalton.[1] I was most interested in the "faster" portion of that book. I had a history of submitting hundreds of resumes to companies all over, looking for work to no avail. Not to mention, the effort often left me feeling empty and with a messy email inbox full of automated rejections. I cannot say I loved everything about this book, but the biggest takeaway I gleaned from it was the most important. I was always told the "networking is key" or "it's not what you know, but who you know" cliches, but no one ever mentions the qualifiers on the "who" part.

Dalton speaks to three types of people we network with: boosters, obligates, and curmudgeons.[2] Boosters are benevolent in their networking as they always desire to help people succeed and have time to do it. They will connect you with whomever they can, whenever they can. Obligates, as the name implies, will only do what they feel obligated to do. Often, they overpromise and underdeliver, because their overactive sense of guilt or disingenuous nature leads them to say one thing and do another. Lastly, curmudgeons are just that. They ain't gon' do nothin' for you.

Let's do a quick exercise. Imagine the faces of the people who have supported you in hard times. Maybe they connected you with a job, took you out to eat, or talked to you when you were depressed. You could be envisioning your parent, teacher, partner, best friend, sibling, boss, colleague, or someone else, but whoever came to mind was most definitely a booster. Boosters are the only people who will lift you up. You and I stand on as many booster's shoulders as we have ever known. Maybe not all of them had the same impact, but each did something to get us to the rope.

Let me give you an example. The second book I picked up was called *Modernize Your Resume: Get Noticed . . . Get Hired* by Wendy Enelow and Louise Kursmark.[2] This book is a resume breakdown tool that has pages of resume examples, which worked perfectly for me since I was concerned that my resume could be preventing me from moving to the next level in my career. I had studied the book and completely redesigned my resume, which landed me a couple jobs starting in 2020, but I still felt like I needed some feedback on it. I reached out to Louise Kursmark with questions on my resume and to my surprise, she responded. She gave a full breakdown on my resume with the pitfalls that could hang up employers and compliments to the new design. I then had action items that I could use on my resume to improve it. Louise Kursmark is 100 percent a booster.

The boosters that we stand on often take various forms though and not every booster is the same. Each person is limited to their own field, network, and knowledge base. From my perspective, I would say there are several different types of boosters that help lift us up. It takes a whole crew of people for you to make it forward. I will give you some examples of ones you have likely met.

## BENEVOLENT CHEERLEADER

Your parents who always believe in you. That best friend who speaks life into you. That teacher who wants to see you pass their class. All of them are benevolent cheerleaders, the type of booster that cheers you to accomplish the goal. You might not be able to grab the rope right now, but the person who is in this role for you will never make you feel like you will stay this way. Often, their positivity and overall belief in you will help motivate you to your goal. This person typically does not do any heavy lifting for you; they are not the ones who dramatically change your circumstances or move roadblocks. Not that they do not want to, but they usually do not have the appropriate connections to do so. For example, your auntie cannot give you a reference for that full-time librarian job you want, but they can give you positive words until you get it.

My mom does this thing that used to drive me insane. When I was in a job I did not like, I would get done with a long day and talk to her to vent. I would get maybe a few sentences into the complaints before she would interrupt and completely derail my conversation into something positive. I could be saying, "I just cleaned up human poop off the floor in the library" and she would interrupt with, "So what new jobs have you applied for this week? Anything exciting?" I would feel completely unheard, but I knew why she was doing it. She would always be my benevolent cheerleader and wanted to cheer for me to reach my goals, even when I saw them as impossible.

Benevolent cheerleaders are important because some of us never truly believe in ourselves. For some, even if the cheerleader said it seventeen times over, you would still be skeptical. Self-doubt and anxiety creep in after constant rejection, but mostly because sometimes we reject ourselves. And in turn, we snap at our benevolent cheerleaders because we just cannot hear "You can do it" when the gatekeepers and naysayers sound so much more believable. Be grateful for those who play this role in your life, if anyone, because having someone who believes in you is not a given.

## FAIRY GODPARENT

The boss who wants to see you shine. The sibling who gives you pointers on interviews. The supervisor who writes you a letter of recommendation. These are all examples of a fairy godparent role that someone can play in your life. Fairy godparents, unlike benevolent cheerleaders, have a skill, ability, or position of power that they can use to help you succeed. Fairy godparents at their worst only support nepotism or maintain a "good ol' boys" club to keep those they like in power, but a true fairy godparent sees you because of you and what you can do, not because you are related or share a similar demographic.

In college, I worked in the admissions department. Everyone who worked there knew the assistant director at the time, Dawn. Dawn was a fairy godparent in the best way, because she had the biggest heart of all. If there was anything she could do for you, she would make it happen. She was always looking for a way to support those whom she came into contact with to help them get to the next level. I remember she invited a student, Brandon, to interview with us. She ran into him when he was making her lunch at a sub shop of all places, but noticed the fact that he was very charismatic. The interview was not a given; if anything, most people on the panel were skeptical since he had not applied for the job, but to be fair, many of our stories were similar where someone saw potential in us. Brandon ended up being one of the best tour guides we hired, and Dawn continued to move up the ranks, mostly because she had a knack for building people up with the tools she had.

Fairy godparents often wield power or influence that the average person does not have access to. They usually are bosses or supervisors who are well connected in their fields. Sadly, those who fall into this category often are not of marginalized backgrounds, not to say they cannot be. It is important to recognize when we are in a position of power and are able to act as fairy godparents to another person. Also, we have to recognize the responsibility that comes with this power, since it is too easy to create nepotism or discrimination as a fairy godparent. In the most Cinderella way possible, sometimes we just need to help get people in the ballroom. The magic they create once they get in the door is all on them.

**PERFECT STRANGER**

The new director who completely supports you. The connection at the conference who is a great contact. The librarian at another library who is an ally. The strongest lifter of the rope net is the perfect stranger. Often, the perfect stranger knows very little about you but is either impressed or genuinely kind and wants to help you out. They will usually have some of the greatest impact on getting you to the next step because out of anyone else, they are likely to know more people and know of opportunities that you do not.

My first job in libraries was in 2016 at my hometown library. I had graduated with an MBA and still needed to find work, but also needed to get out of the house. I was often told that volunteering can lead to job opportunities, so I figured I would volunteer with a place that I was passionate about until I found a full-time role. My perfect stranger would become my supervisor, Amanda. She didn't need help, but given my background in social media, I was a surprise she really couldn't refuse. Within a few months of me helping out occasionally, she would create a role so that she could take me on part time. I crafted many of the design and PR skills I now have at that job, mostly because she taught me.

Perfect strangers are rare in most fields, but for libraries, they are actually fairly common. Librarians are trained in the skill of reference, which at its core is functioning as a perfect stranger. Someone who can help you get what you need or find what you want without the fear that they might take advantage of you or rope you into something you never wanted. Librarians provide services to the public without the expectation of them ever providing something in return. A perfect stranger will be like a librarian for your professional or personal life.

**WING PERSON**

The coworker who goes to events with you. The older cousin who teaches you about life. The best friend who goes out on the town with you. These are all examples of wing people—the kind of person who takes you under their wing in order to instill the experiential knowledge that you need to function at the next level. In the corporate world, these tend to be senior employees, but in libraries, the best wing people you will interact with are veteran librarians who have seen a thing or two.

After being unemployed and finding a new position that also did not work for me, an opportunity fell into my lap. I found my way back into libraries. I entered expecting to be a marketing coordinator but was titled a community engagement librarian. It is well documented that I do not have an MLS, but my boss found it important to still be considered a librarian and do librarian duties such as cataloging, acquisitions, and reference. This made a lot of librarians and library patrons mad, but I did not have much say in the decision, so I needed to be an excellent librarian fast. The person who took me under their wing was Annette. Being months from retirement, she knew that someone needed to learn what she did on the off chance she didn't get to train her replacement. I spent several days shadowing her and learning how she did things until I was comfortable flying solo, but the true test was when she did retire. I did not know everything, but by that point, she had encouraged me to try even if I failed. And if I did fail, she also gave me the resources to fix my mistake.

Wing people are important especially for those who need skill sets that their current schooling has yet to provide. Unlike perfect strangers or fairy godparents, wing people put in a large amount of time investing in your successful outcome instead of a short amount of time that gives you a boost. Having wing people in your life can make the difference between having the skill sets to do the job you want and only having textbook experience. Often, when combined with training or education, the knowledge passed down by wing people can quickly help you to become proficient in a new role. Wing people also can help those who may never consider becoming a librarian to pursue a career. Whom we choose to take under our wing is just as important as providing the support itself.

**WISE ONE**

Examples of wise ones are the best friend with the sage wisdom, the counselor who gives you sound advice, and the partner who helps you understand something better. These are the people in your life who help you download the deep ether that is wisdom and knowledge. Sometimes, wise ones are teachers, helping you learn a skill or task, while other times they're more mental healers, physical coaches, or guides of the soul and spirit. The difference between a wise one and a wing person is typically the relationship. Your wing person typically has a mentor relationship with you while your wise one acts like a counselor.

One of my favorite podcasts to listen to is *Truth Be Told with Tonya Mosley*,[4] where I got this title "wise one" from. She often brings in special experts in different fields like the wise ones to talk about their experiences and answer listener questions. Often, the conversations they have can be raw and revealing, but earnest and soulful. I often found myself being taken back by the small pieces that help inform us, like when Resmaa Menakem broke down the way we can nourish our bodies in resistance to the systemic notions of how Black bodies should present. I remember driving down the road feeling validated when he described the ways our bodies cope with systemic trauma, having never heard someone describe in words what I was experiencing.

Wise ones do not always have to be old, but they have a wisdom that life has taught them and that they can pass along to those who need it. Often, their focus is not just on your professional journey but also your holistic well-being. The wise ones are the kind of people who pull you aside and have that real talk that can help steer your course of life. Wise ones differ from all the other types because of this, as often the wise ones will dive into the mud with you to help pull you out of the mud pit.

## WHO WILL STAND ON YOUR SHOULDERS?

It is easy enough to arrive at a place in life and be thankful to those who helped get you there, but there is no legacy if you take no one with you. After reading these types of boosters, I want you to ask yourself this: Who will stand on your shoulders? What kind of booster will you be? Regardless of where you are in your journey, there is something you have learned that someone else needs to know. If you have the opportunity to help someone else in the field of librarianship, take those steps in their journey, regardless of what that journey looks like; you have been presented with a gift. Just like you may not have made it this far without the support of your boosters, others may not make it without you.

Think about what kind of booster you can be. Can you cheer someone on who needs encouragement? Can you make the impossible become possible for someone who needs it? Are you willing to give an opportunity to someone you know almost nothing about? Will you take someone under your wing and build them up? Will you speak directly to someone's circumstances and give them the wisdom to move forward? You can do any or all of these things for someone, but you have to choose to do so.

Because I was not a traditional library hire, I felt it was important for to me to encourage those who may struggle to see themselves in the field and speak life into them. If you do not see people who look like you or think like you or love like you, you may never decide to pursue something that seems exclusive to others and not you. We can combat that by boosting people to their goal rope. We are ultimately the ones who can help the future generations of library staff. I know that we can only lift so high on the rope net of others, but if we lift hard, we could cause enough inertia for someone to believe they can reach the rope to their goal.

## NOTES

1. Steve Dalton, *The 2-Hour Job Search: Using Technology to Get the Right Job Faster*, 2nd ed. (Berkely, CA: Ten Speed Press, 2020).
2. See Dalton 104-5 for more of a breakdown on boosters, obligates, and curmudgeons in the context of "The 5-Point Email."
3. Wendy Enelow and Louise Kursmark, *Modernize Your Resume. Get Noticed . . . Get Hired*, 2nd ed. (Coleman Falls, VA: Emerald Career Publishing, 2019).
4. Tonya Mosley, *Truth Be Told with Tonya Mosley*. TMI Productions, https://www.deartbt.com/?gclid=EAIaIQobChMI-_z4jcqOgwMVVU1HAR3PUAdVEAAYASAAEgK_DfD_BwE
5. "The Body," *Truth Be Told with Tonya Mosley* from TMI Productions, May 5, 2022, https://www.deartbt.com/episodes/the-body.

## WORKS CITED

Dalton, Steve. *The 2-Hour Job Search: Using Technology to Get the Right Job Faster*, 2nd ed. Berkely, CA: Ten Speed Press, 2020.

Enelow, Wendy, and Louise Kursmark. *Modernize Your Resume: Get Noticed . . . .Get Hired*, 2nd ed. Coleman Falls, VA: Emerald Career Publishing, 2019.

Mosley, Tonya. *Truth Be Told with Tonya Mosley*. TMI Productions. https://www.deartbt.com/?gclid=EAIaIQobChMI-_z4jcqOgwMVVU1HAR3PUAdVEAAYASAAEgK_DfD_BwE.

# 4.24

## Support for Library Support Staff

Robert "C. J." Hall

I spoke with my father one afternoon prior to the beginning of the COVID-19 pandemic, and he asked me about my leadership philosophy. I thought about it for a moment, and told him that I lead by example and jump in to help people as needed and not just dictate what to do. I also try to show my coworkers how to perform a certain task if they are having trouble with it. This can be a challenge, as I am not in a leadership position. Some individuals have not seen this as trying to aid my coworkers, but being more than I should be, in their eyes, and that I should "stay in my place" as a support staff member. But, I have learned that one does not necessarily have to have a formal title to lead. I believe that leadership is more than simply having a managerial or administrative title, as one can lead in whatever position they find themselves. I also think that it is important to put myself in another person's shoes, so to speak, to realize that when I work with library patrons, they may not understand how libraries work, and to help them out to the best of my ability.

I felt like I had a proverbial question mark over my head while growing up when it came to the question, "What do you want to do when you grow up?" When I was younger, I had a fear of working in corporate America, specifically in business, finance, entrepreneurship. I saw corporate corruption in the media in the late 1980s and early 1990s, the 1991 economic downturn, and how it affected individuals and families' financial states at the time. I did not want to work in the typical corporate American job, or what I thought of as a "corporate American job": the stock market, always with a frenzied busyness and a push to "sell, sell, sell" or always sitting behind a computer, typing away and making deadlines. I noticed some of the issues that my father faced in the workplace as a computer analyst, and thought that it was not for me, and felt that I was not the best with computers, thinking that computer science or IT work meant that I had to be like Steve Jobs or Bill Gates (the money would be nice, but I knew that I had to perform exceptionally well to make that much). I did not want to work as a teacher. I noticed the pressures that educators faced in school from unruly students and unsupportive parents, which has only become worse. I also thought that I was too introverted to speak in front of a class every day, along with being a disciplinarian. I was not very good with my hands, fixing broken things, or making crafts, so I figured that a trade would not work for me. So, I felt that getting an education and going to college was the best thing, and that I would find a job when I graduated from college, which my parents emphasized.

I applied to Saint Louis University and was accepted. I grew up in St. Louis, and my parents wanted me to stay in town for my freshman year, but I could transfer to another school afterward if I wanted. It was a good fit for me, and I decided to stay. I learned about the Ronald E. McNair Scholars program, a national educational program for minorities, women, and people in underserved communities, to prepare them for graduate studies in their respective fields, to earn a PhD, and increase their needed presence in academia. I applied to the program and was accepted right after I began my sophomore year and focused on southern African history. Part of the program involved my participation in a summer research internship with a professor in my major. The McNair staff reached out to Dr. George Ndege, a professor in African history, and he agreed to take me on as an intern and mentee for the summer of 2001. Dr. Ndege ran our weekly meetings similarly to Oxford tutorials, going over concepts of traditional African history in KwaZulu Natal and surrounding areas, and introduced me to historical interpretations within the field, historical works from both the colonial perspective and African oral history, and more contemporary interpretations based on African perspectives, to gain an objective view on the history of the region. The research led to a paper, which was later published in 2003.[1] The next summer, I applied for another internship at the University of Missouri and was accepted. I interned with another history professor. I learned more about contextualization using government documents, statistics and figures, to enhance my research. I also learned from the professor what schools to attend to have a stronger advantage in gaining a professorship, and the importance of not resting on my laurels if I were to gain a professorship and tenure, and to "write what speaks to me," because being true to who I am would bring out the best in my research and my career. This research also led to an unpublished paper, which I was able to present at a conference at the end of the internship.

That said, nothing worked out when I went to apply to graduate school. I faced severe burnout prior to graduation, partly from the rigors of the Jesuit curriculum for history majors, which was heavy in philosophy, theology, social sciences, learning a foreign language—I took classical Greek, and tried to take Latin at the same time, which I dropped—besides the rigors of a history degree and elective courses. This, along with my mother's passing from cancer in 2001, after the McNair internship ended, added to the burnout. I also owed money to the university after graduation, and they would not release my transcript before it was paid, and I had difficulty finding work after graduation, other than being allowed to temporarily keep a tutoring job on campus. Both professors that I interned with took extended research sabbaticals: Dr. Ndege traveled between Kenya (his home country), the United Kingdom, and the United States for his work, and the other professor traveled to numerous parts of the United States. I understood completely that it was part of their respective jobs in academia, and that they had to "publish or perish."

I was devastated: I worked so hard for so long, and it was not working out. I began attending a certain church shortly after my mother passed, and on a Sunday that spring, the pastor preached on giving thanks to God when things go wrong, not for the problem but while one endures it. I knew that it was geared toward me, even though he did not know my circumstances. I later learned about an internship with a drum and bugle corps in LaCrosse, Wisconsin, the Blue Stars, and that they needed help driving the corps members, staff, and volunteers during their summer tour. The corps trained me on driving a bus and helped me to obtain a class B CDL driver's license. I helped drive charter buses for the corps, and also help out wherever needed. After it ended that August, I came back home to St. Louis, and two weeks later I learned about a public service position with the St. Louis County Library and immediately applied. I interviewed and started one month after the internship ended, September 6, 2005, exactly four years after my mother passed.

I think about the many challenges, joys, learning experiences, and the people that I have interacted with in the past eighteen years. Many people ask me why I have stayed in this position. There are a number of reasons, the main one being that it has been a varied learning experience. I avoided the traditional corporate sphere, but I ended up working in a corporate environment, learning how to effectively function in the workplace. I feared teaching but was trained by former teachers and academic instructors, and had the chance to train new employees, some managers, and to help numerous individuals in various nonpublic departments.

At times it has felt like I have worked five or six completely different jobs that kept similar titles ("clerk," "circulation assistant," "library associate"). There have been many changes and transitions, and fortunately many supportive employees and friends helped me through them. Some of these transitions were challenging, if not rough, and at times my coworkers and I had to figure out many procedures, with managerial help, and sometimes by ourselves. One example was in 2011 when my department was being remodeled, and the administration placed a returns bin in our redesigned work area. We tested out a function called "direct sorting," which involved placing checked-in library items in their correct order to ideally reduce the number of times each item was touched before shelving. This did not work and was disastrous at first due to the high number of items that circulated and returned, as well as having a much-reduced staff during the 2010–2011 economic downturn (not filling positions when employees retired or resigned, not layoffs). It frustrated me for a long time: trying to keep up with an almost nonstop avalanche of books, audio visual materials, and goodness knows what; examining each item, checking it in, performing snag procedures if needed (for missing items such as missing DVDs or CDs); placing the item in order; checking for damaged items and proper barcodes on each item; answer telephone calls and perform circulation duties for the call center, patrons, managers, other library branches—all during a four-hour block (which was changed years later to a one-hour period). The shallow returns bin amplified the sound of items being dropped into it, sometimes thrown in, sometimes hitting me, and irritated me to no end. The manager at the time was not supportive, which added to the stress, and I had to bottle up a lot of frustration while working at a dizzying pace. I also had to check-in very large amounts of nonrequested items sent back to headquarters from all the other branches, on top of all the other duties while at the returns area. What helped me was quietly playing classical music or BBC news on my cell phone (which many of my coworkers enjoyed because it broke up the silence or the din of returned items), "discovering" Drum and Bass and UKG music (U.K. Garage, similar to House music), or listening to inspirational podcasts, at a time when employees were allowed to wear headphones (usually behind the scenes, and while shelving—I purposely turned the volume down and left one earphone free so that patrons did not think that I was ignoring them). This helped me to make a stressful block into one that was more tolerable.

I endeavored to learn from my working environment, meaning the patrons and other staff in different departments, and not just from the items within the collection. Rebecca Dames, the manager that hired me, introduced me to the employees and managers throughout the building, and part of my duties was to deliver mail from the mailroom to all the different departments—on five floors—and to deliver mail and returned items back to their respective departments. I was able to interact with many employees, and they taught me many of the "ins and outs" of the job, as many of them started in my same position. This helped me to refer employees to different departments and recommend that library patrons contact certain departments if they needed help that was beyond what I or my department could do.

The location which I worked is in a rich, white, section of St. Louis. I quickly noticed how people in that part of town lived and functioned. There is a Starbucks location about two blocks away from the library, and it is packed by 8:00

a.m. with people doing business there, checking their stocks and investments, reading national newspapers, talking to neighbors, and sometimes holding interviews. Many go there: people working at surrounding hospitals, teenage and adult students studying, lawyers and investors meeting with their clients, and even my former congressman. A friend from college remarked on a certain social media platform about how different this location is and the mind-set in this part of town compared to other parts of the St. Louis region. I picked up on this and decided to approach my work in this manner, to try to be as professional as possible, even with the number of tasks that I had to juggle and the different personalities that I had to deal with daily. I also quickly realized that some employees and patrons may not have noticed this, were indifferent to this, or chose to ignore it. I later realized the right people would pay attention and would recognize my efforts. I also learned that my job title does not define who I am. My job titles have changed, but they are basically the same thing, with varying duties. This also goes with the fact that I am an African American male in a mostly white profession and environment: my race is not a liability, but a blessing, no matter what people may think of me.

An important lesson that I have learned is that I do not have to have all of the answers, if any. I was told every single day during my first year, from people in multiple departments, "If you have questions, ask: don't assume that you know the answer, because you probably don't." I realized that the people telling me this were looking out for me, and that I should not make assumptions, which could be very costly. The employees that shared this with me wanted me to succeed. I appreciated their directness, and to not try to be a "hero." I have learned that it is okay to say, "I don't know," and to not pretend, especially with library patrons. I try to direct them to a source that may better help them, be it a manager, administrator (a plus from working at the library's headquarters), another library employee, or a nonlibrary resource. This may seem to be basic knowledge, but I have learned that some employees feel that they need to have to all of the answers, and this can be even more overwhelming. I have also learned that some employees thrive on being braggarts and bullshitters.

A hard lesson that I had to learn was to simply relax as much as I possibly could. Working in environments like the returns area was stressful, and I had to try to relax. I learned from this and from working the desk, where the lines to check out items or ask questions can be very long, if a line even existed (more like a clump of bodies around the desk, waiting to check out the recent Danielle Steel or James Patterson title, or to have me figure out their life for them and get back to them in five minutes, as lines do not necessarily exist for rich people). I could not stop the "lines," so I learned from two older employees, the late Marge Ott and Betty Shepherd, to engage the patrons if they wanted to be engaged, and to keep the transition short if the patron was in a hurry. I also realized that trying to get to the end of the line (or any other library task, including working the returns area) was like trying to stop Niagara Falls: it is beyond me—I am not equipped to do that, and if I did, it would not last long. I trained my mind to only see the patron in front of me, to only take on one request at a time, especially if the patron was not mentally organized or wanted a lot of things done at once. I also learned that mistakes happen when one is hurried, and the adage "Haste makes waste" has been a helpful reminder.

I learned during desk transactions to explain to patrons what I am doing, for those that are interested, so they could better understand procedures and hopefully not think that I have mentally "checked out" or am ignoring them if I am quiet or looking at multiple online resources. I realize that some patrons think that I don't know anything because I am Black. I do this to show that I take their account and their requests seriously. I have also learned to promptly return a patron's library card, ID, or driver's license, so that they do not think that I stole it—even though their contact information is directly in front of me on the computer. One thing that still irritates me is if a white patron throws their library card at me, which happened to me many times a day for many years.

I recognize that I and my coworkers are all on a journey in life, and that I need to give people grace, especially if one is having a bad day or in a bad place in life, which happens a lot in a field that demands so much from us emotionally, physically, and mentally with not a lot of financial gain in it. I am also learning that life's endeavors do not always happen in a straight line, but there are many zigzags, changes, jumps, and sometimes backward movements. I deal with perfectionism, meaning that I feel that I have to do everything just right all of the time, even though it's not realistic. I am learning to see perfectionism when it shows up, usually in stressful times, and to take a step back and try to relax. I wrestled during my first few years with the reality that we as African Americans have to perform many times greater than a white person to gain recognition, which added to the stress that I felt during those first years working in librarianship. A coworker, Johanna Tsifutis, shared a biblical scripture with me that I found helpful: Colossians 3:23 (New King James Version), "And whatever you do, do it heartily, as to the Lord and not to men." The original Greek version uses the phrase "Out of your soul, do your work unto the Lord." I took this to mean simply do the best that I can, do it unto God, and leave it at that. Let others think what they want. I know that others may not share my beliefs, but it has given me a great deal of ease in a difficult working environment.

I have a number of concerns about certain things within librarianship, and I feel that some of these reflect society. I have noticed that librarianship attracts both introverts and people with serious behavioral disorders. I have experienced negative things from certain managers and coworkers, as have a number of my coworkers. I will not go into specifics, but I believe that many library workers, specifically those of color, have had similar experiences (i.e., bullying, suppression, oppression, stalking, belittling behaviors, manipulation, extreme micromanagement, besides outright racism, favoritism, and ageism), no matter their what their library job may be. It takes a toll on individuals, causing anxiety, frustration, illnesses stemming from extreme stress, and workplace-based post-traumatic stress disorder. I spoke with an African American librarian who mentioned that it is common for some people that suffer from Cluster B personality disorders to be attracted to librarianship. If a person that has these disorders does not acknowledge these issues and receive help for them, it can result in a dysfunctional, if not outright toxic, workplace. It is also important to note that there are some African American librarians or other librarians of color who have these disorders and are causing these problems, and not just white library workers or librarians.

I have noticed that many library science programs may not offer courses or training on positive leadership and management skills, and that there needs to be much more. I think that it would help libraries and individual departments to run more efficiently and function in more positive working environments as well as help library managers to make better departmental decisions and be more supportive of their employees. I think that this could be applicable to any type of library setting, and not just public libraries. I also think that supplemental training from leadership experts and organizations such as John Maxwell, Simon Sinek, Les Brown, Brene Brown, and the Dale Carnegie Group, would be beneficial to library science students and library professionals at all levels.

There has been concern about this in the past with the introduction of self-checkout technology, which has actually helped in some libraries with workflow, allowing employees to more one-on-one time with patrons. But, in what ways will AI change library work, and will it be for the better? There are a number of academics that are examining these changes within the workforce, not only in librarianship, and how they may affect the nature of work and the need for ethical ways to approach these innovations. Titles such as Daniel and Richard Susskind's book, *The Future of the Professions*, Daniel Susskind's *A World without Work: Technology, Automation, and How We Should Respond*, and Jamie Susskind's book, *The Digital Republic: On Freedom and Democracy in the 21st Century*, address the current and upcoming changes, challenges, and needs that can and will surface with work. Academics at the Alan Turing Institute, based at the British Library, and Reuben College, the newest college at the University of Oxford, examine how AI and data science will change work, and how to ethically approach change. Some business schools offer programs on disruptive innovation, and how they will affect business. I hope that librarianship and information science is preparing for these innovations and disruptions as well as keeping in mind the people that work in the field, being prepared to help them shift their roles by encouraging training in fields like data science, IT management, and learning the importance of interpersonal relationships, and how they can be used to strengthen libraries as a means of educating patrons, and to become even greater centers of innovation, as well as holding to traditional book collections. I hope that this can be a good time of transition, but I believe that the library administrators have to keep their frontline employees in mind, realizing their value and worth, and that they hold a vital role in the library's well-being, to not only survive change but to thrive in it. This can only occur if they are valued and supported.

**NOTE**

1. Robert Hall. "Images of Shaka: A Modern Approach to Traditional and Revisionist Views." *The McNair Journal*, vol. 1, 2003.

# 4.25

## Issues by Library Professionals without an MLS/MLIS Degree

Carolyn Lawrence

Obtaining a master of library science (MLS) or master of library and information science (MLIS) degree in the library profession is essential in librarianship. Despite having worked in public libraries for numerous years, attending library school provided me with a comprehensive understanding of the complete picture of what it means to be a librarian. Getting my MLIS degree opened up new opportunities for me as a librarian, such as forming partnerships beyond the library, and increasing my pay for the work I was already doing. Furthermore, I also learned that the library is a business that provides free information services to patrons, but still requires various operational functions to be performed, as well as adequate funding to support these services.

As a Garifuna American woman with parents who immigrated from Honduras, I was raised with the understanding of how crucial education is. Seeing my father as the family's primary earner while also attending college and reading books leisurely, while we were living in the Wagner projects in Harlem, New York, motivated me to pursue further education. Meanwhile, my mother worked in caregiving until an injury forced her to become a homemaker. My introduction to the library happened at the tender age of seven when I received my very first library card. While I had no idea that I would eventually become a librarian, working as a teen in the library and shelving books ignited my passion for the field.

I have been working in the public library since 2001, beginning as a page and progressing to roles such as office aide (clerk), information assistant (IA), librarian trainee, and currently, children's librarian. While working as an office aide, I learned the role of processing reserved books and, most importantly, how to communicate with patrons, as this position was the first point of contact when patrons visited the library. While working as a clerk, my primary responsibility was to assist patrons at the circulation desk by providing customer service such as issuing library cards and checking out materials. As a clerk, I aspired to become a senior clerk. However, by the time I became eligible for the position, I learned that it had been phased out and that they were no longer providing any training for it. Being a senior clerk would have given me the opportunity to oversee the pages, volunteers, interns, the scheduling of the circulation desk, and timesheets, as well as to aid the manager as needed.[1]

This would have provided me with valuable experience of managing others. Nevertheless, since the senior clerk position had been phased out, I had to focus on completing my bachelor's degree at that time. Additionally, I would occasionally lead programs such as one-on-one computer help, reading picture books aloud, and singing with children. Although these programs were not mandatory for me at the time, I found them enjoyable because of the positive feedback from patrons, which in turn made me excited to host them. Moreover, I always had the support of an IA or a librarian, which made the experience even more enjoyable.

It took me some time to complete my bachelor's degree as I became pregnant with my first son and then had another one the following year. However, after graduation, I realized that I could no longer sustain myself and my two boys on a clerk's salary, which averages to $33,633.[2] I went through multiple interviews and was eventually able to secure a position as an IA. Once I became an information assistant, I focused on creating, promoting, and hosting programs, and also did some outreach events. During my time as an IA, I facilitated computer classes called Tech Connect, which were held every Friday at 10:00 a.m. I was initially trained to assist with these classes, but when the other IA who typically led them left the library to become a police officer, I was tasked with taking over as the main facilitator. Although I did not have the same level of technical expertise as the other IA, I was able to rely on slides and guides to help me lead the classes. This was beneficial for our manager, as she could report positive attendance numbers for the program.

At first, I enjoyed the opportunity to lead and teach on a larger scale than I had before, but as time went on, the pressure of being the only staff member responsible for Tech Connect began to take a toll on me. In addition to Tech Connect classes, I engaged in other programs as well. I took the initiative to create, promote, and facilitate a crochet group and a monthly book club for adult patrons. When there were no scheduled programs, I would assist the children's librarian by conducting read-aloud sessions and crafts for the children's classes. At that point, I came to the realization that obtaining a master's degree was necessary since I found the most joy in conducting read-alouds and singing with children. While I could have continued leading programs assisting the children's librarian with story time, I recognized that my salary would be restricted to an IA position without an MLIS degree.

In 2017, I enrolled at Pennsylvania Western University in Clarion, Pennsylvania, for their online courses since I had my two small sons at the time, so traveling to classes was not feasible. By attending library school, I was able to become a librarian trainee, so I had the opportunity to combine what I was learning in school to real-life situations that infused the whole library school and experience into one. It is no secret that people who have graduate school degrees are generally paid more than those who do not.[3] Going to school expanded my knowledge of various types of libraries, not just public and school libraries. I believe that because of my years working in the library, plus attending library school, has taught me the importance of building connections with patrons, stakeholders, community leaders, as well as the day-to-day tasks of running a library. Even though I was fortunate enough to have the backing and encouragement to pursue my MLIS degree from my family and friends, I recognize that not everyone is afforded the same privileges. Moreover, the public library where I worked provides several benefits, including a tuition reimbursement program[4] that helped me become a trainee for the children's librarian role, and the union also has a similar program.[5] Additionally, as a children's librarian trainee, I received a pay increase based on the number of credits earned per semester, so I had to submit my transcripts every semester to qualify for the raise. I understand that not all libraries are fortunate enough to have these perks and then some. Lack of financial resources, social support, and other factors may be some of the challenges that professional and support staff may have when it comes to why they may not have hold of an MLS/MLIS degree.

Library professionals who lack an MLS/MLIS face numerous challenges. Prior to becoming a librarian, I was not formally recognized for tasks beyond my job description, such as providing one-on-one tech assistance or assisting the children's librarian with program coordination and collection management. Although my manager acknowledged my efforts during performance evaluations, the institution as a whole did not recognize my skills or offer opportunities for professional development. There were higher-level positions available that only required a bachelor's degree, but the locations were inconvenient for me and my children. Even with these higher positions, there was a limit on how far I could advance without a master's degree. Certain positions still required an MLIS regardless of my ability to perform librarian duties.[6]

As an IA, I was not informed about the training available to enhance my skills in tech support or using other resources when hosting a program. It seems to vary depending on the manager's perspective on whether nonlibrarian staff should receive such training. However, I was fortunate to have previously worked at a location where there were many programs, and I was allowed to participate in promoting or hosting them, as long as it did not interfere with my job duties. This gave me the freedom to learn about other aspects of the library. Even though I did not receive formal training as an IA, I was able to apply what I learned from my previous experience. Unfortunately, not everyone has the same opportunities.

It seems that in the public library realm, your salary will not increase based on your longevity alone, and in order to receive a raise, you need to obtain your master's degree. Pursuing a master's degree can be mentally taxing for some, particularly for those with families and young children who need your attention when you are at home.[7] Therefore, some library professionals may need to take on additional jobs in order to make ends meet while working at the library.

When I was attending library school, I was a participant in the WIC program[8] for my youngest son, which provided me with essential food at home. Additionally, I received childcare assistance, and my situation was further helped by the fact that I lived in a rent stabilized building[9] where my rent was determined by my income as a clerk. As an IA, I earned more than a clerk, but not enough to be financially comfortable while performing additional work responsibilities. Therefore, it was an obvious decision for me to return to school and continue climbing the ladder to earn a higher salary. I have worked with various support staff, including experienced clerks who were more than capable of running the library. However, it seems that those with a master's degree are considered for managerial positions by the higher-ups. There is even a clerk who hosts a weekly program called "Sports with G . . ." and has gained a significant following due to his rapport with patrons. Despite the success of their programs and their ongoing efforts to promote them, these staff members are not recognized by higher management, possibly due to their lack of a master's degree. Their consistency and dedication go unnoticed.

I wish there were a pathway to help professional and support staff to get training so they can move to a higher position like training other staff members on tech support. There are tech-savvy clerks and IAs; they do not get the higher salaries regardless of their ability to keep up with the tech trends. Just recently, the library received their new contract, which gives us a pay increase. However, with inflation and everything else going up, those that do not have an MLS/MLIS degree are just making it. I believe this put us back where we started from.

There are also great IAs who are doing phenomenal programs. During Halloween, there was a program for teens about careers in the mortuary industry. This IA was able to gather job postings, books, websites and to get someone to come to the library to speak to the teens about how they started in that line of work. There was another IA who runs a program teaching basic Spanish every week. She has been consistent with this program since 2021, and it is because of her consistency that her patrons keep coming back.

In my library, the librarians and managers are the ones who get recognition and voices in decision-making processes. A clerk told me that he had inquired from our director about a position as a manager and she quickly asked him if he was planning on going back to school. Another clerk was appointed to the interim manager position, but due to the clerk's academic qualifications, having only a high school diploma, the clerk was promptly substituted by an experienced manager from an alternate location. Subsequently, the clerk was requested to undertake the interim manager position at another site, as there was a need for a manager at that location. This occurrence underscores the recognition by senior leadership of the clerk's prolonged service and aptitude in effectively managing a library. If there had been any uncertainties regarding the clerk's managerial expertise, he would not have been considered for the role of interim manager at another location. Nevertheless, they were able to find an outsider for the manager position he was filling in for instead of just giving him the position.

The negative effects of not acknowledging long-term employees can impact the morale of the job. After the clerk was not given the position of manager, he seemed unmotivated to be productive at work. He would not respond to emails with urgency like he did before. He would relieve staff from the desk casually. Also, this may have led to the library "Great Resignation"[10] with support staff and professionals going to other agencies like the MTA, Department of Sanitation, and JP Morgan Chase & Co., to name a few, with higher pay and possible career growth without having to go back to school to do so. The impact of the library's relationship with its community and stakeholders will be impacted because, for example, the program I mentioned earlier, "Sports with G. . . ." He is leaving to go to the Department of Sanitation, so his program will come to an end since other staff members are not as knowledgeable about sports as he is. This will have an effect on our statistics unless another program takes its place and more importantly, a program that the patrons would enjoy and keep coming back to, otherwise we would lose the program and the attendees. Stakeholders will see a lack in patrons attending programs and reevaluate investing in a library where the community does not utilize it.

I think there should be clear career advancement paths and job descriptions for support staff and professional staff without MLIS/MLS. I believe the years that people stay in a job should count for something. Some people are focused to seek out more opportunities because where they are the opportunities are limited. I also believe that those that are doing more than their position requires, such as doing programs as a clerk, should see their efforts reflected in their pay. Also, clerks and IAs that are able to run the branch as second in charge and acquire years of service should be able to be a part of decision-making process and acknowledged with the library for their hard work, not just a blanket statement congratulating people for working hard but actually highlighting a program of the month and consistency.

So, although there are great benefits to obtaining a master of library science and information degree, the challenge and reality is that not every library professional and support staff can get a MLIS or wants to obtain one. They may not have the finances, support, or time to go back to school. Not acknowledging these challenges can cripple the library supporting the community. Without this degree, staff are being ignored, not heard from, not adequately trained, overworked and underpaid. When staff are supported with adequate pay, proper training, promotions, and acknowledgment, they will continue to excel in their positions and create more people to do the same. And when people feel excited working in the library, patrons will be able to feel and see that the stakeholders would want to support even more because the staff is excited, and the community is even more excited. But this can only happen if the higher-ups can recognize the years that people without degrees are putting into the library. It is just about acknowledging those that are putting in years and increasing engagement in the community.

## NOTES

1. "Overview of Library Support Staff." American Library Association, https://www.ala.org/aboutala/offices/hrdr/librarysupportstaff/overview_of_library_support_staff. Accessed April 30, 2023.
2. "New York Public Library Office Aide Salaries." Glassdoor, https://www.glassdoor.com/Salary?New-York-Public-Library-Office-Aide-Salaries-E5416_D_KO24,35.htm. Accessed April 30, 2023.
3. Korn Ferry. "Should You Go to Graduate School?" *Harvard Business Review*, January 28, 2020, https://hbr.org/2020/01should-you-go-to-graduate-school. Accessed April 30, 2023.
4. "Scholarships." American Library Association, https://www.ala.org.educationcareers/scholarships. Accessed April 30, 2023.
5. "Tuition Reimbursement." District Council 37, https://www.dc37.net/benefits/education/offerings/tuition. Accessed April 30, 2023.
6. "What You Need to Know to Be a Librarian." American Library Association, https://www.ala.org/educationcareers/careers/librarycareersite/whatyouneedlibrarian#:~:text=The%20requirements%20for%20a%20librarian%20position%20can%20span,a%20second%20masters%20degree%2C%20e.g%2C%20a%20law%20degree. Accessed April 30, 2023.
7. Tamar Kirschner. "We All Win—Training and Advancement for Non-MLS Library Workers." Public Libraries Online, January 18, 2022, https//publiclibrariesonline.org/2022/01/we-all-win-training-and-advancement-for-non-mls-library-workers/. Accessed April 30, 2023.
8. "Women, Infants and Children (WIC)." New York State Department of Health, https:www.health.ny.gov/prevention/nutrition/wic/. Accessed April 30, 2023.
9. "Rent Stabilized Building Lists." New York City Rent Guidelines Board, https://rentguidelinesboard.cityofnewyork.us/resources/rent-stabilized-building-lists/. Accessed April 30, 2023.
10. Korn Ferry. "The Great Resignation Didn't Start with the Pandemic," *Harvard Business Review*, March 2022, https://hbr.org/2022/03/the-great-resignation-didnt-start-with-the-pandemic.

## WORKS CITED

Kelly, Michael. "Can We Talk about the MLS?" *Library Journal*, April 29, 2023.

Kirschner, Tamar. "We All Win-Training and Advancement for Non-MLS Library Workers." *Public Libraries Online*, January 18, 2022, publiclibrariesonline.org/2022/01/we-all-win-training-and-advancement-for-non-mls-library-workers/. Accessed April 30, 2023.

Korn Ferry. "The Great Resignation Didn't Start with the Pandemic." *Harvard Business Review*, March 2022, hbr.org/2022/03/the-great-resignation-didnt-start-with-the-pandemic.

Korn Ferry. "Should You Go to Graduate School?" *Harvard Business Review*, January 28, 2020, hbr.org/2020/01/should-you-go-to-graduate-school. Accessed 30 April 2023.

"New York Public Library Office Aide Salaries." *Glassdoor*, www.glassdoor.com/Salary/New-York-Public-Library-Office-Aide-Salaries-E5416_D_KO24,35.htm. Accessed April 30, 2023.

"Overview of Library Support Staff." American Library Association, https://www.ala.org/aboutala/offices/hrdr/librarysupportstaff/overview_of_library_support_staff. Accessed April 30, 2023.

"Rent Stabilized Building Lists." New York City Rent Guidelines Board, rentguidelinesboard.cityofnewyork.us/resources/rent-stabilized-building-lists/. Accessed April 30, 2023.

"Scholarships." American Library Association, www.ala.org/educationcareers/scholarships. Accessed April 30, 2023.

"Tuition Reimbursement." *District Council 37*, www.dc37.net/benefits/education/offerings/tuition. Accessed April 30, 2023.

"What You Need to Know to Be a Librarian." American Library Association, www.ala.org/educationcareers/careers/librarycareersite/whatyouneedlibrarian#:~:text=The%20requirements%20for%20a%20librarian%20position%20can%20span,a%20second%20masters%20degree%2C%20e.g.%2C%20a%20law%20degree. Accessed April 30, 2023.

"Women, Infants and Children (WIC)." New York State Department of Health, www.health.ny.gov/prevention/nutrition/wic/. Accessed April 30, 2023.

# 4.26

## My Contributions to the Library as a Nonlibrarian

Lisa Soler

My career at Queens Library as a nonlibrarian was something I didn't plan, but when I look back, I'm not surprised I'm still here. In the 1990s, I was passionate about corporate America with all the bells and whistles it came with. My mind-set changed when 9/11 happened and I transitioned to survival mode. Queens Library hired me in 2005 as an office aide at the Broadway Community Library. This position quickly transitioned to customer service representative. I learned to prepare books and process library cards. Clocked in, handled my daily duties, clocked out. About a year and a half later, forty-five positions opened for customer service specialists and the library was in dire need. I was fortunate to stay at Broadway and was delighted to contribute to the library in other ways with this change. The position, in its early stages, was called library information assistant, and about five employees had the position. After seventeen years, I can proudly say I'm still a customer service specialist.

"What have I gotten into?" was the first thought I had when I found out that an important part of my duties was to teach technology. I said to myself, "I'm not a librarian and how can this fit with what the library has to offer?" The experience was not there, and I had never taught anything to anyone. I questioned myself, of course. Being able to teach had to come from a desire, a passion from within. One thing about me, I'm willing to try something once and when I did, I realized the sky's the limit. Two important factors came into play: responsibility and purpose. I no longer felt detached from the customers of the library. I could see them as individuals who wanted to succeed and keep up with the times. I was amazed at how easily I could talk about technology and the constant changes with our daily lives every day. Starting at the basic level was my choice because I was also testing myself. I had to make sure I knew what I was talking about and not seem unrelatable to the customers. Programs like Mousing Around and Typing.com were perfect because it would ease the fear of many of our customers. I explained that I was not going to talk throughout the lessons and no, there was no need to take notes. I told them after introducing myself, "You're going to start using a computer today!" I was amused by their expressions, but I reassured them and explained that they would understand by the end of the lesson. I taught once a week and the rest is history. With time, I realized how important it became to teach and how I played a crucial role. Technology was here to stay. I also realized that as the customers learned, I was learning.

The demand became so big that one of our librarians showed interest and asked to teach an intermediate class. The idea was that customers took a beginner's class and continue with our intermediate class. I never thought I could feel so motivated, passionate, and satisfied. The librarian and I would discuss a lesson plan every week. I got a sense of freedom because I decided what to teach and how. We gave each other ideas and advice to make the classes more successful.

One month, Spanish was the first language of all seven students in my class, so I took the position even further by teaching my class in Spanish. The first day of class I explained the importance of learning English but told them that I would agree to teach in Spanish. Although I speak the language well, I had to train myself to speak properly and lay off the slang that I was used to in my daily life. I realized that becoming a student would make me a better teacher. I decided to sign up for Spanish classes that were being offered by our union, D.C. 37. At this point, I understood my responsibility in my role as a customer service specialist.

As I became a seasoned specialist, the introduction to E materials began. Nook and Kindles began to rise in popularity, and I was invited to join training teams to instruct our staff on how to use e-books, e-magazines, and audio book platforms offered by Queens Library. The library introduced public streaming services for movies and music as well. A tablet lending program was launched with the occurrence of Hurricane Sandy. The mobile hot spot launch began soon after.

With the success of the first set of tablets, the library obtained another grant to do it again. The training team worked together to set up training and work on printed materials for the staff and customers. Can you imagine, library staff depending on the training team to provide reliable resources to pass on to the customers of the library? For the first time, librarians are asking for my advice and input. I realize that my purpose is to make a lasting impact.

In 2016 I was working at the Hillcrest Community Library. It's considered a smaller library and doesn't have the traffic like Broadway did. I had to stay busy, so I decided to teach one on one classes. Students had the choice to use our computers with Windows 7 or to bring a device of their own. I was excited because I taught myself to use IOS, Android, and Windows tablets, Mac and Windows laptops, and different cell phones. Believe it or not, customers had flip phones that were difficult to navigate. I had a Sister come every week to learn how to navigate and send emails as well.

I stayed at Hillcrest for about a year and a half because my desire was to transfer to Central Library, one of our largest libraries that had seventy-two public computers and a cyber-center training room dedicated to teaching. I'm currently at Central and have been for the last five years.

Why am I committed? The library has become such a huge part of me. Second in nature, if you will, from the time I started reading Nancy Drew mysteries to improve my English until now. The library is no longer a quiet place just to study. It's a resource to help with job search and training. Programs are offered, like music, art, and poetry to remind us of our diversity. It's a promise that Queens Library has committed to, and this is why I'm still here. Working with the public has its challenges and will never change, but if I can remind one person that Queens Library is for everyone, it's worth it. I embrace every day as a learning experience, and I look forward to what nonlibrarianship has to offer.

# Part IV
# SERVICE TO OUR COMMUNITIES

# Chapter 5
# Academic Libraries

## 5.1

## *On the Other Side of the Tenure Track*

RETENTION AND PROMOTION OF BLACK ACADEMIC LAW LIBRARIANS

Renate Chancellor

Black academic law librarians often find themselves on the other side of the tenure track when working in a university law library and while pursuing tenure[1] at predominantly white institutions (PWIs). Tenure in the United States was developed by the American Association of University Professors (AAUP)[2] as part of the 1940 Statement of Principles on Academic Freedom and Tenure.[3] Achieving tenure is considered as providing a tremendous level of economic security and academic freedom in their teaching and research pursuits. With this condition of employment, a faculty member is expected to continue to give something on an ongoing basis in return for receiving tenure. "Tenure and promotion decisions at most US universities (but not necessarily at primarily teaching colleges) continue to be based on research productivity and teaching effectiveness, with the former weighing more heavily on tenure and promotion decisions."[4]

Black librarians working in academic law libraries may find themselves on the other side of the tenure track in three primary ways: 1) They are hired as nontenured library faculty and are expected to assume similar duties as tenure track faculty. 2) They are hired as tenure-track faculty, but there is little support from deans, directors, and other colleagues for them to obtain tenure. 3) Equity, diversity, and inclusion is a major factor that when absent, leads to racism and/or racial microaggressions.[5] The library profession has long lauded its commitment to equity, diversity, and inclusion and social justice. However, supportive measures are rarely in place to ensure the retention and success of the underrepresented librarians. This often leads to quitting out of sheer frustration, employment termination, and/or experiencing "racial battle fatigue"—a term that describes the psychosocial response to stress from being racially oppressed in society and in universities.[6] Black librarian faculty on the tenure track or promotion track may also encounter the intersection of the burden of care and cultural taxation.[7]

The struggle for Black library faculty acquiring promotion and tenure is not a new concern for librarians working in traditional university libraries. In fact, this topic has been covered extensively in scholarly literature.[8] Moreover, Karin Griffin[9] argues that the path to tenure and promotion in higher education does not provide a fair and equitable process for Black women faculty. Martine Garnar's[10] dissertation examines the experiences of five academic librarians of color and their decisions for remaining or leaving the profession. The second edition of the *Handbook of Black Librarianship*, compiled and edited by E. J. Josey and Marva DeLoach, includes the chapter "African Americans in Special Libraries" but does not offer a deep discussion on the challenges of Black academic law librarians. Nevertheless, Josey was a strong advocate and unwavering supporter of faculty status for Black librarians.[11] This chapter describes the impediments that Black faculty librarians experience while working in law libraries.

### NONTENURED LAW LIBRARIAN FACULTY

Faculty status for academic librarians has been fervently debated ever since its inception in academia. On one side of the debate are those who believe that librarians should not be operating under the title of faculty, and on the other side, there are many who just as fervently assert that librarians rightly deserve the status and must fight hard to maintain it. "Law librarians are often treated in the same manner as clinical professors and legal writing instructors and are not given full faculty status."[12] Black law librarians often undergo extraordinary challenges compared to their faculty counterparts. For example, they may be asked, and are often required, to serve on diversity committees and yet are still required to meet the rigors of tenure. Griffin's[13] autoethnography of her journey through tenure and promotion to becoming a librarian notes that librarians are not always seen as faculty at universities, but those that face challenges regarding research and teaching, as required for any tenure-track position.

Gail Munde[14] outlines the necessity of increasing mentorship in academic libraries and argues that libraries will have to reinvent their leadership to meet the demands of minority librarians. Ione Damasco and Dracine Hodges's[15] study on the tenure and promotion experiences of Black, Indigenous, People of Color (BIPOC) academic librarians focus on retention programs as models for mentorship for BIPOC law librarians. Research on minority retention in academic libraries is scant, and information on overall retention of librarians is low. More research in this important area is needed.

As long as universities continue to question whether academic law librarians should have full-time status, and all the benefits that go along with tenure, Black law librarians will never fully achieve job security. Black law librarian faculty can also be an asset to the university. According to McLaughlin,[16] law librarians offer a tremendous benefit to their schools by utilizing their skills and abilities often without being given the opportunity of a tenurable faculty position. There are a number of benefits to law schools:

> Law librarians as full members of a school's faculty can have a variety of benefits for schools. With the American Bar Association's and hiring attorney's calls for law schools to instill law students with practical skills, law librarians who are placed in faculty positions that allow them to instruct law students in setting such as legal clinics can have a greater chance to help their schools in meeting their education requirements, prepare students for the practice of law, and help those in need access the legal information and services they need. Beyond serving as instructors, law librarians often write on the subjects of legal bibliography, information, and research, but they are also encouraged to write on other legal matters. Without having full faculty or professional status, the publications of law librarians are not given the same weight that publications of other members of their organizations receive, which not only diminishes law librarian's contributions to legal scholarship but also does not allow their school to get the full benefits of having a member of their faculty publish.[17]

## LAW LIBRARIANS SEEKING TENURE

Tenure is typically not an option for librarians working in public, private, or government law libraries. Faculty law librarians who are seeking tenure would share some of the same job responsibilities as those who are nontenured. They provide information, research, and instruction for students and faculty of a law school. Those individuals typically hold two degrees: a master's in library and information science from an American Library Association (ALA) accredited program and a juris doctor (JD) from an American Bar Association accredited law school. A JD is not required for law librarians who choose to work on the technical services section of the library—traditionally acquisitions, cataloging, technology, etc. And, in many law schools, law faculty do not possess a doctoral degree. "The J.D. requirement, is the highest educational level attained by most law professors."[18] Yet most law faculty are hired on the tenure-track and about 95 percent of those hired receive tenure.[19]

The American Association of Law Libraries (AALL) and the Association of College and Research Libraries (ACRL) both support academic librarians' having tenured or continuous appointment status.[20] About 24 percent of nondirector academic law librarians have an opportunity to achieve tenure status at their institutions. Roughly another 44 percent have opportunities to secure some form of continuous appointment.[21]

Tenure is not simply a guarantee of lifetime employment. Appointment to tenure is an unlimited academic employment that can be terminated only for extraordinary conditions such as financial exigency or the discontinuation of a program. The 1940 Statement was supported by the Association of American Colleges and Universities and over 250 scholarly and higher education organizations and is widely adopted into faculty handbooks and collective bargaining agreements at institutions of higher education throughout the United States.[22] It contends that tenure would defend academic freedom on three primary pillars: 1) Teachers are entitled to complete freedom in research and publish their findings subject to the satisfactory performance of their other academic responsibilities. 2) Teachers are entitled to intellectual freedom in the classroom in discussing topics, but they should be careful not to introduce controversial issues which have no relation to their subject. 3) As members of the college or university, teachers are members of a learned profession, and officers of an educational institution. As such, they should be free from institutional censorship or discipline.[23] The AAUP believed that these assertions would allow scholars the freedom to hold diverse perspectives while benefitting society.

## EQUITY, DIVERSITY, AND INCLUSION

Black law librarians comprise only a small percentage of law librarians in the nation. The American Association of Law Libraries (AALL), the premier professional association for law librarians in the United States, has not prioritized collecting demographic data to assess how many law librarians of color are in the profession and in what sector they work. In her 1998 article, "Why Is Diversity Important for Law Librarianship?" Yvonne Chandler[24] emphasized how the demographic shifts in the United States would impact law librarianship. Stating that diversifying the profession "is important because meeting the historical mission that defines the profession—providing services and resources to information users—now, more than ever, requires addressing the information needs of a multicultural population. And, in order to do this, there must be a diverse population of information professionals."[25] Twenty-five years later, this profession continues to struggle with this issue. Alyssa Thursten points out that

> Despite the explosive growth of minority groups in the U.S. population over the past several decades, law librarianship has been slow to reflect the country's diversity in terms of increasing its minority membership. In 1976, the first official AALL survey of minorities in law libraries found that minorities made up only 11.2% of all professional law librarians (those holding an M.L.S. degree), compared to almost 25% of law library support staff.[26]

AALL collected and published demographic data on its membership in their biennial salary survey.[27] Unfortunately, the organization stopped collecting the data in 2005, for reasons unknown, and thereby creating "a gap between what is acknowledged as an issue of concern, and what is being done about it."[28] Currently, the only descriptive data available comes from analysis of the listings contained in the self-reported Minority Law Librarian Directory whose print version ceased in 2015. In 2014, 6.9 percent self-identified as minority law librarians.[29] Data does not reflect a breakdown of the ethnic groups or if they identify as working in public, academic, or government libraries.

It's likely that there is even a smaller number of academic law librarians. There has been a long-standing call for increased diversity, equity, and inclusion in the library profession in general and in law librarianship in particular. Several scholars have written about their experiences as African American academic law librarians[30] where they describe their challenges working in environments that are not always diverse, equitable, or inclusive. BIPOC librarians should feel welcome and that they belong to organizations that hire them. Moreover, they should feel that they are treated equitably and are not marginalized. Racial microaggressions and overt racism have been major factors in the success of Black law faculty librarians.

In 2014, a former librarian with the South Texas College of Law sued on the grounds of racial and gender discrimination.[31] Public facts are unclear as to the motivations for the racial and gender claims of the complaint, but according to the lawyer for the plaintiff, there were other Black employees who experienced discrimination. Ultimately, the claimant lost the lawsuit, but it underscores the point that there is still much work needed toward equity, diversity, and inclusion (EDI) in academic law libraries. Arguably, there are six Historically Black Colleges and Universities (HBCUs) that have law schools: Howard University School of Law, Southern University Law Center, North Carolina Central University School of Law, and Thurgood Marshall. These schools were founded on the belief that every individual deserves access to a college or higher education.

Historically, HBCUs do not share the same challenges that PWIs have when it comes to tenure. However, Black law librarians can find themselves on the other side of the tenure track because of funding or lack of resources to attract and retain talented law librarians. Cheryl Fields[32] argues that faculty at HBCUs may ultimately be in greater danger of losing their tenure privileges than scholars at other institutions due to political and financial constraints. She further contends,

> The main factor threatening tenure at HBCUs is money. Tenured faculty is a big-ticket item on any institutional budget. For HBCUs that are financially strapped, the number of tenure appointments that can be granted is sometimes limited by cost. This explains, in part, why HBCUs have a higher proportion of part-time and non-tenured faculty than do other institutions.[33]

## CONCLUSION

The core principles of democracy that the library profession was founded on has never lived up to its creed. Critics have argued that leaders in the profession conveniently rely on the neutrality stance when asked to tackle difficult issues of equity, inclusion, and social justice.[34] The pervasiveness of racism in American public institutions will not end anytime soon—and maybe never unless radical change occurs. Honma[35] contends that the profession has a deep history of entrenched elitism and thereby will continue to struggle until there is a reckoning with racism.

The recent Supreme Court decision abolishing affirmative action has made it unlawful for colleges and universities to consider race as a special factor in admissions may only be the first step in dismantling initiatives and programs that support African Americans in higher education. There are already many statewide efforts that have been successful in dissolving equity, diversity, and inclusion offices. Legislatures in the states of Florida, Louisiana, North Carolina, North Dakota, and Texas mounted attempts to ban or severely restrict tenure for university faculty. While most of these cases have been withdrawn or defeated, with the exception of North Carolina, it is apparent that the employment of African Americans working in PWIs is threatened. In order for Black law librarians to thrive in academia, they must be fully embraced and treated equitably like their white colleagues. This includes not only working in an environment free of discrimination and subvert and overt racism, but also, they should be offered faculty status and supported throughout the tenure process—all could lead to employment and economic security.

## NOTES

1. The term "tenure" is used throughout the chapter to refer to both tenure and other forms of continuous appointment that require similar processes, procedures, and commitments.

2. American Association of University Professors, 2023, http://www.aaup.org/.
3. "1940 Statement of Principles on Academic Freedom and Tenure with 1970 Interpretive Comments," American Association of University Professors, 1970.
4. Debra Easterly and Cynthia Lee A. Pemberton, "Understanding Barriers and Supports to Proposal Writing as Perceived by Female Associate Professors: Achieving Promotion to Professor," *Research Management Review* 16, no. 1 (2008): 2.
5. Shamika Dalton, Gail Mathapo, and Endia Sowers-Paige, "Navigating Law Librarianship While Black: A Week in the Life of a Black Female Law Librarian," *Law Library Journal*, 110, no. 3 (2018): 429–38, http://works.bepress.com/shamika-dalton/6/.
6. Renate L. Chancellor, "Racial Battle Fatigue: The Unspoken Burden of Black Women Faculty in LIS," *Journal of Education for Library and Information Science*, 60, no. 3 (2019): 182–89, DOI: 10.3138/jelis.2019-0007; William A. Smith, "Black Faculty Coping with Racial Battle Fatigue: The Campus Racial Climate in a Post-Civil Rights Era," in *A Long Way to Go: Conversations about Race by African American Faculty and Graduate Students*, edited by Darrell Cleveland (New York: Peter Lang Publishing, 2004), 171–90.
7. Camille Chesley and Tarida Anantachai, "The Burden of Care: Cultural Taxation of Women of Color Librarians on the Tenure-Track," *University Libraries Faculty Scholarship*, 108 (2018), https://scholarsarchive.library.albany.edu/ulib_fac_scholar/107.
8. TaLisa J. Carter and Miltonette O. Craig, "It Could Be Us: Black Faculty as 'Threats' on the Path to Tenure," *Race and Justice*, 12, no. 3 (2022): 569–87, https://doi.org/10.1177/21533687221087366; Ione T. Damasco and Dracine Hodges, "Tenure and Promotion Experiences of Academic Librarians of Color," *College & Research Libraries*, 73, no. 3 (2012): 279–301, https://doi.org/10.5860/crl-244; Rebecca Hankins and Miguel Juarez, eds., *Where Are the Librarians of Color? The Experiences of People of Color in Academia* (Sacramento, CA: Library Juice Press, 2015).
9. Karin L. Griffin, "Pursuing Tenure and Promotion in the Academy: A Librarian's Cautionary Tale," *Negro Educational Review*, 64, no. 1 (2013): 77–96, 135, http://proxycu.wrlc.org/login?url=http://search.proquest.com/docview/1461359958?accountid=9940.
10. Martin Luther Garnar, "Understanding the Experiences of Academic Librarians of Color," PhD Dissertation, University of Colorado, Colorado Springs, 2021, https://www.proquest.com/dissertations-theses/understanding-experiences-academic-librarians/docview/2618560641/se-2.
11. Renate L. Chancellor, *E. J. Josey: Transformational Leader in the Modern Library Profession* (Lanham, MD: Rowman & Littlefield, 2020).
12. Paul J. McLaughlin, "Advocating for the Law Profession," in *Introduction to Law Librarianship*, edited by Zanada Joyner and Cas Laskowski (Tucson, AZ: Daniel F. Cracchiolo Law Library, 2021), 39–47, https://pressbooks.pub/app/uploads/sites/4509/2021/07/Introduction-to-Law-Librarianship-20210920.pdf.
13. Griffin, "Pursuing Tenure."
14. Gail Munde, "Beyond Mentoring: Toward the Rejuvenation of Academic Libraries," *The Journal of Academic Librarianship*, 26, no. 3 (2000): 171–75. http://dx.doi.org/10.1016/S0099-1333(00)00095-1.
15. Damasco and Dracine Hodges, "Tenure and Promotion."
16. McLaughlin, "Advocating for the Law Profession."
17. Ibid., 40.
18. J. Gordon Hylton, "What Should Be the Prerequisites for Becoming a Law Professor?" *Marquette University Law School*, 2015, https://law.marquette.edu/facultyblog/2011/09/what-should-be-the-prerequisites-for-becoming-a-law-professor/.
19. Adam Chilton, Jonatha S. Masur, and Kyle Rozema. "Rethinking Law School Tenure Standards," Coase-Sandor Working Paper Series in Law and Economics, No. 868 (2020), https://dx.doi.org/10.2139/ssrn.3200005.
20. American Association of Law Libraries. Proceedings of the 80th Annual Meeting of the American Association of Law Libraries, held in Chicago, Illinois, Business Sessions July 6–8, 1987 (Chicago: American Association of Law Libraries, 1987); "Joint Statement on Faculty Status of College and University Librarians (approved June 26, 1972, reaffirmed by the Board June 2007)," Association of College & Research Libraries, 2007, https://www.ala.org/acrl/standards/standardsfaculty.
21. Brian Huddleston, Statistical Summary of the ALL-SIS CST Academic Law Librarian Tenure and Employment Status Survey, updated May 2021, http://www.brianhuddleston.com/CST/summary.html.
22. American Association of University Professors, 2023, http://www.aaup.org/.
23. "1940 Statement of Principles."
24. Yvonne Chandler, "Why Is Diversity Important for Law Librarianship?" *Law Library Journal*, 90 (1998): 545.
25. Ibid.
26. Alyssa Thursten, "Addressing the 'Emerging Minority': Racial and Ethnic Diversity in Law Librarianship in the Twenty-First Century," *Law Library Journal*, 104, no. 3 (2012): 362.
27. James M. Donovan, "Diversity: How Is AALL Doing?" *Law Faculty Scholarly Articles*, 683 (2017), https://uknowledge.uky.edu/law_facpub/683.
28. Ibid.
29. Ibid.
30. Dalton, Mathapo, and Sowers-Paige, "Navigating Law Librarianship"; Griffin, "Pursuing Tenure"; Shamika Dalton, Yvonne Chandler, Vicente E. Garces, Dennis C. Kim-Prieto, Carol A. Nicholson, and Michele A. Villigram, *Celebrating Diversity: A Legacy of Minority Leadership in the American Association of Law Libraries*, 2nd ed. (Getzville, NY: William S. Hein & Company, 2018).
31. Karen Sloan, "Librarian Sues South Texas College of Law for Racial Discrimination," *National Law Journal*, 2016, http://www.nationallawjournal.com/id=1202747729279/Librarian-Sues-South-Texas-College-of-Law-for-Racial-Discrimination?slreturn=20160124093034.
32. Cheryl D. Fields, "Tenure at HBCUs—Historically Black Colleges and Universities," *Diverse Issues in Higher Education*,

2007, https://www.diverseeducation.com/faculty-staff/article/15084441/tenure-at-hbcus-historically-black-colleges-and-universities.
33. Ibid.
34. Amelia N. Gibson, Renate L. Chancellor, Nicole A. Cooke, Sarah Park Dahlen, Shari A. Lee, and Yasmin Shorish, "Libraries on the Frontlines: Neutrality and Social Justice," *Equality, Diversity and Inclusion*, 36, no. 8 (2017): 751-66, https://doi.org/10.1108/EDI-11-2016-0100.
35. Todd Honma, "Trippin' Over the Color Line: The Invisibility of Race in Library and Information Studies," *InterActions: UCLA Journal of Education and Information Studies*, 1, no. 2 (2006): 1-26, http://escholarship.org/uc/item/4nj0w1mp.tes>

**WORKS CITED**

"1940 Statement of Principles on Academic Freedom and Tenure with 1970 Interpretive Comments." American Association of University Professors, 1970. https://www.aaup.org/file/1940%20Statement.pdf.

American Association of Law Libraries. Proceedings of the 80th Annual Meeting of the American Association of Law Libraries, Held in Chicago, Illinois, Business Sessions July 6-8, 1987. Chicago: American Association of Law Libraries, 1987.

American Association of University Professors, 2023. http://www.aaup.org/.

Carter, TaLisa J., and Miltonette O. Craig. "It Could Be Us: Black Faculty as 'Threats' on the Path to Tenure." *Race and Justice*, 12, no. 3 (2022): 569-87. https://doi.org/10.1177/21533687221087366.

Chancellor, Renate L. *E. J. Josey: Transformational Leader in the Modern Library Profession*. Lanham, MD: Rowman & Littlefield, 2020.

Chancellor, Renate L. "Racial Battle Fatigue: The Unspoken Burden of Black Women Faculty in LIS." *Journal of Education for Library and Information Science*, 60, no. 3 (2019): 182-89. DOI: 10.3138/jelis.2019-0007.

Chandler, Yvonne. "Why Is Diversity Important for Law Librarianship?" *Law Library Journal*, 90 (1998): 545.

Chesley, Camille, and Tarida Anantachai. "The Burden of Care: Cultural Taxation of Women of Color Librarians on the Tenure-Track." *University Libraries Faculty Scholarship*, 108 (2018). https://scholarsarchive.library.albany.edu/ulib_fac_scholar/107.

Chilton, Adam, Jonatha S. Masur, and Kyle Rozema. "Rethinking Law School Tenure Standards." Coase-Sandor Working Paper Series in Law and Economics, No. 868 (2020). https://dx.doi.org/10.2139/ssrn.3200005.

Dalton, Shamika D., Yvonne Chandler, Vicente E. Garces, Dennis C. Kim-Prieto, Carol A. Nicholson, and Michele A. Villigram. *Celebrating Diversity: A Legacy of Minority Leadership in the American Association of Law Libraries*, 2nd ed. Getzville, NY: William S. Hein & Company, 2018.

Dalton, Shamika, Gail Mathapo, and Endia Sowers-Paige. "Navigating Law Librarianship While Black: A Week in the Life of a Black Female Law Librarian." *Law Library Journal*, 110, no. 3 (2018): 429-38. http://works.bepress.com/shamika-dalton/6/.

Damasco, Ione T., and Dracine Hodges. "Tenure and Promotion Experiences of Academic Librarians of Color." *College & Research Libraries*, 73, no. 3 (2012): 279-301. https://doi.org/10.5860/crl-244.

Donovan, James M. "Diversity: How Is AALL Doing?" *Law Faculty Scholarly Articles*, 683 (2017). https://uknowledge.uky.edu/law_facpub/683.

Easterly, Debra, and Cynthia Lee A. Pemberton. "Understanding Barriers and Supports to Proposal Writing as Perceived by Female Associate Professors: Achieving Promotion to Professor." *Research Management Review* 16, no. 1 (2008): 1-17.

Fields, Cheryl D. "Tenure at HBCUs—Historically Black Colleges and Universities." *Diverse Issues in Higher Education*, 2007. https://www.diverseeducation.com/faculty-staff/article/15084441/tenure-at-hbcus-historically-black-colleges-and-universities.

Garnar, Martin Luther. "Understanding the Experiences of Academic Librarians of Color." PhD Dissertation, University of Colorado. Colorado Springs, 2021. https://www.proquest.com/dissertations-theses/understanding-experiences-academic-librarians/docview/2618560641/se-2.

Gibson, Amelia N., Renate L. Chancellor, Nicole A. Cooke, Sarah Park Dahlen, Shari A. Lee, and Yasmin Shorish. "Libraries on the Frontlines: Neutrality and Social Justice." *Equality, Diversity and Inclusion*, 36, no. 8 (2017): 751-66. https://doi.org/10.1108/EDI-11-2016-0100.

Griffin, Karin L. "Pursuing Tenure and Promotion in the Academy: A Librarian's Cautionary Tale." *Negro Educational Review*, 64, no. 1 (2013): 77-96, 135. http://proxycu.wrlc.org/login?url=http://search.proquest.com/docview/1461359958?accountid=9940.

Hankins, Rebecca, and Miguel Juarez, eds. *Where Are the Librarians of Color? The Experiences of People of Color in Academia*. Sacramento, CA: Library Juice Press, 2015.

Honma, Todd. "Trippin' Over the Color Line: The Invisibility of Race in Library and Information Studies." *InterActions: UCLA Journal of Education and Information Studies*, 1, no. 2 (2006): 1-26. http://escholarship.org/uc/item/4nj0w1mp.

Huddleston, Brian. Statistical Summary of the ALL-SIS CST Academic Law Librarian Tenure and Employment Status Survey. Updated May 2021. http://www.brianhuddleston.com/CST/summary.html.

Hylton, J. Gordon. "What Should Be the Prerequisites for Becoming a Law Professor?" Marquette University Law School, 2015. https://law.marquette.edu/facultyblog/2011/09/what-should-be-the-prerequisites-for-becoming-a-law-professor/.

"Joint Statement on Faculty Status of College and University Librarians (approved June 26, 1972, reaffirmed by the Board June 2007)." Association of College & Research Libraries, 2007. https://www.ala.org/acrl/standards/standardsfaculty.

McLaughlin, Paul J., "Advocating for the Law Profession." In *Introduction to Law Librarianship*, edited by Zanada Joyner and Cas Laskowski, 39-47. Tucson, AZ: Daniel F. Cracchiolo Law Library, 2021. https://pressbooks.pub/app/uploads/sites/4509/2021/07/Introduction-to-Law-Librarianship-20210920.pdf.

Munde, Gail. "Beyond Mentoring: Toward the Rejuvenation of Academic Libraries." *The Journal of Academic Librarianship*, 26, no. 3 (2000): 171-75. http://dx.doi.org/10.1016/S0099-1333(00)00095-1.

Nicholson, Carol A., Ruth Johnson, and Vicente Garces, eds. *Celebrating Diversity: A Legacy of Minority Leadership in the American Association of Law Libraries.* Buffalo, NY: William S. Hein & Company, 2006.

Sloan, Karen. "Librarian Sues South Texas College of Law for Racial Discrimination." *National Law Journal*, 2016. http://www.nationallawjournal.com/id=1202747729279/Librarian-Sues-South-Texas-College-of-Law-for-Racial-Discrimination?slreturn=20160124093034.

Smith, William A. "Black Faculty Coping with Racial Battle Fatigue: The Campus Racial Climate in a Post-Civil Rights Era." In *A Long Way to Go: Conversations about Race by African American Faculty and Graduate Students*, edited by Darrell Cleveland, 171–90. New York: Peter Lang Publishing, 2004.

Thursten, Alyssa. "Addressing the 'Emerging Minority': Racial and Ethnic Diversity in Law Librarianship in the Twenty-First Century." *Law Library Journal*, 104, no. 3 (2012): 359–81.

Thurgood Marshall College Fund, 2023. https://www.tmcf.org/history-of-hbcus/.

# 5.2

## The Accidental Law Librarian

Melanie E. Sims

The field of law librarianship is often an unchartered career path. Many information professionals find themselves accidental law librarians. One might ask, Why accidental law librarian? The term "accidental" is used because it is not necessarily the first career choice of an individual. There are different paths to one becoming a law librarian who is simply an information professional that specializes in providing legal information. Some people often times confuse law librarians with paralegals or legal secretaries. Law librarians work in a variety of library settings including law firms, law schools, courts, and other government organizations. Law librarians research, analyze, and evaluate legal sources for quality and accuracy. They also teach, train, develop library collections, and manage libraries and information centers. Despite law librarians working in legal settings and with legal information, it is illegal for them to give legal advice to their users. Only licensed attorneys may give legal advice. Law librarians can occasionally walk a thin line between providing research assistance to users and practicing the law. They have to make sure not to interpret the law, select particular forms, or analyze legal issues or points of law for users in an effort to not to be accused of the unauthorized practice of law.

The varying paths to law librarianship may include one simply being recruited to the field, a lawyer transitioning to a second career after practicing law for several years, a law student who realizes they do not want to practice law but enjoys doing legal research, or a temporary position that leads to a full-time position. As a minority, I began my career in law librarianship after being recruited for a position as government documents librarian at Louisiana State University Law Center Library. Otherwise, I would have never considered a job in law librarianship. I am currently the head of Access Services and Government Information. One may be recruited for a position based on their skillsets, ability to work well with colleagues, and the need to increase diversity within an organization. Clarence Robertson II, library and conflicts manager at Jackson Walker LLP, is another example of a minority who was in a temporary position that led to a career in law librarianship.[1]

The requirements to become a law librarian will vary depending on the library setting and the library position. One common misconception about law librarianship is that an individual must have both a master of library and information science (MLIS) degree and a juris doctor (JD) degree. However, most positions generally only require a master's degree from an American Library Association (ALA)-accredited institution. The names of the degrees vary among institutions: MLS, MLIS, or MSIS. Some positions, in addition to the MLS, may also require a JD from an American Bar Association (ABA)-accredited law school. According to the American Association of Law Libraries (AALL), about one-third of all law librarians have a law degree from a law school accredited by the ABA, but fewer than 20 percent of the law librarian positions being filled require both degrees.[2]

There are several advantages as well as disadvantages in having just the MLIS and having dual degrees. Some of the advantages to the MLIS include earning it faster and it's less expensive; the number of online and part-time programs available; and the variety of opportunities that exist, particularly in law firms and as public and technical services librarians in academic and government libraries. Some of the disadvantages of earning just the MLIS include the steeper learning curve to enter the profession; the need to relocate, as fewer non-JD positions are likely to exist in each law library; and the struggle to earn the respect of patrons and even colleagues compared to those who attend law school. The advantages of having the dual degree include salaries that are generally higher; relating well with law students, attorneys, and law school professors; and increased credibility among patrons and colleagues. The disadvantages to the dual degree include high costs and time commitment; only a handful of hybrid online programs exist, but part-time and evening programs are available. You may feel "stuck" in the profession to make use of both degrees.[3] The law degree alone will qualify you for very few professional positions in any kind of law library. It is also worth noting that the opportunities to advance in the field of law librarianship will increase if you possess both degrees.

Law librarians work in three main types of libraries: academic, law firm, and government. Academic law librarians provide information, research, and instruction to faculty and students at law schools. Law school librarians may hold faculty rank and have tenure. They generally require a MLS degree, and a law degree is sometimes required for librarians who work as reference librarians and for some administrative positions. Some of the functions performed by academic law librarians include purchasing, processing, and cataloging new library materials; managing existing collections; teaching courses; and providing reference and research assistance. They may hold specializations in the following areas: foreign and international law, information systems, government documents, patents, taxation, and special collections such as archives and antiquarian books.

Working in a law school library affords me a variety of duties and responsibilities as a law librarian. In my position of head of access services, I oversee the daily operations of opening/closing the library, circulation, reserves, interlibrary loan, and our print center. I also provide reference and research services to faculty, students, and the general public. I serve as a faculty liaison and participate in our collection development by selecting and purchasing materials as well as deselecting materials. I serve as coordinator for both our federal and state depository library programs.

Academic law librarians may be one of three types of employees: at will, nontenure track faculty, or tenure track faculty. There is typically no expectation of scholarship with an employee at will unless explicitly listed in the job description as a duty. There are a variety of nontenure track faculty types, and the job descriptions and promotion guidelines will typically provide guidance about whether scholarship is expected and compensated. A tenure track faculty position requires scholarship for promotion. A librarian who fails to meet the publication and service requirements of their library could be terminated if the requirements are not met.[4]

Each academic institution will vary with what is expected of their faculty to obtain tenure and the timeline. For example, when I first began my position at the LSU Law Library, the tenure timeline was three years to come up for tenure and now it has been expanded to six years. A candidate seeking tenure must receive notable in job performance and notable in either the category of scholarship or service and satisfactory in the other.

The second type of library that law librarians work in is law firms or private law libraries. These libraries are closed to the public and provide legal information to the attorneys and other legal professionals in a law office or legal department of a corporation or association. Like academic librarians, private law librarians also provide a range of services depending on the size of the parent organization. A key role of private law librarians is to provide hard-to-locate information on a timely basis. Typical reference services include database searching, bibliography preparation, client development and marketing support, and current awareness programs. One pitfall of working in a law firm or private library is that you have to be prepared for the possibility of downsizing by the parent organization at any time.

In addition to academic and firm law libraries, many law librarians work in government law libraries that include courts, legislatures, or government agencies at the national, state, or local level. The primary focus of law librarians in government settings is to support the legal information needs of judges, legislators, and their employees. Some court and county libraries also serve the practicing bar and the general public. County law libraries work hard to provide programs to make their materials more accessible to laypeople.[5] Government law librarians generally hold an MLS degree. Some also hold law degrees or public administration degrees.

Law librarians of color face many of the same challenges as librarians of color face in other types of libraries. One particular challenge in law librarianship and higher education is dealing with racial microaggression in the workplace. Racial microaggressions are "brief and commonplace daily verbal, behavioral, or environmental indignities, whether intentional or unintentional, that communicate hostile, derogatory, or negative racial slights and insults toward people of color."[6] An example of microaggression includes a patron coming to the reference desk asking for assistance from someone else because they do not think that you are qualified to answer their question. However, as libraries and other organizations strive to increase their efforts in the areas of diversity, equity, and inclusion some of the challenges faced by librarians of color can be minimized. The key to change is a sense of awareness and to embrace cultural humility. There has to be a concerted effort to make changes in our policies, practices, and collections. You have to place action behind the verbiage.

As the racial and ethnic composition of the country continues to change, there is a need for more diversity within law librarianship as is true with librarianship in general. Statistics indicate librarians of color comprise 22.9 percent of all law librarians while Black or African Americans account for 6.4 percent of that number.[7] Law librarianship can be a rewarding career path and has proven to be the best career decision for some people.[8]

**NOTES**

1. "How a Temporary Position Led to a Law Librarian Career." *AALL Spectrum*, vol. 27, no. 3 (January/February 2023): 28–31. HeinOnline.
2. "Become a Legal Information Professional." American Association of Law Librarians. Accessed March 10, 2023.
3. Aamir Shahnawaz Abudullah, Kaylan Ellis, and Heather J. E. Simmons,. "The Profession of Law Librarianship." In *Introduction to Law Librarianship*, edited by Zanada Joyner and Cas Laskowski (Mountain View, CA: Pressbook (2021): 9. HeinOnline.
4. Margaret Butler, "Scholarship." In *Introduction to Law Librarianship*, edited by Zanada Joyner and Cas Laskowski (Mountain View, CA: Pressbooks (2021): 347. HeinOnline.
5. Aamir Shahnawaz Abudullah, Kaylan Ellis, and Heather J. E. Simmons, "The Profession of Law Librarianship." In *Introduction to Law Librarianship*, edited by Zanada Joyner and Cas Laskowski (Mountain View, CA: Pressbooks (2021): 6. HeinOnline.
6. Shamika Dalton, Gail Mathapo, and Endia Sowers-Paige, "Navigating Law Librarianship While Black: A Week in the Life of a Black Female Law Librarian." *Law Library Journal*, vol. 110, no. 3 (2018): 430.
7. Law Librarian Demographics and Statistics in the US. Zippia.com/law-librarian-jobs/demographics/.
8. See Nichelle Perry, "Leader Profile: Promoting Diversity & Inclusion within the Profession." *AALL Spectrum*, vol. 25, no. 4 (March/April 2021): 24–27.

# 5.3

## *Getting the Job*

BLACK LIBRARIANS IN ACADEMIC LIBRARIES

Rashida Scott Blades and Genevia Chamblee-Smith

The authors of this chapter have experience in different careers and have acquired several librarian positions in the past five years. They strive to "Blacken knowledge" when navigating graduate school and library work because the redlining of information remains in their education;[1] they pass along their knowledge and approach to reach those who need it in a country where the number of Black librarians is detrimentally low.

Black librarians are intentional about creating access to information to address social issues and make a positive impact on their communities. We work for the benefit of the diverse community that encompasses the Black population in the United States. No matter the specialty, we bring the knowledge of our ancestors and elders to our work. This is the Black librarian's special relationship to our libraries. Only 4 percent of all librarians in the United States are Black and this percentage has not increased in decades. E. J. Josey created the Black Caucus of the American Library Association (BCALA) in 1970 to uphold ALA's commitment to supporting Black librarians, which upholds the values of all librarians.[2] However, what we have witnessed is other Black librarians put in overtime to uplift each other. While there are new technologies that allow us to participate in this work, the methods for the twenty-first-century librarian remain largely the same. We position mentoring, interview scheduling, presentation, red flags, green flags, saying yes, the learning curve, and key terms as essential to preparing ourselves for the world of academic librarianship.

The twenty-first-century librarians are seeing many of the same issues our elders fought against. The banning of books by Black authors as described by Stephen Hall; abolishing critical race theory as defined by Richard Delgado and Jean Stefancic; and the dilution of diversity, equity, and inclusion initiatives reflected on by Kate McGee, and affirmative action as written by Elie Mystal are affecting all of us right now.[3] The information presented in this chapter was shared with us by experienced librarians and developed along our personal job search journeys. This is from the perspective of the interviewees: academic librarians in research, instruction, and outreach focus.

## OUR EXPERIENCE

Both their paths to obtaining an MLIS and librarian position began as library staff.

Rashida left a career in finance to pursue something more fulfilling. Through online career research she found that librarianship would perfectly combine her many interests: business, sustainability, art, film, writing, history, books among others. However, you never know what a job will be like until you get there. Rashida began her library career as a part-time library assistant at a public library then soon obtained a full-time position. This process was more competitive than she realized as the end goal of many staff is a full-time staff position. It was important to work in a library before putting in the labor to apply and take classes while continuing to work full time. The following year she was accepted into the University of Arizona iSchool (UA).

It took three years to graduate. In her last year, Rashida left the public library to pursue academic librarianship as a graduate assistant (GA) at Arizona State University (ASU), by way of the Knowledge River (KR) Scholarship Program at the University of Arizona (Knowledge River). KR also paid tuition and included Rashida in a cohort of other students where she no longer felt alone in her struggle to graduate during a global pandemic. While working as a GA, she met with an amazing Black librarian who was tasked with creating a Black library and archive collection on her own. Rashida wanted to help, and together they pushed to create a position where Rashida worked as an intern in Black Collections her last semester. After graduating, she interned at Fidelity Investments to experience corporate librarianship. Librarians become enthusiastic about sharing their experience and project with students. She took advantage of those opportunities by meeting several librarians at every library she worked at or volunteered. In turn they supported her, shared institutional knowledge, and shared opportunities with her that contributed to success in the job market. Rashida took all of her experiences toward her goal of becoming a business librarian. Rashida chose the business subject because of her background in business sustainability and finance. However, most business librarians do not have any background in business. During her last semester and the following summer, she applied for about ten jobs and received interviews for seven of them. After the first phone interview, she declined the second due to low salary ranges and/or daily task arrangement. She received offers from the four institutions where she had second interviews. Due to COVID-19, only one interview was in-person, all others were on Zoom.

Genevia worked as a library paraprofessional in special and academic libraries for ten years before pursuing a master's degree in library science. Although she worked in technical services with the focus on interlibrary loan (ILL) and cataloging, most of her jobs were located in Washington, DC. It was not mandatory to get a master's degree in library science because Washington, DC, salaries for paraprofessionals could pay close to what a degreed librarian would make. She was committed to the library profession but could not afford the tuition. As the world shut down in mid-March 2020 because of COVID-19, Genevia's academic library job in Tennessee was not renewed. The We Here community on social media is a great source to get library news. Someone posted an announcement that their school was offering a paid graduate research assistant (GRA) position with free tuition and a monthly stipend for remote work. Genevia was very motivated to apply because she had a good library experience. As the pandemic shut everything down, she decided to risk going back to school to do the thing she really wanted. North Carolina Central University is the only operating Historically Black College and University (HBCU) with so much history. The archives were always something that Genevia was curious about. After taking the Community Archives course, Genevia knew this was an area to focus on. The classes were vigorous and small. The synchronous and remote approach was the best part about the program.

It took Genevia two years to finish the program going full time and working two part-time jobs. Before graduation, Genevia got hired with the University of Missouri, Kansas City (UMKC) as a Digital Projects Fellow. The job was interesting and remote. Her responsibilities included reviewing ten thousand items in the Islandora collection to check for errors and mistakes. Working with a team of four people felt like they were making progress in the six-month time frame.

## MENTORSHIP IN COMMUNITY

To be successful, you should not try to do it by yourself. The retention of Black students in an iSchool is a national challenge. Rashida and Genevia have discovered that geographic location, peer mentoring, and a wellness plan are essential to completing the MLIS degree. They were not prepared for many of these challenges and unfortunately had to learn them through trial and error.

Mentorship and community is when you get through the entire process and build up the confidence to push through. Rashida and Genevia had several mentorship programs and attended community events. Pairing a tenured librarian with an early career librarian, peer-to-peer mentoring is just as essential. Finding community with other librarians who have the same passion and goals of supporting our community creates an affirmative space for finding mentors who will help you through your journey of iSchool and job searching.[4] There are several scholarship opportunities on the national level such as Spectrum Scholarship, and the American Library Association, there are also state level scholarships, and those with the Black Caucus of the American Library Association (BCALA). The community of librarians and MLIS students help you discover the plethora of resources available to assist you financially and mentally throughout your career.

Rashida and Genevia sought refuge in the BCALA and its Leadership Institute and Breaking Barriers program for MLIS students. Refuge from people who do not value the history, perspectives, and diversity of the work within Black Librarianship. There were a series of virtual meetings and an in-person meeting to discover the needs and issues of Black graduate students. Rashida and Genevia met at the Breaking Barriers virtual meeting. Rashida was a recipient of the Knowledge River Scholarship Program at the University of Arizona.[5] This scholarship program focuses on ethnic and cultural awareness and respect as a core goal. It works to inform the LIS field on the needs, issues, and impact of diversity through research and public information. Genevia was a recipient of the Association of Research Libraries Kaleidoscope Scholarship[6] that involved tuition support, virtual education sessions, attendance to the ARL Annual Symposium, an ARL member site visit, two-year formal mentorship, and professional development support. This program allowed for scholars to build community and develop relationships.

These official programs that received grant funding not only paid for Rashida's and Genevia's participation in these programs but provided a larger network of librarians who share similar interests and goals. The low percentage of Black librarians equates to few tenured and experienced librarians mentoring many LIS students. This creates an imbalance between the time amazing mentors can give to mentees. It is also why peer mentorship is equally valuable.

Our peers have a range of experiences and interests that provide a unique outlook on how they approach librarianship. Peers can combine the wisdom gathered in their separate jobs, previous careers, and what is learned throughout the different MLIS programs. With peers there can be less fear of judgment, which is followed by an increased level of transparency. Traditional and peer mentorship with others outside of your current library system is also beneficial. You get to learn how things operate at other libraries. Every library is different. They can share items to consider that are typically done differently at your library. You can picture creative solutions to various challenges. Another example of peer mentoring involved Genevia becoming active in the North Carolina Central University's Eagle's Memories Student Chapter of Society of American Archivists during her last year in school. She was responsible for getting practitioner archivists to host a session related to learning about their jobs in different sectors and how to get hired using a cover letter. Some advice for graduate students is if you see a need, be the solution. If a solution does not exist, use your librarian/archival skills to be the resource.

While having mentors outside of your library removes some of the manager-employee relationship, it is also important to reach out to the librarians in proximity. This does not need to become a formal interview—I have not met any librarian who does not want to talk about their work and how they contribute to this profession. These librarians who have been working within your organization have institutional knowledge that have explained how to navigate the politics and intricacies of our profession.

**INTERVIEW PREP**

There are many tips online about how to prepare for an academic library interview, this is unique to the twenty-first century. The online presence of every library makes it easier for us to make our case for being the perfect fit for that specific organization. We can also determine whether the library is a good fit for us. After you have submitted your CV, cover letter, DEI statement, you may get an email inviting you to interview. The effort you put forward in preparing for the interview shows what effort you will bring to this role when hired.

Study the university and library's strategic plan. The strategic plan is "used to prioritize efforts, effectively allocate resources, align shareholders and employees on the organization's goals, and ensure those goals are backed by data and sound reasoning."[7] Learn if their priorities align with yours.

It was important to us to work for a student- and community-focused organization with a diverse BIPOC student population. The work of librarians at some universities requires locating specific sources for professors and graduate students. If educating people about how to think critically about the information we have access to is a goal, it should be clearly stated in the strategic plan. Consider why you want to be a librarian.

Outside of the strategic plan, the university website hides much more information. It feels like it's hiding because it takes time to locate the details about this library that makes it different. It's important to take that time to discover it. Place the links to interesting information in a document for easy reference. If there are specific subjects you are interested in or expected to partner with, investigate some of the centers/organizations and professors across campus. Create a short list of maybe five people or centers and describe how you might collaborate and develop relationships with them. Begin with a Black resource center and Black student organizations. If you are applying for a subject librarian position, find the student associations that work with students in that subject area. The specific names of these centers and associations differ across different campuses, but they do exist. There are typically the general Black student union, a business association, engineering student association, creative writing student association, and many more that are run by and for Black students in undergraduate and graduate programs. There are also associations for Black faculty to create a safe space for us to come together. If these do not exist at the university you are applying for, reconsider your application. It is also helpful to apply this same approach to all organizations that support BIPOC and 2SLGBTQIA+ students across campus.

Be prepared to explain your values and unique approach to librarianship in a way that aligns with the library you are interviewing with. Your understanding of Black history in this country in relation to our education system provides needed context for why we do what we do. How would you define librarianship? What articles, authors, librarians, podcasts, blogs, books, inspire you? How do you consider culturally specific key terms in advanced search techniques? What databases have you used that contain these results? How do you provide a critical lens to the results? Typically, when we search for an article or dataset, white authors are the first to populate the results. It takes more time to find Black authors who research any subject. Take cues from the Black Women Collective by "centering Black women's ideas and intellectual contributions" and consider exploited labor.[8]

## THE INTERVIEW

Librarians are leaders. When describing your experience, begin with how you led a project or portion of a project. The phone and in-person interview will have three to five people on a panel asking questions.

The first interview is a fifteen- to thirty-minute phone interview. You will be asked the five standard behavioral interview questions. Question examples are listed on many library blogs across the internet. The arrangement of the questions can vary but the result remains the same. Having a few examples for each of these scenarios will have you overly prepared for any question they give you.

Then you are asked to do a one- or two-day in-person interview. You can decide if after the first interview whether it is worth your time moving forward with the second interview. Have responses ready for a time you recognized a gap or missing piece in a process and how you addressed it. Why do you want to work for that specific library? How do you prioritize projects? How did you handle a difficult situation? Demonstrate how you had to learn a new skill and the steps you took to become proficient at it. What are examples of these skills?

Be prepared to answer questions using specific examples from personal experience using the STAR method.[9] Rashida learned about the STAR method in business school, and it has proved to work in interviews in any industry. "STAR" is an acronym for Situation, Task, Action, Result. Explain the *situation* so the interview panel understands the context behind this specific project. The *task* explains the specific challenges this project is addressing. The *action* describes the actions and skills you took to lead in completing those tasks. *Results* explain the outcomes spawned by your actions. Using this method ensures that you are answering every part of the question and including only important details. This prevents you from rambling on or overexplaining. Be specific. For example, if you worked on a collection development project and moved books from one section of the library to another for weeding or shifting, explain why this was necessary (Situation). How you determined what should be moved and how. In other words, what criteria did you develop (Task)? How did you physically move the items, how did you need to modify or adapt to complete tasks, and what other departments did you have to work with (Action)? How many items were moved within what period of time (Result)? How does all of this work contribute to supporting BIPOC communities that enter your library?

## THE LEARNING CURVE

A steep learning curve is defined as a short period of time that a person has to learn a new skill or knowledge.[10] Some would argue that library school can be difficult for people who have never worked in a library. Or there are some courses that require a student to put in more time to study definitions and concepts. Most library schools require graduate students to have an internship so that they can take the book knowledge and have an experiential learning experience by learning new concepts at the internship. Although the library degree is considered terminal, many library schools offer certificates in areas such as children librarianship, technical services, UX learning, and cataloging. Library Juice Academy and Society of American Archivists offer stand-alone courses and certificates.

Genevia's personal strategy for tackling steep learning curves is to pursue part-time jobs that allow one to develop more knowledge related to libraries. Genevia put this strategy to use by working part time as an adjunct instructor at East Carolina University. It was a great experience working with students and providing support with assignments. It was a rewarding experience as an instructor to watch students discover firsthand experience with basic cataloging principles. Another example of lowering learning curves is to pursue job opportunities where you will need to learn one or two new skills on the job. Genevia chose to pursue a diversity resident librarian position after graduation because she had limited exposure to working in archives. She would be able to learn, discover, and pursue knowledge in a reasonable time frame. Having a steep learning curve to archives and liaison librarianship was positive, which meant that she would complete projects that demonstrate mastery in these areas.

## WHEN TO WALK AWAY

The semester before graduation is a crucial time for all library graduate students. It's a time to focus on what your future library job will look like and to actively apply for jobs. Remember, as libraries interview you, you are also interviewing them. It's important to make a list of jobs that you are interested in and to make time to follow application directions. It is also important to contact your school in advance and ask them to send out copies of your transcripts after you receive your diploma. There are some institutions that request an unofficial transcript as part of the application. I also advise you to order one for your personal records. As you prepare for the interview, please look at the library's website and take notice of the entire library staff. It is also helpful to try and find out about the reputation of a library and its leadership. As for how to determine if a company/institution has red flags, notice if the job description is very vague, if the main interviewer does not appear to be engaging with you, and if you are asked inappropriate questions (i.e., related to race, age, gender, marital status, and religion).[11]

As you interview with potential employers, always have one to two questions to ask them. If the supervisor for the job is on the hiring committee, you can direct questions to them. Example questions can be "How do you describe your management style?" "What are the two main priorities for the person selected for this role?" "How do you describe the work culture?" It can be very telling if no one on the hiring committee answers questions directly. Also, be very familiar with the job posting and ask about a specific job responsibility. This shows the hiring committee that you are very interested in the position. If the institution does not have a strategic plan or a committee on diversity, please ask about it. Depending on what they say will determine if you want to work there. Each of us have specific things we want out of a job, especially as a new graduate. Genevia and I discuss mentorship, instruction practices, faculty connections that you can continue, and strategies they employ to build a better library. Be generous with yourself and recognize that you won't know what it's like working at an institution until you are actually there.

## NOTES

1. Christina Sharpe, *In the Wake: On Blackness and Being* (Durham, NC: Duke University Press, 2016), ProQuest Ebook Central, https://ebookcentral.proquest.com/lib/fullerton/detail.action?docID=4717126.
2. Renate Chancellor, *E. J. Josey: Transformational Leader of the Modern Library Profession* (Lanham, MD: Rowman & Littlefield, 2020); "About BCALA," The Black Caucus of the American Library Association, 2023, https://www.bcala.org/about-bcala.
3. Stephen G. Hall, "Black Librarianship Matters: The Long History of Banned Books," The Good Men Project, July 16, 2023, https://goodmenproject.com/featured-content/black-librarianship-matters-the-long-history-of-book-bans-kpkn/; Richard Delgado and Jean Stefancic, *Critical Race Theory: An Introduction*, 2nd ed. (New York: New York University Press, 2012); Kate McGee, "Texas Lawmakers Find Consensus on Bill Banning Diversity, Equity and Inclusion Offices in Public Universities," *The Texas Tribune*, May 27, 2023, https://www.texastribune.org/2023/05/27/texas-university-diversity-equity-inclusion-dei-bill-conference/; Elie Mystal, "The Supreme Court Has Killed Affirmative Action. Mediocre Whites Can Rest Easier," *The Nation*, June 29, 2023, https://www.thenation.com/article/society/supreme-court-killed-affirmative-action/.
4. Eboni Johnson, *Librarian as Mentor: Grow, Discover, Inspire* (Boston, MA: Mission Bell Media, 2017).
5. Knowledge River, 2023, https://ischool.arizona.edu/kr-circle-friends.
6. "Kaleidoscope Program Components," Association of Research Libraries, 2023, https://www.arl.org/kp-program-components.
7. Catherine Cote, "Why Is Strategic Planning Important?" Harvard Business School Online, October 6, 2023, https://online.hbs.edu/blog/post/why-is-strategic-planning-important.
8. *Cite Black Women: A Critical Praxis*, 2023, https://www.citeblackwomencollective.org/our-praxis.html; Christen A. Smith, *Cite Black Women: A Critical Praxis*, December 21, 2018, https://www.citeblackwomencollective.org/our-praxis.html.
9. Using the Star Method for Your Next Behavioral Interview, https://capd.mit.edu/resources/the-star-method-for-behavioral-interviews.
10. Iwona Adamska, "What Is a Steep Learning Curve? Understanding the Challenges and Strategies for Success." Samelane, May 12, 2023, https://samelane.com/blog/what-is-a-steep-learning-curve/; *Merriam-Webster Dictionary*, https://www.merriam-webster.com/dictionary/pedagogy#dictionary-entry-1.
11. Hunter International, https://www.hirerecruiting.com.

## WORKS CITED

"About BCALA." The Black Caucus of the American Library Association, 2023. https://www.bcala.org/about-bcala.

Adamska, Iwona. "What Is a Steep Learning Curve? Understanding the Challenges and Strategies for Success." Samelane, May 12, 2023. https://samelane.com/blog/what-is-a-steep-learning-curve/.

Chancellor, Renate. *E. J. Josey: Transformational Leader of the Modern Library Profession*. Lanham, MD: Rowman & Littlefield, 2020.

Champine, Robey B., Erin E. Hoffman, Samantha L. Matlin, Michael J. Strambler, and Jacob Kraemer Tebes. "'What Does It Mean to Be Trauma-Informed?': A Mixed-Methods Study of a Trauma-Informed Community Initiative." *Journal of Child and Family Studies*, 31, no. 2 (2022): 459-72. https://doi.org/10.1007/s10826-021-02195-9.

*Cite Black Women: A Critical Praxis*, 2023. https://www.citeblackwomencollective.org/our-praxis.html.

Cote, Catherine. "Why Is Strategic Planning Important?" Harvard Business School Online, October 6, 2023. https://online.hbs.edu/blog/post/why-is-strategic-planning-important.

Delgado, Richard, and Jean Stefancic. *Critical Race Theory: An Introduction*. 2nd ed. New York: New York University Press, 2012.

Hall, Stephen G. "Black Librarianship Matters: The Long History of Banned Books." The Good Men Project, July 16, 2023. https://goodmenproject.com/featured-content/black-librarianship-matters-the-long-history-of-book-bans-kpkn/.

Johnson, Eboni. *Librarian as Mentor: Grow, Discover, Inspire*. Boston, MA: Mission Bell Media, 2017.

"Kaleidoscope Program Components." Association of Research Libraries, 2023. https://www.arl.org/kp-program-components.

Knowledge River, 2023. https://ischool.arizona.edu/kr-circle-friends.

McGee, Kate. "Texas Lawmakers Find Consensus on Bill Banning Diversity, Equity and Inclusion Offices in Public Universities." *The Texas Tribune*, May 27, 2023. https://www.texastribune.org/2023/05/27/texas-university-diversity-equity-inclusion-dei-bill-conference/.

*Merriam-Webster Dictionary*. https://www.merriam-webster.com/dictionary/pedagogy#dictionary-entry-1.

Mystal, Elie. "The Supreme Court Has Killed Affirmative Action. Mediocre Whites Can Rest Easier." *The Nation*, June 29, 2023. https://www.thenation.com/article/society/supreme-court-killed-affirmative-action/.

Sharpe, Christina. *In the Wake: On Blackness and Being*. Durham, NC: Duke University Press, 2016. ProQuest Ebook Central. https://ebookcentral.proquest.com/lib/fullerton/detail.action?docID=4717126.

Smith, Christen A. *Cite Black Women: A Critical Praxis*, December 21, 2018. https://www.citeblackwomencollective.org/our-praxis.html.

Using the Star Method for Your Next Behavioral Interview. https://capd.mit.edu/resources/the-star-method-for-behavioral-interviews/.

# Chapter 6
# Public Libraries

## 6.1

### The Importance of Public Library Youth Services in the Community

Alleta Seales

Maureen Hartman, in her article titled "Out of School and In the Library: Connecting with Resources in the Out of School Time (OST) Field," states youth come to the library after school looking for available computers, to socialize with their friends, and to participate in programs that support their formal education. They also come to wait for their parents to pick them up. Hartman identifies the public library's role as an out-of-school resource; a place where youth have access to technology, an opportunity to learn new skills, "build relationships, and make a difference—all facilitated by a caring, trained adult." Part of the mission of children's and youth services in all public libraries is to serve the needs of school-age children.[1]

I have worked as a library support staff member coordinating an after-school program in the public library. After retirement from the New York City Department of Education, I volunteered in after-school programs as a "homework helper," assisting children with their homework assignments. I'm totally committed to public library services to the community. A homework helper is a paid, trained library support staff worker who assists children with their homework assignments. Volunteers and high school students also serve as homework helpers.

**HISTORY OF HOMEWORK HELP CENTERS**

Intner, in her book titled *Homework Help from the Library: In Person and Online*, credits Cindy Mediavilla's book *Creating the Full-Service Homework Center in Your Library* as "the quintessential guide to the practicalities of setting up a formal homework help center to provide one-on-one homework assistance to student patrons."[2] Librarian and lecturer, Cindy Mediavilla defines a homework help center as "a program dedicated to meeting the curricular needs of students by providing

- Staff or volunteers who are trained to assist students with their homework,
- Space designated for student use during specific days and times, and
- A multiformat collection of materials related to the curricular needs of students."[3]

But what is the history of homework help centers in public libraries? In the 1960s, many libraries across the United States refused to help children with their homework. The thinking was that homework help was the responsibility of the school media library and the public library should not provide that service. Mediavilla states that when she was a young public librarian, she was admonished for providing homework assistance. She was told, "Homework assistance is the purview of the school librarian."[4]

The arguments opposing public library homework assistance for youth changed after the Carnegie Report and due to the success of many after-school homework help programs in public libraries. The Carnegie Council on Adolescent Development indicated that youth needed support after school in order to stay out of trouble. Therefore, the Carnegie Group recommended community after-school programs as a safety net.[5]

By 1989, the Latchkey Enrichment Program at the Queens Borough Public Library in New York was developed through the Library Services and Construction Act (LSCA) grant. The grant funds were used to begin a program in six branches reporting the most severe problems with "latchkey children"—unattended children in the library after school for an extended period of time. The guidelines of the grant were: hire one or two local adults by the hour to offer basic homework help and supervise the recreational side of the program; schedule additional after-school performances by storytellers; craftspeople; science demonstrations and other programmers; order new reference materials; circulate curriculum support books; provide a variety of box games; craft supplies and realia for the children to use after school in the library.

In 1991, librarian Rosellen Brewer established a homework help center in the Seaside branch of the Monterey County Free Libraries in California. With commitment and a donation of $5,000, the Seaside Homework Help Center was opened. She states, "When the center opened, we discovered that many of the students dropping in also needed one-on-one help with math or reading."[6] Therefore, she found volunteer tutors by advertising in the local newspaper and by word of mouth to assist the children in reading and math. Robert Reagan describes how the Los Angeles Public Library (LAPL) gets sponsors for its after-school homework centers. Politicians, library sponsors, and the media realize that homework centers provide direct services to youth. Therefore, the LAPL has been able to get funding for the "newest and best computer equipment available" by highlighting the work they do in their after-school homework centers.[7]

In the article, "Why Library Homework Centers Extend Society's Safety Net," Cindy Mediavilla observed ad photographed library homework help centers across the United States. She concluded that after-school homework help centers provide children with a safe place to be; children develop a relationship with caring adults; children develop stronger social skills; and children receive assistance with homework and work done in class. Partnerships are developed with families, schools, and the community as a result of homework help centers. Additionally, enriching learning activities are offered in some homework programs.[8]

An evaluation of homework help centers is described in Celia Huffman's and Robert J. Rua's article titled "Measuring the Effectiveness of Homework Centers in Libraries." In 2003, the Cuyahoga County Public Library's Maple Heights Branch in Ohio established the Homework Center. The model of homework time, reading time, and educational activities was used. Program attendance was tracked, and the effectiveness of the program was determined by having the parents/guardians of participants fill out exit survey forms. This study followed the pre-experimental research design of one group getting a pretest and posttest. For example, the parents/guardians were given a survey prior to their children entering the Homework Center program. After attending the Homework Center, the parents were given the same survey. However, the exit survey included the phrase, "Since coming to the Homework Center" so that the responses would reflect the child's status after receiving assistance in the Homework Center.

Huffman and Rua had parents/guardians indicate reasons for their child attending the Homework Center at the library. The top reason for parents sending their children to the Cuyahoga County library homework center: to do their homework (95%).[9]

The March/April 2006 edition of Public Libraries identifies all thirteen of the Johnson County Library Locations in Shawnee Mission, Kansas, as having homework-help programs. It is stated in the article that there are volunteer community-trained homework coaches and library staff who provide help with homework. The libraries provide the space and library resources for students to complete their homework.[10]

In addition to homework-help programs, some libraries are providing mentoring and counseling programs for children with the help of youth counselors. The Queens Public Library opened its Queens Library for Teens in December 2007.[11] The teen library offers materials and programs geared toward teens and is staffed with youth counselors. The Queens Public Library describes a youth counselor as someone who mentors and counsels teens during out-of-school hours. Additionally, the youth counselor "facilitates programs with a focus on socio-emotional wellness, relationships, arts and culture, career exploration and planning."[12] Qualifications for the youth counselor position posted by the Queens Public Library are:

> Bachelor's degree in education, Social Work, Sociology, Psychology, or related field required with a minimum of two years of experience in implementing interactive youth programs or a minimum of 60 college credits, in a related field, with a minimum of three years of experience in implementing interactive youth programs required.... Must have excellent attention to detail and familiarity with diverse customers' needs.

The research clearly indicates that after-school programs staffed by a librarian, library support staff and focusing on homework help centers with caring, trained adults and or volunteers from the community benefit children. Parents or guardians from various communities have also indicated that the top reason they send their children to the library after school is to do their homework and to get the help needed to do homework. It is imperative that libraries continue to support and sustain after-school programs to foster a better future for the youth in the communities they serve.

**NOTES**

1. Maureen Hartman, "Out of School and in the Library: Connecting with Resources in the Out of School Time (OST) Field," *Young Adult Library Services*, 9 no. 4 (2011): 10–12.
2. Carol Intner, *Homework Help from the Library: In Person and Online* (Chicago: American Library Association, 2011).

3. Cindy Mediavilla, *Creating the Full-Service Homework Center in Your Library* (Chicago: American Library Association, 2001).
4. Ibid.
5. Carnegie Council on Adolescent Development, *Greater Transition: Preparing Adolescents for a New Century: Concluding Report* (New York: Carnegie Corporation of New York, 1995).
6. Rosellen Brewer, "Help Youth at Risk: A Case for Starting a Public Library Homework Center," *Public Libraries*, 31, no. 4 (2011): 208–212.
7. Susan Woodward, "Briefly: Education: Library Opens Homework Center," *Los Angeles Times,* 23 June 1994, https://www.latimes.com/archives/la-xpm-1994-06-23-cb-7345-story.html.
8. Cindy Mediavilla, "Why Library Homework Centers Extend Society's Safety Net," *American Libraries*, 32, no. 11 (2001): 40–42.
9. Celia Huffman and Robert J. Rua, "Measuring the Effectiveness of Homework Centers in Libraries," *Children & Libraries*, 6, no. 3 (2008): 25.
10. Jennifer Ries-Taggart, "Tales from the Front," *Public Libraries*, 45, no. 2 (2006): 16–18.
11. Maureen O'Connor and Brian Kenney, "Make It New: The Queens Library for Teens and Dallas's Bookmarks," *School Library Journal*, 1 July 2008, https://www.slj.com/story/make-it-new-the-queens-library-for-teens-and-dallass-bookmarks.
12. "Job Posting for Part-Time Youth Counselor Job at Queens Public Library," *Salary.com*, 13 January 2023, https://www.salary.com/job/queens-public-library/part-time-youth-counselor/j202301131744506224296.

## WORKS CITED

Brewer, Rosellen. "Help Youth at Risk: A Case for Starting a Public Library Homework Center." *Public Libraries*, 31, no. 4 (2011): 208–212.

Carnegie Council on Adolescent Development. *Greater Transition: Preparing Adolescents for a New Century: Concluding Report.* New York: Carnegie Corporation of New York, 1995.

Hartman, Maureen. "Out of School and in the Library: Connecting with Resources in the Out of School Time (OST) Field." *Young Adult Library Services*, 9 no. 4 (2011): 10–12.

Huffman, Celia, and Robert J. Rua. "Measuring the Effectiveness of Homework Centers in Libraries." *Children & Libraries*, 6, no. 3 (2008): 25.

Intner, Carol. *Homework Help from the Library: In Person and Online.* Chicago: American Library Association, 2011.

"Job Posting for Part-Time Youth Counselor Job at Queens Public Library." *Salary.com*, 13 January 2023. https://www.salary.com/job/queens-public-library/part-time-youth-counselor/j202301131744506224296.

Mediavilla, Cindy. *Creating the Full-Service Homework Center in Your Library.* Chicago: American Library Association, 2001.

Mediavilla, Cindy. "Why Library Homework Centers Extend Society's Safety Net." *American Libraries*, 32, no. 11 (2001): 40–42.

O'Connor, Maureen, and Brian Kenney. "Make It New: The Queens Library for Teens and Dallas's Bookmarks." *School Library Journal*, 1 July 2008. https://www.slj.com/story/make-it-new-the-queens-library-for-teens-and-dallass-bookmarks.

Ries-Taggart, Jennifer. "Tales from the Front." *Public Libraries*, 45, no. 2 (2006): 16–18.

Woodward, Susan. "Briefly: Education: Library Opens Homework Center." *Los Angeles Times,* 23 June 1994. https://www.latimes.com/archives/la-xpm-1994-06-23-cb-7345-story.html.

---

# 6.2

## *Tribute*

MY NONTRADITIONAL JOURNEY IN LIBRARIANSHIP

Andrew P. Jackson (Sekou Molefi Baako)

The American Library Association cited libraries and librarians as *change agents*, which transform lives and the communities they serve. When I look back on my adult life, I see the Queens Public Library (QPL), the Langston Hughes Community Library and Cultural Center (LHCL&CC), and my undergrad years at York College (CUNY) as my *change agents*, for they surely had a major impact on my professional and personal growth.

Librarianship gave me direction and purpose that allowed me to grow as a cultural advocate. In my youth, I never considered librarianship a career goal. In hindsight, I realize all my earlier experiences prepared me for my directorship and responsibilities at Langston Hughes. I can think of no more rewarding profession than that of a librarian. No better place to work than the library.

In 2016, I retired as executive director at Langston Hughes after thirty-six years. Prior to my appointment in 1980, I served four years in the United States Air Force as an administrative specialist and was honorably discharged in 1968 as a staff sergeant (E-5). After my discharge, I held human resource positions with New York City's Human Resources Administration and Agency for Child Development through 1976. Each served me well with invaluable work experience, improved skills, and managerial development. During my years in human resources, I attended evening classes at Baruch College (CUNY) majoring in business administration. The combined work experience and academic course work provided the perfect germinating experience for me to learn and grow. Afterward, I worked in sales and customer service positions at a large Chevrolet dealership in Northern California for a few years. Here I gained invaluable customer service experience. Upon my return to New York City and a period of job searching, a golden opportunity was offered to me, encouraging me to apply for an assistant supervisor opening at our local Langston Hughes Community Library and Cultural Center of the Queens Borough Public Library.

The unique history of LHCL&CC began in the mid-1960s with residents of Corona-East Elmhurst in Queens County. Residents believed they needed a *community library* that focused on The Black Experience where their children could learn about their history and culture. Community control was one of the new strategies of Mayor Lindsay's Anti-Poverty Program, giving a voice to local neighborhoods on needed services. Out of this came Community Corporations in each of the five boroughs comprised of local leaders and visionaries. As a result, federal, state, and city funding allowed for the creation of day care, family day care, and Head Start programs; community planning boards; and local health centers. The concept of community control had not reached public libraries, and the Langston Hughes library proposal would open that door.

This vision of a Black heritage library was presented to Harold Tucker, director of Queens Borough Public Library, who realized the borough's African American population was indeed underserved and as far as Black heritage materials and programs, unserved. This need fit into the library's overall mission. This new library would serve as the host site for Queens County's Black Heritage Reference Center with an extensive, in-depth *circulating* collection of print and nonprint materials (record albums, cassette tapes, and later VHS tapes and DVDs), unlike Harlem's Schomburg Center for Research in Black Culture that housed *noncirculating* research and reference materials. Our service "community" was not solely Corona-East Elmhurst, but the entire borough. Named for the Harlem poet because of his stature at that time and the scope and breadth of his literary works, Langston Hughes Community Library was the first public institution named for Hughes. This project fit the guidelines of available federal dollars in 1968 through the Library Services and Construction Act (LSCA), Title I and was founded as a *federally funded special project* from 1969 to 1987.

Under the auspices of the Queens Borough Public Library, a board of directors of the newly formed nonprofit, tax exempt community-based organization, Library Action Committee of Corona-East Elmhurst, Inc. (LAC), operated and managed the day-to-day operations of Langston Hughes. During this eighteen-year period, the LAC board was authorized to hire Corona-East Elmhurst residents to fill staff positions. Queens Library assigned senior librarian Evelyn Hall to develop the children's, young adult, and adult collections. Within a decade, librarian Rodney Lee (also from the community) was appointed curator, Black Heritage, a position funded through a State Assembly grant focused on building our Black heritage collections.

In August 1980, I was offered the assistant manager position at Langston Hughes. As a lifelong resident of the community, my youth activism and business background were attractive to the board and deemed beneficial to the growth and development of their library although I had no prior library experience.

One unique feature of the Langston Hughes Library Center as a *special project* was that its manager was not required to be an MLS-degreed librarian but a local resident who possessed skills that would benefit and enhance the library. Six months after my appointment, Library Manager Charlyne Gadsden (also a local resident) took a leave of absence due to a family emergency. I served as acting manager while a search was conducted and was appointed supervisor by the board in January 1981 based on my performance and vision for the future. As a cultural institution, Langston Hughes Community Library offered a blend of programs and services designed to meet the educational, cultural, informational, and recreational interests and needs of residents of all ages.

In 1983, I enrolled in the evening/weekend program at York College (CUNY), located in South Queens, completing my BS degree in business administration in 1990. I considered graduate studies in Black Studies; however, with encouragement from my mentor, Dr. E. J. Josey, I enrolled in the evening program at Queens College's Graduate School of Library and Information Studies (CUNY) in 1993, earning my MLS degree in 1996. In addition to developing practical skills and an understanding of librarianship as a profession, I gained a greater respect for the role and mission of libraries and the librarian as change agent in the lives of library users and for the community at large.

Queens Library provided the autonomy, flexibility, and opportunity to perform extensive outreach. Representing Queens Library, this outreach across the city gave greater public exposure to our extensive Black Heritage collections and the variety of programming including workshops in dance, theater arts, photography, creative writing, video, journalism, and visual arts. I promoted librarianship at public school career days as well as at colleges/universities; participated in programs at city, state, and federal agencies and police and fire department Black history and Kwanzaa programs; and correctional facilities. Around the neighborhood, I spoke at civic and community meetings and churches.

Through ongoing visibility and exposure came invitations to serve on boards of directors at Queens Public Television (QPTV) and The Renaissance Charter School; on community advisory boards of Elmhurst Hospital Center, the Lewis H. Latimer Museum and Louis Armstrong House Museum and Archives; the York College President's Advisory Council; Queens College Arts Advisory Council and cochaired the Queens Borough President's African American Heritage Committee. Each opportunity allowed my voice as a librarian to be heard and represented.

Nationally, I carried the name and reputation of Queens Library and Langston Hughes Library Center to conferences and meetings and served on committees and boards. My active participation in the Black Caucus of the American Library Association, Inc. (BCALA) led to my election as vice president, president-elect, president, and past president from 2002 through 2008 and the executive board through 2016. When ALA scheduled the Annual Martin Luther King Jr. Celebration in their Mid-Winter schedule in 2000, Satia Marshall Orange and Virginia Bradley Moore recruited me. When they retired a few years later, LaJuan Pringle and I became cochairs, and we continue to plan this special event to this day.

The experience and knowledge I gained creating library programs, extensive outreach, and attending design meetings for a new Langston Hughes building led to invitations to serve as library consultant/advisor to libraries in South Sarasota, Florida; Raleigh-Durham and Greensboro, North Carolina; and Roosevelt and Wyandanch Libraries on Long Island, New York.

Directly responsible for the Langston Hughes Cultural Arts Program (CAP), I created all-day cultural celebrations that attracted audiences across the city, from Long Island, Westchester County, New Jersey, and Connecticut. Our first annual Langston Hughes Kwanzaa Celebration was in December 1985, followed by the annual Langston Hughes Celebration in February 1986 featuring live music performances, dance presentations, film screenings, artist exhibitions, poetry and literature readings, craft fairs, and cultural ceremonies. The Langston Hughes Film Series featured independent films and videos, discussions with filmmakers and directors, and highlighted the resources from our circulating VHS and DVD collection. In November 1987, we hosted our annual Langston Hughes Literary Arts Festival highlighting well-known literary figures like Sonia Sanchez and Walter Mosley with up-and-coming poets and writers, panel discussions, and closed with live musical performances.

Between 1991 and 1999, I hosted Open Mic Night on the third Thursday of each month. Our cultural arts calendar drew large audiences and developed a following. In spring and summer months we hosted outdoor craft fairs along our sidewalk that grew into street fairs. On the first Saturday in June, the Annual East Elmhurst-Corona Family Day was an all-day outdoor community "reunion" at a local school playground featuring craft and food vendors, basketball and baseball competition, live cultural entertainment, and activities for all ages. Cosponsored by City Council Member Helen Marshall, Assemblyman Jeff Aubry, and the Langston Hughes Community Library, this was a collaborative community effort with volunteer participation from local civic and political organizations, neighborhood churches, and community groups.

The primary responsibility of the executive director was preparation and submission of grants to the State Department of Education, State Council on the Arts, and City Department of Cultural Affairs and other sources. Grants funded the Black Heritage Reference Center of Queens County (BHRC), the Cultural Arts Program (CAP), and the Homework Assistance Program (HAP). The Library Action Committee's nonprofit 501c3 tax exempt status allowed Langston Hughes greater latitude and flexibility to raise funds to supplement Queens Library's operating budget. This autonomy set LAC apart from Friends of the Library at QPL branch locations.

Over the years, I designed LHCL&CC and BHRC logos for promotional items including bookmarks, pens, note cards, tote bags, caps, T-shirts, sweatshirts, scarves, vests, jackets, shirts, eyeglass cleaner sheets, and pocket calendars, using Black businesses and vendors when possible. Many QPL staff was envious of our autonomy, not realizing that Langston Hughes was created and funded as a "nontraditional" experiment in community library services that did not always conform to traditional practices and standards of librarianship.

In our formative years, Langston Hughes staff generated new service methods such as a color-coded Dewey decimal system; emphasis on paperback collections over hardbound books to stretch the budget; marketing books face out on shelves to highlight the cover design and attract the interest of library users. Information and Referral Services was created in direct response to community queries. Our success was not based solely on book circulation but connecting arts workshops and cultural programs with library services to attract and better serve the needs and interests of our community. In response to student requests for help with daily homework assignments, we secured funding from the City Department of Youth Services for an after-school Homework Assistance Program serving first to seventh grades and hired local high school and college students as tutors.

The Langston Hughes Community Library stood as a new service approach within Queens Library. I remember mumblings at manager meetings: "Well, Langston Hughes is not a 'real' library, so they can do things like that." Langston Hughes was the first location in the Queens system to include *Community* in its name from its inception, connecting library services with the arts as our service design. Through grants, library budgets, and fund-raising, the Library Action Committee enhanced our growth and reputation. Demographics began to change in Corona-East Elmhurst around 1985 from a predominantly Black community to a more diverse neighborhood with a growing Latino and Hispanic presence. In response, the library sought a more diverse staff, expanded our library collections and featured multicultural performances, exhibiting artists, authors, and musicians in our schedule.

In 1985, E. J. Josey requested an article for an edition of *The Bookmark* published by the New York State Library. My essay, "The Langston Hughes Community Library and Cultural Center, A Double-Edged Sword against Illiteracy" became my first published work. Later, "Library Services to Black Americans" appeared in the *Handbook of Black Librarianship Second Edition*, published in 2000. At Dr. Josey's request, I wrote the foreword to the ninth edition of *The African American Almanac*. This was followed by a request from the editor at Thomson/Gale to write the foreword for the tenth edition in 2008.

My first published book, *Queens Notes: Facts about the Forgotten Borough of Queens, New York* (2010), an expanded version of my graduate research project served as a ready reference tool. Since then, numerous essays were printed in the *BCALA News* on Black Caucus events and on Black history. In 2006, Patrick Oliver's book, *Turn the Page and You Don't Stop! Sharing Successful Chapters in Our Lives with Youth* included my essay, "If You Want to Learn the Secrets of the World, Read a Book!" I wrote the preface for public libraries for George C. Grant's 2011 book *In Honor of . . . Libraries Named for African Americans*, and Claudette Spence's *365 Days of Liberation* (2020) includes my foreword. In 2012, I was lead editor for the award-winning book, *The 21st Century Black Librarian in America: Issues and Challenges*, which includes my preface "The Need for Continued Activism in Black Librarianship." *Progressive Librarian* published my tribute essay, "Memories of Dr. Miriam R. G. Braverman (1920–2002)" in 2016.

Over the years, I have received many awards and honors. Several stand out for their uniqueness, including two poems, "What's in a Name?" by empyrean, highlighting my African names and "Sekounificance," George Edward Tait's poetic tribute to my career as a librarian. Three portraits were presented to me by artists expressing their appreciation. One was painted by our assistant library manager, Julia Tan. The other two were from exhibiting artists Peng Hu Qiun and Kay Kelman who exhibited in our gallery. In 2002, the Concourse Village Chapter of Key Women of America commissioned sculptor Wilbur Mapp to create a bust in my likeness as community appreciation for my years of service. It remains on display at the Langston Hughes Community Library. New York senator Jose Peralta nominated and inducted me into the New York State Senate's Veteran's Hall of Fame in 2017 for my military service with the Bronze Star awarded in Vietnam and contributions to the library profession and Queens County. My legacy was cemented by the New York Black Librarians Caucus's creation of the Andrew P. Jackson (Sekou Molefi Baako) Library Support Staff Scholarship, assisting students complete their undergrad degrees and serve as an introduction to librarianship as a profession.

On a cultural level, five African names were given to me in recognition of my promotion of African heritage, history, and culture. New York City musical artists dubbed me *Sekou* (Warrior), *Molefi* (He keeps tradition), *Baako* (first born) at our library's twenty-fifth anniversary celebration in 1994. In 1996, South African performing artists dubbed me, *Bhekizizwe* (take care of your people) and an undergrad student from Sierra Leone gave me the name *Orbai* (teacher). During my second tour to Ghana, West Africa, in 2017, I received two traditional Ghanaian names: *Kwabena* (born on Tuesday) and *Annan* (after the Hon. Kofi Annan, former secretary general of the United Nations, who hailed from Ghana), in a formal naming ceremony by the Antonkwa village elders. Representing Kujichagulia (Self-Determination) the second principle of Kwanzaa, I answer to my American and African names as they represent my American and African heritage.

I serve as an adjunct instructor at both of my alma maters, teaching cultural diversity in 2001–2011 through the history, philosophy, and anthropology department at York College (CUNY) and Black studies in 2011–present. As an undergrad I took Black studies courses at York and was active with an organization called Students for Change, where I conceived of and served as MC for the college's first homecoming in 1985. York's Alumni Association honored me as their distinguished alumni in 1996, and the College's Commemorative Quilt Committee selected me as outstanding alumni in 2006. The Graduate School of Library and Information Studies at Queens College (CUNY) honored me as their 2006 outstanding alum and extended the invitation to serve as adjunct instructor in 2007. Even in semiretirement, I continue to teach, enlighten, and educate our young leaders of tomorrow.

York College, Queens Library, and the Langston Hughes Library Center changed my life. I credit York College and Langston Hughes with connecting me to my African heritage and Queens College GSLIS with equipping me with professional tools. I applaud Queens Library's commitment to staff development that provides a fertile and supportive environment for staff to grow professionally and personally.

The highlight of my career is the appointment to the Queens Library Board of Trustees in 2017 by Queens Borough president Melinda Katz, making me the first librarian and first former staff member to serve on that board. In this capacity, I offer my voice as a librarian. The journey continues.

A colleague once wrote that true activist librarians could only exist where impact is felt nationwide or even globally. I disagree. Many serve as activists on a daily basis at the community level, changing the lives of all ages in large numbers through the library. For me, my nontraditional journey in this most rewarding profession, my outspokenness, extensive outreach, and efforts to expand and grow library services to better meet the changing needs of the community has been that of a proud grass roots *activist librarian*.

My deepest appreciation to Dr. E. J. Josey; Queens Library administrators Constance B. Cooke, Gary E. Strong, and Tom Alford Jr.; and library managers Jewel Nicholson,

Charlyne Gadsden, Evelyn Hall, and Joan Cole; and Marian Glenn Straw, Cultural Arts Director, for their leadership, advice, support, and mentorship throughout my career. Thank you, Josephine Petty and Annie Parker, for encouraging me to apply for the position at Langston Hughes, and Dr. Lenore R. Gall, Grace V. Lawrence, and the LAC board for their unwavering support and community representation over the years. Very special thanks to past and present Langston Hughes staff members for their teamwork and dedication to our mission and purpose.

I did not start out to be a librarian but cannot think of a more rewarding profession.

# 6.3

## African American Research Libraries (Public Libraries)

Andrew P. Jackson (Sekou Molefi Baako)

African American Research Library and Cultural Center
Broward County Library
Opened October 26, 2002
2650 Sistrunk Blvd.
Ft. Lauderdale, FL 33311
(954) 357-6282

Auburn Avenue Research Library on African American History and Culture
Opened May 1994
101 Auburn Avenue NE
Atlanta, GA 30303
(404) 613-4001

African American Research Library of Palm Beach
Opened 2014?
PO Box 173
West Palm Beach, FL 33402
(561) 729-0100

Blair-Caldwell African American Research Library Denver Public Library
Opened April 2003
10 W 14th Avenue Parkway
Denver, CO 80204
(720) 865-1821

Center for Black Literature and Culture Indianapolis Public Library
Opened October 2017
40 E. St. Clair Street
Indianapolis, IN 46204
(317) 275-4100

National Museum of African American History & Culture–Smithsonian Institution
Opened September 24, 2016
1400 Constitution Avenue NW
Washington, DC 20560
(202) 633-7498

Schomburg Center for Research in Black Culture New York Public Library
Opened 1925
515 Malcolm X Blvd
Harlem, NY 10037
(917) 275-6975

## 6.4

## *It Takes a Village*

FORMULATING LIAISONS BETWEEN PUBLIC LIBRARIANS AND AFRICAN AMERICAN HOMESCHOOLING FAMILIES

Raphael Daoud Jackson-Ortiz

I served in various professional roles throughout my career journey. My wife, a former classroom teacher, left the classroom so that we could work together on homeschooling our six children. My eldest two children are currently enrolled in college. The eighteen-year-old is completing his BA in two more semesters, and the second eldest is completing his freshman year at age fifteen. For many, college achievement is the sine non qua evidence of a successful homeschooling experience. Although we are proud of this accomplishment, nonetheless we consider ourselves to still be on a journey. Due to the centrality of librarianship in our home, because of my professional career, I had firsthand knowledge of the essential role that libraries and librarians have had in the success of our homeschooling experience. I hope that by sharing my studies, and my personal and professional experience, I can provide a blueprint for African American librarians and African American homeschoolers to follow that ensures academic and social success for African American homeschoolers, while enriching public library programming[1] for the African American community. The first part identifies who African American homeschoolers are, the recent rapid growth of the movement, and some of the unique challenges they face. The second section describes the mutual benefit African American homeschoolers and African American librarians can experience by working with organized homeschool cooperatives. The conclusion ends with a general guide on how public and academic librarians can create these liaisons to ensure the academic success, college placement, and social development of African American homeschooled students.

### AFRICAN AMERICAN HOMESCHOOL COOPERATIVES

When working with larger organizations, homeschooling families often prefer working in homeschool cooperatives, or co-ops. A homeschool cooperative is a group of families who meet together and work to achieve common goals. The cooperative can be centered around academics, social, arts, physical education, recreation, or all of the above. A common goal of the African American Homeschool Co-op, as organized by the library, can be social and or literary. The quid quo pro between the library and the co-op is that the library provides the community space and contributes to advertising through its preexisting administrative and advertising platforms. In return, the co-op assists in the creation and management of year-round library programming during the nonpeak hours. Because volunteering is at the center of co-op management, the library can incorporate the volunteer services of co-op members into the library programming schedule, specifically with library programming related to the co-op. This ensures the librarian will have appropriate assistance for the increased programming.

### WHO ARE AFRICAN AMERICAN HOMESCHOOLERS?

African Americans represent around 3 percent of the estimated 3.1 million homeschoolers in the United States in 2021–2022. Data before the pandemic shows that the number of US students being homeschooled was approximately 3 percent; however, that number increased by 63 percent in 2020, and only fell by 17 percent in 2021.[2] After the pandemic, the number of African American homeschoolers had risen from 3 percent to 16 percent, the sharpest rise in homeschooling in any singular racial or ethnic group.[3] In terms of family description, 91 percent of African American homeschoolers were brought up in a two-parent household, and the average family consists of 3.2 children. In terms of education, over 80 percent of the mothers and 60 percent of the fathers have an undergraduate college degree or higher.[4] With this rapid rise in a single demographic, librarians of all backgrounds will need to familiarize themselves with the social, literary, and academic needs of this new cohort of homeschoolers.

### WHY SOME AFRICAN AMERICANS HESITATE

I interacted with African American families who were inclined toward homeschooling yet were not ready to make the commitment. Both the literature[5] and my informal observations indicate that many African American families shared personal experiences that confirmed that the school system typically was not acting in their child's best interests.

In my informal conversations with families, I recognized five common things these families tended to overestimate: 1) the educational qualifications of their children's teachers (vis-à-vis their own); 2) the probability of securing meaningful educational reform within their children's scholastic tenure; 3) the likelihood that the problem could be temporarily addressed by changing teachers or transferring schools; 4) the probability that their children's positive interactions would outweigh the negative effects; and 5), many of the families were in awe of the educational and technological resources and programs. In theory these resources were available to all pupils, but in practice these same resources were often denied to their children.

Many African American families who were referred to us were more than willing to compensate us for educating their children. However, despite our reassurances, they were not convinced that they themselves could provide similar educational outcomes in their own homes. My wife and I strongly believe that the family's willingness to project their confidence onto us was partially due to their awareness that we were former teachers. Thus, lack of a teaching license led many otherwise educated African American parents to dismiss their own qualifications, expertise, and talents. It also caused them to overlook perhaps the most valuable resource they had as parents, which the school system lacked: 1) a love for, and intimate familiarity with their children's personality, desires, motivations, talents and 2) an ardent desire to see them succeed that can never be matched by even the most dedicated teacher.

## AFRICAN AMERICAN HOMESCHOOLING SKYROCKET DURING AND AFTER COVID-19

The pandemic lockdowns that forced school closures offered a dual window of opportunity. With parents and children at home, parents had the opportunity to experience the day-to-day schedule of their student's routine and teacher-student interactions. I believe that for many families, the experience served to demystify the public educational system. The second related experience was for parents to contact homeschooling associations, and families, eventually trying homeschooling themselves. And many chose to continue homeschooling after the lockdowns were lifted. Literacy is the foundation of all learning and educational outcomes, as expressed by the average reading language and test scores of African American homeschoolers and is significantly higher than African American public school students. Academic achievement and strengthening of familial bonds are common reasons cited by African American for homeschooling. A third and fourth concern is the desire to use a curriculum that positively reflects African American culture, and avoidance of a Eurocentric curriculum that socializes African American students into low self-esteem and sense of purpose.[6]

## EDUCATIONAL COSTS

Homeschooling families spend an average of $600 per student annually for their education.[7] This is significantly lower than the $12,350 average annual costs of private school tuition.[8] Although the $15,240 annual per pupil costs of public school is spread among the taxpayers. According to the National Retail Federation, the average amount spent on back-to-school costs is $864 per pupil annually. There are indeed other associated costs that must be factored in, namely the costs of forgoing a second income. These costs, however, must also be controlled for hidden costs of two-earner family working couples, which include the costs of being pushed into an elevated tax bracket, day care, and commuting costs to name a few.[9] Unless you live in the handful of states that offer state assistance to homeschooling families, parents must incur the responsibility of funding their own curriculum resources. This places parents in the position to oftentimes focus on some resources at the expense of others. These limitations pose less of a challenge to older children who have narrowed down their interests. For younger students who are still exploring their niches, parents may grow concerned over their inability to have as wide a range of resources at their disposal compared to those that are offered in the public school. This is where the public library bridges the gap.

## PUBLIC LIBRARIANS AS EDUCATION FACILITATORS NOT TEACHERS

The end goal is not to determine whether a handful of professional librarians at a public library can produce the same results of a coordinated team of full-time teachers at the local public school. Rather the goal is for librarians to manage publicly accessible library programming that involves the homeschool cooperative. The homeschool cooperative then seeks to produce proportional results with the small subset of children to which they have been charged. A major designator that distinguishes librarians from schoolteachers is the in loco parentis standard that teachers are held to. In loco parentis is a Latin term that means "in [the] place of the parent." The term refers to the legal doctrine under which an individual assumes parental rights, duties, and obligations without going through the formalities of legal adoption.[10] Public librarians perform a teaching role. Through library programs, they also may interact with, and even teach, minors. However, librarians are not generally subject to the in loco parentis legal doctrine.[11] This enables librarians to provide many of the educational resources available to teachers without the accompanying legal oversight that burdens teachers. Additionally, because the library is not a school, the librarian is not obliged to restrict student access to these resources based upon teacher-assigned educational evaluations (e.g., grades) or enrollment status of the "student." Finally, while collection development may be in harmony with those of the local public school, the library is not held accountable to state-mandated curriculum requirements. Disassociation from the state educational establishment provides the library with a layer of political insulation not usually afforded to public schools, which are often the first target of political agendas. From this perspective, libraries are essentially the second largest educational resource available to school-aged children.

## LIBRARIANS AS TEACHING PARTNERS

Although teaching is not the crux of their responsibility, LIS literature indicates that teaching fairs prominently among the six rules that libraries have adopted across the library spectrum.[12] With the educational and supervisory responsibilities placed back to the parents, the librarian is free to either participate or pull back as their interests or career demands dictate. Thus, the librarian can be directly involved in teaching programs, or simply collaborate with the parent teachers, the same way they would with other community volunteers in the library.

African American homeschool families, on average, have a higher level of education than their non-African American homeschooling counterparts.[13] Thus, college attainment may rank higher in the priorities of African American homeschool families. The co-op coordinator can be charged with educating the group about the qualifications of the librarian coordinator. This would include enabling the library users to distinguish between degreed librarians and library support staff. To build confidence in the co-op, and to educate the public about our profession, it would be worthy to remind the co-op that the minimal entry requirements for professional librarians are generally higher than those of professional teachers.

## AFRICAN AMERICAN HOMESCHOOLERS, HISTORICAL AND CONTEMPORARY CHALLENGES TO INCLUSIVITY

The general homeschooling community consists of a plethora of individual families. Unfortunately, not all homeschool co-ops share the same commitment to inclusivity. In fact, by contrast, some of these families see their ability to segregate from the public school (both racially and socially) as an ancillary benefit to homeschooling. As a result, they can become exclusive in whom they invite as members. In roughly the decade after *Brown v. Board* (1964-1975) scholars estimated that at least half a million white students were withdrawn from publics schools to avoid integrating with African American students. This "white flight" was facilitated by the creation of what sociologists refer to as segregation academies.[14] Thus, despite being founded on facially permissible goals such as teaching religion or a different method of reading instruction distinct from the local public school, in practice these ostensible reasons were thinly veiled means of escaping court-mandated integration. One telltale indicator of whether a school was a segregation academy is that it was founded in the leadup to or immediate aftermath of *Brown*. Another indicator is the contemporary racial makeup of the school, which indicates a grossly imbalanced demographic.[15] Running parallel to white segregationists' newfound interest in Christian education was a newfound interest in homeschooling. Although the mainstream homeschooling movement in the United States is becoming more diverse, the historic strain of Christian segregationists still exists within the movement.[16]

## RESPONDING TO ATTACKS ON CRITICAL RACE THEORY AND AFRICAN AMERICAN STUDIES GENERALLY

African American homeschoolers, who do not patronize public schools, still have reasons to be concerned with actions that affect the majority of children who rely on public school. The concerted push to curtail African American studies is part of the larger campaign to ban the teaching of critical race theory. Since January 2021, forty-four states have introduced bills or taken steps that would restrict the teaching of African American history.[17] Homeschooling has been legal in all fifty states and US territories since 1993. Homeschool laws vary state by state. Many African American homeschoolers are members of the largest homeschool advocacy group, the Home School Legal Defense Association (HSLDA). The HSLDA is an indispensable source of legal guidance and support for homeschoolers, and it is officially a nonpartisan organization. However, HSLDA origins and continuing entanglement with the Christian Right places them squarely in the camp of those who create and or back the initiatives to curtail African American studies programs in public schools under the guise of combating critical race theory. It is essential for African American homeschoolers to seek legal guidance and support throughout their endeavor; membership in a large school advocacy organization such as the HSLDA is the most expedient solution. However, in the long term it is important for African Americans to formulate and rely on advocacy groups that speak directly to our interests as a community.

## CULTURAL RELEVANT AND TARGETED PROGRAMMING

With African American studies under attack in public schools, librarians and African American homeschool cooperatives may need to step up their programming to make culturally available programming to a wider group beyond the cooperative for those cooperative members who may fear that by including general programming their educational curricula may be compromised for broader interests. In response, some cooperative members may want the programming to be tailored toward homeschool members of the co-op exclusively. To them it should be explained that the library cannot exclude patrons from access. However, hosting a youth-centered program during traditional school hours will indeed attract youth who do not generally adhere to a traditional schooling schedule. Thus, those in regular attendance of the co-op-hosted programming are an excellent pool of recruits who can and should be invited to join the co-op. Because librarians are not public schoolteachers, they are not obliged to follow the mandates of local state school boards. Thus, they are generally shielded from the current attacks on African American studies that are occurring at the state and regional levels.

**COLLEGE READINESS**

Statistically speaking, African American homeschooling parents tend to be more educated than their white counterparts. Presumably, stage two of the collaboration process would involve laying the groundwork for preteens and high school-aged students at the local college or university. The librarian can provide information for a co-op volunteer to meet with the dual enrollment coordinators of regional colleges and universities, with the goal of learning how to operate as a dual enrollment coordinator for either their homeschool co-op or individual family. Although the rules and guidelines vary state by state, dual enrollment programs open to public and private high school students are also opened to homeschooled students.

**DUAL ENROLLMENT**

Dual enrollment is when a middle school or high school student enrolls part time at a local college and earns college credit while completing a high school degree. Among the fifty states that have dual enrollment programs at their public universities, virtually all the participating institutions offer options to homeschooled students.[18] Although rules may vary by institution, a dual enrollment student is a registered student who has full access to the academic resources available at the host institution.

A liaison should make inroads with the dual enrollment coordinator at the host college. In a typical dual enrollment program, a full-time student from a sponsoring high school (or middle school) attends classes for part of the school day, at specified classes at a host community college or university. Depending on the host college, their enrollment can range from three credits to upward of twelve credits, and in many dual enrollment programs the student is exempt from paying tuition at the sponsoring university. The student takes a certain number of courses at a host college or university before returning to their sponsoring high school or middle school. Unlike a public or private high school student, a dually enrolled homeschool student is not required to return to their sponsoring high school upon completion of their college courses. This grants them an opportunity to experience campus life outside of classroom hours and an opportunity to utilize the college library resources. The homeschool co-op can arrange for a select few students to offer volunteer services through an informal internship with an academic librarian aligned with their interests. The network serves to make a student-run version of the volunteer network parents established with the local public library. Ideally these older students can reach out to their younger peers involved in the public library programs.

Programming responsibilities can include arranging tours, coordinating volunteer opportunities, or teaching basic research workshops to the younger members of the co-op.

**CONCLUSION**

Libraries and librarians played an integral role in our homeschooling experience. In addition to providing access to much needed education resources, they served as educational partners. These liaisons can start at the community public library and follow the African American homeschool student not only into college and universities but hopefully into their postgraduate life. A commonality of African American homeschoolers is their commitment to family. Thus, by becoming a part of this demographic, librarians can ensure intergenerational library access, participation, and advocacy. These successes will not only benefit the individual students but foster ties in the community and hopefully serve as an impetus to increasing the recruitment, retention, and visibility of African American librarians.

**NOTES**

1. By public librarians I am including all libraries that offer public access due to their receipt of public funds or membership in the Federal Depository Library Program. The early focus is on community public libraries. I also include libraries attached to public academic institutions such as colleges, university, and specialized libraries like law libraries. I generally do not include K-12 school libraries.
2. Jessica Huseman, "Why More Black Parents Are Homeschooling Their Children." February 17, 2015, *Essence*, www.essence.com/education/homeschool-rise-black-families-covid/.
3. Casey Eggleston and Jason Fields, *Census Bureau's Household Pulse Survey Shows Significant Increase in Homeschooling Rates in Fall 2020*, March 22, 2021, census.gov/library/stories/2021/03/homeschooling-on-the-rise-during-covid-19-pandemic.html.
4. Ama Mazama and Garvey Lundy, "African American Homeschooling as Racial Protectionism," *Journal of Black Studies*, vol. 43, no. 7, 2012, https://journals.sagepub.com/doi/full/10.1177/0021934712457042.
5. Ibid.; V. Taylor, "Behind the Trend: Increases in Homeschooling among African Americans Families," *Homeschooling in Full View: A Reader*, edited by Bruce Cooper, Information Age, 2005, pp. 121–34.
6. Mazama and Lundy, "African American Homeschooling."
7. Brian D. Ray, *Homeschooling 2021*, September 15, 2022, nheri.org/how-many-homeschool-students-are-there-in-the-united-states-during-the-2021-2022-school-year/; *Homeschooling: The Research*, March 11, 2023, nheri.org/research-facts-on-homeschooling/.
8. M. Hanson, *Education Data Initiative*, December 27, 2021, educationdata.org/average-cost-of-private-school.
9. Elizabeth Warren and A. W. Tyagim, *The Two-Income Trap: Why Middle-Class Parents Are (Still) Going Broke*. New York: Basic Books, 2013.

10. West's Encyclopedia of American Law, *In Loco Parentis* (Eagan, MN: West Publishing Company, 1998).
11. This is not the case for K–12 library media specialists who are generally considered teaching faculty.
12. E. Vassilakaki and V. Moniarou-Papaconstantinou, "A Systemic Literature Review Informing Library and Information Professionals' Emerging Views." *New Library World*, vol. 116, no. 1-2, 2015, pp. 37–66.
13. Mazama and Lundy, "African American Homeschooling."
14. Andrew Coulson, *Market Education: The Unknown History* (UK: Taylor and Francis, 2017).
15. As late as 2009 schools like the Jackson Academy in Jackson, Mississippi, for instance, had a racial makeup of 98 percent white despite Jackson City public school being 97.6 percent Black. Emily Pettus, "Four Decades Later, Freedom Rider Returns to Mississippi," July 3, 2009, *The Salt Lake Tribune*, archive.sltrib.com/story.php?ref=/news/ci_12748173.
16. Marilyn Grady and Sharon Hoffman, "Segregation Academies Then and School Choice Configurations Today in Deep South States," *Contemporary Issues in Educational Leadership*, vol. 2, no. 2, 2018, digitalcommons.unl.edu/ciel/7.
17. Sarah Schwartz, "Map: Where Critical Race Theory Is under Attack," June 21, 2021, *Education Week*, edweek.org/policy-politics/map-where-critical-race-theory-is-under-attack/2021/06.
18. Paula Penn-Nabrit, *Morning by Morning: How We Home-Schooled Our African-American Sons to the Ivy League* (New York: Villard, 2003).

# 6.5

## *Leading with Knowledge*

PROGRAMS AND SERVICES IN BIPOC COMMUNITIES AND THE IMPORTANCE OF REPRESENTATION
(WHAT PROGRESS HAS BEEN MADE IN SERVING THE BLACK COMMUNITY IN OVER TWENTY YEARS?)

James Allen Davis Jr. and Leslie Williams

It seems there has always been a cycle of revisiting public libraries' service models for serving BIPOC communities.[1]

The desire to provide services relevant to a community's needs and aspirations sometimes falters between perceived service needs and service needs that the community itself has voiced.

Global and national catastrophes have been the catalyst for developing services within several public institutions with libraries sometimes leading the charge. It is imperative that public libraries see themselves as members of the communities they serve, and it is during these pivotal moments in society that the unveiling occurs.

Libraries should build bridges to intellectual freedom by managing their resources, creating programs, and providing space that allows the community to thrive by creating a more inclusive infrastructure that removes barriers to access and build more collaborative spaces.

The question to ask is: What would progress look like as it relates to serving the Black community and how would this differ from previous program models that espoused support for communities of color?

In this chapter we will present a historical analysis of outreach and programming to the Black community and how these programs have changed within public libraries with the hiring of staff who represent the communities the library serves and the importance of Black leadership in building more sustainable programs that are relevant to a Black community that is multifaceted sociopolitically and to some degree economically.

We must move beyond a monolithic culture around ways of meeting the needs of the Black community toward providing spaces that encourage community conversations to highlight shared aspirations within the communities we serve while appreciating the diversity within the Black community.

As we lead with knowledge, we are making a concerted effort to provide programs and services that benefit our communities by unapologetically being an antiracist institution that addresses disparities and builds equitable and inclusive service models. We will address the the history of public library services in Black communities, public library professionals who shifted the focus from biased motivated service models to hearing the voice of the community, programs that remove barriers to access in Black communities, public libraries' response to issues around police brutality, social unrest, health disparities related to the pandemic, and lastly the "knowledge of now!" Where should public libraries go from here?

**HISTORICAL ANALYSIS AND HISTORY OF PUBLIC LIBRARIES IN THE BLACK COMMUNITY**

What are some of the things you remember about your neighborhood library? How often did you visit your neighborhood library? What did the library staff look like and what was your impression of those who worked in the library?

Depending on where people grew up, they could answer these questions in several ways. For some who grew up in rural areas the public library might have been a few miles from where they lived; and others who grew up in an urban setting have a different experience of engaging with the library.

There are some who remember their neighborhood library as a place in the community where they could escape to, a place that held the keys to another world, knowledge of worlds yet to be explored by the inquisitive mind. Aside from checking out a book, listening to story hour, or attending a library event, the library was a great place to explore new things.

Still, there was a time when this service was not available to everyone when certain groups were excluded from the library. The prevailing belief of white supremacy guarded access to information. Intellectual freedom was only offered to some and not to others. The public library was an institution that often reflected the beliefs and practices of other institutions in society, so barriers to services were part of its social structure.

It is important to consider this when we talk about the work of the public library in the Black community, how we can track the service models throughout time, and how they have changed. There are many articles written on the history of library access for Black people, so I will not attempt to restate everything that has already been covered by other scholars. However, I will pull from a few sources to track the timeline of library services and programs led by and for the Black Community.

> The public library can be a source of inspiration and motivation when its resources and staff are diverse, and it is intentional about removing barriers.[2]

I have always enjoyed the works of Jacob Lawrence ever since I became acquainted with his work in college. Lawrence's work provides a glimpse into the journey of what has shaped and developed the Black identity, perspective, and culture. The late Lawrence's work will overwhelm us with emotion through vibrant colorful images, capturing community and shared experiences.

In 1960, Jacob Lawrence created a work called "The Library," which featured an intergenerational scene of Black people reading. According to the Pennsylvania Academy of Fine Arts, "Lawrence represents over thirty-five figures in this vibrant library scene orchestrated through a refined palette of reds, greens, yellows, and blues. Public libraries appear frequently as a subject in Lawrence's paintings, embodying a space where African Americans can access their identity."[3]

It is this image that captures the spirit of intellectual freedom, especially as it relates to the importance of libraries and representation in Black communities. In *Harlem Speaks* edited by Cary D Wintz,[4] Lawrence spent a lot of his time at the library and displayed a passion for his history. "Lawrence became an Independent Researcher who sought out little-known stories of African American life not found in traditional mainstream publications."[5] Lawrence's appreciation for Harlem's Schomburg Library is demonstrated in his series *The Library*.

When we consider the role the public library plays in encouraging and promoting intellectual freedom in the Black community it is clear that the library must shift from being in the community to becoming a part of the community, and there are historical reasons why this shift is important.

Looking at a painting by Jacob Lawrence called *The Library* depicts several images of Black people just soaking in knowledge from several literary sources. The reason this image is so important is because of the history of segregation and the value of learning about one's history, without barriers to information. *The Library* depicted is "the Reading Room" in the Schomburg Library, the former 135th Street Library. According to the Smithsonian American Art Museum, The Schomburg Library was the country's "first significant collection of African American literature, history, and prints opened in 1925."[6]

The influence that libraries have on Black communities regarding the dissemination of information, promoting information literacy, and serving as a meeting space for Black intellectual thought and culture is something that should be infused into the discussion of how libraries can create programs relevant to Black communities. The depiction of the Reading Room in Lawrence's art highlights the value of access to books that highlight a rich culture and history of Black achievement and the quest for Black literature. The figures in this piece are engaging in reading in such a way that it conveys curiosity and pleasure, a sense of community, which is reflective of why we as librarians do this work. The impact that representation and culturally relevant programs have on the community are enormous when it centers on BIPOC voices.

**UNDERSTANDING YOUR "WHY" HELPS YOU BRING THE BEST OF YOURSELF TO WORK**

As a Black male librarian in a field largely occupied by white women, I often communicate my "why" for joining this profession. I realize that not everyone's reason is the same, but what excites me is that it is exactly their reasons for joining the profession that makes the work we do so important.

When I consider the work of Thomas Fountain Blue, "The first African-American to head a public Library,"[7] I often think about the influence this must have had on the community that would visit the Louisville Western Branch Library in Louisville, Kentucky. This library is noted as being the first library made up of exclusively Black library staff and headed by a Black librarian, serving a Black community.[8] Think about the advocacy that took place to bring this library into being, those that saw the need in the community, and collectively worked to address that need.

Throughout my years of working in a public library, I get to see firsthand the impact libraries can have on members of the community. Libraries have provided a space where members of the community can come together to meet, explore, and learn. I have always felt it was important to connect members of the community to resources and spaces that would help strengthen our communities and build bridges toward progress for members within our communities.

I started out pursuing a degree in education and began managing school-age programs while I was pursuing my degree in education. This experience led me to seek more ways to build community beyond working in schools. I participated in mentoring programs and workshops and finally took a job working as a security clerk in the public library. It was then that I noticed the value that the public library had in our community and could have in the community. The programs that we offered were summer reading programs, bookmobiles, and outreach to schools. There was a space that had the potential to bring the community together by collaborating with other community organizations and maximizing these partnerships to address the needs of the community.

## PROGRAMS THAT REMOVE BARRIERS TO ACCESS IN BLACK COMMUNITIES

During my tenure as a librarian, I have always been intrigued by what the library can offer the community, aside from our collection and public computers. As I sit at the reference desk each day, customers always ask me about our services and offer suggestions on what else the library should offer. In Northeast Park Hill, Denver, Colorado, the Pauline Robinson Branch library has historically served a community of 30 percent Black, 30 percent Hispanic, and 30 percent white. In 2013, gentrification started taking place in the neighborhood, and fewer Black families live here now. Staffing at our location looks like this: one library supervisor, one librarian, one library program associate, one circulation/security clerk, one shelver, and one lead clerk. As the library supervisor, I aim to hire staff that mirrors the community in both ethnicities as well as languages spoken. At DPL, we strive to have our programs align with our values: welcoming, connection, curiosity, equity, and stewardship.[9] Programming at the Pauline Robinson Branch ranges from preschool storytime to after-school programs for school-age children to technology and a monthly book club for adults and older adults.

The programs that the Black community attends the most are the technology programs. This makes perfect sense as technology programs reduce barriers to access to our Black community. The reason technology is popular is because of how prevalent it is in everyday life. Our drop-in tech program is where customers get those easy questions answered, like how to do something on their cell phone or how to take photos with it. The nature of the questions must be quick because it is an hour-long program. For more detailed questions and assistance, we have a digital navigator who is at the branch all day one day a week. Customers make appointments and receive one-on-one assistance with learning how to use a computer and other related tasks. Based on observations and customer feedback, our technology programs are very well received by our Black community. Customers get their questions answered and are pleased with the excellent customer service the staff provides.

The staff that facilitates these programs often mirror our community in ethnicity or are bilingual. Being intentional about hiring for these needs is no easy task. Often, once the job is posted, it takes extra time. We are sensitive to the needs of our community and understand that often BIPOC customers feel more comfortable around other BIPOC staff.

## THE FUTURE OF LEADING WITH KNOWLEDGE

During the pandemic, we experienced firsthand the devastating effects of minimizing library services in BIPOC communities. Libraries received a wake-up call toward addressing disparities around technology as it involved BIPOC older adult communities and families who did not have access to internet services and more.

In addition to that, there was an internal awakening that occurred as we had to address the realities of essential workers and those that were privileged to work from home.

Amid this reality was the prevailing social unrest that had a traumatic effect on BIPOC communities and churning of white backlash and political fury.

Libraries must adopt initiatives that build toward a more sustainable service model while addressing the current landscape and the leading disparities that are often polarized socially and politically while clearly defining what neutrality means as a public library.

We want to continue to offer programs that build community and that give everyone access to resources and information by addressing issues that hinder intellectual freedom.

Libraries must unapologetically become antiracist institutions by addressing disparities and building equitable and inclusive service models that will enhance their connection with the communities they serve and will demonstrate an unwavering commitment toward intellectual freedom.

Libraries continue to evolve as institutions that meet the needs of the communities they serve, currently developing partnerships that address food insecurities, connecting with social service agencies, and, as was stated earlier, bridging the technological gap. The future holds many possibilities for a public library that recognizes that it is a part of the community and not just in the community.

**NOTES**

1. Betty L. Jenkins, "A White Librarian in Black Harlem," *The Library Quarterly: Information, Community, Policy*, 60, no. 3 (1990): 216-31, JSTOR, http://www.jstor.org/stable/4308477. Accessed April 15, 2024.
2. "1921,"American Library Association, January 23, 2013., http://www.ala.org/aboutala/1921 (Accessed April 15, 2024).
3. "Jacob Lawrence, 'Dream Series #5: The Library " (1967): Pafa–Pennsylvania Academy of the Fine Arts." PAFA, December 28, 2014. https://www.pafa.org/museum/collection/item/dream-series-5-library.
4. Cary D. Wintz, *Harlem Speaks: A Living History of the Harlem Renaissance* (Naperville, IL: Sourcebooks, 2007).
5. Jacob Lawrence, "The Library," Smithsonian American Art Museum, https://americanart.si.edu/artwork/library-14376. Gift of S.C. Johnson & Son, Inc.
6. 135th Street Branch records, Sc MG 219, Schomburg Center for Research in Black Culture, Manuscripts, Archives, and Rare Books Division, The New York Public Library.
7. Jessica Betit, "In Celebration of Black History Month: Black American Librarians," Gardiner Public Library, November 28, 2022, https://gardinerpubliclibrary.org/in-celebration-of-black-history-month-black-american-librarians/.
8. "Thomas Blue, Librarian, and Minister Born," *African American Registry*, January 2, 2023, https://aaregistry.org/story/thomas-blue-a-first-in-library-services/;
9. Denver Public Library, Mission & Strategic Plan, April 30, 2023, https://denverlibrary.org/about.

**WORKS CITED**

135th Street Branch records, Sc MG 219, Schomburg Center for Research in Black Culture, Manuscripts, Archives, and Rare Books Division, The New York Public Library.

"1921." American Library Association, January 23, 2013. http://www.ala.org/aboutala/1921 (Accessed April 15, 2024)

Betit, Jessica. "In Celebration of Black History Month: Black American Librarians." Gardiner Public Library, November 28, 2022. https://gardinerpubliclibrary.org/in-celebration-of-black-history-month-black-american-librarians/.

Denver Public Library. Mission & Strategic Plan, April 30, 2023. https://denverlibrary.org/about.

"Jacob Lawrence, 'Dream Series #5: The Library' (1967): Pafa–Pennsylvania Academy of the Fine Arts." PAFA, December 28, 2014. https://www.pafa.org/museum/collection/item/dream-series-5-library.

Jenkins, Betty L. "A White Librarian in Black Harlem." *The Library Quarterly: Information, Community, Policy*, 60, no. 3 (1990): 216-31. JSTOR, http://www.jstor.org/stable/4308477. Accessed April 15, 2024.

"Thomas Blue, Librarian, and Minister Born." *African American Registry*, January 2, 2023. https://aaregistry.org/story/thomas-blue-a-first-in-library-services/.

---

# 6.6

## *Being a Youth Services Librarian*

Tahira Ahmad

I became a librarian because of my passion for reading and community development. I've always found it interesting to learn about other people and cultures. My curiosity and passion for community development has given my job a deeper meaning through the years. Within this deeper meaning has evolved my passion for community projects that brings about collaboration.

I started my career as a children's librarian in 2015 at the Queens Public Library, Far Rockaway Branch. Thanks to Mr. Andrew Jackson, who encouraged all his students to apply to Queens Public Library. I remember sending in my application in 2015 and Mr. Jackson telling me to followup with it. I remember starting out at the Cambria Heights Branch for two weeks of training and getting my first real experience of everything outside my own world. I remember how hard it was for me to understand why a child's behavior could be so aggressive or destructive, or why so many young patrons would find it uninteresting to paint or take part in educational programs. I remember how I would go back and forth about my frustrations because I felt so much concern for these young patrons. I felt it was my duty to solve their problems and make things better. I felt if I could not make things right for them then I was a failure!!! What was Mr. Jackson's response each time? "Meet these kids where they are and not where you want them to be." Of course, this was the most difficult thing for me to accept, yet Mr. Jackson, your words became my "'Strength," it showed me the most important reason not to give up. So, I never did and probably never will!!! THANK YOU!!!

Between 2015 and now (2023), I've had the opportunity to work in both Nassau and Suffolk County Public Libraries. I've developed and evolved ten times better than I ever imagined I would. Yes, I've had my doubts about my future within the profession, but this has not stopped me from researching the profession from a broader perspective.

As a Black, female youth services librarian, I have had the unique opportunity to serve, learn from, and empower young children and teens in every community I've worked in. The role of a librarian is often associated with books and literacy, but it goes far beyond that. We are agents of change, advocates for diversity and inclusion, and facilitators of lifelong learning.

I believe being a Black youth services librarian is a unique and challenging opportunity that requires passion, dedication, and a strong commitment to serving the community. This role is essential in providing useful access to information, resources, and programs that promote literacy, learning, and personal growth for Black youth in particular.

One thing I've observed through the years is that the most interesting and sometimes difficult aspect of my job is ensuring that Black youth in particular have access to materials that reflect their experiences, histories, and cultures. In a society that has historically marginalized and excluded Black voices, it is essential to provide young people with representation in literature and other forms of media. By doing so, we can help them develop a sense of pride in their identity and help them understand the richness and diversity of their community. This was something I discovered when I took Mr. Jackson's graduate class at Queens College, The Importance of Cultural Representation in Books.

Beyond curating a diverse collection of materials, I also create programs that engage and inspire our youth. This can take many forms—from book clubs and author visits to cultural celebrations and community service projects. By providing a safe and welcoming space for young people to connect, learn, and grow, we can help them develop the confidence and skills they need to succeed.

As a youth services librarian, I am keenly aware of the challenges that Black youth in particular face within our societies. Many of these challenges, such as systemic racism and poverty, can impact their access to proper education and essential resources. A public library should be a place where everyone feels welcome, safe, and supported, regardless of their background or circumstances.

In addition to providing resources and programming, I also see my role as an advocate for social justice and equity. This means being vocal about issues that affect our community and advocating for policies and practices that promote equity and inclusion. It also means partnering with community organizations and stakeholders to address the root causes of social inequality.

In conclusion, my experiences through the years have shaped the way I advocate for diversity and inclusion, which as we all know, is critical in community development. By creating an inclusive environment and providing access to diverse materials and programs, librarians can help promote understanding, respect, and empathy among members of the community.

Being a Black youth services librarian is a multifaceted and rewarding job that requires a deep commitment to social justice and equity. By providing our youth with access to diverse resources, engaging programming, and a supportive community, we can help them develop the skills and confidence they need to succeed in life. It is an honor to be able to serve and empower the next generation of diverse leaders, thinkers, and changemakers.

# 6.7

## *Land of Endless Dreams & Possibilities!!!!!*

Judi Belle Raines

As far back as I can remember, the library was that special place where dreams were possible—even for a kid from Queensbridge! My Mother was an only child who grew up loving to read. She passed this passion on to her three children by agreeing, along with Dad, to have my sisters and I consistently spend time surrounded in the land of endless possibilities. It was only natural that I viewed the library as that special sacred place. Afterall, where else were you not allowed to speak above a whisper, dare drink, or eat anything without exception.

The day finally came when the librarian handed me my own library card. At that moment I realized this was definitely an experience that would impact my life in more ways than I could have ever imagined. It wasn't just the fun activities or special contests making us feel like we could escape to worlds unknown, fantasy full of endless, boundless journeys, but much more! You could be royalty, a sports star, doctor, superstar and even as I grew up to see my biggest dream seep into reality, the president of the United States!!! I wanted to bathe in the sea of knowledge. Quench my thirst every chance I got. The library allowed me to do this and more.

Fourth grade presented me with a test that would enhance all I obtained from my early years in the library and propel me closer to my dream of one day becoming a teacher in a public school just like the one I was attending. The statewide reading exam known as the Iowa Reading Test was all ingredients poured into me by every librarian I had ever met in that small Queens Bridge library. Librarians encouraged me to read different genres, explore outside my comfort zone to the unfamiliar, and continue on my journey of reading. I listened intently, determined to understand, develop, and mostly grow up to be somebody. Along with my parents, the library had resources that encouraged, tested, supported, and embraced who I was and later was destined to become. Three of us were summoned to the principal's office, with my mind racing. What was I in trouble for? Seconds later, I discovered my crime was solely that of reading so much that I, along with the two boys standing beside me, scored the highest on this special statewide reading test and as a result, were being transferred to a school for IGC (intellectually gifted children).

The power of the library began. I was exposed to places and opportunities I had only dreamed of, but now as a maturing young adult realized was more than possible. Throughout my educational experience I was catapulted to countries where libraries were adorned by children in such beautiful islands as Anguilla, St. Kitts, and Jamaica. Reading flyers posted and often on desks in the library informed me of programs similar to the Peace Corps, like Operation Crossroads Caribbean where I created and directed a summer camp program.

Visits to the Schomburg Library offered an unbelievable extensive summer program for teachers in 1993. For half the summer I was presented with top historians passionately sharing their knowledge on topics such as the language of hieroglyphics by Maulana Karenga to one of my most favorites, the language of cartography by Ward Kaiser. This seminar delved into the significance and principles behind the Peters' Projection Map and its impact on the world, which expanded my perspective of existence to a new level. Not always realizing the relevance of how countries are portrayed in size in proportion to each other allowed me throughout the duration of the class to understand the necessity of accurately representing for sake of fairness, all countries across the globe.

As a guidance counselor at Flushing High School, I was informed by a student visiting my office of her recent pleasure from reading the memoir *The Color of Water* by James McBride. Reading an article in the newspaper allowed me to alert the principal, Mrs. Cornelia Gutwin, of the fact that the author would be speaking just a few blocks away from the school, at the Flushing Library in Queens, New York. Once again, the library had proven to be the pinnacle of rewarding experiences. The comments and questions asked by the students went beyond the imaginable. With giggles of enthusiasm two students waited to walk up to the podium and present James McBride with a bouquet of flowers for his family in gratitude for sharing his story. They along with myself were fully engaged in a memorable program presented free at the Queens Public Library. I will never forget the smiles on their faces as they stood next to this renowned author for a photo op and book signing.

As I was called to stand with Mr. James McBride proudly, my mind reached back to many years prior upon seeing a large sign in the front window of the Queens Central Library across the street from the Jamaica bus terminal in Queens, New York, that read author Claude Brown of *Manchild in the Promised Land* will be our guest! Such joy resonated through my entire body. I would meet someone I idolized for half my lifetime. Thanks once again to the priceless, free opportunity provided by the Queens Public Library. I not only had the opportunity to experience an outstanding event but was blessed after inviting Mr. Brown to Andrew Jackson High School to accept my invitation to come and speak to the students about his life experiences. Needless to say, without hesitation he graciously agreed. Today, I reminisce through the countless photos taken with him and my precious students. As I shop for groceries, a typical day for a retiree, and walk quietly down the aisle, a voice will surface saying, "Thank you Ms. Raines for that trip to Elmhurst, Queens, New York. I truly enjoyed meeting Sistah Souljah during that time when you took us to the Langston Hughes Library. We sure had fun!"

It seems no matter the location or uniqueness of the building, the library has never failed to provide a space where people can receive educational resources and infinite amounts of knowledge and entertainment. This was certainly the case when I filled out my application to participate in the Gilder Lehrman Teachers Summer Seminar Program and fortunately was once again accepted for a third time, as a participant in the summer of 2000. I was to spend two weeks on Harvard University's campus with access to the library every single day while attending the Words of Liberty: Rhetoric and American Democracy Seminar.

Ever since seeing the motion picture *Glory*, I knew I wanted to read the actual letters Colonel Shaw wrote his parents about the participation of the first all-Black volunteer group of soldiers known as the Fifty-Fourth Massachusetts Infantry Regiment who fought the Confederates during the

Civil War. As I learned more about the Fifty-Fourth Regiment from seeing the letters in print within a book titled *Blue-Eyed Child of Fortune* by Colonel Robert Gould Shaw, I became obsessed with the notion that one day I would firsthand witness the actual letters on exhibit at Harvard University's Houghton Library. I wanted the experience of holding those letters in my hands while examining Colonel Robert Gould Shaw's handwritten style and grace. At last, the opportunity through the Gilder Lehrman Summer Teachers Seminar made my dream a reality.

Even though the letters were removed from the exhibit, I was informed by a librarian that if I visited the library the following day during lunch, that I might be able to view the letters. After hours of restless sleep, the time I had patiently awaited had finally arrived. I was escorted to a reading room within the library and handed a pair of white cotton gloves. As I sat in a huge mahogany leather chair, I was handed a metal box. Once instructed to place the box carefully on the wooden table, I opened it with delicate care. To my utter amazement, the letters were simply in a neat pile awaiting my intense reading of the repaired fragile documents by Vicki Denby, curatorial assistant and assisted by Susi Barbarossa, conservation technician for the Houston Library, along with Christopher Sokolowski, project paper conservator, and Karen Walter, senior paper conservation technician of the Weissman Preservation Center who spent more than ninety days carefully working with the letters before presenting them to the public. Sitting and reading each letter was beyond any experience I had known. I realized at that unparalleled moment that my perspective of how I viewed and interpreted the Civil War would be changed forever. I left the library and returned to class knowing once again this privilege was only made possible because of my great respect and reverence over the years for the library. From that day on I enthusiastically shared my experience with students, colleagues, and family who shared my interest in these documents that helped reveal the gallant, skillful contributions of men determined to fight for freedom. I am so grateful for Shaw's neatly written ninety-eight letters addressed to his mother, along with thirty-one written to his father with others to his sisters and brothers-in-law. I'm sure being the colonel of the first Black regiment was an arduous task that Col. Shaw accepted willingly.

Presently, I'm thinking of writing a book describing the bravery, commitment, and patriotism shown by female soldiers who disguised as men and fought in the Civil War. As I ventured out seeking information, the suggestion was made to inquire about help doing such research from librarians who worked at the Thomas Jefferson Building in Washington, DC. Without hesitation I had made an appointment, filed for the necessary time-entry pass, and now boarded the Accela train to begin my historical project venture. Of all the libraries I had visited, the Library of Congress was definitely the one to take my breath away. I loved the way the front of the building faced the Capitol with its height of four stories, gold-designed dome covering the main reading room. I was truly consumed by the fancy décor of marble and bronze doors opening up to the granite exterior on the lower level. The portrait busts of famous writers were framed by the grandeur of circular fine windows. According to many of them, I could see why they regarded the Thomas Jefferson building as an impressive educational palace. All materials I had required for my project needed to be requested a minimum of one week in advance. Upon entry to the library, I realized it was necessary to obtain a Library of Congress Reader Registration Card at the entrance of the Central Reading Room in order to access entry into any of the seventeen reading rooms to use the collections. As I slowly approached one of the reference librarians on duty, I began to ease into a less anxious existence. I was thankful to have gone over the rules of the library beforehand, which suggested that I request a research appointment. This proved vital to ensuring that the materials I was seeking would be available during the time spent on my visit.

The reference collections were available in all of the reading rooms, which made it easy to search out even the most difficult information anywhere else. Before I could even settle into my study mode, I had to decide which of the seventeen reading rooms would best serve my purpose. Fortunately for me I began my research by browsing catalogs and venturing through various research guides with the help of a librarian by telephone and my computer. I was directed to the Main Reading Room as a first timer to ensure the best results. I was pleased with the primary sources expediently made available regarding the lives of such female soldiers not easily found in general libraries or even school textbooks. Why weren't these women regarded as significant contributors to American history? Periodicals and textbooks noted hundreds of women like Frances Clain, who fought under the alias of Jack Williams; she enlisted and fought alongside her husband until his death right beside her during the battle of Stones River. Women studies specialist Kristo Conkle contributed so much to assisting and ensuring the success with my research regarding those women that fought and died alongside the men. Reading about how female soldiers maintained being undetected as a woman and behaving like all the other soldiers was remarkable, especially during that time period while on the battlefield. Some lasted years, while other female soldiers were unfortunately discovered sooner. All in all, my five days in Washington, DC, proved to be a huge success. The exposure to vast amounts of primary resources was definitely worth the trip.

As I recall each venture with pride and fond memories, I look toward the future when once again I'll visit my favorite place with hope of fulfilling my dreams and possibilities!

# 6.8

## *The Great Escape*

C. Atterbury

What can be said of a child whose existence is thoroughly dependent on parents or extended family members? Isn't this normal for an average child to have this limited experience of independence in the world? It usually is, but couple this with a child who has physical or medical disabilities, and the dependency grows exponentially. This was my experience.

For some reason it appeared my legs were not as strong as other children's legs, and I would often be perceived as being clumsy when my knees buckled under me for no apparent reason. I can still remember receiving a tricycle for an early birthday and I would muster all my strength to just get the pedal to go down after a painful rotation. Now mind you, this was not outside, but in my granduncle's basement while the adults surrounded me saying, "What's wrong with her? She can't even push the pedal down? What a shame!" Whoever thought children could not understand grown folk's conversations was truly misinformed. I understood every word they said, but for the life of me I could not get that tricycle to move around that circle of peering adults with faces of sorrow and lament. I'm not sure what happened, but I never saw the tricycle again.

It is important to share at this juncture my parents were experiencing a prolonged divorce and my mother decided to leave our Harlem apartment with me in tow. Off to Corona, Queens, we went, to the land of private houses and pets. This was an emotional time for me. I missed my father and now had difficulty breathing because of acute asthma caused by a collie and a house cat. Illness became so much my normal I had to carry an inhaler wherever I went, developed bronchitis, and had to have my tonsils removed. All of this caused my mother to be even more protective of me, limiting my freedoms to nonexistent.

My family members, especially my uncles, began giving me books when I was still teething. I remember chewing the book corners, much to my mother's chagrin. It wasn't because I was hungry. I just needed to gnaw on something. Even with this, the books kept coming and my mother kept reading to me, developing my vocabulary and opening my imagination, which was endless.

After picture books and chapter books such as the Nancy Drew and Hardy Boy series, two books stand alone from the pack—a children's Golden Press Edition of *The Iliad and the Odyssey* (adapted from Homer) and *Little Lame Prince and His Travelling Cloak* by Dinah Maria Mulock Craik. The *Iliad and the Odyssey* were printed together in one hardcover book, beautifully illustrated and eloquently written so children could either read to themselves or an adult could read to them. By the time I received this book I was already reading to myself and imitating my mother's theatrics, while being transported to ancient Greece. The *Little Lame Prince and His Travelling Cloak* introduced me to a small English boy who had been physically challenged since birth, but after a visit from his godmother with magical powers he adapted the ability to fly on his cloak and see the world. I could instantly identify with this book. This is what happened to me when I read. Books did this for me. They allowed me to encounter strange lands, people, and situations unknown to me until I opened the pages to find a new adventure.

Being an only child is a lonely existence, unless you had cousins or other young relatives who visited often. Unfortunately, this was not my experience, so those monthly visits from my cousins who I knew lived in Jackson Heights, Queens, just one town away from me was extremely important. I waited with bated breath for those Sunday visits and when they did occur, I was overwhelmed with glee. When they moved to New Jersey we children naively thought the monthly visits would continue. We were thoroughly mistaken. Our "once a month" visits turned to three times a year: Easter, Thanksgiving, and Christmas. When my cousins finally moved again, this time to California, all physical contact ended. Loneliness won the battle, but throughout disappointment, trips to the library and purchasing my own books sustained me. There was a way to escape the loneliness.

Now you may wonder a few things. Why I didn't just go outside and play with the neighborhood children, or why children in the family didn't just pick up the phone and call each other. My mother, grandaunt, and granduncle were extremely strict (Caribbean strict), so the thought of me leaving the house unattended with my poor health was out of the question. The inquiry about using the phone is simple. Many children of lower income families were not awarded the privilege of using the phone. Phone calls cost money (especially long-distance calls). I had to ask permission to call anyone, and it had to be school related. Also, I was not allowed to answer the phone as a child. That was "grown folk business."

The one thing I could do with permission was go to the Corona Branch of Queens Public Library because it was within walking distance from my house and my elementary school. It was considered a lengthy walk, but it was a reason to leave the house or not come home directly after school. I can remember one summer there was a contest to see who read the most books and complete book reports. This would seem like work for some, but it was fun. Having thrown myself into the assignments, I diligently wrote as many book reports as were needed. Looking forward to the award I knew I would win but was devastated when I fell ill and could not attend the final session where all the reports were submitted and awards presented. Even without the award, I still knew I would have won, and I enjoyed the assignments and books read.

It was imperative that I found an outlet to maintain my sanity. Reading was the escape. All through my early life I have memories of my mother reading to me. Whether it was the Sunday comics or the encyclopedia, she read. Not only did my mother read, but she also performed. Every comic character found in the Sunday news—Blondie, Brenda Starr, Dick Tracy, Dondi, Gasoline Alley, Little Orphan Annie, Moon Mullins and Pogo—all had their unique style and voice. She even gave their voices a different tonality, but there was a comic strip that was never read by my mother, Lil' Abner. The absence of academic English was blatant, and the southern jargon was inappropriate for my mother's professionalism.

Along with this there were somethings that my mother refused to do, enter in the back door of any building, sit in the back of any bus, attend performances where we would not be hired, that is, Rockettes at Radio City Music Hall, or movies without people of color employed, etc. The movies she chose were mostly Sidney Pointier, or any other movie with Black characters that did not have a person of color in a buffoon role. That was just thoroughly unacceptable.

My mother worked a "dreaded job" (her words) for the Special Procedures Department of the Internal Revenue Service in New York City throughout my elementary, high school, college years, and even afterward. Every weekday she left home dressed in a corporate suit, stockings, and heels to travel on the subway downtown. At the time of her employment, she was the only person of African descent in her department and quietly dealt with the covert institutional racism and misogyny on a daily basis. It is difficult for me to believe my mother was quiet about anything, because she was known to speak her mind at any time, to anyone, but she must have used some digression because she maintained her employment for three decades. When she retired from her government job, she earned her great escape and acquired her dream job of working at our neighborhood library, Langston Hughes Community Library and Cultural Center (QPL)! With the differences of staff demographics, not having to take the subway, and being employed where she wanted to be, it became the first time I ever saw her anxious and excited to go to work.

Needless to say, as a child I needed an outlet for escape. Reading became that for me. Libraries became my friends. To obtain a library card was the means to go places and meet people I would never be exposed to in my everyday activities, but having my own book collection was my goal. Scholastic book sales at school became the purpose for me to save money. Since I wasn't allowed to work until I was fourteen years of age during the Summer Youth Program, I had to figure out a way to save something from the miniscule allowance that was granted me when I did my household chores. I needed books!

Unfortunately, as a young child I never had a book where I could racially identify with the characters. My first doll looked like me, being born in Harlem accommodated this, but books were a different story. My imagination would have to account for that, focusing on other aspects of the characters instead of race, whether it be emotion, gender, physicality, or socioeconomic level, I would find a way to emerge myself into the characters, whether they be Austrian, Greek, Irish, Italian, Jewish, or Polish. Their commonality was their race, but I had to use my imagination to find something with which I could identify. I never had the desire to be someone else, but I did wonder how it would be to be athletic, healthy, and strong as a child. It wasn't until I went out of state to college, away from furry animals that I was able to survive without an inhaler. My athleticism developed and I experienced a more physical life, but my love for books and libraries never diminished.

Now I was introduced to writers of African descent, and I became insatiable and literally sought to feed my hunger. I found Langston Hughes Community Library and Cultural Center (QPL) and could easily spend hours examining the shelves to see what I had been missing throughout my educational experience. Now I would have to reprogram myself to view the characters to look like me regardless of genre, theme, plot, and even when they were from other communities, or ethnicities, they looked like me! I could easily relate to Ann Frank as a youth, but now I learned about Maya Angelou in *I Know Why a Caged Bird Sings* and James Baldwin in *Go Tell It on the Mountain*, Alice Walker's character Celie in *The Color Purple*, and so many others. Time frames and locations would transverse, and I would find myself during the Harlem Renaissance with Langston Hughes, Nella Larsen, Zora Neale Hurston, and Countee Cullen. W. E. B. Du Bois, and Booker T. Washington could be pictured in a debate in early 1900s, while Octavia Butler would take me on a science fiction journey to travel to past or future times. Toni Morrison would cause one to reread her passages several times to digest the gist of her thought processes while Malcolm X and Rev. Dr. King could debate for months. I could stay in the library all day, every day, but one has to work.

So, I taught! After college I taught American and world literature, American and world history, and African American literature on the high school level. Now I had more time to discover all I had missed when I was in elementary and high school. Now I had the power to choose the authors and I made sure to make the assignments multicultural to match my student population. Gone were the days of only European culture and literature. The schools' libraries were finally attempting to become inclusive. My students would at least receive somewhat of an ethnically balanced literary education. Some of our field trips would include The Apollo, The Schomburg Center for Research in Black Culture in Harlem (NYPL), The Studio Museum, and bookstores throughout the New York City area. We also traveled to Central Park where we found the plaque identifying the location of Seneca Village where people of African, Indigenous, and European descent lived together in harmony sharing similar socioeconomic levels during the nineteenth century as landowners. My students' excitement was overwhelming as they looked for the area and finally found proof of what they had previously researched at the school library.

It is interesting to note the phenomenal spaces for academic learning we have in New York City. Many pass by without even a regard to the wonders of academia right under their noses. Through a Department of Education program, I had the opportunity to attend Columbia University in pursuit of my second master's degree. I had attended Fordham University at the Lincoln Center campus earlier because of its proximity to my full-time job at Martin Luther King Jr. High School. I could walk to classes during spring semester and the summer courses worked well with my schedule. There I completed a MS in special education. Now I had an opportunity to attend Columbia in pursuit of an American studies MA degree. I would be allowed to enter the Butler stacks and be propelled back in time just through the architecture alone. The solemnity found there precedes itself, and many in academia appreciate these hallowed halls.

All those books, but not enough time. Notes would be taken by hand and time would halt. Before I realized it, several hours had passed. Hardly any distractions took place. It was as if everyone was on a personal mission. For an academic, it is a slice of heaven on earth. I felt welcomed in the Butler stacks. I experienced a feeling of belonging.

I must admit, I am in possession of two library cards, one for each of my favorite locations: Langston Hughes Community Library and Cultural Center in Queens and libraries in Harlem. You are not required to have a library card to visit New York Public Library's Schomburg Center for Research in Black Culture, but if you want to borrow a book you can always go around the corner to the 136th Street Library off Lenox Boulevard. Langston Hughes Community Library and Cultural Center (QPL) is a circulating library, and I can take out books while utilizing the Black Heritage Reference Center. I can also enjoy the numerous live musical and theater performances with other special events such as literary panel discussions and yearly Kwanzaa celebrations. The Schomburg offers a multiplicity of art pieces shown at various times, historical artifacts, photograph exhibits, and a plethora of multi-generational activities for family and friends. Even though it is a noncirculating library, the wealth of knowledge housed there is unique and priceless. Truly, I have found the best of both worlds here in New York City!

Now I must transfer this passion for reading and the importance of libraries to the next generation. The challenge now becomes teaching the children to develop an imagination. How is it possible to enjoy reading if you just see words across a page? You have to be able to see what you are reading, imagine the setting, become the characters. Then and only then will you experience the love of literature the library can offer you. Developing imagination does not come easy to those who need external stimulation to experience something. Bright lights and moving pictures across a screen will diminish the ability to imagine. Imagination is a gift used to visualize and create the arts. Without imagination people lose part of their humanity. Libraries allow us to imagine. This is a special gift to pass on to others. Let us not take this for granted and let us teach those who have difficulty accessing this inner sphere of our existence as humans—the ability to imagine, the ability to escape.

From a small library in Corona, Langston Hughes Community Library and Cultural Center (QPL) to the Schomburg Center of Research in Black Culture New York Public Library, to the Butler Stacks at Columbia University, I say,

O library, library, where would I be without you, O library?

# 6.9

## *Black Male Librarians*

ADVOCATING FOR CHILDREN AND LITERACY

Tiffeni Fontno

In an increasingly diverse and interconnected world, the need for representation across all professions and fields becomes ever more apparent. The role of a librarian, often regarded as a guardian of knowledge and a facilitator of learning, is no exception. Within this context, the demand for Black male librarians has gained considerable significance.

Their presence in libraries is crucial not only to counter the historical underrepresentation of Black individuals in the profession but also to offer diverse perspectives, inspire young minds, and foster a sense of inclusivity in library spaces. Black male librarians serve as role models, educators, and advocates, bringing unique insights that enrich the library experience for patrons of all backgrounds.

Cultural responsiveness is the cornerstone of fostering an inclusive library environment that resonates with the diverse identities and needs of its users. In this context, Black male librarians emerge as catalysts for transformative change, particularly in library outreach and literacy efforts, with a profound impact on young Black children.

Their presence as relatable and aspirational figures not only challenges stereotypes but also bridges cultural gaps, making literature and learning more accessible and engaging for marginalized communities. By curating collections that authentically represent the experiences of Black individuals, these librarians can instill a sense of pride and belonging in young readers, while also dismantling barriers that have historically limited their engagement with literature.

Through interactive programs and mentorship initiatives, Black male librarians offer more than just information—they provide guidance, encouragement, and a platform for young Black children to see themselves as valued participants in the world of knowledge. In this way, these librarians stand as a dynamic force, propelling library outreach and literacy efforts into a realm of enriched cultural understanding and empowered learning.

In this chapter, we share the crucial role of representation and diversity within the realm of librarianship through a compelling video interview from September 23, 2021, with four dynamic and diverse Black male librarians: Andrew Sekou Jackson, AJ Allen, Mr. John, and Mychal Threets. This conversation stands as a powerful testament to the transformative potential of inclusive library spaces. As advocates for change, these Black male librarians bring their unique experiences, perspectives, and insights to the forefront of library service. With varied backgrounds and experiences with literacy and their entry into librarianship, they engage in an exploration of the challenges, triumphs, and aspirations of Black male librarians in today's society.

Delving into their personal journeys, the interview unpacks the ways in which representation impacts library patrons, particularly young Black individuals seeking relatable role models and a sense of belonging. Through their narratives they shed light on the pivotal role that Black male librarians play in reshaping the library landscape and fostering literacy among diverse communities. As we navigate the transcript of this illuminating dialogue, readers are invited to witness the vital conversations and insights that have the power to drive change and inspire those within their communities.

Tiffeni Fontno: Today we're going to talk about Black male librarians and children's librarianship, and I wanted to introduce our guests, our panelists.

The first panelist I want to introduce is Mychal Threets. He grew up in Solano County, California. He earned his MLIS from San Jose State University in 2018. He has worked for Solano County Library since 2013. He's worked as a children's librarian and now is currently a digital community librarian, and his main duties include monitoring and editing the library's website, social media, and other forms of digital marketing. Thank you, Mychal.

Next, we have Mr. John Light, who is known as Mister John. He's an author, storyteller, librarian, genealogist. He's from Richmond, but now lives in beautiful Savannah, Georgia. He received his bachelor's degree in history at Old Dominion and got his master's degree at Syracuse. Mister John has published four books and has performed as a storyteller many times with young people, and he loves to empower others to discover who they are through books, stories, and family. And next on the list, we have Mister Billy, who is a librarian who is focused on youth services. He is currently the youth services supervisor at North Regional Library at Broward County.

AJ Allen is also the founder of Three King Vision and Educational Storytime Platform. This platform features the YouTube show *Storytime Adventures with Mister Billy*. Mister Billy is a proud alumni graduate of two HBCUs: Lincoln University and North Carolina Central.

We have our esteemed Andrew Sekou Jackson, who's here with us. Mr. Jackson was the executive director of Queens Library, the Langston Hughes Community Library and Cultural Center for thirty-six years. He is the one of the past presidents of Black Caucus of the American Library Association. Nationally from 2004 to 2006. He chairs the BCALA Affiliates Committee.

He earned his business administration degree from York College. An MLS, from the Graduate School of Library and Information Studies at Queens College. He is an adjunct professor in Black studies and cultural diversity. He teaches library science at Queens College Library, School of Library, and Information Studies. Mr. Jackson is on the board of trustees of Queens Public Libraries. Most notably, he's also the recipient of a Bronze Star medal for his service in Vietnam and also given several African names for his commitment to teaching and sharing African history and culture.

Andrew Sekou Jackson: My introduction to reading. My mother is a teacher, my sister's a teacher. And I was surrounded by teachers all my life. I'm the oldest of a set of triplets. So, when we were kids, my mother enrolled us in the Book of the Month Club, and every month we got books. I still got my Roy Rogers book from when I was a kid. I still have my Robin Hood book. When I was a kid, we had to read and not only did we have to read the books as a teacher, we had to write book reports about what we read and we had to discuss around the dinner table on Sundays what we were reading and why we thought these books were important. So, the whole analysis of reading it and really, not just scanning it and saying, "Oh, this book was a good read. I enjoyed the book." It was a lot of activities. You had to really talk about what the book was about. That was my introduction to reading as opposed to going to the library. We actually built our library at home, so it was always material to read around the house and having a mother as a teacher always meant that you had to deal with things from the teacher's perspective and not just as the kid that was reading the book.

AJ Allen: Well, my introduction to reading was kind of funny. I'm an avid basketball junkie, so my mother would order a lot of *Sports Illustrated*, *Slam Basketball* magazines, and I grew up on hip-hop. My parents were hip-hop junkies, so my mom was ordering the *Jet* magazines, *The Source* magazines. I was always infused with reading about the current events in the hip-hop community and in sports. But I thought it was funny, my very first book I can vividly remember was when I'm in the third grade and it was from Scholastic, and it was a book based on the show *Family Matters*. I was reading all about Urkel. That was like some of the most vivid memories with me, and it always stuck with me because my mother always made me read to my sisters. I guess I just got story time embedded in me. You know, it's all about just having an influence in reading what you're interested in, and that creates a thirst for reading. Those are my first-time experiences.

Mr. John: All right. Hello, everybody. I'm kind of like AJ, I read *Sports Illustrated*. I loved football. My mom was like, "I'ma get you these *Sports Illustrated* magazines." I probably was like, seven or eight. And I got them until I left the house till I was eighteen. I was getting them every week. You know, I went from a point where, I'm really only looking at the pictures, to now I'm reading the whole magazine from cover to cover. That was my main thing, my main piece of literature, if you will, that I've read as a child.

I had a couple of books that from the He-Man and the Masters of the Universe. I read this book and funny story about this book. I had this book and the one that was called *The River of Run*. I read this book over and over and over again. I got till I was about seventeen years old, and I found a book in a crate somewhere. I was like, Oh, man, you know, I'm looking at my book. Oh, they got my He-Man book. And I was like, *The River of Ruin*. I have been calling that book *The River of Run* for eleven years. I'm like, "Oh, that must be a little bit dyslexic." But and that was even with me reading like *Sports Illustrated* the whole time. Yeah, that's what I did as well. I read a lot of *Sports Illustrated*, that was really it. Besides going to school, I never went to the library. I don't even know what the inside of a Richmond library looks like, to tell the truth.

Mychal Threets: I think reading has always been a part of my life. My mom was also my teacher. I was homeschooled all the way up until high school. I've always read. My parents always had us reading for an hour a day. They didn't care what we read. We read *Wayside School*, *Junie Jones*, *Bud, not Buddy*. First book I ever remember reading was *Where the Wild Things Are*. I ended up having i tattooed it on my arm, so that tells you how much I ended up loving that one. But I love sports too. I love basketball. I love football. So I started reading Matt Christopher all the way up until high school. Even when we were playing video games, we would mute the video games and we would listen to *Chronicles of Narnia* and other things on audiobook. I've always been into reading, but the library was a big part of my life. I've had a library card since I was five years old and I now work for the library where I got my first library card from. I'm a true lifelong reader.

Tiffeni Fontno: Tell us about your childhood and adolescent experiences in public and school libraries. What was that like for you all?

Andrew Sekou Jackson: I was just saying that the school library was just a place to hang out for me because I didn't have to go to the library to read because I did so much reading at home. But I got to know the library from my school library. And then when I would go to the local public library, the Dewey decimal system drove me crazy. So, I was always asking questions of the librarian and pestering them to find what I needed to find. Plus, it was a place where all the girls were, so that was the place to hang out.

Mr. John: We went to the school library from time to time in school. You know, just like with your class. The only thing I can really remember about the library is I always, always did feel safe in the library. I could say that there was always this aura in the library when you come in. For me, I felt safe in that space more than I think any other place in the school. It was just a nice place to be. So, I mean, that's really what I remember the most about it.

AJ Allen: I think what I remember is going inside of the media center and them having book fairs. The books I wanted from the book fair. My mom said, "No, I can't get no more video game books." And always seeing older white women telling me and my friends to be quiet because we were too loud in the library. Ironically, you know, this is what we're doing now, telling the kids to be quiet in the library.

It's always been a positive experience. The only times we actually went was when we were at school. I thought it was pretty interesting, just listening to everybody else's stories and even seeing how I see the teens and tweens and the elementary kids coming to the library. It was a different experience, but you see how important the library is for the youth.

Mychal Threets: It was interesting for me to grow up in a public library. Even now, because I work for the same library system, it's very weird to see my childhood librarian still in the library system that I work for. But I always love to like the librarian Mr. Johnson. It was a safe place for me is where I hung out, where I felt safe. We got to know the librarians. They always would greet us when we come in and grab our holds. They would teach us how to use a self-checkout machine. And then I never had any experience in school libraries being homeschooled. I think I got to go to a Scholastic book fair somehow. I don't even remember how we got invited to this Scholastic book fair when we were homeschooled, but we made it. Otherwise, my first true experience with school libraries was as a children's librarian visiting the kids throughout Vallejo and Fairfield. So that was definitely an interesting experience for me growing up and then coming full circle as an actual librarian.

Tiffeni Fontno: What was your library use? Do you remember what might have caused you to go or stay away from school and public libraries? And how were the librarians? How do you feel like were they there for you? Please share those experiences.

Andrew Sekou Jackson: You know, to be honest, I can't remember any of the librarians in my neighborhood when I was growing up. I guess because I did so much reading, I didn't rely on the library to do the reading. I do know the impact that the library had once I got involved with libraries at Langston Hughes Library. I know the impact that the library had on children in our community.

As most of the Brothers said, it was a safe haven for the children to come to after school. Once we got them in the library there were two things that children asked for. The first thing they did when they came into the library was to ask where was the bathroom? And the second was, Can somebody help me with my homework? That got us started in creating an after-school homework assistance program at our library. Initially it started from third to seventh graders and we would hire local high schools and college students to be the paid tutors. It provided job opportunities as well. And over the thirty-six years that I was at Langston Hughes, we now have great grandparents bringing their great grandchildren to that same homework assistance program. Students will still come there. And that will be the place that Mom says, "After school, you go to the library, I'll pick you up on the way home. But that's where I expect you to be when I come out of come from work, you be at the library." The library is that safe haven for a lot of our children.

Mr. John: I'm glad to hear that, Mr. Sekou, where I am right now, my library is like right, right around three schools, the middle school, the high school, and the elementary school. We get a lot of students at the library and most of them are sitting there, waiting for their parents to come pick them up. They're trying to do their homework. They're trying to decompress from the day from being in high school and wearing a mask all day. This is something that's needed. Like it was needed when you first started your program and it's still needed today. So, I'm glad to hear. As far as for me, like, the library was kind of around even when wasn't, I wasn't even thinking about trying to be in the library. I got to Old Dominion and my work study was at the library. I went to try to find a real job. And, you know, eventually I was like, oh, well, you know, I was working at the library for two years, but let me go try the library. I ended up at the library, left the library again after like seven years, and I did all kinds of crazy stuff, I ended back at the library again. That third time was a charm, and it was like, look this is where you're supposed to be. That's been my experience with the library is almost like this is always like a home. It's always a safe, a safe space for me.

AJ Allen: Me growing up, I think it was a disconnect. Probably after elementary school, like middle school and high school, I wasn't in the library like that. But once I got back into college and I was at Lincoln University of Missouri, one of my friends, when I was trying to get into the nursing program, I needed the job. And he was like, "Look, man, come work for the library." So, when I started working in the library, I noticed how active the library was. I didn't even know libraries had cafes. I didn't know you can get DVDs from the library. When I was introduced to this world and I was like, "Oh, people look like us in here, okay, this is dope." Even now, like at my current library and my previous library, where we had partnerships with a middle school and an elementary school, when you see all these kids come in it's a beautiful thing because I think times have changed. Parents don't trust their kids at home, so they need somewhere to go. They need to be in a safe haven spot like the other Brothers mentioned, where we can provide program, educational resources, and just introduce them to a different element. Because I don't remember or recall any interactions with the librarians I had when I was younger. When I'm connecting with them, asking them how their day was, they go a long way as far as establishing rapport and getting them interested in what they want to read, what type of programs versus me just going to Baker and Taylor, just ordering whatever, I've got the source right there. It's a really, really dope experience to engage with the youth because you'd be so surprised how much information you get because guess what? That's our job anyway, is to get information.

Mychal Threets: I was always really close with my with my local librarians. They meant a lot to me. They always knew who I was. We'd see them in Costco and they'd recognize you. And even though we thought we, we always thought they lived in the library. So we were shocked to see them in Costco shopping with all of us. But they always greeted us by name. They always knew who we were, and that meant everything to me. And I was luckily lucky enough to be a children's librarian in a in a small neighborhood library, which I think small libraries are the best libraries just because they are able to connect with everybody who visits. The same thing as everyone else was saying, I use my childhood librarians' influence on me, knowing who I am to connect with all the kids in middle schoolers and high schoolers who came into the library, and I was able to get to know them and get them to trust me. And even when the middle schoolers are showing off for all the girls, as soon as they're done, they come back and they're like, all right, where was that book you were talking about? Now we can get down to business and all that good stuff. So yeah, the library definitely had an impact on me growing up. I don't think there was ever a time where I didn't go to the library. Maybe I went through some things for a few years before I became a library worker. So maybe that two-year window and other than that, the library has been in my life for twenty-nine of thirty-one years.

Tiffeni Fontno: Did you all have reading role models? If so, who was it like Sekou mentioned his mom was a teacher, but who was that reading role model and what did they do to model, you know, your literacy practices?

Andrew Sekou Jackson: My first role model for reading was my was not necessarily my mother, who was the one that made sure we did our reading as the mother teacher. But my father was my first role model one. He was always reading the Bible, but he read the newspapers, he read the magazines he read. So, the example of it was cool to read came from my father. And then the second role model was my older brother. Who was who was in college when we were in elementary and middle school and him always having books around him and reading. And then, of course, him having all these good-looking girlfriends. I figured there must be a connection between going to school, reading, and girls. So that was always the model that I had that I wanted to emulate. And I'll tell you a short story. When I graduated from middle school, my older brother Walter gave me this book. It was Langston Hughes *Simple Stakes, a Claim*. And written in the cover of the book, 1960, "Dear Press, he called me by my middle name Preston. I hope you find out who Langston Hughes is. Your brother, Walt." That was in 1960. Twenty years later, I started working at Langston Hughes Library. And then I really started learning who Langston Hughes was because I started reading all the works of Langston Hughes. So that was my that was my role models to, reading and that was cool to read and cool to be around books.

AJ Allen: I would say my role models were obviously my parents. My father, you know, he was a die-hard Laker fan like me. But, you know, we were checking out the box scores and Michael Jordan, even when Magic left the Lakers, we were checking out the Lakers before Kobe came with Nick Van Exel. We always reading the box scores because back then, social media wasn't around, or we didn't have NBA league pass. We had to read the newspapers to get hold and stay updated on what was going on in the NBA world. Also my mother, she was going to school while she was help raising me and my sister. She was in nursing school, so she was always throwing books at me. She's like, "AJ, what do you need to read? What are you interested in?" She stayed and risked, you know, her money financially as far as subscribing to, like *Mr. Jones* said, *Sports Illustrated*, basketball magazines, video game magazines, hip-hop magazines. When she was reading and studying, me and my sister were at the table reading with her. That obviously established a culture of reading and it never left me. I'm just thankful for that.

Andrew Sekou Jackson: You just reminded me of it. In the summertime, when you're ready to go out there and spend the whole summer out in the park playing ball. My mother would say, "I know you're going to go out to the park and I'm not going to see you until dinnertime. But before you go out, you got to sit down and read for an hour." That was a teacher in her over the summer. She said, "You're not going to use your reading skills over the summer. You're going to read at least an hour every day before you go out and play."

Mr. John: I would say I really didn't have a mentor per se. My mentor was boredom. So I'm the only child and my mama's only child. I lived with my mama. When I got in trouble, the TV got shut down, the video games got shut down. What did I had left . . . He-Man and *Sports Illustrated*. So I would read them and I read them over and over and over again. But secondly, just like Mr. Sekou, I think he said your dad was reading the Bible. My mom got to a point later in life where she started reading the Bible, and, and so she was reading a lot. One time I did something I was doing, did something foolish. I stayed in trouble, but I felt like I didn't do that much that was bad. But she was like, "Boy, you need some wisdom. Go read Proverbs." I was like, okay and so I started reading Proverbs. That would be the other major book that I started reading because I read Proverbs and then I just like kept reading because I was like, "What is this big book? Let me just keep reading this, you know? And that way maybe I'll stay out of trouble."

Mychal Threets: I think I had three different role models for reading role models. Growing up, my mom was my biggest one. She would always read to us when we were kids. Every single day she would read to us. She would read. She even read for school. She read the Homer. She read *Odyssey*. She even read *A Child Called "It"* by Dave Pelzer, which I don't know if you read that book, but it should not have been read aloud to kids. But she still did it and it had an impact. We weren't scarred, so kudos to her for that. I think the second one was my grandfather, my mom's dad. He was he's the biggest Stephen King fan in the world. And then he and I read the Harry Potter as kids and grandpa. We would just talk about that after every single book. That was big. I think that's the that's the closest thing I am to my grandfather is reading Harry Potter. And then third is LeVar Burton. I love LeVar Burton and *Reading Rainbow*. If I hear the *Reading Rainbow* theme song, it just makes my soul awaken a little bit. Just the style and energy he had reading books, and it meant the world to me. And some of you guys may not know, but I do too many TikTok's and I love using the *Reading Rainbow* theme song and LeVar Burton. So those are my three reading role models. They made me who I am today.

Mr. John: I just want to point out, like, I hope. I hope young people get to see this or hear this or at least, some portions of this, because you are, you're hearing and seeing the many different environments of people who consider themselves to be readers. You know what I'm saying? You have someone who's been reading all their life and then you got others that, you know, kind of like read sporadically, or read like things that weren't necessarily considered to be reading.

The parents to come in and will say "I want my child to read *War and Peace*. Where are the *War and Peace* books." And you're like, "What? What are you talking about?" So it's just good to hear. I hope people get to see that you don't have to have the perfect, or you know, what we call it kind of consider like the perfect upbringing to be a reader. All you got to really do is like, just read the things that you really love and, and, you know, and just go from there.

Andrew Sekou Jackson: I have to piggyback off that as well. One of the things that I remember having conversations, not only with kids that came to the library with the homework program, which was on the same floor as my office. So outside my office, the big open floor had the homework program there. Whenever the kids would act up, especially the little boys. When they would act up, they had to go to see Mr. Jackson. So I would sit down and talk to them about why don't you like to read? What's wrong? What's going on? and befriend them. They all knew me because I came from the neighborhood. It wasn't like I was a stranger. I grew up in that same neighborhood that I worked in for thirty-six years. So that was home. They would sit there and be good because it was Mr. Jackson and they knew their mother or their grandmother knew who Mr. Jackson was. Then I'd start talking to him and then I would start talking to him about things that dealt with Black history. And that was the other thing that happened with this library, is that it introduced me to my history and culture, but I would start asking the questions to try to find out what they were interested in.

Then I would take them downstairs and take them to the children's room and let them see books about what they were interested in, whether it was the Lakers or whether it was the Knicks. In New York, it wasn't the Lakers, it was the Knicks or the Nets, or it was the Mets or the Yankees. Then it start them looking at things. The other thing that got them interested was the fact that there were books in the library that dealt with Black people. It was because they didn't get that in school. It wasn't in their curriculum. They got introduced to the history and culture. Once I got them interested in things, they would calm down, they would sit down, they would listen, and then I could get them to go back out and sit out there and do their homework on a regular basis.

Tiffeni Fontno: How could the relationship have been improved and what difference would that have made to have a librarian that knew the young patron? Mychal had a librarian who knew who knew his name. What difference would that have made with the kids that people see coming into libraries? What are your thoughts?

AJ Allen: I would like to comment on that. That is a big thing when you talk about librarians in general, when they always talk about all the kids coming into the library. The reason why I've been successful dealing with the kids, I tell them because I talk to them. I treat them like they're adults, especially the middle school and high schoolers. You're developing that rapport with them that goes a long way when they do probably need homework assistance or just someone to talk. Because they're going through puberty or they like girls or they ask Mr. Billy, Could you do a program? I'll make it happen, you know, because I'm getting that information from them. You have to engage with the youth. You can't shy away from them. I'm telling you get so much energy. I think the dopest thing about it is you get to see them grow up. I mean, literally, when I left Pembroke Pines Library, I literally was doing programs and providing resources for kids in elementary school and in middle school. I've seen them driving now. Some of them are going to college. Having teens wanting to come back to volunteer at the library. You don't understand how much impact that you have, especially when they see someone that looks like them. It's a different type of language. A lot of my librarians, I hate to say it, some of my librarians I used to manage, they were White and they used to look at me and they would say, "How are you having this connection?" I tell them look, I mean, it's something that you can't teach, but I am engaging with them. I'm going to always say that word because it's so important. I mean, that's just a little food for thought, you know, as far as engaging with the teens.

Andrew Sekou Jackson: There's another links that may be invisible to everybody listening to this or watching this, but there's two different links that I've heard so far that cannot be overlooked from my generation to Michael's generation. You see that gap in time, but you see the commonality.

One of the common factors I see because I did an extensive amount of outreach into my community schools, organizations, churches, city agencies, Rikers Island for fourteen years, going back and talking to inmates. One of the things that always shocked them was that I was a Black man and I was a librarian. The impact that had on young brothers that librarians could be men, changed their perspective. In fact, the first librarian director at Langston Hughes Library was a man because the woman who was selected to be the director said, no, no . . . in fact, the Black Panther Party said we need a man to be a role model for brothers to read and libraries as a cool thing to do. So having men in librarianship like E. J. Josey, who is my mentor, was part of that catalyst, that impact you can't even understand what that impact is on younger generations.

The second is all of us talked about books and reading from home before we even got to the library. So, the impact that the family has, seeing Dad read, seeing Mom read, seeing books be cool, seeing libraries at the home, that is part of that lexicon that a lot of children don't have. But that was the purpose that the library served, because if you couldn't afford to buy books and have them at home, you could borrow them at the library and learn how to be responsible and take them back.

Tiffeni Fontno: How did you find out about and become librarians? Tell that story.

AJ Allen: I'll go first. Well, first and foremost, I flunked out of college initially, trying to chase all the girls, and my dad made me enlisted in the Air Force. I had to mature, traveled the world. When I got out of the military, I was twenty-two, trying to figure out what I wanted to do. I ended up going back to school to work on my bachelor's at twenty-five. I was following Mom's footsteps as becoming a nurse. Midway through my undergrad, shout out to my homeboy Bradley Kirkendall and Lincoln University. He was like, "Yo man, I'm about to be a librarian." The first question that I asked him is the same question I get to this day. I said, "What the hell does a librarian do?" He introduced me to the field of librarianship. He introduced me to our mentor, Jerome Offord. And then we got introduced to Kelvin Watson and Makeeba Foster. I did not know how big this field was, and I thought it was pretty dope. I never saw Black male librarians before, like Mr. Jackson said, so I ended up changing my bachelor's degree and getting my bachelor's degree in biology with a minor in library science.

And then when I moved back home to North Carolina, I got my MLS from NCCU in 2016. I'm five years in the game and haven't looked back. I always felt like I was an entertainer, hosting talent shows and stuff like that. My ability to engage with the youth was kind of natural. I ended up falling into being a youth librarian. Everybody loves engaging with the little ones. I love storytelling, but I also like impacting the older ones too, because that is so important. Representation is so important. I say this all the time. What we're doing right here on this panel is so important for the younger ones because it's more to Black men than becoming an athlete or a rapper. You could do some positive things. Librarianship has changed my life. I'm just trying to spread the word, bring more brothers into the field because it's much needed. It's a dope field. You have a lot of career advancement. I've been blessed and I just love seeing brothers like everyone on this panel practicing the field of librarianship.

Mr. John: I'll go after AJ after he gave that rousing rendition of why you should be a Black librarian. I'll use this example because AJ loves basketball. I love to help people. If I was playing basketball, I would be a point guard. I would rather pass the ball into somebody else, score, and then be the one that had to go and try to score myself. That's always how I've been. I was just out there, man. I didn't know what I really wanted to do. I majored in history. I got my degree in history, but I still couldn't figure out like how I wanted to do it. All of these other little jobs that I was finding it was always kind of in like the service field. The last job before I got the librarian before I really began to be a librarian was in insurance. All of that's like kind of like customer service, like helping people. When I was able to get back into the library in 2015 I was looking at it like, I love to help people. I love the library. I'm gonna go full steam ahead with this. When I went, when I got back in there. Oh, my goodness. It's like I haven't been working since, like, 2015. I haven't been working. I've just been going somewhere and get paid because, really, I would do it for free, you know what I'm saying? If I had ten million dollars, I would go and just volunteer at the library all day. I would do it for free, but thank God, they paid me. I appreciate that. I was working with the youth. It was just wonderful, man. Just to see their eyes, man. When they look at you, when you're doing story time or you're telling a story or you're doing the craft and you're on the floor with them. Both of y'all trying to color something or put something together. It's just wonderful. It's just wonderful.

And those experiences are what led me to go ahead and get this degree and stop playing. And I love it. I mean, I finally found a place where I was supposed to be after being out there, not really knowing what I wanted to do.

Mychal Threets: For me, I think I kind of stumbled upon becoming a librarian. Again, I grew up in libraries, but I think in the back of my mind, I never knew that I could become a librarian. I never saw a male librarian. I don't even think I ever saw a Person of Color librarian, even growing up in libraries. And then I experienced severe depression, panic disorder, and anxiety and then I somehow returned to the library. I was just reading books every single day. I went up to the front desk and I asked the person there how can I apply for a job at the library? I don't think I thought they were going to say no. People like you can't apply to become a librarian, but I'm sure somewhere in the back of my mind it was there. But no, she said, you can apply. I went to the county site. I applied to be a shelver. I got hired. I was a shelver for two years. I saw a posting for library aid. I said, "Hey, I like this job. Maybe I'll apply. Maybe if I get it, maybe librarianship is for me." They showed me some kindness and they gave me the library aid job. I became a library assistant. I went to library school while I was working full time, became a library associate briefly, and then got hired as a librarian, as a children's librarian. Loved it for a year. So yeah, I stumbled upon becoming a librarian.

Andrew Sekou Jackson: My introduction to becoming a librarian was by accident. The irony is, as active as I am with this profession now with BCALA and the executive board and past president. I didn't go into it knowingly. I had worked in human resources for eight years. I'd worked in when I was up in Novato, California. I worked with Robinson Chevrolet, so I was in sales and in customer service. Then I came back to New York. I was out of work looking for work for eighteen months. And then the members of the community board at our library said, Andrew, you need to apply for this job as the assistant supervisor wasn't directing. It's called the assistant supervisor because they need somebody with some background in business. They need somebody who's from the community and who's been an activist in the community, and we need you at the library. So I said, "Look, I'm looking for work. I need to pay my bills." I worked there for a couple of years, and then I'll go back to California. The rest is history. Because once I got at Langston Hughes, I started understanding the difference between what that library was about. It was a library that was focused on the Black experience for the borough of Queens and not just a local community. And after I'd been there for a couple of years and got settled in the job, they said, Andrew, you need to go back and finish your undergraduate degree.

I transferred to York College here in Queens, and the first class I took was a Black studies class. So taking Black history, that just opened my eyes to this history I'd never known about. But all this history about people and then having access to the library as the supervisor on Sunday when nobody was there, I'd come in the library, spend the whole day doing all my research and studies at the library, and the more I got ingrained in the library, the more I got ingrained in history and culture. That's what started the transition from my life, and it just changed completely.

E. J. Josey was the one that said "You need to become a librarian" because I really had gotten so immersed in Black studies that I wanted to get my master's in black studies and Africana studies, and even think about going to get a PhD, which is a whole story in itself. But the only two campuses that had graduate programs was Temple University in Philadelphia and Cornell University, in upstate New York. And I wasn't going to leave my job at Langston because I was so committed to what I was doing there to take time off for a year or two years to go and work on a graduate degree. So E. J. I said, "Well, why don't you get your library science degree? You're in the profession." That was how I got involved in the library in Black studies and the transition. The transition it made in my life came from being at Langston Hughes Library.

Tiffeni Fontno: Let's talk about children's librarianship. Share the positives and barriers of being a Black male librarian as a children librarian.

Andrew Sekou Jackson: I guess I'll open that up because I'm probably the only one here that wasn't a children's or young adult librarian. I came in as a manager, but my outreach, I participated in readings. I participated in career days. I would go to the schools and do talks on Black history. I would introduce the students to Kwanzaa. My interaction with the schools, they thought I was a children's librarian and then I would bring them to the library and introduce them to the librarian.

But as the manager, I had the ability to do all of that outreach to the total community and even go to parent organizations and talk to them about the importance of libraries. Talk to them about the importance of them sitting down and reading with their children and not leave it to the responsibility of the teacher. My impact was as a manager, but the impact was that I was representing the library profession and not just Langston Hughes Library.

AJ Allen: I would say my experience being a youth librarian has been amazing. It's been life changing. Like Mr. Jackson said, outreach is so important. Every library has its own community, and that's the dopest thing about being a children's librarian, is you're going to engage in different diverse communities. I learned this term a couple of years ago, and I really believe youth librarians should abide by that. It's the three Cs: creation, curiosity, and community. Like, you have to have those three Cs as far as trying to adapt and assess what the community needs. We have an uptick and an uprise of young adult parents coming up right now. You have a lot of single parents. You have a lot of stay-at-home moms, depending on what type of community. I've worked in communities where you had stay-at-home moms, people had money. But guess what? Just because they had money, they didn't have nothing to do with their kids. They needed resources. They needed programs, especially during the summertime. Storytime was so important into developing their early literacy skills and also giving the parents a break and then exposing them to other resources. I think that is the most fulfilling thing as far as introducing families and communities every day to what the library has to offer.

This past Saturday, I dressed up as a pirate and convinced my staff to dress up as pirates for Talk like a Pirate Day. I was doing that and I'm managing the library. But guess what? Every time I see families coming around, I'm giving them spontaneous storytimes. Because the best thing about being a youth librarian is you can create an experience every time you come into the library. It's going to be an experience when you come in there, and that's the most gratifying thing. I don't think it's any negative things that's happened to me as far as being a youth librarian, maybe the challenges of transitioning into management, but also mean I'll never forget my first librarian job in Jacksonville. Meeting all the higher-ups and the library administration, and it was an older White man. He had been at least by eighty-five, so he was just staring at me at orientation like this, and I knew what he was getting at. He said, "Do you know how rare you are?" I said, "Sir, I'm just happy to be here." I knew what he was getting at. We are considered unicorns in this field. I'm not worried, I consider it a badge of honor because I know we're impacting the youth.

Mr. John: But as far as for me being a youth librarian. By the time, by the time I got back into the library in 2015, I was like, so comfortable with who, who I am as a person. I had a nice long journey. By the time I got there I really had like knowledge of who I am, knowledge itself. I took it for granted that I was in this space doing what I was doing and helping. I was in a library that had all ethnicities and all ethnicities, came to our library, all ages, came to our library. And so, you know, I was there and I was just working. I was just having a good time. And my wife, she said something, "You know, them kids ain't never seen a Black librarian before."

I started thinking about my early library experiences I think about a school librarian. I think about this old woman. That's like when you think about librarians, that's the person that I think about. It kind of dawned on me after a while that, I'm giving me I'm showing these children, the young people here, something that I never saw in my life. I was kind of taken aback from it. But at the same time, I love what I was doing.

I know who I am. I was always comfortable wherever I am. The other day one of the teens came and dapped me up. I was like, "How are you doing?" He was like, "Oh, Mr. John is here today, I can check out a book." I was like, "You can check out a book any day, man." He was like, "Nah, nah, I'll check out a book when you here." That statement says two different things. I'm just appreciating my presence and understanding that I'm needed, especially, for Black boys. I'm needed and we're needed to be in that space for them to be comfortable. I always felt comfortable no matter who was in the library. But that's not always going to be the same situation for other people.

Mychal Threets: I think someone in the chat had mentioned how it's hard for kids to get to the library sometimes because their parents are tired after work or whatever circumstances are happening. And I think in my experience, that is one of the biggest challenges as a children's librarian is accessibility for kids and families to the library. I'm going to echo everybody else and say, that's why outreach is so important. I was always doing outreach. I would spend eight hours at a school talking to every single class if I could. I was blessed with super cool, friendly, kind coworkers who were willing to take extra desk hours so I could talk to as many people as possible. I would always agree to any school, any center, anyone who asks for me to come and talk to their kids about the library, about library cards, about the importance of books, any books, regardless of their level, just the joy of reading. I was more than happy to talk to them about that. Outreach always created some of the coolest opportunities, the coolest moments for me. I remember I would go to a lot of the same centers, same child starts, same locations.

One of my favorite memories is this little girl. I saw her every single time and she was about two. She was about to leave. She was telling me she was like, "I'm not going to see you anymore, Mr. Michael." First she came in and she said, "Mr. Michael, my Brown librarian, I want to be a Brown librarian. I'm going to be leaving soon. Someday I'm going to be a Brown librarian and I will see you again." And then she sat down and her little friend next to her, who was White said, "Well, I want to be a Brown librarian." And she leaned next to me and she said, "Well, we can all be Brown librarians." So because kids don't see my color, they just see me as a crayon, they see my skin color. And so just like that, because of outreach, because of being out there, because of just showing the joy of books, I'm not the smartest librarian. I don't know everything at all. I will admit that every single time. But I just have sheer library and book joy, and I think that's what the kids saw. That's why I tried to show them every single time. And that's why maybe she and her little friend want to be Brown librarians someday, even if one of them is not. It doesn't have to be Brown, right?

Andrew Sekou Jackson: I have to piggyback off that because that to two instances I can think of. The most recent was, I think in 2019 when I had to go back to Atlanta to close out my brother's affairs. When he passed away, I'm sitting in the airport getting ready to come back to New York, and this young, good looking tall brother sits across from me. I'm sitting there reading and he keeps looking up and I'm watching him and I'm seeing that this is a probably going to be a lawyer or a doctor one day. And he looks at me and he says, "Excuse me, can I ask you a question?" I said, "Yes." He says, "Aren't you from Langston Hughes Library?" And this is in Atlanta, Georgia, and the Langston Hughes Library is located in Corona,

Queens, New York. He says, "I thought I remembered you." He said, "I was in the homework program and you always made us want to read. You always made us want to do the right thing and do our homework. And you always made us proud that you were a Black man running that library." And so you never know the influence that you have on children that come into the library and what that impact can mean years later.

The other story was a young brother who was one of those reluctant readers that sat down one day, and I introduced him to Langston Hughes poetry and I introduced him to Black history. He now is a father of, I think, three or four boys. He lives in Florida. He's got his own business in southern Florida. He's down in southern Florida. He says he to this day, he sits down with his children, reads Black history books to them. Talks about Black history as he makes sure he takes them to the library. They all have their library cards and they circulate books because he said, "I learned that from you when I was a kid that was reluctant reader. You made me want to learn how to read." So those things stay with you when you hear about them years later.

Tiffeni Fontno: What barriers do you see for engaging Black males with literacy and what needs to happen to engage Black males with literacy?

AJ Allen: From my experience, the main barrier is the communication. Once again, I keep saying, you have to communicate with the youth. They'll tell you everything, what they want to read. It's just like us as an adult. I can't assume what Mister John likes to read as an adult. Your job is supposed to assess the needs. It's time to change. You got to get creative with reading. I always tell the teens, you ain't never going stop reading. If you say "You don't like reading that book. Well, let me find something you want to read." I know most of the young men either like sports or let's say they're into graphic novels. I like to talk to them and I'll indirectly be kind of getting the feel of what they're into. That's when I go to my book ordering or if I'm trying to create a program for them. I remember what James (a young patron) said or I remember what his homie said, what they wanted to read. They didn't see any books when Kobe Bryant died. I said, "Oh, no, this is all bad." So I made that happen. It's all about interacting with the youth. I think that eliminates the barrier as far as trying to get the information and resources you need to give to them.

Mr. John: To add on top of that, is the representation. It's the seeing it at home. Seeing it in your community, in your sphere, so seeing people read, when they see this, see that you're reading, then they're more apt to read. When you have books at home and you have that access to books, then they're going to be readers. If they have the books at home. I'm just piling on top of what AJ said. But representation. If you're a parent, a guardian, or educator just let them see you read sometime. Just hold the book. That way they were like, "Oh, you know what, Dad's reading or my mom's reading or whatever. Let me go and see what's going on with reading."

Andrew Sekou Jackson: I think the two things. One thing, one of the principles I picked up from Kwanzaa is self-determination. One of the things that I started doing when it got introduced to Kwanzaa in the 1980s is every time I give a gift, my niece, when she was an infant, my triplet sister brought her off the plane in a bassinet. The first thing I did was give her a book of children's folktales from Africa. She couldn't read then she was too small. But from that day on, every time I gave her a gift, no matter what the gift was for graduation, birthday, whatever it is, she always got books.

Now I'm helping her build her own library. And I think that is one of the things we need to do, because reading and books are not part of our natural lexicon. We need to make sure that children feel that books are accessible. And also that it is cool to read. Every time you give them a gift for any purpose, include a book as part of that gift for something that they love, whether sports or fashion or history or American history, whatever it is. Give them books so that they can develop their own library and feel comfortable around books.

Mychal Threets: Some barriers that I've seen for reaching, for reaching Black boys and Black men with books and literacy is at an early age, is showing them that representation, showing them a person. I remember finding out how often kids would tell you that they didn't have a dad either. Their dad had unfortunately passed away or they knew that their dad was in jail. But then they would see me and then they would see my tattoos on my arm, and they'd be like, "Hey, you have tattoos? Like my dad, you have tattoos like my uncle." And they would connect to me, and they would see me liking and appreciating reading. And again, the cool factor of books is the hard part. Like those others were saying, showing them that there's something for everybody. There's Black Panther books. There's books that Kobe Bryant wrote. I live in the Bay Area. There are a bunch of Warriors fans who just found out that Steph Curry has a book club. I would get to know them, and they would mess with me. I'd mess with them. They'd find out I'm a Lakers fan. They'd be like, "Why are you always cheering for the Lakers? Why isn't it the Warriors?" And I'd be like, "That's because the Lakers are seventeen-time champions. I'm sorry, what do you want me to tell you?" And then from there, you make that connection, and it just grows from there. I think the way that we can keep on going forward is just reaching kids where they're at. I'm a big proponent of using social media to reach Black boys, Black men, even. That's why I keep on using TikTok. My library has a TikTok. I have a TikTok. I don't dance on TikTok. That's my only rule. But using their using their Instagram, asking them what they want to see, letting them set your content for you because they're the ones who are going to provide you with the answers. If you talk to them, they'll let you know how you can reach them to get them engaged with literacy.

Tiffeni Fontno: Thank you so much, panelists. I really do appreciate this. If anybody in the audience has a question, please feel free to ask.

Roosevelt Weeks: Austin Public Library. Mr. Sekou, have been inspired by you guys, but I do want to make a couple statements. Yeah, I do want to make a statement. And that's to Mr. Threads and Mr. Allen. If you ever want to come to Austin to work, please let me know; you got a job and mean that. But thank you, guys. Y'all been really inspiring. All the stuff we go through. This was inspiring. Midweek manna. This is absolutely wonderful. Thank you all for inspiring me to keep going on.

Andrew Sekou Jackson: I have to tell you, one of the hardest decisions I've had to make was retiring from day-to-day librarianship. I mean, that was really a very difficult decision. But I'm still so involved in the profession, I don't feel like I'm retired because my activity with BCALA and what I do.

The other thing I wanted to say that the inspiration of what we get from our children can turn out to be something that elevates your life as well. I was at a high school in Brooklyn doing a presentation trying to encourage young people during library week to read and use books and introduce them to Langston Hughes. They could not connect with Langston Hughes. I started comparing at that time, Tupac Shakur's book came out, *The Rose That Grew from Concrete*. I had read that and read the poetry in there. And I started to compare Tupac's life with Langston Hughes's life and the themes in their poetry and that started to connect him to who Langston Hughes was. Eventually I started writing about it and wrote a whole essay entitled "In the Tradition: The Legacy of Cultural Messages from Langston Hughes to Tupac Shakur." And it actually got published. I've been using that essay to interact with young people and connect them to students and reading and Langston Hughes since then.

You never know what the impact of what you do as a librarian is going to do on your life as a professional librarian and as an author and reader as well. I love this profession. I also feel that all of us are doing what we do because the creator set that path for us. I never thought about being a librarian. When I look back, I could never think of anything that I would have done other than being a librarian. And everything I did before that was preparing me to be a librarian.

AJ Allen: I want to answer the question about how we bridge the gap between the importance of growing up seeing Black male librarians and actually getting to work in libraries. As far as like, information and college, honestly, I lived through it. I went through it when I was at Lincoln University of Missouri. My mentor, Jerome Offord, created the only information library information science minor, and this is at an HBCU. He had me and my homies. It was seven of us, and then it was ten other brothers and sisters that was enrolled into this program. Only six of us actually went through it. He put us in internships at WashU when we was in Saint Louis to get exposed to different fields of librarianship, where I met Makeeba Foster and Kelvin Watson, where we went to ALA for the first time, went to BCALA for the first time in 2012.

Those are the type of experiences and mentorship is everything as far as getting young Black men into libraries. I want to adopt that same program that Mr. Offord did for me. And the ultimate way I can do that, I've been giving back. I've put on six of my homeboys that three of them are already in library school and three of them just got their MLS this past year. I think us as Black men just continue to give back promoting the profession and that's going to stand out alone. Because they see us. Once they see us, a Black male librarian, they know the elephant in the room. Just continue to advocate for the profession and I feel like we're going to be fine.

Through their representation as Black men, they bridge the gaps between literature and lived reality, ensuring that every young member of the community finds their own reflection in the stories they encounter. This profound connection not only fosters a love for literacy but also nurtures a sense of identity, pride, and cultural awareness that transcends the library walls. As custodians of both knowledge and heritage, Black male librarians open doors to dialogue, growth, and a renewed understanding of the rich mosaic that is the Black experience. Their significance for our youth lies in their representation in library spaces, the empowerment of voices, their service to community, and commitment to literacy and diversity.

# 6.10

## From Badge to Books

A JOURNEY OF COMMUNITY CARE AND LIBRARY LEGACY

Kelly Richards

I grew up in a close-knit family. My eight siblings and extended family were all close particularly on both sides of the family because my dad was the oldest of his siblings. He raised his youngest brothers and sisters because his father was working in the steel mill and their mother had passed. He brought them the basic items they needed, and they looked to him as their father. As they grew up and started their own families, they all stayed close. My dad was the go-to person when they had problems or needed help with their own families. We were taught to look out for each other and our neighbors.

As I was growing up and thinking about college, I wanted to do something to take care of the community and improve people's lives. Criminal justice was the best fit because it would allow me to do social work or legal work. I graduated with a BS in criminal justice. My first job out of college was as an administrator for a daycare center. Then, I became a foster care social worker but determined that wasn't what I really wanted to do.

After speaking with people in a barbershop, I connected with the head of HR for the city of Flint. He encouraged me to apply for a police officer position. After applying, I removed my name from consideration. The police chief called me and said they wanted me to keep my name in. I became an officer. My idea of a police officer came from *Mayberry RFD*, and I wanted to follow that model. Get cats out of trees and helping kids was my goal as a community police officer. I was an officer in Flint for a long time. Flint was ranked number one for murders for multiple years. I couldn't help people the way that I wanted, and I had second thoughts about this career.

One day, I was chasing suspects from a B&E. One partner caught one suspect. Me and my other partner didn't catch the other suspect. When I was doing my report at the precinct, I saw a childhood friend sitting in a cell. I started talking to him and wondered how he ended up in this situation. I asked him how he was doing and how was our other friend, Phil. He told me that Phil got away. I realized that Phil was the other suspect that I had been chasing. That was the moment where I decided that I wanted to help people before they got into trouble.

I moved to Vegas and did state policing while I figured out what job would help me achieve that goal. One day I was looking at the job board in a library. It was serendipity. I struck up a conversation with the library administrator. We talked about how I wanted to help kids and strengthen communities. She wanted me to apply for a vacancy she had. I applied, didn't get the job, and was pretty bummed out. She called me and told me she wanted my name in the queue because a friend at another library across town needed a children's librarian. Her friend interviewed me and hired me. I put my gun down and started doing story time. I had no idea what I was doing, but I started observing my peers. It helped me not knowing because it attracted kids to the library.

As time went on, programs and attendance increased. We received media attention. I was the manager of the Young People's Department in a historically Black community and enjoyed outreach to the schools and communities. One day, a guy came in to do an Upward Bound program from Virginia Union University and my boss introduced us. We began chatting and exchanged numbers. I went to my part-time job at K-mart later and saw him again there. He asked why I was there, and I said I work here too.

A month or so later I received a call from the University of Pittsburgh. That phone call was from a guy I didn't know named Dr. Josey. He said, "I was sitting in an airport next to this guy and we struck up a conversation. I told him that I was a prof of library science and trying to get more Blacks in library science." The Upward Bound guy gave my name to Dr. Josey. He called me and asked if I wanted to go to library school. He told me about a scholarship, but said I needed to go to PA and work there for two years.

Not too long ago, I'd recently moved to Vegas and was adjusting there. I liked the library system there and built friendships. I wasn't prepared to spend two years in Pennsylvania. We talked and Dr. Josey said he'd get back with me. He called me and said he was offering something he doesn't offer in these circumstances: a graduate student assistantship position. I didn't know what that meant. He said it was a full graduate assistantship with a stipend, full tuition, and medical insurance for me and my family. I couldn't turn that down. Vegas also counteroffered with a stipend, but I knew I needed to do this. I accepted Dr. Josey's offer, and we packed up and moved to Pittsburgh. Got an apartment not far from campus. I was amazed at the city. It was such a cool place. It was the first time I had a sandwich with French fries and a salad with French fries.

Now, I'm in library school and I still don't know who Dr. Josey is. As I spend time with him, talk to him, and help him research his books, I learn that I'm working with a civil rights activist. I had no idea that he was an editor for a newspaper during the Montgomery bus boycott. It was mind-boggling to me that I was working with the founder of the BCALA. We became friends. I learned a lot from him as we went to ALA and other conferences. I'd sit with him, as this green library student, and the greats/trailblazers of Black librarianship, including Andy Venerable, Hardy Franklin, and others of that ilk. They discussed their trials, tribulations, and successes regularly with Dr. Josey. Our connection continued throughout the years. I flew Dr. Josey into Vegas when we had to remodel a building there and Dr. Josey was the keynote speaker for the grand opening.

There was a group of students of color who always hung out, studied, talked, and joked together. We had unspoken communication during some questionable comments in class from our professors. One special event we had on campus was the showing of *Eyes on the Prize* and *Mississippi Burning* in the lobby area. I still keep in touch with them now with random phone calls. We pick up the conversation as if we're still at Pitt. These friends still give me guidance and help in my career.

Pitt was the beginning of my move into professional librarianship. While in school, one of my projects was to develop an African American collection for a library. I wrote a plan for that and the librarian in Vegas used this plan to create a collection that is still there today.

I worked with Jim Wilborn, who ended up as the director of the New Haven Public Library, as a graduate student intern at the Carnegie Library. He oversaw community partnerships and outreach at Carnegie. This opened my eyes to building synergy between libraries, nonprofits, and government agencies. This informed my efforts for literacy, social work, and entrepreneurship programs. I did the internship for the entire academic year instead of one semester. He had a pulse on the community and knew how to grow the library's impact in the community. When I graduated, Mr. Rogers was the keynote speaker and Aisha, a classmate, introduced him. I believe she went on to work for Mr. Rogers after that.

I went back to Vegas as a reference librarian/head of periodicals for one year. Next, the administrator position that I left opened up in an African American neighborhood. I interviewed for it and got it. I did outreach, programs, and rites of passage programs (I developed a series of trainings for youth with an Afrocentric focus to navigate growing up with topics that included health, politics, conflict resolution; youth crossed over into adulthood at the end of the program). Then, I had an opportunity to work in one of the wealthiest communities in Las Vegas. Sun City was one of the largest retirement communities in the country. Here is where I came to understand the term "senior moment." It was interesting to see the difference between a Black and Brown community in poverty and a rich, homogenous community. Turns out there isn't much difference in their needs. They both wanted computers, VHS tapes, and programs. I was the first librarian to start collecting popular videos. Other libraries were mad and said we'd be competing against Blockbuster. I said that we're not competing against Barnes & Noble, or Waldenbooks. I was the only one with popular VHS tapes and it exploded from there.

I worked there for some years, and you never know who's watching you. I got a call from a library director who wanted me to apply for an assistant director position in Flint. She'd been watching me when she visited Sun City. I interviewed and she hired me. It gave me an opportunity to move back to my hometown and spend time with my family, friends, and church members. I worked in Genessee County and loved it as it served rural, suburban, urban, and diverse communities. Engaging elected officials to make sure they are in time with the happenings of the library was a learning experience.

Then, I was recruited to apply for a position in Muskegon. My parents grew up there and it's a place I love. I applied and was offered the position of director, which I accepted. Muskegon had polarizing communities of the far right and far left, which required a good working relationship with both, in terms of communications, outreach, finding out their needs and concerns, building coalitions, heading off political issues before they grew, meeting 1:1 with people, learning to navigate, and bringing people together. We focused on early literacy issues because Muskegon was ranked last for testing for third grade proficiency. We saw Storyville in Baltimore and emulated that in Muskegon. We worked hard to get them in several libraries; got elected support and business support. Put these elaborate playful learning areas in three libraries.

Muskegon's budget was extremely low when I arrived. Six classes in Michigan; we were class 6, which is the largest class. I was able to get the budget increased by two-thirds.

There was a proposed .75 to 1.25 percent budget increase. When it failed, I was crushed. After we lost, I hired a well-known consultant to do a survey of the community and found out what the community wants from their library. I learned that they wanted literacy efforts for youth, a library for the blind, and more services. In our next campaign, we focused on that, and we won by the same percentage of the survey given to residents. We instituted all of the changes that the community wanted, including a millage increase and early literacy programming, more books and materials, a full remodeling of all eleven libraries, and a bookmobile. I was excited about the direction that the system was going. While looking for the next opportunity, I received a call about Philadelphia. I told the recruiter that I thought they were one of my library friends playing a joke on me, but I was interested. It was a long interview process (May through September) until the job was offered. I went through many interviews, including one with friends, staff, board members, and had several with the search firm alone. It was challenging and invigorating. The Free Library needed to find the right person.

I arrived in Philly to learn that my entire administrative team was gone. The interim director was promoted up two levels to support the system. When I came onboard, I needed her to stay in place to help me. There was a lot she knew and a lot she didn't know. We learned together and worked together. It was an unusual position, but I like challenges. We worked together as a great team to make change happen. My experiences in Muskegon and Flint taught me the importance of building political bridges. I worked with our boards to build these relationships. I shared with the City Council and the mayor that the system had critical budget issues and was hurting, not only due to the pandemic, but due to staffing challenges. They gave us a budget increase of $13 million.

I'm here and it's a new beginning. We're trying to reignite the system, address the racial strife, and staff concerns. We're building up our new team, looking at the organization and seeing where we need to perform better. That's where we are now.

Strengthening five-day service across the city through hiring is necessary to restore trust and stability to our communities. Once this is established, our next goal is to add six-day service, which will provide more hours for patron access and programs, followed by seven-day service at several libraries.

We will begin a strategic plan process to learn how community interests and needs have changed and how we can position our library system to further engage our residents. This will involve various stakeholders and set the library system's trajectory for the next ten years. Dr. E. J. Josey's support contributed significantly to my success, and I look forward to leading the continued growth of the Free Library of Philadelphia.

# Chapter 7
# School Libraries

## 7.1

### *The Game Changer*

BECOMING A SCHOOL LIBRARIAN

Sandra Michele Echols and Eboni M. Henry

The role of a school librarian has been evolving over the years. From being a mere custodian of books to becoming an integral part of the educational process, school librarians have become an invaluable asset to the school system. However, despite the importance of this role, there is still a lack of diversity in the profession. This is especially true when it comes to school librarians of color. The lack of diversity in the profession has a direct impact on the quality of education that students receive. It is essential for students to have access to a diverse range of resources and perspectives in order to gain a comprehensive understanding of the world around them.

By having a school librarian of color, students can gain access to a unique set of resources and perspectives that can help them to better understand the world. In addition to providing students with a diverse set of resources and perspectives, a school librarian of color can also serve as a role model for students. By seeing someone of their own race and background in a position of authority, students can gain a sense of empowerment and motivation to pursue their own educational goals. This can be especially beneficial for students of color who may not have had access to such role models in the past. Finally, a school librarian of color can also help to bridge the gap between the school and the community. By having a librarian of color, the school can create a more welcoming environment for students from diverse backgrounds. This can help to foster a sense of community and encourage students to become more involved in the school's activities.

Becoming a school librarian of color can be a game changer for both the school and the students. It can provide students with access to a diverse set of resources and perspectives, serve as a role model for students, and help to bridge the gap between the school and the community. It is essential for schools to recognize the importance of having a school librarian of color and to make the necessary steps to ensure that they are represented in the profession.

Libraries are often seen as a cornerstone of education and learning, providing a wealth of knowledge and resources. However, did you know that having more Black librarians in schools can significantly impact students' academic success? With the lack of representation of Black librarians in the industry, many students are missing out on meaningful cultural connections and mentorship opportunities. Black librarians bring a unique perspective, offering diverse literature, history, and cultural resources to help students better understand and appreciate their identities and those of others. In this chapter, we'll explore why Black librarians are the game changers schools need and the positive impact they can have on students' academic and personal growth.

Black librarians act as cultural liaisons, providing students with a connection to their cultural heritage, something that is often lacking in traditional classrooms. Many students in urban settings come from diverse ethnic backgrounds and may not see their cultures represented in school curriculums. However, Black librarians can bridge this gap by incorporating literature and educational materials representative of different cultures. This is important because students who see their cultures reflected in their available resources are more likely to feel a sense of belonging and pride in their cultural identity.

Moreover, Black librarians can help students explore and understand different cultures, religions, and traditions. They can use their knowledge of diverse cultures to guide students in understanding and appreciating differences, promoting respect, and empathy. Black librarians can also help students inculcate a sense of curiosity and appreciation for the diverse world around them.

However, many schools still lack representation despite the clear benefits of having Black librarians as cultural liaisons. This is due to a lack of diversity in the field and systemic barriers that hinder the hiring and retention of Black librarians.

As Black librarians we are always viewed as mentors and role models for students of color, particularly those from disadvantaged backgrounds. Many students do not have role models or mentors who reflect their ethnic background, making it difficult for them to envision themselves in certain professions or positions of leadership. Black librarians can change this by serving as positive role models and mentors, providing guidance and support to help students achieve their goals.

Moreover, Black librarians can help foster a love of learning among students, demonstrating the value of education and the importance of knowledge. They can serve as academic advisors, helping students with research and study skills and providing guidance on college and career paths.

However, the lack of diversity in the field means many students miss out on the benefits of Black librarians as mentors and role models. This lack of representation is particularly harmful to students from underrepresented communities, who may need access to positive role models or mentors in their personal lives.

One of the most significant benefits of having Black librarians in schools is the diverse literature and resources they can provide. Students with access to various literature and educational materials are likely to engage with learning, develop critical thinking skills, and build empathy and understanding for others.

Black librarians can help diversify the resources available to students, incorporating literature that reflects a variety of ethnic and cultural backgrounds. This can help students better understand and appreciate the experiences and perspectives of others, developing a sense of empathy and respect for different cultures.

Moreover, Black librarians can help fill gaps in the school curriculum, providing resources on topics not covered in traditional classrooms. For example, Black librarians can provide resources on African American history, literature, and culture often overlooked in mainstream curriculums.

However, the lack of diversity in librarianship means many schools need access to diverse literature and resources. This lack of representation can have a significant impact on a student's academic success, as well as their personal growth.

Despite the clear benefits of having Black librarians in schools, some significant challenges and barriers hinder the hiring and retention of Black librarians. One of the most significant barriers is the need for more diversity in librarianship. Many schools and libraries struggle to recruit and retain Black librarians, as there are not enough qualified candidates.

Moreover, systemic barriers such as discriminatory hiring practices, low salaries, and inadequate training opportunities can also hinder the hiring and retention of Black librarians. This lack of representation can significantly impact the quality of education and resources available to students.

The lack of diversity in librarianship also means that Black librarians often face isolation and discrimination in the workplace. This can lead to feelings of burnout and frustration, making it difficult for Black librarians to continue working in the field.

## SUCCESS STORIES OF SCHOOLS WITH BLACK LIBRARIANS

Despite the challenges and barriers Black librarians face, many success stories of schools have embraced diversity and hired Black librarians. These schools have seen significant improvements in student learning outcomes, as well as increased engagement and enthusiasm for learning.

Many urban cities have committed to hiring more Black librarians, recognizing the importance of diversity in education. These school districts have seen significant improvements in student engagement and academic success and increased access to diverse literature and resources.

Moreover, schools that have hired Black librarians have seen improvements in student self-esteem and confidence and a greater sense of belonging and connection to their cultural heritage. This highlights the significant impact that Black librarians can have on students' academic and personal growth.

In conclusion, having more Black librarians in schools can significantly impact students' academic success and personal growth. Black librarians act as cultural liaisons, mentors, and role models, providing diverse literature and resources to help students better understand and appreciate different cultures and perspectives.

However, the lack of representation of Black librarians in librarianship remains a significant barrier to achieving these benefits. Schools and libraries must make a concerted effort to recruit and retain Black librarians, recognizing the importance of diversity in education and the value of having positive role models and mentors for students.

We must also address systemic barriers and discriminatory practices that hinder the hiring and retention of Black librarians. Doing so can create a more inclusive and equitable education system that provides all students with the resources and support they need to succeed.

# 7.2

## The Pivotal Role of Black School Librarians in Promoting Diversity, Equity, and Inclusion in Education vis-à-vis Culturally Responsive Pedagogy

Miriam Thomas and Chanelle Maynard

### THE EVOLUTION OF THE BLACK LIBRARIAN

The evolution of Black librarians has had a storied past post–Civil War. "Throughout their history, African-American librarians have been pioneers, visionaries, risk-takers, hard-workers, innovators, organizers, and achievers."[1] As the annals of time have exemplified, the struggle of Black women and men becoming librarians has been marked by underrepresentation and systemic barriers. Nonetheless, Historically Black Colleges and Universities led the way in teaching library service to those individuals pursuing professional employment in libraries who, in addition, would be serving their community as a cultural center. After World War I, Hampton Institute Library School opened its doors to Black students interested in studying librarianship.[2] A few years later in the early twentieth century, with the shortage of Black librarians across a variety of public libraries and schools, "several Negro institutions became interested in offering professional library training" to Black students.[3] This training served to provide librarians with jobs to service Black patrons in school libraries and public libraries.

At a librarian convention in Virginia during the 1930s, Miss T. Vivian Tucker, a high school librarian in Norfolk, stated that trained school librarians were needed. "It is necessary for scholastic and social purposes. It is the heart of the school."[4] By the mid-1940s in Alabama, an emphasis would start being placed on recruiting and training school librarians for Black students in public schools. During these early years of school library service, Black librarians were trained to teach minority students who were not allowed in the school of the majority population.[5] This helps us to understand the important position Black school librarians have held for almost a century. As early as the 1960s, Maurie Hillson posited,

> One can assume that no particular way of life is superior, but rather that all culture is functional in nature (including lower-class or minority group culture), it is legitimate to expect nay insist, that the public school of America meet the expectations of the youth of any given social class. These expectations can be "aspirationally" middle class in nature, or they can be those that will enable youth to cope better, in a highly relevant way, with their present life situation. If the lifestyles of minority groups and the lower class are granted functional validity, and if the school as a social institution creates programs based on the environmental and motivational correlates of this culture, then by this action the school would truly reflect the most cherished wishes of an operational democracy. The simple truth is that, with rare exception, the American school has discriminated against the lower-class and minority group youth from early childhood education programs on through to all areas of higher education where the so-called enlightened and leadership community should have known better.[6]

It is through this historical lens, viewed across the decades, that we can acknowledge the pivotal role of Black school librarians teaching in a culturally responsive approach that has safeguarded diversity, equity, and inclusion in public school libraries.

### BLACK SCHOOL LIBRARIANS AND CULTURALLY RESPONSIVE TEACHING

Culturally responsive pedagogy is an educational approach that recognizes and values the cultural backgrounds, experiences, and perspectives of students, particularly those from marginalized communities.[7] When teachers can integrate their student's background knowledge and cultural heritage into their instruction as a means of realizing academic achievement, this concept is known as culturally responsive teaching (CRT).[8] CRT aims to create an inclusive and empowering learning environment by incorporating culturally relevant materials, pedagogical practices, and community engagement. In the context of urban school libraries, school librarians of African descent play a crucial role in implementing CRT principles to support the academic and cultural development of students. It is important for Black school librarians to actively engage in their cultural competence training and education to assist and facilitate the learning of the various groups they serve. Librarians are trained to stay informed about current issues and topics related to diversity, equity, and inclusion to ensure collection development and that library services are provided for their demographics. This knowledge enables them to engage with students sensitively, provide appropriate resources, and address any concerns for conflicts that may arise in the library space. Black school librarians' endeavor to provide multilingual resources that cater to the linguistic diversity of their student body. They stock books, magazines, and other resources in different languages spoken by students, fostering a sense of inclusivity and promoting literacy across cultures. The school library cultivates a sense of community by collaborating with families, community organizations, and local authors. These activities illustrate how Black school librarians prioritize fashioning a space that celebrates diversity, promotes cultural understanding, and ensures that all students feel welcome and represented; and are efforts that contribute to a positive and inclusive educational experience for students of all backgrounds.

Culturally responsive teaching methods can support academic achievement. Research consistently demonstrates a positive correlation between the presence of a certified librarian and improved academic performance. Students in schools with certified librarians tend to have higher standardized test scores, improved reading proficiency, and enhanced critical thinking skills.[9] A certified school librarian of African descent can collaborate with teachers to support differentiated instruction and demonstrate how library resources and varied educational strategies will meet diverse student needs. They assist in identifying materials at various reading levels, offering resource for English language learners, and promoting inclusive literature that reflects the backgrounds and experiences of all students.

A colleague, a Black assistant professor teaching preservice teachers, discussed the importance of diverse literature for all students. As students begin her Reading Through Children's Literature course, they are introduced to Rudine Sims Bishop's windows, mirrors, and sliding glass doors metaphor, and throughout the course, students interpret it and reflect on their relationships with books. This metaphor is still regarded as important to "inspire more culturally relevant practices."[10] Among the books shared recently were *I Am Enough* by Grace Byers and *I Am Every Good Thing* by Derrick Barnes and Gordon C. James. Both books feature African American children as the main characters. There were no African American students in those classes, but when the students had to choose books for their demonstrations, those were two of the books they chose. They shared that the books were engaging, and the themes resonated with them. These themes included self-awareness and acceptance, the importance of families and communities, and the significance of having aspirations. The preservice teachers discussed why it was important their future students saw themselves both reflected in the books they read; however, just as importantly, they saw and learned about other cultures.

As a certified school librarian of African descent, and currently an instructor for teachers aspiring to become certified school librarians in Texas, I have witnessed firsthand the positive impact a Black K–12 certified school librarian can have on enriching the school curriculum and in promoting academic success for students. School librarians who identify as Black can provide distinct perspectives and contribute invaluable insights to the field of education based on their background, experiences, and culture. Early in my librarian career, I worked with a ninth grade young man in a Title I urban school who would never check out a library book. In talking with him, he asked if I had a book about Tupac. I did. He checked the book out and several weeks later when the class returned to the library, he told me that was the first book he had ever read. He asked for another book on Tupac, which I did not have. However, I was able to get an interlibrary loan from another school. He read that one also and continued to hold on to it. Eventually, I personally gifted him with a different book on Tupac to read at his leisure. Being culturally responsive also includes making connections with student patrons so that they feel comfortable in opening up. Understanding how my background, experiences, and culture have molded me as a librarian of African American heritage, I believe that the educational efforts of Black school librarians will tend to focus on diversity, equity, and inclusion by embracing culturally responsive teaching methods within the school library program. Black school librarians achieve this by curating collections offering access to an assorted range of diverse literature, creating welcoming and inclusive library environments, and building empathetic relationships with patrons through discussions.

A diverse range of books in the library can benefit all students, irrespective of their background, by providing them with characters they can relate to and identify with culturally, socially, or experientially. This, in turn, can boost their self-confidence and self-esteem while encouraging a positive self-image. When students learn about different characters and cultures, they are presented with diverse viewpoints that can broaden their understanding of the world and help prepare them to be global citizens. As a group that has historically been in the minority,[11] Black school librarians can identify with and acknowledge the cultures and histories of underrepresented groups, or those groups overlooked in mainstream literature. As a teacher of future librarians, by ensuring course materials encompass diverse and inclusive literature and stressing the importance of an equitable collection, I illustrate how librarians can incorporate culturally responsive instruction into their library program. As a past high school librarian, I readily worked to ensure a representative library collection for the various demographics of students I served. Culturally responsive teaching is reinforced when integrating these resources into the curriculum and collaborating with teachers on unit lessons.

## BLACK SCHOOL LIBRARIANS AS CHANGEMAKERS

Although there has been an increase in book banning and censorship,[12] it is crucial that students continue to have access to a wide range of diverse books that promote inclusivity, foster empathy, and provide global understanding. Such books provide valuable perceptions of people from various cultures and circumstances. By providing diverse literature for exploration, students can develop a global perspective and gain insight into prejudices and biases that they can then analyze and challenge using critical thinking skills. Developing critical thinking skills can aid students in gaining a more comprehensive understanding of intricate issues like discrimination, social justice, and equity. Students can scrutinize and question their beliefs by examining various viewpoints and tackling challenging topics, promoting critical thinking skills. Social issues and disparities are often addressed in diverse books, providing students with a glimpse into the lives of marginalized communities. These books can initiate conversations about justice, equality, and social reform, enabling students to become champions for positive change in their communities.

Unfortunately, some parents, school districts in response to parent challenges, and state governments are seeking to ban and censor many diverse books.[13] This, however, does not deter the Black school librarian from creating a welcoming and inclusive environment for their patrons. They actively seek out books, magazines, and resources that feature diverse authors, characters, and topics, including those from different racial, ethnic, and cultural backgrounds. By providing a diverse collection, Black school librarians help students see themselves and their experiences reflected in the materials available. Organizing cultural programming and celebrations throughout the year to honor and highlight the rich diversity of their student population is another way to make their patrons feel welcome. Other planned programming events include author visits, book clubs, storytelling sessions, or film screenings that showcase different cultures and perspectives that create opportunities for students to learn about and appreciate various backgrounds, fostering a sense of inclusivity.

Librarians of African descent frequently act as champions for fairness and social justice in their schools and communities. They establish environments where discussions about diversity, inclusivity, and the trials of underrepresented communities can occur by organizing thought-provoking events, book discussions, and dialogues with authors; they nurture critical thinking, empathy, and comprehension, cultivating a cohort of knowledgeable and socially aware individuals. It is crucial that when these conversations are conducted they are facilitated with sensitivity and impartiality.

In the Young Adult Literature course I teach, my graduate students read *The Hate U Give* by Angie Thomas and then group themselves to have a video conversation about its themes and other literary elements. They can incorporate this practice into a lesson also applied in the classroom. It is important, however, that this practice is done open-mindedly and respectfully. Other books providing insights into marginalized communities and that can serve as an impetus for critical conversations are *Wonder* by R. J. Palacio, *Inside Out and Back Again* by Thanhha Lai, *George* by Alex Gino, *The House on Mango Street* by Sandra Cisneros, or *Out of My Mind* by Sharon Draper. This is a small representation of the wide selection of diverse age-appropriate books Black school librarians can curate for K–12 students to read. Books that represent various identities, cultures, experiences, and viewpoints provide students with rich literature to absorb, which broadens their horizons as conveyors of information literacy.

## BLACK SCHOOL LIBRARIANS AS INFORMATION LITERACY SPECIALISTS

A. Peter Bailey addressed the Black Caucus of the American Library Association in 1986 stating, "One thing we lack as a people is awareness of the absolute critical importance of information. Information is the most important thing you can possess. Information is POWER!"[14] As part of information literacy, it is crucial to teach students how to evaluate information critically. In public schools, it is essential to develop these skills as they enable students to find, evaluate, and use information effectively to support their learning, decision-making, and problem-solving processes. According to Thomas and Haas,[15] using a sociocultural method to assess research skills that study students' cultural experiences can help identify skill deficiencies more accurately. By incorporating students' background knowledge and experiences, we can help them better understand how to integrate that information into their research processes and practices. Given today's digital age, this is particularly important in media literacy, which makes an abundance of information available online. Black school librarians can play a vital role in guiding students in evaluating the reliability, bias, and cultural context of different online sources. They can also help students identify and challenge stereotypes and misinformation present in texts. By introducing students to primary sources that highlight the experiences and voices of Black individuals and other underrepresented groups, librarians of African descent can deepen students' understanding of various histories and cultures. These librarians can provide access to documents, oral histories, photographs, videos, and other primary sources that help students develop a well-rounded perspective of their respective culture and others. Additionally, Black school librarians can guide students in researching and understanding social issues relevant to their communities, such as systemic racism, social justice movements, cultural heritage, and contemporary challenges faced by marginalized groups. They can recommend reputable sources, facilitate discussions, and encourage critical thinking. Finally, Black school librarians can empower students to become critical consumers and creators of media by teaching them about cultural misrepresentations and helping them analyze and question media representations of Black people and other diverse communities.

## A PAUCITY OF BLACK SCHOOL LIBRARIANS

A study by Lance, Kachel, and Gerrity[16] found that access to school librarians from pre-K through high school is inequitable when it comes to race and ethnicity. In districts where the majority of students are nonwhite, defined as having 50 percent or more of any minority group or a combination thereof, nearly 40 percent of districts reported having no librarian, certified or not. This lack of a librarian was consistent regardless of poverty indicators.[17] The Houston Independent School District released a Facts and Figures Report for 2022–2023, which revealed that out of the 274 schools in the district, 69 of them had school librarians. The district has around 190,000 enrolled students, including 18,000 who identify as white, while the rest come from diverse ethnic backgrounds.[18] The absence of a school librarian limits the availability of curated resources and media that reflect the diversity and inclusivity of preK–twelfth grade schools' students and communities, especially for minority students. As of 2021, Zippia The Career Expert's website indicates the percentage of school librarians who identify as Black or African American is only 6.29 percent, which has remained comparable as far back as 2010.[19] This is a small representation of Black school librarians considering the multitude of school libraries across the United States. This nominal percentage makes it challenging to support various races, cultures, and ethnicities with the strengths Black school librarians can bring.

As a teacher-librarian of African descent, I aim to provide all students with an empowering and liberatory learning experience by providing an array of resources where students can see themselves and appreciate other groups and minorities as they gain a global perspective of the world in which they live. Additionally, I strive to serve as a positive example for students of color to demonstrate the myriad possibilities available to them as global citizens. Black school librarians are great role models for students from diverse backgrounds as they incorporate culturally responsive approaches that undergird their students' academic success. They inspire and cultivate a sense of belonging to the students they serve. Black school librarians play a pivotal role in education by recognizing and acknowledging the diversity, equity, and inclusivity of their student populations by validating that academic success and intellectual pursuits are attainable for all.

## NOTES

1. Alma Dawson, "Celebrating African American Librarians and Librarianship," *Library Trends*, 9, no. 1 (2000): 49.
2. E. J. Josey and Ann Allen Shockley, *Handbook of Black Librarianship* (Littleton, CO: Libraries Unlimited, 1977), 35.
3. Ibid., 38.
4. Ibid., 63.
5. Ibid., 47–48.
6. Maurie Hillson, "The Reorganization of the School: Bringing about a Remission in the Problems Faced by Minority Children," *Phylon*, 28, no. 3 (1967): 231–32.
7. Geneva Gay, *Culturally Responsive Teaching: Theory, Research and Practice*, 2nd ed. (New York: Teachers College Press, 2010).
8. Ibid.
9. Keith C. Lance, Marcia J. Rodney, and Christine Hamilton-Pennell, *Measuring Up to Standards: The Impact of School Library Programs & Information Literacy in Pennsylvania Schools* (Harrisburg: Pennsylvania Citizens for Better Libraries, 2000).
10. Alina O'Donnell, "Windows, Mirrors, and Sliding Glass Doors: The Enduring Impact of Rudine Sims Bishop's Work," *Literacy Today*, 36, no. 6 (2019): 18.
11. "School Librarian Demographics and Statistics in the US," Zippia, www.zippia.com/school-librarian-jobs/demographics/.
12. Kasey Meehan and Jonathan Friedman, "Banned in the USA: State Laws Supercharge Book Suppression in Schools," Pen America, April 2023, https://www.pen.org/report/banned-in-the-usa-state-laws-supercharge-book-suppression-in-schools/.
13. Ibid.
14. E. J. Josey, *The Black Librarian in America Revisited* (Lanham, MD: Scarecrow Press, 1994), 182.
15. Miriam Thomas and L. Haas, "Information Literacy Skills Proficiency and Academic Achievement of Select 12th-Grade Students at a High-Minority High-Poverty School: A Mixed Methods Study," *Journal of Texas Association of Black School Educators-JTABSE* (Fall 2020): 126, https://www.tabse.net/wp-content/uploads/2021/02/TABSE-Journal-2020.pdf.
16. Keith C. Lance, Debra E. Kachel, and Caitlin Gerrity, "The School Librarian Equity Gap: Inequities Associated with Race and Ethnicity Compounded by Poverty, Locale, and Enrollment," *Peabody Journal of Education*, 98, no. 1 (2023): 85–99, https://doi: 10.1080/0161956X.2023.2160112.
17. Ibid., 88.
18. "Facts and Figures," Houston Independent School District, 2022–2023, https://www.houstonisd.org/site/handlers/filedownload.ashx?moduleinstanceid=48525&dataid=395205&FileName=Pace-60711_2022-2023_Facts-Figures_7583c.pdf.
19. "School Librarian Demographics and Statistics in the US."

## WORKS CITED

Banks, James A. *Cultural Diversity and Education: Foundations, Curriculum, and Teaching*, 4th ed. Boston: Allyn and Bacon, 2001.

Dawson, Alma. "Celebrating African American Librarians and Librarianship." *Library Trends*, 49, no. 1 (2000): 41–50.

"Facts and Figures." Houston Independent School District, 2022–2023. https://www.houstonisd.org/site/handlers/filedownload.ashx?moduleinstanceid=48525&dataid=395205&FileName=Pace-60711_2022-2023_Facts-Figures_7583c.pdf.

Gay, Geneva. *Culturally Responsive Teaching: Theory, Research, and Practice*. 2nd ed. New York: Teachers College, 2010.

Hillson, Maurie. "The Reorganization of the School: Bringing about a Remission in the Problems Faced by Minority Children." *Phylon*, 28, no. 3 (1967): 230–45.

hooks, bell. *Teaching to Transgress: Education as the Practice of Freedom*. New York: Routledge, 1994.

Johnson, Aisha. "Dr. Virginia Lacy Jones: The Blueprint for Relentless Advocacy for Black Librarianship." *Libraries: Culture, History, and Society*, 6, no. 1 (2022): 63–80.

Josey, E. J., and Ann Allen Shockley. *Handbook of Black Librarianship*. Littleton, CO: Libraries Unlimited, 1977.

Ladson-Billings, Gloria. "But That's Just Good Teaching! The Case for Culturally Relevant Pedagogy." *Theory into Practice*, 34, no. 3 (1995): 159–65. http://www.jstor.org/stable/1476635.

Ladson-Billings, Gloria. "Reading between the Lines and beyond the Pages: A Culturally Relevant Approach to Literacy Teaching." *Theory into Practice*, 31, no. 4 (1992): 312–20. http://www.jstor.org/stable/1476313.

Lance, Keith Curry, Debra E. Kachel, and Caitlin Gerrity. "The School Librarian Equity Gap: Inequities Associated with Race and Ethnicity Compounded by Poverty, Locale, and Enrollment." *Peabody Journal of Education*, 98, no. 1 (2023): 85–99. https://doi.org/10.1080/0161956X.2023.2160112.

Lance, Keith Curry, Marcia J. Rodney, and Christine Hamilton-Pennell. *Measuring Up to Standards: The Impact of School Library Programs & Information Literacy in Pennsylvania Schools*. Pennsylvania Department of Education Office of Commonwealth Libraries, 2000. https://files.eric.ed.gov/fulltext/ED446771.pdf.

Meehan, Kasey, and Jonathan Friedman. "Banned in the USA: State Laws Supercharge Book Suppression in Schools." Pen America, April 2023. https://www.pen.org/report/banned-in-the-usa-state-laws-supercharge-book-suppression-in-schools/.

O'Donnell, Alina. "Windows, Mirrors, and Sliding Glass Doors. The Enduring Impact of Rudine Sims Bishop's Work." *Literacy Today*, 36, no. 6 (2019):16–19. https://www.Literacyworldwide.org.

"School Librarian Demographics and Statistics in the US." Zippia The Career Expert, updated July 21, 2023. https://www.zippia.com/school-librarian-jobs/demographics/.

Thomas, Miriam, and Lory Haas. "Information Literacy Skills Proficiency and Academic Achievement of Select 12th-Grade Students at a High-Minority High-Poverty School: A Mixed Methods Study." *Journal of Texas Association of Black School Educators (JTABSE)*, 5, no. 1 (2020): 105–55. https://www.tabse.net/wp-content/uploads/2021/02/TABSE-Journal-2020.pdf.

Welton, Anjalé D., and Melissa A. Martinez. "Coloring the College Pathway: A More Culturally Responsive Approach to College Readiness and Access for Students of Color in Secondary Schools." *The Urban Review*, 46 (2014): 197–223. https://doi.org/10.1007/s11256-013-0252-7.

Wlodkowski, Raymond, and Margery B. Ginsberg. *A Framework for Culturally Responsive Teaching*. San Francisco, CA: Jossey-Bass, 1995.

# Chapter 8
# Special Libraries

## 8.1

### Counternarratives in Practice

Jina Duvernay

*Counter Narratives in Practice* is a series of podcasts centered around storytelling and multicultural heritage collections that are found in archives, libraries, special collections, and museums.[1] The librarians, archivists, and curators who participated in the podcasts are all fellows of The Andrew W. Mellon Fellowship for Diversity, Inclusion & Cultural Heritage.[2]

The fellowship was created by Rare Book School, a nonprofit institute that supports the study of history of the book and related topics, after being awarded a $1.5 million grant from The Andrew W. Mellon Foundation in 2019. It was designed to fulfill four specific goals: "1) [develop] skills for documenting and interpreting visual and textual materials in special collections and archives; 2) [raise] awareness within professional communities about the significance of inclusive, multicultural collections, including their promotion, development, and stewardship; 3) [build] connections with diverse communities and publics through strategic programming, outreach, and advocacy; and 4) [advance] careers by establishing new pathways and skills for professional growth."[3]

Forty-five fellows "who identify with diverse racial or ethnic communities and/or who work primarily with collections that document minority, immigrant, and non-Western cultural traditions" were selected to be a part of one of three cohorts within the fellowship. During the two-year period, each cohort is to advance multicultural collections by focusing on innovation, leadership, and curation. One way in which fellows achieved the goals of the fellowship was through a podcast series. Groups of fellows worked together to create a podcast that highlighted the archival collections of people from varying ethnic communities. The aim was to provide counternarratives by amplifying interesting but lesser-known collections housed at various institutions.

With the help of a facilitator, three working groups created episodes that included an array of topics such as manuscript collecting, archival gaps, and farmworkers. I served as a host in my working group by opening and closing two episodes, introducing each fellow and asking relevant questions to facilitate the fellow's presentation of content. Fellows contribute to the podcast to fulfill one of the requirements of the fellowship. I worked with accomplished and passionate fellows, who held the following positions at the time of the creation of the podcast, to produce two dynamic episodes:

- Margarita Vargas-Betancourt, Latin American and Caribbean Special Collections Librarian at the University of Florida
- Patrice Green, the inaugural Curator for African American Collections at Penn State University
- Meaghan Alston, project archivist with the Southern Historical Collection at the University of North Carolina at Chapel Hill's Wilson Special Collections Library
- Victor Betts, Student Success Librarian for Special Collections at North Carolina State University Libraries

In our first episode, titled "Hidden Histories: Immigrant Farm Workers and Black Intellectual Histories," both Margarita Vargas-Bethancourt and Patrice Green share collections that they each wanted to highlight. Margarita discussed the COVID-19 Florida Farmworkers Collection. Digital content that captured content from social media platforms, videos, websites, petitions, as well as University of Florida Institute of Food and Agricultural Sciences documents, are included in the collection. The collection documents the impact of the experiences and voices of Mexican, Haitian, and Central

American Florida farmworkers who are frequently underrepresented and marginalized.

Patrice Green enlightened listeners about the Charles Blockson Collection, which is housed at Penn State University. The Charles L. Blockson archival collection contains materials that depict Black art, history, and culture. Although the majority of the collection pertains to African Americans from 1900 to 2006, Blockson also collected material related to the Black diasporic experience, particularly those in the Caribbean.

Patrice also talked about the special collections newer digital collection, The Black History and Visual Culture Collection, which includes a variety of materials reflecting such topics as Black life in Pennsylvania and the Black student experience. Patrice also shared her desire to mentor others to work in special collections and encouraged them to do the work of preserving history and culture. Moreover, she mentioned that she and her colleagues hope to obtain important oral histories in the near future.

The second episode, titled "Hidden Histories: African American, Asian American, and Afro-Asian Relationality," featured Meaghan Alston and Victor Betts. Meaghan discussed the origins of the Southern Historical Collection at UNC-Chapel Hill's Wilson Library and its collections. She focused on material in the collection that documents the history and experience of Black people who were enslaved, and focused on the fact that much of this vital information is rarely spotlighted. Meaghan concluded by mentioning some ways in which she is contributing to ensuring that their story is not overlooked.

Victor Betts highlighted Justina Harris Williams, the first African American to be hired at North Carolina State on the academic staff. Furthermore, she was the first African American to be hired at the university over the level of a custodial worker. In 1958, Williams worked in the genetics department as a research technician.

Betts also discussed Dr. Kenichi Kojima, a Japanese American population geneticist who also worked at the university. Through his research, Betts learned that Williams worked in Dr. Kojima's lab. Betts talked about how infrequently stories of Asian and Asian Americans are highlighted and how he hopes to continue to do the work to change that.

Once completed, the episodes were uploaded to the dedicated site provided by Rare Book School. Each episode included supplemental keywords and links that were referenced during the podcast. Photographs for a couple of the collections also accompanied the episodes. In addition, each fellow offered and committed to promote the podcast in a number of ways including sharing the link and information on listservs as well as social media library and archives groups.

Based on The Andrew W. Mellon Fellowship for Diversity, Inclusion & Cultural Heritage components, I along with my working group fulfilled the fellowship stipulation of participating in one of the three required working groups. An overview of the fellowship's components are:

- Orientation: Fellows will participate in a two-day orientation seminar to include a series of seminars, guided conversations, and workshops, with a focus on skills-based mentoring.
- Courses at RBS: Fellows will attend three of Rare Book School's five-day seminar-style courses, one per year for three years. During these courses, fellows will have the opportunity to handle, analyze, and interpret materials from RBS's approximately one hundred thousand-item collection, from the University of Virginia's Special Collections, and, in some cases, from the Beinecke Rare Book & Manuscript Library, the Library of Congress, the Morgan Library & Museum, and other major special collections in the United States.
- RBMS conference and customized career advancement workshops: During their first year in the program, fellows will receive funding to attend the annual conference of the Rare Books and Manuscripts Section (RBMS) of the Association of College and Research Libraries.
- Additional conference funding: In their second and third years of the program, fellows will receive funding to attend conferences of their choosing, whether RBMS or other professional conferences or specialized workshops.
- Community symposia: Each fellow will hold inclusive, public-facing events that will advance understandings of cultural heritage, archives, and/or special collections. These symposia will be held at the fellows' home institutions and will enable fellows to promote aspects of their archives or collections to broader publics. Fellows will receive instruction and training on program design and planning both during and after their orientation.
- Working groups: The fellowship program will include three working groups, the aims and objectives of which will be shaped by the fellows with the aid of facilitators. Each group will conduct project-based work designed around one of the four goals of the fellowship program: education, advocacy, outreach, and advancement. Fellows will choose one working group each year.
- Cultural heritage field schools: Each fellow will participate in one cultural heritage field school, a targeted visit to libraries and archives in a major metropolitan area designed to provide fellows with the opportunity to meet prominent curators, archivists, librarians, conservators, and preservationists working with multicultural collections, who are active leaders in their respective fields.

Working on the podcast with the other fellows was a great experience. We all collaborated well with one another and were very supportive of each other. We all enjoyed learning about the various collections and participating in the creation of a podcast with Allie Alvis, book historian and cataloguer at Type Punch Matrix, and our podcast media consultant Kelsey Brown. The episodes were made possible with sponsorship from Rare Book School and The Andrew Mellon Foundation.

## NOTES

1. "Counter Narratives Podcast Series," *Podcasts of the Andrew W. Mellon Fellows for Diversity, Inclusion, & Cultural Heritage*, https://chfellowspodcasts.pubpub.org/.
2. "The Andrew W. Mellon Fellowship for Diversity, Inclusion & Cultural Heritage," *Rare Book School*, April 2020, https://rarebookschool.org/admissions-awards/fellowships/mellon-diversity/.
3. Ibid.

## WORKS CITED

"Counter Narratives Podcast Series." *Podcasts of the Andrew W. Mellon Fellows for Diversity, Inclusion, & Cultural Heritage.* https://chfellowspodcasts.pubpub.org/.

"The Andrew W. Mellon Fellowship for Diversity, Inclusion & Cultural Heritage." *Rare Book School*, April 2020. https://rarebookschool.org/admissions-awards/fellowships/mellon-diversity/.

# 8.2

## *The Blair-Caldwell African American Research Library, Denver, Colorado*

Jameka B. Lewis

### THE FOUNDATION

In the early 1980s, a small, one-room branch of the Denver Public Library was located in the heart of the historically Black Five Points neighborhood. This branch library, shared with Denver Human Services, served the neighborhood with nonfiction paperbacks and magazines but was not able to showcase or celebrate the contributions of neighborhood residents, including a rich collection of African Americans who defined the Five Points area.

Fast-forward seventeen years, and plans for a new branch library were set in motion by former Denver mayor Wellington E. Webb and his wife, Wilma, to not only replace the tiny Five Points Branch Library but also give the community a modern, updated, and interactive facility that captured the unique history of the neighborhood. The Webbs had a shared vision of a research library and museum to preserve and showcase the many contributions of African Americans in Colorado and the West. Much of that history was in private hands—those of political leaders, community organizations, churches, and individuals. Other history was unwritten, still in the heads and hearts of those who had lived it.

In 1999, a commission was formed to lead in developing plans for this new Five Points branch library. Black librarians Charleszine "Terry" Nelson and Gwendolyn Crenshaw joined with community members and the Webbs to lead the charge to collect the history of the historic neighborhood of Five Points. Mayor Webb remarked, "There's so much history, and we need to capture that for young people."[1] "So much of it is in boxes, in basements, or in our heads." And so, the journey of gathering that history began. With diligence and community support, they acquired nearly two hundred collections from Black community leaders, politicians, families, community organizations, business owners, and others to curate the archives and special collections for the new library. Some key leaders whose materials are located in this library include Harold Jacobs (an officer of the American Woodmen), Omar Blair (the first Black president of the Denver School Board), John Mosley (one of the original Tuskegee Airmen of World War II) and his wife Edna Mosley (the first Black city councilwoman for the city of Aurora, Colorado), Marie Greenwood (the first Black teacher to receive tenure in the Denver Public Schools), and many others who contributed to the Black history of Denver and the Rocky Mountain West.

By 2000, the Denver Public Library had engaged consultants and a community advisory committee to help plan the Blair-Caldwell African American Research Library. Public meetings were held with neighborhoods that would use the facility, and library staff began to collect personal and professional papers, publications, photographs, works of art, and other memorabilia of distinguished African Americans from all walks of life. Finally, groundbreaking for the new library took place in early 2002.

Former mayor Wellington Webb and First Lady Wilma Webb proposed the name, which combines the last names of Omar Blair, the first Black president of the Denver school board, and Elvin Caldwell, the first Black city council member.

"Omar Blair and Elvin Caldwell made major contributions to our community and are fitting namesakes for this unique addition to the Library system," said Landri C. Taylor, Denver public library commissioner at the time. "We unanimously approved the proposed name for the Library because Blair and Caldwell are prominent African Americans who have given of their time and talents to bring about significant change in Denver and the West."[2]

Terry Nelson and Gwendolyn Crenshaw served as the first managers for the Blair-Caldwell Library. Terry focused on community engagement, outreach, acquisitions of collections, and supervision of the Western Legacies Museum (located on the third floor). Gwendolyn was placed in charge of branch services, including circulation, community partnerships, collection development, and other public services.

## THE PRESENT

The Blair-Caldwell African American Research Library is the gateway to the historical cultural district of Five Points and the Welton Street Historic District. The building merges with Sonny Lawson Park via a plaza connecting the two. The library has three spacious levels, each with its own unique purpose.

## LEVEL ONE: A FULL-SERVICE BRANCH LIBRARY

Entering level one is an inviting experience. This space was recently renovated (renovations were completed in August 2023) and features a 5,800-square-foot gallery where Black art and artists host featured exhibitions throughout the year. The first floor also features two conference rooms that the public can reserve for free: The Links, Inc. large conference room with seating for one hundred people and the Black Chamber of Commerce Board Room with seating for twenty people. Other features of the first floor include two circulating collections: One collection is a general public library circulating collection that includes books, magazines, CDs, DVDs, and public computers with internet access. The second circulating collection is a new feature added through the renovation, which is a collection of Black history and culture books that mirrors the noncirculating collection located in the research library on the second floor. The branch area of this library also features individual areas for children, teens, and adults, along with many items available in English and Spanish.

Branch services at Blair-Caldwell are unique in that every service or resource specifically highlights and celebrates the Black experience. While programming and outreach are done with a variety of community input and feedback, along with longtime community partnerships, the focus and mission of Blair-Caldwell is the acquisition, preservation, promotion, and celebration of Black accomplishment and achievement. The programming offered by Blair-Caldwell is Black-focused, in accordance with its mission.

## LEVEL TWO: SPECIAL COLLECTIONS ARCHIVES AND RESEARCH LIBRARY

The archives provide a wide range of primary sources including photographs, manuscript collections, letters, and diaries. It also features audio and video oral histories, including the Trailblazers series: a collection of oral histories from a cross-section of Coloradans. There are nearly three hundred collections in the archives, all related to different individuals, organizations, and movements led by Black people in the Rocky Mountain West. The research library is a favorite of all types of researchers; from children to adults, researchers who are interested in the historical contributions of Black people in the West utilize the archives and special collections for all types of research.

## LEVEL THREE: THE WESTERN LEGACIES MUSEUM AND CHARLES R. COUSINS GALLERY

From early pioneers to present-day heroes, visitors to the Western Legacies Museum are invited to follow the footsteps of African Americans who settled the West. This exhibition space spans more than seven thousand square feet and includes an African American Legacy corridor, a leadership hall, and a replica of the office of former Denver mayor Wellington E. Webb. Exhibits featured in the museum include an overview of Black settlement in the West, information about the Black Seminoles, an area dedicated to Robert Smith (a formerly enslaved man who established a business in the Five Points area), celebration of the unique history of the Five Points neighborhood, spotlights on Black celebrities and others who are from the Denver area, and the history of everyday local heroes like Dr. Henry Westbrook, Sam Cary, and Dr. Justina Ford. The Charles R. Cousins changing art gallery highlights local Black artists and exhibits throughout the year. Artists have the opportunity to host receptions and sell their art in the gallery free of charge. Tours, school visits, research appointments, speaker requests, and limited classes are all offered by the staff at Blair-Caldwell by request.[3]

## THE FUTURE

The year 2023 marked the twentieth anniversary of the opening of the Blair-Caldwell Library. Currently led by Branch Supervisor Jameka B. Lewis and Archives & Museum Supervisor Dexter Nelson II, Blair-Caldwell is entering a new era of commitment and contributions to the preservation and promotion of the history of Black people in the West. Lewis and Nelson agree that they are building on a firm foundation of achievement and accomplishment created by the Webbs, Nelson, and Crenshaw and are in constant communication with the community and other supporters of the library. Plans after renovation and reopening include the expansion of staff (twenty-five in total); more broad and intentional outreach and community engagement with community organizations, businesses, and other partners; expanding the on-site digitizing program; a refresh of the museum (including the creation of more traveling exhibits for community use); promotion of Black history in schools and other institutions that Blair-Caldwell hasn't worked with before; reaching out to underserved populations; and broadening Blair-Caldwell's visibility nationally and internationally. Other future plans include reestablishing the Blair-Caldwell volunteer program, continued partnerships with the Smithsonian National Museum of African American History and Culture, and a potential internship program that will allow Black students the opportunity to collaborate with librarians and archivists behind the scenes as an introduction to library and museum work. More information about the library can be found at https://history.denverlibrary.org/blair.

## NOTES

1. "About the Blair-Caldwell African American Research Library," n.d., *Denver Public Library,* https://history.denverlibrary.org/about-blair-caldwell-african-american-research-library.
2. Ibid.
3. "Blair-Caldwell African American Research Library," n.d., *Denver Public Library,* https://history.denverlibrary.org/blair.

## WORKS CITED

"About the Blair-Caldwell African American Research Library," n.d., *Denver Public Library.* https://history.denverlibrary.org/about-blair-caldwell-african-american-research-library.

"Blair-Caldwell African American Research Library," n.d., *Denver Public Library.* https://history.denverlibrary.org/blair.

# 8.3

# *The Auburn Avenue Research Library on African American Culture and History*

A RICH HISTORY LEADING THE WAY IN THE SOUTH

Victor E. Simmons Jr.

## A RICH HISTORY

The Auburn Avenue Research Library on African American Culture and History (AARL) is a special library of the Fulton County Library System, and for the entire Southeast of the United States. Located on the corner of Courtland Street and Auburn Avenue in the historic Sweet Auburn district of Atlanta, Georgia, The Auburn Avenue Research Library is dedicated to collecting, preserving, and providing access to the documentation and materials that reflect the experiences, history, and culture of people of African descent throughout the world. The institution is also committed to supporting research, education, and public programming that promote the understanding and appreciation of African American culture and history.

The library is also a cultural center that celebrates and preserves the legacy of Black people in Atlanta and beyond. It is the first public library in the Southeast to offer specialized reference and archival collections dedicated to the study and research of African American history and culture. The research library's story began in the early twentieth century, when a group of visionary librarians, educators, and activists fought for the right of Black citizens to access public library service in a segregated city. This chapter will explore the history of the library and its core collection, which reflects the struggles and achievements of African Americans in Atlanta and the nation.

The Auburn Avenue Research Library's core collection was formed decades before the research library was even an idea. It started at the Auburn Branch of the Carnegie Library of Atlanta, which was located at 333 Auburn Avenue, just a few minutes' walk from the current research library. Since its inception in 1902, the Carnegie Library of Atlanta excluded its African American citizens from utilizing its library system under the Jim Crow laws of the era. The Auburn Branch officially opened its doors on July 25, 1921, becoming Atlanta's first public library branch for African Americans.

The collection that is the backbone of the Auburn Avenue Research Library's collection is the Auburn Branch's Negro History Collection, which was developed in part by two extraordinary librarians of color: Alice Dugged Cary and Annie L. McPheeters.

Alice Dugged Cary was a prominent African American educator and librarian who made significant contributions to the advancement of Black education and culture in the late nineteenth and early twentieth centuries. She was born in Indiana in 1859 and graduated from Wilberforce University in 1881. She taught in public schools in Kansas and Missouri before moving to Atlanta, Georgia, where she became the second principal of Morris Brown College, an institution founded by the African Methodist Episcopal Church. She also established the first free kindergarten for Black children in Atlanta, Macon, and Charleston. In 1921, she was appointed as the first librarian of the Auburn Branch of the Carnegie Library of Atlanta. She was also a leader of several women's organizations, such as Zeta Phi Beta Sorority, Inc.

Annie L. McPheeters was a pioneer in library science and a champion of civil rights for African Americans. She was born in 1908 in Georgia and graduated from Clark Atlanta University and Hampton University. She worked as a librarian and educator in various institutions, including the Auburn Branch of the Carnegie Library of Atlanta. She also served as the first African American faculty member at Georgia State University and a consultant at Pergamon Press. She was active in several civic and professional organizations, such as Alpha Kappa Alpha Sorority, Inc.

Together Alice Dugged Cary and Annie L. McPheeters created The Negro History Collection, which collected special noncirculating materials that focused on the African American experience. The collection was formally organized in 1934. The collection began to grow as it incorporated titles received from the American Library Association, the American Association of Adult Education, the Julius Rosenwald Fund, as well as volumes already owned by the Auburn Branch. The collection was then further expanded with the inclusion of bound periodicals that included W. E. B. Du Bois's *The Crisis* and the *Atlanta Daily World*.

The west side of Atlanta witnessed a rise in the population of African Americans during this time. Along with this, the residents also demanded better public library service. The city responded by funding the construction of a new library branch for the Black community. The West Hunter Branch, which opened on December 6, 1949, at the intersection of West Hunter Street and Morris Brown Drive, became the second location of the Negro History Collection. McPheeters worked as the librarian there until she retired in 1966, and the collection stayed there for twenty years, even after the now Fulton County Library System integrated in 1959.

In 1970, the collection moved to the Carnegie Library building in downtown Atlanta, near Peachtree Street, where it was officially named the Samuel W. Williams Collection on Black America, in honor of Samuel W. Williams, a local educator and theologian. In 1994, the collection was moved into its new home at the Auburn Avenue Research Library, where it currently resides. In 2008, a fifty thousand-square-foot, four-story building was approved for a complete remodel/renovation due to Fulton County voters approving a library bond referendum, which included funds to improve and enlarge the facility. The facilities at Auburn Avenue closed for renovations in 2014, with a portion of the staff and collection moving to the Fulton County Library Systems' Central Library. On Thursday, August 4, 2016, the Auburn Avenue Research Library on African American Culture and History reopened after a $20 million renovation that saw the building size increase to fifty-six thousand square feet, programming spaces moved from the top floor down to the first floor, numerous gallery spaces added (including a children's gallery that focuses on art created for and/or by children), temperature controlled book storage spaces, numerous study rooms with audio/visual capabilities, and an amazing two-part sculptural installation designed by renowned artist Radcliff Bailey. Named "From the Cabinet," the two-part sculptures are located at the front and back entrances of the library. The sixteen-by-fourteen-foot sculpture, located at the north entrance, is comprised of two-tiered steel, wall-mounted shelves, each holding symbolic sculptural components:

- Sculptural elements include symbolic imagery associated with the movement and growth of the people of the African diaspora, as well as the artist's family history.
- Sculptural silhouettes include musical instruments, ships, African sculptures, doorways, picture frames, a soldier, a nineteenth-century Garveyite, an oar, and a connecting ladder that transforms from a railroad track to a DNA strand.
- A second sculpture of a Victrola/phonograph, located at the south entrance, incorporates sound works and recordings curated from the library's audio archives.

The library boasts one of the largest collections of African American literature, art, music, film, and periodicals in the southeastern United States. It also holds over one hundred archival collections that document the lives and works of prominent African American individuals and organizations, such as civil rights leaders, activists, politicians, educators, artists, writers, and religious figures. Some of the notable collections include the papers of Donald Lee Hollowell, Andrew J. Young, Annie L. McPheeters, and Hosea L. Williams.

## COLLECTION HIGHLIGHTS

### Hosea L. Williams

Hosea L. Williams[1] was a multifaceted American civil rights leader, activist, minister, entrepreneur, philanthropist, scientist, and politician. Born in 1926 in Georgia to blind teenage parents, he faced poverty, racism, and violence. He served in World War II and earned a Purple Heart. He became a chemist and a member of the National Association for the Advancement of Colored People (NAACP). He joined Martin Luther King Jr., the SCLC, and led many protests and marches for racial justice.

Williams also had a political career as a state senator and a city council member in Georgia. He fought for the rights and welfare of marginalized groups. He founded Hosea Feed the Hungry and Homeless, a large social service organization. He also ran several businesses, such as a soft drink company, a radio station, and a newspaper. He transitioned in 2000 after battling cancer.

The Hosea L. Williams papers at the AARL in Atlanta document his life and work from 1926 to 2000. The collection contains various materials that reflect his activities and impact in the civil rights movement, his political career, his business ventures, and his involvement in several organizations. The collection also reveals his personal and family life. Additionally, the collection is a valuable source of information and insight into Williams's role and contributions to African American culture and history.

Some examples of specific items or documents from the collection that illustrate or demonstrate Williams's work, vision, or personality are:

- Hosea Feed the Hungry and Homeless documents
- Army Discharge Papers and Civil Service Ratings, 1960
- *The Crusader* newspaper(s)
- wall calendars, 1970-1973

## Andrew J. Young

Andrew J. Young[2] is a prominent figure in American politics, diplomacy, and activism. He has made significant contributions to the civil rights movement and African American culture and history. He was born in 1932 in New Orleans, Louisiana. His mother was a teacher and his father a dentist. He studied at Howard University and became a minister in the United Church of Christ. He married Jean Childs in 1954 and they had four children. He later married Carolyn Watson in 1996. Young joined the Southern Christian Leadership Conference (SCLC) in 1961 and became a close associate of Martin Luther King Jr. He participated in many civil rights campaigns, such as the Selma to Montgomery marches, the Chicago Freedom Movement, and the Poor People's Campaign. He was a Georgia congressman from 1972 until 1977, when he was appointed by President Jimmy Carter as the US ambassador to the United Nations. He resigned from this position in 1979 after meeting with the Palestine Liberation Organization (PLO) leader Yasser Arafat.

Young then became the mayor of Atlanta from 1982 to 1990, overseeing the city's economic growth and social development. He also ran for governor of Georgia in 1990 but lost to Zell Miller. After his political career, Young cochaired the 1996 Atlanta Olympic Games and founded GoodWorks International, a consulting firm that promotes business and humanitarian interests in Africa and the Caribbean. He also served as the chair of the Southern Africa Enterprise Development Fund and received numerous awards and honors for his achievements. The Andrew J. Young Papers are a valuable collection of materials that document his life and work over more than fifty years.

The collection is housed at the Auburn Avenue Research Library on African American Culture and History. It consists of various types of documents, such as minutes, scrapbooks, photographs, reports, personal papers, books, artifacts, artwork, posters, programs, manuscripts, notes, sermons, and audiovisual material. The collection covers the period from the 1910s to 2007 and reflects the activities of Young during his various roles as a minister, civil rights activist, congressman, ambassador, mayor, cochair of the Olympic Games, businessman, philanthropist, and family man. The collection provides a rich source of information and insight into Young's role and impact in the civil rights movement and African American culture and history. It reveals his contributions to the struggle for racial justice, social change, and economic empowerment. It also shows his challenges, controversies, and achievements as a leader, an activist, a diplomat, a politician, a businessman, a philanthropist, a husband, and father.

Some examples of specific items or documents from the collection that illustrate or demonstrate Young's work, vision, or personality are:

- poems (handwritten)
- childhood photographs
- Holy Bible, 1951
- speech, "Dynamics of a Movement, Birmingham in the Sixties," undated

## Donald L. Hollowell

Donald Lee Hollowell[3] was a prominent civil rights lawyer and leader who fought for racial justice and equality in Georgia. He was born in 1917 in Kansas and faced poverty and discrimination. He served in the US Army during World War II and earned a Purple Heart. He became a lawyer in Atlanta in 1952 and joined the NAACP. He led many cases and campaigns to end segregation and discrimination in education, transportation, and public facilities. He also freed Martin Luther King Jr. from prison, mentored other civil rights lawyers, and defended civil rights activists in the Albany Movement. King called him "the chief counsel of the civil rights movement."

Hollowell also worked in public service and became the first Black regional director of the Equal Employment Opportunity Commission (EEOC) in 1966. He held the position for twenty years. During his final years, Hollowell was honored by many institutions for his contributions, including the University of Georgia, which honored Hollowell with an honorary Doctor of Laws. He passed in 2004 in Atlanta, Georgia.

The Donald L. Hollowell papers are a collection of materials that document his life and work of over more than five decades. The collection is housed at the Auburn Avenue Research Library on African American Culture and History (AARL) in Atlanta. It consists of various types of documents, media, and artifacts that reflect Hollowell's role and impact in the civil rights movement and African American culture and history.

Some examples of specific items or documents from the collection that illustrate or demonstrate Hollowell's work, vision, or personality are:

- civil rights cases (files, case documents)—Preston Cobb
- sixtieth wedding anniversary photograph, Donald and Louise Hollowell
- speeches by Donald L. Hollowell
- The US Equal Employment Opportunity Commission Length of Service Certificate Awarded to Donald L. Hollowell in Appreciation and Recognition of Twenty-Nine Years of Dedicated Service to the Federal Government, April 25, 1985

**Annie L. McPheeters**

Annie L. McPheeters (1908–1994)[4] was an African American librarian and civil rights activist who played a pivotal role in developing and promoting the study and research of African American culture and history in Atlanta, Georgia. She was one of the first African American professional librarians in the Atlanta Public Library and an influential proponent of African American culture and history. She was also a founder and leader of several civic, educational, and cultural organizations that served the African American community.

McPheeters was born in Berwin, Georgia, to Josephine and William A. Watters, who instilled in her the importance of education. She graduated from Clark University (later Clark Atlanta University) in 1929 with a degree in English and a minor in education. She then earned a BS degree in library science from the Hampton Institute School of Library Service in 1933 and an MS degree in library science from Columbia University in 1940. She married Alphonso McPheeters, an educator, in 1940.

McPheeters began her career as a teacher-librarian at St. Albans County Training School, a Rosenwald school in Simpsonville, South Carolina, where she witnessed the desire of many African Americans to learn despite the lack of resources and opportunities. She then served as the city and county librarian at the Phillis Wheatley Branch of the Greenville Public Library, where she drove the bookmobile throughout the rural areas to provide library services to segregated communities.

In 1934, McPheeters was appointed as the assistant librarian at the Auburn Branch of the Carnegie Library of Atlanta, which was the first public library branch for African Americans in Atlanta. She developed the core collection of the library, known as the Negro History Collection, which comprised books, magazines, newspapers, and scholarly journals by, for, and about African Americans. She also organized educational programs for children and adults, such as story hours, book reviews, lectures, exhibits, and film screenings. McPheeters was also an active participant and leader in various civic, educational, and cultural endeavors that aimed to improve the social and economic conditions of African Americans and to promote their heritage and achievements. She collaborated with prominent African American leaders and organizations, such as John Wesley Dobbs, William Holmes Borders, Clarence A. Bacote, Warren Memorial United Methodist Church, Alpha Kappa Alpha Sorority, Inc., Utopian Literary Club, Atlanta University Center Library Council, and Atlanta Negro Voters League.

In 1956, McPheeters became the head librarian of the West Hunter Branch Library, where she continued to expand and enrich the Negro History Collection and to serve the needs and interests of the African American community. She retired from the library system in 1966 after over thirty years of service.

McPheeter's career in library services didn't end in 1966 as she was offered and accepted a position with Georgia State University and became the first African American faculty member in the university's history.

The Annie L. McPheeters papers collection at the AARL contains various materials that document her life and work from 1926 to 1994. Some examples of specific items or documents from the collection that illustrate or demonstrate McPheeters's work, vision, or personality are:

- Auburn Branch Library photographs
- certificates awarded to Annie L. McPheeters
- political advertisements
- Auburn Avenue booklets

The Auburn Avenue Research Library on African American Culture and History is not only a library but also a cultural center that offers a variety of programs and services to the public. AARL hosts lectures, workshops, exhibitions, film screenings, book signings, and performances that celebrate and explore various aspects of African American culture and history. The library also collaborates with local and national institutions and organizations to promote scholarly research and community engagement on issues related to African American culture and history.

As a valuable resource and asset for anyone who is interested in learning more about the diverse and dynamic contributions of people of African descent to the world, The Auburn Avenue Research Library on African American Culture and History is open to everyone wishing to discover the wealth of information and inspiration that awaits them at 101 Auburn Avenue in Atlanta, Georgia.

## NOTES

1. The Editors of Encyclopaedia Britannica, "Hosea Williams," *Encyclopedia Britannica*, https://www.britannica.com/biography/Hosea-Williams; W. Kirkland, "Hosea Williams," *New Georgia Encyclopedia*, August 14, 2020, https://www.georgiaencyclopedia.org/articles/history-archaeology/hosea-williams-1926-2000/; "Hosea Williams," Wikipedia, August 10, 2022, https://:en.wikipedia.org/wiki/Hosea_Williams; Reverend Hosea L. Williams Papers, Archives Division, Auburn Avenue Research Library on African-American Culture and History, Fulton County Library System, Atlanta, GA. https://aspace-aafa.galileo.usg.edu/repositories/2/resources/122.
2. The Editors of Encyclopaedia Britannica, "Andrew Young," *Encyclopedia Britannica*, https://www.britannica.com/biography/Andrew-Young; J. Moye, "Andrew Young," *New Georgia Encyclopedia*, August 12, 2020, https://www.georgiaencyclopedia.org/articles/government-politics/andrew-young-b-1932/; "Andrew Young," Wikipedia, August 10, 2022, http://en.wikipedia.org/wiki/Andrew_Young; Andrew J. Young Papers, aarl98-005, Auburn Avenue Research Library on African-American Culture and History, Atlanta, GA, https://aspace-aafa.galileo.usg.edu/repositories/2/resources/30.
3. "Donald L. Hollowell," Wikipedia, August 10, 2022, https://en.wikipedia.org/wiki/Donald_L._Hollowell; Donald L. Hollowell Collection, aarl012-002, Auburn Avenue Research Library on African-American Culture and History, Atlanta, GA. https://aspace-aafa.galileo.usg.edu/repositories/2/resources/108.; Edward Hatfield, "Donald Hollowell," *New Georgia Encyclopedia*, April 5, 2021, https://www.georgiaencyclopedia.org/articles/history-archaeology/donald-hollowell-1917-2004/.
4. Annie L. McPheeters Papers, Archives Division, Auburn Avenue Research Library on African-American Culture and History, Fulton County Library System, Atlanta, GA. https://aspace-aafa.galileo.usg.edu/repositories/2/resources/91, accessed August 10, 2023; Kerrie Williams, "Annie L. McPheeters," *New Georgia Encyclopedia*, May 4, 2021, https://www.georgiaencyclopedia.org/articles/education/annie-l-mcpheeters-1908-1994/; "Annie L. McPheeters," Wikipedia, August 10, 2022, https://en.wikipedia.org/wiki/Annie_L._McPheeters.

## WORKS CITED

"Andrew Young." Wikipedia, August 10, 2022. http://en.wikipedia.org/wiki/Andrew_Young.

Andrew J. Young Papers. Auburn Avenue Research Library on African-American Culture and History. Atlanta, GA.

"Annie L. McPheeters." Wikipedia, August 10, 2022. https://en.wikipedia.org/wiki/Annie_L._McPheeters.

Annie L. McPheeters Papers. Archives Division, Auburn Avenue Research Library on African-American Culture and History, Fulton County Library System, Atlanta, GA.

Britannica, The Editors of Encyclopedia. "Andrew Young." *Encyclopedia Britannica*. https://www.britannica.com/biography/Andrew-Young.

Britannica, The Editors of Encyclopaedia. "Hosea Williams." *Encyclopedia Britannica*. https://www.britannica.com/biography/Hosea-Williams.

"Donald L. Hollowell." Wikipedia, August 10, 2022, https://en.wikipedia.org/wiki/Donald_L._Hollowell.

Donald L. Hollowell Collection. Auburn Avenue Research Library on African-American Culture and History. Atlanta, GA.

Hatfield, Edward. "Donald Hollowell." *New Georgia Encyclopedia*, April 5, 2021. https://www.georgiaencyclopedia.org/articles/history-archaeology/donald-hollowell-1917-2004/.

"Hosea Williams." Wikipedia, August 10, 2022. https://en.wikipedia.org/wiki/Hosea_Williams.

Kirkland, W. "Hosea Williams." *New Georgia Encyclopedia*, August 14, 2020. https://www.georgiaencyclopedia.org/articles/history-archaeology/hosea-williams-1926-2000/.

Moye, J. "Andrew Young." *New Georgia Encyclopedia*, August 12, 2020. https://www.georgiaencyclopedia.org/articles/government-politics/andrew-young-b-1932/.

Reverend Hosea L. Williams Papers. Archives Division, Auburn Avenue Research Library on African-American Culture and History, Fulton County Library System, Atlanta, GA.

Williams, Kerrie. "Annie L. McPheeters." *New Georgia Encyclopedia*, May 4 2021. https://www.georgiaencyclopedia.org/articles/education/annie-l-mcpheeters-1908-1994/.

# Chapter 9
# State and Federal Libraries

## 9.1

*Twenty Years a County Librarian*

A LEGACY

Jos N. Holman

March 2022 marked my twenty-year anniversary as the county librarian of the Tippecanoe County Public Library (TCPL) in Lafayette, Indiana. I did not see myself working in the same position in the same library system in the same city for over two decades. Overall, it has been a good and rewarding career move. During these two decades I have seen quite a bit of change in public library services and programs. I have also seen quite a bit of change in the community that my library serves. What I have not seen enough of is a change in the attitudes of some Indiana citizens who still allow their unconscious bias to serve as the de facto guide for their behavior as they interact with people of color and more specifically, Black males. As a Black library director, seeing good changes and unconscious bias on full display initiates complex dynamics between what my responsibilities are and who I am. In a previous published article, I made the following statement, "[I] hope one day, I will have more flexibility entering a new directorship, and that historical racism doesn't have to be the guiding principle for how I approach the job."[1] Unfortunately, I have yet to see that day. Yet I maintain that hope with the same confidence I have with the lyrics from the well-known civil rights song "We Shall Overcome" someday.[2]

There are several items that might point to a successful career here at TCPL. Over the span of thirteen years, TCPL has built three new 1,400-square-foot library branches without any increase to the tax rate for property owners in the library district. Additionally, twenty years apart, TCPL purchased two "mobile library-type" vehicles that serve outlying areas while raising visibility with visits to local schools and festivals. TCPL transitioned to streaming materials collections, migrated to a new ILS (integrated library system) with a total RFID (radio frequency identification), and implemented a new accounting software system. TCPL strengthened partnerships with local businesses and agencies that continuously support its summer reading and winter reading programs. TCPL regularly collaborates with financial supporters like the Community Foundation of Greater Lafayette and the McAllister Foundation, two local granting agencies that funded multiple projects over a span of twenty years. Within Indiana, it is well-known that TCPL has one of the most successful friends group in the state and its own foundation with over $1.5 million in monetary assets.

The average person would likely agree that this is a successful career for a library director. Yet the question remains, Has there been enough success that an individual can see the whole of me, and my professional librarianship first as opposed to seeing my Blackness first?

This is not in any way to discount or not be proud of my Blackness, because I am certainly proud of being Black and my positive self-esteem remains intact. Certainly, being a Black male plays a role in everything I do because of the cultural heritage that comes with it. What I question is when do my skills, experience, strengths, education, integrity, creativity, out-of-the box thinking, determination, and fortitude become the qualities and characteristics that are seen first? When does my Blackness not become the major and sometimes only thing that individuals see?

Dare I say this visual blind spot is just coincidental? I think not. I will say, this blind spot (a lack of visible assessment) is not the starting point with other local Black professionals who see the whole of me and my librarianship when I interact with them. Yet I dare say these professionals face the same challenge I do when it comes to others seeing their Blackness first and their core qualities and characteristics second. For some of us as Black library directors, this aspect of our work can be overwhelming, frustrating, and downright disappointing. In my stage of work and life itself, it is just disappointing. I got past the other two feelings in the same way I have dealt with racist attitudes most of my life. It is their attitude and therefore their problem! I choose to not allow another person to make their racist attitude my problem.

As a former youth librarian and administrator, one of my greatest challenges in living and working in a majority community is not enough well-designed targeted programs for our Black youth. Thirty-five years ago, when I came into the profession, it was specifically to work with young Black boys who I thought needed to be able to express themselves. I was enthusiastic about doing programs that could help with this—that is, reading poetry out loud, doing creative dramatics, and performing reader's theater scripts. At TCPL today, we only have younger white female youth librarians who are planning programs for our younger clientele. It is challenging for them to consider programs with a male focus. It is even more challenging for them to develop programs for young Black males. Over the years, I have made suggestions for program ideas but somehow, we just don't succeed in this area. I suppose I could develop and do these programs myself, but they would only happen while I continue my tenure here. What is required is for TCPL as an institution and the youth librarians to see this type of specific program as needed, relevant, and doable.

In the last five years, I have begun to wonder how unconscious bias plays a role in TCPL not having these programs. Is it the unclear leadership on my part? I believe the unconscious bias is playing a greater part than my leadership. I partly think it is because I see unconscious bias demonstrated toward me. Though the amount of it may be limited, I still see it. I see unconscious bias in the tone of a handful of staff members who disagree with my interpretation of personnel policies but never address it with me. I see it in the actions of some staff members who often utilize the passive-aggressive approach with basic communication to me, including some who think they can choose not to speak to me. This can occur with a new staff member until I call them on it. Over the years, I have had to call several of them on it.

More recently I saw unconscious bias in my board of trustees who mishandled their attempt to find a resolution to a situation involving a former staff member's assessment of my work. As you can imagine, this use of unconscious bias on the part of appointed individuals who should be working on governance and strategic goals for our community would be somewhat daunting and discouraging. And yes, it is. However, my approach has always been that the institution is bigger than any one of us or any single facet of us. TCPL as an institution has to keep moving forward by making progress in its commitment to serve its community. So, I look past, "waaaaaay past," the attitude, discouragement, and daunting negativity of unconscious bias toward me as a Black male library director, whether by staff or the board. Why, might you ask? Mostly, because in all three examples cited above, I do not believe it is everyone (everybody) who projects this unconscious bias. More so, it is because I just want to do my job. If I am always stopping to think how this will be perceived through the lens of unconscious bias and historical racism, I would get very little accomplished and as someone who likes to make things happen, that is not me.

Speaking of making things happen, my involvement in the community provides many opportunities for me to build collegial relationships that either avoid unconscious bias or allows me to call an individual on it. One example is related to my term on the board of directors of a local arts organization. As planning ensued for a future retreat, board members were asked to complete a skills assessment test as the organization determined the strengths of the full board. Specifically, everyone needed to take the CliftonStrengths test conducted through a Gallup online survey.[3] In the survey, you identify your top five strengths and learn more about how you can utilize them to be successful in various areas of your life.

Frankly, I wasn't interested in taking the time to complete the test and I anticipated I would be cynical of its results. Neither the lack of interest nor my cynicism kept the test from affirming what I have long known to be my strengths: connectedness, achiever, strategic, communication, and arranger. I was delighted that connectedness was identified as my number one strength. Though I absolutely use several of these strengths in my everyday work, these same strengths are used repeatedly in every other aspect of my life.

Considering how I am perceived with regard to involvement in the community, it is readily and routinely seen that I have these strengths as I am called upon to use them. In some instances, my being a Black male adds to the idea that someone wants me to be involved. An example of this is when someone from the majority group has an idea for people of color in our community but are unsure how to connect with them. What CliftonStrengths called "connectedness," I identify as networking and there are innumerable times I have done this in my life. There is quite a bit of personal satisfaction in connecting individuals who end up accomplishing mutually benefiting goals.

I also like to think that in some instances the strength itself overrides my Blackness and I am just called upon to use the strength. This is the case with our local diversity round table where I have been called upon time and again to moderate or facilitate a group discussion. About eight years ago, I was asked to go on as the keynote speaker for our biannual diversity summit because the invited keynoter fell ill the morning of the event. It is because of my communication strength that I was asked to serve in this capacity. Because of these two strengths combined, I was recognized with the inaugural Diversity Leader Award given in 2012 by Greater Lafayette Commerce.

I often wonder what I contribute for the individual Black person who regularly visits the library. Performing my administrative job day by day, but not directly involved in public service, it is sometimes difficult to gauge what impact, if any, I actually make on an individual. Better yet, it is more difficult with library customers who are Black males.

Years ago, I was told, it makes a world of difference in a very positive way when Black community members walk into the library and see you serving as the director. At the time I did not perceive the same observation. Recently, I interacted with one Black male who indicated my being at the library helped him tremendously in his life when he moved to the community. He encouraged me to keep up the good work. Numerous other times, a young adult Black male has repeatedly said he makes sure he doesn't misbehave in the library because of the respect he has for me, and he does not want his misbehavior to reflect on me. Other than my stating my appreciation to them, neither of them truly knows how much their verbal sharing meant to me. I have always been an individual who wants to make a difference in someone's life and their statements indicate I did just that.

Another way I have tried to make a difference in the lives of younger Black males and generally in our community is being involved in various organizations that help to speak to the Black experience, especially experiences for youth. One such organization is the Greater Lafayette Chapter of the Indiana Black Expo (GLIBE). My involvement with GLIBE spans a decade as I have served on its board of directors as treasurer three different times. Over the past four years I have done something more meaningful by coordinating our local backpack giveaway a couple of weeks before school starts each year. The activity includes buying backpacks, stuffing them with school supplies, and giving them away in a carnival-type atmosphere. The Saturday morning activity also includes local not-for-profit agencies that provide various services for families on the lower economic spectrum. This is a rewarding activity that assists children on day one of their school year. Serving on its scholarship committee, we provided fourteen scholarships to high school and undergraduate students. Time and time again, GLIBE has been told what a difference it makes in awarding these scholarships.

One of the most satisfying activities was an after-school mentoring program named Success Academy for fourth through six grade students. Several of us as Black men met with Black male students to introduce them to various cultural topics and intrinsic values to ensure they had a Black experience as part of their education. This direct one-on-one experience prompted and facilitated much needed conversation for young Black males who often did not have a consistent positive Black male role model in their lives. Mothers of these students constantly expressed their appreciation for the work we were doing. The administrative personnel of the elementary and middle school also expressed gratitude for the work as these students had no Black male educators in their schools.

As you might guess, making a difference in the lives of young Black males along with involvement in the community goes a long way in giving me personal satisfaction. Also, as you might guess, the frustration with unconscious bias does not produce the same personal satisfaction. Reflecting on twenty years as county librarian, people start talking about your legacy. The fact is I am the first Black library director for TCPL. That fact and legacy won't change. There is a legacy in having built three branches with Jos N. Holman on all three dedication plaques. That fact won't change, and those plaques will remain even if the buildings are torn down for future progress. More importantly is the potential legacy and impact I will leave with the young Black male students I have mentored and worked with. That potential legacy brings the ultimate satisfaction. Parallel to any legacy and more challenging is the development and implementation of interesting, creative, and appropriate programming for young Black males at TCPL. This legacy is yet to be accomplished. As a Black male this challenge is really important to me as it is my duty to find a way to accomplish it before I retire. Another legacy challenge is the duty to continue to work on training for TCPL staff to help them learn how to relegate their unconscious bias in order to offer the best customer service in better serving everyone in our community. Thurgood Marshall once said, "What you have to do—White or Black—you have to recognize that you have certain feelings bout the other race, good or bad. And then get rid of 'em. But you can't get rid of them until you recognize them."[4] When as professional librarians we personally accept and employ this inspiring initiative, public librarianship will better serve everyone who accesses the library's resources.

## NOTES

1. Jos N. Holman, "Making the Grade as an African American Library Director in a Majority Community," in *The 21st-Century Black Librarian in America: Issues and Challenges*, ed. Andrew P. Jackson, Julius Jefferson, and Akilah Nosakhere (Lanham, MD: Scarecrow Press, 2012), 67–70.
2. Bryan Collier, *We Shall Overcome* (New York: Orchard Books, an Imprint of Scholastic Inc., 2021).
3. "Cliftonstrengths," Gallup Topic, https://www.gallup.com/topic/cliftonstrengths.aspx. Accessed August 1, 2023.
4. Janet Cheatham Bell, *Till Victory Is Won: Famous Quotations from the NAACP* (New York: Washington Square Press, 2002), 118.

## WORKS CITED

Bell, Janet Cheatham. *Till Victory Is Won: Famous Quotations from the NAACP*. New York: Washington Square Press, 2002.

"Cliftonstrengths." Gallup Topic, accessed August 1, 2023. https://www.gallup.com/topic/cliftonstrengths.aspx.

Collier, Bryan. *We Shall Overcome*. New York: Orchard Books, an Imprint of Scholastic Inc., 2021.

Holman, Jos N. "Making the Grade as an African American Library Director in a Majority Community." In *The 21st-Century Black Librarian in America: Issues and Challenges*, edited by Andrew P. Jackson, Julius Jefferson, and Akilah Nosakhere. Lanham: Scarecrow Press, 2012.

# Chapter 10
# Collaborations with Museums

## 10.1

*Louis Armstrong as Archivist*

Regina Bain

**LOUIS ARMSTRONG, WORLD ICON**

Louis Armstrong was born in New Orleans, Louisiana, one generation post the Emancipation Proclamation and into stark poverty. He never finished the fifth grade, but he honed his craft playing the trumpet through a music program in a youth detention center in the early 1900s. By the time he was a teenager, he was performing with the best bands in the city, his life forever changed through the power of arts education. Many elements of jazz, like improvised solos, swing, and scat singing were first perfected and made popular by Armstrong. He helped make the trumpet into a solo instrument, hitting improbable high notes with consistency, bending notes to suit the mood and playing with time, moving in and around the metronome. By the 1930s, he was famous as a musical virtuoso and on his way to becoming a world icon.

Perhaps best known for the song "What a Wonderful World," Armstrong had hit songs for five decades. He was the first African American to have featured billing in a Hollywood film and one of the first to have written in his contract that he would not play in a hotel unless he could stay there. Armstrong entertained millions, from heads of state and royalty to the kids on his stoop in Corona, Queens, where he and his wife, Lucille, resided for three decades. That national and New York landmarked home is now the Louis Armstrong House Museum (LAHM), a three-building campus with signature programming supporting the legacy of Louis and Lucille Armstrong. No one has lived in the home since the couple and all the furnishings and memorabilia are theirs, a unique occurrence for any house museum, but especially for one belonging to Black artists.

In addition to the remarkable home, the Armstrongs left behind a vast personal collection of 1,600 recordings, 700-plus home recorded reel-to-reel tapes, many in hand-decorated boxes, scrapbooks, photographs, trumpets, 270 sets of band parts, twelve linear feet of papers, letters, manuscripts, and more. Donated by the Louis Armstrong Educational Foundation and cared for through Queens College for decades, these personal materials, plus several extraordinary additional collections, make up the Armstrong Archives, a sixty-thousand-piece assemblage that is the largest archive of any single jazz musician. The collection now resides in the Armstrong Center, a fourteen-thousand-square-foot building erected across the street from the historic home. The center holds a seventy-five-seat performance space, is the permanent home for the Armstrong archives, and features the landmark interactive exhibition *Here to Stay*, curated by pianist and visual artist Jason Moran.

Both the house and the archives have been open to the public for decades and have become an invaluable resource for researchers, publishers, historians, and jazz fans around the world who can now study and interpret Armstrong's materials for themselves. In 2018, the archives were completely digitized and made accessible to the public 24/7 through a searchable database. That year, *The New York Times* recognized the impact of this digitization with a front-page article in the Sunday Arts & Leisure Section. In that article, Giovanni Russonello wrote

> Behind his blistering trumpet solos, revolutionary vocal improvising and exuberant stage persona, how did Louis Armstrong see himself? What was it like to be the

first pop virtuoso of the recorded era—the man whose earliest releases set the tune for America's love affair with modern black music, and who went on to become one of history's most famous entertainers? Those questions aren't rhetorical. There's actually a deep well of resources on hand to help answer them.[1]

## PERSONAL AUDIO RECORDINGS: THE REEL-TO-REEL TAPES

The bulk of the resources to address questions about Armstrong's experiences and philosophy come from Armstrong himself. He was his own archivist. Between 1950 and 1971, the legendary trumpeter personally recorded more than seven hundred reel-to-reel tapes. The recordings feature Armstrong practicing his trumpet, playing along with albums, talking with friends in his home, recording the audio of television programs he found particularly important, and more. One reel contains an audio recording of the entirety of Martin Luther King Jr.'s televised funeral. He would then index the recordings, writing on lined paper the itemized contents of the reel. He kept the index in a notebook he could reference. In one reel he explains to his friends, "Now I got a Den, I can look at all my tapes around the walls and just pick out what I want to hear. [Lucille] know that would be my life in music, so when I can hear every record I ever made, all I got to do is look in the little book and put my finger on it. My interviews I got 'em all on tape."[2]

The "little book" he references is of his own creation, his archival index, creating a record of his accomplishments as well as the in-between moments of rehearsal, conversation, and contemplation that made up his life. In March 2020, the digitized archives were brought to life through a series of curated online exhibits by LAHM's director of research collections, Ricky Riccardi, and featured in *The Washington Post*.[3] The online exhibits dive deep into a selection of the reels, giving the reader the ability to review Armstrong's handwritten index and hear some of its content. I personally enjoy the many times Armstrong speaks directly into the microphone and says he's here talking to "you." It's unlikely anyone was in the room with him when he made many of these comments. The "you" he references are all of us who, decades later, are reviewing his recordings. He knew we would want to hear them, and he provided us with a personal greeting.

## TAPE BOX COLLAGE ART

Perhaps equally as significant as the reel-to-reel tapes are the tape boxes themselves. Armstrong used the boxes as a palette onto which he designed collages out of photographs, newspaper clippings, correspondence, and other materials on hand in the den of his Corona, Queens, home. In September 1953, Armstrong wrote to a fan, "My hobby is to pick out the different things during whatever I read and piece them together and make a little story of my own."[4]

The national significance of the collages has been articulated by several prominent writers. In 2008, *The Paris Review* included several collages in a photo spread and noted that collage "became a visual outlet for [Armstrong's] improvisational genius."[5] In his foreword to Brower's 2008 coffee-table compendium of collages, Hilton Als, longtime theater critic of *The New Yorker*, wrote,

> Collage, like drawing, is as the poet Marianne Moore had it in another context, "a radiograph of the soul." These images reveal Armstrong's soul to have been writerly in its density. They became a visual autobiography made from his pen and paper and scissors to cut up the way he saw the world, and to represent—accurately—how Americans are cut up but insist on being put back together, with dreams.[6]

## ARMSTRONG'S MANUSCRIPTS

In addition to the reels and the collage tape box covers, the archive contains Armstrong's manuscripts. Louis Armstrong was a prolific writer. Like his singing voice, his writing voice was unique and unapologetic. For me, it's reminiscent of the language and cadence I might find in a Zora Neale Hurston novel. In an archival photograph of him at his typewriter, his aspect is focused and studious—descriptors too often neglected when describing his artistic genius. His writings came in the form of two autobiographies—*Swing That Music* in 1936 and *Satchmo: My Life in New Orleans* in 1954—and the thousands of letters he wrote to fans and friends, some of which have been donated back to the museum.

In a series curated by staff member Sandrine Frem, Adrianna Carrillo, LAHM's Director of Guest Experience wrote about another manuscript in the archive, The Armstrong Story, an unpublished biography which was acquired by the museum in 2016 and shared a line from the manuscript: "I give you the sound and you go on from there, Wow, you dig?"[7]

## THE OBJECTS

In addition to the reels, collages, and manuscripts, there are a number of objects in the archives that LAHM has collected throughout the years. Some of them were personally amassed by the Armstrongs and others were acquired through collectors and fans. They include the handrail from the Colored Waif's Home in New Orleans where he was sent from January 1913 to June 1914 after firing a gun.[8]

In this ongoing museum series about the archives, Junior Armstead, LAHM's facilities assistant, writes about the bronze trumpet sculpture from Armstrong's grave. Jake Goldbas, program director, writes about a picture of Louis practicing his horn backstage. Pedro Espinoza, managing director, writes about Samuel Countee's portrait of Lucille Armstrong. Sandrine Frem and Charanya R., two Fulbright alumni on staff, write about Armstrong's passport. They write,

[I]ssued on December 14, 1956 and used until 1961, [the passport] is filled with stamps from all over the world—England, France, Jamaica, Italy, Lebanon, Kenya, Brazil, Chile, Switzerland, Belgium, Uruguay, Turkey, Congo, Ghana, Trinidad and Tobago, to name a few, and is a testament to his global impact and the lives he touched. . . . To us, his passport is more than just a travel document; it's a powerful symbol of his impact. It represents not only his musical achievements but also his role as a cultural ambassador and advocate for peace and understanding. As Fulbright scholars at the Louis Armstrong House Museum, we feel a deep connection to this archival piece. We are inspired by Louis and share his mission to promote cultural exchange and global understanding. Today, we continue to draw on his message of unity and love and envision a world where boundaries are bridges and music connects us in solidarity.[9]

The archives have had a significant effect on Armstrong scholarship, impacting books (*Louis Armstrong In His Own Words*), documentaries (Sacha Jenkins's *Black and Blues* and Ken Burns's *Jazz*), academic articles (Ben Alexander on Louis Armstrong in the *American Archivist*), other museums (the Smithsonian exhibit of archival materials), recordings (Grammy-winning collections of Armstrong's 1920s recordings used archival materials), conferences, symposia, plays, and more. In addition to these major texts and events, the effect of these artifacts on the staff, docents, visitors, and young people who access them is clear through their own words.

## DEEPENING THE STORY THROUGH ARCHIVAL ACCESS

Louis Armstrong is an icon as an entertainer. His relationship to matters of social justice are complex—many view him as a civil rights pioneer while others are unfamiliar with his connection to equity in America and beyond. Armstrong's smile, his humor, and his performative demeanor have been both a spoken and unspoken barrier of engagement. Despite his role as a central figure in the story of the Little Rock Nine (1957), his distinguished record of international humanitarian outreach, and his position as a mentor and touchstone for subsequent generations of musicians, for too many people the perception of Louis Armstrong is one-dimensional. The archives allow us to dive into stories like the formation of the All Stars, a famously racially integrated band that Armstrong insisted upon. The band's composition forced promoters throughout the United States to reckon with their segregation policies. Louis Armstrong was a pioneer at a time when a misplaced word or gesture could mean a lynching. He stepped forward into those fractious arenas with a smile and with a quiet insistence in the quality and nature of his art. He made outspoken comments about President Eisenhower's lack of swift action when nine Black students in Arkansas attempted to enroll in Central High School after the 1954 Supreme Court ruling of *Brown vs. Board of Education* and were met with an angry mob. What followed landed in Armstrong's FBI file, prompted questions about his suitability to represent America abroad, and led to his blackballing from American television. The archives tell these stories from Armstrong's perspective, allowing us to delve behind closed doors and deepen our understanding of his life and work.

## ARMSTRONG NOW! CONTEMPORARY ARTISTS RESPONDING TO THE ARCHIVES

The archives allow us to contextualize Armstrong's story within history and place his achievements among the pantheon of Black artists and thinkers such as Langston Hughes and James Baldwin who were his near contemporaries. LAHM's ongoing goal is to place Armstrong in proper context and share his story more fully for all audiences, including for the artists that are directly in his legacy. The manuscripts, recordings, collage, objects, and the stories of the pursuit of civil rights are part of the birthright of today's artists and audiences.

Armstrong Now reintroduces audiences everywhere to his legacy of artistry and innovation. The program features artists responding creatively to the digitized Armstrong archives. The result of these residencies and engagements are the development of new collaborative projects, art works, and a suite of short films. Armstrong Now brings these artists into intimate proximity to his legacy and gives them the opportunity to learn, to interpret, and to respond in ways that reflect the issues of today and their own artistic values.

In a 2023 *New York Times* article, Melena Ryzik quotes Moran:

> I think that this will do something that we haven't quite seen in a jazz space. . . . That's also something that my community needs to witness, too. It needs to watch, how can we take care of an artist's history? And what else can it unleash in a community that might not even care about the art, but might care about something else related to it? Armstrong gives us all those opportunities to do that.[10]

Ryzik continues, "Even a longtime Armstrong devotee like Marquis Hill . . . was moved by these personal mementos. . . . A half-century-old recording of Armstrong discussing how important it was to listen to all kinds of music inspired a Hill composition for Newport, commissioned by the Center. Its jazz club, he said, is 'going to be a new space for what Louis Armstrong wanted, to keep pushing the music forward.'"[11]

Daniel J Watts, performer and Armstrong Now artist says, "For me, Armstrong Now is simply a reminder that Louis and his legacy have never left. His imprint is woven, printed, and embossed in all that we do."[12] Amyra León, performer and Armstrong Now artist, shares, "I cannot wait to get to know the self-documented version of Louis Armstrong—the person behind the brass and grit, the melody and sway."[13]

**THE FUTURE**

We've developed a practice that when an artist comes through our doors, we ask them to consider, "Where are your archives?" Only rarely do we receive a clear and definitive answer: "My papers are with the university" or "I'm in talks with two institutions." More often we hear, "Well I'm not Louis Armstrong," intimating that their stars are not bright enough to warrant a collection of items chronicling their life and work. We ask them to reconsider. Years from now, when stories are told about them through books, films, and recordings, we want their voices to be at the table.

Armstrong Now is part of the Louis Armstrong House Museum's signature programs, designed to ensure that future generations learn about Louis and Lucille Armstrong, have access to the highest-quality arts education programming, and have the space to innovate and create new works. We are thankful to Armstrong, our first archivist; Mrs. Armstrong, our first preservationist; and to the staff, volunteers, and community members who have worked diligently to ensure this legacy.

**NOTES**

1. Russonello, Giovanni, "Louis Armstrong's Life in Letters, Music, and Art," *New York Times*, November 16, 2018, https://www.nytimes.com/2018/11/16/arts/music/louis-armstrong-archive.html
2. "Virtual Tour," *That's My Home*, https://videopress.com/v/i4lrjUwt , at 20:06.
3. Edger, Geoff, "Louis Armstrong's Museum Has Gone Silent, but 'Pop's is Still Talking," *The Washington Post*, April 13, 2020, https://www.washingtonpost.com/entertainment/museums/louis-armstrongs-museum-has-gone-silent-but-pops-is-still-talking/2020/04/13/3d6ef176-7cd8-11ea-a3ee-13e1ae0a3571_story.html
4. Armstrong, Louis. *Letter to Marili Morden*, September 1953, https://collections.louisarmstronghouse.org/asset-detail/1000843
5. "Reel to Reel: Louis Armstrong," *The Paris Review*, Issue 184, Spring 2008.
6. "Foreword," in Brewer, Steven, Satchmo: *The Wonderful World and Art of Louis Armstrong*, New York: Abrams, 2009, page 6.
7. Armstrong, Louis, *The Armstrong Story*, unpublished typescript.
8. "Railing," *Louis Armstrong House Museum Online Catalog*, https://louisarmstrong.pastperfectonline.com/webobject/C03D8248-D53C-4C55-B420-244636335052; Ratliff, Ben, "Visitor Center Planned for Louis Armstrong House and Museum," *New York Times*, December 21, 2010, https://archive.nytimes.com/artsbeat.blogs.nytimes.com/2010/12/21/visitors-center-planned-for-louis-armstrong-house-and-museum/ ; Koppel, Niko. "Collector Shares Mementos and Memories of Jazz Legend." New York Times, 29 Sept. 2008, p. B4(L). Gale Academic OneFile, link.gale.com/apps/doc/A185704540/AONE?u=anon~64c55369&sid=sitemap&xid=737e8fe0. Accessed 13 June 2024. ; Lobdell, Linda, "At Home with the Armstrongs: Field Trip to Queens with Jazz Station WBGO," Jersey Jazz, vol. 36, no. 8, September 2009, p. 30, https://njjs.org/files/2009/3708%20web%20archive%20files/3708_JerseyJazzFullIssue.pdf
9. "Louis Armstrong House Museum Welcomes Back Archives," *Queens Gazette*, April 20, 2023, https://www.qgazette.com/articles/louis-armstrong-house-museum-welcomes-back-archives/
10. Ryzik, Melena, 'Satchmo's Wonderful Word: Louis Armstrong Center Amplifies an Artist's Vision," *New York Times*, August 3, 2023.
11. Ibid.
12. Watts, Daniel J. "Armstrong Now," https://www.louisarmstronghouse.org/armstrong-now/
13. "Esperanza Spalding Announces Livestream from Louis Armstrong House," Bass Magazine, https://bassmagazine.com/esperanza-spalding-announces-livestream-from-louis-armstrong-house/

# Chapter 11
# Library Trustees

## 11.1

*Experiences as a Library Trustee*

Laura Ellis

Hello Everyone,

My name is Laura Ellis, and I am currently serving as a trustee on the Anne Arundel County Board of Trustees. Thank you for allowing me to be part of your publication.

1. How were you appointed?

    I was nominated by my Maryland state delegate, Mr. Mark Chang.

2. How long is your term of office?

    My term of office is three years with a two-term limit.

3. How many members are on the board? Committee assignments.

    We have eighteen members on our board. We were twenty-four members, then we went down to seventeen members, but recently added a student member, so we are a total of eighteen members. All board members are on one committee.

4. Why did you accept membership on the board?

    I wanted to serve my committee. I have also been an election judge. Service is important to me. As a member, I believe it brought more diversity to the board, even though there were already four other African American women on the board when I joined. I believe we have the same number now, but two members are new. I am no longer the new member on the board.

5. Anything else you would like to share?

    I am a career librarian. My thirty years of service have been in educational libraries. I have worked at a four-year university, a community college, and K–12 schools. The vast majority of my career has been in K–12. I have used, but never worked in, a public library. The experiences are not exactly the same. In a public school setting the librarian has to have a master's degree in library science. We are also responsible for the safety of the students in our spaces.

    I never thought about being on the board of anything, or even what boards do, how people get on boards, and how boards impact their institutions, so I am very grateful to Delegate Chang for nominating me for this opportunity. I have learned so much and I have been able to have a direct impact on what our citizens have access to as far as materials and services.

    When I joined the board there were members that had served for twenty-nine years, but now we have term limits, which I think is good because it gives more people an opportunity to serve and different types of people who truly reflect the communities where the libraries are.

    One drawback is that board members are invited to a lot of events during the day, or in the evenings, which I simply cannot attend because I work full time. I have often wondered if past members were individuals who could set their own schedules, which I do not.

# 11.2

## *Being a Library Trustee*

Andrew P. Jackson (Sekou Molefi Baako)

By the time this edition of the *Handbook of Black Librarianship* will be published, I will be in my third term as a library trustee with the Queens Public Library. The invitation to serve as a trustee was offered by then Queens Borough president Melinda Katz in 2016 upon my retirement as executive director of Queens Library's Langston Hughes Community Library and Cultural Center after thirty-six years. Library trustees are appointed by the mayor of the City of New York or the president of the borough they reside in. Each term is three years.

When the notice of my retirement became public news, Borough President Katz called me to her office at Queens Borough Hall for a brief meeting. I had no idea what our discussion would be about, even though we knew each other very well over her tenure in office. I actually hoped this meeting was not to offer me a position in our staffing as I did not want to replace my work at the library with another full-time position. To my surprise, Ms. Katz thanked me for my years of "invaluable service to Queens Library and the residents of the borough"[1] and said, "'We can't just let you ride off into the sunset, we still need your services. Would you accept an appointment to the Queens Public Library board of trustees."[2] Her question caught me as a complete surprise and a happy one at that. It only took a few seconds to realize the magnitude of this invitation, and I accepted.

With my appointment in 2017, I am extremely proud to be the first librarian and first former staff member to serve on the Queens Public Library board of trustees. There are nineteen mayoral and borough presidential appointments to the board, each representing a city council district in the borough. I represent Community Board #3, the Corona-East Elmhurst community where I have resided most of my life.

As a librarian, I bring a unique lens to each discussion in our trustee meetings based on my legacy as a staff member and as a library professional whereas the other members are lawyers, businesspeople, or active citizens. I take this vantage point seriously and often add some historical or opinion on a topic that stems from my thirty-six-year librarian experience. Two examples of this were presented at our September board meeting. I serve as chair of the board's programming committee and made two proposals to the board. The first related to our current promotion and support of banned and censored books and the fact that most library staff and our public have no idea who the members of the board of trustees are.

My first proposal comes from a news report I heard over the summer announcing that the city of Hoboken, New Jersey, was designated unanimously by the City Council an official sanctuary for banned and censored books, meaning it will not ban or remove any books from the city's library shelves. With that news, I recommended that the Queens Public Library encourage the New York Public Library and Brooklyn Public Library to each make it official that they are sanctuaries for books and encourage the mayor and the New York City Council do the same for New York City and with that official designation, encourage the governor of New York to do the same. That news report also cited Chicago as another city whose City Council had "declared itself a sanctuary for endangered and endangered stories and established Book Sanctuaries across 77 distinct neighborhoods and 81 library branches."[3] Why not New York?

My second proposal to the board was to take a most successful program idea I designed many years ago to invite elementary school, middle school, and community residents to a community read-in with elected officials, business leaders, school principals, ministers, and other residents to read to our children. Using that model, I proposed that the members of the board of trustees participate in a community read-in during the month of April celebrating National Library Month (I extended the week to a month.). This provides a very visible programmatic opportunity for our residents to meet their trustee members. Both of my program proposals were received warmly, and I am excited at the possibilities.

Being a library trustee has been most enlightening for me to see and learning and being involved in oversight of the Queens Public Library; the separation from the duties of the trustee board from that of library administration and the work of each of the seven working committees of the board. In addition to the programming committee, I am also a member of the building and grounds committee. This has been a most rewarding experience and another level of growth for me as a library professional, semiretired where my active years can influence my voice as a trustee. I thank Ms. Katz for offering me this golden opportunity and will continue to serve as long as I am asked to do so.

It has been a privilege collaborating with the other members of the board of trustees to provide oversight of the library for the residents of Queens County. The board has been extremely fortunate to be working in concert with a dynamic and visionary president/CEO in Dennis M. Walcott; our knowledgeable chief librarian, Nick Buron; and their skilled and talented administrative team.

**NOTES**

1. Melinda Katz, personal communication, 2016.
2. Ibid.
3. Laura Rodriguez Presa, "As Attempts to Ban Books across the Country Increase, Chicago Establishes 'Book Sanctuaries': 'Encouraging and Alarming,'" *Chicago Tribune*, 26 September 2022, https://www.chicagotribune.com/2022/09/26/as-attempts-to-ban-books-across-the-country-increase-chicago-establishes-book-sanctuaries-encouraging-and-alarming/.

**WORKS CITED**

Katz, Melinda Katz. Personal communication, 2016.

Presa, Laura Rodriguez. "As Attempts to Ban Books Across the Country Increase, Chicago Establishes 'Book Sanctuaries': 'Encouraging and Alarming.'" *Chicago Tribune*, 26 September 2022. https://www.chicagotribune.com/2022/09/26/as-attempts-to-ban-books-across-the-country-increase-chicago-establishes-book-sanctuaries-encouraging-and-alarming/.

# 11.3

## *Empowerment, Representation, and Leadership*

A REFLECTION ON JOINING THE QPL BOARD

Cloyette Harris-Stoute

When Queens borough president Donovan Richards bestowed upon me the honor of joining the board of trustees at the Queens Public Library (QPL), it was a call that resonated deeply with my values and mission. Having founded a nonprofit focused on nurturing leadership qualities in teen girls, especially those from underprivileged and immigrant backgrounds, I deeply understand the transformative power of access to knowledge. The Queens Public Library, serving as a beacon of information and resources for community empowerment, aligns with the ethos of my organization, Guyanese Girls Rock Foundation.

Serving on the board of QPL is not just a professional duty but a personal commitment. It embodies my mission to empower young women by connecting them to the very resources that can catalyze their growth. It is about ensuring the library remains not just a place of books but a sanctuary of dreams and empowerment. Further, as a Black female leader, my presence on the board stands as a testament to the possibility of leadership and influence, underscoring the importance for young Black and minority girls to witness women who reflect their own identities and aspirations. Representation has the profound ability to shift paradigms and uplift communities. My acceptance of this role is, in part, to be that guiding light for them.

My childhood in Guyana is a testament to the power of books. Without the distractions of television, books became my solace, my education, and my escape. They were the portals through which I traveled the world, from the romance-filled corners of Harlequin novels to the intriguing mysteries of the Hardy Boys and Nancy Drew. These stories instilled in me a sense of wonder, a passion for learning, and a relentless spirit of inquiry. The library, albeit miles away from home, was a treasure trove that shaped my worldview.

In the same way that books and the library became a pillar of support and growth for me, QPL is a place where countless young people discover their potential, ignite their passions, and envision brighter futures. Libraries are more than repositories of books, they are hubs of growth, curiosity, and learning. They offer environments where young individuals can recognize and magnify their potential. By accepting a seat on the board, I saw a chance to make the library a bridge to opportunity for countless teen girls.

Service, to me, is an extension of one's purpose, and being a member of the board of trustees at QPL is a harmonious blend of my personal experiences, professional aspirations, and passion for empowerment. In this role, I hope to champion the library as an institution that nurtures dreams, fosters leadership, and amplifies voices. For in the pages of books and the aisles of libraries, we can find reflections of who we are, who we can be, and the world we hope to shape.

# 11.4

## *The Importance of the Public Library*

A TRUSTEE PERSPECTIVE

Earl G. Simons

The public library played a role in my growth and development as a youth in New York City. It was a quiet place where you were there to do your homework, research, work on a group assignment, or discover new information. It was also a safe place for students to go after school to get a jump-start on assignments. These experiences hold true today with the current library with enhanced opportunities for all ages in-person and virtually.

Years before knowing I would be affiliated with the Queens Public Library (QPL), my interest, passion, and support was demonstrated through community engagement. As an active member of the Cambria Heights Civic Association, I supported the seasoned elders and public officials in the community who identified the need for a new larger full-service branch library to replace the small storefront at the time. Following great collaboration and focus, a new branch was built to serve the growing community. It is at that same branch where our children would go to do their homework, research, and assignments. It was also the place where they would go to read off their fines and fees for overdue books. A lesson learned to return books on time.

In 2015, the then Queens borough president, Melinda Katz, ask me to join the Queens Borough Public Library (that was the name at the time) as one of her new appointees. My appointment came at a pivotal time in the history of the library. There were Queens public officials on the local and state levels of government actively engaged in supporting the library at that time. There were new governance laws and policies enacted that impacted the library in a positive way. As a resident of Queens, I accepted the borough president's appointment to the board of trustees and on day one rolled up my sleeves and got to work.

As a member of the board of trustees, I had the pleasure of experiencing the transition of executive leadership and the growth and enhancement of the library. I participated in the development of the strategic plan led by a professional consultant as well as the process related to the library's branding. The marketing and branding process led to the logo change and the change from Queens Borough Public Library to Queens Public Library.

It continues to be a blessing to serve as chair of the Queens Public Library board of trustees. This is an energetic, committed, and inclusive group of professionals who volunteer their service to Queens County and the City of New York. We have been working collaboratively to address important issues and services provided by QPL to the residents and patrons of the library. It continues to be important for us to embrace and acknowledge the growing and evolving role of the library and role in the tapestry of the community, county, and city.

It is also a pleasure and a privilege to serve on a board at an institution serving one of the most diverse counties in the nation. It is with this backdrop that I am sensitive to the need to be increasingly open to exploring creativity to address the services and needs of patrons, while balancing history and traditions in the middle of local, state, and federal fiscal challenges.

The library continues to be a place close to the community where resources are easily accessible. As a result, the partnerships established over the years, such as serving as a cooling center during the hot summer days for senior citizens and families; access for municipal IDs, COVID-19 testing sites; early voting sites, teen centers, and job readiness workshops are a few examples of critical areas of collaboration to serve the community. All services provided while continuing to be the place in the neighborhood where individuals of all ages and languages can go and seek information, read a book, and/or enhance their life skills.

The Queens Public Library has a dedicated staff with sixty-six locations and continues to be a special place uniquely positioned to serve the community in-person and virtually beyond its walls. I am proud to be a part of this service to the community.

# Part V
# LIBRARY TECHNOLOGY AND BLACK LIBRARIANSHIP

# Chapter 12

# Open Pedagogy as the Intersection of Digital Skills and Community

Willa Liburd Tavernier and Maria E. Hamilton Abegunde

Libraries and the academy should pay greater attention to processes for equitable participation in scholarly communication, coproduction of knowledge, and community. Digital community engagement holds promise for this, if we start with humans, not technologies and tools.[1] This chapter provides a review and analysis of an open pedagogy project at Indiana University as an example of community building through coconstruction of knowledge in the classroom, using digital methods as one of the tools.

In March 2022, Indiana University Libraries launched the public open digital scholarship resource Land, Wealth, Liberation: The Making and Unmaking of Black Wealth in America (LWL) to counterbalance decisions and priorities in collections, libraries, and the academy that have historically marginalized the experiences, histories, and traditions of people of color, and to disrupt the replication of this marginalization in the digital sphere.[2] The launch was not only well received, but it was also timely, relevant to, and resonant with the ongoing changes happening in public, community, and university libraries.

Library services and access to information have traditionally been tied to the needs of particular and well-defined populations, for example, disciplinary, campus, spatial, or ethnic communities. With the turn toward digital information and the open access movement, many academic libraries advocate for open access to scholarly information, support open access publication of scholarship through policies and mandates, library publishing, transformational agreements, and funds for publishing open access articles.

Such initiatives position libraries as providers of access to knowledge to anyone in the world with an internet connection, even as libraries work within a complex system of publishers, vendors, platform developers, and others to form a global knowledge commons. This positioning is not without its risks: different actors in the scholarly communication system have differing motivations, as starkly outlined in the ongoing case *Hachette Book Group, Inc. vs Internet Archive*.[3] This raises three questions: Does the pivot to open access risk losing a sense of community? What implications may this have for libraries and communities? What should libraries do about any of it?

Although the public has access to increasing amounts of scholarly information through open access publication, distrust in scholarly and scientific information continues to rise.[4] This distrust is not a new phenomenon as many communities have historically, and with good reason, been distrustful of those who claim to hold authoritative scientific information.[5]

Scholars studying the sharing of information resources observe that a key attribute of systems that successfully manage shared resources is trust, and one of the evaluative criteria to assess the robustness of such systems is legitimacy and participation.[6] McGinnis[7] notes that participation tends to increase legitimacy with coproduction being a particularly effective method of participation and trust building. Similarly, Dempsey, Malpas, and Sandler's[8] case study of consortial activities in the Big Ten Academic Alliance also notes that "trust develops through shared practices" and is an important prerequisite to success. Wilson[9] suggests that a Black feminist approach to distrust in science, which begins with community and is undergirded by "the idea that we are all interdependent on one another," appropriately shifts the responsibility to institutions to act in a trustworthy manner. Community is of key importance in scholarly communication.

The Land, Wealth, Liberation (LWL) digital resource offers one way to shift and transform the relationships between libraries and different communities, in this case disciplinary. At the LWL launch, Dr. Abegunde, a creative scholar and poet who works in multiple genres and is a faculty member in the Department of African American and African Diaspora Studies (AAADS) at Indiana University, expressed keen interest in using the digital resource in her classroom. In July 2022, Dr. Abegunde invited IU librarians Willa Tavernier and Deloice Holliday to join her in applying for the inaugural cohort of the American Library Association (ALA) Civic Imagination Stations (CIS) grant program. Such a grant would leverage the LWL resource in the fall 2022 iteration of her A263-Contemporary Social Issues in the African American Community course.

Willa Tavernier, Deloice Holliday, and Dr. Abegunde successfully applied for the grant as a teaching team to fund an open pedagogy project that would integrate with the Black studies and contemplative practices methodologies she uses in her classroom. The addition of the open pedagogy project would deepen both approaches by inviting students to interrupt and make meaning of what they learned about the marginalization of Blackness through digital literacies, the arts, and the humanities. We situated our work at the intersections of social issues, Black expressive traditions, and digital technology, designed to address the need to construct space within the public sphere and the academy to unmask racialized systems' effects on contemporary social issues—in this case Black environmental experiences with water.

Open pedagogy is an experiential, hands-on pedagogical practice that leverages digital scholarship. It is a student-centered practice that goes beyond using open access materials in teaching to position students as knowledge creators. Chiappe and Adame[10] describe it as putting "learners into a position of sharing their learning, adapting products created by their peers or constructing collaboratively their knowledge with people far beyond the limits of the regular classroom."

Open digital scholarship benefits the public by providing access to, and engagement with, educational and culturally enriching material beyond the boundaries of university courses or restricted library material. Open pedagogy can allow faculty and students to tackle issues of public importance in new formats, and "capitalize on this relationship between enrolled students and a broader public by drawing in wider communities of learners and expertise to help our students find relevance in their work, situate their ideas into key contexts, and contribute to the public good."[11]

The ALA Civic Imagination Station Grant allowed the teaching team to expand and enhance Dr. Abegunde's course by including digital resources and pedagogy that were not part of the original course. While the course focused on the historical, cultural, socioeconomic, emotional, psychological, and political dimensions that surround water and its safety, affordability, and accessibility in Black and African diasporic communities, it did not have a digital component or utilize digital humanities resources.

Using the short science fiction film *Pumzi*[12] as the starting point for dialogue about current and future worlds, the inclusion of the digital components was ideal in demonstrating to students the importance of digital humanities in the future—especially the need for digital libraries and archives if the current physical forms become unavailable.

The LWL digital resource served as an additional textual resource in the A263 syllabus; students could reference and explore its timelines and topics as well as the digital methods used. LWL presents a counternarrative that challenges the dominant narrative about the racial wealth gap and presents a wealth of research by Black studies scholars and other researchers, about the targeted destruction of thriving Black communities, contextualizing this history against the backdrop of government action and inaction, and presents history using media-rich digital timelines. As their final project, students created digital projects, collectively titled Letters to Ourselves: The A263 Water Epistles, which then became a subpage of the LWL digital resource.

## PROCESS

The strength and value of collaboration and cocreation was evident from the outset of the planning process. Cohort participants attended a two-day virtual institute and two workshops hosted by the ALA Civic Imagination Stations coaching team, Michael Rohd and Willa Taylor, which provided nineteen hours of process development work. We explored broad concepts, including public engagement, listening, and democracy, and responded to questions about artistic process, disparate working styles, joyful and productive artist-librarian collaboration, impact, and the definition of success.

Willa, the research impact and open scholarship librarian, expressed concerns that library administration would be seeking metrics for success that did not necessarily align with the goals of the teaching team. With her work in research impact, she knew that not everything that has value can be counted, and that not everything that can be counted has value. She referenced notes from another draft grant application where the team envisaged multiple assessment-based tools to define success:

1. Student pre- and postproject assessments to evaluate perspectives on community, experience with dialogue and empathy toward persons from different communities, and familiarity with the topic of Black histories, communities, and wealth. The postproject assessment will also include questions about building knowledge and skills to have meaningful conversations on difficult topics inside and outside the classroom and building digital competencies through the open pedagogy project.
2. Instructor feedback will be gathered throughout the program and during a final working session in spring 2023, about instructors' experience with open pedagogy, digital skills they gained, and student engagement in the classroom. Instructors will reflect on if/how they will reuse open pedagogy as an instructional method in future courses.
3. Success will be measured by student growth evidenced by pre- and postproject assessment divergence, student digital competency development, and the instructors' positive rating of their own likelihood to reuse open pedagogy in the future.

Deloice, the multicultural outreach librarian, head of the NMBCC Library and collection manager for African American and African Diaspora Studies, said, "My approach has always been that the success is in the offer. I offered this to the campus or the community. Whether I get ten people, or one hundred people, success is in the offer. I think that our team should decide what success looks like, not administration or other external forces."

Dr. Abegunde noted that members of the teaching team come from different areas, so they each must define success. For Dr. Abegunde what the students say, what they got out of it, whether they are able to work together to get what they wanted out of it, whether they can articulate their own engagement, whether they are able to share their knowledge with their families and communities, and what this means for them, is what drives success. She highlighted that learning objectives for the class include that students will be able to develop and articulate concepts around Black history and culture, so it was not very different from point 1 above.

Deloice and Dr. Abegunde, as longtime collaborators, were able to provide reassurance that the teaching team could define success on their own terms. This collaborative approach laid the groundwork for how we would work throughout the project.

The workshop sessions also helped cohort participants develop and refine the questions the project would address. For the A263 project these questions were:

1. How can we share information about the global water crisis in Black communities with our peers and home communities?
2. How can combining Black studies and digital humanities strengthen arts-based research practices and lead to relevant, resonant, and accessible outcomes for participants and targeted audiences?
3. How can libraries be a site for collaboration with different communities inside/outside the university?
4. How can we use our new digital knowledge to research this topic further and impact change?

The grant allowed the teaching team to hire a Public Open Digital Scholarship (PODS) fellow to provide additional hands-on support in the classroom. The teaching team was very intentional in writing the job description emphasizing that the "PODS Fellow will need to be a flexible and imaginative thinker as students enrolled in A263 will have a significant amount of latitude in thinking about their research projects. Therefore, the approach the PODS Fellow will need to take is to adapt digital methodologies to meet student needs and enhance student literacy, rather than attempting to fit student goals into a particular digital vehicle." Preferred qualifications were an academic background in Black studies, African studies, African American studies, or African diaspora studies, and an awareness of or interest in current digital humanities trends and projects or digital project development.

We specified that we would provide digital humanities training in collaboration with Indiana University's Institute for Digital Arts & Humanities (IDAH), which the Office of the Vice Provost for Research and the IU Libraries finances. This was to redress previous practice in the Scholarly Communication Department of focusing on specific types of experience, which had the effect of restricting the pool of potential applicants to the detriment of candidates of color. By offering on-the-job training we hoped to encourage individuals with the skills and aptitude for the position to apply, even if they lacked specific qualifications or experience.

The successful applicant, Dhakir Abdullah, a PhD candidate in AAADS and a HASTAC scholar, had some digital humanities exposure, and worked with Deloice in the NMBCC library. In this role he split his hours between the Scholarly Communication Department, IDAH, and the A263 classroom.

We planned six coteaching sessions, four with the librarian team and two with the PODS Fellow and IDAH. We designed the librarian coteaching sessions to stimulate discussion, make space for coconstruction of knowledge and of the parameters of the A263 digital project, and ensure that students could make informed decisions about whether and how to share their work. The A263 syllabus dedicated five additional days for students to work solely on their projects in the final weeks of the semester, where the teaching team and PODS Fellow answered student questions and provided technical, content, and research support.

Session 1 introduced the LWL digital resource, focusing on erasure, archival silence, and silenced narratives, starting with a personal experience with water in the Black community of Jasper County, Mississippi, shared by Deloice. Large farms surrounded the community that relied on well water. Crop dusters would frequently spray these farms with insecticide, and there was never any advance warning. As soon as the women heard the plane engines in the distance, women and girls in the community would grab their quilts and rush to cover the wells to avoid contamination by the crop dusters.

This prompted stimulating student discussions, some of whom shared their own stories surrounding amenities in communities of color. Discussions are an important part of coconstruction of knowledge. Our approach was to center student views and to let them interpret and reinterpret events by providing contextual information, rather than trying to impart our own viewpoints.

Storytelling is a particularly effective way of eliciting discussion. Deloice's story is also the subject of Dr. Abegunde's featured poems in the Water Epistles, and we displayed Deloice's family quilts at Black Arts + Digital, our community event featuring the A263 Water Epistles. At the end of this lesson, we asked students to complete the Center for Digital Dannelse's Digital Competence Wheel and submit their results for IDAH and the PODS Fellow to help plan digital humanities teaching sessions.

Session 2 was at the IU Libraries IQ Wall. Students were able to use the IQ Wall to interact and play around with digital project examples and start thinking about their own projects. Digital engagement librarian, Leanne Nay, introduced the makerspace and explained the equipment that students could access and borrow. The class collaboratively developed a name for the project (Water Epistles), brainstormed the landing page, and, though we did not plan for it, students shared what the term "epistles" evoked for them. We intended to have students work on their thesis statement, but we converted this to an assignment because of time constraints.

Session 3 was the first instruction session with Dhakir and Vanessa Elias, the IDAH program and project manager, covering the field of digital humanities, the parallels and differences between digital and traditional scholarship, and providing an overview of digital methods.

For session 4 we split the class, with half the students visiting the makerspace and the other half remaining at the IQ Wall to work through the IDAH template project charter and refine their thesis. At the midpoint of the class the students switched places. The goal was to widen students' views of their relationship with digital technology from solely being consumers to being creators.

Session 5 was the second digital humanities instruction session, led by Dhakir the PODS Fellow. He showed students how to communicate narrative arguments through appropriate placing of multimedia elements within digital spaces such as websites, immersive digital maps, or podcasts. Students learned writing for digital projects versus traditional writing forms.

Before the final coteaching session, Dr. Abegunde used the class time to hold a breakfast for students at the Neal-Marshall Black Culture Center Bridgwaters lounge. Students identified their target audience and the digital method they would use. Dr. Abegunde advised us that ongoing discussions with the students led to redesigning the final project to give students more latitude. Students were no longer required to tie the project temporally to *Pumzi* although they would need to reflect on the film as part of the project. As the class continued to progress, the specifics of the assignment were fleshed out in continued discussion with students.

Session 6 started with the A263 Contemporary Social Issues in the African American Community—Digital Project Resources Library Research Guide (the LibGuide), which incorporated the teaching materials and digital tools covered in previous sessions, and instructions for adding their project to the LWL digital resource. Willa provided a step-by-step explanation of copyright and licensing using creative commons licenses, and had students consider whether to share their project publicly, and what license to apply to their project by working through the creative commons license chooser on their own.

Dhakir and Willa then distributed a brief survey to assess students' levels of confidence with digital tools, asked students to specify whether their project would be public or private, and what license they would apply for publicly shared projects. We made this survey available on Canvas for students who missed that class session. The focus was on having students make an informed choice about the work they created and how they wanted to share it. Students could also change their choices prepublication.

The project included three community events.

1. A community-built physical word cloud during the October 2022 Arts & Humanities Council First Thursdays using a poster featuring a drop of water with A263 students' reflections on water. We invited community members to write their thoughts about what water means to them on blue wave-shaped sticky notes and affix them to the poster and provide video responses.
2. A panel discussion as part of the IU Libraries Open Access Week Symposium. The faculty speakers explained that they published open access so that the communities they researched would have access to the publications. Featured speaker Melanie Chambliss, an intellectual historian who researches Black libraries in the early twentieth century, emphasized the strong community connections of Black libraries. The teaching team discussed the ongoing A263 work and the questions projects like these raised for pedagogy, community, and Black studies. Deloice also invited participants to share their "water words," and this stimulated a lively discussion.
3. A Black Arts + Digital Showcase held as part of IU Libraries' Black History Month 2023, featuring talks by community artists displaying work in textiles, print, and digital formats. A panel featuring four A263 students alongside the teaching team was the feature presentation.

**CONCLUSION**

With the help of the teaching team, the PODS Fellow, and IDAH, students created unique digital projects surrounding the historical, cultural, socioeconomic, emotional, psychological, and political dimensions on the safety, affordability of, and access to water in Black communities to provide a collaborative and cocreated educational resource.

The Water Epistles can serve as one model for bridging access and opportunity divides through arts and digital community engagement. This project helps increase the library's visibility as a place of educational persistence as the Land Wealth and Liberation digital resource is a living online archive that maintains communal accessibility and perpetual alterability.

Students' confidence in using digital technology as creators increased over the course, as well as their ability to understand their role in recognizing and addressing social issues, and their confidence in using technology to raise awareness about social issues. Students also felt that the format prioritized student learning and allowed them to think critically about issues while acquiring new knowledge and practical skills.

Dhakir notes that the emergent and process-oriented design and praxis of the class challenged him to understand and develop ways to support students who were working on vastly different projects with varying methods (e.g., topics, formats, styles, number of people), a task with a higher level of complexity, in comparison to a similar scenario in which all students are working on more uniform projects. However, he feels that he is better prepared for similar challenges in the future. The teaching team notes that this emergent practice worked for them because of a high level of trust built during prior collaborations.

Most telling is that students have proudly shared this information with their families, communities, and friends, a core tenet of Black studies. Family members attended the Black Arts + Digital showcase, participated in the event, and made sure to introduce themselves to the teaching team.

In their mission to provide access to all, libraries should take a values-based approach with community as a core value. Open pedagogy and digital community engagement hold promise for an equitable, trustworthy, scholarly communication system. If we use reciprocal cocreative processes, strive for equitable civic engagement, and center community, libraries will remain foundational to society as spaces for knowledge production and acquisition, as sites that offer opportunities for cocreation and collaboration, and as ways to engage different worlds and ways of being across multiple times and places.

## NOTES

1. Rebecca S. Wingo, Jason A. Heppler, and Paul Schadewald, "Introduction," *Digital Community Engagement: Partnering Communities with the Academy* (Cincinnati: University of Cincinnati Press, 2020), 12–13. Project MUSE, https://muse.jhu.edu/pub/330/oa_edited_volume/book/75900.
2. Safiya Umoja Noble, "Toward a Critical Black Digital Humanities," in *Debates in the Digital Humanities 2019*, edited by Matthew K. Gold and Lauren F. Klein (Minneapolis: University of Minnesota Press, 2019), 28, JSTOR, https://doi.org/10.5749/j.ctvg251hk5.5; Moya Bailey, "All the Digital Humanists Are White, All the Nerds Are Men, but Some of Us Are Brave," *Journal of Digital Humanities*, 1, no. 1 (2011), https://journalofdigitalhumanities.org/1-1/all-the-digital-humanists-are-white-all-the-nerds-are-men-but-some-of-us-are-brave-by-moya-z-bailey/; Kim Gallon, "Making a Case for the Black Digital Humanities," in *Debates in the Digital Humanities 2016*, edited by Matthew K. Gold and Lauren F. Klein (Minneapolis: University of Minnesota Press, 2016), 42–49, JSTOR, https://doi.org/10.5749/j.ctt1cn6thb.7.
3. Roger C. Schonfeld, Karin Wulf, Rick Anderson, Lisa Janicke Hinchliffe, Joseph Esposito, and Roy Kaufman, "The Internet Archive Loses on Controlled Digital Lending," *The Scholarly Kitchen*, March 28, 2023, https://scholarlykitchen.sspnet.org/2023/03/28/internet-archive-controlled-digital-lending/.
4. Emilija Stojmenova Duh et al., "Publish-and-Flourish: Using Blockchain Platform to Enable Cooperative Scholarly Communication," *Publications*, 7, no. 2, 2 (2019): 33–55, www.mdpi.com, https://doi.org/10.3390/publications7020033.
5. Alice Marwick, Rachel Kuo, Shanice Jones Cameron, and Mora Weigel, "Critical Disinformation Studies," Center for Information, Technology, and Public Life (CITAP), https://citap.unc.edu/research/critical-disinfo/.
6. Madelyn Sanfilippo et al., "Privacy as Knowledge Commons Governance: An Appraisal," in *Governing Privacy in Knowledge Commons*, 1st ed., edited by Madelyn Rose Sanfilippo et al. (Cambridge: Cambridge University Press, 2021), 268–90, DOI.org (Crossref), https://doi.org/10.1017/9781108749978.012.
7. Michael D. McGinnis, "An Introduction to IAD and the Language of the Ostrom Workshop: A Simple Guide to a Complex Framework," *Policy Studies Journal*, 39, no. 1 (2011): 176, Wiley Online Library, https://doi.org/10.1111/j.1541-0072.2010.00401.x.
8. Lorcan Dempsey et al., "Operationalizing the BIG Collective Collection: A Case Study of Consolidation vs Autonomy," *OCLC Research*, 2019, 23, https://doi.org/10.25333/JBZ3-JY57.
9. Yolanda Wilson, "Is Trust Enough? Anti-Black Racism and the Perception of Black Vaccine 'Hesitancy,'" *Hastings Center Report*, 52, no. S1 (2022): S15, Wiley Online Library, https://doi.org/10.1002/hast.1361.
10. Andrés Chiappe and Silvia Irene Adame, "Open Educational Practices: A Learning Way beyond Free Access Knowledge," *Ensaio: Avaliação e Políticas Públicas Em Educação*, 26 (2017): 216, SciELO, https://doi.org/10.1590/S0104-40362018002601320.
11. Robin DeRosa and Scott Robison, "From OER to Open Pedagogy: Harnessing the Power of Open," in *Open: The Philosophy and Practices That Are Revolutionizing Education and Science*, edited by Rajiv Jhangiani and Robert Biswas-Diener (London: Ubiquity Press, 2017), 117, https://doi.org/10.5334/bbc.i.
12. Wanuri Kahiu, writ., dir., *Pumzi*, 2009, 21:00.
13. DeLoice Holliday, personal conversation, August 5, 2022.

## WORKS CITED

Bailey, Moya. "All the Digital Humanists Are White, All the Nerds Are Men, but Some of Us Are Brave." *Journal of Digital Humanities*, 1, no. 1 (2011). https://journalofdigitalhumanities.org/1-1/all-the-digital-humanists-are-white-all-the-nerds-are-men-but-some-of-us-are-brave-by-moya-z-bailey/.

Chambliss, Melanie. "Black Libraries and the Diffusion of Knowledge: Decolonizing Access in the Early Twentieth Century." *Open Access Week Symposium 2022*. Oct. 2022. scholarworks.iu.edu, https://scholarworks.iu.edu/dspace/handle/2022/28618.

Chiappe, Andrés, and Silvia Irene Adame. "Open Educational Practices: A Learning Way beyond Free Access Knowledge." *Ensaio: Avaliação e Políticas Públicas Em Educação*, 26 (2017): 213–30. SciELO, https://doi.org/10.1590/S0104-40362018002601320.

Dempsey, Lorcan, Constance Malpas, and Mark Sandler. "Operationalizing the BIG Collective Collection: A Case Study of Consolidation vs Autonomy." *OCLC Research*, 2019. https://doi.org/10.25333/JBZ3-JY57.

DeRosa, Robin, and Scott Robison. "From OER to Open Pedagogy: Harnessing the Power of Open." In *Open: The Philosophy and Practices That Are Revolutionizing Education and Science*, edited by Rajiv Jhangiani and Robert Biswas-Diener, 115–24. London: Ubiquity Press, 2017. https://doi.org/10.5334/bbc.i.

Gallon, Kim. "Making a Case for the Black Digital Humanities." In *Debates in the Digital Humanities 2016*, edited by Matthew K. Gold and Lauren F. Klein, 42–49. Minneapolis: University of Minnesota Press, 2016. JSTOR, https://doi.org/10.5749/j.ctt1cn6thb.7. Accessed April 7, 2023.

Holliday, DeLoice. Personal conversation, August 5, 2022.

Kahiu, Wanuri, writ., dir. *Pumzi*. 2009.

Marwick, Alice, Rachel Kuo, Shanice Jones Cameron, and Mora Weigel. "Critical Disinformation Studies." Center for Information, Technology, and Public Life (CITAP). https://citap.unc.edu/research/critical-disinfo/.

McGinnis, Michael D. "An Introduction to IAD and the Language of the Ostrom Workshop: A Simple Guide to a Complex Framework." *Policy Studies Journal*, 39, no. 1 (2011): 169–83. Wiley Online Library, https://doi.org/10.1111/j.1541-0072.2010.00401.x.

Noble, Safiya Umoja. "Toward a Critical Black Digital Humanities." In *Debates in the Digital Humanities 2019*, edited by Matthew K. Gold and Lauren F. Klein, 27–35. Minneapolis: University of Minnesota Press, 2019. JSTOR, https://doi.org/10.5749/j.ctvg251hk.5.

Sanfilippo, Madelyn, Brett Frischmann, and Katherine J. Strandburg. "Privacy as Knowledge Commons Governance: An Appraisal." In *Governing Privacy in Knowledge Commons*, 1st ed., edited by Madelyn Rose Sanfilippo, Brett Frischmann, and Katherine J. Strandburg, 268–90. Cambridge: Cambridge University Press, 2021. DOI.org (Crossref), https://doi.org/10.1017/9781108749978.012.

Schonfeld, Roger C., Karin Wulf, Rick Anderson, Lisa Janicke Hinchliffe, Joseph Esposito, and Roy Kaufman. "The Internet Archive Loses on Controlled Digital Lending." *The Scholarly Kitchen*, March 28, 2023. https://scholarlykitchen.sspnet.org/2023/03/28/internet-archive-controlled-digital-lending/.

Skov, Anders. *The Digital Competence Wheel*. https://digital-competence.eu/.

Stojmenova Duh, Emilija, Andrej Duh, Uros Droftina, Tim Kos, Urban Duh, Tanja Simonic Korosak, and Dean Korosak. "Publish-and-Flourish: Using Blockchain Platform to Enable Cooperative Scholarly Communication." *Publications*, 7, no. 2, 2 (2019): 33. www.mdpi.com, https://doi.org/10.3390/publications7020033.

Tavernier, Willa Liburd. *Library Research Guides: A263 Contemporary Social Issues in the African American Community—Digital Project Resources: Home*. Accessed April 7, 2023. https://guides.libraries.indiana.edu/A263/DigitalProjects.

Wilson, Yolonda. "Is Trust Enough? Anti-Black Racism and the Perception of Black Vaccine 'Hesitancy.'" *Hastings Center Report*, 52, no. S1 (2022): S12-17. Wiley Online Library, https://doi.org/10.1002/hast.1361.

Wingo, Rebecca S., Jason A. Heppler, and Paul Schadewald. "Introduction." *Digital Community Engagement: Partnering Communities with the Academy*. Cincinnati: University of Cincinnati Press, 2020. Project MUSE, https://muse.jhu.edu/pub/330/oa_edited_volume/book/75900.

# Chapter 13

# Libraries' Part in Solving Problems of Inclusive Online Education during the Pandemic

Ahalya Sudev

COVID-19 is an agonizing pandemic that hit during the twenty-first century. In the wake of this pandemic, people around the world experienced pressure in their daily life. Although the spread of COVID-19 has decreased, many people are still unable to get back to normal. In every sphere of human existence, this epidemic has caused chaos including healthcare, manufacturing, agriculture, education, and so on.

Among these, the education sector is one of the most severely impacted. Students with special education needs, their teachers, and their parents have suffered the most. Therefore, this chapter describes what libraries can do to facilitate online inclusive education for students with special education needs.

## COVID-19 AND EDUCATION

Educational institutions are places where people come together. As a result, they were forced to close during lockdown to prevent the rapid spread of COVID-19. This crisis shifted the traditional, in-class education system to a virtual education system. It helped to reduce the spread of COVID-19 to some extent. In addition, the online education system has helped students to continue their learning during the pandemic period. However, this transition is detrimental to all those associated with educational institutions.[1] Numerous strategies have been implemented worldwide to make online education a reality. The most common were broadcasting instructors' lessons via radio and television and giving real-time classes to students via online meeting platforms and various applications. However, many students lacked the requisite infrastructure to have access to this. To address this, various authorities have supplied students with devices, internet access, and other resources to enable them to attend lessons online.

However, the transition from the traditional educational system to the virtual educational system has had a significant impact on students with special education needs (SEN). Many SEN students are studying in special schools and mainstream schools. They were experiencing a lot of challenges even in the traditional education system. So, each of these students deserves special consideration. Identifying the special needs of this group and satisfying these needs through online and virtual setup was a challenging task for their educators. As part of inclusive education, special educators in mainstream schools have a significant challenge when attempting to implement online inclusion of SEN students with other students.

## WHAT WAS THE STATUS OF SEN STUDENTS DURING THE COVID-19 PANDEMIC?

SEN students who had difficulty even in the traditional education system have not been able to cope with the online education system during the COVID-19 pandemic. They are also one of the most distressed groups during the COVID-19 pandemic. No matter what education system was followed, the special requirements of SEN students were not fully met. Furthermore, many school authorities were reluctant to enroll SEN students in their schools. In their case, often the right to education was neglected. They are excluded from their peer groups and mainstreaming, even if they have the right to inclusive education.

Online education practices were not differently-abled-friendly. Online classes do not work for children with hearing impairment because they cannot hear what their teachers are saying. They can only understand sign language. But there is no provision for sign language in online meeting platforms. Visually impaired students face similar challenges in online classes. They cannot see the content presented by the teacher on the screen. Students with intellectual disabilities and mental behavioral disorders have a hard time with both traditional and online education systems. They cannot pay attention to a small screen for a long time. Moreover, SEN students were isolated during the COVID-19 pandemic period. It is challenging for special educators in online classrooms to meet the particular demands of each SEN student.

SEN students that share the same disability are enrolled in a certain school. For example, schools for students with intellectual disabilities only accept students with intellectual disabilities. Likewise, schools for students with hearing impairments only accept students with hearing impairments. Therefore, the special educators there only need to engage with students who fall within the same category. So, special educators can make virtual classes by making adaptations according to their special needs. However, as part of inclusive education, various categories of students are enrolled in mainstream schools, such as students with visual impairment, hearing impairment, intellectual disability, autism, and so on. As a result, there are many challenges for both teachers and students when an online education system encompasses a wide range of learners with and without special education requirements.

When learning activities are conducted for students of both categories, general education teachers often need the help and cooperation of special educators to address SEN students from different categories. However, in a virtual setup conducting lesson activities with the cooperation of both general education teachers and special educators is a difficult task. Generally, in a virtual setup remedial classes were provided by special educators along with the main lessons prepared and provided by general education teachers for SEN students.

### SPECIAL EDUCATORS' CHALLENGES IN PROVIDING LEARNING ACTIVITIES FOR SEN STUDENTS

Special educators have encountered several obstacles in giving lessons, learning activities, and instructions to SEN students enrolled in mainstream schools because it's more difficult to give individualized teaching to SEN students in an e-learning situation for special educators.[2] As mentioned earlier, a mainstream school includes different categories of SEN students like students with visual impairment, hearing impairment, intellectual disability, and so on, and each of these distinct groups has unique special education requirements. For example, students with visual impairment need classes in audio form instead of visual content, students with hearing impairment need classes in sign language and more visual content, and students with attention deficit hyperactivity disorder need classes in more interesting formats, and students with intellectual disability need classes in more simplified form. So, addressing all these needs under the same roof is a challenging task for special educators in mainstream schools.

Another significant problem that special educators encounter is the inaccessibility of technology and sources required for delivering virtual classes for SEN students. For conducting virtual classes both special educators and SEN students required more reliable internet connection and digital devices. However, in a developing country a majority of the people lack internet connection and reliable devices for making their life easy. If a SEN student is from an economically challenged family, they may not be able to access the internet or digital devices to attend the virtual classes provided by their teachers. Moreover, educators conducted the classes from their homes. It does not mean that educators should get the same infrastructure for teaching at their homes as the school. There may be challenges like network issues and inaccessible devices and technology. From the point of view of the school authorities, they cannot provide adequate devices for home use for all teachers as every teacher in a school is engaged in virtual classes. So special educators also suffer from the inaccessibility of reliable internet connection and fully equipped devices for handling virtual classes for their students.

During the pandemic, many groups came to the aid of students who did not require special education by providing them with lessons, study materials, and assistance. But it is lacking in the case of SEN students. So, making online inclusive education effective, the needs of each category of students must be addressed properly and they must be satisfied in their learning process. Moreover, both students and teachers need well-equipped infrastructure for attending virtual classes.

### WHAT CAN LIBRARIES DO FOR ONLINE INCLUSIVE EDUCATION

Libraries are for the prosperity of our society. Both academic and public libraries have an important role in our society. However, libraries were also closed as part of the lockdown. Due to this, potential readers were unable to access the libraries. During the pandemic, readers were only able to access e-reading materials in libraries that provide remote access. Readers could not access printed or physical reading materials from the libraries. During the lockdown, no one utilized digital devices in digital libraries, including computer systems and laptops. Under such conditions, library resources could be used effectively for the education of both mainstream students and SEN students.

As the libraries were closed and the readers were not coming, the workload of the library professionals was less to some extent and the skills of library professionals were not properly utilized. Many creative librarians were not able to do anything at that time. At the same time, SEN students struggled with study materials. Students with visual impairment need more audio textbooks, instructions, and other study materials, but students with hearing impairment mostly need visual content. Special educators struggled to address the unique needs of each SEN student. To solve this issue, we can use the skills of library professionals. Most librarians are familiar with e-books and audiobooks. They can be assigned the work of making audiobooks and e-books, especially for SEN students by the education department.

Many schools and educational institutions have prioritized the education of students without special education needs. They regarded that providing learning instructions and study materials for SEN students is the duty primarily of special educators. They used the computer lab and other infrastructure for recording classes for students without special educational needs. For teaching SEN students, most of the special educators didn't get access to computers and other devices from the schools. Since computers and other devices in most digital libraries were not in use during the pandemic, if special educators were granted access to digital libraries, they could follow COVID protocols and come to the libraries to prepare and record lessons for their pupils as well as conduct live classes.

Most of the teachers, including special educators, do not have the experience of conducting classes virtually. To successfully host virtual classes, teachers need a high level of digital competency. However, the sudden shift from the traditional teaching method to the virtual one adversely affected most of the teachers. To combat this, libraries can host workshops to equip both instructors and students with the necessary digital skills for successful participation in online learning environments.

The main virtual education method adopted in most countries was the broadcasting of recorded lessons through radio and television. But many students were not equipped to access them. Using the COVID-19 protocols, public libraries can identify students who are having trouble gaining access to these broadcasted classes in their region and invite them to use the library's study space and avail the use of libraries' television, radio, and computer facilities.

Instead of being approachable and inclusive for SEN students only during a pandemic, libraries should always be differently-abled-friendly and inclusive. An inclusive library should be accessible to everyone irrespective of age, sex, religion, caste, color, or physical and mental abilities. In the case of people with disabilities, the library should be accessible in all manner. From the entrance itself, the library should be accessible. There should be provisions for ramps, rails, and wheelchairs. If a library has several floors, there should be provision for lifts and escalators. For assisting the patrons with hearing impairments, there should be at least one staff who knows sign language and there should be guide maps to different sections in the library. Likewise, the library authority should address all categories of disabilities and should provide adequate services and adaptations in libraries. It is ranged from arranging disability-friendly furniture to adaptive toilets. Library authorities should not forget to make adaptations in collection management also. There must be braille books and other important books dealing with disabilities that can provide information for these kinds of patrons.

## CONCLUSION

Libraries are the storehouse of information and the powerhouse of technologies. They can assist society in any adverse situation with the pool of information. If we were to make effective use of libraries during the pandemic, we would be able to alleviate some of the challenges that are being experienced in the educational system. Many libraries, from public libraries to special libraries, were closed during the pandemic. During that time, we were not able to make economic use of libraries and their library professions. If we face such a crisis in the future, we can make use of libraries properly and ensure that no one's education has been interrupted.

## NOTES

1. Seble Tadesse and Worku Muluye, "The Impact of COVID-19 Pandemic on Education System in Developing Countries: A Review," *Open Journal of Social Sciences*, 8, no. 10 (2020): 159–70, https://doi.org/10.4236/jss.2020.810011.
2. Cathy Mae Dabi Toquero, "'Sana All' Inclusive Education Amid COVID-19. Challenges, Strategies, and Prospects of Special Education Teachers," *International and Multidisciplinary Journal of Social Sciences*, 10, no. 1 (2021): 30–51, https://doi.org/10.17583/rimcis.2020.6316.

## WORKS CITED

Tadesse, Seble, and Worku Muluye. "The Impact of COVID-19 Pandemic on Education System in Developing Countries: A Review." *Open Journal of Social Sciences*, 8, no. 10 (2020): 159–70. https://doi.org/10.4236/jss.2020.810011.

Toquero, Cathy Mae Dabi. "'Sana All' Inclusive Education amid COVID-19: Challenges, Strategies, and Prospects of Special Education Teachers." *International and Multidisciplinary Journal of Social Sciences*, 10, no. 1 (2021): 30–51. https://doi.org/10.17583/rimcis.2020.6316.

# Chapter 14

# Digital Access and Historically Black College and University Libraries

Dawn Kight and Maletta Payne

Libraries continue to transform lives through their various offerings of information resources, spaces, services, technology tools, and expertise. Libraries at Historically Black Colleges and Universities (HBCUs) are instrumental in ensuring that students of color have access to resources that not only shape their college experiences but help prepare them for future endeavors in this technology-driven world. In 1964, the Higher Education Act established HBCUs with the mission of educating Black Americans.[1] These schools continue to be significant in educating, empowering, and graduating African American students. According to the National Center for Education Statistics, as of 2021, there were 102 HBCUs in nineteen states, the District of Columbia, and the Virgin Islands.[2] Many HBCUs rely heavily on federal funding and have limited endowments compared to predominantly white institutions (PWIs). About "52% of HBCUs received funding from federal, state, and local governments in 2020, amounting to $9 billion in revenue."[3] Due to this gap in funding between HBCUs and PWIs, financial disparities have impacted organizational advancements, retention, and research. Historically Black Colleges and Universities also face specific technological funding needs. This funding is needed to upgrade and support technology infrastructure, including campus-wide high-speed internet connectivity, Wi-Fi coverage, and computer labs. A robust and reliable technology structure is required to support online learning and research activities at HBCUs in the twenty-first century. By effectively leveraging technology, HBCUs can overcome information and digital literacy training barriers for students and educators. Furthermore, technology enables the broader dissemination of knowledge and facilitates collaboration, supporting the success of open access, open educational resources (OER), and digital preservation initiatives. HBCU librarians' expertise in information instruction, organization, preservation, and accessibility, combined with their commitment to promoting openness and knowledge-sharing, makes them invaluable contributors and campus supporters in the advancement of open access initiatives at HBCUs.

## OPEN ACCESS AT HBCUS

Open access initiatives are transforming academic and scholarly communities. Open access removes financial barriers by making research publications and educational resources freely available to students, faculty, researchers, and the public. The rising cost of textbooks is a significant concern for students and academic institutions worldwide, particularly for HBCU students. In "2020–2021, a first-year college student's average cost of books and supplies was $1,226."[4] The traditional textbook publishing industry has experienced substantial price increases, leading to financial challenges that can hinder students' academic success. In addition, about "70% of HBCU students are Pell grant recipients indicating they are from households below poverty level."[5] Many academic libraries offer textbook reserves for short-term borrowing, which relieves students of some financial burden. However, many students still lack access to class textbooks due to the limited number a library can purchase. Academic libraries are increasingly investing in e-textbooks and digital resources that can be accessed online. College libraries are expanding their digital collections and ensuring that e-books and other digital resources are accessible to all students. These resources are often more cost-effective and easily accessed by multiple users simultaneously. Although access to e-textbooks does offer students access, HBCU libraries often have limited budgets compared to predominantly white institutions. Allocating funds for electronic resources while ensuring other library services and collections are adequately supported can be challenging for most HBCU libraries. While e-books provide students access to course content, not all college students can afford the necessary devices to access and read them. Technologies such as laptops and tablets can be expensive, and students from low-income families may prioritize other essential expenses over acquiring such technology.

To bridge the digital divide for HBCU students, many academic libraries have implemented computer labs and programs to provide affordable or loaner devices for students. For the HBCU college student, the digital divide can significantly affect access to educational resources and learning opportunities. Often times, students requiring access to technology and reliable internet need help to fully participate in virtual classrooms or accessing online educational resources. However, "Access to high-speed broadband is not evenly distributed, and this can exacerbate existing economic disparities, particularly in rural and underserved communities."[6] With technology, students can access various digital open access resources, including research articles, journals, books, and educational materials. Additionally, access to online repositories, institutional repositories, and open access platforms provides a wealth of scholarly information that can enrich students' learning experiences and research opportunities at no cost to them.

The establishment of open access initiatives allows HBCUs to actively promote OER to reduce reliance on expensive commercial textbooks and materials.

Another benefit for HBCUs related to open access resources is that it allows faculty the opportunity to create, publish, and create content utilized in their courses to advance the use of open education and making it more accessible to students to achieve positive learning outcomes. These faculty-created resources equally support pedagogical innovation, collaboration among educators, and the development of a more equitable and inclusive education system. As the use of OER continues to grow, HBCU faculties' contributions to this movement will continue to enrich teaching and learning experiences worldwide. Furthermore, open access aligns with the mission of HBCUs to promote equity and inclusivity in education. By providing free access to knowledge, HBCUs can ensure that all students, regardless of their financial background, have equal opportunities to learn and engage with scholarly works. HBCU students can access scholarly materials without the burden of expensive subscription fees or paywalls. In addition, having open accessible research publications allows scholars to receive higher visibility and citations, potentially increasing the impact and recognition of HBCU researchers' work created within the academic community. Open access technology also promotes collaboration among researchers at HBCUs and beyond. Researchers can easily share their findings and data, leading to potential global collaborations and partnerships. Another example of how open access publications impact institutional scholarship is that it can reach a broader audience, including researchers, policymakers, and the public worldwide, fostering community engagement and knowledge dissemination on a global scale. By actively participating in open access initiatives, HBCUs contribute to the global open scholarship movement, advocating for the open sharing of knowledge and the democratization of education. HBCUs can leverage institutional repositories, open access journals, and collaborative initiatives to support adopting open access practices.

**OPEN EDUCATIONAL RESOURCES AND HBCUS**

Extending entry from open access activities to OER is a natural progression that builds on the principles of openness and free access to knowledge for all people. While open access primarily focuses on making research and scholarly works freely available, OER takes the concept further by encompassing the creation and dissemination of educational materials, such as textbooks, lecture notes, quizzes, and multimedia resources, to support equitable access. "Open Educational Resources are teaching, learning, and research materials in any medium, digital or otherwise, that reside in the public domain or have been released under an open license that permits no-cost access, use, adaptation, and redistribution by others with no or limited restrictions."[7]

The overarching benefit of OER is that the learning content is freely accessible and can significantly reduce the financial burden on students, who often struggle with the high costs of commercial textbooks and educational materials. Moreover, students from diverse backgrounds, including low income or those in remote areas, can have equitable access to educational resources regardless of their geographical location. Another benefit of OER is that they are typically published with open licenses, allowing educators to adapt, remix, and customize the content to suit specific learning objectives and student needs. This flexibility enables personalized and relevant learning experiences for all students. OER encourages innovative teaching practices, as educators can incorporate multimedia elements, interactive activities, and real-world examples into their teaching materials. By incorporating culturally relevant materials for African Americans in HBCU settings, student learning outcomes and interest in the subject matter can be customized to reflect African Americans' diverse history, culture, and contributions. OER also promotes a culture of collaboration and knowledge sharing among educators and institutions. Educators can freely share their instructional materials and benefit from the collective expertise of the global educational community. Another benefit of OER is that information can be continually updated and improved, ensuring educational resources remain current and relevant. This agility is particularly valuable in rapidly evolving fields where traditional textbooks may become outdated quickly. OER is not limited to formal education settings. They can also support informal and lifelong learning. Anyone with internet access can use OER for self-directed learning and professional development. Open licenses like Creative Commons' challenge traditional copyright models and foster a more open and collaborative approach to knowledge creation and dissemination. OER has a global impact, transcending geographical boundaries and benefiting learners and educators worldwide. They promote cross-cultural understanding and collaboration, fostering a diverse and interconnected global educational community.

OER practices are essential in creating an inclusive, accessible, innovative educational ecosystem. By leveraging OER use at HBCUs, educators can improve student access to quality resources, enhance teaching practices, and foster a culture of knowledge sharing and collaboration, leading to better educational outcomes. Additionally, the library can play a significant role in supporting OER. Librarians can assist faculty in locating and evaluating them, provide copyright guidance, and manage the institutional repository for hosting and preserving locally created resources. Evaluating OER through assessments is essential for HBCUs. Evaluations help quantify the cost savings achieved through their adoption. Therefore, assessing the monetary impact of OER can demonstrate the tangible benefits of open resources in reducing the financial burden on students and families. Equally important, educators can identify the most effective OER materials and instructional strategies that align with specific learning objectives. This information can guide future OER selection and creation efforts. Technological enhancements that support their creation have advanced and are now competitive with for-profit learning management solutions. New technologies support evaluations that ensure OER materials are high quality and pedagogically sound. Assessing the content for accuracy, relevance, and alignment with learning objectives helps maintain the integrity of the educational resources. Accordingly, evaluations offer opportunities for continuous improvement of OER. Feedback from students and faculty provides criticism to support updates to refine existing OER materials, ensuring they remain current, relevant, and impactful. By conducting assessments of OER use, HBCUs can gather valuable data to understand the importance of OER and its impact on students, faculty, and the broader educational community.

This data-driven approach allows for evidence-based decision-making, continuous improvement, and the promotion of OER as an essential component of an inclusive and accessible education system. As awareness and understanding of OER increase, more institutions should strive to collect data to assess its impact on student success, cost savings, and teaching effectiveness. Fostering collaborative initiatives and partnerships can also play a role in sharing best practices and experiences, contributing to a more robust dataset on OER use within the HBCU community.

**INSTITUTIONAL REPOSITORIES AND HBCUS**

The term "institutional repository" (IR), was first documented by the Scholarly Publishing for Academic Resources Coalition as "digital collections capturing and preserving the intellectual output of a single or multi-university community."[8] IRs offer a secure and centralized location for HBCUs to preserve and archive various institutional materials, such as theses, dissertations, student projects, faculty publications, data sets, and administrative documents. By making content available in the IR, HBCUs can increase the visibility of their scholarly and institutional works. Open access materials in the repository can be freely accessible to the public, promoting knowledge-sharing and research dissemination. Institutional repositories can highlight the research and scholarly contributions of HBCU faculty, researchers, and students, enhancing the institution's reputation and recognition within the academic community. IRs provide tools for organizing and categorizing content, improving the discoverability of resources. Users can search and access materials based on metadata, keywords, authors, and other relevant information. Research offices now require researchers to make their publications and data openly accessible. IRs help HBCUs comply with these policies by providing a platform to share funded research outputs.

IRs offer digital preservation features, ensuring that scholarly and institutional materials are archived and accessible long term, safeguarding valuable research and institutional heritage for future generations. Institutional repositories can host OER created by faculty and students at HBCUs, making them openly accessible to learners worldwide, supporting OER adoption, and contributing to the open education movement. IRs also facilitate collaboration among researchers and institutions by providing a space for sharing data, preprints, and other research materials. Furthermore, IRs provide usage metrics, downloadable statistics, and citation counts for content, enabling HBCUs to assess the impact of their research outputs and institutional materials. The effect of institutional repositories, open access, and OER on HBCUs can be significant and transformative.

Library support plays a crucial role in establishing and maintaining institutional repositories. Librarians can work with faculty, researchers, and students to collect, review, and upload scholarly content to the institutional repository ensuring that materials meet quality standards and adhere to copyright and open access policies. Additionally, libraries can provide training and support to faculty, researchers, and students on using the institutional repository effectively by offering workshops, tutorials, and one-on-one consultations to encourage and facilitate content submission. Student usage statistics and analytics to assess the impact and usage of the institutional repository's content are equally important as these insights help demonstrate the value of the repository and inform future development strategies. By providing comprehensive support for institutional repositories, HBCU libraries can contribute to disseminating scholarly knowledge, promoting open access principles, and enhancing the visibility and impact of their institution's research outputs.

Promoting the institutional repository to the academic community and raising awareness about open access may require marketing and outreach efforts. Institutional repositories serve as valuable tools for highlighting and preserving the intellectual contributions of the academic community. The cost of IRs can significantly impact HBCUs. Establishing and maintaining a repository involves various financial considerations. While IRs offer several benefits, there are budgetary constraints that can influence the decision to implement and sustain an institutional repository. However, HBCUs can explore collaborations and partnerships with other institutions or join consortia to share resources, expertise, and costs related to IR implementation and maintenance. Another strategy is open source repository platforms, which can reduce software licensing fees and allow customization based on specific needs. Grant funding provides an excellent opportunity for HBCUs to pursue external funding sources that support open access initiatives and repository development. Finally, developing sustainable planning to ensure the ongoing financial support of IR campus buy-in is essential to preserving the OER initiatives at HBCUs. By carefully considering the cost implications and adopting cost-effective strategies, HBCUs can successfully implement and sustain institutional repositories, enhancing the visibility and impact of their academic output while promoting open access and scholarly communication.

## DIGITAL LITERACY SKILLS AND HBCUS

Digital literacy refers to using, understanding, and navigating digital technologies effectively and responsibly. It encompasses a range of skills and competencies that enable individuals to interact, communicate, create, and critically evaluate information in digital environments. Digital literacy goes beyond simply knowing how to use specific tools or devices; it involves a deeper understanding of the digital world and its impact on various aspects of life. Digital literacy is becoming increasingly important in today's technology-driven world.

Fostering digital literacy skills enables HBCU students to navigate online resources, conduct research, and effectively use digital tools for learning. As job markets demand proficiency in digital technologies across various disciplines, equipping HBCU students with digital literacy skills helps with preparation for the modern workforce, making graduates more competitive and adaptable in their careers. As technology becomes increasingly integral to education and professional success, HBCUs are taking proactive measures to promote digital literacy on their campuses. Some HBCUs include digital literacy training as part of their orientation programs for incoming students. This early introduction to digital skills sets a foundation for their academic journey.

Digital literacy skills are crucial for survival in today's society. Information and communication technology rapidly changed the world and how information is shared.[9] Whether completing job applications, submitting resumes online, achieving academically, using telehealth options, or simply shopping online, having digital skills is a requirement. The impact of the digital divide is even more noticeable in communities of color where there is a disproportionate number of households in need of digital skills training and development. HBCUs are being proactive in producing digital navigators who take skills learned in digital literacy programs and share knowledge by training others in their communities.

The need for digital training was greatly exposed in 2020. Faculty and students in higher education had to expediently transform teaching and learning when institutions swiftly moved to online learning so that the academy could continue through the COVID-19 pandemic. Libraries played critical roles in supporting access to learning management systems, resources, and digital devices, along with providing campus-wide digital training at some HBCUs. Information literacy skills for students and faculty became even more important in supporting teaching, learning, and research by enabling users to find, assess, and navigate online resources effectively. However, even when digital skills are mastered, access to high-cost licensed resources and learning systems presents barriers to the learning community, highlighting the need for HBCUs to consider open access technology options. Overall, digital literacy skills empower students and faculty to engage, innovate, inspire, create, and produce in this technologically sophisticated environment.

## SOCIAL MEDIA TECHNOLOGY AND HBCUS

Cloud computing technology in education has relieved campuses of large server rooms that require enormous on-campus human support. This technology also supports popular social media applications that higher education institutions, including HBCUs, are using to reach their audiences. From Facebook to blogs, these technologies have replaced traditional models of recruitment and services, including those offered by libraries. Librarians face challenges and opportunities of offering reference and research services through nontraditional modes. The reference interview is moving more from in-person to using e-chat, Twitter, Zoom, or MS Teams. Access anytime and anywhere (AAA) has become expected and not considered a privilege. Social media platforms and learning technologies utilizing information and communication technologies facilitate AAA and eliminate barriers of time and space communication methods.[10] HBCU librarians are promoting resources, events, and guides via social media channels instead of using print.

While websites are still popular and provide more static information, students tend to check their social media accounts more often and pay closer attention to information presented on those applications. The faculty are designing courses that utilize applications such as YouTube, Instagram, and TikTok. Therefore, libraries are hiring social media librarians or including those duties in library roles. Southern University and A&M College, an HBCU in Louisiana, recently announced the hiring of a reference librarian and noted 50 percent of the duties would be using social media applications to promote reference and instruction services. The interaction, engagement, library promotion, training, and assessment opportunities are readily available to meet the needs of users via social media. Furthermore, most of the applications are free to use and support transferable technology skills. While social media technology apps are generally low to no cost, some HBCU libraries still have roadblocks of having enough staff to fully utilize these resources. Of course, librarians are creative, and many engage students and graduate assistants, who are knowledgeable about apps, to assist libraries in offering services and marketing resources using social media technology.

## CONCLUSION

While the twenty-first century has presented many technological changes, HBCUs are forging ahead and taking advantage of opportunities to remain competitive as they recruit, retain, and graduate students to be productive and contributing members of society. Truthfully, the digital gap exists and can often be noted in various ways. Additionally, for several years the HBCU Affordable Leaning Solutions initiatives have helped thousands of students save money on textbooks.[11] Therefore, the mission for HBCU librarians is to remain true to their core values of librarianship and encourage campuses to embrace technologies that promote open access and diminish the digital divide. Utilizing open access, OER, social media apps, learning and library management systems, and providing information and digital literacy training have become part of HBCU librarians' strategies as partners in the path to academic success, especially with a focus on elevating students from underserved, underrepresented communities.

**NOTES**

1. "What Is an HBCU?" White House Initiative on Advancing Educational Equity, Excellence, and Economic Opportunity through Historically Black Colleges and Universities, accessed August 4, 2023, https://sites.ed.gov/whhbcu/one-hundred-and-five-historically-black-colleges-and-universities/.
2. "Digest of Education Statistics, 2022," National Center for Education Statistics, accessed August 4, 2023, https://nces.ed.gov/programs/digest/d22/tables/dt22_313.10.asp.
3. Jessica Bryant and Lyss Weldingread, "HBCU Facts and Statistics," Bestcolleges.com, January 5, 2023, https://www.bestcolleges.com/research/hbcu-facts/.
4. Melanie Hanson, "Average Cost of College Textbooks," Education Data Initiative.org, July 15, 2022, https://educationdata.org/average-cost-of-college-textbooks.
5. Abigail Grimshaw, "The Facts on HBCUs: Top 10 Facts about Historically Black Colleges and Universities," The Century Foundation, September 19, 2022, http://tcf.org/content/commentary/the-facts-on-hbcus-top-10-facts-about-historically-black-colleges-and-universities.
6. Luis Angel Lucendo-Monedero et al., "Measuring the Digital Divide at Regional Level. A Spatial Analysis of the Inequalities in Digital Development of Households and Individuals in Europe," *Telematics and Informatics*, 41 (2019): 197–217, https://doi.org10.1016/j.tele.2019.05.002.
7. "Open Educational Resources," Unesco.org, May 22, 2023, https://www.unesco.org/en/open-educational-resources.
8. Raym Crow, ed., *The Case for Institutional Repositories: A SPARC Position Paper* (Washington, DC: SPARC—Hosted by the Association of Research Libraries, 2002).
9. Gloria J. Holbrook, ed., *Academic and Digital Libraries: Emerging Directions and Trends* (New York: Nova Science, 2018).
10. Kiran Bala Nayar and Vikas Kumar, "Cost Benefit Analysis of Cloud Computing in Education," *International Journal of Business Information Systems*, 27, no. 2 (2018): 205, https://doi.org10.1504/ijbis.2018.089112.
11. "From Open Access to Educational Equity," Mit.edu, Accessed August 4, 2023, https://openlearning.mit.edu/news/open-access-educational-equity.

**WORKS CITED**

Bryant, Jessica, and Lyss Weldingread. "HBCU Facts and Statistics." Bestcolleges.com, January 5, 2023, https://www.bestcolleges.com/research/hbcu-facts/.

"COE–Price of Attending an Undergraduate Institution." National Center for Education Statistics, updated May 2023. https://nces.ed.gov/programs/coe/indicator/cua.

Crow, Raym, ed. *The Case for Institutional Repositories: A SPARC Position Paper*. Washington, DC: SPARC—Hosted by the Association of Research Libraries, 2002.

"Digest of Education Statistics, 2022." National Center for Education Statistics, accessed August 4, 2023. https://nces.ed.gov/programs/digest/d22/tables/dt22_313.10.asp.

"From Open Access to Educational Equity." Mit.edu, accessed August 4, 2023. https://openlearning.mit.edu/news/open-access-educational-equity.

Grimshaw, Abigail. "The Facts on HBCUs: Top 10 Facts about Historically Black Colleges and Universities." The Century Foundation, September 19, 2022. http://tcf.org/content/commentary/the-facts-on-hbcus-top-10-facts-about-historically-black-colleges-and-universities.

Hanson, Melanie. "Average Cost of College Textbooks." Education Data Initiative.org, July 15, 2022. https://educationdata.org/average-cost-of-college-textbooks.

Holbrook, Gloria J., ed. *Academic and Digital Libraries: Emerging Directions and Trends*. New York, Nova Science, 2018.

Lucendo-Monedero, Angel Luis, Francisca Ruiz-Rodríguez, and Reyes González-Relaño. "Measuring the Digital Divide at Regional Level: A Spatial Analysis of the Inequalities in Digital Development of Households and Individuals in Europe." *Telematics and Informatics*, 41 (2019): 197–217. https://doi.org10.1016/j.tele.2019.05.002.

Nayar, Kiran Bala, and Vikas Kumar. "Cost Benefit Analysis of Cloud Computing in Education." *International Journal of Business Information Systems*, 27, no. 2 (2018): 205. https://doi.org10.1504/ijbis.2018.089112.

"Open Educational Resources." Unesco.org, May 22, 2023. https://www.unesco.org/en/open-educational-resources.

Smith, Denise A. "The Facts on HBCUs: Top 10 Facts about Historically Black Colleges and Universities." The Century Foundation, September 19, 2022. https://tcf.org/content/commentary/the-facts-on-hbcus-top-10-facts-about-historically-black-colleges-and-universities/.

"What Is an HBCU?" White House Initiative on Advancing Educational Equity, Excellence, and Economic Opportunity through Historically Black Colleges and Universities, accessed August 4, 2023. https://sites.ed.gov/whhbcu/one-hundred-and-five-historically-black-colleges-and-universities/.

# Chapter 15

# How Tech Has Enhanced the Jobs of Library Professionals

Kelvin Watson

"A library outranks any other one thing a community can do to benefit its people," said philanthropist and steel tycoon Andrew Carnegie. "It is a never-failing spring in the desert."[1]

The Las Vegas-Clark County Library District fulfills the greatest aspirations of Carnegie, who in his wildest dreams could never have imagined how libraries would evolve into centers for cutting-edge tech experiences, job training, language learning, and direct outreach to populations of low income residents striving to uplift their lives and serve as oases of technology.

A prescient and savvy businessman who made his fortune in the railway, oil, and steel industries during the Industrial Revolution, Carnegie's steel empire funded his renowned philanthropic endeavors laying the financial foundation for some three thousand libraries to be built in the United States and across the world. "It was from my own early experience that I decided there was no use to which money could be applied so productive of good to girls and boys who have good within them and ability and ambition to develop it as the founding of a public library," explained Carnegie of his belief in the empowerment libraries had on underserved communities.[2]

A child immigrant from Scotland, Carnegie and his family made their way to Allegheny City, Pennsylvania, where his first job was as a bobbin boy in a textile mill. He was determined to improve his lot and found that his local library staff would provide him with a place to self-educate, but he couldn't pay the two dollar subscription for a local library that was available only to apprentices and he certainly couldn't afford to buy books.[3]

Carnegie sent a letter to the library administrator asking for access to the library, but the administrator turned him down flat. So, seventeen-year-old Andy got the letter published in *The Pittsburgh Dispatch*. "He made his case so well that the administrator backed off immediately," explains Carnegie biographer David Nasaw. "And the library was opened to working men as well as apprentices. He got what he wanted." One could argue that this was the beginning of open access to all in America's library system![4]

Eventually leading the expansion of the American steel industry in the late nineteenth century, Carnegie made a vast fortune and donated $60 million in the early 1900s (which today would be worth approximately $2.2 billion adjusted for inflation) to fund thousands of public libraries in cities across the United States and throughout the world. He singlehandedly established the library as a community anchor for all Americans, rather than a luxury for the wealthy. "There is not such a cradle of democracy upon the earth as the Free Public Library, this republic of letters, where neither rank, office, nor wealth receives the slightest consideration," said Carnegie. But he could not have envisioned the evolution/revolution that would come with the advent of digital information management, which has exponentially expanded the ease and speed with which the public can find what they are seeking.[5]

As all librarians know, this digital evolution/revolution has also created a sea change within our profession. This seismic shift from the physical to the virtual has opened unlimited opportunities to librarians with new ways to think about how technology can be brought to bear for the needs of the underserved in our communities.

I have been fortunate to serve in leadership roles in major library systems, and in each case, I have worked to meet library customers "where they are," by leveraging technology and creating strategic partnerships.

The miracle of technology is that it is the great equalizer. It empowers all who use it and prepares both young people and adults for good-paying twenty-first-century jobs. The challenge, though, is *access*. The key to this, again, is to meet people where they are, on city buses and cruise ships, in hospitals and rehab centers, through free Wi-Fi and cell phone checkouts—the possibilities are unlimited! My library teams have achieved these new delivery systems by reaching out to community partners and businesses that seek to provide unique and unexpected benefits to those they serve. This, in turn, gives our library staff opportunities to develop and enhance their technological skills, interests, and knowledge—and to serve as advocates for bridging the digital divide.

Librarians are expanding the range of programs and services in ways that were unthinkable just a decade ago. At the Las Vegas-Clark County Library District's twenty-five branches, technology has enabled us to transform our branches into community hubs, offering classes, cultural events, historical exhibits, art galleries, live performance spaces, teen tech centers, DJ labs, makerspaces with robotics and 3D printing, podcasting booths, music and sound production studios, video production with green screens, and so much more that is to come. Our goal at the Library District is to educate people that the word "library" means so much more than books—though literacy will always be our core mission.

In Las Vegas, we have a rapidly growing Hispanic population. To serve this important demographic, we offer our promotional materials in Spanish and feature a robust Spanish language collection in our catalog. We have hired more bilingual staff, and we support our librarians as they work with this community to offer ESL classes, workforce training, and where possible, bilingual tutoring. By 2030, the US Census predicts that immigration will become our primary source of population and economic growth, putting greater pressure on our schools to teach literacy and tech skills. We already know that our local school district will not have the funding needed to meet this challenge and that our libraries will be called upon to fill this void. Technology is the answer to every one of these needs and the key to jobs of the future—from machine learning to virtual reality to robotics and coding.

Technology will continue to empower libraries and library professionals to enhance information access, expand their services, and adapt to the evolving needs of our customers. While the future of AI is uncertain, there is no question that with the right guardrails, it will help us to improve efficiency, increase the scope and reach of our resources, and transform traditional library roles, making them even more exciting and valuable. But, of course, all of this takes ample financial support.

Funding, through revolutionary partnerships, will make all this possible for public libraries. Going forward, libraries must step up their efforts to find new and innovative funding streams, forge impactful partnerships, and advocate for intellectual freedom.

The following are four innovative programs that illustrate how my team across the Las Vegas-Clark County Library District has melded technology with smart, strategic partnerships for the betterment of the community we serve—living up to our promise as a wellspring of possibilities in the desert home.

**REACHING THE DISENFRANCHISED WITH A CELL PHONE LENDING PROGRAM**

Access to technology is the key to unlocking opportunities for the underserved populations in the United States. The Las Vegas-Clark County Library District has taken technology outreach a step further with a program created for the community's most vulnerable residents. In April 2022, we launched the groundbreaking Cell Phone Lending Program that provides life-enriching and educational resources, as well as critical social and community services.[6]

Our new Cell Phone Lending Program is a pilot initiative that put internet connectivity into the hands of local adults and teens who are low income or experiencing homelessness. These devices are a lifeline, reconnecting these folks with family, social resources, educational and employment assistance, and so much more.

In partnership with the Nevada Homeless Alliance (NHA) and Nevada Partnership for Homeless Youth (NPHY), the Library District provided more than four hundred smartphones, preloaded with Library District apps, to low-income residents and those experiencing homelessness. Premier Wireless provided unlimited domestic calls and 5G hotspots, loaded library apps for education and workforce services, and contact information for employment, social service agencies, and job skills training. The program was funded with a $200,000 grant provided by the federal 2021 LTSA ARP Act through the Institute of Museum and Library Services and the Nevada State Library. The Library District later received an additional $20,000 grant from the ALA COVID Library Relief Fund, which funded an additional thirty-five phones. NHA and NPHY selected individuals to participate in this eighteen-month program. At the end of the lending period, recipients will be permitted to keep their phone and phone number, and they are encouraged to arrange a contract with any telecom provider to continue service.[7]

"Many people may not realize the barriers that individuals experience when they don't have access to a phone or Wi-Fi," said Catrina Grigsby-Thedford, NHA executive director. "In this post-pandemic era, services are accessed via the Internet or platforms such as Zoom. The Library District's Cell Phone Lending Program will fill some of those gaps. We are proud to collaborate with the Library District on this barrier-busting partnership."

We knew that receiving a new phone could be overwhelming for those who are not tech savvy, so we held an event to distribute the phones and provide one-on-one training sessions, plus a vendor fair with social service providers, library card sign-ups, immunizations, and a mobile shower truck.

A subsequent survey with Cell Phone Lending Program recipients found that 82 percent said their new phone is their only personal access point to the internet. Furthermore, 80 percent of recipients use the phone to access social services and 78 percent use it to apply for employment.

**ACCESS TO THE WORLD WITH FREE WI-FI**

Thousands of southern Nevadans can now get free personal Wi-Fi access through a new program formed by the Las Vegas-Clark County Library District and Cox Communications, which launched on August 18, 2023. Introduced just as kids were heading back to school, families who are currently without access to Wi-Fi in their homes now have a resource made possible by the library. Congresswoman Susie Lee (NV-03) helped kick off the program by presenting the Library District with a check for $3.8 million from the Federal Emergency Connectivity Fund, part of the American Rescue Plan.[8]

Our mission is to contribute to the elimination of the digital divide and this program is taking a huge step in this direction. I believe that access to connectivity and technology should be a right that is available to everyone, and access in the home is especially important for children to be successful at school. This partnership with Cox Communications is another example of how public libraries are creating powerful programs using public funding to erase barriers and unlock opportunities.

The Wi-Fi access program enables fifty thousand low-income residents to use their library cards to borrow a user ID and password from participating library branches. The user ID and password provide free access to the Cox Wi-Fi hotspot network for up to three devices until June 30, 2024. This allows parents to share their credentials with family members, thereby expanding the service to as many as 150,000 southern Nevada residents with new access.

"The Library District's innovative American Rescue Plan investment in hotspot access reflects President Biden's belief that access to high-speed internet is now essential for any young person, worker, or small business owner to be able to thrive educationally and economically," said Gene Sperling, White House American Rescue Plan coordinator and senior advisor to the president. "President Biden is deeply appreciative to the members of the Nevada Congressional delegation who voted for the American Rescue Plan and made possible for the people of Nevada this step forward toward universal, affordable broadband."

The program is the first of its kind in Nevada and possibly in the nation. Traditionally, library programs in other states lend physical hotspot devices to customers, which then must be returned at the conclusion of the lending period, typically three weeks. With the Library District program, there is nothing to return when service ends in 2024.

### DRIVING THE WHEEL OF CHANGE

With a fleet of four hundred Wi-Fi-enabled city buses, averaging three million passengers per month, the Regional Transportation Commission (RTC) was the ideal partner for the Las Vegas-Clark County Library District to target lower income customers who may have never had a library experience. The goal of the partnership between the RTC and Library District is to introduce bus riders to the many free programs and services that the library offers to uplift and enhance their lives, encouraging them to discover our branches and website and become lifelong customers. As a result of this collaboration, we launched "Bringing the Library to Transit Riders" on September 16, 2021, to both English- and Spanish-speaking residents of the Las Vegas Valley.[9]

The program enables transit riders to use the RTC's onboard Wi-Fi to instantly sign up for the Library District's Libby app. Once downloaded, the app instantly verifies the new account through the rider's cell phone number and allows them to begin borrowing e-books, e-audiobooks, magazines, and movies at no cost, on the bus, at home, or anywhere on the go. The service is also available to Las Vegas visitors who can receive temporary access via a seven-day pass.

Through this initiative, we are making the library more accessible to folks who may have never experienced a library before, helping them to discover the life-changing resources we provide in this new and unexpected environment. As I said before, we meet people where they are! The RTC's fleet of buses made more than thirty-five million passenger trips in 2021, introducing riders to a wonderful world of discovery.

"The RTC is committed to increasing equity and accessibility for our customers, and this innovative partnership has allowed us to support our riders with tools and resources to grow, learn, and enrich their lives," said M. J. Maynard, RTC chief executive officer. "We are excited about this meaningful collaboration with the Library District to bring all of the services the library has to offer in a simple, accessible, and equitable way directly to our riders during their daily commute."

The service is compatible with all major computers and devices, including iPhones, iPads, Androids, and Chromebooks. Users can download titles for offline use and have the option of sending them to their Kindle. All digital items are automatically returned at the end of the lending period, which guarantees no late fines.

Since launching "Bringing the Library to Transit Riders" in September 2021, the program has recorded 319,981 digital material check-outs and had 21,889 users through August 2023.

### ONE-STOP SHOPPING LIBRARY AT THE BOULEVARD MALL

And speaking of wonderful worlds of discovery, the newest attraction at the Boulevard Mall dispenses books with the mere swipe of a free library card. It's a user-friendly book vending machine that uses familiar technology to put English and Spanish language books into the hands of kids, teens, and adults. The Boulevard Mall targets the Spanish language market and they have become another crucial partner in our service to this demographic. They gave us a premiere location for our book vending machine, right across from the movie theater and snack bar.[10]

This new remote library represents an exciting next step in the Library District's quest to bring the power of our libraries directly to the people, to places where they gather to make new connections in their communities. As I said, access to technology is a basic human right and this new library vending machine is a noteworthy example of how we are using technology to serve underserved communities.

Dubbed the Library at the Boulevard Mall, the 2.5-ton machine houses 235 books in both Spanish and English. Situated inside this 1,180,000-square-foot indoor mall, the book vending machine has a colorful exterior and stands seven feet high and ten feet wide. The mall gave us easy-to-follow banner signage to help guide people to find it, and the machine is extremely simple to use. Library patrons just follow the instructions (available in English and Spanish) to check out a book using their library card. There is a twenty-one-day check-out period, and books can be returned to the vending machine or any library branch. Library cards are always free and can be obtained at any of the Library District's twenty-five branches.

The Library District unveiled the book vending machine on May 5, 2023, with the help of Nevada governor Joe Lombardo, who cut the ribbon on the new library. "In partnership with the Library District and the Latin Chamber, we are coming up with solutions in the State of Nevada for early literacy," Governor Lombardo said at the ribbon-cutting ceremony. "Education opens up opportunities, and the ability to do with your life what you want instead of what someone else is telling you to do."

Latin Chamber of Commerce president Peter Guzman said the new library at the Boulevard Mall represents an important economic investment in the neighborhood. "Libraries are a critical community resource for services, such as job training, ESL classes, tutoring, and reminding us of our cultural roots," Guzman explained. "Under Kelvin Watson's leadership, the Las Vegas-Clark County Library District is at the forefront of creating far-reaching educational efforts and developing original programming that touches the lives of so many people. The library serves as an economic engine, by providing educational opportunities for everyone."

You may not have an Andrew Carnegie in your community, ready to step up and write a million-dollar check, but I believe that every community, no matter how small, can find these kinds of partnerships to bring new, innovative thinking to our library spaces. If you have any questions about these programs, I encourage you to reach out to me at kelvin.watson@thelibrarydistrict.org.

**NOTES**

1. Rachel Heydecker, "Engaging Libraries: Inspiring and Encouraging," Medium, March 27, 2019, https://carnegieuktrust.medium.com/engaging-libraries-inspiring-and-encouraging-6475c6d45057.
2. "Andrew Carnegie: Pioneer. Visionary. Innovator," Carnegie Corporation of New York, 2015, https://www.carnegie.org/interactives/foundersstory/#!/.
3. Vartan Gregorian, "Can Libraries Save America?" *Carnegie Reporter*, September 27, 2019, https://www.carnegie.org/news/articles/can-libraries-save-america/
4. "Remembering Andrew Carnegie's Legacy," *American Libraries*, September 9, 2019, https://americanlibrariesmagazine.org/2019/09/30/remembering-andrew-carnegies-legacy/.
5. "Andrew Carnegie: Pioneer. Visionary. Innovator"; Andrea Q. Jemison, "More Than a Coffee Shop: How Libraries Support Civil Liberties," *Intellectual Freedom Blog, The Office of Intellectual Freedom of the American Library Association*, August 8, 2018, https://www.oif.ala.org/more-than-a-coffee-shop-how-libraries-support-civil-liberties/.
6. Matt Ennis, "Las Vegas Library Provides Smart Phones, Unlimited Data to Unhoused Persons," *Library Journal*, September 8, 2022, https://www.libraryjournal.com/story/las-vegas-library-provides-smartphones%2C-unlimited-data-to-unhoused-patrons.
7. Kelvin Watson, "Libraries on Call," *American Libraries*, March 1, 2023, https://americanlibrariesmagazine.org/2023/03/01/libraries-on-call/.
8. Lisa Jacob, "Las Vegas-Clark County Library District Teams Up with Cox Communications to Provide FREE Personal WiFi to 50,000 Qualified Households," Globe News Wire, August 21, 2023, https://www.globenewswire.com/news-release/2023/08/21/2728890/0/en/Las-Vegas-Clark-County-Library-District-Teams-Up-with-Cox-Communications-to-Provide-FREE-Personal-WiFi-to-50-000-Qualified-Households.html.
9. Las Vegas-Clark County Library District, "Urban Library Council Honors Las Vegas-Clark County Library District and RTC for Innovation," PR News Wire, January 24, 2022, https://www.prnewswire.com/news-releases/urban-libraries-council-honors-the-las-vegas-clark-county-library-district-and-rtc-for-innovation-301466756.html.
10. Kyndell Kim, "Mobile Library Now Open inside the Boulevard Mall," 3 News, https://news3lv.com/news/local/mobile-library-now-open-inside-the-boulevard-mall-las-vegas-southern-nevada-latin-chamber-of-commerce-governor-lombardo.

**WORKS CITED**

"Andrew Carnegie: Pioneer. Visionary. Innovator." Carnegie Corporation of New York, 2015. https://www.carnegie.org/interactives/foundersstory/#!/

Gregorian, Vartan. "Can Libraries Save America?" *Carnegie Reporter*, September 27, 2019. https://www.carnegie.org/news/articles/can-libraries-save-america/.

———. "Remembering Andrew Carnegie's Legacy." *American Libraries*, September 9, 2019. https://americanlibrariesmagazine.org/2019/09/30/remembering-andrew-carnegies-legacy/.

Ennis, Matt. "Las Vegas Library Provides Smart Phones, Unlimited Data to Unhoused Persons." *Library Journal*, September 8, 2022. https://www.libraryjournal.com/story/las-vegas-library-provides-smartphones%2C-unlimited-data-to-unhoused-patrons.

Heydecker, Rachel. "Engaging Libraries: Inspiring and Encouraging." Medium, March 27, 2019. https://carnegieuktrust.medium.com/engaging-libraries-inspiring-and-encouraging-6475c6d45057.

Jacob, Lisa. "Las Vegas-Clark County Library District Teams Up with Cox Communications to Provide FREE Personal WiFi to 50,000 Qualified Households." Globe News Wire, August 21, 2023. https://www.globenewswire.com/news-release/2023

/08/21/2728890/0/en/Las-Vegas-Clark-County-Library-District-Teams-Up-with-Cox-Communications-to-Provide-FREE-Personal-WiFi-to-50-000-Qualified-Households.html.

Jemison, Andrea Q. "More Than a Coffee Shop: How Libraries Support Civil Liberties." *Intellectual Freedom Blog, The Office of Intellectual Freedom of the American Library Association*, August 8, 2018. https://www.oif.ala.org/more-than-a-coffee-shop-how-libraries-support-civil-liberties/.

Kim, Kyndell. "Mobile Library Now Open inside the Boulevard Mall." 3 News, May 5, 2023. https://news3lv.com/news/local/mobile-library-now-open-inside-the-boulevard-mall-las-vegas-southern-nevada-latin-chamber-of-commerce-governor-lombardo.

Las Vegas-Clark County Library District. "Urban Library Council Honors Las Vegas-Clark County Library District and RTC for Innovation." PR News Wire, January 24, 2022. https://www.prnewswire.com/news-releases/urban-libraries-council-honors-the-las-vegas-clark-county-library-district-and-rtc-for-innovation-301466756.html.

Watson, Kelvin. "Libraries on Call." *American Libraries*, March 1, 2023. https://americanlibrariesmagazine.org/2023/03/01/libraries-on-call/.

# Part VI
# PEARLS OF WISDOM FROM OUR RETIREES

# Chapter 16

# BCALA Pearls of Wisdom: Phyllis Green Mack, Retired Librarian, New York Public Library

AS TOLD TO S. MICHELE ECHOLS

Sandra Michele Echols and Phyllis Green Mack

For many people, libraries are synonymous with books and a quiet space to read. However, the role of a librarian goes beyond shelving books and maintaining a quiet environment. As a librarian we are instrumental in fostering a love for learning and providing access to information for all members of the community we service. In the words of Marian Wright Edelman, "Service is the rent we pay for being. It is the very purpose of life, and not something you do in your spare time." As a retired librarian, my passion for learning and service never truly faded away.

Throughout my career I faced many challenges as a Black librarian in the twentieth century. I was a career librarian with the New York Public Library, retiring in 2002 after thirty-nine years of service. I only spent one year as a paraprofessional at Hunter College Library, CUNY. After graduating cum laude with a bachelor's degree in education from an HBCU, West Virginia State College now University, I knew that I wanted to become a librarian. I obtained a student assistant job in my college library performing various duties in cataloging and circulation. The library director and the reference librarian (both Black males) encouraged me to pursue a library degree, MLS. They observed that I enjoyed the detailed cataloging work and also working with students at the circulation desk.

The sixties were a turbulent age, remembered for demonstrations, protests, riots, and assassinations. Education was paramount if Black women were to be successful. Even though I held a BS degree, I was unsuccessful in securing a position at my local West Virginia County library; there was no Black staff in the early 1960s. Teaching positions were also difficult to obtain. Shortly afterward, I decided to relocate to New York City and reside with maternal family members. Having written a letter to the president of the NYPL, on the advice of my college advisor, I received a pleasant acknowledgment. I did apply for a position at the NYPL and was informed that only clerical positions were available to me with a bachelor's degree. Within a two-week period and after passing a simple test, I was hired as a clerk in the cataloging office. Realizing that this position was not my goal, I applied to library school and was accepted to Pratt Institute, Brooklyn, New York. At that time in the early 1960s, there were only three accredited library schools in the New York area: Columbia University, Pratt Institute, and Rutgers University in New Jersey. Although Columbia University was closer to me, the GRE requirement and costs were prohibitive to me at the time. I enrolled part time, worked full time, and was a young wife and mother of one daughter. I persevered and completed the MLS degree requirements in the summer of 1967. I consequently received my MLS degree in the spring of 1968 when I attended commencement. Finances were a challenge, only small amounts of money from NYPL were available for tuition. No full scholarships or other perks as there are now.

Libraries are often referred to as the "heart of the community," and for good reason. Librarians are responsible for providing access to information and resources that help individuals to pursue their educational and personal goals. As a young librarian, I was assigned to a South Bronx branch library in what was then called "Fort Apache" with gangs and unruly teens. It was a real culture shock, but the staff and the public liked and admired me, and I survived. In a large public library system, when vacancies occur, you may apply for positions, therefore I did apply and became a branch librarian (manager) in a few years. There were not many Black librarians as branch managers then, especially young ones. The MLS and passing other internal seminars were required. As a result, this experience taught me to navigate the racism and discrimination I experienced with grace and tenacity.

Looking back, I was somewhat amazed at the progress I made to obtain higher positions by working harder, smarter, strategically planning my moves, and being more qualified than others. The majority of my career was spent working in minority neighborhoods. Many of my assignments were difficult and not desired by other staff members. I remember being passed over for positions that I was overqualified for; maybe it was assumed that I would not fit in certain neighborhoods. Similar to what new librarians are facing today with experiencing knowledge assault by some employers. I recall one interview with the director, I was told to consider getting more education. Soon an opportunity presented itself as an EEOC doctoral fellowship in library services at Columbia University. I applied as a candidate with recommendation letters from Dr. E. J. Josey and Dr. Robert B. Ford Jr., the chief librarian of Medgar Evers College, CUNY and I was a successful candidate and extremely elated. The fellowship recipients, two of us, were recommended not to work, therefore I was granted an education leave during a NYC budget crisis. After the one-year fellowship and stipend for the required course work, you were on your own financially to enroll until you completed the dissertation. While taking courses, a professor stated that having a doctor in library science enabled you to teach in library school or work in an academic library, neither of which I wanted to pursue at that time. I also had an advisor who said that she would be my sponsor if I did a historical biography on a librarian that I really did not wish to spend my time and money pursuing. I wanted to contribute by writing on Black librarians' contributions to the profession. I know there are many, but there were no willing sponsors.

Therefore, after much thought, family considerations, and my health, I decided to get the advanced certificate in library services. In hindsight, with the technological advances today and diversity, equity, and inclusion, I would have breezed through it. It is my hope that future librarians do not endure the microassaults I experienced. However, if you do remember with the advent of technology and improvement within our field you have a plethora of tools available for you to use to advocate for yourself and thrive as a librarian.

As a Black librarian, advocating for myself and my colleagues has been an ongoing process. One of the most effective strategies I have used is networking. Building relationships with other professionals in the industry has not only provided me with valuable career opportunities but also a support system. Through networking, I have been able to connect with other Black librarians and become part of a community that shares similar experiences and challenges. This has allowed us to come together to develop strategies to promote diversity and inclusion in the field.

I was overjoyed to learn that the New York Black Librarians Caucus and the Black Caucus of the American Library Association were formed in 1970. I became a member of both as soon as possible and still hold membership today. I'm also a member of the American Library Association and the New York Library Association. The NYBLC provided an opportunity to meet and network with librarians in similar New York City library positions and other metro librarians from the academic, school, and private sector to discuss problems, solutions, and just talk about being minorities in the library profession. I'm an editor of the newly self-published, *Looking Back, Moving Forward: Celebrating 50 Years of the New York Black Librarians Caucus, 1970–2020*. Since 2018, the NYBLC has been a roundtable of the New York Library Association to open and invite membership in the entire state of New York. The book details much of what was done to advocate for Black librarians, including giving yearly scholarships to library school students.

As a member of the NYBLC, I was encouraged to become the president in 1981 and with the assistance of a hard-working scholarship and fund-raising committee, we presented scholarships to two library school students in 1981. Many in the library systems in New York became aware of the Caucus's existence.

Being a member of BCALA was very enlightening. Meeting Black librarians from all over the United States at BCALA conferences and ALA meetings really widened my scope. Of course, whenever possible, I conveyed this information to the staff and other librarians I would encounter. I was once asked by a supervisor if only Black librarians attended these conferences and meetings, and I thought back to why Dr. E. J. Josey started BCALA in 1970. I gave a succinct and courteous reply.

I was fortunate to serve as a board member of BCALA for two terms and become a member of the proceedings committee for three of the National Conference of African American Librarians, NCAAL. I encouraged my fellow librarians and family to attend the first five conferences and they thoroughly enjoyed the experience. Some made presentations at the conference.

I retired in 2002, before diversity, equity, and inclusion became a prominent buzzword. In a large system I was able to make suggestions to human resources about who was needed in the branch libraries I supervised, and my advice was rarely if ever taken. Communities needed to see librarians that looked like them and were knowledgeable about the community the library served. However, I do believe in the importance of diversity and inclusion in libraries. Gathering from my past experience, today's librarians can glean from the initiatives that occurred during the latter part of the twentieth century.

Support the development of diverse collections, the offering of multicultural activities, and the hiring of diverse personnel. All staff members must receive diversity and inclusion training in order for them to be aware of any unconscious biases and to be able to work together to create a welcoming workplace for all customers. Also, by collaborating with neighborhood community organizations, librarians may better understand the wants and requirements of various demographic groups and design services and programs that are tailored to their needs. Libraries may become more representative of the communities they serve and give all users a more equitable and inclusive experience by establishing a priority on diversity and inclusion.

My position as regional librarian in Central Harlem, where I spent the final eighteen years of my library career, was quite challenging. Being a library advocate in the community was essential along with other administrative duties. We were encouraged to have library advocates, known as "library support groups," at the time. The group at my library was well-known for its letter writing to elected officials during budget time, book sales, and being willing observers (acting as a guard) in the children's room when necessary. Many were retired teachers who had taught their parents, this was very helpful and useful. I attended community board meetings to inform the community of the library's programs and services in my region, and as a library advocate on budget issues. As a result, I applied for and was appointed by my local elected official to Community Board #10 Manhattan (serves Central Harlem) and shortly afterward elected president. Many library budget requests became a priority for the community board as a result. The elected officials also gave some much needed discretionary funds to libraries in the Central Harlem region as a result of my lobbying, which I later learned were diverted to other library needs. One elected official asks if we were getting our fair share of what was allocated. This was a very legitimate question.

I lived in the community where I worked, which was a definite plus and I was a constituent of the elected officials. I was also recognized by community people as "the librarian" wherever I would go and am still to this day recognized as such.

My advice for anyone currently pursuing a degree in library science or early career librarians—my past experience supervising and training numerous young librarians in my lengthy career, it's obvious that I learned they must decide what type of library they want to work: public, academic, special, or school. Having a mentor is ideal if one is available. In my experience many did not like the atmosphere in a public setting or working with the general public. Others wanted a shorter workday and summers off; thus, the school library was their choice and most children's librarians enjoyed working with children. Others preferred a corporate setting and others liked working with students and publishing articles. I met a few at library conferences who had left the public library for greener pastures, and they told me they were so happy in their choices; some positions were more lucrative, others met their needs. Black librarians are still in the minority today in most settings. Coping with "code-switching, "imposter syndrome," "microaggression," "cultural competency," etc. are still daily issues. Retired librarians dealt with these issues also, but it was not so named back then.

The most important issue facing libraries today is staying relevant in these days of constant technological advances. I have observed that the media projects libraries as being obsolete or a thing of the past, but some media have portrayed libraries today as a "new golden era for libraries." Newly renovated libraries offer a plethora of innovation including stunning reading rooms, community rooms, they are eco-friendly, cafes, music production facilities, business centers, rooftop terraces, and inventive programming to mention a few. These upgrades should entice all ages of patrons to visit libraries instead of solely relying on digital information.

My views as a Black librarian regarding collection development stems from working in a large system, books were preselected, and the librarian in each specialty was able to select from these preselections. Many of the controversial books, Black authors, Black-themed books, etc. were not ordered by the mainstream branches with larger book budgets, but they were bought by my library and immediately reserved by those who did not live in the neighborhood until a new policy was initiated. Reserves were first honored by the library that purchased the book. I do understand that many policies have changed since my retirement over twenty years. I also found and experienced that libraries were understaffed in minority communities and staffed with problem incompetent librarians sent to be reformed. I stayed in my position for the long haul because I was constantly told that I was the bright light for many who used the library by providing the information they needed.

According to the current research and many library theorists I most definitely agree with the many sources and the American Library Association statements on the most important role of libraries in society.

a. lifelong learning (tops the list for me)
b. support for literacy
c. meeting spaces for the community, book clubs, reading groups
d. technology provider, free source of computer and internet access
e. job searches
f. Access to government information on the federal, state, and local levels
g. health and wellness—find doctors; research illnesses for themselves or for relatives, friends, colleagues; Medicare and Medicaid
h. GED instruction/information, ESL classes for new populations

I'm certain there are other roles that libraries provide.

Today, despite the many benefits that libraries provide to their communities, librarians face a range of challenges in their work. One of the most significant challenges is budget cuts. Libraries often have to do more with less, which can result in reduced staffing, fewer resources, and less programming.

The role of librarianship has evolved significantly over the years. In the past, librarians were primarily focused on providing access to books and other print materials. However, with the advent of the digital age, libraries have had to adapt to keep up with changing technology and consumer needs.

Despite the challenges, being a librarian can be incredibly rewarding. Librarians have the opportunity to make a positive impact on their communities every day. They help people to find the information they need to succeed, support literacy and lifelong learning, and create programming that brings people together. We as librarians also have the satisfaction of knowing that we are contributing to a greater good. We are helping to promote the idea that access to information and knowledge is a fundamental human right. For many retired librarians and me, we feel this sense of purpose and fulfillment is what made our work so meaningful.

In conclusion, I have enjoyed being a career librarian despite its challenges, ups and downs, joys and pains. My type A personality kept me grounded and focused during those years. Ending with a quote by many, "Was very active in her profession and community, she earned a reputation of being reliable, dependable, businesslike, competent and fair minded which led to her election to various leadership positions."

# Chapter 17
# Statements from Retirees

IDA D. MCGHEE, MLS

Ida D. McGhee

I am still in awe of the fact that May 2023 marked twenty years that I am officially retired from the Hartford Public Library (HPL), Hartford, Connecticut, as manager of the Library on Wheels Department.

Retired? Hmmm. I have had to stay connected to the library world. It's in my soul. I know no other career. I have always wanted to be like my mentor, Mrs. Mary Oliver, the school librarian at Fred D. Wish Elementary School in Hartford. She was one of two African Americans at the school when I first attended in third grade. Mrs. Nelson, a first grade teacher was the other. I volunteered at the school library until I graduated and went on to volunteer for four years at my high school.

When I was nine, every day after school, I would walk to the public library and browse the large collection of children's books before deciding what to borrow. I recall the wonderful summer programs at the library and could not wait to be hired as a library page. Finally, upon graduating from eighth grade in June 1970, I was hired at HPL Barbour Branch where I worked until leaving for college in August 1974.

It was bittersweet but I knew I had to attend college as I was the first one in my family to do so. During my four years of undergraduate studies at Southern Connecticut State University, not only did I work four years in the Technical Services Department, but I also worked at the New Haven Public Library in the Children's Department and also at the reference desk. After I graduated, I decided to go back South (I was born and raised in Alabama) to attend Atlanta University for my master's degree in library science. I fondly look back over my many years and still believe that librarians must always be in the forefront in society. Retired librarians like me must keep abreast of the newest developments and technologies in the field, the new concepts and ideals, and by all means, continue to read library literature and attend affordable library conferences, nationally and local.

I am very much committed to the profession as I continue to work to ensure the word "library" is a household word. It is extremely important that our children have libraries in their schools and communities—and that books, computers, and databases are available to them.

Having retired and relocated to Rhode Island in 2004, I am one of the founders of Cornucopia of Rhode Island: Serving the Library Community of Color, a diverse group of librarians and library support staff that presents free community workshops during the year as well as presenting at our state's annual library conference, advocating for library services. I am also still the facilitator of a monthly book discussion group in the Hartford area that I established in December 1998 while working at HPL. Our main focus is reading and discussing titles by African American authors or African American genre.

In essence, yes, I am retired, but I can never retire from the field. It is imperative that I continue to strive and commit to promoting the field of library science. I must continue to mentor students of color to encourage them to enter and enrich the diversity of our profession. Just as importantly, I must continue to ensure that libraries are purchasing books that reflect their communities as well as their professional staff. No more *Dick and Jane* books, the titles that I remember from my childhood Barbour Branch library.

My fifty-three plus years in the library profession have been most rewarding. I am still in touch with many patrons and families that I served. I will always remember the joy of summer story hours on the bookmobile with a farmer and his potbellied pig; the many parades the bookmobile participated in throughout the years; the collaboration between community organizations and the library for the benefit of the public; and my bragging rights that "although we were not a building, the circulation of the Library on Wheels Department each year was often higher than many of the HPL's nine branches." The bookmobile offered full library services, just on wheels.

I will always be grateful for Mrs. Oliver, the first teacher and librarian of color I met. I later became her sorority sister when I was one of the original members to establish an interest group and become a general member of Alpha Kappa Alpha Sorority, Inc. at Southern Connecticut State University.

As a constituent and retiree, I will continue to be a strong library advocate. I remain engaged in the library world and strive to inspire others along the way. Hopefully, my epitaph will read, "She immensely loved the library profession. Low pay, but always rewarding."

# Chapter 18
# Pearls of Wisdom

IN CONVERSATION WITH MARCIA SMITH-WOODARD

Michele Fenton and Marcia Smith-Woodard

In this chapter, Michele Fenton interviews her esteemed mentor and colleague Marcia Smith-Woodard. Before retiring in 2014, Smith-Woodard spent thirty-four years as an advocate, mentor, consultant, and leader in the library profession. In 2013, Smith-Woodard received the BCALA Advocacy Award for helping bring diversity to the library profession through her work with the IMLS-funded Indiana Librarians Leading in Diversity (I-LLID) Fellowship Program.

Michele Fenton: Please share your reflections on librarianship today. Include encouragements and/or struggles in your work in librarianship.

Marcia Smith-Woodard: It would have been nice to have had mentors earlier in my career. Black mentors would have been helpful. It was a struggle to get hired. My first place of employment had never had a Black librarian with an MLS. They only had a Black librarian with a BLS. She retired by the time I left library school, so I did not get a chance to sit down and talk with her.

    I didn't know at the time how to reach out to librarians in the local community. I wish I had reached out to the Gary Public Library, which has a better history as far as Black librarians.

MF: How are your reflections related to Black librarians?

MSW: I feel fortunate to have worked at a statewide level which allowed me to come to know, meet, and network with Black librarians across Indiana. I also had an opportunity to meet librarians in libraries other than public libraries. In addition, I got to meet a variety of Black librarians I would have never met were it not for the Indiana Black Librarians Network (IBLN) and the Black Caucus of the American Library Association (BCALA).

MF: What are your views on challenges and/or triumphs on librarianship in general and Black librarianship specifically, over the last twenty years?

MSW: It has been very enlightening to see more and more Black librarians in positions of authority and leadership in libraries these past twenty years. Despite the negativity from non-Black librarians, Black librarians continue to successfully contribute to the library profession through their outreach and programming efforts, mentoring, educating, and recruiting other Black librarians, research and writing, and advocating for library services.

MF: Identify any challenges and/or triumphs that remain.

MSW:

- There is still room for more advancement.
- Especially with COVID, it has been more acceptable for people to express racism more vocally. Librarianship has suffered because of the increased racism, and this affects promotion and inclusion in the profession.
- Racism has also affected access to materials. Black literature is under attack. We know that not having access to that information does not help the public.

MF: Do you have pearls of wisdom and encouragement to share with librarians today—for example, advice for current or future librarians?

MSW:

- When you are in library school, really spend some time getting to know the subject matter(s) you are interested in and networking with people who are involved in the areas you're passionate about. This will influence your papers, research, programming, etc.
- When you graduate and begin looking for a job, don't just look for a job. Look for employment in an area of librarianship that you enjoy working in and are passionate about.
- Don't just be a member of a library association, be actively involved. You can see librarianship from different perspectives but grow your own perspective.
- Get continuing education. Don't pass this up even if what you are learning is not something you are interested in today; it may come in handy later.
- Find other librarians and network with them. Build your network of people who can help you and of people whom you can help.

- I encourage Black library science students to be memorable. Make sure your instructors know who you are, what your capabilities are, and what your contributions are.
- Don't just stay in your Black world.
- Don't just do the job; stop and have fun doing what you do. If it becomes drudgery, look for your next move. Change your work environment. If it gets to the point where you are dreading going to work, it is time to make a change. You may have to change the type of library you work in.
- Don't work in a toxic environment. Be in a place where you are supported and appreciated.
- Don't be afraid to go somewhere different. Be willing to stretch out to areas that may give you better opportunities. Don't be afraid to go out there and see what the options are. I don't know how it would have turned out, but fear caused me to pass on my first opportunity out of library school. It would have sent me to the Upper Peninsula of Michigan to an environment totally foreign to me. I regret being shortsighted.
- Give back. Support where you were supported and beyond if you are able.

MF: Is there anything else you would like to say?

MSW: Thanks for the opportunity to be included. Hopefully I said something that will be helpful.

# Chapter 19

# Pearls of Wisdom by Joyce C. Wright as Relayed to Marva L. DeLoach

Joyce C. Wright and Marva L. DeLoach

Marva L. DeLoach: Please share your reflections on librarianship today. Include encouragements and/or struggles in your work in librarianship.

Joyce C. Wright: Librarianship has changed drastically over the last three decades. The advent of technology has brought librarians from various backgrounds into the field of information science. During my library school's days at the library school of the University of Michigan most of my classmates had undergraduate degrees in the humanities and social sciences. Technology has brought librarianship into a new arena domestically and globally.

Librarians are adept at technology with great aplomb. Technology has enhanced librarians with a greater scope of the vast field of informational resources they impart to users.

As a retired librarian I often visit the local public library in my area. I am intrigued by how much today's reference librarians know about technology, they are good at explaining all types of technological resources one can use such as Box, Google, Google Scholar, numerous online databases like JSTOR, Word, PowerPoint, and many other resources.

MD: How are your reflections related to Black Librarians?

JCW: On the outside looking in, I think Black librarians are thriving in the field. Many are taking on nontraditional positions in digital librarianship, metadata librarianship, and informatics. I have mentored several Black librarians over my forty-year career in librarianship. I offer them the same advice I received early on in my profession. They are appreciative of what I impart to them. I've mentored two academic librarians who were in tenured track positions. Both received tenure.

MD: What are your views on challenges and/or triumphs in librarianship in general and Black librarianship specifically over the last twenty years?

JCW: As a librarian of color, I feel that Black librarians have faced the challenges in the field extremely well considering all the odds that were against them early in the field. Many have pursued further education or training beyond the MLS as well as in other fields of study.

Using myself as an example, in 1974 I received a master's degree. Upon completion of my studies, I was immediately employed. From 1974 through 1984 I worked in the following types of libraries: academic, community colleges, and public libraries. After ten years it was time for me to return to renew my skills. I enrolled in the CAS (Certificate of Advanced Studies Program) at the University of Illinois at Urbana-Champaign. The technology world was buzzing.

MD: Identify any challenges or triumphs that remain.

JCW: In an ever-changing world with such a vast amount of information today, I think challenges will always be present. The triumphs of reaching everyone through the printed word and digital resources will forever remain prevalent.

MD: Do you have pearls of wisdom and encouragement to share with librarians today—for example, advice for current or future librarians?

JCW: I would advise librarians today to stay abreast of all the innovative techniques in the field. Become involved in professional organizations; network, network, network; participate in conferences and workshops; be an activist leader-role model as you advance professionally; pursue increasingly challenging and upwardly progressive positions; seek mentorship early and mentor others along the way; contribute to professional research and publishing in the field; be an outspoken advocate for equity, diversity, inclusion, and multiculturalism; be inquisitive; learn your history; and give back/provide services to your communities.

As mentioned earlier, I've worked in academic, community colleges, and public libraries. Pearls of wisdom may be gleaned from the increasingly challenging and upwardly mobile positions that I have held during my career:

- Trident Technical College, Charleston, South Carolina, Reference/Documents Librarian, 1974–1976
- Hampton Public Library, Hampton, Virginia, Reference Librarian, 1976–1978

- Memphis/Shelby Public Library and Information Center, Memphis, Tennessee, Head of General Reference/Information Department, 1978–1980
- Voorhees College, Denmark, South Carolina, Administrative Librarian, 1980–1985
- University of Illinois at Urbana-Champaign, Urbana, Illinois, Undergraduate Librarian, Coordinator of Reference and Instructional Services, 1985–January 1989; appointed Acting Head of IRRC (Illinois Research and Reference Center), February 1988–November 1988; Assistant to the Director of Departmental Library Services, January 1989–March 1992; Acting Head of Undergraduate Library, March 1992–June 1994; Director of Undergraduate Library, June 1994–2006; Head of Agricultural Communications Documentation Center, Agricultural Library, June 2006–January 2014

MD: Is there anything else that you'd like to add or share?

JCW: Throughout my career I found librarianship a rewarding profession. I never had any regrets about my decision to enter the field. Working in different types of libraries has forever broadened my concepts.

# Chapter 20
# Stephanie Tolson, Retired Librarian

Stephanie Tolson

Curiosity has always opened doors for me. I was fortunate to love reading, which is why I ended up at the library often during my childhood. Book after book allowed me to learn and explore new things. I attended a midwestern college and was intrigued to see military officers returning to get their college education. When I realized they were studying business administration, I decided that I would take up that major as well. They encouraged me to persevere despite the lack of females in this field. While in college, I worked and studied in the library. When I finished my degree ahead of schedule in December 1974, I wanted to go to graduate school, but found that the University of Missouri would not allow me to enter library school until the fall. I shared my dismay with Dr. Smith, the head librarian. He encouraged me to explore other options. Emporia Kansas State University also had a library program. They granted me an interview and before you knew it, I was enrolled in the spring. I was young, curious, and willing to pursue a degree in library science.

The combination of my undergraduate and graduate degrees opened many doors for me. During my career, I worked in public, corporate, and academic libraries. I was afforded membership in professional organizations and assumed leadership roles in the American Library Association, Special Libraries Association, and the Missouri Library Association. Early on, I remember my supervisor asking me, "Why do you always expect the organization will send you to library conferences?" I was surprised and responded, "I can only ask, it is up to you to grant or deny my requests." Perhaps this taught me to always be ready to justify my pursuits. At conferences and workshops, I sought out programs that would teach me something new. I took detailed notes and wrote reports highlighting the benefits for my colleagues and superiors.

Membership has its benefits. Before I assumed leadership roles in library organizations, I took my membership seriously. I attended local chapter meetings, volunteered, and presented at conferences. I also became a book reviewer after sitting next to an editor at a national conference. When asked to run for Chapter Council office by the Missouri Library Association, I accepted the challenge. However, I experienced comradery when I joined the Black Caucus of the American Library Association (BCALA). Black librarians from all over the country came together during BCALA meetings at the American Library Association's annual conference. I had worked over twenty years as a librarian, library director, and dean before I felt comfortable enough to ask my employer to send me to the Black Caucus of the American Library Associations' National Conference of African American Librarians (NCAAL). Never had I seen so many librarians of color. I felt empowered to face challenges of being one of the few, if not the only Black librarian in my organization thanks to my newfound network. I believe that some opportunities came my way because I was Black and there were not enough Black librarians with similar exposure. I believe most of my fortune came from God.

# Chapter 21
# The Joy in Retirement

Jessie Carney Smith

Among the great joys that one can experience in retirement is to enter that phase of life with the satisfaction that they met their professional goals and dreams. My story is an example of a dream fulfilled. I spent most of my library years as a top administrator of the library at Fisk University. My appointment came in 1965 with the rank of full professor; later Fisk added the title Camille Cosby Distinguished Chair in the Humanities; and still later, Fisk promoted me to dean of the library. Upon retiring in 2020, Fisk rewarded me with the distinguished title of Librarian Emerita. This leaves me with the comfort of knowing that the institution recognized and appreciated my administrative efforts and my research and published works.

Neither Fisk nor members of the library profession realize how much satisfaction I achieved during my professional life. Our library's rich Special Collections fed my joy. The longer I stayed the more I wanted to do something special and enduring with two of our holdings. They were the *Slave Bible: Let the Story Be Told* (reprint of the 1807 work published in London in 1807 on behalf of the Society for the Conversion of Negro Slaves) void of all passages related to freedom, and our Julius Rosenwald Rural Negro Schools Collection. My joy was intensified just before retirement and continues. The Museum of the Bible, in Washington, DC, displayed *Slave Bible* in a special, prominent, and choice location, and it gained national and international attention. My proposal to the Andrew W. Mellon Foundation just before retirement resulted in a successful planning grant to make the Rosenwald collection more publicly accessible. This introduction of the Rosenwald schools to Mellon led to a sizable grant following my retirement. Although this success filled my dream, the desire to have that dream fulfilled was my primary focus, bringing immense joy in retirement. With persistence, insistence, dedication, and hard work, retirees can meet their goals and desires. Retirement can be joyful, and one's legacy can be enduring. Yes, there is joy in retirement. While we acknowledge the popular saying, "Joy comes in the morning," for those who at some point will enter their twilight years, Joy also comes in the evening.

# Chapter 22
# My Life's Work in Academic and Public Librarianship

Gloria J. Mims

My professional career as a librarian began at the Atlanta University Graduate Library as head of Special Collections shortly after having received my MSLS degree from the Atlanta University School of Library Service. It was an ideal position that enabled me to use my African American studies background, which proved to be an asset when providing research and reference services to the students, faculty, and scholars who frequented the library. When the Atlanta University Center Libraries were merged into the newly constructed Atlanta University Center Robert W. Woodruff Library, as head of the Division of Special Collections and Archives, this position afforded me the opportunity to continue in academic librarianship where contacts, research assistance, and interactions with renowned local, national, and international artists, authors, historians, professors, and writers in addition to the students and faculties benefited greatly from having access to the various collections.

My transition to public librarianship with the Atlanta-Fulton Public Library System was quite easy since having been a user of their resources within the Special Collections Department at the Central Library over the years. While still providing research and reference services to the public, much time was devoted to acquiring and preparing collections and resources for the newly constructed Auburn Avenue Research Library on African American Culture and History, a special library of the Atlanta-Fulton Public Library System. During my forty-plus years in librarianship, I have experienced much joy and satisfaction because it was a career that I enjoyed helping others locate information that enhanced the success of their personal or academic achievements. Additionally, librarianship is a noble profession!

# Chapter 23
# "When You Become a Librarian . . ."

Marshelle Berry

"When you become a librarian . . ." were the words spoken to me on a regular basis when I was a full-time clerk shelving books and assisting visitors with utilizing the public library where I had been working for almost five years. My branch manager would always make comments like, "Marshelle, when you become a librarian, make sure your displays include books for boys, as well as for girls." Or "Marshelle, when you become a branch manager, be sure to get suggestions from full-time and part-time staff, because you never know where the best ideas will originate." I heard my manager's words of wisdom, but every time she said, "When you become a librarian . . . ," I thought she was being quite silly. I had never said anything about becoming a librarian. I did not know where she had gotten that information. It was a complete mystery to me.

However, as time passed, I returned to school, obtained my master's degree, and yes, I became a librarian and later a branch manager. It was at this time that I began to understand and embrace the true power and meaning of leadership. Being a librarian means serving as a leader who steers individuals toward successfully accomplishing personal, professional, educational, and even recreational goals. My manager's words led me in the direction of achieving great results for myself and countless others. I took advantage of leadership training opportunities and moved progressively up the ranks within the library to becoming a library administrator and member of the executive leadership team. I served as a mentor and supervisor for numerous people who also excelled in library careers.

As a library retiree, it is very fulfilling to have been recognized by the Florida Library Association with the 2022 Lifetime Achievement Award. It is also quite rewarding to hear staff and library customers say I had a positive impact on their lives. Librarians have the noble responsibility to embrace roles as leaders, seeking to make a favorable difference one person at a time. In this manner, libraries will have a lasting impact on their visitors and the communities they serve. Moreover, the librarian profession will continue to thrive as others are led to become librarians.

# Chapter 24
# What Librarianship Has Meant to Me

Irene Owens

It was a fall day in Washington, DC, and happenstance that drew me in, but it was the love of the profession that kept me in my work and service in librarianship. A chance meeting with Judy, a former classmate at Barber-Scotia College on G Street who was working at the Library of Congress, suggested that I apply for a job there, which was, unknowingly, the beginning of my career. Judy remembered that I worked in the library as an undergraduate, which fueled her query. At the time, that did not signal there was an undergraduate connection with my later profession. Within less than a two-year period at the Library of Congress (where I really fell in love with the profession), I was recruited for the master of library science degree program at the University of Maryland, which was the next step in my career. While attending Maryland, I had the honor of serving as an assistant to the dean who was also my advisor. That experience didn't signal that I would one day be recruited as a dean.

Not having decided while a student what type of library environment I wanted to work in, I decided *where* I wanted to work and that was at Howard University. During that time, I served as the browsing librarian, head of the Reference Department both in Founders Library, where I enjoyed preparing exhibits, planning and presenting author talks and receptions, helping students with reference questions, mentoring students, and enjoying the proximity of the work of the Moorland Spingarn Research Center. Seeing and speaking with the doyenne of Black bibliography, Dr. Dorothy Porter Wesley, remains an awesome honor. I later served as the librarian for the Divinity Library and also earned a master of arts degree as was expected of a subject specialist. It was at Howard that I also learned the importance and the art and craft of writing grants. I took part in obtaining two very successful grants and have since secured others.

After serving for thirteen years as the director of the Divinity Library and having planned and moved into a new library for the school, I decided that I needed another mountain to climb. That decision led me to the PhD program at the University of North Carolina at Chapel Hill (1995) and then being hired as the first African American in a tenure track position at the University of Texas at Austin. Shortly afterward, I was nominated for the deanship at North Carolina Central University and served in that capacity for eleven wonderful and challenging years. I have no regrets. I am still working in the profession I love because of its meaning to society for all people and especially African Americans. I have no idea and would not want to ponder where we as a people would be without the documentation of our heritage, which has been curated and made accessible by librarians and libraries!

# Chapter 25

# Pearls of Wisdom by Linda Jolivet as Relayed to Marva L. DeLoach

Marva L. DeLoach and Linda Jolivet

Marva L. DeLoach: Please share your reflections on librarianship today. Include encouragements and/or struggles in your work in librarianship.

Linda Jolivet: Today, there are many challenges we thought we had overcome. Book bans, fewer middle, high school, and college students using libraries for reading and reference uses, etc. Learning new technology and new social media platforms is also a challenge for librarians (especially librarians who have been in the profession fifteen years or more). They often are not as familiar with these platforms as younger librarians and need support for hands-on training.

I personally miss the days when people would ask for assistance in finding information from print reference books. Some still ask for help in using online reference sources, but this has been greatly reduced with two years of the pandemic and increased online use, and the last two generations of Americans becoming more and more inclined to do almost everything on their phones.

Regarding book challenges, right-wing groups are increasingly imposing their beliefs on what the general public and school communities should be allowed to read. This reminds me of the days of the civil rights movement when these types of self-righteous folks wanted to dictate who was allowed to go to certain public schools based on race.

Implicit bias and White privilege continue to affect librarians of color, especially African American librarians. As someone who has over two decades of experience in the profession, I do not see much progress in this area.

MLD: How are your reflections related to Black librarians?

LJ: My reflections are related to Black librarians in the above thoughts that apply across the board to librarians of color.

MLD: What are your views on challenges and/or triumphs in librarianship in general and Black librarianship specifically over the last twenty years?

LJ: Over the last twenty years, we have seen an increased number of African American librarians move into leadership roles as library directors, and also in positions of high responsibility at local, state, and federal levels. Recently we welcomed the first African American head of the Library of Congress appointed (Carla Hayden), for example.

MLD: Identify any challenges and/or triumphs that remain.

LJ: Bias against African American librarians in promotions and fair evaluations continue to exist. This often shows up on a day-to-day basis in the form of small insults and other microaggressions.

MLD: Do you have pearls of wisdom and encouragement to share with librarians today—for example, advice to current or future librarians?

LJ: My advice for current and future librarians is as follows:

Don't be surprised that you are treated unfairly on jobs.
Always keep a revised resume on hand and don't hesitate to explore a wide range of options.
Don't feel guilty about leaving a job for a better opportunity.
Constantly add to your skills and expertise.
Actively participate in Black librarians' organizations.
Seek out mentors.

I have realized the aforementioned pearls in positions that I have held within and tangential to librarianship since becoming a librarian. I retired from the Oakland (California) Public Library (OPL) System after nineteen years of service. Prior to employment at OPL, I worked at St. Mary's College in Moraga, California, and at Kentucky State University, Frankfurt, Kentucky.

After retiring from OPL in 2014, I worked as an AmeriCorps volunteer as a reading tutor at an elementary school in East Oakland for a year, then as a literacy specialist for Girls Inc. at two elementary schools. Since 2017, I have worked part-time as a reference librarian for the Peralta Community College District (California) at Laney Community College in Oakland and at Berkeley City College in Berkeley,

MLD: Is there anything else that you'd like to add or share?

No response given.

# Chapter 26
# Customer Service

A MANY SPLENDORED THING

Sharon D. Banks

My first interaction with a librarian was in the late 1950s when I visited the public library for the first time. The white librarian stood up, looked down at me, and asked, "What could you possibly want from here?" Not understanding either the coldness of her attitude or the question asked, I simply said, "A book." So much for customer service. Decades later, I became a librarian as a midcareer change of course. That embedded memory returned. I knew I never wanted anyone to feel as I had for having visited a library that day many years ago. And as a professional, I learned that customer service done right was way more than simply asking "How may I help you?"

1. A woman left her child in the library while she shopped in the supermarket across the street. After a while her child became restless and decided to find her mother at the store. He was hit by a car while crossing the street. His mother returned to the library in time to see her child being placed in the ambulance. She was hysterical. We calmed her down so she could call both her husband, who was at work, and a friend who would take her to the hospital. I reassured her that her groceries, including the perishables, were safe. I called security and was given permission to keep the building open until her friend arrived. We found out the next day that her son had not been seriously injured.
2. An elderly gentleman was a regular visitor, and when I was not busy, he would reminisce about his late wife. One afternoon he shared how much they loved ballroom dancing and how much he missed it, especially the waltz. Inspired, I asked him if he could hum the music to which they had danced. He said yes. I then asked for his hand to dance. Surprised, he finally stood up. And we waltzed around the library to applause. He died not too long afterward.
3. As a librarian, I quickly learned that if you had an affinity for working with teens, you were gold to your manager. But one incident threw me for a loop. I had two tables of teens, the regular crowd who came every day and with whom I interacted on a daily basis. This particular day, they were seated at two tables—boys at one and girls at the next table. They were intensely interested in their phones. They were so engaged, they did not realize I had quietly circled the room so I could get a glimpse of what they were watching. They were all looking at the same video. It was of one of the boys and one of the girls seated at the tables engaged in sex with each other. I quietly walked back to the staff room and prayed for guidance. By now things were winding down and the teens were leaving. I call the young lady over and asked if she was coming back the next day. She said yes.

   The next day I told her to come to the staff room with me. I calmly told her about the day before. It was not my place to give her sex education, but without judgment, I asked if she had considered the consequences to her reputation if the pictures were circulated beyond her circle of friends. I asked if she were aware that her video could end up on the dark web. What if she and her boyfriend broke up and he circulated their video together with other boys? Their intimacy was very personal, a shared experience meant for the two of them only. I ended by suggesting she see a school nurse in whom she could confide. The nurse could be helpful if she needed contraceptives. None of this had ever entered her mind.
4. Within days I was promoted to another library, and we lost touch. Several years later our paths crossed again. She excitedly told me she had graduated from high school and had not gotten pregnant! I was so happy. I have had countless parents brag about their children's college acceptances. But at that moment, remembering her as I knew her when she was younger with no one to guide her, I could not have been prouder.

I love the memories I hold of the many customers I was honored to serve. My continuous admonishment to the staff was that customers should always leave the library feeling better than they felt upon entering. We might not be able to solve their concerns, but we can be pleasant, respectful, and mindful about the reason(s) they are standing before us.

# Chapter 27
# Are You Thinking about... Mission? Value? Staff?

Thomas Alford

In recent years we all have lived through a global pandemic, civil unrest, and other crises. At the same time, the last four years were marked with fortitude and innovation, from development of COVID-19 vaccines in record time, to emerging technologies that have reprioritized methods and practices. In response to these recent events and earlier challenges, many libraries have made several changes to collections and services. For over the past decade, I've read about and observed many library changes and improvements in services to library customers in all types of libraries.

As we continue with these changes into this new era as a service provider, mission and vision statements are a couple of important library documents that should be given a review in order to ensure that the library board, management, and staff are on the same track. Thus, now is an excellent time to conduct these reviews. Such reviews bring depth, experience, and great expertise in service, building management, operations, and finances as well as processes and procedures, and identifying areas where staff training and development may be needed.

The library's mission should be to provide customers with the highest-quality library service that it can. To accomplish this goal, the library needs to know what it's doing right and what needs to be changed or improved. The board and management mission and vision documents should create the right culture that drives staff in that direction and identify areas where more training is needed. Identifying and restating the purpose helps library administration and staff to focus and reaffirm what's important. Purpose-oriented statements help staff persist through challenges and go the extra mile. They also help to build trust in servicing our users. Also, clearly stated values may lead to better decisions in times of uncertainties and should to the development of sets of values with staff who understand well and better follow.

When a library works as a team, it can accomplish many things. Written documents are an essential part of that team. They can help the library tackle society's biggest challenges, from misinformation and social injustice to the future of climate control, and so much more. Ready, Set, Go!

# Chapter 28
# Challenges and Triumphs

PERSONAL REFLECTION ON MY CAREER IN THE ATLANTA PUBLIC LIBRARY SYSTEM

Carolyn Lowe Garnes

Before I speak to my personal reflections it is important to capture the essence of Atlanta's role in the civil rights movement and the desegregation of the library system. The two events set the stage for the social and political environment of the city.

## ATLANTA: THE MECCA OF THE CIVIL RIGHTS MOVEMENT

The civil rights movement was a nonviolent social movement and campaign that took place from 1954 to 1968 in the United States to abolish legalized racial segregation, discrimination, and disenfranchisement.[1]

Atlanta was considered the mecca of the civil rights movement, the home of Dr. Martin Luther King Jr., the drum major for social justice. During less than thirteen years of Dr. King's leadership of the modern American civil rights movement, from 1955 until 1968 African Americans achieved more genuine progress toward racial equality in the United States than the previous 350 years. Dr. King is widely regarded as America's preeminent advocate of nonviolence and one of the greatest nonviolent leaders in world history.[2]

The Atlanta student movement was formed in 1960 by students of campuses of the Atlanta University Center (AUC). It brought social change to Atlanta. Students mobilized to launch a series of demonstrations to end legalized segregation in public facilities. The movement greatly impacted both racial tensions not only in Atlanta but nationally. These sit-ins also helped to engage America's youth, bringing a younger generation of leaders to the fore. Thanks to the Atlanta student movement, Atlanta began to live up to its slogan, "A City Too Busy to Hate."[3]

These events provided an open opportunity for progressive mayors like William B. Hartsfield and Ivan Allen Jr. to collaborate with local African American leaders to move Atlanta toward inclusion.

## EARLY LIBRARY SERVICES TO AFRICAN AMERICANS AND DESEGREGATION OF ATLANTA PUBLIC LIBRARY

During the twentieth century, library service to African Americans paralleled the civil rights progress. In the thick of the civil rights movement most public libraries were as segregated as was the rest of the country.

In its early history of library services to African Americans, Atlanta Public library had three facilities operating exclusively for Black citizens. Atlanta's first public library branch for African Americans was the Auburn Avenue Branch, officially opened on July 25, 1921, in the red brick Carnegie building.[4] It closed in 1959. It was only the fourth southern public library system to have constructed a Black branch with Carnegie funds.

From 1937 to 1962 library service was provided in the University Homes Public Housing projects. During the same period, increasing numbers of African Americans migrated to Atlanta's west side. Accompanying this growth were residents' demands for expanded public library service. In response, the city allocated funds for the construction of another library branch to serve the needs of Black citizens. On December 6, 1949, the newly built West Hunter Branch opened.[5]

The individuals who served as librarians at that time were not master's degree certified professionals. Several of the librarians did, however, hold the Bachelor of Science in Library Science (BSLS) degree from the Hampton School of Library Service. The first African American librarian with a master's degree was Annie McPheeters, receiving her MSLS in 1957 from Columbia University. She became the first African American to serve as a department head promoted as the head of the Negro Department in 1950, which was headquartered at the West Hunter Branch where she also served as branch manager. McPheeters remained at the West Hunter Branch until 1966.[6]

Public access to libraries in Atlanta came by influence and efforts of prominent African Americans. Atlanta Black elites waged a constant battle to obtain library services, eventfully forcing the library system to open its doors to all citizens. The true heroes in this desegregation effort were the pioneer Black librarians who played a vital role in laying the foundation for the success of African American librarians today.[7]

Although they experienced prejudice and discrimination, it was their perseverance that provided inspiration for a new generation of Black librarians. Credit must be given to those who endured a racist environment to bring the rich world of libraries to people of color.

The Atlanta Public Library was formally desegregated in 1959. Irene Dobbs Jackson, mother of the former mayor of Atlanta, requested a library card from the central library. After threat of a lawsuit by the Atlanta Council of Human Rights, the library board voted to allow Black people full access to the library on May 19, 1959.[8]

Staff integration, as well as employing more African Americans, slowly proceeded over the next decade. In their efforts to integrate the library staff at the central library between 1966 and 1968 service staff were promoted to library clerk positions. By 1968, African Americans constituted 18 percent of APL employees.[9] Regarding professional librarians, several were hired during the period: reference librarians, children's library coordinator, head of the mobile unit, and head of African American collection.

The next several years the library made significant advances in diversifying its workforce. The influx of African American librarians throughout the library system began in the early 1970s. Ella Yates was hired in 1972 as branch services administrator, promoted to deputy director, and in 1976 became the first African American library director. As racial transition occurred through the library system, it was during the administrations of Carlton Rochelle (1968-1976) and Ella Yates (1976-1981) that African Americans rose to powerful administrative positions. Today, the Atlanta Public Library, presently named Fulton County Library System, has the second African American woman its helm.

## REFLECTIONS ON MY CAREER IN ATLANTA PUBLIC LIBRARY SCHOOL EDUCATION

From 1970 to 1972, I was Carnegie Scholar at the University of Illinois. My classmates included Samuel Morrison, Bobby Player, Edith Fisher, Sylvia Moses, Jewel Armstrong Player, and Gwendolyn Weaver. Dr. Nicole Cooke recounts the journey of our group: "During the late 1960s and early 1970s the University of Illinois took many risks in an effort to diversify the ranks of their student body. One such initiative was the Carnegie Scholars experiment; thirty minority students were recruited to the Graduate School of Library Science, twenty-nine graduated, and many went on to become leaders in their profession."[10]

## CAREER REFLECTIONS

I knew I wanted to work in Atlanta. I had a husband prospect and family support awaiting me there. At the time I applied for employment, there were no vacancies. Since I had planned to spend my 1971 Thanksgiving holiday in Atlanta, my advisor, Dr. Terrence Crowley, suggested I call and make an appointment for an interview. I followed through, was granted an interview, and was offered a job during the Christmas holidays.

In February 1972, I began my career in the Atlanta Public Library as interim branch manager covering a maternity leave at the West Hunter Library. Upon the return of the branch manager, I requested to stay as the children's librarian since there was only one professional librarian at the branch. My request was denied, and I was assigned to a branch where I was the fourth professional. Although my daily tasks were those of a library clerk, I welcomed an opportunity to conduct school visits to the neighborhood high school because the white YA librarian was afraid to visit a Black school. Later, I requested a meeting with the library director to discuss my future with the library system. Shortly after the meeting I was assigned to the South Branch. This move was not based on my innate ability, but I was replacing a librarian after a tragic incident, unbeknownst to me. It was my fail-or-succeed moment.

The majority of my career, I managed numerous branch libraries in African American communities executing successful community initiatives that resulted in new services and increased public awareness and launching aggressive outreach and community engagement programs revitalizing library service in communities of color. I improved operating systems, resulting in more efficient operations, improved staff morale, and enhanced customer service. I built community-relevant collections and introduced young people to African American literature. Other work highlights included:

1972-1975    Manager, South Branch
The implementation site for a US Department of Education grant that developed a "Neighborhood Information Center" providing information referral to critical community services, also provided free notary and voter registration services.

1975-1981    Manager, Georgia-Hill Branch

I opened the first branch of APL to be in the neighborhood community center housing various public and private agencies that provided services ranging from day care to youth and social services program engaging in community outreach programs.

### Manager, West Hunter Branch: 1981-1986

When I returned to the historic West Hunter Branch, the library program was failing. From 1949 to 1959, the branch had served as the only branch Black people could use. I welcomed the opportunity to bring this branch back to its grandeur, launching an aggressive outreach program revitalizing the library and increasing usage. I reinvigorated public interest by planning a thirty-fifth anniversary celebration. I was awarded a grant to develop a "Black Image in Children's Book Collection" that was unveiled at the celebration.

### Manager, Community Outreach Services: 1986-1995

I designed, developed, implemented, and directed the library system's outreach program—a department mandated by a $35 million bond referendum designed to reach special populations not served through traditional branch libraries, including public housing residents, geographically isolated, senior citizens, and "at-risk" preschoolers. I conceptualized and coordinated Senior Stop and Story Caravan, programs designed to provide books and programs for senior citizens and "at-risk" preschoolers. I directed the move-in and organized a unit at headquarters that served as a resource and training center.

I staffed the start-up of this outreach department from an initial staff of two at inception to a team of forty within the second year of operation. I determined staffing requirements and qualifications; developed job descriptions; conducted interviews; selected employees; hired, trained, and directed staff; as well as built a productive, responsive, and dedicated team.

I reestablished the bookmobile program after an eleven-year absence, including developing vehicle specifications, service criteria, stop selection, and scheduling.

I administered the opening of six libraries in public housing communities, including site selection, facility design, move-in coordination, and opening day collections.

### Branch Manager East Point Branch: 1995-2000

I led the transition of an independent library into the Atlanta Library System, including establishing timelines, conducting task analysis, and designing an effective library program, doubling usage in the first six months of operation.

I served as project manager in all aspects of the new East Point Library—facility design, layout, materials collections, staff recruitment, promotions, and grand opening coordination.

### Deputy Director: 2000-2003

I promoted library services, functioned as a goodwill ambassador, successfully encouraged use of library services, and interacted with government officials to increase library awareness.

I collaborated with the library director in planning and directing all major activities and functions of an urban library system with a four-hundred-plus staff and a $30 million budget. I unveiled a new interior design and look for the library system's Central Library, providing a more attractive and welcoming environment for the staff and public. I facilitated the development of a more innovative service-delivery model at the library system's Central Library. User feedback was extremely positive and overall usage greatly increased.

I administered the planning of new libraries, including community needs assessment, consultation with architects and building construction managers, developing building programs and timelines, and planning ground-breaking and opening day ceremonies.

### CHALLENGES OF BEING AN AFRICAN AMERICAN LIBRARIAN

Once the APL integrated in the mid-twentieth century, racial tensions among library staff members became especially pronounced as Black women challenged white privilege by attempting to climb the administrative hierarchy and make their voices more widely heard.[11]

At some point between 1974 and 1980, the APL's African American employees formed a caucus to address perceived discrimination. Here are a few of our triumphs:

1. Professional Children's Librarians in Libraries Serving Black Communities

    During the early 1970s, the staffing patterns in Atlanta Public were structured for inequitable access. There were noteworthy differences—the branches on the south side serving Black communities had one professional librarian while on the northside branches serving white communities had multiple librarians. All the branches on the northside had dedicated children's librarians. Black branch managers protested this obvious gap in service delivery to children on the south side. We emphasized the importance of having a full-time children's librarian at our branches. As a result, tremendous research, and justification. A celebrated victory for Black librarianship was the hiring of seven energetic children's librarians. The impact of hiring these librarians cannot be overstated. They helped ignite an enthusiasm for reading, introduced African American literature, and facilitated enrichment programs that would have positive effects for decades.

2. Pay Equity

    Pay inequity remains a persistent and pervasive problem in the library profession. African Americans have a long history of fighting for pay equity. In the Atlanta Public Library, a difference in pay existed between African American librarians and their white counterparts. In 1975, when Atlanta considered classifying the APL's workers as civil service, African Americans made up 44 percent of the library's workforce. Still, as Emma Darnell, Atlanta commissioner of administrative services, pointed out, most of Atlanta's Black library workers were in the lowest pay brackets. Only 17 percent of Black library employees were in the higher pay ranges.[12] After much protest, it was through a pay-and-class study conducted by an independent consultant that brought some parity in pay for African American librarians and staff.

3. Equitable Performance Standards

    During the early twentieth century, Atlanta, like other public libraries, tended to evaluate their activities entirely by circulation statistics, program attendance, and visits. While these indicators demonstrate a certain level of activity, they do little to express the true value of the library experience. As racial transition rapidly occurred in Atlanta neighborhoods, Black branch managers had to identify clear measures to assess their impact and effectiveness on their library users. Branches now open to Black citizens were not available to them in the past. We had to eliminate the stigma of nonlibrary use, which required aggressive outreach and community engagement. These efforts had to be included in our measure of success. Over time, following constant resistance and vigorous debate, we were able to validate our success as outreach data was added to performance measures.

**LOOK TO THE FUTURE!**

Black librarianship has steadily decreased. Just over 82 percent of librarians identified as white in 2022. Library technicians and assistants were slightly more diverse. Among library assistants, 77 percent identified as white in 2022. In 2022, only 4.3 percent of librarians identified as Black or African American, a steep decline from 9.5 percent in 2020.[13]

We cannot be dismayed. We must be steadfast and resilient just as those brave African American librarians who came before us. We must stand up and fight for the right of African American literature to be freely and abundantly available.

I close with words of the first African American and woman Librarian of Congress: "This is a profession that is dedicated to providing accurate information and checking sources," says Hayden, who also wants to eliminate the stereotype of the meek librarian. "Our superpower, if you will, is empowering others."[14]

**NOTES**

1. "Civil Rights Movement," Wikipedia, The Free Encyclopedia, June 29, 2023, https://en.wikipedia.org/wiki/Civil_rights_movement.
2. "Martin Luther King Jr/About Dr. Martin Luther King, Jr.," The King Center, http://www.thekingcenter.org/about martinlutherkingjr.
3. "Atlanta Student Movement," City of Atlanta, https://www.atlantaga.gov/visitors/history/atlanta-student-movement.
4. "Auburn Avenue Research Library: History," Fulton County Library System, https://www.fulcolibrary.org/auburn-avenue-research-library/aarl-history/.
5. Annie McPheeters, *Library Service in Black and White: Some Personal Recollections, 1921-1980* (Metuchen, NJ: 1988).
6. Kerrie Williams, "Annie L. McPheeters," *New Georgia Encyclopedia*, https://www.georgiaencyclopedia.org/articles/education/annie-l-mcpheeters-1908-1994.
7. Akilah Nosakhere and Sharon Robinson, "Library Service for African Americans in Georgia: A Legacy of Learning and Leadership in Atlanta," *Georgia Library Quarterly*, 35, no. 2 (1998): 9-12, http://www.libsci.sc.edu/histories/georgia/statehistory/Service_For_African_Americans.pdf.
8. Annie McPheeters, *Library Service in Black and White*.
9. Amato Nocero, "Dallas Hanbury. *The Development of Southern Public Libraries and the African American Quest for Library Access, 1898-1963*," *The American Historical Review*, 127 (2022): 1520-21.
10. Nicole Cooke, "The GSLS Carnegie Scholars: Guests in Someone Else's House," *Libraries: Culture, History, and Society*, 1, no. 1 (2017): 46-71.
11. Dallas Hanbury, *The Development of Southern Public Libraries and the African American Quest for Library Access, 1898-1963* (Lanham, MD: Lexington Books, 2020).
12. Ibid.
13. "Library Professionals: Facts, Figures, and Union Membership," Department for Professional Employees, AFL-CIO, 2023, https://www.dpeaflcio.org/factsheets/library-professionals-facts-and-figures.
14. Marva Hinton, "Black Librarianship: Stories of Impact and Connection," *School Library Journal*, February 2, 2023, https://www.slj.com/story/Black-Librarianship-Stories-of-Impact-and-Connection.

**WORKS CITED**

"Atlanta Student Movement." City of Atlanta. https://www.atlantaga.gov/visitors/history/atlanta-student-movement.

"Auburn Avenue Research Library: History." Fulton County Library System. https://www.fulcolibrary.org/auburn-avenue-research-library/aarl-history/.

"Civil Rights Movement." Wikipedia: The Free Encyclopedia, June 29, 2023. https://en.wikipedia.org/wiki/Civil_rights_movement.

Cooke, Nicole. "The GSLS Carnegie Scholars: Guests in Someone Else's House." *Libraries: Culture, History, and Society*, 1, no. 1 (2017): 46-71.

Hanbury, Dallas. *The Development of Southern Public Libraries and the African American Quest for Library Access, 1898-1963*. Lanham, MD: Lexington Books, 2020.

Hinton, Marva. "Black Librarianship: Stories of Impact and Connection." *School Library Journal*, February 2, 2023. https://www.slj.com/story/Black-Librarianship-Stories-of-Impact-and-Connection.

"Library Professionals: Facts, Figures, and Union Membership." Department for Professional Employees, AFL-CIO, 2023. https://www.dpeaflcio.org/factsheets/library-professionals-facts-and-figures.

McPheeters, Annie. *Library Service in Black and White: Some Personal Recollections, 1921-1980*. Metuchen, NJ: Scarecrow Press, 1988.

"Martin Luther King Jr/About Dr. Martin Luther King, Jr." The King Center. https://thekingcenter.org/about-tkc/martin-luther-king-jr/.

Nocero, Amato. "Dallas Hanbury. *The Development of Southern Public Libraries and the African American Quest for Library Access, 1898-1963*." *The American Historical Review*, 127 (2022): 1520-21.

Nosakhere, Akilah and Sharon Robinson. "Library Service for African Americans in Georgia: A Legacy of Learning and Leadership in Atlanta." *Georgia Library Quarterly*, 35, no. 2 (1998): 9-12. http://www.libsci.sc.edu/histories/georgia/statehistory/Service_For_African_Americans.pdf.

Williams, Kerrie. "Annie L. McPheeters." *New Georgia Encyclopedia*. https://www.georgiaencyclopedia.org/articles/education/annie-l-mcpheeters-1908-1994.

# Chapter 29
# Reflections, Remembrances, and Ramblings

Sandy Bright

Many professionals assert that they've had a wonderful career—the best. For me that is absolutely the truth! My awesome experiences cannot be matched by many. I've had unprecedented opportunities and exposure to mentors and advisors who were masterful. For the most part, I never thought of the positions I held or my work as "my dream job!" Looking back over the years at the big picture, I just didn't realize it. My career dreams surely did come true. I went from being a junior high school student, who when my class visited the school library was allowed to approach the shelves or handle any of the books on display. The librarian selected and placed four books in the center of each table before we entered the library. Those were the only books we had to choose from during our class visits. This happened on a weekly basis. The librarian didn't know it, but I was already a library user. I visited the Eastern Parkway Branch of Brooklyn Public Library regularly. There I was able to browse library shelves and displays and choose which books I wanted to borrow, take home, and read!

Now, picture this, that junior high schooler, years later, became the director of the Office of School Library Services for the New York City Department of Education. Who could have predicted this? I knew at thirteen years old I wanted to be a school librarian. I could do the job much better. I felt I was being shortchanged, discriminated against, and racially profiled. I knew those feelings; I just didn't have the proper words to describe it at the time. Just to backtrack a little, I was so young when Mom wasn't home to take me to the library on Eastern Parkway. I had to promise to go down the subway steps to cross the parkway underground and pass the subway token booth. I wasn't allowed to cross Eastern Parkway's four lanes of traffic in each direction. My mom was very strict about that promise. I don't remember having a librarian while in elementary school, but I do remember there was a library. I remember it was there, that I went to my first book fair. I remember to this day one of my first book purchases there, *Toby Tyler or Ten Weeks with the Circus*. Strange the things we remember!

My high school had a fantastic library and three very good librarians. One in particular became my first mentor. And she wrote me my first letter of reference ever! I was a high school senior. I worked on the high school library squad for years. It was my first taste of clerical library work. I loved my tasks. I witnessed library professionals modeling behaviors that would follow me throughout my library career: how to conduct a reference interview, plan author studies, and provide reading guidance. They were into service! I was a reader at an early age, and I was the daughter of readers. My father read paperback westerns by Louis L'Amour. And my mother read mysteries and romance novels.

So many memories of my early and humble librarianship interests. On to college where I continued student work in the college library. It was one of my early part-time positions. After undergraduate school it was on to library school where my concentration was school librarianship. My coursework was illuminating with the history and philosophy of librarians and librarianship, but I didn't see much that reflected my own culture and experience. Multicultural programming and collection development were in their infancy. In addition, there was very little study of the application of technology, including computers, for information. This was a new world to be discussed and explored. I graduated with an MLS degree: a master's in library service. The word "service" was the key word as we were sent out into the world.

My first professional school library media specialist position was at PS 21, in Bedford-Stuyvesant, Brooklyn. There I was supervised by a strong educational leader who was multiculturally centered in her demands for excellence. The students were to be educated in an historical context of Black success. I was finally seeing myself in the student body, the staff, and the community. Approaches to teaching reflected authentic awareness of history. I was encouraged to fully develop the library's collection to reflect the ethnicity of the students, staff, and surrounding community. As a Black school library media specialist, I finally felt at home professionally. Ready to grow and be a role model for others. My professional identity was growing too.

All of my early history being covered, forty-seven years later and fully retired, here are my thoughts about how to define librarians and librarianship. The most basic definition is trained professionals providing arrangement and access to materials and information, with equal access and free of cost. For Black library professionals this presents multilevel challenges. To list just a few challenges, think about the following: The first challenge is that there is such a small number of Black librarians. Statistics say less than 7 percent of library professionals in the United States are Black. The second challenge is the issue of appropriate materials. The third challenge is the technology and tech training for the communities to be served. The fourth challenge is understanding what patrons expect from libraries. The greatest challenge is free and equal access to collections without barriers.

For current and retired Black librarians the challenges continue. I was once told that each of us should work toward attracting at least two new people into the profession of librarianship. Recruitment is a key activity for the future: locally and nationally. You should be responsible to replicate yourself twice. I've successfully encouraged at least twelve people to join the profession.

For the twenty-first century, experienced Black librarians in all types of libraries are vital to the future of the profession. If you're still working you should be modeling the possibilities of what the profession has to offer. Talk about how the individual interests may be broadened by library work. Talk about the different types of libraries: school libraries, public libraries, academic libraries, and the many special libraries. Many have a narrow view of what a librarian does. We need to show the many possibilities of joining one's interest with library work and the profession of librarianship as a career goal.

We should also remember that archivists go to library school. Sometimes we meet someone looking for a career that speaks to their special interests in local or world history, science, art, music, or other special subjects for collections.

My mentors, advisors, and cheerleaders over the years were strong leaders who didn't take any prisoners. They were fearless, opinionated, and well-versed in what being a true professional would look like. They are listed here in alphabetical order because it would take up too much space to list the many areas of their wisdom and experience:

Ms. Geraldine Clark
Dr. Jean Coleman
Dr. Phyllis Fisher
Mercedes Rowe
Dr. Adelaide Sanford
Ms. Aletta Seales
Dr. Lucille C. Thomas

The impact of technology and the costs of postgraduate education are challenges for students who may be considering library studies. As working and retired Black librarians we may be conduits to fellowships, grants, scholarships, and other financial incentives for study. And we may also assist in finding internships for students to get a look at librarianship in working situations that are real and significant. Internships can be invaluable experiences toward a professional career. Whether paid or unpaid, internships are an awesome experience in the real world of work.

My mentors encouraged me in many ways. Black librarians should remember four things in particular that have stayed with me over the years:

1. Plan ahead.
2. Continue to study.
3. Don't expect thanks for doing your job.
4. Look for the "JOY."

# Part VII
# GLOBAL ISSUES IN LIBRARIES

# Chapter 30

# Unlocking Libraries' Potential to Improve the Lives and Prospects of the Members of Our Communities

Loida Garcia-Febo

Libraries are strengthening the backbone of our societies and contributing to the social and cultural capital of nations through the work they do daily providing information in different formats. In this chapter, we will learn about the United Nations (UN) sustainable development goals (SDGs) and how all types of libraries can unlock their potential to serve communities deeply affected by different socioeconomic aspects. The chapter includes background of the SDGs, work by library associations, examples of library programs, triumphs and challenges, areas in need of improvement, and closes with a call to librarians to contribute to development.

## UNITED NATIONS SUSTAINABLE DEVELOPMENT GOALS BACKGROUND

UN SDGs were adopted in 2015 by all the United Nations Member States. Governments from countries in all regions of the world use SDGs to guide their development efforts and infrastructure strategies during the period 2016–2030.

SDGs built on the Millennium Development Goals were adopted by the UN in 2000 to reduce extreme poverty by 2015.[1] SDGs were crafted by a UN working group established in 2013. This group had participation from civil society organizations including the International Federation of Library Associations and Institutions (IFLA). After years of negotiation between the UN member states, SDGs were adopted during the UN General Assembly in September 2015. The UN declared the seventeen SDGs to be the 2030 agenda for the development of the world and the life on land and life below water. They include:

Goal 1: No Poverty
Goal 2: Zero Hunger
Goal 3: Good Health and Well-being
Goal 4: Quality Education
Goal 5: Gender Equality
Goal 6: Clean Water and Sanitation
Goal 7: Affordable and Clean Energy
Goal 8: Decent Work and Economic Growth
Goal 9: Industry, Innovation, and Infrastructure
Goal 10: Reduced Inequalities
Goal 11: Sustainable Cities and Communities
Goal 12: Responsible Consumption and Production
Goal 13: Climate Action
Goal 14: Life below Water
Goal 15: Life on Land
Goal 16: Peace, Justice, and Strong Institutions
Goal 17: Partnerships for the Goals

## LIBRARY ASSOCIATIONS AND UN SDGS

IFLA has led library advocacy at the UN and has encouraged its members to advocate for libraries to be included in the development plans of their countries. The American Library Association (ALA) has joined these efforts.

## INTERNATIONAL FEDERATION OF LIBRARY ASSOCIATIONS AND INSTITUTIONS

IFLA started advocating on behalf of libraries at the United Nations in 2014[2] presenting a joint event with the United Nations Development Programme entitled "Dialogue on Data and Accountability for the Post-2015 Development Agenda" to promote access to information provided by libraries.[3] This was the first event hosted by IFLA at the UN. Loida Garcia-Febo, IFLA governing board member at the time, represented IFLA speaking about "Closing the Information Gap in the Post-2015 Framework: Libraries as Champions of the Data Revolution."[4]

The UN features IFLA's commitment to work with its members to support implementation of SDGs in their countries on one of its webpages.[5] IFLA often organizes workshops to help library associations understand the importance of SDGs and how libraries are contributing to development.

The *IFLA Toolkit: Libraries, Development and the United Nations 2030 Agenda* is a resource to help library associations to advocate for access to information inclusion on their country's development agenda.[6]

IFLA's Library Map of the World (LMW) is a database where library associations can enter stories to show how libraries are supporting development efforts in their countries, advocate for libraries, and partner with local governments and organizations.[7] Recent IFLA work at the UN includes presenting programs at the High-Level Political Forum (HLPF) on Sustainable Development in New York in July 2022. ALA past presidents and members of IFLA committees, Loida Garcia-Febo and Julius C. Jefferson, were part of a delegation from IFLA speaking at programs and meeting with UN members to share how libraries are already supporting development.[8]

The Management of Library Associations Section (MLAS) of IFLA developed a webinar series to support efforts from library associations in different regions of the world. The series, "Sustainable Development Goals and Library Associations," is presented in collaboration with IFLA's Regional Divisions, the New Professionals Special Interest Group, and the Environment, Sustainability and Libraries Section.[9] The first webinar on March 6, 2023, featured the North American region. MLAS presented events with other regions in 2023.

**AMERICAN LIBRARY ASSOCIATION**

The ALA Task Force on the 2030 United Nations Sustainable Development Goals was established as part of ALA past president Julius C. Jefferson's presidential initiatives. The Task Force, chaired by Loida Garcia-Febo, worked during the term of 2020–2021 developing a multiyear strategic plan to increase participation by libraries in efforts to achieve the goals.[10] The members of the Task Force developed free downloadable bookmarks, charts, and templates for all types of libraries to show how they support the goals. The Task Force produced webinars to provide information about the SDGs and how libraries can support development in their communities. Some webinars were presented in collaboration with international library associations such as the German Library Association and the Philippines Library Association. The recordings of the webinars are available on the Task Force webpage on the ALA website.[11]

The strategic plan crafted by the Task Force was sent to the ALA executive board. As a result, in January 2023, ALA established the ALA International Relations Committee's United Nations Sustainable Development Goals Subcommittee, chaired by Loida Garcia-Febo. The subcommittee charge is to "collaborate with ALA divisions, round tables, committees and membership, and US library associations in the implementation of the multi-year strategic plan developed by the ALA UN 2030 SDG Task Force to increase participation by libraries in efforts to achieve the Goals."[12]

To date, the subcommittee has collaborated consulting on speakers for an event by the Public Library Association entitled "Capturing Library Contributions to Sustainable Development Goals with Project Outcome."[13]

The chair of the subcommittee was invited to moderate the panel "Reforming Scientific Publishing" during the 3rd Open Science Conference by the United Nations Dag Hammarskjöld Library in New York.[14]

Future plans include presenting a poster during the ALA ODLOS Diversity Fair at the ALA 2023 Annual Conference and following on IFLA steps, applying for consultative status to the UN Economic and Social Council.

**UNLOCKING LIBRARIES' POTENTIAL**

The *Sustainable Development Report 2022* indicates that a confluence of various worldwide crises such as the pandemic, wars, and financial instability have resulted in no progress across the seventeen SDGs.[15] Five SDGs in which libraries serving communities deeply affected by different socioeconomic aspects traditionally focus are: Goal 1, No Poverty; Goal 2, Zero Hunger; Goal 3, Good Health and Well-being; Goal 8, Decent Work and Economic Growth; and Goal 10, Reduced inequalities. Services developed by libraries, per these five goals, support development in communities served by the libraries. Examples of services that can be adapted by libraries include:

Goal 1—Zero Poverty: Los Angeles Public Library in California provides a Career Online High School program to enable adults to earn a free accredited high school diploma that could lead to higher paying jobs.[16]

Goal 2—Zero Hunger: Belk Library's Food Pantry located in the Appalachian State University Library in North Carolina provides a food hub open during the day and night for students in need.[17]

Goal 3—Good Health and Well-being: The New York Public Library created a web page dedicated to providing information about COVID-19, where to get vaccinated, free tests for at-home testing, community resources, and information about city services.[18]

Goal 8—Decent Work and Economic Growth: Denver Public Library provides a myriad of services for entrepreneurs and those seeking to start their own business including a special library card for groups or businesses to be used for business purposes and renewed every four years. The library's Bizboost is a program for these individuals to make an appointment with a reference librarian to find information to support their business or marketing plan.[19]

Goal 10—Reduced Inequalities: The Jefferson Academy Library, part of the District of Columbia Public Schools, provides students with reading experiences including print, e-books, and digital resources. The library participates of efforts to promote reading such as National Read a Book Week. Additionally, the library designs its own programs to motivate students to read with the creation of videos and reader's moments and celebrates reading about holidays and monthly designations such as Women's Month.[20]

## LIBRARIES AND SDGS IN DIFFERENT REGIONS OF THE WORLD

Libraries worldwide are developing programs and services that support development. As libraries in the United States serve populations coming from different countries, it is valuable to be informed about library services in different regions of the world. For purposes of this chapter, the classification of regions used by IFLA is used to share examples:

Africa: The Laterbiokorshie Library in Ghana carried out a campaign to provide "access to sexual and reproductive health education in the library to curb teen pregnancy." The first time it conducted the initiative, a total of two thousand school-aged children benefited. The project continues with monthly events. The library partnered with the Ghanian Ministry of Education and Health, members of Parliament, Planned Parenthood of Ghana (PPAG), the Directorate of Public Health, Mamprobi Polyclinic, Ghana Education Services, churches, and nongovernmental organizations. This is an example of an SDG story in the IFLA LMW.[21]

Asia and Oceania: My Tree House is a green library for kids inside the National Library of Singapore. The goal of the library, built with a sustainable efficient and eco-friendly system, is to teach about green values and caring for the environment. To this effect, library collections, storytelling, and varied programming feature themes of sustainability for the little ones. The library bookmobile also features these themes when carrying out outreach in communities in Singapore.[22]

Europe: Pozega Public Library in Serbia, in collaboration with the school Gymnasium Sveti Sava, hosts the SDGs Book Club Serbia to promote SDGs and improve the reading skills of high school students. The students create lists of books on hunger and poverty, prepare summaries of the books they read and translate them into the languages taught in school, and give presentations to other students.[23]

Latin America and the Caribbean: BibliotStreet is an outreach project from Chile designed by Antofagasta Health Services in partnership with the Antofagasta Regional Library and the VIVA Library to help the homeless. The five-month program targets at-risk alcohol and drug users to bring them back to health networks, employment, and to expand their opportunities within the community. Participants receive digital literacy classes, reading and writing workshops, reflective analysis, and storytelling. At the conclusion of the program participants can share their stories with their community. This is another example of an SDG story in the IFLA LMW.[24]

## TRIUMPHS AND CHALLENGES

Triumphs include featuring "access to information," a core activity of librarianship as part of Goal 16 Peace, Justice, and Strong Institutions, specifically on Target 16.10: "Ensure public access to information and protect fundamental freedoms, in accordance with national legislation and international agreements." It represents the first time a phrase conveying libraries is included in such a document by the UN.[25]

Another notable achievement, per IFLA's Library Map of the World, is that many librarians are empowered to reach their local governments to advocate for libraries sharing facts anchored on SDGs about how libraries are bettering education and lifelong learning in communities.

Unfortunately, halfway into the 2030 Agenda, development has not progressed as expected due to the pandemic and other ongoing crises. Additionally, efforts by libraries to support development are not always documented and libraries are forced to re-create the proverbial wheel again and again.

Other challenges, anecdotally gathered, include politician's turnover, libraries' budgetary constraints, and notions that countries are already developed and do not need to join UN SDGs.

However, these challenges represent an opportunity for libraries to establish themselves as development accelerators, and partner with other agencies and organizations to design services to help move forward development in their communities.

### How Can We All Contribute?

Everyone can contribute from where they are. First, it is key for librarians to understand what SDGs are. Additionally, libraries are already contributing to development with programs and services provided to promote reading, critical thinking, and research. Then, it is crucial for librarians to learn what the needs of the communities served are to meet them.

It is imperative that libraries either create or increase services to support development in the communities they serve at academic, public, school, or any other type of libraries. As development impacts all areas of life on land and life under water including human lives, it concerns all types of libraries.

The strategy should be long term. Don't leave anyone behind. We must promote policy transformation. Collaborate with all sectors, not just in our library ecosystem. Embrace efforts as multidimensional processes. Show the value of our proposals: the value of libraries.

Everyone deserves basic needs contemplated in SDGs. Libraries are essential for development; they are key to social cohesion. We can all contribute to the society we deserve.

### NOTES

1. "The 17 Goals," United Nations, https://sdgs.un.org/goals.
2. "IFLA Annual Report 2014," IFLA, https://www.ifla.org/wp-content/uploads/2019/05/assets/hq/annual-reports/2014.pdf.
3. "Governance, Access to Information on the Agenda at Open Working Group 8," IFLA, February 12, 2014, https://www

4. "Closing the Information Gap in the Post-2015 Framework: Libraries as Champions of the Data Revolution," IFLA, 2014, https://www.ifla.org/wp-content/uploads/2019/05/assets/hq/topics/libraries-development/documents/bridgingtheinformationgap_final.pdf.
5. "Contribution of Libraries to the SDGs," United Nations, March 2023, https://sdgs.un.org/partnerships/contribution-libraries-sdgs.
6. "Toolkit: Libraries, Development and the United Nations 2030 Agenda," IFLA, March 2021, https://www.ifla.org/wp-content/uploads/files/assets/hq/topics/libraries-development/documents/libraries-un-2030-agenda-toolkit-2017.pdf.
7. "Library Map of the World," IFLA, https://librarymap.ifla.org/map.
8. "UN High Level Political Forum 2022," IFLA, 2022, https://hlpf.un.org/2022.
9. Loida Garcia-Febo, "IFLA MLAS + Regions: Supporting Strong Library Associations," IFLA, March 16, 2023, https://www.ifla.org/news/ifla-mlas-regions-supporting-strong-library-associations/.
10. Robin Kear and Loida Garcia-Febo, "ALA UN 2030 Sustainable Development Goals Task Force," *International Journal of Librarianship*, 5, no. 2 (2020): 94-97, https://doi.org/10.23974/ijol.2020.vol5.2.173.
11. "ALA Task Force on United Nations 2030 Sustainable Development Goals." About ALA, June 18, 2021, https://www.ala.org/aboutala/ala-task-force-united-nations-2030-sustainable-development-goals.
12. "IRC UN Sustainable Development Goals Subcommittee," About ALA, March 7, 2023, https://www.ala.org/aboutala/irc-un-sustainable-development-goals-subcommittee.
13. "Capturing Library Contributions to Sustainable Development Goals with Project Outcome," Public Library Association (PLA), March 15, 2023, https://www.ala.org/pla/education/onlinelearning/webinars/sustainable.
14. "Open Science Conference 2023," United Nations, February 2023, https://www.un.org/en/library/OS23.
15. *The Sustainable Development Goals Report 2022*, United Nations, July 7, 2022, https://unstats.un.org/sdgs/report/2022/.
16. "Career Online High School," Los Angeles Public Library, https://www.lapl.org/diploma.
17. "Food Pantry," Appalachian State University, October 12, 2022, https://library.appstate.edu/services-search/food-pantry.
18. "COVID-19 Vaccine Resources," The New York Public Library, https://www.nypl.org/about/remote-resources/community-resources/covid-19-vaccine-resources.
19. "Colorado Small Business Resources," Denver Public Library, https://www.denverlibrary.org/content/small-business.
20. Jefferson Academy Library, March 2, 2023, https://www.smore.com/xj2m7-jefferson-academy-library.
21. "Access to Sexual and Reproductive Health Education in the Library to Curb Teenage Pregnancy," IFLA Library Map of the World, March 25, 2019, https://librarymap.ifla.org/stories/Ghana/ACCESS-TO-SEXUAL-AND-REPRODUCTIVE-HEALTH-EDUCATION-IN-THE-LIBRARY-TO-CURB-TEENAGE-PREGNANCY/130.
22. "My Tree House Kids Library—City Developments Limited," National Library Board Singapore, https://www.nlb.gov.sg/main/partner-us/give-to-us/Highlights/my-tree-house.
23. Yinuo Chen, "SDG Book Club Serbia at Pozega," United Nations, May 5, 2020, https://www.un.org/sustainabledevelopment/blog/2019/12/sdg-book-club-serbia-at-pozega/.
24. "Bibliostreet Programme Helps to Integrate People Experiencing Homelessness," IFLA Library Map of the World, April 12, 2019, https://librarymap.ifla.org/stories/Chile/BIBLIOSTREET-PROGRAMME-HELPS-TO-INTEGRATE-PEOPLE-EXPERIENCING-HOMELESSNESS-/132.
25. "Goal 16," United Nations, https://sdgs.un.org/goals/goal16.

## WORKS CITED

"Access to Sexual and Reproductive Health Education in the Library to Curb Teenage Pregnancy." IFLA Library Map of the World, March 25, 2019. https://librarymap.ifla.org/stories/Ghana/ACCESS-TO-SEXUAL-AND-REPRODUCTIVE-HEALTH-EDUCATION-IN-THE-LIBRARY-TO-CURB-TEENAGE-PREGNANCY/130.

"ALA Task Force on United Nations 2030 Sustainable Development Goals." About ALA, June 18, 2021. https://www.ala.org/aboutala/ala-task-force-united-nations-2030-sustainable-development-goals.

"Bibliostreet Programme Helps to Integrate People Experiencing Homelessness." IFLA Library Map of the World, April 12, 2019. https://librarymap.ifla.org/stories/Chile/BIBLIOSTREET-PROGRAMME-HELPS-TO-INTEGRATE-PEOPLE-EXPERIENCING-HOMELESSNESS-/132.

"Capturing Library Contributions to Sustainable Development Goals with Project Outcome." Public Library Association (PLA), March 15, 2023. https://www.ala.org/pla/education/onlinelearning/webinars/sustainable.

"Career Online High School." Los Angeles Public Library. https://www.lapl.org/diploma.

Chen, Yinuo. "SDG Book Club Serbia at Pozega." United Nations, May 5, 2020. https://www.un.org/sustainabledevelopment/blog/2019/12/sdg-book-club-serbia-at-pozega/.

"Closing the Information Gap in the Post-2015 Framework: Libraries as Champions of the Data Revolution." IFLA, 2014. https://www.ifla.org/wp-content/uploads/2019/05/assets/hq/topics/libraries-development/documents/bridgingtheinformationgap_final.pdf.

"Colorado Small Business Resources." Denver Public Library. https://www.denverlibrary.org/content/small-business.

"Contribution of Libraries to the SDGs." United Nations, March 2023. https://sdgs.un.org/partnerships/contribution-libraries-sdgs.

"COVID-19 Vaccine Resources." The New York Public Library. https://www.nypl.org/about/remote-resources/community-resources/covid-19-vaccine-resources.

"Food Pantry." Appalachian State University, October 12, 2022. https://library.appstate.edu/services-search/food-pantry.

Garcia-Febo, Loida. "IFLA MLAS + Regions: Supporting Strong Library Associations." IFLA, March 16, 2023. https://www.ifla.org/news/ifla-mlas-regions-supporting-strong-library-associations/

"Goal 16." United Nations. https://sdgs.un.org/goals/goal16.

"Governance, Access to Information on the Agenda at Open Working Group 8." IFLA, February 12, 2014. https://www.ifla.org/news/governance-access-to-information-on-the-agenda-at-open-working-group-8.

"IFLA Annual Report 2014." IFLA. https://www.ifla.org/wp-content/uploads/2019/05/assets/hq/annual-reports/2014.pdf.

"IRC UN Sustainable Development Goals Subcommittee." About ALA, March 7, 2023. https://www.ala.org/aboutala/irc-un-sustainable-development-goals-subcommittee.

Jefferson Academy Library. March 2, 2023. https://www.smore.com/xj2m7-jefferson-academy-library.

Kear, Robin, and Loida Garcia-Febo. "ALA UN 2030 Sustainable Development Goals Task Force." *International Journal of Librarianship*, 5, no. 2 (2020): 94–97. https://doi.org/10.23974/ijol.2020.vol5.2.173.

"Library Map of the World." IFLA. https://librarymap.ifla.org/map.

"My Tree House Kids Library—City Developments Limited." National Library Board Singapore. https://www.nlb.gov.sg/main/partner-us/give-to-us/Highlights/my-tree-house.

"Open Science Conference 2023." United Nations, February 2023. https://www.un.org/en/library/OS23.

"The 17 Goals." United Nations. https://sdgs.un.org/goals.

*The Sustainable Development Goals Report 2022*. United Nations, July 7, 2022. https://unstats.un.org/sdgs/report/2022/.

"Toolkit: Libraries, Development and the United Nations 2030 Agenda." IFLA, March 2021. https://www.ifla.org/wp-content/uploads/files/assets/hq/topics/libraries-development/documents/libraries-un-2030-agenda-toolkit-2017.pdf.

"UN High Level Political Forum 2022." IFLA, 2022. https://hlpf.un.org/2022.

# Chapter 31
# Brazilian Black Librarianship

PATHS, STRUGGLES, AND RESISTANCE

Franciéle Carneiro Garcês-da-Silva[1]

(Re)existing and not giving up in a country where Black people are placed at the bottom of Brazilian society is a constant challenge. The struggle is against the hegemonic, colonial, capitalist, patriarchal, and racialized system that exists, which has relegated (and still relegates) Black people to the fallacious narrative of being "people without knowledge."

My understanding is that this narrative is present in our personal, interpersonal, work, and intellectual and scientific production relationships, and that it gained strength during the Bolsonaro government: a government of science denial, dissemination of fake news, genocide of Black and Indigenous people. This compelled me, as a Black librarian and researcher, to think and seek ways that we can choose to assist our society in being committed to social, racial, gender, informational, and epistemic justice[2] and to highlight plural knowledge and diverse epistemes, seeking to reduce inequalities and promote equitable opportunities for all people. Among the paths to transform this system, and as a Black woman in the world, I chose the university as a space for educational-scientific emancipation and political action for my people.

The university was an unknown and inaccessible world until 2013 when I decided to enroll in the library science course at the Universidade do Estado de Santa Catarina (UDESC). At twenty-five years old, I was part of the statistics of late entry of Black people in undergraduate studies, while at the same time, I found myself in a privileged position compared to my ancestors, many of whom did not even have the opportunity to attend school, finish elementary education, or enroll in a public university.

My perception is that I completed two undergraduate degrees over four years, one in library science and another in Black, African and Diaspora Studies, at the Núcleo de Estudos Afro-Brasileiros (NEAB–Afro-Brazilian Studies Center). At NEAB, I understood the world from the perspectives of Abdias Nascimento, Lélia Gonzalez, Milton Santos, Nilma Lino Gomes, Angela Davis, Frantz Fanon, W. E. Du Bois, Aimé Cesáire, among many others. Their counternarratives stood out as a decolonial option[3] to the hegemonic discourse present in my professional and intellectual training environment, while also demonstrating that a Black person can be recognized for their intellectual capacity and considered an epistemic authority on a particular subject.

Moreover, it was through reading the works of these scholars that my gaze turned critically toward the library science program at my university. Under the guidance of Professor Daniella Camara Pizarro, my undergraduate research project presented the teaching discourse on the inclusion of ethnic-racial issues in the librarian education at that institution.[4] Together with the undergraduate research projects carried out by Black scholarship students from NEAB who studied library science at UDESC, the work developed by NEAB for over ten years toward raising awareness of ethnic-racial diversity and promoting equity in the university environment, as well as the role of antiracist professors in the program. This research was one of the factors responsible for the creation of the mandatory Ethnic-Racial Relations course, which is now part of the curriculum of said program.

In my master's thesis, this time at the Instituto Brasileiro de Informação em Ciência e Tecnologia (IBICT), in partnership with the Universidade Federal do Rio de Janeiro (UFRJ) and under the guidance of Professor Gustavo Saldanha, I arrived at a diagnosis of the inclusion of African and Afro-Brazilian cultures in Brazilian librarianship education, based on the perception of teachers and evaluation of normative instruments of undergraduate courses.[5] Also in my master's program, I discovered the world of American Black librarianship and the contributions of librarians and intellectuals such as E. J. Josey, Dorothy Porter Wesley, Clara Stanton Jones, Daniel P. Murray, and many others. Inspired by these Black librarians, I sought to defend a Brazilian Black librarianship and its main actors, historical and epistemological aspects in the information and library field.

In my doctoral thesis, guided by Professors Dr. Rubens Alves da Silva and Dr. Fabrício José Nascimento da Silveira at the Universidade Federal de Minas Gerais, I addressed some of the thoughts that had been troubling me for years. These concerns emerged during my journey as a Black woman in the field of library and information science, linked to an activist science of recognition of the intellectuality of my people: Black people. This research allowed for an in-depth study of Black-African epistemologies produced by Black librarian theorists, through the lens of critical race theory.

Throughout my academic journey, there have been many intellectual figures that inspired me to look at library and information science (LIS)—especially regarding library education and the historical and epistemological studies of the field—and feel the "present absences." Among such absences were, above all, the gaps of Black and African knowledge in the composition of what we understand today as the theory of knowledge—also known as epistemology—and in Brazilian library and information science.

The pursuit of a broad understanding of what epistemology is has directed scientific research in various fields within the Brazilian context. For some time now, studies in the field of library and information science have highlighted epistemologies and schools of thought originating from white, European, and/or North American men. What we understand as knowledge in Brazil historically comes from scientific practices that do not belong to Black, Indigenous, and other marginalized groups, but rather to those belonging to hegemonic groups who construct narratives, theoretical and discursive references that prevail in contemporary academia.

I understand that in any field of knowledge, scientific research is permeated by the worldviews of those who conduct the research, the intellectual figures they read, the context in which they are embedded, among other facets that make up our humanity. In this sense, I believe that scientific research and praxis in Brazilian library and information science are generated from conscious and unconscious political choices that are built throughout our existence.

In the field of library and information science, it is no different. Informed by various intellectuals, I have argued that coloniality—divided here into the coloniality of being, knowing, power, and nature[6]—as well as the omission of race within the field are (some of) the driving forces behind a formation and practice of Brazilian librarians that are distant from the humanities and increasingly close to a professional project that reinforces a colonial, mercantilist, technicist, and neoliberal perspective on practice, education, and epistemes.[7] Thus, the profession promotes epistemicide[8] and memoricide[9] of knowledge based on non-Westernized perspectives and transforms them through a univocal narrative of being, existing, and understanding the world.

The contributions of ethnic-racial groups to the construction of Black and African epistemes in diaspora within the field would be fruitful in pointing out how the colonial and the racial are present in the genesis, construction, and development of scientific research in Brazilian librarianship. Such a colonial-racial perspective is a guarantee of control over everyday thought and the production of scientific knowledge from a racialized standpoint, which is hidden behind a supposed academic neutrality, using research methods that exclude knowledge understood as nonuniversal.

The discussion about power relations within and outside academia, and the resulting effects of the intellectual segregation[10] of Black-African epistemes on the field of library and information science, as well as on the social and political world of societies, are important approaches for critical analysis and identification of instances of epistemic apartheid[11] in the history and construction of Brazilian librarianship. At the same time, it allows us to understand the comprehensive effects of epistemic, racial, social, economic, and gender injustices[12] on Brazilian knowledge production within the field throughout the centuries.

Thinking about this, I set out in search of what I understand as Black-African epistemologies in Brazilian library and information science. As a concept, I have established Black-African epistemologies as the theoretical-practical reflections produced by Black people, African people, and those in the African diaspora in the LIS field that are decolonial counternarratives to hegemonic, colonialist, and racialized perspectives. Such epistemologies place race at the center of the debate in library and information science and the power instruments linked to it, such as whiteness, racism, the myth of racial democracy, the ideology of white supremacy, racial colorblindness, epistemicide, memoricide, among other racial power instruments present in Brazilian society.

From the reflection on the centrality of race in the field, these epistemes of African and Black origin establish relations and intersections between subjects of marginalized ethnic-racial groups in Brazil and the social and informational injustices they suffer. Furthermore, such Black epistemes make it possible to identify the consequences of the exclusion of these groups in the professional formation in library science, in libraries, in the curriculum, and in research in LIS.

As one of the countries formed within the process of Western racial formation and with influence from the African diaspora, Brazil is a country marked by racism (and its facets) that feeds deep levels of inequality and injustice. Therefore, in the nineteenth and twentieth centuries, the absence of the debate about race and racism in Brazilian library and information science, libraries, professional education, and librarianship during this period is noticeable.[13]

The construction of the history of libraries, library science courses, and postgraduate programs in information science in Brazil is inexorably linked to the historical and social contexts experienced during the nineteenth and twentieth centuries worldwide. Historically, there is a relationship between the scarce literary production and typographical activity of the Portuguese Royal Press between the sixteenth and nineteenth centuries, which influenced reading formation and typographical production activities in colonial Brazil. This legacy of the Portuguese tradition resulted in the absence of technical and scientific knowledge production, maintaining a predominantly poetic and theological culture in the country. Another important factor is the elitist character of reader formation, as only a certain public had access to reading rooms in the country during the colonial period until the nineteenth century. Thus, if access to libraries, books, and reading was already restricted for white people, imagine the Black populations who were under the control of a slave regime and far from access to the epistemic goods of social emancipation.[14]

Moving on to the emergence of library science courses, historically the Brazilian National Library was a pioneer in offering library education through a course created in 1911. After this event, other milestones in the field followed, such as the development of library science achools in the country, the regulation of the library profession, the creation of professional organizations, the elaboration of a code of professional ethics, the construction of formal and informal scientific communication channels, the increase in scientific production, the creation of the first master's degree program in information science, and the differences and similarities between information science and library science, among other markers.[15]

During this period, although there were hegemonic forces, racist theories, instruments of racial power, and colonial narratives that may have influenced the possible distancing of the race-and-racism debate in the Brazilian library-informational field, the contribution of Black intellectuals in various social spheres and areas of knowledge, including LIS, is unquestionable. As an example of this Black presence, we can cite the foundation of the Teatro Experimental do Negro (Experimental Theater of the Negro, 1944), the Convenção Nacional do Negro (National Convention of the Negro, 1945–1946), Conferência Nacional do Negro (National Conference of the Negro, 1949), Congresso do Negro Brasileiro (1st Congress of the Brazilian Negro, 1950), the foundation of Instituto de Pesquisas e Estudos Afro-Brasileiros (IPEAFRO; Institute of Afro-Brazilian Research and Studies, 1981), all under the activism and leadership of Abdias Nascimento; the foundation of the Movimento Negro Unificado contra a Discriminação Racial (MNU; Unified Black Movement against Racial Discrimination, 1978) by Lélia González and other Black activists; the creation of Geledés–Instituto da Mulher Negra (Institute of Black Women, 1988) by Sueli Carneiro and other Black intellectuals and activists; the launch of the documentary Ôrí, by Beatriz Nascimento, among other Black protagonist milestones. In addition to these previously mentioned intellectuals, others such as Alberto Torres, Manoel Bomfim, Kabengele Munanga, Oracy Nogueira, and Petrônio Domingues promoted discussions about the racial issue and produced works that still fuel racial debates today, and which are part of the theoretical foundation of Black, African, and Afro-diasporic studies in the Brazilian context.

However, it is necessary to make a caveat: depending on their time, context of work, and the reflection they were engaged in, Black librarians used broader terms (multiculturalism, diversity, social protagonism, human rights, social justice, etc.) as a way of triggering the ethnic-racial debate within the library and information science field. Such terms, beyond being derived from various schools of thought and theoretical currents, served as a survival strategy against the oppressions experienced in their professional work environments, scientific production, teaching, and other spheres in which Black people were inserted.

In my master's research, I addressed the Brazilian Black librarianship and its constitution through a chronology of events considered markers of Black and antiracist epistemic agencies. Conceptually, I understand Brazilian Black librarianship as a theoretical-critical-reflexive movement that discusses the formation in the field, the librarian work of Black professionals, and the scientific production carried out by Black and non-Black librarians on ethnic-racial issues. The movement involves aspects that respond to the social condition of populations of African origin in Brazil through the theoretical-methodological lenses of librarianship. This movement initially uses the theory and techniques of bibliography as an instrument of resistance, visibility, and representation of the identity of the Brazilian Black population.[16]

Some events can be considered as markers of this Black librarianship in Brazil. I found the first bibliographic material about African-origin populations published by the National Library to be the book titled *Para uma história do negro no Brasil* (For a History of Blacks in Brazil), released in 1988. With sixty-four pages, this work addresses slavery in Brazil, the end of the African slave trade, the abolitionist movement, and the search for citizenship and equality by the Black population.[17]

Over the years of development of Black Brazilian librarianship, Black corporeality has served as a counterpoint to whiteness demarcated by privilege, and its action has brought epistemic-academic representativeness to the Black population. This is the case of Black librarians Regina Santos Silva Tonini, Julieta Carteado, Ana Virginia Teixeira da Paz Pinheiro, Mirian de Albuquerque Aquino, Joselina da Silva, Iara Conceição Bitencourt Neves, Maria Aparecida Moura, Izabel França, Marcos Luiz Cavalcanti de Miranda, among others. Despite structural, institutional, and epistemic racism, all these Black librarians promoted representativeness of the Black group in historically white spaces of power, while also providing critical racial education for a new generation of Black Brazilian librarians.

Regarding librarian education, Regina Santos Silva Tonini was the first Black woman to graduate with a degree in library science and documentation in 1966 from the Universidade Federal da Bahia, followed by Julieta Carteado who graduated in 1967 from the same institution. After them, other Black librarians emerged and became involved in the academic antiracist struggle and the library association movement. Among these actions within the association movement, we highlight the creation of the Grupo de Trabalho Relações Étnico-raciais e Decolonialidades (Working Group on Ethnic-Racial Relations and Decolonialities) linked to the Brazilian Federation of Associations of Librarians, Information Scientists and Institutions (FEBAB); the Grupo de Trabalho 12—Informação, Estudos Étnico-Raciais, Gênero e Diversidades (Working Group 12—Information, Ethnic-Racial Studies, Gender, and Diversities) linked to the National Association of Research and Post-Graduation in Information Science (Ancib); and the creation of the Encontro Nacional de Bibliotecários Negros e Antirracistas (ENBNA—National Meeting of Black and Antiracist Librarians) in 2018 and the Encontro Internacional de Bibliotecárias Negros e Antirracistas (EIBNA—International Meeting of Black and Antiracist Librarians) in 2022.

In recent years, the movement of Brazilian Black librarianship has been seeking to strengthen agendas and struggles for a more critical and antiracist formation and practice in librarianship. The scientific production led by Black librarians has expanded the debates on racism, critical epistemology, and antiracist practices, marked by works such as the collection *Bibliotecários Negros* (Black Librarians, volumes 1–4) published between 2018 and 2021, and books such as *O negro na Biblioteca: mediação da informação para construção da identidade Negra* (The Black in the Library: Information Mediation for the Construction of Black Identity, 2015); *Repertório Bibliográfico sobre a Condição do Negro no Brasil* (Bibliographic Repertoire on the Condition of Blacks in Brazil, 2017); *Mulheres negras na Biblioteconomia* (Black Women in Librarianship, 2019), *Epistemologias Negras: Relações Raciais na Biblioteconomia* (Black Epistemologies: Racial Relations in Librarianship, 2019), *Fundamentos da Biblioteconomia Negra* (Foundations of Black Librarianship, 2023), and *Biblioteconomia Negra: das epistemologias negro-africanas à teoria crítica racial* (Black Librarianship: From Black-African Epistemologies to Critical Race Theory, 2023).

A future project to collaborate with this memorial and historiographical reconstruction of Brazilian Black librarianship is to conduct interviews with various Black librarians from the past and present, aiming to highlight the various voices, narratives, contexts, and actors who have contributed (and continue to contribute) to this Black presence and (re) existence in the field. I understand that this is a responsibility, including with these ancestral agents and with library and information science, so that Black history does not remain only in the individual or collective memories of those who contributed to the emergence, development, and transformation of Black librarianship in the country.

Regarding this, I agree with Dorothy Porter[18] when she reminds us that the way to claim the achievements, memories, stories, and actions of Black people is by recording them so that they can be preserved, recovered, accessed, and interpreted by future generations. I understand that this is one way to combat the absence of Black Brazilian librarians from the history of LIS, the invisibility of their narratives, actions, and efforts, as well as the constant application of epistemicide, memoricide, epistemic apartheid, and epistemic racism in their contributions, reflections, and experiences.

## NOTES

1. E-mail adress: francigarces@yahoo.com.br; Cell number: +55 (21) 9 99391968. Bio: Black librarian and researcher in Black librarianship. PhD in information science from the Universidade Federal de Minas Gerais. Professor in the graduate program in information management at the Universidade do Estado de Santa Catarina (PPGInfo/UDESC). Creator and manager of Quilombo Intelectual and coordinator of the Nyota Publishing. Vice-leader of the Núcleo de Estudos e Pesquisas sobre Recursos, Serviços e Práxis Informacionais (Research Group on Resources, Services, and Information Practices) at the Universidade Federal de Minas Gerais (NERSI-UFMG).
2. Bharat Mehra, Kendra S. Albright, and Kevin Rioux, "A Practical Framework for Social Justice Research in the Information Professions," *Proceedings of the American Society for Information Science and Technology*, 43, no. 1 (2007): 1–10, doi https://doi.org/10.1002/meet.14504301275; Franciéle Carneiro Garcês da Silva, Dirnéle Carneiro Garcez, Rodrigo de Sales, and Gustavo Silva Saldanha, "Dorothy Porter Wesley e a Organização do Conhecimento Negro na Coleção Especial Moorland-Spingarn Research Center," *Liinc em Revista*, 17 (2021): 1–23.
3. Walter D. Mignolo, "Desobediência epistêmica: a opção descolonial e o significado de identidade em política," *Cadernos de Letras da UFF*, no. 34 (2008): 287–324, http://professor.ufop.br/sites/default/files/tatiana/files/desobediencia_epistemica_mignolo.pdf.
4. Franciéle Carneiro Garcês da Silva, *A inserção da temática Africana e Afro-brasileira no ensino de Biblioteconomia da Universidade do Estado de Santa Catarina* (Florianópolis: Universidade do Estado de Santa Catarina, 2016).
5. Franciéle Carneiro Garcês da Silva, *Representações Sociais acerca das Culturas Africana e Afro-Brasileira na Educação em Biblioteconomia no Brasil* (Rio de Janeiro: Instituto Brasileiro de Informação em Ciência e Tecnologia, 2019).
6. Aníbal Quijano, Colonialidad del poder, eurocentrismo y America Latina. *La colonialidad del saber: eurocentrismo y ciencias sociales: perspectivas latinoamericanas*, edited by Edgardo Lander (Buenos Aires: Clacso/Unesco, 2000); Edgardo Lander, "Ciências sociais: saberes coloniais e eurocêntricos," *A colonialidade do saber: eurocentrismo e ciências sociais*, edited by Edgardo Lander, Perspectivas latino-americanas, Ciudad Autónoma de Buenos Aires, Argentina: CLACSO, 2005); Joaze, Bernardino-Costa and Ramón Grosfoguel, "Decolonialidade e perspectiva negra," *Revista Sociedade e Estado*, 31, no. 1 (2016): 15–24, doi https://doi.org/10.1590/S0102-69922016000100002.
7. Franciéle Carneiro Garcês da Silva, "Colonialidade do saber e dependência epistêmica na biblioteconomia: reflexões necessárias," *Epistemologias Latino-americanas em Biblioteconomia e Ciência da Informação: contribuições da Colômbia e do Brasil*, edited by Natalia Duque Cardona and Franciéle C. Garcês da Silva (Florianópolis: Rocha; Nyota, 2020).
8. Beth Patin, Melinda Sebastian, Jieun Yeon, Danielle Bertolini, and Alexandra Grimm, "Interrupting Epistemicide: A Practical Framework for Naming, Identifying, and Ending Epistemic Injustice in the Information Professions," *Journal of the Association for Information Science and Technology*, 72, no. 10 (2021): 1306–18, doi https://doi.org/10.1002/asi.24479; Sueli Carneiro, *Dispositivo de racialidade: a construção do outro como não-ser como fundamento do ser* (Rio de Janeiro: Zahar, 2023).
9. Leandro A. F. Missiatto, "Memoricídio das populações negras no Brasil: atuação das políticas coloniais do esquecimento," *Revista Memória em Rede*, 13, no. 24 (2021): 252–73.
10. Reiland Rabaka, *Against Epistemic Apartheid: W. E. B. Du Bois and the Disciplinary Decadence of Sociology* (Lanham, MD: Lexington Books, 2010).

11. Ibid.
12. Miranda Fricker, *Epistemic Injustice: Power and the Ethics of Knowing* (Oxford: Oxford University Press, 2007); Coady, David. "Two Concepts of Epistemic Injustice," *Episteme*, 7, no. 2 (2010): 101-13. doi https://doi.org/10.3366/E1742360010000845; Gaile Pohlhaus Jr., "Relational Knowing and Epistemic Injustice: Toward a Theory of Willful Hermeneutical Ignorance." *Hyatia*, 27, no. 4 (2012): 715-35, *JSTOR*, http://www.jstor.org/stable/23352291.
13. Daniella Camara Pizarro, *Entre o saber agir e o saber fazer: o que professam os docentes de Biblioteconomia em Santa Catarina* (Florianópolis: Universidade Federal de Santa Catarina, 2017).
14. Ibid.
15. César A. Castro, *História da Biblioteconomia brasileira: perspectiva histórica* (Brasília: Thesaurus, 2000); Edson N. Fonseca, *Introdução à Biblioteconomia*, 2nd ed. (Brasília: Briquet de Lemos, 2007); Francisco das Chagas de Souza, *A Biblioteconomia no Brasil: profissão e educação* (Florianópolis: ACB, 1997); Pizarro, *Entre o saber agir e o saber fazer*.
16. Silva, *Representações*.
17. Brazilian National Library, *Para uma história do negro no Brasil* (Rio de Janeiro: BN, 1988).
18. Dorothy B. Porter, "Of Me and Records in the History of the Negro," in *Dorothy Porter Wesley (1905-1995): Afro-American Librarian and Bibliophile*, edited by James A. (Findlay, Broward County Library, 200 p1), 13-29.

## WORKS CITED

Bernardino-Costa, Joaze, and Ramón Grosfoguel. "Decolonialidade e perspectiva negra." *Revista Sociedade e Estado*, 31, no. 1 (2016): 15-24. doi https://doi.org/10.1590/S0102-69922016000100002.

Brazilian National Library. *Para uma história do negro no Brasil*. Rio de Janeiro: BN, 1988.

Carneiro, Sueli. *Dispositivo de racialidade: a construção do outro como não-ser como fundamento do ser*. Rio de Janeiro: Zahar, 2023.

Castro, César A. *História da Biblioteconomia brasileira: perspectiva histórica*. Brasília: Thesaurus, 2000.

Coady, David. "Two Concepts of Epistemic Injustice." *Episteme*, 7, no. 2 (2010): 101-13. doi https://doi.org/10.3366/E1742360010000845.

Fonseca, Edson N. *Introdução à Biblioteconomia*. 2nd ed. Brasília: Briquet de Lemos, 2007.

Fricker, Miranda. *Epistemic Injustice: Power and the Ethics of Knowing*. Oxford: Oxford University Press, 2007.

Lander, Edgardo. "Ciências sociais: saberes coloniais e eurocêntricos." *A colonialidade do saber: eurocentrismo e ciências sociais*, edited by Edgardo Lander. Perspectivas latinoamericanas. Ciudad Autónoma de Buenos Aires, Argentina: CLACSO, 2005.

Mathiesen, Kay. "Informational Justice: A Conceptual Framework for Social Justice in Library and Information Services." *Library Trends*, 64, no. 2 (2015): 198-225. doi https://doi.org/10.1353/lib.2015.0044.

Mehra, Bharat, Kendra S. Albright, and Kevin Rioux. "A Practical Framework for Social Justice Research in the Information Professions." *Proceedings of the American Society for Information Science and Technology*, 43, no. 1 (2007): 1-10. doi https://doi.org/10.1002/meet.14504301275.

Mignolo, Walter D. "Desobediência epistêmica: a opção descolonial e o significado de identidade em política." *Cadernos de Letras da UFF*, no. 34 (2008): 287-324. http://professor.ufop.br/sites/default/files/tatiana/files/desobediencia_epistemica_mignolo.pdf Accessed April 30, 2023.

Missiatto, Leandro A. F. "Memoricídio das populações negras no Brasil: atuação das políticas coloniais do esquecimento." *Revista Memória em Rede*, 13, no. 24 (2021): 252-73.

Patin, Beth, Melinda Sebastian, Jieun Yeon, Danielle Bertolini, and Alexandra Grimm. "Interrupting Epistemicide: A Practical Framework for Naming, Identifying, and Ending Epistemic Injustice in the Information Professions." *Journal of the Association for Information Science and Technology*, 72, no. 10 (2021): 1306-18. doi https://doi.org/10.1002/asi.24479.

Pizarro, Daniella Camara. *Entre o saber agir e o saber fazer: o que professam os docentes de Biblioteconomia em Santa Catarina*. Florianópolis: Universidade Federal de Santa Catarina, 2017.

Pohlhaus, Gaile, Jr. Relational Knowing and Epistemic Injustice: Toward a Theory of Willful Hermeneutical Ignorance. *Hyatia*, 27, no. 4 (2012): 715-35. *JSTOR*, http://www.jstor.org/stable/23352291. Accessed April 30, 2023.

Porter, Dorothy B. "Of Me and Records in the History of the Negro." *Dorothy Porter Wesley (1905-1995): Afro-American Librarian and Bibliophile*, edited by James A. Findlay, 13-29. Broward County Library, 2001.

Quijano, Aníbal. Colonialidad del poder, eurocentrismo y America Latina. *La colonialidad del saber: eurocentrismo y ciencias sociales: perspectivas latinoamericanas*, edited by Edgardo Lander. Buenos Aires: Clacso/Unesco, 2000.

Rabaka, Reiland. *Against Epistemic Apartheid: W. E. B. Du Bois and the Disciplinary Decadence of Sociology*. Lanham, MD: Lexington Books, 2010.

Silva, Franciéle Carneiro Garcês da. *A inserção da temática Africana e Afro-brasileira no ensino de Biblioteconomia da Universidade do Estado de Santa Catarina*. Florianópolis: Universidade do Estado de Santa Catarina, 2016.

Silva, Franciéle Carneiro Garcês da. *Representações Sociais acerca das Culturas Africana e Afro-Brasileira na Educação em Biblioteconomia no Brasil*. Rio de Janeiro: Instituto Brasileiro de Informação em Ciência e Tecnologia, 2019.

Silva, Franciéle Carneiro Garcês da. "Colonialidade do saber e dependência epistêmica na biblioteconomia: reflexões necessárias." *Epistemologias Latino-americanas em Biblioteconomia e Ciência da Informação: contribuições da Colômbia e do Brasil*, edited by Natalia Duque Cardona and Franciéle C. Garcês da Silva. Florianópolis: Rocha; Nyota, 2020.

Silva, Franciéle Carneiro Garcês da, Dirnéle Carneiro Garcez, Rodrigo de Sales, Gustavo Silva Saldanha. "Dorothy Porter Wesley e a Organização do Conhecimento Negro na Coleção Especial Moorland-Spingarn Research Center." *Liinc em Revista*, 17 (2021): 1-23.

Souza, Francisco das Chagas de. *A Biblioteconomia no Brasil: profissão e educação*. Florianópolis: ACB, 1997.

# Chapter 32
# Understanding the Journey

EXPLORING INFORMATION CHALLENGES FACED BY MIGRANTS IN INDIA AND LIBRARY INTERVENTIONS

Aysha Zakiya A

Interstate migrants, especially migrant laborers, are a marginalized community in their corresponding host states. India is a country with diverse cultures and traditions. Hence, when people from one state travel to another, they are migrating to new and unfamiliar settings even though they are traveling within one country. This makes them vulnerable, and it takes them time to adjust to their new surroundings.

There are many reasons for the people to migrate from their native place to another, mostly for employment reasons, for a better living environment, and marriage in the case of most women. There are forced migrations too. Due to natural calamities, riots, etc. the native people are forced to leave their home and take shelter in another state that feels safe.

In recent years, the COVID-19 pandemic is also one of the major causes of migration. The pandemic left many people in confusion, and migrants, mainly those without a proper shelter for living, were strongly affected by this.

Even though migrants arrive in new places hoping for a comfortable and more relaxed lifestyle, it is not always promised. The situation and nature of people in host states affect their life very much.

## INDIAN MIGRATION SCENARIO

The latest government data on migration comes from the 2011 census. Per the census, India had 456 million migrants in 2011 (38% of the population) compared to 315 million migrants in 2001 (31% of the population). Between 2001 and 2011, while the population grew by 18 percent, the number of migrants increased by 45 percent. In 2011, 99 percent of total migration was internal and immigrants (international migrants) comprised 1 percent.[1]

## MIGRATION PATTERN

Internal migration can be categorized based on origin and destination states:

1. Rural-Rural
2. Rural-Urban
3. Urban-Rural
4. Urban-Urban

According to the 2011 census, 210 million people moved from rural-to-rural areas, constituting 54 percent of classifiable internal migration. Each of the two migration patterns, rural-urban and urban-urban, involved about 80 million people. About 30 million people moved from urban to rural areas (7% of classifiable internal migration).

Another way to classify migration is:

1. Intrastate
2. Interstate

Nearly 88 percent (396 million people) of all internal migration in 2011 was intrastate travel. When it comes to interstate migration, there are differences between states. There were 54 million interstate migrants, according to the 2011 census. The major origin states were Uttar Pradesh and Bihar, while the biggest receiving states were Maharashtra and Delhi. Bihar's population of 6.3 million and Uttar Pradesh's population of 8.3 million had both relocated temporarily or permanently to other states. By 2011, over 6 million individuals from all over India had moved to Maharashtra.[2]

## EXISTING INFORMATION NEEDS, ACCESSING PATTERN, AND SOURCES OF MIGRANTS

It goes without saying that migrants will have a lot of questions and confusions when they move from their home state to a new one, and they will require information to clear those up. They have a variety of means to get the information they need, but most of them rely heavily on migrants who have already gotten settled in the host state.

## INFORMATION NEEDS

Information needs arise out of the migrants' adaptations to the new society. An individual has two types of information needs: one that is personal to them and one that is related to a group to which they belong, like students, laborers, etc.[3] The major information needs of migrants are for work, language, housing, schooling, health, driving, banking, legal issues, etc.

**INFORMATION ACCESSING PATTERN**

According to studies, social networking is one of the primary ways in which information demands are met. They may passively gather knowledge when conversing with friends or family. At times, they actively gather information from the internet. If there is a significant time between the decision and the actual migration, a family will typically take their time gathering information. Only as the departure date nears do they aggressively gather as much particular information as possible. The migrants have been searching the internet for information and contacting people who have already gone through the process.[4]

**INFORMATION SOURCES**

Migrants rely on information from agencies, contractors, and, most significantly, friends. Some began reading and listening to news from destination states, as well as attending gatherings of potential migrants. Even though they can rely on the internet for information, it is impossible for them to get details necessary for survival in host states. Also, the internet may result in misleading them, so unless for official works, like websites, the main sources of information for migrants are their friends or other migrants who have already gone through the process.

**PROBLEMS FACED BY MIGRANTS**

Migrants can be considered as marginalized communities. Everything about the surroundings, the language, the culture, and the people is foreign to them. The process of adjusting to a new circumstance takes time. They must rely on others during these periods to grasp things. They must deal with a number of challenges, like discrimination, misinformation, lack of proper registration, etc. as they move through the process of settling in host states (temporarily or permanently).

**DISCRIMINATION**

On many occasions, migrants are treated as second-class citizens, which results in failure of enabling proper and deserved rights for them. Unfortunately, many migrants are so used to discrimination that they detach themselves from social events most of the time. They live in their own space and will only socialize with others if and only if their work demands it. It is simply because they think they are not welcomed into this new society. The important reason for the discrimination could be language. The language and culture the natives follow is entirely different from that of migrants. Hence, the migrants will often feel like outcasts. Also, that natives think that migrant laborers are of a lower-class division as they are not from privilege makes the situation even worse. There are incidents where migrants are used for political agendas. Using them as either victimizers or culprits for many cases have been recorded. Even attacks against migrants are used for creating panic among both migrants and locals.

**PANDEMIC AFFECT**

The COVID-19 pandemic hit everyone hard, even the migrants. But, unlike locals, their lives were put on hold. They could neither work due to the shutdown of industries nor go back home as all transportation was stopped. Hence, they were stranded. They also lived in clusters, which increased the risk of spreading the virus. Also, proper awareness about the pandemic, vaccines, preventive measures, etc. did not reach many migrant spaces, and even if it did, it was impossible to follow strict rules such as social distancing taking their situations into consideration.

**MISINFORMATION EFFECT**

The unwanted and unconfirmed news was spread among the migrants, which resulted in mass panic. Social media played a very important role in this. Even though social media was really useful in reaching out to people, some irrelevant and wrong information was shared and went viral. This made the situation worse, as people were already in a panic. There is a possibility that when the migrants look for information online, they will stumble upon websites that deceive them and disseminate misleading information. Even some locals in the host countries spread false information to migrants in order to take advantage of them. Since migrants are unfamiliar with the area and the language, it will be difficult for them to tell the difference between what's true and false. Due to this, they are impacted mentally as well as monetarily. They will feel let down and find it difficult to trust anyone at work. This will make it more difficult for locals and migrants to live in harmony.

**HEALTH INFORMATION**

Information regarding health is very important anytime, but it is necessary and essential while we are going through something huge like a pandemic. Improper or lack of relevant information will gradually lead to one getting misinformed. The huge language barrier caused migrants to stay uninformed about major realities. It took time to reach them, but it arrived too late. The pandemic spread at a rising speed, and everyone was left in lockdown.

**LACK OF PROPER REGISTRATION**

The major reason officials could not reach out to migrants was lack of proper registration of migrants. It was challenging to consider everyone involved in the process because of the undefined population of migrants. The government should take the necessary steps to ascertain the precise number of migrants in order to introduce various initiatives for suitable housing, financial assistance, transportation, and healthcare. When they enter the country, immigrants should feel responsible for registering themselves as well, and it is the responsibility of officials to inform immigrants of these processes. Lack of proper registration will prevent immigrants from obtaining the government advantages set aside for them.

## HOW MIGRANTS PLAY KEY ROLES AS GAME CHANGERS

Migration has significant economic advantages, such as a more flexible labor market, a wider pool of skills, and increased demand. Most of the host state experiences a shortage of unskilled laborers when residents of metropolitan centers relocate to other countries/states in quest of skilled (white-collar) work. Migration aids in most significant developments by assisting the state in closing this gap. Social change is influenced by migration, and progressive ideas from big cities (such as women's education) will also spread to rural areas. Migration aids in the blending of diverse cultures, which actually encourages individuals to embrace one another despite cultural differences and even kickstarts the creation of composite cultures. The government of host states benefits greatly from the presence of migrant groups, particularly in the previously mentioned economic sector.[5]

## WHAT LIBRARIES CAN DO FOR MIGRANTS

Sometimes things happen that are unpredictable or unexpected and no matter how prepared a person is there is nothing that could have been done to help or change the situation. Public library programs and services can assist migrants in navigating daily living in foreign surroundings and learning a new language. Language classes, for example, address social determinants of health by encouraging social participation and community bonds and assisting in the development of friendships.[6]

Because migrants face misinformation even about fundamental requirements and many natives take advantage of their unfamiliarity with new surroundings, it is critical for libraries to stand up and develop a solution to this problem. They can add a new section, or even a subsection, to provide information valuable to migrants. The informant must be aware of the basic needs that a migrant may require. In addition, libraries should provide sections for newspapers in their native tongue. Most importantly, migrants should understand that they may seek information from libraries rather than being victims of misinformation.

## CONCLUSION

People migrate from their home state to another for many reasons: education, including employment opportunities, new beginnings, etc. Whatever the reason, they must deal with the unfamiliarity of the host state to which they have moved. Information needs are a significant demand for migrants. They require information about the location they transmit—about the settlement, access to healthcare, employment options, educational prospects, the character of the populace, etc. They will feel lost in their new state if they lack the right information. To help their doubts, there are multiple ways to access information from friends, families, and authorities. The libraries, as a responsible public service center and information source, should initiate facilities for migrants to access information. It is crucial to inform the migrants that they may go to libraries for reliable information. They can protect themselves from deceit and misinformation in this way.

## NOTES

1. "Census Tables," *Office of the Registrar General, India Ministry of Home Affairs, Government of India*, 2021, https://censusindia.gov.in/census.website/data/census-tables#.
2. Madhunika Iyer, "Migration in India and the Impact of the Lockdown on Migrants," *PRS Legislative Research*, October 6, 2020, https://prsindia.org/theprsblog/migration-in-india-and-the-impact-of-the-lockdown-on-migrants.
3. Snunith Shoham and Sarah Kaufman Strauss, "Immigrants' Information Needs: Their Role in the Absorption Process," *Information Research*, 13, no. 4, paper 359 (2008), https://informationr.net/ir/13-4/paper359.html.
4. Ibid.
5. Balaji, "What Are the Advantages and Disadvantages of Migration?" *BYJU'S Exam Prep*, February 12, 2023, https://byjusexamprep.com/upsc-exam/what-are-the-advantages-and-disadvantages-of-migration.
6. Suzanne Grossman et al., "How Public Libraries Help Immigrants Adjust to Life in a New Country: A Review of the Literature," *Health Promotion Practice*, 23, no. 5 (2022): 804–16, https://doi.org/10.1177/15248399211001064.

## WORKS CITED

Balaji. "What Are the Advantages and Disadvantages of Migration?" *BYJU'S Exam Prep*, February 12, 2023. https://byjusexamprep.com/upsc-exam/what-are-the-advantages-and-disadvantages-of-migration.

Grossman, Suzanne, Denise E. Agosto, Mark Winston, Rabbi Nancy E. Epstein, Carolyn C. Cannuscio, Ana Martinez-Donate, and Ann C. Klassen. "How Public Libraries Help Immigrants Adjust to Life in a New Country: A Review of the Literature." *Health Promotion Practice*, 23, no. 5 (2022): 804–16. https://doi.org/10.1177/15248399211001064.

Iyer, Madhunika. "Migration in India and the Impact of the Lockdown on Migrants." *PRS Legislative Research*. October 6, 2020. https://prsindia.org/theprsblog/migration-in-india-and-the-impact-of-the-lockdown-on-migrants.

Shoham, Snunith, and Sarah Kaufman Strauss. "Immigrants' Information Needs: Their Role in the Absorption Process." *Information Research*, 13, no. 4, paper 359 (2008). https://informationr.net/ir/13-4/paper359.html.

# Part VIII
# BANNED BOOKS AND CENSORSHIP ISSUES

# Chapter 33
# Racial Colorblind Theory and Book Acquisition

Elizabeth Jean Brumfield

This chapter examines racial colorblind theory as perpetuated through textbook acquisition or purchasing policies in state and local governments, school boards, universities, and K–12 schools. Racial colorblindness is the ideology that to end discrimination is to not see "color" in individuals and to treat individuals without regard to race, culture, or ethnicity.[1] Persons who say, "I don't see color," use this statement to justify their interactions with persons of color. They claim "colorblindness" to skin color acts as their excuse to blindness to the disparities, inequities, injustice, mistreatment, and historical discrimination that person of color experience. White people who support the ideology of a colorblind society ignore racism and deny the existence of white privilege.

This chapter discusses the theory of colorblindness as a lens to explain how the production, selection, and acquisition of books often contribute to pervasive barriers to equitable education for students of color. School textbooks reflect the depictions of cultural/racial conflict, popular media, hate speech, and environmental science discourses. Textbooks convey the author's imagination and thoughts and can be problematic if overemphasizing one group's conflicts while minimizing another. A predominant theme found in discourses and policies following the election of President Barack Obama is the view that after the election of a Black president, the United States is now a postracial, colorblind society, where race doesn't matter. Colorblindness as a theory allows white dominance to disregard racial inequities as irrational or baseless. Thus, colorblindness theories are uniquely presented in educational settings and state policies for school boards and publishers regarding the adoption and acquisition of textbooks. Ideologies such as colorblindness can impact purchase decisions and censorship of culturally relevant books, thus continuing the oppression of people of color. This chapter examines the impact of these theories on textbook acquisition policies, especially as it relates to African American students.

## TEXTBOOKS AS OPPRESSORS

Education is not, and never has been, neutral, impartial, unbiased, or innocent. Historically, education has served the role in society of directing minds in a specific way, indoctrinating, instructing, and reinforcing cultural values and modes of behavior.[2] Textbooks, a primary pedagogic resource used in most K–16 schools, nationwide, are not mere reading material, repositories of knowledge, blameless contributors and provocateurs of words. The choices made by state governments, universities, libraries, publishers, authors, and all others related to the production, selection, and acquisition of books comprise complex thought processes. The selective gathering and interpreting of evidence, highlighting certain issues and events, while deemphasizing or omitting others serve to reinforce ideologies and narratives that contribute to racial, gender, sexual orientation, and class inequities.[3] Children from very early ages are presented images in popular literature that reinforce racial and sexual stereotypes. Many adults, who look back on their favorite authors, such as Dr. Seuss, fail to recognize the racism that was boldly displayed and accepted as education or entertainment. The famous *Cat in the Hat*, used to teach reading, is based on racial stereotypes and was inspired by traditions of blackface minstrels.[4] Few see the irony of these cultural traps and subtle expressions of racism.[5]

School textbooks combine various thoughts, discourses, and religions and can perpetuate the ideologies of those dominant in a society. Books have a great potential to reveal practices resonating between the domains of formal, practical, and political ideologies. What a student reads remains in their mind long after the class is over. Textbooks may not blatantly discriminate or encourage racism or sexism; for some, the unequaled representation and lack of positive role models of people of color promote racial ideologies. One teacher stated, "I teach white history to Black kids."[6] He added, "In addition, to teaching racism, I teach sexism and discrimination. I do not mean . . . that I personally indoctrinate students . . . but the textbook that I use (and that nearly every public school in every state uses) indirectly leads teachers into teaching students to be racist, sexist and discriminatory to their peers."[7]

## COLORBLIND RACIST THEORY

Colorblind racist theory is defined as the denial, distortion, or minimization of race and racism. Colorblind beliefs deny that racism or white privilege exists. Proponents of this belief suggest that race does not matter in the way people experience the world.[8] Colorblindness upholds the notion of meritocracy in the United States, denying relevant cultural differences and silencing the narrative of true accounts of racial discrimination. Colorblindness maintains the structural status quo of white dominance by allowing whites to ignore their position of privilege.[9] Colorblind racism as a theory emerged after the civil rights movement in the 1960s and 1970s.[10] Racism in the postcivil rights era was largely promoted as a biological construct. As society looked for ways to justify differences in power and resources and legitimize existing ideologies, other theories about race surfaced.[11] Proponents of the colorblind theory suggest that the ideology resulted from society's increasingly complex arguments about race and discrimination in three legal cases.[12] Southern school districts and courts use colorblindness as an attempt to deny integration by suggesting that the Constitution was "race neutral." In South Carolina a school board pleaded, "The Constitution is colorblind; it should no more be violated to attempt integration than to preserve segregation." Some incorrectly argue that Martin Luther King's speech was a desire for a colorblind society, "judged not by the color of skin but by the content of their character," and a justification to abolish policies that considered race as a deficit, such as affirmation action.[13]

Colorblind rhetoric is often used to legitimize silencing persons of color, effectively aiding in perpetuating a normalized white hegemony in education. Many White Americans don't experience discrimination due to race. They can disregard racism and feel contented with their relatively privileged status in society. However, many African Americans regularly experience difficulties due to race; their perspective is quite different. Colorblind ideologies deny people of color their racially negative experiences; it rejects their cultural heritage and invalidates their unique perspectives in society.

**COLORBLIND RACISM AND SCHOOL BOARDS**

The First Amendment of the Constitution guarantees the right of Americans to voice their beliefs without government approval. The First Amendment has a role in providing access to ideas, discussions, and debates and guarantees the right to read. Texas Education Code (TEC, Ch. 31) and Texas State Board of Education Rules (19 TAC Chapter 66) defend the right of free speech in their guide for the inclusion of instructional material for school districts. State review boards are appointed to oversee the acquisition of instructional resources, including textbooks, to ensure that purchases meet the requirement of providing "essential knowledge and skills" (TEC Ch 31, Sec 66). The code also outlines procedures for residents to challenge material adopted by the state and/or request corrections to data or language found in a textbook. For the adoption of materials, a two-person review and a majority vote are required from a quorum of fifteen members. Statistically, throughout the United States the representation of people of color on school boards is very low, in larger districts the highest number, according to a National School Board Association, was 21 percent African American and 6 percent Latino.

State acquisition policies permit residents and nonprofit organizations to request the removal of books in school libraries and classrooms. *To Kill a Mockingbird* is a popular book that school board members in many states receive complaints from residents and request for its removal from school districts. Proponents of racial colorblindness reject the use of the language in the book and the depiction of whites as racists. Arne Duncan, who was education secretary during the Obama administration said concerning the removal of the book in the Biloxi, Mississippi, school district, "When school districts remove 'To Kill a Mockingbird' from the reading list, we know we have real problems (Chandelis quoting Duncan)." Members of the school board said the book made people feel "uncomfortable."[14] The colorblind racial attitudes of the school board members would rather eliminate materials that make racial discrimination uncomfortable than to articulate an authentic discourse on racism. Blatant racist behavior is condemned in most discourses, but ignoring and deidentifying the realities of a people is just as harmful. The flawed perception of a nontoxic racial United States continues to marginalize people of color and contributes to white privilege and power.

**COLORBLIND RACISM IN TEXTBOOKS**

Giroux maintains that to change schools, we have to create a nonexploitative, nonracist, and a gender-equalitarian society. He argues that education in Western society expresses oppressive ideologies and only the views of the dominant, privileged class.[15] Scholars argue that education is part of a hegemonic process, where the world is taught from the point of view of dominant groups while ignoring the knowledge of marginalized groups.[16] In this way, students learn that only certain types of knowledge are legitimate.[17] "Through this process of legitimation, 'schools reproduce the social organization of inequality at multiple levels.'"[18]

Colorblind racism in textbooks fail to give students a full representation of people of color, perpetuate racial stereotypes, and limit the scope of the achievements of African Americans and a complete understanding of the complexities of Black history. Without an accurate historical perspective, both the oppressed and those privileged continue to be defensive and protective of their historical social issues.[19] School boards in some states have as a requirement for addressing diversity in textbooks, a mention of slavery, or the civil rights movement (Kansas Standards for History). Colorblind ideologies in textbooks limit the teaching of Black history by treating racism like an issue of the past and framing slavery as a moral consequence, not a power and an economically controlled institution. Textbooks create the impression that racism ended after the civil rights movement. The focus placed on the civil rights era forces students to believe that racial injustice no longer exists. Textbooks neglect to highlight the achievements of people of color, causing students to believe that the civil rights movement was the only achievement for African Americans. Additionally, the wording used in textbooks uses descriptors designed to evoke emotion and perpetuate negative stereotypes. For example, a high school textbook recalling the history of sit-ins during the civil rights movement described the participants as "angry black students," implying that by their protests, they were the violent aggressors. The failure of textbooks to adequately portray African Americans as achievers and successful contributors to society has a negative effect on students. When students identify with the portrayal of persons of color as inferior and unsuccessful, many Black students succumb to the self-fulfilling prophecy of the Pygmalion effect. As Tanner notes, "When there is a preconceived cultural perception of a group, as being inferior . . . students can enter the system with a Pygmalion-self that is ill equipped to break down those stereotypes (p. 33)."[20] The students struggle with their self-esteem and racial identity, they give up on education because they think they will fail no matter what.[21]

Some textbooks focus solely on the degrading conditions of slavery and the enslaved, stressing it as a moral narrative of the strong master and weak subjugated victims. Educators are no stranger to language that blames the victims for their oppression. The implication is that something is wrong with the oppressed and that caused their own marginalization. Slavery is framed only as morally wrong, something happening to powerless individuals. Slaves are presented as lacking any meaningful political action, and the historical processes that lead to and enforced slavery, economic and political independence are negated as side stories. Slavery is thus framed as an emotional experience that all can empathize with, white or African American, but the structural role of colonialism and oppression is glossed over. Texas, as one of the leaders in textbook publishing, recently made changes in K-12 textbooks so that "the slave trade" would be renamed the "Atlantic triangular trade," essentially removing slavery out of the history books. It is important to note that the states with the largest populations of African Americans have the least amount of influence in what gets published. Texas and California are the largest publishers of textbooks. These states having a large amount of control over textbook content are likely to omit many achievements that Black people have made in favor of supporting their constituents.

**COLORBLIND RACISM AND PUBLISHERS**

Texas Education Code (TEC Ch. 31) and Texas State Board of Education (Rules 19 TAC Chapter 66) outline the procedures for the selection of instructional resources for school districts. State curriculum development policies require administrators to purchase books, including e-books, which are educationally appropriate and consistent with the district's educational philosophy, goals, and law (2017). Administrators have a duty to ensure that selection decisions are not made to advance an ideological, political, or religious viewpoint. For purchases, The Texas Code advises publishers to provide an electronic sample copy of their textbook to the Texas Education Agency (TEA) and a copy to each of twenty regional education service centers; the books selected then become district-wide purchases.

Publishers have as their goal to make money. Colorblindness, for publishers, is profitable on many levels. Colorblindness reinforces racial patterns of white dominance perpetuated for generations in history books and popular literature. Publishers perceive the white race to be the dominant race in society, in prestige, achievement, wealth, and power; there is little incentive to challenge the status quo. Publishers have a stable market and a loyal audience. Years ago, there was speculation that the internet would replace the need for books; however, these speculations were far from the truth. Statistics from the Nielsen reports indicate that the US book market is stable. Since 2004, the overall book market grew 52 percent, accounting for increases in e-books and digital markets. According to the report, as of 2016, children and young adult book sales show steady growth, with board books and graphic novels topping the list in sales. The United States has the world's largest market for books and journals, generating approximately $27.78 billion in net revenue yearly. Publishers of college textbooks charge exorbitant amounts for books because they know students must buy the required textbooks for their courses. They also try to publish new editions frequently to keep the old books from being sold by other students or cheaper vendors. University administrators contribute to the problem. The more books sold, the more universities earn from their bookstore contracts.

Colorblindness also serves publishers as a justification for standardization. The standards enforced by publishers are rarely examined and hardly questioned. Yet many of these standards restrict free expression and cultural narratives from African Americans and people of color around the globe. In the United States, the standard language for published manuscripts is English. The globalization of English as the language of commerce is profitable to textbook publishers. Research from foreign scholars may not be published if the manuscript submitted is not translated correctly or the reviewer has a problem understanding the content. The APA style of writing is a standardized form used in publishing by the American Psychological Association and publishers in the United States. The European Union publishes an interinstitutional style guide that encompasses twenty-four languages across the European Union and the United States. Many other countries have style guides that are required in various disciplines. We rarely use these other writing styles because the United States has dominance in the field of publishing and as such can set the requirements. The same publishers of journals are now also the leading database providers of educational materials, which create a monopoly in the industry. Having a monopoly in a noncompetitive market allows publishers to promote the dominant cultural perspective that has been institutionalized in American schools. Racial colorblindness ensures that people of color remain disenfranchised and lacking basic resources, and books that confirm their achievements and acknowledge historical inequities.

The first step in correcting a problem is admitting there is a problem. Publishers, school boards, and university administrators must challenge racial colorblindness in textbooks and establish communication channels to discuss the realities of white privilege. Describing and analyzing racial colorblind theories in book acquisition policies assists in eliminating a toxic school environment and promotes inclusiveness.

Textbook acquisitions need to emphasize diversity in all areas including race, language, physical challenges, same-sex relationships, transgender identity discussions, and lesbian and gay expressions. Textbooks that misrepresent history and the historical experiences of the marginalized and oppressed should be examined, and purchase decisions should reflect acceptance that racial and other biases exist and need to be discussed. Librarians have the responsibility to ensure that information is accurate and marginalized communities are not slighted or ignored.

**NOTES**

1. Monnica T. Williams, "Colorblind Ideology Is a Form of Racism: A Colorblind Approach Allows Us to Deny Uncomfortable Cultural Differences," *Psychology Today*, December 27, 2011, https://www.psychologytoday.com/us/blog/culturally-speaking/201112/colorblind-ideology-is-form-racism.
2. Paulo Freire, *Pedagogy of the Oppressed* (New York: Bloomsbury, 2018).
3. James A. Banks, "Race, Knowledge Construction, and Education in the USA: Lessons from History," *Race Ethnicity and Education*, 5, no. 1 (2002): 7–27; James A. Banks, *Educating Citizens in a Multicultural Society* (New York: Teachers College Press, 1997).
4. Richard H. Minear, *Dr. Seuss Goes to War: The World War II Editorial Cartoons of Theodor Seuss Geisel* (New York: New Press, 2001).
5. Randall B. Lindsey, Kinkanza Nuri Robins, Raymond D. Terrell, and Delores B. Lindsey, *Cultural Proficiency: A Manual for School Leaders* (Thousand Oaks, CA: Corwin Press, 2018).
6. Nicholas Ferroni, "We Teach Racism, Sexism and Discrimination in Schools," *Huffington Post*, October 24, 2012, https://www.huffpost.com/entry/teaching-education-discrimination_b_1826113.
7. Ferroni, "We Teach Racism."
8. Helen A. Neville, Roger L. Worthington, and Lisa B. Spanierman, "Race, Power, and Multicultural Counseling Psychology: Understanding White Privilege and Colorblind Racial Attitudes," in *Handbook of Multicultural Counseling*, ed. Joseph G. Ponterotto, 2nd ed. (Thousand Oaks, CA: Sage Publications, 2001), 257–88; Thandeka K. Chapman, "You Can't Erase Race! Using CRT to Explain the Presence of Race and Racism in Majority White Suburban Schools," *Discourse: Studies in the Cultural Politics of Education*, 34, no. 4 (2013): 611–27.
9. Eduardo Bonilla-Silva, *Racism without Racists: Colorblind Racism and the Persistence of Racial Inequality in the United States* (Lanham, MD: Rowman & Littlefield Publishers, 2006).
10. Ibid.
11. Ibid.
12. Ibid.
13. Amy E. Ansell, "Casting a Blind Eye: The Ironic Consequences of Colorblindness in South Africa and the United States," *Critical Sociology*, 32, no. 2–3 (2006): 333–56.
14. Chandelis R. Duster, "Mississippi School Board Pulls *To Kill A Mockingbird* from Reading List," NBC News, October 16, 2017, https://www.nbcnews.com/news/nbcblk/mississippi-school-board-pulls-kill-mockingbird-reading-list-n811136.
15. Henry A. Giroux, "Schooling as a Form of Cultural Politics: Toward a Pedagogy of and for Difference," in *Critical Pedagogy, the State, and Cultural Struggle*, ed. Henry A. Giroux and Peter McLaren (Albany: State University of New York Press, 1989), 125–51.
16. Michael W. Apple, *Official Knowledge: Democratic Education in a Conservative Age*, 2nd ed. (New York: Routledge, 2000); Giroux, "Schooling," 125–51.
17. Tyrone Tanner and Mary E. Frank, *Culturally Responsive Educational Theories: Practical Guide with Case Studies for Improving the Academic Performance of Diverse Learners* (Cypress, TX: Educational Concepts, 2013); Apple, *Official Knowledge*; Giroux. "Schooling," 1989.
18. Dorothy E. Smith, "Schooling for Inequality," *Signs: Journal of Women in Culture and Society*, 25, no. 4 (2000): 1147–51.
19. Ibid.
20. Ibid.
21. Ibid.

**WORKS CITED**

Ansell, Amy E. "Casting a Blind Eye: The Ironic Consequences of Colorblindness in South Africa and the United States." *Critical Sociology*, 32, no. 2–3 (2006): 333–56.

Apple, Michael W. *Official Knowledge: Democratic Education in a Conservative Age*. 2nd ed. New York: Routledge, 2000.

Banks, James A. *Educating Citizens in a Multicultural Society*. New York: Teachers College Press, 1997.

———. "Race, Knowledge Construction, and Education in the USA: Lessons from History." *Race Ethnicity and Education*, 5, no. 1 (2002): 7–27.

Bonilla-Silva, Eduardo. *Racism without Racists: Colorblind Racism and the Persistence of Racial Inequality in the United States*. Lanham, MD: Rowman & Littlefield Publishers, 2006.

Chapman, Thandeka K. "You Can't Erase Race! Using CRT to Explain the Presence of Race and Racism in Majority White Suburban Schools." *Discourse: Studies in the Cultural Politics of Education*, 34, no. 4 (2013): 611–27.

Duster, Chandelis R. "Mississippi School Board Pulls *To Kill A Mockingbird* from Reading List," NBC News, October 16, 2017. https://www.nbcnews.com/news/nbcblk/mississippi-school-board-pulls-kill-mockingbird-reading-list-n811136.

Ferroni, Nicholas Ferroni. "We Teach Racism, Sexism and Discrimination in Schools." *Huffington Post*, October 24, 2012. https://www.huffpost.com/entry/teaching-education-discrimination_b_1826113.

Freire, Paulo. *Pedagogy of the Oppressed*. New York: Bloomsbury, 2018.

Giroux, Henry A. "Schooling as a Form of Cultural Politics: Toward a Pedagogy of and for Difference," in *Critical Pedagogy, the State, and Cultural Struggle*, ed. Henry A. Giroux and Peter McLaren, 125-51. Albany: State University of New York Press, 1989.

Lindsey, Randall B., Kinkanza Nuri Robins, Raymond D. Terrell, and Delores B. Lindsey. *Cultural Proficiency: A Manual for School Leaders*. Thousand Oaks, CA: Corwin Press, 2018.

Minear, Richard H. *Dr. Seuss Goes to War: The World War II Editorial Cartoons of Theodor Seuss Geisel*. New York: New Press, 2001.

Neville, Helen A., Roger L. Worthington, and Lisa B. Spanierman. "Race, Power, and Multicultural Counseling Psychology: Understanding White Privilege and Colorblind Racial Attitudes," in *Handbook of Multicultural Counseling*, 2nd ed., ed. Joseph G. Ponterotto, 257-88. Thousand Oaks, CA: Sage Publications, 2001.

Smith, Dorothy E. "Schooling for Inequality." *Signs: Journal of Women in Culture and Society*, 25, no. 4 (2000): 1147-51.

Tanner, Tyrone, and Mary E. Frank. *Culturally Responsive Educational Theories: Practical Guide with Case Studies for Improving the Academic Performance of Diverse Learners*. Cypress, TX: Educational Concepts, 2013.

Williams, Monnica T. "Colorblind Ideology Is a Form of Racism: A Colorblind Approach Allows Us to Deny Uncomfortable Cultural Differences." *Psychology Today*, December 27, 2011. https://www.psychologytoday.com/us/blog/culturally-speaking/201112/colorblind-ideology-is-form-racism.

# Chapter 34
# Always Been There

THE CULTURAL POLITICS OF CHILDREN'S BOOKS AND BLACK LIBRARIANS

Edith Campbell

*Sweet land of Liberty. Home of the Free.*
*The Melting Pot. The American Dream.*
*The Tooth Fairy. Adam and Eve. The Virgin Birth.*
The more time I spend in the library,
The less sure I am about everything.

—Marilyn Nelson[1]

Children's books reflect the times in which they are published. Through a sort of political maneuvering, particular perspectives become dominant in each era, inserting themselves through each nuance of a book's creation. Politics, after all, is a display of power, and whose story gets told is its reward. All books are political. It may seem odd to reflect on children and librarians in relation to power because each seem to have so little, but it's through their positionality to literacy that either of these groups gains and maintains any sense of liberation, and it's through books and the stories they contain that freedom is manifested.

We can trace how Black librarians have resisted the perpetual impact of white imperialism on children's literature by considering the interplay between Black librarians, Black children's books, and the dominant white society in the United States. Black children's books, those that are historically written for Black children, and highlight the lived experience of Black children,[2] have historically censored the actual Black child through constraints that are placed upon both the quantity and quality of these stories. In more contemporary times, as the books have come to present more authentic representations, they become the objects of censorship to alleviate white guilt.

As the 1960s began, Augusta Baker became the head of the New York Public Library's children's department. Baker, an African American and a noted storyteller, was quite critical of the representations in children's literature that were based upon false scientific thinking and prejudicial thoughts. She reflected in the *Horn Book* that there was

> no wonder it was an accepted fact in children's books that blacks [sic] were lazy, shiftless, lived in shanties, had nothing and wanted nothing, sang and laughed all day. Black writers for children were practically nonexistent, and the few who had written—such as Arna Bontemps and Langston Hughes—reached a very small audience. Consequently, few children knew that blacks [sic] lived just as other people lived, having the same aspirations and hopes.[3]

Baker was quite aware of books published over the decades with images of Black children depicted as unclean and unkept, speaking barely recognizable dialects, uneducated, clumsy, and often appearing as less than human. She also read the works of Lorenz Graham, Dorothy Sterling, and Jesse C. Jackson and knew they offered what was needed. Black children's librarians have always known that we need Black-authored books.

Nancy Larrick, a white educator, made this quantifiably obvious in her 1965 article "The All-White World of Children's Books." This article was published five months after the passage of the Elementary and Secondary Education Act, legislation that provided millions of dollars to schools that serviced large numbers of children from low-income families. When many of the schools intended to use the funds to acquire books for classroom and library use, it quickly became apparent that there were not enough books available that offered any representation of the Black and Brown children in these communities.[4] In 1966, Rep. Adam Clayton Powell convened a hearing on Books for Schools and the Treatment of Minorities with its purposes being to

> explore (1) the role of the publishing industry in producing books suitable for the needs of educationally disadvantaged, low income, and what is variously referred to as culturally deprived schoolchildren; (2) the treatment of minority groups and their role in American society in the basic reading texts used in all schools; (3) official school and library selection policies.[5]

In 1967, Black librarians Charlemae Hill Rollins and Augusta Baker responded to the call for books with Black representation for children with the third edition of *We Build Together: A Reader's Guide to Negro Life and Literature for Elementary and High School*.[6] Rollins was well poised to do this work, having surveyed books and developing three criteria in 1941 for use when selecting Black books: illustrations, language, and theme.[7] Rollins's and Baker's work to improve representation by identifying books by authors who were making contributions to Black children's literature would no doubt be what Kara Keeling would term "stewardship": taking care and responsibility for cultural forms.[8]

Black librarians Mabel McKissick and Glyndon Geer chose to create a pathway to highlight and honor authors and illustrators of outstanding youth literature in 1969 by establishing the Coretta Scott King Book Awards.[9] Creators honored with this award set standards for representation through their "expression of the African American experience via literature and the graphic arts, including biographical, historical and social history treatments by African American authors and illustrator."[10] The first award was given in 1970. It began to seem that a new era was beginning. "By the end of the decade, combined social, political, and economic forces had begun to propel the field of children's literature toward greater diversity."[11]

The 1970s, with reforms in education, advances in civil rights, and self-empowering movements that reinforced positive images of Blackness lulled us into believing there had been a true revolution in children's literature. From 1973 to 1975, the number of books with one or more Black characters more than doubled from what Larrick found a decade earlier.[12] Books about Blacks were still most often written by people outside the Black experience who focused on smiling, fun-loving enslaved people, or with historical contributions lacking authenticity[13] alongside a few more books by Black authors with Black characters placed in more contemporary settings, such as *A Hero Ain't Nothing But a Sandwich* (1973) and *The Young Landlords* (1979). Librarians became part of the Council on Interracial Books for Children to address what Larrick had missed: the quality of representation. The organization was highly critical of books such as *Sounder* (1969), *Dr. Doolittle* (1920), and *The Slave Dancer* (1973), among others.[14] Their work resulted in texts being altered as was the case with *Mary Poppins* (1934),[15] and *Charlie and the Chocolate Factory* (1964),[16] and Jane Addams Award recognition being questioned for *The Cay* (1969).[17] Augusta Baker transitioned librarians into the 1970s positing that perpetual question of Black children's literature, "Does one have to live the Black experience in order correctly to portray it?" Could stories with Black characters written by those outside the Black community ever be sourced in bias-free communal histories rather than being mired in whiteness? As that sentiment continued to fester, Black authorship grew with contributions from Sharon Bell Mathis, Virginia Hamilton, Eloise Greenfield, and John Steptoe.

But you know the saying: One step forward, two steps back.

Ronald Reagan moved the country into the 1980s, the era of Reaganomics. Before he was sworn into office, political shifts were setting in most noticeably to the world of youth literature in 1978 when lists of books were beginning to be banned in communities across the country.[18] The 1980s was time for white supremacists to seek retribution for the nascent voices proudly and openly expressing Black cultural identity. The American Library Association received about one hundred complaints directed at books per year in the early 1970s, but by 1981 there were over one thousand for that year alone.[19] Book bans were being situated to focus on the moral and social values taught to children rather than the historical precedence of profanity and obscenity. *A Hero Ain't Nothing But a Sandwich* (1973) was one of the challenged texts, as was the *American Heritage Dictionary*.[20]

The year 1984 had half the number of books published with Black characters as compared to 1974. The realities of the publishing business led Walter Dean Myers to opine in *The New York Times*,

> I no longer feel that the industry has any more obligation to me, to my people, to my children, than does, say a fast-food chain. It's clear to me that if any race, any religious or social group, elects to place its cultural needs in the hands of the profit makers then it had better be prepared for the inevitable disappointments.[21]

Myers's article continued to surface some forty years later with the politics of consumerism rather than that of the people dominating publishing. In the early 2000s, youth literature was heavily critiqued through social media outlets. Blogs maintained by Black librarians, booksellers, and literature enthusiasts such as *Reading in Color*, *The HappyNappyBookseller*, *Multiculturalism Rocks*, and my own blog, *Cotton Quilts*,[22] often challenged the status quo in youth literature. Blogs gave a public presence to voices that had long gone unheard. Concepts once discussed only among academics became part of the lexicon of practitioners: anticolonialism, intersectionality, critical literacy, systemic racism, and white fragility. These voices were being heard with such might that they were able to enact changes to book covers, and amendments to content or force withdrawals of entire books from publication. The anti-Blackness expressed in imagery (*The Bad Mood and the Stick*, 2017; *Liar*, 2009), simianization (*If I Ran the Zoo*, 1950; *Hi Jack*, 2019), language (*When We Was Fierce*, 2016), and historical inaccuracies (*A Birthday Cake for George Washington*, 2016) was confronted directly and eliminated.

This growing awareness in youth literature was paradoxical to the trauma that continued to be perpetrated upon Black bodies. Young girls were thrown out of desks at school by safety officers, the insult "liar" was hurled at President Barack Obama while he was delivering the State of the Union address to a joint session of Congress, and unarmed Black men and women continued to be killed by police officers.

An important outgrowth of social networking was We Need Diverse Books (WNDB). This inclusive movement brought a new sense of hope as it began facing the exact same constrictions as those from previous *centuries*: a lack of marginalized people employed throughout the publishing industry, stereotypes that reduce the efficacy of minoritized literacy, and an inability to navigate shared histories. With social media as its driving impetus, WNDB solidified voices of parents, teachers, librarians, and students across boundaries of race, ethnicity, sexual orientation, gender, and disabilities to grapple with those constrictions, and demanded not only more, but more accurate representations both in books and in the publishing houses themselves. Black mentorships, workshops, and symposiums were created within WNDB while imprints such as Make Me A World, Versify, and Freedom Fire were established in the publishing world specifically for marginalized voices. Award committees began realizing, and awarding, the artistic merit of books written by Black, Indigenous, and authors of color. Barak Obama had been elected president in 2008 and anything was possible in reaction to that.

Even the election of Donald J. Trump in 2016.

Could Black books still matter? Just like in the early 1980s, retribution for gains made were enacted through book challenges, but this time they were heavily directed at books by Black and LGBTQIA+ authors. The ALA reported more than 1,200 challenges in 2022, doubling from the year prior.[24] Black librarians K. C. Boyd, Lakeisha Darden, and Cicely Lewis are tirelessly among those working to protect libraries and their collections. Dr. Emily Knox engages her scholarship on book bans and censorship to educate the public on issues of intellectual freedom.

With a love of both children and literature, we enter the field of children's librarianship. "There is a dedication in this work which beams with love for African American children and a heartfelt obligation to provide them with positive images through the words, the themes, and the images."[23] We've done this for over a hundred years, Black men and women who hope to cultivate young minds for opportunities that they may not yet even imagine. It's been done by so many generations with so much grace and eloquence, that we've not always noticed the weathering on our beings. But we have a collective spirit that transcends politics of the moment, and it will not be eroded because the power we can acquire through literacy is critical to our liberation.

**NOTES**

1. Marilyn Nelson, *How I Discovered Poetry* (New York: Dial Books, 2014).
2. Judy Richardson, "Black Children's Books: An Overview," *The Journal of Negro Education*, 43, no. 3 (1974): 380.
3. Augusta Baker, "The Changing Image of the Black in Children's Literature," *The Horn Book*. February 1, 1975. https://www.hbook.com/story/the-changing-image-of-the-black-in-childrens-literature.
4. Paul Cornelius, "Interracial Children's Books: Problems and Progress," *The Library Quarterly: Information, Community, Policy*, 41, no. 2 (1971): 108, https://www.journals.uchicago.edu/doi/abs/10.1086/619932.
5. United States Congress House Committee on Education and Labor, Ad Hoc Subcommittee on De Facto School Segregation, *Books for Schools and the Treatment of Minorities: Hearings before the Ad Hoc Subcommittee on De Facto School Segregation of the Committee on Education and Labor, House of Representatives, Eighty-ninth Congress, Second Session on Books for Schools and the Treatment of Minorities. Hearings Held in Washington, D.C. August 23, 24, 30, 31; and September 1, 1966* (Washington, DC: United States Government Printing Office, 1966), 2.
6. Charlemae Hill Rollins and Augusta Baker, *We Build Together: A Reader's Guide to Negro Life and Literature for Elementary and High School Use*, 3rd ed. (Champaign, IL: National Council of Teachers of English, 1967).
7. Cass Mabbott, "The We Need Diverse Book Campaign and Critical Race Theory: Charlemae Rollins and the Call for Diverse Children's Books," *Library Trends*, 5, no. 4 (2017): 516, https://doi.org/10.1353/lib.2017.0015.
8. Wesley Morris, "We're Never Going to Get That Top 40 Out of Us," *Still Processing*, April 14, 2022. https://www.nytimes.com/2022/04/14/podcasts/still-processing-american-top-40.html.
9. "The History of the Coretta Scott King Book Awards," *American Library Association*, September 8, 2022, https://www.ala.org/rt/cskbart/about.
10. "The Coretta Scott King Book Awards for Authors and Illustrators," *American Library Association*, January 19, 2009, http://www.ala.org/rt/cskbart/cskbookawards/slction.
11. Rudine Sims Bishop, "Reflections on the Development of African American Children's Literature," *Journal of Children's Literature*, 38, no 2 (2012): 5-13.
12. Jeanne S. Chall, Eugene Radwin, Valerie W. French, and Cynthia Hall, "Blacks in the World of Children's Books," *The Reading Teacher*, 32, no. 5 (1979): 532. https://www.jstor.org/stable/20194821; Nancy Larrick, "The All-White World of Children's Books." *Saturday Review*, September 1965, 63-65, 84-85, https://brichislitspot.files.wordpress.com/2017/08/384larrick.pdf.
13. Chall, "Blacks in the World of Children's Books," 531-32.
14. Judith Stinton, *Racism & Sexism in Children's Books* (London: Writers and Readers Publishing Cooperative, 1979); Paula Fox, *The Slave Dancer* (Scarsdale, NY: Bradbury Press, 1973); Hugh Lofting, *Dr. Doolittle* (Philadelphia: Frederick A. Stokes, 1920); William H. Armstrong and James Barkley, *Sounder* (New York: HarperCollins, 1969).
15. Stinton, *Racism & Sexism in Children's Books*, 31; P. L. Travers and Mary Shepard, *Mary Poppins* (London: HarperCollins, 1934).
16. Stinton, *Racism & Sexism in Children's Books*, 42; Roald Dahl, *Charlie and the Chocolate Factory* (London: George Allen & Unwin, 1964).
17. Susan C. Griffith, *The Jane Addams Children's Book Award: Honoring Children's Literature for Peace and Social Justice Since 1953* (Lanham, MD: The Scarecrow Press, 2013); Theodore Taylor, *The Cay* (New York: Avon, 1969).
18. Colin Campbell, "Book Banning in America," *The New York Times*, December 20, 1981, Section 7, 1, https://www.nytimes.com/1981/12/20/books/book-banning-in-america.html.
19. Ibid.

20. Ibid.
21. Walter Dean Myers, "I Actually Thought WE Would Revolutionize the Industry," *The New York Times*, November 9, 1986, Section 7, 50, https://www.nytimes.com/1986/11/09/books/children-s-books-i-actually-thought-we-would-revolutionize-the-industry.html.
22. Ari Valde, *Reading In Color*. http://blackteensread2.blogspot.com/; Doret Canton, *The HappyNappyBookseller*, http://thehappynappybookseller.blogspot.com/; N. J. Mvondo, *Multiculturalism Rocks*, https://multiculturalism.rocks/; Edith Campbell, *Cotton Quilts*, https://edicottonquilt.com/.
23. "American Library Association Reports Record Number of Demands to Censor Library Books and Materials in 2022," American Library Association, March 22, 2023, http://www.ala.org/news/press-releases/2023/03/record-book-bans-2022.
24. Nancy Tolson, "Making Books Available: The Role of Early Libraries, Librarians, and Booksellers in the Promotion of African American Children's Literature," *African American Review*, 32, no. 1 (1998): 9–16, https://doi.org/10.2307/3042263.

**WORKS CITED**

"American Library Association Reports Record Number of Demands to Censor Library Books and Materials in 2022." American Library Association, March 22, 2023. http://www.ala.org/news/press-releases/2023/03/record-book-bans-2022.

Armstrong, William H., and James Barkley. *Sounder*. New York: HarperCollins, 1969.

Baker, Augusta. "The Changing Image of the Black in Children's Literature." *The Horn Book*. February 1, 1975. https://www.hbook.com/story/the-changing-image-of-the-black-in-childrens-literature.

Bishop, Rudine Sims. "Reflections on the Development of African American Children's Literature." *Journal of Children's Literature*, 38, no 2 (2012): 5–13.

Campbell, Colin. "Book Banning in America." *New York Times*, December 20, 1981, Section 7, 1. https://www.nytimes.com/1981/12/20/books/book-banning-in-america.html.

Campbell, Edith. *Cotton Quilts*. https://edicottonquilt.com/.

Canton, Doret. *The HappyNappyBookseller*. http://thehappynappybookseller.blogspot.com/.

Chall, Jeanne S., Eugene Radwin, Valerie W. French, and Cynthia Hall. "Blacks in the World of Children's Books." *The Reading Teacher*, 32, no. 5 (1979): 527–33. https://www.jstor.org/stable/20194821.

Cornelius, Paul. "Interracial Children's Books: Problems and Progress." *The Library Quarterly: Information, Community, Policy*, 41, no. 2 (1971): 106–27. https://www.journals.uchicago.edu/doi/abs/10.1086/619932.

Dahl, Roald. *Charlie and the Chocolate Factory*. London: George Allen & Unwin, 1964.

Fox, Paula. *The Slave Dancer*. Scarsdale, NY: Bradbury Press, 1973.

Griffith, Susan C. *The Jane Addams Children's Book Award: Honoring Children's Literature for Peace and Social Justice Since 1953*. Lanham, MD: The Scarecrow Press, 2013.

Lofting, Hugh. *Dr. Doolittle*. Philadelphia: Frederick A. Stokes, 1920.

Mabbott, Cass. "The We Need Diverse Book Campaign and Critical Race Theory: Charlemae Rollins and the Call for Diverse Children's Books." *Library Trends*, 5, no. 4 (2017): 508–22. https://doi.org/10.1353/lib.2017.0015.

Morris, Wesley. "We're Never Going to Get That Top 40 Out of Us." *Still Processing*, April 14, 2022. https://www.nytimes.com/2022/04/14/podcasts/still-processing-american-top-40.html.

Mvondo, N. J. *Multiculturalism Rocks*. https://multiculturalism.rocks/.

Myers, Walter Dean. "I Actually Thought WE Would Revolutionize the Industry." *New York Times*, November 9, 1986, Section 7, 50. https://www.nytimes.com/1986/11/09/books/children-s-books-i-actually-thought-we-would-revolutionize-the-industry.html.

Larrick, Nancy. "The All-White World of Children's Books." *Saturday Review*, September 1965, 63–65, 84–85. https://brichislitspot.files.wordpress.com/2017/08/384larrick.pdf.

Nelson, Marilyn. *How I Discovered Poetry*. New York: Dial Books, 2014.

Richardson, Judy. "Black Children's Books: An Overview." *The Journal of Negro Education*, 43, no. 3 (1974): 380–400.

Stinton, Judith. *Racism & Sexism in Children's Books*. London: Writers and Readers Publishing Cooperative, 1979.

Taylor, Theodore. *The Cay*. New York: Avon, 1969.

"The Coretta Scott King Book Awards for Authors and Illustrators." American Library Association, January 19, 2009. http://www.ala.org/rt/cskbart/cskbookawards/slction.

"The History of the Coretta Scott King Book Awards." American Library Association, September 8, 2022. https://www.ala.org/rt/cskbart/about.

Tolson, Nancy. "Making Books Available: The Role of Early Libraries, Librarians, and Booksellers in the Promotion of African American Children's Literature." *African American Review*, 32, no. 1 (1998): 9–16. https://doi.org/10.2307/3042263.

Travers, P. L. and Mary Shepard. *Mary Poppins*. London: HarperCollins, 1934.

United States Congress House Committee on Education and Labor, Ad Hoc Subcommittee on De Facto School Segregation. *Books for Schools and the Treatment of Minorities: Hearings before the Ad Hoc Subcommittee on De Facto School Segregation of the Committee on Education and Labor, House of Representatives, Eighty-ninth Congress, Second Session on Books for Schools and the Treatment of Minorities. Hearings Held in Washington, D.C. August 23, 24, 30, 31; and September 1, 1966*. Washington, DC: United States Government Printing Office, 1966.

Valde, Ari. *Reading In Color*. http://blackteensread2.blogspot.com/.

*Part IX*

# BOOKS, PERIODICALS, AND OTHER RESOURCES RECOMMENDED FOR BLACK COLLECTIONS

# Chapter 35
# Selected Bibliography of Works by Dr. E. J. Josey

Andrew P. Jackson (Sekou Molefi Baako)

Josey, E. J. *The Black Librarian in America*. Metuchen, NJ.: The Scarecrow Press, Inc., 1970.

Josey, E. J. *The Black Librarian in America Revisited*. Metuchen, NJ: The Scarecrow Press, Inc., 1994.

Josey, E. J. "The Civil Rights Movement and American Librarianship: The Opening Round." In *Activism in American Librarianship, 1962-1973*, edited by Mary Lee Bundy and Frederick J. Stielow, 13-20. New York: Greenwood Press, 1987.

Josey, E. J. "Foreword." In *Educating Black Librarians*, edited by Benjamin Speller Jr., vii-xiii. Jefferson, NC: McFarland & Company, Inc., 1991.

Josey, E. J. *Libraries, Coalitions & the Public Good*. New York: Neal-Schuman Publishers, Inc., 1987.

Josey, E. J. *Libraries in the Political Process*. Phoenix, AZ: Oryx Press, 1980.

Josey, E. J. *New Dimensions for Academic Library Service*. Metuchen, NJ: The Scarecrow Press, Inc., 1975.

Josey, E. J. "The Role of the Black Library and Information Professional in the Information Society: Myths and Realities." In *Educating Black Librarians*, edited by Benjamin Speller Jr., 51-59. Jefferson, NC: McFarland & Company, Inc., 1991.

Josey, E. J. *What Black Librarians Are Saying*. Metuchen, NJ: The Scarecrow Press, Inc., 1972.

Josey, E. J., and Marva L. De Loach, eds. *Ethnic Collections in Libraries*. New York: Neal-Schuman Publishers, Inc., 1983.

Josey, E. J., and Marva L. DeLoach, eds. *Handbook of Black Librarianship*, 2nd ed. Lanham, MD: The Scarecrow Press, Inc., 2000.

Josey, E. J., Sidney L. Jackson, and Elinor B. Herling, eds. *A Century of Service: Librarianship in the United States and Canada*. Chicago: American Library Association, 1976.

Josey, E. J., Clara Stanton Jones, and American Library Association President's Commission on the Detroit Conference. *The Information Society: Issues and Answers*. Phoenix, AZ: Oryx Press, 1978.

Josey, E. J., and Kenneth E. Peeples Jr., eds. *Opportunities for Minorities in Librarianship*. Metuchen, NJ: The Scarecrow Press, Inc., 1977.

Josey, E. J., and Ann Allen Schockley, eds. *Handbook of Black Librarianship*. Littleton, CO: Libraries Unlimited, Inc., 1977.

Josey, E. J., and Kenneth D. Shearer, eds. *Politics and the Support of Libraries*. New York: Neal-Schuman Publishers, 1990.

# Chapter 36
# Brief Bibliography of Essays and Journal Articles by Dr. E. J. Josey

Marva L. DeLoach

Jordan, Casper L., and E. J. Josey. "A Chronology of Events in Handbook of Black Librarianship." In *Handbook of Black Librarianship*, edited by E. J. Josey and Anne Allen Shockley, 15-24. Littleton, CO: Libraries Unlimited, 1977.

Josey, E. J. "The Absent Professors." *Library Journal*, 87, no. 2 (1962): 173-75, 181.

Josey, E. J. "All Shades of Colors." *Library Journal*, 123, no. 12 (1998): 8.

Josey, E. J. "The American Library Association: Then and Now." In *Culture Keepers: Enlightening and Empowering Our Communities: Proceedings of the First National Conference of African American Librarians September 4-6, 1992, Columbus, Ohio*, edited by Stanton F. Biddle, 15-19. NJ: Black Caucus of the American Library Association, 1993.

Josey, E. J. "Black Caucus of the American Library Association." In *Handbook of Black Librarianship*, edited by E. J. Josey and Ann Allen Shockley, 66-77. Littleton, CO: Libraries Unlimited, 1977.

Josey, E. J. "Black Caucus of the American Library Association: The Early Years." In *Handbook of Black Librarianship* 2nd ed., edited by E. J. Josey and Marva L. DeLoach, 83-99. Lanham, MD: Scarecrow, 2000.

Josey, E. J. "Can Library Affirmative Action Succeed?" *Library Journal*, 100, no. 1 (1975): 28-31.

Josey, E. J. "The Challenges of Cultural Diversity in the Recruitment of Faculty and Students from Diverse Backgrounds." *Journal of Education for Library and Information Science*, 34, no. 4 (1993): 302-11.

Josey, E. J. "The Civil Rights Movement and American Librarianship: The Opening Round." In *Activism in American Librarianship*, edited by Mary Lee Bundy and Fredrick J. Stielow, 13-20. New York: Greenwood Press, 1987.

Josey, E. J. "Coddling Segregation." *School Library Journal*, 18 (1971): 40-41.

Josey, E. J. "College Library Accreditation: Boom or Burst." *Wilson Library Bulletin*, 32, no. 3 (1957): 233-34.

Josey, E. J. "The College Library in New York's 3R System." *College & Research Libraries*, 30, no. 1 (1969): 32-38.

Josey, E. J. "A College Library's Cultural Series." *Wilson Library Bulletin*, 30, no. 10 (1956): 767-68.

Josey, E. J. "Community Use of Academic Libraries-Symposium-Introduction." *College & Research Libraries*, 28, no. 3 (1967): 184-85.

Josey, E. J. "Diversity: Political and Social Barriers." *Journal of Library Administration*, 27, no. 1 (1999): 191-202.

Josey, E. J. "Diversity and Information Services." *DttP*, 23 (1995): 46.

Josey, E. J. "A Dreamer with a Tiny Spark." In *The Black Librarian in America*, edited by E. J. Josey, 297-23. Lanham, MD: Scarecrow Press, 1970.

Josey, E. J. "Education for Library Services to Cultural Minorities." *Education Libraries*, 15, no. 3 (1991): 16-22.

Josey, E. J. "Edward Christopher Williams: A Librarian's Librarian." *The Journal of Library History*, 4, no. 2 (1969): 107.

Josey, E. J. "E. J. Josey." In *Notable Black American Men*, edited by Jessie Carney Smith, 670-72. Detroit, MI: Gale Research, 1999.

Josey, E. J. "Enhancing and Strengthening Faculty-Library Relationships." *The Journal of Negro Education*, 33, no. 2 (1964): 191-96.

Josey, E. J. "Full Faculty Status This Century." *Library Journal*, 97, no. 6 (1972): 984-89.

Josey, E. J. "The Future of the Black College Library." *Library Journal*, 94, no. 16 (1969): 3019-22.

Josey, E. J. "The Future of the Black Library." *Library Journal*, 94, no. 16 (1969): 3019-4022.

Josey, E. J. "Giving Disadvantaged Negro Children a Reading Start." *Negro History Bulletin*, 29, no. 7 (1966): 155.

Josey, E. J. "Josey's Greatest IFLA Moment." *American Libraries*, 20, no. 11 (1989): 1062.

Josey, E. J. "Libraries and Adult Learners." *The Bookmark (Albany)*, 40, no. 3 (1982): 1.

Josey, E. J. "Libraries and Emancipation Centennial." *Negro History Bulletin*, 26, no. 7 (1963): 219-21.

Josey, E. J. "Libraries and the Liberation of Black Folk." *North Carolina Libraries*, 35, no. 2 (1977): 3-9.

Josey, E. J. "Libraries, Reading, and the Liberation of Black People." *Library Scene*, 1, no. 1 (1972): 4-7.

Josey, E. J. "Library and Information Services for Cultural Minorities: A Commentary and Analysis of a Report to the National Commission on Libraries and Information Science." *Libri*, 35, no. 4 (1985): 320-32.

Josey, E. J. "Minority Representation in Library and Information Science Programs." *The Bookmark*, 48, no. 1 (1989): 54-57.

Josey, E. J. "More Than Two Decades Later." In *The Black Librarian in America Revisited*, edited by E. J. Josey, 357. Lanham, MD: Scarecrow Press, 1974.

Josey, E. J. "A Mouthful of Civil Rights and an Empty Stomach." *Library Journal*, 90, no. 2 (1965): 202-5.

Josey, E. J. "Negro Youth's Quest for Certainty." *Negro History Bulletin*, 27, no. 7 (1964): 159.

Josey, E. J. "'Out in the Cold: Academic Boycotts and the Isolation of South Africa '" by Lorraine J. Haricombe and F. W. Lancaster (Book Review). *Libraries and Culture*, 31, no. 3/4 (1996): 672-74.

Josey, E. J. "Race Issues in Library History." In *Encyclopedia of Library History*, edited by Wayne A. Wiegand and Donald G. Davis, 533-37. New York: Garland Publishing, 1994.

Josey, E. J. "Radical Badge of Honor." *Library Journal*, 122, no. 17 (1997): 8.

Josey, E. J. "Reading and the Disadvantaged." *Negro History Bulletin*, 28, no. 7 (1965): 156.

Josey, E. J. "Recruitment of International Students: The Pittsburgh Model." *Journal of Education for Library and Information Science*, 32, 3/4 (1991): 216-21.

Josey, E. J. "Remarks on Racism, International Relations and Librarianship." *Progressive Librarian*, 15 (1998): 62-64.

Josey, E. J. "The Role of the College and Research Library Staff in the Instruction in the Use of the Library." *College and Research Libraries*, 23, no. 6 (1962): 492-98.

Josey, E. J. "The Role of Trustees in Helping Eradicate Illiteracy." *The Bookmark (Albany)*, 43, no. 1 (1984): 41-43.

Josey, E. J. "Silence of the Drums: A Survey of the Literature of the Harlem Renaissance." *Afro-Americans in New York Life and History (1977-1989)*, 3, no. 2 (1979): 80.

Josey, E. J. "Social Responsibility and the Library Bill of Rights: The Berninghausen Debate." *Library Journal*, 98 (1973): 32-33.

Josey, E. J. "The State of Diversity." *The Reference Librarian*, 21, no. 45-46 (1964): 5-11.

Josey, E. J. "Use of Libraries: Key to Negro Process." *Negro History Bulletin*, 25, no. 7 (1962): 161-63.

Josey, E. J. "Using Grass Roots Organizations to Support Library Services." *Public Libraries*, 22, no. 1 (1983): 14-16.

Josey, E. J., and Fay M. Blake. "Educating the Academic Librarian." *Library Journal*, 95, no. 2 (1970): 125-30.

Josey, E. J., and Ismail Abdullahi. "Why Diversity in American Libraries." *Library Management*, 23, no. 1/2 (2000): 10-16.

Josey, E. J., and Marva L. DeLoach. "Discrimination and Affirmative Action: Concerns for Black Librarians and Library Workers." In *Librarians' Affirmative Action Handbook*, edited by John F. Harvey and Elizabeth M. Dickinson, 177-99. Metuchen, NJ: Scarecrow, 1983.

Josey, E. J., Marva L. DeLoach, and Alex Boyd. "Shorter Notice—Handbook of Black Librarianship, 2nd ed." *Library Quarterly* 71, no. 4 (2001): 549-50.

Schubert, Joseph F., and E. J. Josey. "Clarifying and Defining Library Services." *The Bookmark (Albany)*, 9, no. 2: n2.

Schubert, Joseph F., and E. J. Josey. "College and University Libraries." *The Bookmark (Albany)*, 45, no. 1 (1986): 1.

Schubert, Joseph F., and E. J. Josey. "Library and Information Education for the Information Society." *The Bookmark (Albany)*, 48, no. 1 (1989): 1.

Schubert, Joseph F., and E. J. Josey. "The New York Library Association Centennial." *The Bookmark (Albany)*, 49, no. 2 (1990): 2.

# Chapter 37
# Spring Reading List 2023

Carol Gilliam

National Library Week 2023 was celebrated April 23–29. The theme was "There's More to the Story." Libraries are full of stories in a variety of formats from picture books to large print, audiobooks to ebooks, and more.

Library infrastructure advances communities by providing interest and technology access as well as a variety of literacy skills. National Library Week is a great time to tell your library's multifaced story . . . and do not forget the celebration of jazz, poetry, Black Music Month, and Juneteenth!

*The Color Line* by Igiaba Scego
Inspired by true events, this haunting novel intertwines the lives of two Black female artists in Italy.

*Concentrate: Poems* by Courtney Faye Taylor
These poems demand an absolute focus on Black womanhood.

*Conversations in Jazz* by Ralph J. Gleason
Gleason recorded many in-depth interviews with some of the greatest jazz musicians of all time.

*Driving the Green Book, A Road Trip through the Living History of Black Resistance* by Alvin Hall
This book is a vital work of national history, as well as hopeful chronicles of Black resilience and resistance.

*Famous Black Quotations*
First published in 1986, this new edition includes the Obamas, John Legend, and others.

*Historically Black American Icons Who Attended HBCUs* by Alonzo Vereen
A vibrant collection of biographies and illustrated portraits that capture the brilliance and excellence in many fields from politics to STEM.

*I'm Always So Serious* by Karisma Price
A debut collection on Blackness, family, and loss.

*Invisible Boy* by Harrison Mooney
An unforgettable coming-of-age memoir about a Black boy adopted into a white, Christian family.

*The Meaning of Soul: Black Music and Resilience since the 1960s* by Emily J. Lordi
Lordi offers a vision of soul that foregrounds the intricacies of the musical craft.

*Plant Power* by Dr. Ian K. Smith
An essential guide to the power of plants and the benefits of a plant-forward diet.

*A Quiet Teacher* by Adam Oyebanji
A teacher trying to hide in the shadows finds himself embroiled in a murder investigation.

*Serving Herself, the Life and Times of Althea Gibson* by Ashley Brown
A compelling narrative of the trials and triumphs of tennis champion Althea Gibson.

*Still Rising, Famous Black Quotations for the Twenty-First Century* by Janet Cheatham Bell

# Chapter 38
# Bibliotherapy

AFRICAN AMERICAN YOUTH AND MENTAL HEALTH

Mitzi Mack

This bibliography contains journal articles, books, edited anthologies, and other resources representing the nexus of mental health and bibliotherapy in the lives of African American youth. Bibliotherapy is based on the premise that books can serve as potential change agents. Exposure and discussion to books with particular words, themes, and experiences in a story has been known to impact attitudes, skills, and behaviors. With the increased demand for mental health services in the schools, bibliotherapy can be considered an individual or a school-based therapy providing preventive treatment.[1] In fact, in the early 1800s, libraries were of significant value in mental health institutions. Born out of ancient Greek history of libraries, bibliotherapy captured the essence of words as a balm or medicine for the soul as lists of books were curated for therapeutic purposes. In today's current climate of unrest, counselors and librarians have collaborated in the use of bibliotherapy in school settings to address bullying and aggression. Addressing mental health literacy through bibliotherapy has created key opportunities to support students with responsive and preventive services in an affordable and familiar environment.

**BOOKS FOR YOUTH/TEENS**

Alexander, Kwame. *The Crossover*. Houghton Mifflin Harcourt, 2014.

*The Crossover* is one of three books in a trilogy devoted to honoring sports and family. Twin brothers are faced with a family tragedy and the woes of coming of age.

Comrie, Courtne. *Rain Rising*. First edition. Harper, 2022.

When her older brother suffers a near-fatal beating from members of an all-White fraternity, thirteen-year-old Rain Washington's struggle with depression goes from bad to worse. Her emotional health is in dire straits when her favorite teacher invites her to join a group of students who support each other in after-school counseling sessions. Written in dazzling verse, this novel tells a somber yet inspiring story of healing.

Draper, Sharon M. *Forged by Fire*. First edition. Atheneum Books for Young Readers, 1997.

*Forged by Fire* tells the story of Gerald, haunted by family struggles, child abuse, and the loss of a parent. Gerald finds refuge in basketball and learns to survive trauma through the love and strength of family and friends.

Harrison, Vashti. *Big*. First edition. Little Brown and Company, 2023.

Size is addressed in this picture book as it tells the story of a young girl that is often praised for being a 'BIG' girl, until the meaning changes context.

Mbalia, Kwame, et al. *Black Boy Joy*. First edition. Delacorte Press, 2021.

An anthology packed full of stories and poems about the beauty of Black boy joy.

Myers, Walter Dean, and Christopher Myers. *Monster*. Revised Harper Teen edition. HarperTeen/Amistad, 2008.

Written as a screenplay, *Monster* delves into the life of a young Black boy replaying the story of his life through prison and courtroom drama.

Percival, Tom. *Ruby Finds a Worry*. Bloomsbury Publishing, 2021.

This delightful picture book tells the story of Ruby and how she learns to identify and cope with anxiety.

Rhodes, Jewell Parker. *Ghost Boys*. First edition. Little Brown and Company, 2018.

Jerome, a seventh grader, is killed by a police officer in a tragic mishap. In the aftermath of his death, Jerome joins a host of other Black boys killed too early in life.

Reynolds, Jason, and Brendan Kiely. *All American Boys*. First edition. Atheneum Books for Young Readers, 2015.

The right place at the wrong time is the premise of this story of Rashad, a young Black male with a promising future and the impact of police brutality.

Stone, Nic. *Chaos Theory*. First edition. Crown Books for Young Readers, 2023.

Shelby and Andy meet at a time in life when they are both at a crossroad of indecision. Their bond becomes one that could be lasting.

Stone, Nic. *Dear Martin*. First edition. Crown, 2017.

Justyce MacAlister begins a journey of self-discovery as he writes in a journal to Dr. Martin Luther King to express his discontent living life between two worlds.

Woodson, Jacqueline, and López Rafael. *The Year We Learned to Fly*. Nancy Paulsen Books, 2022.

In this story, a brother and sister use their grandmother's advice to help them move beyond a frustrating time and situation.

## BOOKS FOR ADULTS

Alderson, Sarah Louise. "Books: The Novel Cure: Books as Therapy." *The British Journal of General Practice: The Journal of The Royal College of General Practitioners*, vol. 66, no. 648, 2016, p. 379. doi:10.3399/bjgp16X685993.

This text is chock-full of suggested books to support a variety of mental health issues. Organized in alphabetical order according to mental health issues, the authors provide a multitude of novels that speak to the promotion of health and happiness.

Cacchioli, Serena, et al. "The Healing Power of Books: The Novel Cure as a Culturally Tailored Literary Experiment." *Reading Today*. UCL Press, 2018, pp. 145-56. JSTOR, https://doi.org/10.2307/j.ctt20krxjt.15.

The authors of this article candidly capture the importance of the healing power of books by walking through the various translations of the text *The Novel Cure* and making a case for the power of words. Each translated version of the book *The Novel Cure* had to be represented in an appropriate context and manner according to the adaptation of the new language translation.

Green, Kelda. *Rethinking Therapeutic Reading: Lessons from Seneca Montaigne Wordsworth and George Eliot*. Anthem Press, 2020.

Using examples from literary artists, the author makes a connection to dealing with life's situations and troubles through worthy reads from George Eliot, Wordsworth, and other notable literary writers.

## JOURNAL ARTICLES

Byrd, Janice A., et al. "Reading Woke: Exploring How School Counselors May Use Bibliotherapy with Adolescent Black Boys." *Professional School Counseling*, vol. 25, no. 1, part 4, 2021, pp. 1-12.

An investigation into the use of "woke" books with bibliotherapy techniques is the focus of this article. The writers consider bibliotherapy as a therapeutic approach to address student trauma by using select books including African American boys as the protagonist. This approach was selected in the study in hopes of garnering identity development through the relationship students make with the main character. One caveat for the investigators of the study was a recommendation for individuals implementing the bibliotherapy to come to terms with their own implicit bias.

De Vries, Dawn, et al. "Healing with Books: A Literature Review of Bibliotherapy Used with Children and Youth Who Have Experienced Trauma." *Therapeutic Recreation Journal*, vol. 51, no. 1, 2017, pp. 48-74.

Previous studies from 2014 demonstrated proven success using bibliotherapy with students to build coping skills after experiencing a trauma. In this article, the writers expound on the two types of bibliotherapy—cognitive and affective—and methods of following the steps to ensure techniques are implemented with fidelity. A thorough explanation of the process is provided within the article, in addition to recommendations for further consideration on different angles of the study.

Freeman, J. C. "Bibliotherapy as a Bullying and Aggressive Behavior Intervention in Schools." *International Journal of Nursing & Clinical Practices*, vol. 3, 2016, pp. 202-5.

Bullying and aggression are key concerns in school settings. The author addresses ways in which bibliotherapy has been successfully implemented in school settings to deal with bullying.

Gladding, Samuel T., and Claire Gladding. "The ABCs of Bibliotherapy for School Counselors." *The School Counselor*, vol. 39, no. 1, 1991, pp. 7-13. JSTOR, http://www.jstor.org/stable/23901529.

Various types of bibliotherapy examples are addressed in this article to provide step-by-step considerations when seeking to implement either strategy in a school setting.

Mumbauer, Janyna, and Viki Kelchner. "Promoting Mental Health Literacy through Bibliotherapy in School-Based Settings." *Professional School Counseling*, vol. 21, no. 1, 2017, pp. 85-94. JSTOR, https://www.jstor.org/stable/90023519.

Shepherd, Terry, and Lynn B. Iles. "What Is Bibliotherapy?" *Language Arts*, vol. 53, no. 5, 1976, pp. 569-71. JSTOR, http://www.jstor.org/stable/41404208. Accessed 13 November, 2023.

An explanation of bibliotherapy is offered in this article and a discussion of the practical value of bibliotherapy when implemented in the lives of children.

Tukhareli, Natalia. "Bibliotherapy in a Library Setting: Reaching Out to Vulnerable Youth." *Partnership: The Canadian Journal of Library and Information Practice and Research*, vol. 6, no. 1, 2011, pp. 1-18.

This project sought to investigate the use of bibliotherapy techniques in the library with individuals dealing with HIV/AIDS. Bibliotherapy was defined as the practice of using books to impact the lives of individuals facing various traumas. The candidates for the study were between the ages of five and eighteen and twenty and fifty-eight living in Johannesburg at a care facility. Socioeconomics contributed a major factor in the lives of study candidates and was perpetuated by stigmatization. Since the library setting was used for the study, group storytelling sessions served as the main source of the process.

**NOTE**

1. Janya Mumbauer and Viki Kelchner. "Promoting Mental Health Literacy through Bibliotherapy In School-Based Settings." *Professional School Counseling*, vol. 21, no. 1, 2017, pp. 85-94. *JSTOR*, https://www.jstor.org/stable/90023519.

# Chapter 39

# Bibliography of Select African and African American Films for Collection Development and Academic Course Instruction

Monique Threatt

Media librarians face many challenges to provide access to films in either a physical format or via streaming for classroom use. For the media librarian, building a media collection in support of teaching, research, and learning is a delicate art within itself. Media librarians rely heavily on collection development policies to help guide acquisitions, budget, format, scope of coverage, subject boundaries, preservation, and more. However, the majority of available films used for course instruction in academic institutions are in alignment with an arts and humanities curriculum versus those in support of STEM majors.

Listed here is a select, and subjective, list of films depicting Africans in the diaspora that are heavily used for course instruction on the Indiana University Bloomington campus. Also included are a few supplemental external archive and database resources. You may find these resources useful as they can serve as learning tools for faculty, staff, and students. The annotations listed below are written primarily by catalogers and via distributor web pages. However, the contributor provides additional text. The list is by no means complete.

**TOP TWENTY RECOMMENDED TITLES FOR COLLECTION DEVELOPMENT AND COURSE INSTRUCTION**

McQueen, Steve, et al. *12 Years a Slave*. Beverly Hills, CA: Twentieth Century Fox Home Entertainment, 2014.

Based on the true story of Solomon Northup. It is 1841, and Northup, an accomplished, free citizen of New York, is kidnapped and sold into slavery. Stripped of his identity and deprived of all dignity, Northup is ultimately purchased by ruthless plantation owner Edwin Epps and must find the strength within to survive. Filled with powerful performances by an astonishing cast including Chiwetel Ejiofor, Michael Fassbender, Benedict Cumberbatch, Brad Pitt, and newcomer Lupita Nyong'o, *12 Years a Slave* is both an unflinching account of slavery in American history and a celebration of the indomitable power of hope. Subject areas: African American studies, comparative literature, human rights, slavery. —Indiana University Catalog

*13th*. Directed by Ava DuVernay, Forward Movement, Kandoo Films, Netflix, 2016. Netflix, youtube.com/watch?v=krfcq5pF8u8

(Permission granted by filmmaker to show this Netflix original in class.) Director, filmmaker, producer, and writer Ava DuVernay takes an in-depth look at the prison system in the United States and how it reveals the nation's history of racial inequality. Subject areas: African American studies, law and legal, prisons. —imdb.com

Dixon, Thomas, et al. *The Birth of a Nation*. Image Entertainment [distributor], 1994, originally released in 1915.

This film is in the public domain. A Civil War spectacular. It portrays life in the South during and after the Civil War as revealed in a story depicting the war itself, the conflict between the defeated Southerners and emancipated renegade Negroes, the despoiling of the South during the carpetbagger period, and the revival of the Southern white man's honor through the efforts of the Ku Klux Klan. Subject areas: African American studies, history, law, slavery, stereotypes. —Indiana University Catalog

Coogler, Ryan, et al. *Black Panther*. Multiscreen edition. Marvel Studios, 2018.

Based on the Marvel comics by Stan Lee and Jack Kirby, King T'Challa returns home to the isolated, technologically advanced African nation of Wakanda to serve as new leader. However, T'Challa soon finds that he is challenged for the throne from divisions within his own country. When two enemies conspire to destroy Wakanda, the hero known as Black Panther must join forces with CIA agent Everett K. Ross and members of the Wakandan Special Forces, to prevent Wakanda from being drawn into a world war. Subject areas: African American studies, comparative literature, comics, English, superheroes. —Indiana University Catalog

Johnson, Broderick, et al. *The Blind Side*. Widescreen version. Distributed by Warner Home Video, 2010.

Michael Oher is a homeless African American teenager. Mike is taken in by the Touhys, a well-to-do white family who help him fulfill his potential. At the same time, Oher's presence in the Touhys' lives leads them to some insightful self-discoveries of their own. Mike faces a completely different set of challenges to overcome—as both a football player and student. Subject Areas: African American studies, Adoptees, homeless teenagers, introduction to reading, writing, and inquiry (English), ethics, sports. —Indiana University Catalog

Kantayya, Shalini, et al. *Coded Bias.* Women Make Movies, 2020.

*Coded Bias* explores the fallout of MIT media lab researcher Joy Buolamwini's startling discovery that facial recognition does not see dark-skinned faces accurately, and her journey to push for the first-ever legislation in the US to govern against bias in the algorithms that impact us all. Subject areas: African American studies, artificial intelligence, facial recognition, gender studies, psychology. —Coded Bias website

Walker, Alice, et al. *The Color Purple.* Wide screen ed. Warner Home Video, 1992.

An uneducated woman living in the rural American south who was raped by her father, deprived of the children she bore him, and forced to marry a brutal man she calls "Mister" is transformed by the friendship of two remarkable women, acquiring self-worth and the strength to forgive. Subject areas: African American literature, comparative literature, English, gender studies. —Indiana University Catalog

Dash, Julie, et al. *Daughters of the Dust.* Deluxe ed. Kino International, 1999.

*Daughters of the Dust* tells the story of a large African American family as they prepare to move north at the dawn of the twentieth century. It explores the unique culture of the Gullah people, descendants of slaves who lived in relative isolation on the Sea Islands off the Georgia coast. As the generations struggle with the decision to leave, their rich Gullah heritage and African roots rise to the surface. Subject areas: African American studies, Georgia Sea Islands, Gullah culture and language. —Indiana University Catalog

Lee, Spike, Danny Aiello, and St. Clair Bourne. *Do the Right Thing.* MCA Universal Home Video, 1995.

This powerful visual feast combines humor and drama with memorable characters while tracing the course of a single day on a block in the Bedford-Stuyvesant area of Brooklyn. It is the hottest day of the year, a scorching twenty-four-hour period that will change the lives of its residents forever. Subject areas: African American studies, film and filmmaking analysis and criticism (Media School), introduction to reading, writing, and inquiry (English), music in film, racial tension. —Indiana University Catalog

von Wangenheim, Annette. *Josephine Baker: Black Diva in a White Man's World.* Kanopy Streaming, 2015.

A tender, revealing documentary about one of the most famous and popular performing artists of the twentieth century. Her legendary banana belt dance created theater history; her song "J'ai deux amours" became a classic, and her hymn. The film focuses on her life and work from a perspective that analyses images of Black people in popular culture. It portrays the artist in the mirror of European colonial cliches and presents her as a resistance fighter, an ambulance driver during World War II, and an outspoken activist against racial discrimination involved in the worldwide Black consciousness movement of the twentieth century. Subject areas: African American studies, activism, dance, music in film, theater, racism. —Indiana University Catalog

Spielberg, Steven, et al. *Lincoln.* Universal City, California: DreamWorks Pictures, 2013.

A revealing drama that focuses on the sixteenth president's tumultuous final months in office. In a nation divided by war and the strong winds of change, Lincoln pursues a course of action designed to end the war, unite the country, and abolish slavery. With the moral courage and fierce determination to succeed, his choices during this critical moment will change the fate of generations to come. Subject areas: African American studies, Civil War, public law and government relations, slavery. —Indiana University Catalog

Walker-Canton, Roxana, et al. *Living Thinkers: An Autobiography of Black Women in the Ivory Tower.* Women Make Movies, 2013.

"Living Thinkers . . . examines the intersection of race, class and gender for Black women professors and administrators working in U.S. colleges and universities today. Through their diverse narratives, from girlhood to the present, Black women from different disciplines share experiences that have shaped them, including segregated schooling as children, and the trials, disappointments and triumphs encountered in Academia. Though more than 100 years have passed since the doors to higher education opened for Black women, their numbers as faculty members are woefully low and for many still, the image of Black women as intellectuals is incomprehensible. And while overtly expressed racism, sexism and discrimination have declined, their presence is often still often unacknowledged. Through frank and sometimes humorous conversations, this documentary interrogates notions of education for girls and women and the stereotypes and traditions that affect the status of Black women both in and out of the Academy. A perfect companion film for any classroom discussion on the intersection of racism, sexism and/or feminism." Subject areas: African American studies, education.—Indiana University Catalog

Lee, Spike, et al. *Malcolm X.* Warner Home Video, 2000.

Screen version of the life of Malcolm X, who through his religious conversion to Islam, found the strength to rise up from a criminal past to become an influential civil rights leader. Subject Areas: African American studies, activism, civil rights, music in film, racism, religion. —Indiana University Catalog

Jenkins, Barry, et al. *Moonlight*. Lionsgate, 2017.

This Academy Award–winning film highlights a young Black man who struggles to find his place in the world while growing up in a rough neighborhood of Miami. Subject areas: African American studies, bullying, LGBTQ+, young adults. —Indiana University Catalog

Peele, Jordan, et al. *Nope*. Collector's edition. Universal Studios Distribution Services, 2022.

As the horses on their ranch mysteriously go missing, two siblings struggling to run their father's ranch and business outside of L.A. need to discover what is happening or forfeit their legacy. As they observe phenomena that defy explanation, they involve an esoteric filmmaker and their sometimes-business partner, the child star turned owner of the theme park down the road. Subject areas: African American studies, film and filmmaking analysis and criticism (media school), horror, introduction to reading, writing and inquiry (English), science fiction. —Indiana University Catalog

McQueen, Steve, et al. *Small Axe: A Collection of 5 Films from Steve McQueen*. BBC, 2020.

*Small Axe* is based on the real-life experiences of London's West Indian community and is set between 1969 and 1982. *Mangrove* tells the true story of The Mangrove Nine who clashed with London police in 1970. The trial that followed was the first judicial acknowledgment of behavior motivated by racial hatred within the Metropolitan Police. *Lovers Rock* is about a single evening at a house party in 1980s West London. It develops intertwined relationships against a background of violence, romance, and music. *Red, white and blue* spotlights the true story of Leroy Logan, who at a young age saw his father assaulted by two police officers, motivating him to join the Metropolitan Police and change their racist attitudes from within. *Alex Wheatle* follows the true story of award-winning writer Alex Wheatle from a young boy through his early adult years. Having spent his childhood in a mostly white institutional care home with no love or family, he finally finds not only a sense of community for the first time in Brixton, but his identity and ability to grow his passion for music and DJing. When he is thrown in prison during the Brixton Uprising of 1981, he confronts his past and sees a path to healing. *Education* is the coming-of-age story of twelve-year-old Kingsley, who has a fascination for astronauts and rockets. When Kingsley is pulled to the headmaster's office for being disruptive in class, he discovers he is being sent to a school for those with "special needs." Distracted by working two jobs, his parents are unaware of the unofficial segregation policy at play, preventing many Black children from receiving the education they deserve, until a group of West Indian women take matters into their own hands. Subject areas: activism, West Indians in London, music in film, racism. —Indiana University Catalog

Riley, Boots, et al. *Sorry to Bother You*. Twentieth Century Fox Home Entertainment, 2018.

In an alternate present-day version of Oakland, telemarketer Cassius Green discovers a magical key to professional success, propelling him into a macabre universe. Subject areas: African American studies, introduction to reading, writing, and inquiry (English), telemarketing. —Indiana University Catalog

Fruchtman, Rob, Lisa Fruchtman, and Lex Fletcher. *Sweet Dreams*. Liro Films, 2014.

Powerful sounds pierce the silence of the Rwandan countryside. Curious children gawk outside the gate. This is something new in Rwanda, a group of women, sixty strong, pounding out rhythms of power and joy. They are Ingoma Nshya, Rwanda's first and only women's drumming troupe, open to women from both sides of the conflict in which close to a million were killed by neighbors, friends, and even family. When, with the help of Brooklyn ice cream purveyors, the troupe decides to open the country's first ice cream shop, this spirited film evolves into a surprising and joyful tale of courage, ingenuity, and hope in the face of the unthinkable. *Sweet Dreams* follows this remarkable group of women as they emerge from the devastation of the genocide to create a new future for themselves. Subject areas: African and African American studies, genocide, music in film. —Indiana University Catalog

McCullough, David G. *That Rhythm—Those Blues*. GTN production; presented by WGBH/Boston, WNET/New York, and KCET/Los Angeles, 1989.

Deals with rhythm and blues music performed by Black musicians during the 1940s and 1950s in small towns and rural areas of the American South, and their aspirations of performing in the Apollo Theater. Subject areas: African American studies, music in film, racism. —Indiana University Catalog

Dunye, Cheryl, et al. *The Watermelon Woman*. Restored twentieth anniversary edition. First Run Features, 2017.

Set in Philadelphia, *The Watermelon Woman* is the story of Cheryl (Cheryl Dunye), a twenty-something Black lesbian struggling to make a documentary about Fae Richards, a beautiful and elusive 1930s Black film actress popularly known as "The Watermelon Woman." While uncovering the meaning of Fae Richards's life, Cheryl experiences a total upheaval in her personal life. Her love affair with Diana (Guinevere Turner, *Go Fish*), a beautiful white woman, and her interactions with the gay and Black communities, are subject to the comic yet biting criticism of her best friend Tamara (Valerie Walker). Meanwhile, each answer Cheryl discovers about the Watermelon Woman evokes a flurry of new questions about herself and her future. Subject areas: African American studies, LGBTQ+, interracial dating, music in film. —Indiana University Catalog

**TOP TEN RECOMMENDED ARCHIVES, CATALOGS, AND DATABASES**

In addition to the resources listed below, numerous academic institutions curate their own African American film collections such as Emory, Harvard, Princeton, and Yale. Most collections provide open access; however, some collections are restricted to campus use. Abstracts provided below are from distributor websites with minor editing from the author.

African American Home Movie Archive (https://www.aahma.org/)

Users will need to request login instructions. The African American Home Movie Archive was created to serve as an online resource for researchers, educators, students, archive and library professionals, and other interested parties. The main feature of the website is the Black Home Movie Index, an aggregate of African American home movie collections from the early 1920s through the mid-1980s.

Black Film Archive (https://blackfilmarchive.com/). Open access.

Black Film Archive celebrates the rich, abundant history of Black cinema dedicated to making historically and culturally significant films made from 1898 to 1989 about Black people.

Black Film Center & Archive (https://bfca.indiana.edu/index.html). Open access.

Forty years of Black cinema and media scholarship, the Black Film Center & Archive at Indiana University at Bloomington, Indiana, aims to not only address the longstanding underrepresentation and absence of Black voices within film history and curricula, but also to create a local hub for Black cinema resources in the center of the Midwest. To date, the BFC&A remains the only repository in the world solely dedicated to the collection, preservation, and promotion of Black cinema.

Black Studies in Video Catalog (a product of Alexander Street Press [ASP]) (https://alexanderstreet.com/discipline/black-studies). Database fee.

The Black Studies in Video database is an award-winning video collection of archival footage, powerful interviews with leading figures in the civil rights movement, and documentaries examining the Black experience in the arts, history, politics, public, and private life, and much more. The collection contains five hundred hours and is the exclusive streaming source for the SNCC Legacy Video Collection. Additional subject areas provided by ASP include, but are not limited to: anthropology, art and architecture, border and migration studies, dance, education, ethnographic studies, fashion, health, human rights, American and world history, Indigenous studies, LGBT, music, news archives that include CNN, nursing, opera, psychology, theater, silent film, sports medicine, and much more.

California Newsreel Catalog (https://newsreel.org/)

Film and video for social change since 1968. Includes titles on African American perspectives and the Library of African Cinema.

HistoryMakers Digital Archive (https://da.thehistorymakers.org/home). Database fee.

An African American oral history video collection. Includes interviewees from across the United States, from a variety of fields, and with memories stretching from the 1890s to the present. Rather than focus on one particular part of a person's life or a single subject, such as a career or participation in the civil rights movement, the interviews are life oral histories covering the person's entire span of memories as well as their family's oral history.

Internet Archive (https://archive.org/about/) and Library of Congress Public Domain Films (https://www.loc.gov/film-and-videos/?q=african+americans)

The Internet Archive and the Library of Congress Public Domain Films are both open access digital repositories containing both films and film clips related to African American history and culture.

Schomburg Center for Research in Black Culture (https://www.nypl.org/locations/schomburg)

The Schomburg Center for Research in Black Culture in Harlem, one of the New York Public Library's renowned research libraries, is a world-leading cultural institution devoted to the research, preservation, and exhibition of materials focused on African American, African diaspora, and African experiences.

Third World Newsreel Catalog (https://www.twn.org/tidy default.aspx)

Third World Newsreel (TWN) is an alternative media arts organization that fosters the creation, appreciation, preservation, and dissemination of independent film and video by and about people of color and social justice issues.

Women Make Movies Catalog (https://www.wmm.com/)

A collection of nearly seven hundred films is used by thousands of cultural, educational, and community organizations across North America and throughout the world. Its long-standing commitment to diversity shows in its catalog, more than half of which is produced by women from different cultures, as well as by LGBTQI women, older women, women with disabilities, and women of color.

# Chapter 40
# Black Heritage Reference Collection

LANGSTON HUGHES COMMUNITY LIBRARY AND CULTURAL CENTER

Christine Zarett

At the beginning of 2023, we reviewed the Collection Development Policy for the Black Heritage Reference Center of the Langston Hughes Community Library and Cultural Center, which was approved in February 1997 and has not been updated since.

Overall, we found the policy solid, but some language needed to be updated. The collection development policy guides the selection of materials that maintain a comprehensive reference and circulating collection, reflecting the study and interpretation of Black history and culture.

The collection "serves as a deterrent against cultural deprivation, historical misconceptions, misinformation and image distortion."[1] The Black Heritage collection provides the "informational, educational, cultural, recreational, and research needs of the user community, including students, researchers, educators, historians, all other interested users; and any individual or organization that seeks access to the specialized materials in the collection."[2]

In 1969, the Langston Hughes Community Library and Cultural Center was established as a place for the predominantly Black community to come to learn about Black history and culture, as this was not represented in schools and other public library branches. The Langston Hughes Library received its initial funding from the Library Services and Construction Act, which provided funding to underserved libraries and was inspired by the civil rights movement of the 1950s and 1960s. It is the first public institution named after Langston Hughes. This was appropriate because Langston Hughes was an eloquent interpreter of the Black experience and a relentless social activist. It is a testament to community activism that the mission of the library remains steadfast.

What has changed over time is the demographics of the community and material formats. Today, the community has a large Hispanic community, as well as Asian, South Asian, and Middle Eastern populations and a still active Black presence.

The importance of Black history and culture to United States history cannot be overstated. US history centers around Black history and Black history transforms US history. It is necessary for the collection to convey this sentiment to all people, not solely to the Black community. Many members of the community discovered and learned about Black history and culture by reading material from the collection and is central to their community activism.

The breadth and depth of the collection is comprehensive. This allows reference questions to be answered accurately, and authoritative information with context is provided. Material is accessible for Black studies classes on an array of subjects and students and researchers are able to find material related to their work.

The list of subjects below illustrates the scope of the collection and demonstrates how the collection is able to provide a careful and correct history.

Popular subjects held in the BHRC are:

- History: Africa, African diaspora, America
- Slavery
- Slave Trade
- Slave Narratives
- Civil Rights Movement
- United States—History—Civil War
- Black Power Movement
- Black Arts Movement
- Black Lives Matter
- Harlem Renaissance
- Literature including Heinemann Caribbean Writers Series, Heinemann African Writers Series, classics by Toni Morrison, James Baldwin, a collection of Langston Hughes writings, and others.
- Critical Race Theory
- Law
- African American: Biographies
- African American intellectuals
- Racism: United States
- African American: Poetry
- African American: Athletes
- African Americans: Music
- African American Art
- Dance
- African American: Photographers
- Black Panthers
- African American: Women

Other notable Black Heritage Reference Collection resources include:

- Encyclopedias: *Encyclopedia of Race and Crime, Race and Racism in the United States An Encyclopedia of the American Mosaic, Encyclopedia of African American Education, The Greenwood Encyclopedia of African American Folklore, Encyclopedia of the Middle Passage, The Jim Crow Encyclopedia, Encyclopedia of Slave Resistance and Rebellion, Encyclopedia of African American Politics, Encyclopedia of Race and Ethnic Studies, Encyclopedia of Rap and Hip-Hop Culture,* and *Encyclopedia of Negro League Baseball*.
- Writings, letters, and speeches: Martin Luther King Jr., Malcolm X, Marcus Garvey, Langston Hughes, Charles W. Chestnutt, Alice Walker, Arna Bontemps, Captain Paul Cuffe, Jackie Robinson, June Jordan, C. L. R. James, Ralph Ellison, Zora Neale Hurston, George Jackson, Bayard Rustin, Wynton Marsalis, Tupac Shakur, Audre Lorde, W. E. B. Du Bois, and Barack Obama.

Encyclopedias and primary source documents provide valuable starting points and introductions to a topic when commencing research or browsing out of curiosity. The subjects noted provide suggestions for representation in a Black Heritage collection. And critical to any Black Heritage collection is Literature and the Heinemann African Writers Series and Caribbean Writers Series, which are collections of reissued and translated books of recognized authors and early works by previously unknown authors. They are widely acclaimed and have been used by researchers for articles and author studies.

Oppression, discrimination, and violence are omnipresent in Black history. Reading stories about resistance to slavery, Jim Crow, lynching, and other forms of oppression like red lining and incarceration and understanding these lived experiences shifts one's thinking about Black history and culture and one can see their life as part of the larger human experience. Black history is about combating racism through achievement in the arts, sciences, and literature. Notable is how much Black achievement is documented and held in the collection. Achievement is resistance. Resistance is a theme throughout.

Discovering that Black resistance to oppression existed from the first day Africans were forced into slavery presents a true accounting and dismisses historical misconceptions.

**BLACK HERITAGE MATERIAL AND ITS USEFULNESS**

When the library locked down during the pandemic, virtual programs were created using material from the collection. A wonderful book from the collection, *Reminiscences of My Life in Camp: An African American Woman's Civil War Memoir* by Susie King Taylor published in 1902, was read aloud and discussed as a group virtually. (This book was typed into a Google Docs and screen shared with a virtual group.) This memoir is a moving narrative. Ms. King Taylor, born into slavery in Georgia, writes about her time traveling with the Union Army and the 33rd United States Colored Troops as a teen. Ms. King Taylor describes nursing wounded soldiers, shares details about the Civil War and her time living and traveling in the South. She also describes teaching and opening schools only to have them closed because of racism, witnessing a lynching, having to work as a domestic, and her time living in Boston, Massachusetts. She praises Black men and women's work to create better lives free from slavery and keeps the memory of these men and women alive.

Each chapter in this memoir has so much to unpack, from life in the antebellum South, recollections from the Civil War, and personal recollections of life as a Black woman in nineteenth-century America. This book, like all the materials in the collection, inspires one to look deeper into Black history. Another important point is that this memoir, like other writings in the collection, allows the reader into the interior lives of Black men and women, demonstrating the transformative power of literature. Reading stories evokes empathy and provides the student, researcher, and reader the ability to ask better questions.

Black Presence in New York is a Black studies college course taught at Baruch College, CUNY. The following bibliography was created listing titles that chronicle the experience and history of the Black presence in New York, how slavery shaped both Black and white New Yorkers, the abolitionist movement in New York, the move from slavery to freedom, the treatment of Blacks in New York, and Black activism in New York.

**BLACK PRESENCE IN NEW YORK BIBLIOGRAPHY**

Alexander, Leslie M. *African or American?: Black Identity and Political Activism in New York City, 1784–1861*. Urbana, University of Illinois Press, 2008.

From 1784 to the eve of the Civil War in New York, this book provides a detailed account of Black activism and the founding of the African society in response to inequality through examination of Black newspapers, speeches, and organizational records. (Call Number: 305.896 A)

Bascom, Lionel C., editor. *A Renaissance in Harlem: Lost Essays of the WPA by Ralph Ellison, Dorothy West, and Other Voices of a Generation*. New York: Amistad, 2001. (Call Number 810.8 R)

Berlin, Ira and Leslie M. Harris. *Slavery in New York*. New York: New Press, 2005.

Published to accompany a major exhibit at the New York Historical Society. (Call Number 974.7049 S)

Dodson, Howard. *The Black New Yorkers: The Schomburg Illustrated Chronology 400 Years of African American History*. New York, John Wiley, 1999. (Call Number 974.7004 A)

Hodges, Graham Russell. *David Ruggles: A Radical Black Abolitionist and the Underground Railroad in New York City*. Chapel Hill: University of North Carolina Press, 2010.

David Ruggles (1810–1849) was a heroic and often overlooked figure of the early abolitionist movement in America. (Call Number: B Ruggles H)

Hodges, Graham Russell. *Root and Branch: African Americans in New York & East Jersey 1613–1863*. Chapel Hill: University of North Carolina, 1999.

From the arrival of the first African on Manhattan Island in 1613 to bloody draft riots of 1863, an all-inclusive history of Black life, including work, religion, activism, resistance. (Call Number: 974.71 Hodges)

Johnson, James Weldon. *Black Manhattan*. New York: Arno Press, 1930.

This book traces the Black experience in New York from the prerevolutionary period to the Harlem Renaissance of the 1920s. (Call Number: 326 Johnson)

Peterson, Carla L. *Black Gotham: A Family History of African Americans in Nineteenth-Century New York City*. New Haven, CT: Yale University Press, 2011.

This book counters the notion that not all African Americans were enslaved. (Call number 305.896 P)

White, Shane. *Stories of Freedom in Black New York*. Cambridge, MA: Harvard University Press, 2002.

Black New Yorkers experience moving from slavery to freedom. (Call Number 974.71 W)

The class also accessed poems from an anthology, *In Search of Color Everywhere* by E. Ethelbert Miller, that included artists from New York or who lived in New York. As part of the Black Presence in New York course, students read poems for a Langston Hughes Day Celebration, an annual event at the Langston Hughes Library.

Essays from the Black Heritage collection were shared digitally for online classes. Examples include:

- *From #BlackLivesMatter to Black Liberation* by Keeanga-Yamahtta Taylor
- *A Renaissance in Harlem: Lost Essays of the WPA*, by Ralph Ellison, Dorothy West, and Other Voices of a Generation edited by Lionel C. Bascom
- WPA Slave Narratives.

The WPA (Works Progress Administration) Slave Narratives are an essential resource held in the collection. The WPA Slave Narratives are first-person accounts of formerly enslaved people and compiled in seventeen states from 1936 to 1938. This collection provides life histories told by those who experienced slavery. The WPA slave narratives have been accessed by many Black studies classes for presentations, papers, and class visits. The narratives shift one's thinking, reject any impulse to diminish the brutality of slavery, and makes clear that slavery was morally wrong.

Other examples of bibliographies requested and created for Black studies classes, students, and researchers include:

- The Black Press
- The Great Migration
- African Free Schools in New York
- Harlem Renaissance Writers of Caribbean Descent
- Environment, Health, Land, Earth
- Celebrating the Harlem Renaissance
- African Methodist Episcopal Church Doctoral Research Project

Material from the collection is also used for programming and displays, and feedback is always positive. Community members often respond saying, "Why didn't I know this?" or "Thank you, I did not know this."

This response demonstrates some of the gaps in knowledge and understanding United States history. History can be ugly and unpleasant. Unless the population is equipped with the knowledge of history, we cannot have a conversation about the present.

As W. E. B. Du Bois wrote:

> Nations reel and stagger on their way; they make hideous mistakes; they commit frightful wrongs; they do great and beautiful things. . . . And shall we not best guide humanity by telling the truth about all this so far as the truth ascertainable?[3]

Black history is ascertainable. The highest circulation titles reveal a range of subjects in the collection and validate the necessity to develop and hold a comprehensive collection. Physical books present numerous topics for further exploration and learning, reinforcing the purpose of developing a collection that meets the needs and interests of students, researchers, and the general public. Holding a physical collection versus online resources allows for browsing and serendipitous and authoritative discoveries of history and culture. As you can see, publication dates range from the 1930s to the present and have been evolving since 1969 (the Langston Hughes Library's founding). Titles acquired come from the Queens Public Library collection development division and independently by the curator selected from reading book reviews, updates from literary organizations, attending book festivals, and subscribing to literary newsletters. Old and damaged titles are replaced if titles still available for purchase.

Here is a list in order of highest circulation by subject and title:

| Subject | TITLE/AUTHOR |
|---|---|
| African Americans—Mental Health | *Post Traumatic Slave Syndrome: America's Legacy of Enduring Injury and Healing* by Joy DeGruy Leary (2005) |
| African American Musicians—Interviews | *Notes and Tones: Musician to Musician Interviews* by Arthur Taylor (1982) |
| Nkrumah, Kwame, 1909-1972 | *Ghana: The Autobiography of Kwame Nkrumah* (1971, c1957) |
| African Americans—Poetry | *And Still I Rise* by Maya Angelou (1978) |
| Psychological Fiction | *Passing* by Nella Larsen; with an introduction by Ntozake Shange (2000) |
| Historical Fiction | *Things Fall Apart* by Chinua Achebe: with an introduction by Kwame Anthony Appiah (1958) |
| France—Colonies—Africa | *Toward the African Revolution: Political Essays* by Frantz Fanon; translated from the French by Haakon Chevalier (1988, c1967) |
| United States—Race Relations | *Black Lies / White Lies: The Truth according to Tony Brown* by Tony Brown (1995) |
| African Americans—Illinois—Chicago—Fiction | *Only Twice I've Wished for Heaven: A Novel* by Dawn Turner Trice (1997) |
| African Americans—Religion | *The Cross and the Lynching Tree* by James H. Cone (2011) |
| Santeria | *Santeria: An African Religion in America* by Joseph M. Murphy (c1988) |
| Bildungsromans | *For the Love of Money: A Novel* by Omar Tyree (c2000) |
| Finance, Personal—United States | *Zero Debt: The Ultimate Guide to Financial Freedom* by Lynnette Khalfani-Cox (2009) |
| African American Women—Fiction | *The Color Purple* by Alice Walker (1992) |
| Dagaaba (African people)—Rites and ceremonies | *The Healing Wisdom of Africa: Finding Life Purpose through Nature, Ritual, and Community* by Malidoma Patrice Somé (1998) |
| Feminism—United States—Evaluation | *Feminist Theory from Margin to Center* by bell hooks (1984) |
| Coltrane, John, 1926-1967 | *Clawing at the Limits of Cool: Miles Davis, John Coltrane and the Greatest Jazz Collaboration Ever* by Jasmine Griffin and Salim Washington (2008) |
| African Americans—Economic conditions | *Collective Courage: A History of African American Cooperative Economic Thought and Practice* by Jessica Gordon Nembhard (2014) |
| Critical pedagogy | *Pedagogy of the Oppressed* by Paulo Freire; translated by Myra Bergman Ramos (1993) |

The top twenty highest circulating titles are listed here to demonstrate a real-world example of how developing a special collection can have longevity and diversity. All these titles have circulated within the past four years with many being checked out in 2021 and 2022 and many older titles still circulating.

The Reference Collection, in addition to books and DVDs, holds:

- Microfilm from Black newspapers, Black magazines, and other works from Black writers and publications about slavery, abolitionism, and Africa.
- Some of the Black newspapers on microfilm include *Atlanta Daily World*, *Chicago Defender*, *City Sun*, *Forward Times*, and *The Gary Crusader*. Years of publication range from the 1930s to the 2000s.
- Black magazines include *Black Scholar*, *Black World*, *Ebony*, *Freedomways*, and *Negro Digest* just to name a few.
- The Adele Cohen Music Collection contains musical settings of original works by Langston Hughes set to music.
- A collection of Theses and Dissertations concerning Africans and African Americans in the Diaspora. The focus of the collection is on criticisms of works by Black writers,

with special emphasis on the work of writer and poet laureate of the Harlem Renaissance, Langston Hughes.

The largest percentage of materials held in the circulating collection are in the 300s classification, social science, sociology, and anthropology of the Dewey decimal system, with other classifications fairly proportioned. The circulating collection is audited regularly, and out-of-print or material that has not circulated moves to the reference collection in order to meet possible future requests from students, researchers, or the general public. The circulating collection is 40 percent of the Black Heritage Reference Collection, and the reference or noncirculating materials are 60 percent of the collection.

It is the inclusion of an array of resources that is vital for presenting a holistic history, and that the collection acts as a "deterrent against cultural deprivation, historical misconceptions, misinformation and image distortion"[4] as noted at the beginning of this chapter. The Black Heritage Reference Collection distinguishes the Langston Hughes Community Library and Cultural Center as a unique branch of the Queens Public Library system and characterizes the history of the library and community. It is essential to maintain a physical collection that is inclusive, accessible, and discoverable when developing a Black heritage special collection in a library.

## NOTES

1. Andrew Jackson and Gary E. Strong, *Collection Development Policy: Black Heritage Reference Center of the Langston Hughes Community Library and Cultural Center* (Queens, NY: Queens Borough Public Library, 1997), 6.
2. Ibid.
3. W. E. B. Du Bois, *Black Reconstruction in America: 1860-1880* (New York: Atheneum, 1992), 714.
4. Jackson and Strong, *Collection*, 6.

## WORKS CITED

Du Bois, W. E. B. *Black Reconstruction in America: 1860-1880.* New York: Atheneum, 1992.

Jackson, Andrew, and Gary E. Strong. *Collection Development Policy: Black Heritage Reference Center of the Langston Hughes Community Library and Cultural Center.* Queens, NY: Queens Borough Public Library, 1997.

# Chapter 41

# Selected US Bookstores by State That Are Black-Owned and/or Specialize in Black Books and Other Black Resources

Marva L. DeLoach

Bookstores have played vital roles in Black/Africana history and promotion of Black literature, culture, and knowledge. They have been significant places for Black people to get access to books and other resources, as well as being spaces for them to engage in intellectual and cultural discussions.

A look at the Harlem Renaissance, civil rights movement, Black power movement, and the more contemporary Black bookstores movement address how instrumental they have been and continue to be instrumental in preserving and promoting Black literature, history, and culture. Black bookstores are pillars of knowledge, activism, economic enrichment, empowerment, and community building within the Black community and beyond.

Black bookstores are cultural archives. They have played multifaceted roles resisting censorship, nurturing emerging writers, being educational resources for children and the community at large, in addition to promoting social and racial justice and equity for all.

As long ago as when David Ruggles, a Black freeman and abolitionist, opened the first black-owned bookstore in 1834, the Mirror of Liberty, in New York City, to the National Memorial African Bookstore (aka African National Memorial Bookstore) established in Harlem in 1969 by Lewis H. Michaux, to when Marcus Books opened nearly sixty-four years ago by the Drs. Richardson in the Fillmore District of San Francisco, California (now owned by their daughter Karen Johnson and her siblings in Oakland since 1970) until today's more contemporary edifices, bookstores have played key roles in our communities and beyond. Black bookstores' contributions can't be overstated in the major role they have had in advancing and promoting Black literature, history, culture, and voices.

Black bookstores have surged and ebbed over time. In the 1990s, there were an estimated 325 Black bookstores, which decreased to 149 in 2023. Dimirije Curcic's chronicles in "Black-owned Bookstore Statistics—WordsRated" that Troy Johnson, founder and president of the African American Literature Book Club (AALBC), recounted that Black bookstores increased to at least 200 in the 1990s before decreasing to 54 in 2014. Statistics for over the last few years are charted below:

| Year | Number of Bookstores |
|------|---------------------|
| 2023 | 149 |
| 2022 | 143 |
| 2021 | 100 |
| 2019 | 117 |
| 2018 | 110 |

Reasons for the ebbs have been attributed to increasing competition from larger online retailers, ebooks, and other digital technology, for example. Rising costs for operations, limited resources for Black owners, changing consumer preferences, and the COVID-19 pandemic are other reasons cited for this decline.

Despite such decline, there has been a 30 percent increase in the number of Black bookstores since 2018 that represents 6 percent of the independently owned bookstores in the United States. Fortunately, some places still demand physical books and resources for their tactile experience, aesthetic appeal, and sense of community that physical bookstores offer. Black-owned bookstores' increased presence on Facebook, Instagram, TikTok, YouTube, X (formerly Twitter), email, and other digital entities are examples cited for the uptick in Black-owned bookstores. Other issues cited for the uptick in Black bookstores are the Black Lives Matter movement and unprecedented unrest following several high-profile deaths in the last few years. What does this have to do with Black librarianship?.

Black librarianship and Black bookstores have a symbiotic relationship. They work together to uplift voices and experiences of Black communities. They are interconnected and complementary to each other as they both play significant roles in supporting and promoting Black literature, culture, knowledge, and history.

Black librarianship and Black bookstores support each other's efforts through creating powerful networks that amplify Black voices, promote cultural representation, and foster a place of community and pride within the Black community. Some ways that they can support each other include collection development with diverse collections and book, author, or other resource recommendations, Black history programs, open mic nights, in-person author events/presentations, resource sharing, engaging the community through spelling bees, education, outreach, advocacy, and regular support of each other.

Collective efforts can change how the publishing industry thinks about being more inclusive and diverse. Efforts can impact the thinking of library systems also.

Restraints remain, however, for Black bookstores. We must all work together to consciously support Black-owned bookstores and bookstores specializing in Black resources.

Although Black bookstores specialize in Black/Africana literature, BIPOC or other marginalized groups are represented also. We must support Black-owned businesses because when they are in high demand, the companies tend to become more profitable. Supporting Black businesses contributes to creating entrepreneurial opportunities that fuel economic prosperity. Black businesses are more likely to hire Black workers, and disparity can have ripple effects that impact the broader community, especially increasing more job opportunities for Black people.

It is important to be a minority-owned business because of the economic role it plays in the growth and development of our communities. Black Americans have high stakes in the success of Black-owned businesses because of the impact they have in the Black community and beyond. Black bookstores are essential for promoting representation, fostering community, supporting education, and empowering the Black community. They are spaces for celebrations, thus ensuring that Black voices and stories are valued and shared.

The selected list of bookstores that follows is designed to assist the process of celebrating Black bookstores. Please note that there a few pure bookstores. Bookstores combine galleries, toys, cafes, bars, art stores, accessories, and other types of businesses. Bookstores are dynamic. As always, they are forever changing.

Bookstores in this list are arranged alphabetically within states and the District of Columbia. The selected list includes bookstores that are found in key listings online and/or that I am personally aware of or that have been recommend to me. NOTE is listed if that criteria did not typically prevail.

Complete information was considered as follows: bookstore's name, address, phone number, the owner/proprietor/founder, email address, and when the bookstore originally opened or was founded or most recently updated. As much information as available was documented as of November 2023.

More bookstores are leaning into combined brick-and-mortar, online only, mobile, or pop-up businesses. When conflicting data were located, the latest data are documented, sometimes combining data from several sources, including me contacting bookstores directly, as a single entry.

**Alabama**
NOTE

**Alaska**
NOTE

**Arizona**
Grassrootz Bookstore
1145 E. Washington St., Suite 200
Phoenix, AZ 85034
M. Ali Nervis, owner
info@grassrotzbookstore.com
(480) 442-0293
Opened 1998

**Arkansas**
Pyramid Art, Books & Custom Framing
1002 Wright Ave.
Little Rock, AR 72206
G. Hearne, owner
(501) 372-5824
pyramidartbooks@gmail.com
Originally opened 1988

**California**
Ashay by the Bay
157 Albertross Way
Valley, CA 94589
Deborah Day, owner
(844) 543-7732
ashaybythebay@gmail.com
Online since 2002

Malik Books, Gifts & Calendars
3560 W. Martin Luther King, Jr. Blvd.
Los Angeles, CA 90008
Malik and April, owners
(323) 389-8040
realmalikmuhammad@gmail.com
Opened 1990

Marcus Books
3900 Martin Luther King, Jr. Way
Oakland, CA 94609-2316
Johnson Family, owners
(510) 652-2344
info@marcusbooksoakland.com
Opened 1960 in San Francisco; Opened 1970 in Oakland
PLEASE NOTE: This is the oldest Black bookstore in US

Multicultural Bookstore & Gifts
260 Broadway
Richmond, CA 94805
Tamara Shiloh, owner
(510) 422-5304
multiculturalbookstore@gmail.com
Opened 2019

Reparations Club
3054 S. Victoria Ave.
Los Angeles, CA 90016
Jazzi McGilbert, owner
(323) 591-0012
info@reparations.club
Opened 2019

Underground Books
2814 35th St.
Sacramento, CA 95817
Georgia "Mother Rose," owner
(916) 737-3333
gwest@undergroundbooks.com
Opened 2003

### Colorado
Shop at Matter
2134 Market St.
Denver, CO 080206
Rick Griffith and Debra Johnson, owners
(303) 893-0303
shop@matter.com
Opened

Tattered Bookshop
1701 Wynkoop St.
Denver, CO 80202
Bended Page LLC, owners
info@tatteredcover.com
Opened 1971

### Connecticut
People Get Ready Books
119 Whalley Ave.
New Haven, CT 066511
Doris and Lauren, owners
(203) 446-2070
peoplegetteady@gmail.com
Opened 2019

Reader's Block
2420 Main St., Suite 7
Stratford, CT 06615
Tondrea Mabbins, owner
(203) 345-3298
readersblock@outlook.com
Opened 2021

### Delaware
Mejah Books, Inc.
2083 Holly Oak Plaza, 2099A
Philadelphia Pike
Claymount, DE 19703
Emlyn Q. DeGannes, owner
(302) 793-3424
mejahinc@yahoo.com
Opened 2000

### District of Columbia (Washington, DC)
Loyalty Bookstores Pentworth
843 Upshur St.
Washington, DC 20011
Hannah Oliver Depp, owner
(240) 863-2087
loyaltybookstores.com
Opened 2019

Mahogany Books (Anacostia)
1231 Good Hope Rd., SE
Washington, DC 20020
Derrick, Ramunda, and Mahogany Young, owners
(202) 844-2062
customerservice@mahoganybooks.com
Opened 2017

Sankofa Video, Books and Cafe
2714 Georgia Ave., NW
Washington, DC 20001
Shirikiana Germia, owner
(202) 234-4755
sankofa@gmail.com
Opened 1998

### Florida
African American Literature Book Club (AALBC)
15310 Amberly Dr., Suite 250
Tampa, FL 33647
Troy Johnson, owner
(347) 692-2522
troy@aalbc.com
Opened 1997
Largest, most referred-to list

Best Richardson African Diaspora Literature and
    Culture Museum
83 Washington St.
St. Augustine, FL 32084
Skip Richardson and Gigi Best Richardson, owners
(904) 217-8255
bradlcmuseum@gmail.com
Opened 1997

A Better Life Bookstore
869 Derbyshire Rd.
Daytona Beach, FL 32117
Derek Triplett, owner
fdazit@hopefellowship.org
Opened 2014

DareBooks
245 N. US Highway (17-92)
Longwood, FL 32750
Desmond A. Reid, owner
(407) 673-3273
desmondr@darebooks.com
Opened 1982, relocated from Brooklyn, NY

**Georgia**
All Things Inspiration Giftique
1400 Veterans Memorial Hwy SE, Suite 140
Mableton, GA 30126
LaVonya Tensly, owner
(678) 671-0270
help@allthingsinspirationgift.com
Opened 2019

Black Dot Cultural Center and Bookstore
6984 Main St., Suite A
Lithonia, GA 30058
Kazemde Ajamu, owner
(770) 305-6373
info@blackdot.com
Opened 2017

Medu Bookstore
2841 Greenbriar Pkwy. SW, n426
Atlanta, GA 30331
Nia Damali, owner
(404) 346-3263
medubooks@bellsouth.ney
Opened 1989

Nubian Bookstore
1540 Southlake Pkwy, Suite 7A
Morrow, GA 30260
Marcus Williams, owner
(678) 422-6120
marcus3x@yahoo.com
Opened 1999

Shrine of Black Madonna
946 Ralph D. Abernathy Blvd., SW
Atlanta, GA 30310
Aminika Covington, GA
(404) 549-8676
byer@shrinebookstore.com
Opened 1975

**Hawaii**
NOTE

**Idaho**
NOTE

**Illinois**
Afriware Books Co.
1701 S. 1st Ave., Suite 503
Maywood, IL 60153
Nzingha Nomma, owner
(708) 223-8081
afriwarebooks@afriwarebooks.com
Opened 1993

Da Book Joint
350 E. 51st St., #9
Chicago, IL 60615
Verlean Singletary, owner
(773) 655-3146
verlean@dabookjoint.com
Opened 2007

Frontline Bookstore
5206 S. Harper Ave.
Chicago, IL 60615
Sekou, owner
info@frontlinebookpublishing.com
Opened 1987

Semicolon Bookstore & Gallery
515 M. Halstead St., Suite A
Chicago, IL 60642
Danielle L. Mullen, owner
(312) 324-4464
info@semicolonchi.com
Opened 2019

The Underground Store
1727 E. 87th St.
Chicago, IL 60617
(773) 768-8869
TheUndergroundBookstore@gmail.com
Opened 1993

**Indiana**
Akoma Novelties and Books
936 Judson St.
Evansville, IN 47713
(812) 449-8593
Brittney "Aya" Odum, owner
info@akomalife@gmail.com
Opened 2015

Beyond Barcodes Bookstore
3139 E. 10th St.
Indianapolis, IN 46201
DeAndra Beard, owner
(765) 201-03883
beyondborderslanguage@gmail.com
Opened 2013

The Brain Lair Bookstore
714 E. Jefferson Blvd.
South Bend, IN 46617
(547) 400-5572
info@thebrainlair.com
Opened 2018

Loudmouth Books
212 E. 16th St.
Indianapolis, IN 46202
Leah Johnson, owner
Opened 2023

**Iowa**
Soul Book Nook Bookstore
110 E. 4th St
Waterloo, IA 50703
(319) 232-2188
Amber Collins
soulfoodbookstoreofficial@gmail.com
Opened 2020

**Kansas**
NOTE

**Kentucky**
Wild Fig Coffee & Books
726 N. Limestone
Lexington, KY 40508
Cooperatively owned
(859) 739-3207
wildfigworkercooperative@gmail.com
Opened 2011

**Louisiana**
Baldwin & Co. Bookstore
1030 Elysian Fields Ave.
New Orleans, LA 70117
D. J. Johnson, owner
(504) 354-1741
info@baldwinandcobooks.com
Opened 2021

Community Book Center
2523 Bayou Rd.
New Orleans, LA 70119
Vera Warren-Williams, owner
(504) 948-7323
readcbc@gmail.com
Opened 1983

Umoja Books and Products
1006 Surrey St.
Lafayette, LA 70501
Michael Malveaux
(337) 781-5758
umojabooksandproducts@yahoo.com
Opened 2002

**Maine**
NOTE

**Maryland**
Everyone's Place
1356 W. North Ave.
Baltimore, MD 21217
Tabia and National, owners
(410) 728-0877
everyonesplacestore@gmail.com
Opened 1986

Mahogany Books (National Harbor)
121 American Way
Oxon Hill, MD 20745
Derrick and Ramunda Young, owners
(202) 844-2062
customerservice@mahoganybooks.com
Opened 2021

Urban Reads Bookstore
3008 Greenmount Ave.
Baltimore, MD 21218
Tina Hamilton, owner
info@oururbanreads.com
Opened 2019

Wisdom Book Center
5116 Liberty Heights Ave.
Bro. Tehuti and Bro. Elliot, owners
(410) 664-1946
wisdombookcenter@verizon.net
Opened 1997

**Massachusetts**
Footprints Café
127 W. Rodney French Blvd.
New Bedford, MA 02744
Robert "Bobby" Gordon, owner
footsprintscafellc@gmail.com
(774) 473-9537
Opened 2001

Olive Tree Books-n-Voices
97 Hancock St.
Springfield, MA 01109
Zee Johnson, owner
(413) 737-6400
olivetreebooks@msn.com
Opened 2004

**Michigan**
Blackstone Bookstore and Cultural Center
214 W. Michigan Ave.
Ypsilanti, MI 48197
Kip Johnson and Carlos Franklin, owners
(734) 961-7376
blackbookstoneproject@gmail.com
Opened 2013

Detroit Book City Bookstore
272608 Southfield Rd., Suite 201
Southfield, MI 48076
Janeice and Reginal Hayes owners
(248) 993-3844
janeice@detroitbookcity.com
Opened 2016/brick and mortar 2023

Shrine of Black Madonna
13535 Livermore Ave.
Detroit, MI 48238
Nkenge Bishop Abi, owner
(313)) 491-0777
anika@shrinebookstore.com
Opened 197

Source Booksellers
4240 Cass Ave., Suite 105
Detroit, MI 48201
Janet Jones, owner
(313) 832-1155
info@sourcebookdetroit.com
Opened 1989

**Minnesota**
Planting People Growing Justice Press & Bookstore
1832 E. 35th St.
Minneapolis, MN 55407
Dr. Artika R. Tyler, owner
info@ppgjbooks.com
Opened 2019

Strive Bookstore
IDS Center
80 S. 8th St., Suite 254
Minneapolis, MN 55402
Mary Taris, owner
(763) 270-5738
info@strivepublishing.com
Opened 2022

**Mississippi**
Marshall's Bookstore
618 N. Farish St.
Jackson, MS 39020
Maati Jane Prime, owner
(601) 355-5335
info@marshallsbookstore.com
Opened 1938

**Missouri**
BLK+BRWN
104½ W. 39th St.
Kansas City, MO 64111

Cori Smith, owner
(816) 945-7736
blkbrwnkc@gmail.com
Opened 2023

EyeSeeMe
7872 Olive Blvd.
University City, MO 63130
Pamela and Jeffrey Blair, owners
(314) 349-1122
customerservice@eyeseeme.com
Opened 2015

Willa's Books & Vinyl
5547 Troost Ave.
Kansas City, MO 64110
Willa Robinson, owner
(816) 419-1051
willasbooks@gmail.com
Opened 1994

**Montana**
NOTE

**Nebraska**
Aframerica Bookstore
3226 Lake St.
Omaha, NE 68111
Annette, owner
(402) 455-9209
aframericabookstore@yahoo.com
Opened 2000

**Nevada**
The Analog Dope Store
205 E. Colorado Ave.
Las Vegas, NV 89104
Rachelle Luster, owner
(702) 483-1567
adstore@analogdope.com
Opened 2021

Multicultural Bookstore Las Vegas
Las Vegas, NV 89106
Tamara Shiloh and Carol Santiago, owners
mcblasvegas@mail.com
Opened 2023

R. D. Talley Books. LLC
4882 W. Lone Mountain Rd.
Las Vegas, NV 89130
Roderick D. Talley, owner
roderickdtalkey@rdtalleybooks.com
Opened 2018

**New Hampshire**
NOTE

**New Jersey**
Ida's Bookshop
734 Haddon Ave.
Collingswood, NJ 08108
Jeannine A. Cook, owner
info@idasbookshop.com
Opened 2021

La Unique African American Books & Cultural Center
111 N. 6th St.
Camden, NJ 08102
(856) 338-1958
launiquebooks@gmail.com
Opened 1992

The little Boho Bookshop
164a Broadway
Bayonne, NJ 07002
Sandra Dear and Rod Johnson, owners
(201) 258-4499
info@thelittlebohobookshop.com
Opened 2017

Source of Knowledge
867 Broad St.
Newark, NJ 07102
Dexter George and Masani Barnwell, owners
(973) 824-2556
sourceofknowledge867@yahoo.com
Opened 1992

**New Mexico**
NOTE

**New York**
Blenheim Hill Books
698 Main St., Suite A
Hobart, NY 13788
Cheryl Clarke and Barbara Balliet, owners
(607) 538-9222
Blenheimbooks1@gmail.com
Opened 2005

Café con Libros
724 Prospect Pl.
Brooklyn, NY 11216
Kalima DeSuze, owner
(347) 460-2838
info@cafeconlibrosbk.com
Opened 2019

Grandma Dawn aka Grandma's Place in Harlem
84 W. 120th St.
New York, NY 10027
Grandma Dawn Harris-Martinez, owner
grandmasplaceinharlem@gmail.com
Opened 1999

Sister's Uptown Bookstore & Cultural Center
1942 Amsterdam Ave.
New York, NY 10032
Janifer P. Wilson, owner
(212) 862-3608
info@sistersuptownbookstore.com
Opened 2000

Zawadi Books
1382 Jefferson Ave.
Buffalo, NY 14208
Kenneth and Sharon Holley, owners
(716) 903-6740
holleykenneth@yahoo.com
Opened 1976

**North Carolina**
Liberation Station Bookstore
208 Fayetteville St., Suite A-130
Raleigh, NC 27601
Victoria Scott—Mills, owner
(919) 867-6604
info@liberationstationbookstore.com
Opened 2023

The Urban Reader Bookstore
440 E. McCullough Dr., SuiteA-130
Charlotte, NC 28262
Sonyah Spencer, owner
(980) 938-5767
info@urbanreaderbook.com
Opened 2021

**North Dakota**
NOTE

**Ohio**
Black Art Plus
43 Parsons Ave.
Columbus, OH 43215
Mike Miller, owner
(614) 469-9980
blackstoneplus@att.net
Opened 1987

A Cultural Exchange
12624 Larchmere Blvd.
Cleveland, OH 44120
Deborah McHamm, owner
(216) 229-8300
info@aculturalexchange.org
Opened 1991

**Oklahoma**
Fulton Street Books & Coffee
210 W. Latimer St.
Tulsa, OK 74106
Onikah Asana-Caesar, owner
(918) 932-8646
info@fultonstreet918.com
Opened 2020

Nappy Roots Books
3705 Springlake Dr.
Oklahoma City, OK 73111
Landry Camille, owner
(405) 896-0203
nappyrootsbooks@gmail.com
Opened 2018

**Oregon**
Sunrise Books
4605 NE 23rd Ave., Suite 208
Edith Johnson, owner
(503) 309-4287
Sunrisebooks.shine@gmail.com
Opened 2020

Third Eye Books, Accessories & Gifts
3439 Hawthorne Blvd.
Portland, OR 97214
Michelle Lewis and Charles Hannah, owners
(503) 688-7008
sales@thirdeyebag.com
Opened 2019

**Pennsylvania**
The Black Reserve Bookstore
319 W. Main St., Suite 8
Lansdale, PA 19446
Shaykh Anwar Muhammad, owner
(267) 221-3090
theblackreservebookstore@gmail.com
Opened 2017

Harriett's Bookshop
258 E. Girard Ave.
Philadelphia, PA 19125
Jeannine A. Cook, owner
info@harriettsbookshop.com
Opened 2020

Hakim's Book Store and Gift Shop
210 S. 52nd St.
Philadelphia, PA 19139
(215) 474-9495
Yvonne Blake, owner
bookstorehakims@gmail.com
Opened 1959

Uncle Bobbie's Coffee & Books
5442 Germantown Ave.
Philadelphia, PA 19144
Mark Lamont Hill, owner
(215) 403-7058
info@unclebobbies.com
Opened 2017

**Rhode Island**
NOTE

**South Carolina**
Turning Page Bookshop
604 St. James Ave., Suite I
Goose Creek, SC 29445
VaLinda, owner
(843) 640-3164
info@turningpagebookshop.com
Opened 2019

**South Dakota**
NOTE

**Tennessee**
Alkebu-Lan Images Bookstore & Gift Shop
217 Jefferson St.
Nashville, TN 37208
Jordan Harriss, owner
(615) 321-4111
alkebulanimages@gmail.com
Opened 1986

The Bottom
2340 E. Magnolia Ave.
Knoxville, TN 37917
El-Amin, owner
(865) 444-5915
TheBottomKnox@gmail.com
Opened 2019

De Moir Books & Things
739 White Station Rd.
Memphis, TN 38122
Jeremee Demoir, owner
demoirbooksandthings@gmail.com
Opened 2021

**Texas**
African Imports Houston
12300 N. Fwy St.
147 Greenspoint Mall
Houston, TX 77060
Obi, owner
(281) 875-0056
donbasel@yahoo.com
Opened 1997

BLACKLIT Bookstore
4050 McEwen Rd., Suite 9105
Farmers Branch, TX 75244
Nia-Taylor Clark, owner
info@supportblacklit.com
Opened 2022

Black Pearl Books
7112 Burnet Rd.
Austin, TX 78757
Katrina Brooks, owner
(512) 902-9717
blackpearlatx@gmail.com
Opened 2020

The Dock Bookshop
6637 Meadowbrook Dr.
Fort Worth, TX 76112
Donna and Donya Craddock, owners
(817) 457-5700
info@thedockbookshop.com
Opened 2008

Edna's Boutique
428 N. Main St.
Duncanville, TX 75116
E. Jean Pemberton Jones, owner
(972) 460-6362
ednasbotique@gmail.com
Opened 2019

Shrine of the Black Madonna (Houston)
5309 Martin Luther King Jr. Blvd.
Houston, TX 77021
Nailah Nelson, owner
(832) 408-1071
nilah@shrinebookstore.com
Opened 1986

**Utah**
NOTE

**Vermont**
NOTE

**Virginia**
Harambee Books and Artworks
1132 Prince St.
Alexandria, VA 22314
(703) 299-2591
info@harambeebooks.org
Opened 2016

House of Consciousness Bookstore
633 W. 35th St.
Norfolk, VA 23508
Andrea Wilson, owner
(757) 314-1943
hocbookstor@gmail.com
Opened 1986

Mahogany Books (Reagan National Airport)
2401 Smith Blvd.
Arlington, VA 22202
Derrick and Ramunda Young, owners
(202) 844-2062
customerservice@mahoganybooks.com
Opened 2023

Positive Vibes
6220 Indian River Rd., B1
Virginia Beach, VA 23464
Partnership, owners
(757) 523-1399
bhewitt985@aol.com
Opened 1992

**Washington**
Parable
3502 McKinley Ave., Suite A
Tacoma, WA 98404
LeEcia Farmer, LaKecia Farmer, and Deatria Williams, owners
info@parabletacoma.com
Opened 2021

**West Virginia**
NOTE

**Wisconsin**
Mahogany Gallery & Cultural Center
1422 Washington Ave.
Racine, WI 53403
Scott Terry, owner
(262) 865-7971
mahoganygalleryinfo@gmail.com
Opened Originally, 1979; Opened 2020

**Wyoming**
Mad Dog and The Pilgrim Booksellers
4176 WY-789
Sweetwater Station, WY 82520
Polly Hinds and Lynda German, owners
(307) 330-4127
booksellers@wbaccess.net
Opened 1990

## SOURCES

Curcic, Dimirije. "Black-Owned Bookstores." *WordsRated*. 14 Feb. 2023. wordsrated.com.

Green, Alex. "A New Generation of African-American-Owned Bookstores." *Publishers Weekly*. 6 Apr. 2018. publishersweekly.com.

Guyton, Jessica A. "The Historic Black Book Fight for Survival against the COVID 19 Pandemic," *USA Today*. 7 Sept. 2020. usatoday.com.

"The History and Legacy of Black-Owned Bookstores." *Cross Cultural Solidarity: History, in the Service of Solidarity*, 2023. https://crossculturalsolidarity.com/.

Jackson, Ashawanea. "The First Black-Owned Bookstores and the Fight for Freedom. *JSTOR Daily*, July 10, 2020. https://daily.jstor.org/the-first-black-owned-bookstore-and-the-fight-for-freedom/.

Johnson, Troy. "157 Black-Owned Bookstores in the United States." AALBC.com LLC. 2021. https://aalbc.com/bookstores/list.php.

Johnson, Troy, founder and president, "African American Literature Book Club" 2021. AALBC has the largest, oldest, most frequently visited website dedicated to books by, and about, people of African descent. It was opened in 1997 and is a recognized source of information on Black-owned bookstores in the United States. Sites should be reviewed for the latest data. AALBC also has a less comprehensive list of Black publishers.

Marva L. DeLoach accessed bookstores websites or called bookstores to ascertain data available as of November 2023.

NOTE indicates search online for "_____ Black Bookstores. " Include name of state in blank with quotes (e.g., Maine Black Bookstores).

Phillippe, McKenzie. "127 Black-Owned Bookstores in America That Amplify Literature." *Oprah Winfrey Daily*, 27 Aug. 2020. https://www.oprahdaily.com/entertainment/books/a33497812/black-owned-bookstores/.

# Index

*The 1619 Project*, 14

AASLIG. *See* Association of College and Research Libraries, African American Studies Interest Group
A, Aysha Zakiya, 32, 325-27
Abegunde, Maria E. Hamilton, xxxi, 269-74
Academic Cultural Enrichment Scholars Program (ACE), 13
*Access to Public Libraries*, 7
Adams, Elaine P., 11, 47, 50, 61
Affirmative Action, xxix, 38, 105, 145-48, 156, 193, 198
Aframerica Bookstore, 364
African American(s), 3, 4
*The African American Almanac*, 209
African American Authors, 74-78
African American Education and Librarianship, 4
African American Subject Funnel Project, 94
African American Home Movie Archive, 353
African American Homeschool Cooperatives, 211
African American Literature Book Club (AALBC), 361
African American Materials Project (AAMP), 9
African American Medical Library Alliance (AAMLA), 166-70
African American Publishers, xxx, 74-78
African American Research Libraries, 210
African American Research Library of Palm Springs, 210
African Americans in Special Libraries, 191
African Diaspora, xvi, xix, xxix-xxxii, 13, 17, 25, 36, 39-40, 65, 71, 131, 143-44, 160, 250, 269-71, 320-21, 350, 353, 354, 357
African Imports Houston, 366
African Libraries and Information Associations and Institutions (AfLIA), 14; AfLIA Conference, 14
The African Library Project, 13
African Library Summit, 13-14
*African or American? Black Identity and Political Activism in New York City, 1784-1861*, 355
Afriware Book Co., 362
*Afro-American Women Writers 1746-1933*, 11
Ahmad, Tahira, xxxi, 218-19
AI. *See* Artificial Intelligence
Alabama A&M College, 4. *See also* Alabama A&M University
Alabama A&M University, 8, 107
Alabama A&M University School of Library Media, 8-9
Allen, AJ, 225-34
Alexander, Leslie M., 355
Alford, Jr., Thomas, v, xxxi, 18, 45, 50, 61, 209, 306
Alkekbu-Lan Images Bookstore & Gifts Shop, 366
Alire, Camila, 13
All Things Inspiration Giftique, 362
Allen, Richard, 3
"The All-White World of Children's Books," 336
Alston, Jason, xxx, 17, 20, 110-14
Alston, Meaghan, 245-46
Aman, Mohammed M., 11
American Association of School Librarians (AASL), 11
American Association of Law Librarians (AALL), 192
American Association of University Professors (AAUP), 191
The American Civil Liberties Union (ACLU), xxi, 35
American Diabetes Association, 173
American Library Association (ALA), xvii, xviii, xix, xxi, 5, 15, 337; *American Library Association Bulletin*, 4; Annual Conference, xxi, 5, 7, 11-12, 14-16; Centennial Award, 9; Council, xvii, 8-9, 15;
Children's Services Division, 7; Civic Imagination Stations Grant Program (CIS), 269-70; Committee on Opportunities for Negro Students in the Library Profession, 7; Coretta Scott King Book Awards Round Table, 16; COVID Library Relief Fund, 284; Equality Award, 11, 15; Graphic Novels & Comics Round Table, 68; Grolier Foundation Award, 11; Family Focus Initiative, 13; Intellectual Freedom Round Table 16; *Library Bill of Rights*, 10, 92, 147, 156; Library History Round Table, 16; Literacy Nation, 16; Martin Luther King, Jr. Sunrise Celebration, 208; Medal of Excellence, 16; Melville Dewey Award, 12; Rally to Read, 16; Spectrum Scholarship Program, 12; Work with Negroes Round Table, 5
American Negro Academy, 4
American Rescue Plan Federal Emergency Connectivity Fund, 284
Aminu, Alisha, xxx, 125-28
The Analog Dope Store, 364
Anderson, Jill, xxx, 171-75
Andrew W. Mellon Foundation, 108, 245, 300; Fellowship for Diversity, Inclusion & Cultural Heritage, 245
Angelou, Maya, 223, 357
Arizona State University, 199
artificial intelligence, 99, 102
Armstrong, Louis, 257-60; "Swing That Music," 258; *My Life in New Orleans*, 258; *The Armstrong Story*, 258; *Louis*

**369**

*Armstrong in His Own Words*, 259; "Black and Blues," 259; *Ken Burn's Jazz*, 259; Armstrong Now, 259
The Arthur Spingarn Collection of Black Authors, 6
Ashay by the Bay, 360
Ashby, Charmaine, 13, 76
Ashby, Richard, xxx, 13-14, 16, 20, 76-77
Association for the Study of African American Life and History (ASALH), 5, 134
Association of College and Research Libraries (ACRL), 192; African American Studies Librarians Interest Group (AASLIG), 89; Kaleidoscope Scholarship, 199; Rare Books and Manuscripts Section (RBMS), 246-47
Association of Research Libraries (ARL), 86, 200
Atkins, Hannah D., 8
Atlanta University, 4, 6, 11, 14; School of Library Science, 6, 8, 10; The Henry Proctor Collection, 6
Atlanta University Press, 4
Atterbury, C., xxxi, 222-24
Auburn Avenue Research Library on African American History and Culture, 210, 249-53; Hosea L. Williams Collection, 250-51; Andrew J. Young Collection, 251; Donald L. Hollowell Collection, 251-52; Annie L. McPheeters Collection, 252
Aubry, Jeffrion L., xxx, 164-65, 208

Bain, Regina, xxxi, 257-60
Baker, Augusta, 7, 9-10, 336
Baldwin, James, 65, 223, 260, 354
Baldwin & Co. Bookstore, 363
Banks, Sharon D., xxxi, 305
Barksdale-Hall, Roland, xxx, 46, 48, 51, 61, 129-33
Bartley, Kelsa, xxx, 166-70
Bascom, Lionel C., 356
Baylor, Jazmyne, xxx, 159
Beinecke Rare Book and Manuscripts Library, 246
Bell, Gladys Smiley, xxx, 12, 19-20, 45-46, 48-51, 61, 64, 67, 71
Bellwether Publishing Company, 8
Benedict College, 4
Berkeley (California) Public Library, 7
Berlin, Ira, 355
Berry III, John, 92
Berry, Marshelle, xxxi, 302
Best Richardson African Diaspora Literature and Culture Museum, 361
A Better Life Bookstore, 361
Betts, Victor, 245, 246
Biblioboard, 14
*Bibliographical Checklist of American Negro Poets*, 5
*The Bibliography of the Negro in Africa and America*, 5
Bibliotherapy, xxxii, 5, 25; African American Youth and Mental Health, 347-49; Tuskegee VA Hospital, 5, 25
Biddle, Stanton, v, xxx, 18-20, 45-51, 61, 64, 66, 67, 69-70
Biden, Joseph, 15
Bingham, Rebecca T., 9-10, 12
BIPOC (Black, Indigenous, and People of Color), viii, ix, xxx-xxii, 13, 15, 65, 86-88, 92-93, 111-12, 125 138-41, 146-48, 168-70, 192-93, 200-01, 215-17, 360
*The Birth of a Nation*, 35
Black/African American Librarians, xvi, xviii, 4-6, 36, 63, 68, 82, 84-85, 91-92, 96-97, 99, 106, 108, 110-18, 120-21, 130-31, 139, 143, 145-48, 159-60, 173-74, 191, 198, 200, 209, 238-40, 247, 291-93, 295, 297, 299, 304, 307, 311-12, 320, 322-23, 336-38
Black Arts + Digital Showcase, 272-73
Black Caucus of the American Library Association (BCALA), xv-xvii, xix, xxi, 196, 199, 208; BCALA Membership Directory, xix; BCALA Panel of African American Deans, 10; BCALA Trailblazer Award and the DEMCO/BCALA Award for Excellence in Librarianship, 18-19; BCALA Virtual Summit 2020: Connecting Cultivating and Collaboration, 15; Black History Month (BHM) Programming in Libraries, 15, 64; Breaking Barriers: The Future of Black Librarianship National Forum, 15; Distinguished Service to Librarianship Award, 10; Film 'The Speaker' violated ALA Bill of Rights, 10; Co-Sponsored Kenya Library Association Joint Conference of IFLA, 10; DEMCO Award, xxix, 12, 18-19, 67; iBlackCaucus, 15, 108; *Newsletter of the Black Caucus of the American Library* Association, xix; Professional Development Committee, 10; Reading is Grand, 13; The Satia Marshall Orange Spectrum Scholarship Endowment Fund, 16; Services to Children of African Descent Committee, 13; Self-e Literary Award, 14; Trailblazer Award, 18; 20th Anniversary Gala Reception, 11; 25th Anniversary, 12; Leadership Institute, 199; Literary Awards, 71-73
Black Caucus of the American Library Association Affiliates: BCALA Connecticut, 12, 71; California Librarians Black Caucus, 71; Chicago Chapter of BCALA, 71; Colorado Black Librarians Association, 14, 71; Georgia Library Association—Black Caucus, 14, 71; Indiana Black Librarians Network, 13, 15, 68, 71, 121, 295; Maryland Library Association Black Caucus, 71; Metro Atlanta Black Librarians Network. See Georgia Library Association Black Caucus; Missouri Chapter—BCALA, 14, 71; New York Black Librarians Caucus, 71, 209; Pennsylvania Black Librarians' Caucus, 15, 71; South Carolina Black Librarians Caucus, 71; St. Louis Regional Librarians. See Missouri Chapter-BCALA; Tennessee Network of Black Library Employees, 71; Virginia Library Association Librarians of Color, 71
Black Art Plus, 365
Black Health and Healing Summit, 172-73
*The Black Librarian in America*, xvii, xviii, 8
*The Black Librarian in America: Reflections, Resistance and Reawakening*, 15
*The Black Librarian in America Revisited*, 28
The Black Reserve Bookstore, 366
Black Dot Cultural Center and Bookstore, 362
Black, Estelle M., 11
Black Film Archive, 353
Black Film Center & Archive, 353
*Black Gotham: A Family History of African Americans in Nineteenth-Century New York City*, 356
BLACKLIT Bookstore, 367
Black Male Archives, 15
*Black Panther*, 16, 131, 233, 350
Black Panther Party, 230
Black Pearl Books, 367
Blackstone Bookstore and Cultural Center, 363

Black Studies in Video Catalog, 353
Blades, Rashida Scott, xxxi, 198-203
Blenheim Hill Books, 365
*The Blind Side*, 350-51
BLK & BRWN, 364
Blue, Thomas Fountain, 4-5, 24, 26, 106, 115-16, 119, 217
*Blued Eyed Child*, 220
Bond, DJ, xxx, 176-79
Bond, Julian, xx
Bond, Rebecca, 5
Bontemps, Arna W., 6, 336, 355
Book Bans: Examining How Censorship Limits Liberty and Literature, 16
Booker, Libre (Latrice), 15
*The Bookmark*, xv, 209
Books for Adults, 348
Books for Schools and the Treatment of Minorities, 336
Books for Youth/Teens, 347-48
Boston Public Library West End Branch, 3
The Bottom, 366
Boyd, K.C., 15-16, 338
Bradshaw, Chris, 13
The Brain Lair Bookstore, 363
Brazil, xxxii, 142-43, 145, 259, 320-23
Brewer, Rosellen, 204
Bright, Sandy (Sandra), xxxi, 311-12
Broadside Press, 7
Bronx Community College, xvi
Brooks, Gwendolyn, xx, 6, 9
Brooks, Hallie Beacham, v, 5-6, 26, 118, 120-21
Brooklyn Public Library, 13, 27, 140, 262, 311
Broughton, Jason, 14-15
Brown, Charles, 11
Brown, Claude, 220
Brown, Lorene, 10
Brown, Michael, 14
Brown, Paula Edme, xx
*Brown vs Board of Education (1954)*, 3, 7, 213, 259
Brown, Wanda K., 13-14, 17, 19-20, 46, 48-49, 52, 61, 64, 67
Brumfield, Elizabeth, xxxii, 49-50, 52, 61, 331-35
Bunch III, Lonnie G., 15
Burns-Simpson, Shauntee, 15, 17, 19, 46, 50, 52, 61, 63-68
Burton, LaVar, xxi
Butler, Octavia, 223
Byam, Milton, 8-9

Cafe con Libros, 365
*California Newsreel Catalog*, 353
Cambria Heights Civic Association, 264
Campbell, Edith, xxxii, 336-39
Cannon, Tyrone, 13
Capers, Kim McNeil, xxx, 171-75
The Caribbean, 22, 39, 220, 222, 245-46, 251, 317, 354-56
Carnegie, Andrew, 283
Carnegie Corporation, 5-6; General Education Board Library Conference, 6; Field Service Program to Enrich African American School Libraries in the South, 6
Carnegie Institute of Technology, 5
Carnegie Library, 4-5

Carnegie Non-European Library Service (Transvaal), South Africa, 6
Carroll, Kathy, 15
Carter, Jimmy, 10
Catholic Library Association, 10
Cataloging, 27, 38-39, 77, 93-94, 107, 178, 192, 197, 199, 201, 291
*Catalogue of the African Collection in the Moorland Foundation*, 7
Cawthorne, John, 15
*The Cay*, 337
Cecil B. Moore Library, xxi
Center for Digital Dannelse's Digital Competence Wheel, 271
The Challenges, Changes and Conflicts Facing American Libraries, xx
Chambers, Tamela, 13, 19, 50, 52, 62, 67
Chamblee-Smith, Genevia, xxxi, 196-93
Chambliss, Melanie, 272
Chancellor, Renate, xxx-xxxi, 191-96
Chandler, Sue P., 9
Chandler, Yvonne, 192
Charles Blockson Archival Collection, 246
*Charlie and the Chocolate Factory*, 337
Cheatham, Bertha, 11
Charlotte (North Carolina) Public Library, 4
Charlotte-Mecklenburg County Public Library. *See* Charlotte (North Carolina) Public Library
Charleston County (South Carolina) Public Library, 14
Chicago Public Library, 11-12, 27, 34-35
Churchwell, Charles D., 9, 11, 12
Clack, Doris Hargrett, v, 27, 47, 52, 62
Clay, Rudolph, xxx, 19, 49-50, 53, 62, 67, 71
Clinton, William, 12
Colbert-Lewis, Danielle, xxx, 99-105
College of New Rochelle, xvi
Cole, Joan, 209
Coleman, Carolyn Q., xx
Collection Development, xxxii, 84, 143, 197, 201, 212, 241, 248, 293, 311, 350, 354, 356, 360
*The Color of Water*, 220
*The Color Purple*, 223, 351
Columbia University, 10, 11, 224
Columbia University Library School, xv
The Commission on Interracial Cooperation Education and Race Relations, 6
The Committee on Scientific and Technical Information (COSATI) Subcommittee on Negro Research Libraries, 8
Common Cause, xxi
Community Book Center, 363
Conference for the Evaluation of Materials About Black Americans (CEMBA), 8
The Conference on the Use of Microphotography and Black Studies, 8
*Constitution of the United States of America, First Amendment*, 332
Cooke, Constance B., 209
Cooke, Nicole, xxx, 16, 20, 88, 150-54, 308
Coogler, Ryan, 350
Cooperative College Library Center, 8
Cornucopia of Rhode Island, 13, 294
Corbett, Kizzimekia S., 173

Coretta Scott King Book Award, xx, 337
Cossitt Library, 4
*Cotton Quilts*, 337
Council on Interracial Books for Children, 337
Council on Library Resources, 11
*Counter Narratives in Practice*, 245-47
COVID-19 Pandemic, xxix, xxx, xxxi, xxxii, 15, 18, 65-66, 77, 83, 129, 131, 134-36, 140, 144, 160, 169-71, 176, 180, 199, 211-12, 216-17, 237, 275-77, 281, 284, 304, 306, 316-17, 325-26, 355, 359
Craft, Jerry, 16
Creating the Full-Service Homework Center in Your Library, 204
Critical Race Theory (CRT), 147, 155, 198, 213, 320, 354
Cronquist, Michelle, 94
Crummel, Alexander, 4
Cruzat, Gwendolyn, 167-68
Cullen, Countee, 25, 223
A Cultural Exchange, 365
culturally responsive teaching, 240-44
Curry, Eboni, 46, 49, 53, 161
Curtis, Florence Rising, 5, 115
Cuyahoga County Public Library Maple Heights Branch, 205
Cynthia Graham Hurd St. Andrews Regional Library, 14

De Moir Books & Things, 366
Dancy, Billie E., 11
Darden, Lakeisha, 50, 53, 62, 338
DareBooks, 362
Dash, Julie, 351
*Daughters of the Dust*, 351
Davis, Angiah, xxx, 134-37
Davis, Hillis, 8
Davis, Hiram L., 1, 11
Da Book Joint, 362
Davis, Denyvetta, 14, 17, 46, 49, 53, 62, 64
Davis, Jr., James Allen, xxxi, 66, 215-18
Dawes, Trevor, 14, 49, 53, 62
Dawson, Alma. *See* Dawson, Alma E.
Dawson, Alma E., vii, 30-33
decolonization, 93-94, 320-22
Delaney, Sadie Peterson, 5, 25-26
Delgado, Richard, 198
DeLoach, Marva. *See* DeLoach, Marva L.
DeLoach, Marva L., vii, viii, xxi, 12, 29, 191, 344-45, 359-68
Delta Sigma Theta Sorority, Inc., 68
DEMCO/BCALA Award for Excellence in Librarianship, 11, 18
Detroit Book City Bookstore, 364
Detroit Public Library, 11
The E. Azalea Hackley Memorial Collection on Black Music, Dance and Drama, 6
Denver Public Library, 13
Dhlomo, Herbert Isaac Ernest, 6
"Digital Access and Historically Black College and University Libraries," 278-82
*Directory of Ethnic Professionals in Librarianship*, xix
Distinguished Service to Librarianship, 10
Distinguished Service to the Library Profession, 10
Diversity, Equity, and Inclusion (DEI), xvii, xxix, xxx-xxxi, 15, 87, 92, 99, 138-42, 146, 155-57, 169, 174, 193, 197-98, 200, 240-42, 292

Dixon, Thomas, 350
Dobson, Naomi Willie Pollard, vii, 30
The Dock Bookshop, 367
Dodson, Howard, 10, 355
*Do The Right Thing*, 351
Douglass, Frederick, xviii
*Dr. Doolittle*, 337
Drexel University Library Science Program, 8-9
Du Bois, W. E. B., 223
Dunye, Cheryl, 352
Durham School and Library School, Chapel Hill, 6
DuVernay, Ava, 350
Duvernay, Jina, xxxi, 245-47

*Ebony Magazine*, 357
*Ebony Man Magazine*, 12
Edna's Boutique, 367
Echols, Sandra Michele, xxxi, 238-39, 291-93
Economic Opportunity Authority Savannah-Chatham County, xxi
EEOC. *See* Equal Employment Opportunity Commission
E. J. Josey Foundation for Justice and Peace, xxi
E. J. Josey Scholarship Fund, xviii
Ellis, Laura, xxxi, 261
Elmhurst Hospital Center, 208
Emerging Technologies, xvi, xxv, xxix, xxxi, 5, 8, 27, 71, 87, 93, 98, 102-03, 107, 132, 172, 177, 183, 187, 192, 204, 217, 267, 270, 272-73, 276, 278-79, 281, 283-85, 292-93, 297, 304, 311-12, 346, 359
Emmanuel African Methodist Episcopal Church, 14
empyrean, 209
Enoch Pratt Free Library Pennsylvania Avenue Branch, 14
Equal Employment Opportunity Commission, 88, 251, 291
*An Enquiry Concerning the Intellectual and Moral Facilities and Literature of Negroes*, 3
Ethiopia Reads, 14
Evansville (Indiana) Public Library, 5, 26, 118-20
Evansville-Vanderburgh County (Indiana) Public Library. *See* Evansville (Indiana) Public Library
Everyone's Place, 363
EyeSeeMe, 364

Faison, Vernice, xxx, 99-105
Fellowship of the American Guild of Organists, xx
Fenton, Michele, v, xiii, xxix-xxx, 3-16, 18-30, 46, 49, 54, 62, 117-24, 295
Ferguson (Missouri) Municipal Public Library, 14
Ferguson, Octavene Beachem, 118
First Conference on Black Oral History, 9
The First Negro Library Conference, 5
Fisk University, 5-6
Fisk University Library, 8-9, 24; Summer Institute on Black Studies-Librarianship, 8
Floyd, George, 72, 134, 161
Fletcher, Lex, 352
Florence, Virginia Proctor Powell, 5
Folger Shakespeare Library, 100
Fontno, Tiffeni, xxxi, 20, 49-50, 54, 62, 225-34
Footprints Café, 363
Forbes, George Washington, 3

Ford, Sylverna, 12
Fortune, Amos, 3
Foster, Makeeba, 230, 234
Franklin, Hardy, 11, 236
Franklin, Sandra, 166, 168
Free Library of Philadelphia, 8, 16, 140, 237
Freeman, Rodney E., xxx, 15, 95-97, 121
Frontline Bookstore, 362
Fruchtman, Lisa, 352
Fruchtman, Rob, 352
Fulton Street Books & Coffee, 366

Gadsden, Charlyne, 207, 210
Gaines Yates, Ella, 9, 11, 308
Gall, Lenore R., 210
Galveston, Texas, 4
Garcês-da-Silva, Franciéle Carneiro, xxxii, 320-24
Garcia-Febo, Loida, xxxi, 315-19
Garner, Martine, 191
Garnes, Carolyn Lowe, xxxi, 17, 48, 54, 62, 307-10
Gaskin, Etka Braboy, 5, 26, 118
Gebregeorgis, Yohannes, 14
General Education Board, 4, 6, 115, 119
George Peabody Collection of the Negro, 4
"The Georgia Child's Access to Materials Pertaining to American Negroes," 8
Georgia Library Association's Black Caucus Interest Group, 15
Ghana Library Authority, 6
Gilder Lehrman Summer Teachers Seminar, 220
Giles, Louise, 9
Gilliam, Carol, xxxii, 346
Gilton, Donna, 13
Ginga, 142-45
Gleason, Eliza Atkins, v, 6, 13, 27, 115, 120
*Go Tell It On The Mountain*, 223
Graham, Clarence R., 6
Grandma Dawn aka Grandma's Place in Harlem, 365
Grant, George C. *See* Grant, George
Grant, George, xviii-xix, xxxii, 98
Grassrootz Bookstore, 360
"The Great Escape," 222-24
Green, Patrice, 245-46
Greenfield, Eloise, 337
Gregory, James H., 4
Greguire, Henri, 3
Greene, Belle Da Costa (born Belle Marion Greener), 5
Greener, Richard T., 3
Greenfield, Eloise, xx
Gray, Freddie, 14
Griffin, Karin, 191-92; *The Guiding Light*, 11
Guinier, Lani, xx
Guyanese Girls Rock Foundation, 263

*Hachette Book Group, Inc. vs Internet Archive*, 269
Hakim's Book Store & Gift Shop, 366
Haley, Alex, 10, 36
Hall, Evelyn, 207, 210
Hall, Lillian Haydon Childress, v, 5, 26, 118
Hall, Robert "C. J.", xxx, 180-83

Hall, Stephen, 198
Hall, Tracie D., vii, 15-16, 29-30
Hamilton, Virginia, 337
Hampton Institute (University), xx, 5; Library School, 5, 6, 24, 240
Hampton Institute Library, 4

*Handbook of Black Librarianship*: first edition, 10; second edition, 12, 191, 209
The Happy/Nappy Bookseller, 337
Harambee Books & Artworks, 367
Harriett's Bookshop, 366
Harris, Leslie M., 355
Harris-Stoute, Cloyette, xxxi, 263-64
Harris, Kamala, 108
Harris, Rachel Davis, 5, 26
Harris, S. D., 46, 49, 55, 62
Harris-Stoute, Cloyette, xxxi, 263-64
Harrison, Talisha, xxx, 33-38
Hartman, Maureen, 204
Harvard University, 3, 220-21, 356
Hayden, Carla, 11, 13-14, 29
Hayden, Carla D. *See* Hayden, Carla
Hayes, Ernest, xx
Hayes, Nichelle M., xxx, 14-16, 20, 46, 50, 55, 62, 63-68, 120
Havener, Michael, 13
Health Information Literacy, 129, 131, 166, 168, 172-73, 326
Hennepin County (Minnesota) Library, 11
Henry, Eboni, xxxi, 16, 238-39
*A Hero Ain't Nothing But a Sandwich*, 337
Hewitt, Vivian Davidson, xix, 10, 16, 27, 120
*Hi Jack*, 337
*Hidden Histories: Immigrant Farmworkers and Black Intellectual Histories*, 245
Hightower, Monteria, 11
Hillson, Maurie, 240
Historically Black Colleges and Universities (HBCUs), 278-82
HistoryMakers Digital Archive, 353
Hodges, Graham Russell, 356
Holiday, Deloice, xxix, 3-16, 269-72
Holly, Ellen, 11
Holman, Jos N., xxxi, 13, 17, 20, 46, 48-50, 55, 62, 64, 254-56
Home School Legal Defense Association (HSLDA), 213
*Homework Help from the Library: In-Person and Online*, 204
Hooks, Benjamin, xx
Hopkins, Diane McAfee, 11
House of Consciousness Bookstore, 367
Houston, Charles Hamilton, xix
*Houston Independent School District Facts and Figures Report 2022-2023*, 243
*How To Be Anti-Racist*, 16
Howard University, xx, xxi, 4, 5, 8; Conference on Black Bibliography, 8; Moorland-Spingarn Collection, 6; School of Law, 192
Huffman, Celia, 205
Hughes, Langston, 223, 259; *Simple Stakes a Claim*, 228
Hunton, Margaret Reynolds, 6
Hurd, Cynthia, 14
Hurston, Zora Neale, 223, 258, 355

I. C. Norcom High School, xxi
Ida's Bookshop, 365
The IDEAL Conference, 14. See also National Diversity in Libraries Conference
*If I Ran the Zoo*, 337
*If You Want to Learn the Secrets of the World Read a Book!*, 209
*I Know Why The Caged Bird Sings*, 223
*In The Heat of the Night*, 11
"In The Tradition: The Legacy of Cultural Messengers from Langston Hughes to Tupac Shakur," 234
India, xxxii, 325-27
Indiana Black Expo, Greater Lafayette Chapter, 2
Indiana Historical Bureau, 16
Indiana Historical Society, 118, 120
Indiana Librarians Leading in Diversity (I-LLID) Fellowship Program, 13, 117, 120, 295
Indiana Library Association, 26, 121. See also Indiana Library Federation
Indiana Library Federation, 15, 26, 68, 120-21
Indiana Public Library Commission Summer School for Librarians, 5, 26,118-19
Indiana State Library, 117-21
Indiana State Library Summer School. See Indiana Public Library Commission Summer School for Librarians
Indianapolis Public Library, 5, 14, 16, 26, 66, 118-20, 210; Center for Black Literature and Culture, 14; Paul Laurence Dunbar Branch, 5, 16
Indianapolis Public School No. 26 (John Hope School), 16
Indiana University: *A263 Contemporary Social Issues in the African American Community-Digital Project Resources Library Research Guide (the LibGuide)*, 272; Bloomington, 350; Department of African American and African Diaspora Studies (AAADS), 269; Institute for Digital Arts & Humanities (IDAH), 270; Libraries, 269; Libraries IQ Wall, 271; Libraries Open Access Week Symposium, 272; Scholarly Communication Department, 270
Information Literacy, 136, 147-48, 216, 242, 281
Institution of Museum and Library Services (IMLS), 284; Laura Bush 21st Century Librarian Program, 15; National Leadership Grants for Libraries Program, 15
Intellectual Freedom Committee, xviii; *The Speaker* (film), xviii, 10
The International African American Museum, 16
International Federation of Library Associations and Institutions (IFLA), xvi
International Research Association, Inc., 7
Internet Archive, 353
Ivory, Edrice G., 12

Jackson, Andrew P., vii, 13, 206-210, 218, 225-234, 262-263, 343
Jackson, Andrew P. (Sekou Molefi Baako). See Jackson, Andrew P.
Jackson, J. Arthur, 5
Jackson, Rev. Dr. Curtis, xx
Jackson, Lorin, xxx, 159-64
Jackson, Miles, 11
Jackson-Brown, Grace, 15, 20, 64
Jackson-Ortiz, Rafael Daoud, xxxi, 211-215
Jacobs, Alma, 7-8

Jacobs, James, 7
Jefferson, Jr., Julius C., xxv, 14-16, 20, 49, 55, 62, 316
Jenkins, Althea H., 11
Jenkins, Barbara Williams. See Barbara Williams
Jenkins, Cynthia, 10-11
Johns Hopkins School of Medicine, 173
Johnson, Beatrice Bethel, 9
Johnson, Broderick, 350-51
Johnson, James Weldon, 356
Johnson, Joan, 15
Johnson-Perkins, Brenda, xxix, 3-16, 46, 50, 56, 62
Joint Conference of Librarians of Color (JCLC), 13-14, 16
Joint Council of Librarians of Color, Inc., 77, 110
Jolivet, Linda, xxxi, 304
Jones, Absalom, 3
Jones, Clara. See Jones, Clara Stanton
Jones, Clara Stanton, v, xxiii, 8-10, 18, 343
Jones, Jacqueline, xxix, 30-33
Jones, Michelle E., xxx, 134-37
Jones, Nikole Hannah, 14
Jones, Shannon, xxx, 166-70
Jones, Thomas J., 5
Jones, Virginia Lacy, 6-10
Jordan, Casper L., xxix, 3, 10-11, 20-30, 46-47, 56, 62
Jordan, Casper LeRoy. See Jordan, Casper L.
*Josephine Baker: Black Diva in a White Man's World*, 351
Josey E. J. (Elonnie Junius Josey), vii, xv-xix, xxi, 7-13, 191, 196, 207-08, 231, 235-37; ALA Equality Award, 11; ALA Lippincott Award for Distinguished Service to Library Profession, 10; ALA President, 10; Chair, Association of Cooperative Library Organizations (ACLO), 9; Chief, Bureau of Academic and Research Libraries New York Education Department, 8; DEMCO/BCALA Award for Excellence in Librarianship, 11; E.J. Josey Scholarship Award, 11; Formation of BCALA (1970), 8; Georgia Library Association, 7; *Handbook of Black Librarianship, First Edition*, 9-10; *Handbook of Black Librarianship, Second Edition*, 12; John Ames Humphrey/OCLC/Forest Press Award, 12; Journal of Library History Award, 8; Pennsylvania Library Association Distinguished Service Award, 12; Tenured Professor, University of Pittsburgh, School of Library and Information Science, 11
Josey, Frances Bailey, xx
Josey, Willie, xx

Kantayya, Shalini, 351
Karenga, Maulana, 220
Katz, Melinda, 209, 262-64
Kendi, Ibram X, 16
Kendrick-Samuel, Syntychia, xxx, 142-45
Kenya Library Association, xviii, 10
Key Women of America (Concourse Village Chapter), 209
Kight, Dawn, xxxi, 278-82
Killens, John Oliver, xx
King, Coretta Scott, xx
King, Jr., Martin Luther, xviii, xx, 223
Klein, Arthur, 5
Knowledge River (KR) Scholarship Program,199-200
Knowles, Em Claire, 15, 20, 46-49, 56, 62
Knox, Emily, 16, 20, 338

Knoxville College, 4
Kuykendall, Bradley, 50, 56, 62, 230
Kwanzaa, xxiv-xxv, 231

La Unique African American Books & Cultural Center, 365
Lamkin, Burton E., 8
"Land of Endless Dreams and Possibilities," 219-21
*Land, Wealth Liberation: The Making and Unmasking of Black Wealth in America (LWL)*, 269-70
Lane, William Coolidge, 91
Langston Hughes Community Library and Cultural Center (LHCL & CC), 206-10, 222, 232; A Double-Edged Sword Against Illiteracy, 209; Black Heritage Reference Center, 354-58
Larrick, Nancy, 336
Larsen, Nella, 223
The Las Vegas-Clark County Library District, 283-87; Cell Phone Lending Program, 284; Bringing the Library to Transit Riders, 285; Library at the Boulevard Mall, 285
Latimer, Catherine Allen, 5, 82
Law, W. W., xx
Lawrence, Carolyn, xxx, 183-86
Lawrence, Grace, 210
Lawrence, Jacob, 216
Lee, Rodney, 207
Lee, Spike, 351
Lee, Susie, 284
Lemmons, Karen, 13, 49, 50, 56, 62, 67
Lenox, Mary F., 4, 6, 10
*Letters to Ourselves: The A263 Water Episcoples*, 270
Lett, Rosalind, 166
Lewis, Cicely, 338
Lewis, Jameka B., xxxi, 247-49
Lewis, John, 14, 91, 107
The Lewis H. Latimer House Museum, 208
LGBTQIA+, 126, 151, 168, 338, 352-53
*Liar*, 337
Liberation Station Bookstore, 365
Librarian of Congress, 3, 220
*Libraries: Culture, History and Society*, 16
Library Action Committee of Corona-East Elmhurst, Inc. (LAC), 207; The Library Company of Philadelphia, 3
Library of Congress, xviii, xxi, 3, 5, 8
Library Services and Construction Act (LSCA), 204; Title I, 207
library services to students with special needs, 275, 352
Library Trustees, x-xxi, xxiv, xxxi, 5, 13, 32, 71, 83-84, 100, 106, 140, 144, 155, 209, 226, 255, 345
Light, John, 225-34
*Lincoln*, 351
LiteracyNation, xxx, 13, 16, 76-78
The Little Boho Bookshop, 365
*Little Known Black Librarian Facts*, 13
*Living Black American Authors: A Bibliographical Directory*, 9
*Living Thinkers: An Autobiography of Black Women in the Ivory Tower*, 351
Los Angeles Public Library, 5
Louis Armstrong: as archivist, 257-60; The Louis Armstrong House Museum and Archive, 208
Louisiana State University Law Center Library, 196
Loudmouth Books, 363

Loyalty Bookstore Pentworth, 361
Lumumba, Malikah Dada, xv-xvii, xxxii, 48, 57, 62

Mack, Mitzi, xxxii, 347-49
Mack, Phyllis Green, xxxi, 48, 57, 62, 291-93
*Mad Dog and the Pilgrim Booksellers*, 367
Mahogany Books: Anacostia, 361; National Harbor, 363; Reagan National Airport, 367
Mahogany Gallery & Cultural Center, 367
Malcolm X, 351-52
Malik Books, Gifts and Calendars, 360
*Manchild in the Promised Land*, 220
Mapp, Wilbur, 209
Marcus Books, 360
Marblehead, Massachusetts, 4
Marshall, Albert P., 7, 64
Marshall, Helen, 164-65, 208
Marshall, Mary Louise, 167
Marshall, Thurgood, 256
Marshall's Bookstore, 364
Martin Luther King, Jr. Holiday, xxi
Martin, Sandra, 166
*Marvel Super Stories*, 16
*Mary Poppins*, 337
Mathis, Sharon Bell, 337
Matthews, Miriam, vii, 5, 30
Maude Hill Family Foundation, 8
Maynard, Chanelle, xxxi, 240-44
McBride, James, 220
McDonald, Antoine Ajani, xxx, 81-86
McGee, Kate, 198
McGhee, Ida, xxxi, 13, 294
McLin, Claudette, 13, 67
McNeil, Brandy, 16, 46, 57, 62
McQueen, Steve, 350, 352
Mediavilla, Cindy, 204
Medical Library Association, 166-67
Medu Bookstore, 362
Mejah Books, Inc., 361
mental health, 65, 148, 168-69, 172-73, 347-49, 357
Memphis, Tennessee, 4, 24, 298, 366
Mendez, Manuel, xxx, 39-41
Michel, Tamara, xxx, 171-75
microaggressions, 15
migrants, xxxii, 325-27
Miller, Helen M., 8
Mims, Gloria J., xxxi, 301
misogynoir, 86, 88-89
Missouri Library Association, 7
Milwaukee Public Library, 15
Mobley, Emily R., 11
Montana Library Association, 7
Monterey County Free Libraries Seaside Homework Help Center, 205
Moore, Ginnie. *See* Virginia Bradley Moore
Moore, Virginia Bradley, v, 76, 208
Moore, Wilma Gibbs, 120
The Moorland Foundation Collection, 5
Morehouse-Spelman Summer School, 5
The Morgan Library and Museum, 246

Morris, Effie Lee, xv-xvi, 3, 5, 7-8, 10-11, 13
Morton, Josephine G., 166
Moses, Sybil, 11, 20
Mosley, Tonya, 179
Multicultural Bookstore and Gifts, 361
Multicultural Bookstore Las Vegas, 364
Multiculturalism Rocks, 337
Munde, Gail, 192
Murray, Daniel Alexander Payne, 3-5
Myers, Walter Dean, 337
Mystal, Elie, 198

Nappy Roots Books, 366
*A Narrative of the Proceedings of Black People During the late Awful Calamity in Philadelphia*, 3
National Archives (U.S.), 10
National Association for the Advancement of Colored People (NAACP), xx-xxi, 28, 131-32, 251; NAACP Georgia State Conference, xx; NAACP NC State Conference, xx; North Carolina NAACP, 98; Sioux City (Iowa) NAACP, 35
National Center for Education Statistics, 278
National Conference of African American Librarians (NCAAL), xviii, 5, 11, 12, 13, 14, 15, 17-18; National Diversity in Libraries Conference, 13
National Museum of African American History and Culture, 14, 210, 249
The National Network of Libraries of Medicine (NNLM), 172-73
National Sankofa Council on the Education of Black Children Conference, xxi
National Urban League, xxi, 5, 21, 26, 131
Navesink Library, 92
Ndege, George, 180-81
Ndumu, Ana, xxx, 15, 39-41, 50, 57, 62, 64, 105-10
Neal-Marshall Black Culture Center Bridgewaters Lounge, 272
"The Need for Continued Activism in Librarianship," 209
*The Negro Almanac, First Edition*, 8
*Negro Education, A Study of the Private and Higher Schools for Colored People in the United States*, 5
Negro History Week, 5
Negro Library Conference, 24, 26
Negro Society for Historical Research, 4
*The Negro in the United States: A Selected Bibliography*, 8
*The Negro Yearbook*, 4
Nelson, Marilyn, 336
Nevada Chamber of Commerce, 285
Nevada Homeless Alliance (NHA), 284
Nevada Partnership for Homeless Youth (NPHY), 284
Nevada State Library, 284
New Haven (Connecticut) Public Library, 12, 236
New York Public Library: 135th Street Branch, 5; African American Research Collection, 6
New York City Department of Cultural Affairs, 208
New York City Education Department, 204
New York State Education Department, 208; Division of Library Development, Bureau of Specialist Library Services, xv; New York State Library School, 4
Nicholson, Jewel, 209
Njoku, Eboni. *See* Curry, Eboni
*Nope*, 352

Normal College, xx
*North American Negro Poets: A Bibliographic Checklist of Their Writing*, 6
North Carolina Central University, 199; Colloquium on Southeastern Black Librarians, 9; Eagle's Memories Student Chapter of Society of American Archivists, 199; School of Law, 192; School of Library Science, 6, 9
Nnaso, Sylvestor, 14
Nosakhere, Akilah, 14, 49, 58, 62
Nubian Bookstore, 362

Oakland (California) Public Library, 12
Obama, Barack, 15, 331, 337, 355, 337-338
Obama, Michelle, 14
OCLC WorldCat, 77
Offord, Jr., Jerome, 14, 17, 19, 46, 49, 58, 64, 67, 230, 234
Ohio Library Association, 11, 23
Olive Tree Books-n-Voices, 363
Oliver, Patrick, 209
*One Life to Live*, 11
Orange, Satia Marshall, v, 16, 19-20, 48, 50, 58, 62, 67, 208
Ott, Marge, 182
*Out of School and In the Library: Connecting with Resources in the Out of School Time (OST) Field*, 204
Owens, Candace, xxx, 91-95
Owens, Irene, xxxi, 19, 67, 98, 101, 106, 303
Owens, Major, v, 10-11, 27-28

Pacific Northwest Library Association, 7
*Parable*, 367
Payne, Maletta, xxxi, 278-82
pedagogy, 30, 106, 240, 269-73, 357
Peele, Jordan, 352
Pegues, Conrad, xxx, 145-49
Pembroke Pines Library, 228
Pennsylvania Western University, 184
People Get Ready Books, 361
Perry, Katie, xxx, 114-17
Peterson, Carla L., 356
Phinazee, Annette Hoage, 7, 9-10
Pierpont Morgan Library, 5; The Division of Negro Literature, History and Prints, 5
Piper, Gemmicka, xxx, 86-91
Planting People Growing Justice Press & Bookstore, 364
Player, Bobby, 13, 17, 19, 67, 308
*Plessy vs Ferguson* ("Separate but equal"), 3
Porter, Dorothy B. *See* Wesley, Dorothy B. Porter
Positive Vibes, 367
Powell, Jr., Adam Clayton, 336
*Preliminary List of Books and Pamphlets by Negro Authors for the Negro Exhibit Paris Exhibition*, 4
Pringle, LaJuan, 208
*The Problems of Negro High School Libraries in Selected Southern Cities*, 6
*Progressive Librarian*, 209
Public Library Association (PLA), 8, 11, 13, 16
*Pumzi*, 270
Purdue University Black Culture Center Library, 13
Pyramid, Art, Books and Custom Framing, 360

Queens Borough President's African American Heritage Committee, 208
Queens Borough Public Library, 10, 171-75; Black Heritage Reference Center, 354-58; Board of Trustees, 209; Latchkey Enrichment Program, 204
Queens College (CUNY): Ethnicity and Librarianship II Institute, xv; Graduate School of Library and
Information Studies (GSLIS), 207; Louis Armstrong Educational Foundation, 257; Louis Armstrong House Museum and Archives, 257-60
Queens County's Black Heritage Reference Center, 207
*Queens Notes: Facts About the Forgotten Borough of Queens New York*, 209
Queens Public Library: Cambria Heights Branch, 219; Corona Branch, 222; Far Rockaway Branch, 218; Library Trustees, 262-65; Queens Library for Teens, 205. *See also* Queens Borough Public Library, 206-10, 218
Queens Public Television, 208

*A Radical Black Abolitionist and the Underground Railroad in New York City*, 356
Radical Self-Care and Wellness, 168-69
Raines, Judi Belle, xxxi, 219-21
Randall, Dudley, 7
Rare Book School, 245
R. D. Talley Books, LLC, 364
Reader, Sylvia Lyons, 9
Readers Block, 361
Reading In Color, 337
Reason, Joseph H., 8
Reese, Gregory, 11, 17
Regional Transportation Commission, 285
The Renaissance Charter School, 208
*A Renaissance in Harlem: Lost Essays of the WPA by Ralph Ellison, Dorothy West, and Other Voices of a Generation*, 355
Reparations Club, 361
Riccardi, Ricky, 258
Rice, Estes, 7
Richards, Donovan, 263
Richards, Kelly, xxxi, 16, 235-37
"The Right to Information Access," xix
Riley, Boots, 352
Roberts, Othella, 5
Robertson II, Clarence, 196
Robinson, Deborah, 15, 64
Robinson, Gleniece, 12
Rohd, Michael, 270
Rollins, Charlemae Hill. *See* Rollins, Charlemae
Rollins, Charlemae, xxx, 7-9, 33-34, 37, 336
Rollins, Tina D., xxx, 105-110
*Root and Branch: African Americans In New York and East Jersey 1613-1863*, 356
*The Rose That Grew From Concrete*, 234
Rosenberg Library, 4
Rosenwald Fund, 5
Rua, Robert J., 205
Ruggles, David, 356

San Jose State University, 225
Sankofa, 129-30, 132

Sankofa Video, Books and Café, 361
Savannah, Georgia, 4; The Second Negro Conference, 5
Scholarly Publishing for Academic Resources Coalition, 280
Schomburg, Arturo Alfonso, 5, 6, 353; African American Research Collection, 6; The Schomburg Collection, 5
Schomburg Center for Research in Black Culture, 5, 10, 205, 210, 220, 224
*School Daze*, 11
School District of Philadelphia, 9
*School Library Journal*, 11, 15
Scott-Branch, Jamillah, xxx, 99-105
Seat of Wisdom Library, 14
Seales, Aletta, xxxi, 204-06, 312
segregation, xvi, xvii, xxiii, 6-7, 22, 34, 40, 64, 92, 94, 99, 115, 146-47, 213, 216, 251, 259, 307, 332, 352
*Sekounificance*, 209
*A Select Bibliography of the Negro American*, 4
Semicolon Bookstore and Gallery, 362
Shaker Heights (Ohio) Public Library, 12
Shakur, Tupac, 234
Shapiro, Karl, xx
Shareef, Courtney, xxx, 154-59
Shaw, Robert Gould, 220
Shockley, Ann Allen, 9-11, 29
Shepherd, Betty, 182
Shop at Matter, 361
Shores, Louis S., 5-6
Shrine of the Black Madonna: Atlanta, 362; Detroit, 364; Houston, 367
Simmons, Jr., Victor E., xxxi, 66, 249-53
Simons, Earl G., xxxi, 264-65
Sims, Melanie E., xxix, xxxi, 30-33, 196-98
Sister's Uptown Bookstore & Cultural Center, 365
*The Slave Dancer*, 337
*Slavery In New York*, 355
*Small Axe: A Collection of 5 Films from Steve McQueen*, 352
Smith, Jessie Carney, v, xxxi, 8-10, 20, 33, 47, 59, 62, 300
Smith-Woodard, Marcia, xxi, 120, 295-96
Smithsonian Institute, 15, 100
social media, xxix, 64, 75, 77 97, 127-28, 135, 144, 147, 161 173, 176, 178, 182, 199, 225, 228, 233, 245-46, 281-82, 304, 326, 337
Solano County (California) Library, 225
Soler, Lisa, xxx, 187-88
*Sorry to Bother You*, 352
Soul Book Nook Bookstore, 363
*Sounder*, 337
Source Booksellers, 365
Source of Knowledge, 365
*The Southern Negro and the Public Library*, 6
The Southern Poverty Law Center, xxi
Southern University and A&M College, 281
Southern University Law Center, 192
Soyinka, Wole, xx
Special Libraries Association (SLA), 8, 10, 16, 27, 299
Speller, Benjamin F., 10
Spence, Claudette, 209
Spielberg, Steven, 351
Spofford, Ainsworth Rand, 3
Starks, Samuel W., 4, 22, 82-3

**Index**     377

State Librarian of West Virginia, 5
Stefancic, Jean, 198
Steptoe, John, 337
*Stories of Freedom in Black New York*, 356
Straw, Marian Glenn, 210
Strive Bookstore, 364
Strong, Gary E., 209
The Studio Museum of Harlem, 224
Sudev, Ahalya, xxxi, 275-77
Sunrise Books, 366
*The Survey of Negro Colleges and Universities*, 5
*Sweet Dreams*, 352
Syracuse University Library Science Program, 6

Tait, George Edward, 209
Talladega College, 4
Tattered Bookshop, 361
Tavernier, Willa Liburd, xxxi, 269-74
Taylor, Madelyn V., 168
Tambo, Oliver, xx
*Texas Education Code*: TEC, Ch 31, 332, 333; *TEC, Ch 31, Sect 66*, 332, 333
Texas Higher Education Opportunity Board, 11
*Texas State Board of Education Rules (19 TAC Chapter 16)*, 332, 333
Third Eye Books, Accessories & Gifts, 366
*Third World Newsreel Catalog*, 353
13th (film), 350
Thomas, Lucille C., 9, 11, 13
Thomas, Miriam, xxxi, 240-44
Thompson, Karolyn S., 13, 46, 49, 60, 62, 64
Threatt, Monique, xxxii, 350-53
The 3M Corporation, 8
Threets, Mychal, 225-34
Thurgood Marshall, 193
Tippecanoe County (Indiana) Public Library, 246-48
*To Kill A Mockingbird*, 332
Tolson, Stephanie, xxxi, 299
Totten, Herman L., 9, 11
*Truth Be Told*, 179
Tucker, Harold, 207
Tucker, T. Vivian, 240
*Turn the Page and You Don't Stop! Sharing Successful Chapters in Our Lives with Youth*, 209
Turner, Amina, v, xvii, xix-xxi, xxx, xxxii, 98
Turner, Amina Josey. *See* Turner, Amina
Turning Page Bookshop, 366
Tuskegee Airmen, 164, 247
Tuskegee Institute, 4, 20-22, 73, 164, 171; The Department of Records and Research, 4
Tuskegee University. *See* Tuskegee Institute
Tuskegee Veterans Hospital, 5
*12 Years a Slave* (film), 350
*The 21st Century Black Librarian in America: Issues and Challenges*, 14, 209

Ubuntu, xxx, 129, 131-32
Umenta, Janet, xxx, 171-75
Umoja, xxiv, 144-45, 363
Umoja Books and Products, 363
Uncle Bobbie's Coffee & Books, 366

Underground Books, 361
The Underground Store, 362
United States Bureau of Higher Education, 5
United States Office of Education, Department of Health, Education and Welfare, 5, 8, 9
United States Supreme Court, 3; *Brown vs Board of Education* (school segregation), 7; *Brown vs Louisiana 383 US 131* (peaceful protest of illegal segregation in libraries), 7
University of Arizona: iSchool, 199; Knowledge River, 199
University of Hawaii, 11
University of California-Berkeley, 7
University of Chicago, 6
University of Florida Institute of Food and Agricultural Sciences, 245
University of Maryland Library School, xviii
University of Missouri, 11
University of Missouri-Kansas City (UMKC), 199
University of New York at Albany, xxi
University of North Carolina at Chapel Hill, 6, 94, 106, 245-46, 303, 356
University of North Carolina Greensboro, 13
University of North Texas, 11
University of Rhode Island, 13
University of South Africa, 14
University of Southern Carolina, 3
University of Virginia Special Collections, 246
University of Washington, 15
University of Wisconsin-Milwaukee, 11
The United Negro College Fund, 8
Urban League. *See* National Urban League
The Urban Reader Bookstore, 365
Urban Reads Bookstore, 363

The Vaccine Research Center of the National Institute of Allergy and Infectious Diseases at the National Institutes of Health, 173
Van Jackson, Wallace, 9
Van Vechten, Carl, 6
Vargas-Bethancourt, Margarita, 245
Venable, Andrew, 47, 60, 62
Virginia Union University Upward Bound Program, 235
Von Wangenheim, Annette, 351

Walcott, Dennis M., 65, 263
Walker, Alice, 68, 223, 351, 355, 357
Walker, Shaundra, 15, 19, 64, 66-67
Walker-Canton, Roxana, 351
Washington, Booker T., xviii, 223
*The Watermelon Woman*, 352
Watson, Kelvin, xxxi, 14, 16-17, 19-20, 67, 230, 234, 283-87
*We Build Together: A Reader's Guide to Negro Life and Literature for Elementary and High School*, 336
We Need Diverse Books (WNDB), 14, 337
Wedgeworth, Robert, 9-11
Weeks, Roosevelt, 234
Weissman Preservation Center, 220
West Baden, Indiana, 5
West Baden Springs Hotel, 5
Wesley, Dorothy Burnett, vii, xxx, 6, 18, 30, 33-34, 36, 105, 303, 320

West Indies, 20, 39
West Virginia State Librarian, 4
Westchester Library System, xv
Western Reserve University-Adelbert College, 3
*What Black Librarians Are Saying*, 9
"What of the Black and Yellow Races," 4
*What's In A Name?*, 209
Wheeler, Maurice B., 12
Whisenton, Andrew Carl, xxx, 38-39
Whisenton, Vera N., xxx, 38-39
White, Carl, 6
White, Shane, 356
"Why is Diversity Important for Law Librarianship," 192-93
Wilberforce University, 4
Wilburn, James, 236
Wild Fig Coffee & Books, 363
Wiley College, 4
Wilkin, Binnie Tate, xxxii, 20, 45, 47, 60, 63
Willa's Books & Vinyl, 364
Williams, Barbara, 11
Williams, Edward Christopher, xxiii, 3-5, 20, 23-24, 82, 105, 114, 118-19, 344
Williams II, James F., 11

Williams, Jamia, xxx, 166-70
Williams, Leslie, xxxi, 215-18
Winston-Salem State University, xxi
Wisdom Book Center, 363
Women Make Movies Catalog, 353
Woodson, Carter G., 5
Work, Monroe Nathan, 4-5
World Library and Information Congress (WLIC), xvi, 14
World War II, xx
Wray, Wendall, 10, 129, 132
Wright, Joyce C., xxxi, 297-98

Yale University James Weldon Johnson Collection, 6
York College (CUNY), 206, 231; Alumni Association, 209; Commemorative Quilt Committee, 209; President's Advisory Council, 208; Students For Change, 209
Young, Courtney, 14
*The Young Landlords*, 337
Yust, William R., 4

Zarett, Christine, xxxii, 354-58
Zawadi Books, 365

**Index** 379

# About the Contributors

**Aysha Zakiya A** is a PhD student at the Department of Library and Information Science, University of Calicut, Kerala. Her areas of interest include human information behavior, digital humanities, and social media.

**Maria E. Hamilton Abegunde**, PhD, uses the arts, contemplative practices, and ritual to explore ways to heal trauma through community, collaborative, and co-creative processes. Her award-winning poetry, creative nonfiction, and essays have been recently published in the journals *North Meridian Review and Obsidian*; in the books *SO WE CAN KNOW: Writers of Color on Pregnancy, Loss, Abortion, and Birth*, *ASHE: Ritual Poetics in African Diasporic Expressivity*, and *Trouble the Waters: Tales from the Deep Blue*; and in the exhibition Sister Song: The Requiem. Dr. Abegunde is a Cave Canem, Sacatar, and Black Earth Institute fellow. She is a faculty member in the Department of African American and African Diaspora Studies at Indiana University Bloomington.

**Tahira Ahmad** is a Youth Services Librarian with a passion for outreach and community development. Ahmad loves undertaking big projects and building partnerships with local stakeholders. In addition, Ahmad likes writing children's short stories, poetry, painting, and tennis. She lives in Suffolk County.

**Thomas Alford** a recipient of the 2015 BCALA Trailblazer Award. A retired Public Library Administrator, Alford worked at the Los Angeles Public Library, the San Bernardino County (CA) Library, and the Queens Public Library.

**Jason Alston**, PhD, MLS, holds a PhD in library and information science from the University of South Carolina, as well as an MLS from North Carolina Central University and a bachelors in English from the University of North Carolina-Wilmington. Alston has taught for the LIS program at Mizzou since 2018. He also has experience as the University of North Carolina Greensboro's first Diversity Resident Librarian, a Business Librarian for Coastal Carolina University, and as a Reference Librarian for Forsyth County (NC) Public Library, Midlands' Technical College, and the University of Missouri–Kansas City. Alston's dissertation focused on diversity residency programs. Alston is originally from Soul City, North Carolina, and can be found on Twitter and Instagram under the username "SoulCitySigma."

**Aisha Aminu**, MI, is a computer science liaison librarian at the University of Toronto Engineering & Computer Science Library. Originally from Lagos, Nigeria, they have a BSc in computer science from the New Jersey Institute of Technology and an MI from the University of Toronto Faculty of Information. They are an active member of the Toronto Ballroom scene and the Toronto Kiki Ballroom Association (TKBA).

**Jill Anderson** is assistant director of Jail, Prison, Reentry, and Youth Justice Services in the Queens Public Library Outreach team. She loves working in outreach and bringing library services to the community in innovative ways.

**Richard Ashby Jr.**, Sharon Hill Public Library director, is a trailblazer in the literary world. As the past president of the New York Black Librarians Caucus and the Black Caucus of the American Library Association, current president and cofounder of the Pennsylvania Black Librarians Caucus, he has been a driving force for diversity and inclusion in library leadership. In addition to his advocacy, he is the president and cofounder of Literacy Nation, the American Library Association's newest affiliate.

**C. Atterbury**, having graduated from Fordham and Columbia Universities, obtained both MS and MA degrees while teaching and securing a special education dean position at Martin Luther King High School Campus in New York City. Also, as a former American studies and sociology lecturer at the College of New Rochelle, South Bronx, Brooklyn Campuses and later an adjunct professor of American history and sociology at BMCC, CUNY, her scholarship is plentiful. Currently she is on the Board of the Library Action Committee, a community board organization for Langston Hughes Community Library and Cultural Center (QPL).

**Jeffrion L. Aubry** serves the 35th A.D. of Queens County since being elected to the New York State Assembly in a special election on January 3, 1992. He is the current speaker pro tempore and former chair of the Correction Committee.

**Regina Bain** is the executive director of the Louis Armstrong House Museum and recently opened the Armstrong Center, a new performance and education space. Bain's ongoing work spans college access, leadership, and artistic excellence. Bain is cochair of Culture @3's antiracism working group and recently served on the Yale Board of Governors.

**Sharon D. Banks** was a Queens Public Librarian for seventeen wonderful years. She served as assistant manager of the Richmond Hill Library, and manager of Pomonok and Cambria Heights libraries. She received her MLIS from Queens College and earned a Certificate of Advanced Studies in Public Library Administration from The Palmer School of Library and Information Science, LIU.

**Roland Barksdale-Hall** is the Branch Manager of the Farrell Library Branch of the Community Library of Shenango Valley. Barksdale-Hall wrote a blog, "Making Ubuntu Spaces, Addressing Inequalities, and Peopling the Commons."

**Kelsa Bartley**, MSI, AHIP Kelsa Bartley (she/her/hers) is the Education and Outreach Librarian in the Learning, Research & Clinical Information Services Department at the Louis Calder Memorial Library, University of Miami Miller School of Medicine. Her interests include diversity, equity, and inclusion in libraries, library marketing and outreach, social media, and mobile technology for health information promotion, and library instruction and instructional design. Kelsa graduated with her master of science in information degree at Florida State University in December 2018.

**Jazmyne Baylor**, MLS, is a Research and Instruction Librarian at Western Carolina University. She attained her BS in communication broadcasting from Western Carolina University, and her MLS from North Carolina Central University. Jazmyne's professional passions are grounded in promoting information literacy, social justice in libraries, and community outreach.

**Gladys Smiley Bell** is currently the Peabody Librarian at Hampton University. She manages the Peabody collection of rare and classical books by and about African Americans. Ms. Bell is a life member of BCALA and served as president from 2000 to 2002. She also helped found the Joint Conference of Librarians of Color.

**Marshelle Berry** is a retiree of the Jacksonville Public Library in Jacksonville, Florida. Berry worked with the public library for thirty-five years starting in 1986 as a clerk and retiring as a library administrator in January 2022.

**Stanton F. Biddle**, PhD, is a retired Academic Library Administrator. He has been a continuously active member of BCALA since 1973, having served a total of twenty-eight years on the Executive Board in a variety of capacities including president, treasurer, and at-large board member. He is a graduate of Howard, Atlanta, and New York Universities and the University of California, Berkeley. He is from Rochester, New York, and now lives in New York City.

**Rashida Scott Blades**, MLIS, is the tenure-track business and communications librarian at San Diego State University. Her research focuses on DEI in business and communication librarianship. She provides research support, instruction, and outreach to SDSU's students and faculty, and San Diego's greater community, tying in specifically Black, Indigenous, Latinx, and gender-inclusive practices in everything library.

**DJ Bond**, MBA, is a writer, graphic designer, and marketing specialist focused on the library field. He has a master's in business administration with a concentration in marketing and a bachelor's in English, both from Oakland University. He currently serves as the Member Engagement Coordinator at The Library Network in Michigan, using his skills to help provide marketing support to libraries in the cooperative. When he is not working, Bond is typically writing and producing his graphic novels.

**Sandy Bright** is Director Emeritus, Office of School Library Services, New York City Department of Education. Bright is also adjunct instructor and Internship Site Visit Manager at Queens College, Graduate School of Library and Information Studies. In addition, she is the adjunct instructor at Long Island University, Palmer School of Library and Information Science.

**Elizabeth Jean Brumfield**, PhD, CAS, MLIS, is Distance Services Librarian and head of the Northwest Houston Center Library, at Prairie View A&M University. She received a BA in communications and legal studies, a MLIS and CAS in library and information science from the University of Pittsburgh, and a PhD in educational leadership-higher education from Prairie View A&M University. She is a graduate of the Harvard Institute for Academic Librarians and is certified in Microsoft Digital Accessibility Training.

**Shauntee Burns-Simpson** served as the 2020–2022 president of the Black Caucus of the American Library Association (BCALA). She is the associate director of the Center for Educators & Schools for the New York Public Library. An ambassador for libraries and youth librarian, Simpson enjoys connecting people to the public library and its resources. She works closely with at-risk teens and fosters a love of reading and learning with her innovative programs. In addition to leading BCALA, she chaired ALA's Committee on Diversity of the American Library Association.

**Edith Campbell** has worked both as a school librarian in Indianapolis and as an Associate Librarian at Indiana State University. Campbell served on the WNDB's Walter Award committee, YALSA's Printz and ALSC's Sibert award committees. Her research interests include the representation of Black children in youth literature and implementation of critical literacy practices in libraries. Campbell is a founding member of See What We See and the We Are Kidlit Collective Summer Reading List. Most recently, Campbell organized Black Cotton Reviewers, a group of Black librarians and educators committed to reviewing middle grade and young adult books written by Black authors about the Black experience.

**Renate Chancellor**, PhD is associate professor and associate dean for Diversity, Equity, Inclusion, and Accessibility at the School of Information Studies at Syracuse University. She is affiliate faculty at the Syracuse Lender Center for Social Justice. She has published widely in the areas of critical cultural information studies; Equity, Diversity, and Inclusion (EDI); and social justice in library and information science. She serves on the editorial boards of *Library Quarterly* and *Education for Information*. She also serves on the American Library Association's Publishing Committee. Dr. Chancellor received the Association for Library and Information Science Education's (ALISE) Excellence in Teaching Award in 2014 and was recipient of the ALISE Norman Horrocks Leadership Award in 2012.

**Rudolph Clay**, MLS, MA in human resources, serves as head of Inclusion, Diversity, Equity, and Access (IDEA) for the Washington University in St. Louis Libraries, leading the library's diversity initiatives, which support the information needs of an increasingly diverse university community. In the role as a subject librarian, he assists students, staff, and faculty working in the areas of African and African American studies and urban studies. He also manages an internship program that seeks to encourage undergraduate students of color and other marginalized students to consider academic librarianship as a career.

**Danielle Colbert-Lewis**, MLIS, MEd, serves as the head of Research and Instructional Services at the James E. Shepard Memorial Library of North Carolina Central University (NCCU). She is a seasoned librarian with extensive experience in various areas such as reference services, information literacy, outreach, first-year experience, government documents, institution repositories, sustainability, and scholarly communications.

**Nicole Cooke**, PhD, is the Augusta Baker Endowed Chair and a professor at the University of South Carolina. Her research and teaching interests include human information behavior, critical cultural information studies, and diversity and social justice in librarianship. She was the 2019 Association of Library and Information Science Education (ALISE) Excellence in Teaching Award recipient, and she has edited and authored several books, including *Information Services to Diverse Populations* and *Fake News and Alternative Facts: Information Literacy in a Post-Truth Era*. Her forthcoming titles include the second edition of *Information Services to Diverse Populations* and *Foundations of Social Justice*, both of which will be published by ALA Editions|-Neal-Schuman.

**Angiah L. Davis**, MLIS, is the director of Library Services at Gordon State College in Barnesville, Georgia. She earned an MLIS from Florida State University. Her research interests include library leadership and management, organizational culture, and the information needs and information access of diverse groups.

**James Allen Davis Jr.** has worked in public libraries for over twenty years and has developed programs and outreach to several communities. He is an advocate for the professional development and advancement of Black librarians and actively works to mentor and assist in recruiting and retention of librarians of color.

**Marva L. DeLoach**, PhD, retired professor/head of Technical Services and Collection Development Librarian, Diablo Valley College, Pleasant Hill, California, and former adjunct professor San Jose State University/SIS; coeditor with E. J. Josey of *Handbook of Black Librarianship, Second Edition*.

**Jina DuVernay**, MLIS, is a librarian and archivist. She advocates for the collection, stewardship, accessibility, and discoverability of resources related to Black history and culture and has served on the BCALA board, the Archivists and Archives of Color Section of the SAA, as well as ASALH committees to name a few. She holds an MLIS from the University of Alabama.

**Sandra Michele Echols** is a native New Yorker, a thought-leader librarian, and works as a school media specialist and reference librarian. An unrelenting passion for empowering people has fueled Michele's journey to excellence. She enjoys reading and participating in community service and lives by the words of late activist Helen Keller: "Life is either a daring adventure or nothing at all."

**Laura Ellis** is a professional librarian. She has her Master of Library Science from the University of Alabama and has spent her career in educational libraries from universities to elementary schools. She currently also serves as a Board of Trustees member for her local county public library system.

**Taina K. Evans**, MLS, is a Regional Director at Brooklyn Public Library and oversees a portfolio of twelve library branches. She is the outgoing chair of both the RSS Library Services to Aging Population and the User Services in Public Libraries Committees of Reference and User Services Association (RUSA). She is also active in New York's Library Association, serving as the president of the New York Black Librarian Caucus. As an adjunct professor in the Division of Library and Information Science Program at St. John's University, Evans teaches the Collection Development and Management course. She has a BA in government and politics and a Master of Library Science from St. John's University.

**Vernice Faison**, MLS, is the Head Librarian for the Music Library at North Carolina Central University, overseeing daily operations including cataloging, outreach, and information literacy. She established and chairs the Marketing Committee at the James E. Shepard Memorial Library since 2007. Faison was part of the first digital library class at NCCU's School of Library and Information Sciences and helped produce the first digital collection on NCCU's campus. She led the creation of the James E. Shepard Memorial Library's first two digital collections: NCCU Digital Collection and NCCU: The Early Years.

**Michele Fenton**, MLIS, is a monographs catalog librarian at the Indiana State Library in Indianapolis, Indiana. She received her Master of Library and Information Studies degree from the University of North Carolina Greensboro and is the blogger for *Little Known Black Librarian Facts*. Fenton is a member of BCALA, ALA, ACRL, CORE, EMIERT, LHRT, IRRT, and the Indiana Black Librarians Network. In addition, she is a member of the Association for the Study of African American Life and History, the Indiana African American Genealogy Group, and the Afro-American Genealogical and Historical Society.

**Tiffeni Fontno** is the director of Peabody Library at Vanderbilt University. She has a doctorate from the University of Dayton's Leadership for Organizations program and is an active member of the American Library Association. Tiffeni's professional background includes teaching in Durham Public Schools, North Carolina, and at a single-gender African American elementary school for the Cleveland Metropolitan School District in Cleveland, Ohio. She has also served as a school librarian and technology teacher in Ohio. Tiffeni is an experienced academic librarian with expertise in government documents, business, education, and curriculum librarianship. Her research interests include literacy, African American children's literature, and curriculum development.

**Rodney Freeman** has worked over thirteen years in the library field at various levels, building digital collections, working with databases, and taxonomy. Freeman started his career working with digital archives and collections. He has worked in academic, public, and government libraries and in multiple positions, from a library page to a library administrator. Freeman is currently working as an archivist in the special collections department of the Atkins Library at the University of North Carolina-Charlotte.

**Franciéle Carneiro Garcês-da-Silva**, PhD, is a researcher in Black Librarianship and a professor in the graduate program in information management at the Universidade do Estado de Santa Catarina (PPGInfo/UDESC) in Florianopolis, Brazil. Garcês-da-Silva is also the creator and manager of Quilombo Intelectual and coordinator of Nyota Publishing. In addition, she is vice-leader of the Núcleo de Estudos e Pesquisas sobre Recursos, Serviços e Práxis Informacionais (Research Group on Resources, Services, and Information Practices), at the Universidade Federal de Minas Gerais (NERSI-UFMG). Garcês-da-Silva received her PhD in information science from the Universidade Federal de Minas Gerais.

**Loida Garcia-Febo** is an international library consultant advocating at the United Nations on behalf of libraries since 2014. She is a past president of the American Library Association and REFORMA who served two terms on the Governing Board of the International Federations of Library Associations and Institutions. She was born, raised, and educated in Puerto Rico.

**Carolyn Lowe Garnes**, during her storied thirty-year tenure with the Atlanta-Fulton Public Library, emerged as an entry-level librarian to Deputy Director of one of the major library systems in the country. Renowned for her successful community outreach initiatives and progressive work with the underserved and as a respected children's literature advocate, Garnes has labored on the front lines of the struggle to advance, identify, and cultivate books that promote and affirm the rich historical perspective of African Americans, receiving the 2015 Zora Neal Huston Award. She has been actively involved Coretta Board Awards Round Table, serving as chair (1990–1994) and the BCALA, serving on the Executive Board, cochair of the 10th National Conference of African American Library as well as receiving the 2022 Appreciation Award, 2021 Retiree of Year, and Advocacy Award, 1994.

**Carol Gilliam** is a retired school library Media Specialist from The Freeport Public Schools (Long Island, New York), Caroline G. Atkinson Middle School, and Freeport High School. Gilliam is presently at Roosevelt Public Library as the Black Heritage Librarian. Prior to her jobs in Long Island, Gilliam worked for the New York Public Library, Harlem branches, including the Schomburg Center for Research and Black Culture. Gilliams received a BA in sociology and education from Fisk University, a BA in early childhood education and an MA in education from Adelphi University, and an MLS from Queens College (CUNY).

**George C. Grant**, PhD, is a retired academic library administrator with more than fifty-five years of service. He has been an active officer and member of the Black Caucus of ALA and served as its president from 1978 to 1980 and its *Newsletter* editor and publisher from 1980 to 2000. He is also the founder and CEO of GrantHouse Publisher Inc., with more than 190 book titles published for over 150 authors since 1989. He continues to write and publish.

**Robert "C. J." Hall** is a library associate with the St. Louis County Library, St. Louis, Missouri. Hall holds a Bachelor of Arts in history from Saint Louis University.

**Cloyette Harris-Stoute** is an accomplished tech professional, nonprofit leader, teen mentor, and entrepreneur, deeply committed to empowering Guyanese women and girls globally through her organization, Guyanese Girls Rock Foundation, Inc. A Guyana native turned proud Queens resident, she balances her roles as an IT manager at Mount Sinai Digital Technology Partners and the creative force behind Twin Elegance, a boutique jewelry brand. Cloyette also serves as a member of the Board of Trustees for Queens Public Library and Unity of Brooklyn Church and is the Georgetown, Guyana, Region Chair for G100 Youth Leadership & Entrepreneurship. Additionally, she champions diversity in the Women's Jewelry Association, contributing actively to the DEI committee.

**Talisha Harrison** is an MLIS student and soon to be graduate from San Jose State University (Fall 2023) as well as a Library Public Services assistant of eleven years at Seminole State College. Talisha is also a Blerd, a self-published author, and cat mom who enjoys reading, arts, and crafting. Her career goal is to be a research/reference librarian.

**Nichelle M. Hayes**, MLS, is the current president of the Black Caucus of the American Library Association. She has been instrumental in leading the Indianapolis Public Library and serves on several community boards throughout the state of Indiana, including the Indiana Black Librarians Network (IBLN), NAACP, and Association for the Study of African American Life and History (ASALH). She is a member of Delta Sigma Theta Sorority Inc. and is a blogger at https://thetiesthatbind.blog/ where she discusses genealogy and keeping families connected.

**Eboni M. Henry** is a native New Yorker and has been in the library profession for twenty-five years. She has worked in academic, special, public, and school librarianship. She is a certified school librarian within the District of Columbia Public School System.

**DeLoice Holliday** is a librarian at the Indiana University Libraries, Neal-Marshall Black Culture Center Library. She serves as the Multicultural Outreach Librarian and the Head of the Neal-Marshall Black Culture Center Library. She has worked at Indiana University Bloomington since 2001 and has worked in various departments during her tenure. She specializes in African American studies and has been active in state, local, national organizations, and groups. Holliday has a library science degree from Indiana University Bloomington.

**Jos N. Holman** is the County Librarian of the Tippecanoe County Public Library, Lafayette, Indiana. He previously served as the Library Director of the Alexandrian Public Library, Mt. Vernon, Indiana, from 1996 to 2002. His library career began as a Branch Manager and Children's Librarian, and he has presented public performances for the past forty years. His MLIS is from the University of Texas at Austin and he has a BFA in theater from Roger Williams College.

**Cheryl Willis Hudson** is vice president and editorial director of Just Us Books. Her published titles include the classics *AF-RO-BETS ABC Book* and *Bright Eyes, Brown Skin* (with Bernette G. Ford, illustrated by George Ford), and *Brave. Black. First:50+ African American Women Who Changed the World*, illustrated by Erin K. Robinson. Wade and Cheryl are coeditors of the anthologies *We Rise, We Resist, We Raise Our Voices* and *Recognize! An Anthology Honoring & Amplifying Black Life* and *The Talk, Conversations about Race, Love and Truth.*

**Wade Hudson** is president of Just Us Books, Inc., an independent publisher of Black-interest and multicultural books for young readers, which he and his wife Cheryl founded in 1988. He has written more than thirty-five books for young readers. His most recent is the coming-of-age memoir *Defiant: Growing up in the Jim Crow South,* which *Kirkus Reviews* called a "powerful testimony from a children's literature legend." *Defiant* is a 2022 Malka Penn Award winner, a Junior Library Guild selection, and a New York Historical Society Children's History Book Award finalist.

**Andrew P. Jackson (Sekou Molefi Baako)** is an adjunct instructor at Queens College Graduate School of Library and Information Studies (CUNY) and at York College, Black Studies Program, History, Anthropology & Philosophy Department (CUNY). Jackson is a member of the Queens Public Library's Board of Trustees.

**Lorin Jackson** is the Executive Director of the Region 2 Regional Medical Library, which is a part of the Network of the National Library of Medicine (NNLM) and is located at the Medical University of South Carolina (MUSC). Lorin mentors BIPOC LGBTQ+ students/alumni alongside promoting the expansion of valuable healthcare information to communities throughout the southeastern United States.

**Raphael Daoud Jackson-Ortiz**, MLS, earned his MLS at the University of South Florida and his JD from the Interamerican University-College of Law in Puerto Rico. He is an experienced teacher, School Media Specialist, and Academic Librarian. He is currently a librarian assistant professor at the University of Miami School of Law teaching Florida legal research in addition to his reference duties. He and his wife, Shantel, homeschool all six of their children.

**Brenda Johnson-Perkins** is a Community Engagement Coordinator in the Adult and Community Engagement Department of Baltimore County Public Library. She has a passion for community outreach and promoting equitable services to underserved groups. She received an MA degree in Black comparative literature from the University of Maryland-Baltimore County in 1996 and an MLIS from the University of Maryland-College Park in 2019. She is a 2015 Spectrum Scholar and a Library Journal Mover & Shaker.

**Linda Jolivet** worked at the Laney College Library, the Berkeley City Library, and the Oakland Public Library. Jolivet is a member of the California Black Librarians Caucus as well as the Black Caucus of the American Library Association (BCALA). In addition, Jolivet assisted BCALA in planning its National Conference of African American Librarians (NCAAL) and has authored several articles for the *BCALA Newsletter*.

**Jacqueline Jones**, MLIS, is Library Director at Baton Rouge Community College. Jones received her Master of Library and Information Science degree from Louisiana State University (LSU), Baton Rouge, in 2000. Jones holds memberships in ALA, BCALA, and LLA. Jones is an active community volunteer who has special interests in African American history, literacy for young African American children, and promoting children's books by Black authors and about the Black experience.

**Michelle E. Jones**, MSLS, currently serves as Head of Reference Services and professor at Columbus State University in Columbus, Georgia. She earned an MSLS from Clark Atlanta University. She has authored a guest forum article for *The Informed Librarian* (2020) and a chapter in *Promoting African American Writers: Library Partnerships for Outreach, Programming, and Literacy*.

**Shannon Jones**, EdD, MEd, MLS, AHIP, FMLA, is the Director of Libraries for the Medical University of South Carolina Libraries in Charleston. She is also the Director of Region 2 of the Network of the National Library of Medicine. Her educational background includes an EdD in educational leadership from Charleston Southern University, an MEd in adult learning with a concentration in human resources development from Virginia Commonwealth University, and a Master of Library Science from North Carolina Central University.

**Syntychia Kendrick-Samuel**, MLS, is the Assistant Director at Uniondale Public Library. She began her librarian career as a Young Adult Librarian in 2004 when she received her MLS from CUNY Queens College. Over the years, she created dynamic programming for the young adults in Uniondale that led to the creation of the Teen Services Department. In 2016, she was named a Library Mover & Shaker in the category of Innovation by *Library Journal*.

**Dawn Kight**, PhD, is the dean of libraries at Southern University in Baton Rouge, Louisiana. She has a PhD in science and mathematics education and a master's degree in librarian and information science. Most of her career has been dedicated to improving access through library technology services.

**Carolyn Lawrence** is a children's librarian with a passion for self-discovery and healing her inner child. In her free time, she enjoys dancing for Budari Dance Company where she performs Garifuna-style dances such as Punta, Chumba, and Wanaragua. She recently wrote a blog titled "Beyond Self-Care for Library Staffers" for *Public Libraries Online*.

**Jameka B. Lewis** is the Branch Supervisor at the Blair-Caldwell African American Research Library in Denver, Colorado. An experienced educator in the areas of Black history and culture, Jameka enjoys discovering, presenting, and preserving information pertaining to Black representation in pop culture and history.

**Malikah Lumumba** is a retired librarian with almost sixty years of library experience from a public library page, IBM Special Library Intern, to Head of YA, Library Consultant, to adjunct college professor. World traveled, she is married for over thirty-five years to Shaka Lumumba with two sons: Eddie and Ptah. Bergen Volunteers (New Jersey) awarded her a Lifetime Achievement Award in 2022 for all her volunteer services.

**Mitzi Mack** serves as a media specialist for a local magnet middle school in the School District of Hillsborough County. In this role, Mitzi collaborates, leads, coordinates, and develops plans for successful integration of technology, curriculum, and literature. Mitzi is an accomplished teacher/curriculum specialist for twenty-nine years and currently serves on several American Library Association committees in support of "FREADOM," the right to read banned books. Writing has always been a secret passion, so, whether writing grants, poems, or book reviews, Mitzi enjoys putting pen to paper to inform and transform. Though often buried in a book, Mitzi is also a community-conscious volunteer that feeds her passion and drive by helping others and participating in continuing education courses at the local university.

**Phyllis Green Mack** retired from the New York Public Library as the Regional Librarian, Central Harlem Region, after thirty-nine years of service. She holds a BS degree from West Virginia State College (now University) an HBCU; Pratt Institute, MLS, and an advanced certificate in library science, Columbia University. She holds membership in and has held leadership positions in professional and community organizations including but not limited to ALA, BCALA, NYBLC, and NYLA. She is a Golden Life member of Delta Sigma Theta Sorority, Inc. and is a Golden Delta Dear and a charter member of the North Manhattan Alumnae Chapter. She is the editor and compiler of *Looking Back, Moving Forward, Celebrating 50 Years of the New York Black Librarians Caucus, 1970–2020*, which was recently published

**Chanelle Maynard** is an assistant professor of education at Schreiner University in Kerrville, Texas. Dr. Maynard teaches in the EC-6 teacher preparation and MEd programs with an emphasis on literacy instruction. Previously, Dr. Maynard spent over twenty-five years in K–12 education serving as a special education and reading teacher, a reading specialist, and an instructional coach. She is currently an associate editor of the *Texas Association of Literacy Education Yearbook*. Her research interests include technology integration and literacy instruction.

**Antoine Ajani McDonald** is a native Rochesterian, and double HBCU graduate from Lincoln University and North Carolina Central University's School Library and Information Science. As the only African American male librarian in his public library system, McDonald is the Reference Librarian in the Local History and Genealogy Division where he serves as project manager for the Archive of Black History and Culture, implements programming, and provides reference services with a passion for youth education. McDonald first began acquiring professional library experience as a graduate assistant while interning at the Law Library of Congress and the George W. Bush Presidential Library and Museum. McDonald is a member of Omega Psi Phi Fraternity Incorporated by way of BETA Chapter, and in his spare time he enjoys reading, traveling, working out, and developing his recent literacy start-up company, the Total Wellness, Academic and Advocacy Network (T.W.A.A.N).

**Ida D. McGhee** is enjoying retirement after working for over fifty years in the library field. Ida is very passionate about making "library" a household word. She continues to mentor to ensure that future librarians will be librarians of color. When not working or traveling to attend her two granddaughters' STEM and sports activities, she is home repotting her plants. Ida enjoys shopping for creative cards of encouragement to mail to the sick and homebound. BCALA awarded Ida the 2021 Library Advocacy Award, and she is a 2020 recipient of the Rhode Island Library Association's Library Champion Award.

**Kim McNeil-Capers** is the Director of Community Outreach and Hip-Hop Programs at the Queens Public Library. She oversees correctional services, mobile library outreach, hip-hop programs, and special outreach initiates. In 2018, Kim received the Advocacy Award from the Third National Joint Conference of Librarians of Color (JCLC) and in 2017 was *Library Journal's* Mover & Shaker recipient known as the human bridge of connectivity. Aside from being an outreach expert and hip-hop advocate, Kim believes in the importance of education and the power of hip-hop to connect with people in a meaningful way.

**Manuel Mendez** is a University of Maryland PhD student (College of Information Studies) whose scholarship focuses on Afro-Latino history in the Washington, DC, metropolitan region. A documentary producer and archival activist, Manuel is a frequent invited panelist and speaker on Latino identity, Black cultural memory and heritage, and anti-Black racial oppression among Spanish-speaking and/or white supremacist communities. Manuel's scholarship draws from his experience with youth organizing, bilingual public library service, and grassroots oral history work. His work has been recognized and utilized by Politics & Prose; Hola Cultura; Univision; the Office of the Washington, DC, mayor; and various universities across the United States.

**Tamara Michel**, MPH, has worked at Queens Public Library since 2007. She serves as the library's Deputy Health and Wellness Officer. Prior to holding that role, while cocoordinating the Black Health and Healing Summit, she was the library's Community Health Coordinator. Tamara has an MPH in sociomedical sciences with a focus on urbanism and the built environment from Columbia University's Mailman School of Public Health and a BS in psychosocial and physiological studies from the University of Connecticut. She lives in Queens, New York.

**Gloria J. Mims**, MSLS, is a retired librarian and a graduate of the Atlanta University Library School. Mims began her career as Head of Special Collections at the Atlanta University Graduate Library. Mims also served as Head of the Division of Special Collections and Archives at the Atlanta University Center Robert W. Woodruff Library. In addition, Mims worked as Senior Librarian at the Fulton County Public Library System in Atlanta, Georgia.

**Ana Ndumu** is an assistant professor at the University of Maryland College Park's College of Information Studies. She researches and teaches on library services to immigrants—particularly, Black diasporic immigrants—along with methods for promoting racial realism and representation in LIS. Dr. Ndumu's experience as an HBCU librarian on a distinctly majority-immigrant campus inspired her interest in the cross between Black identity, libraries, and social inclusion. A proud Afro-Latina, Dr. Ndumu works actively with the Black Caucus of the American Library Association (BCALA), the National Association for Library Service to Latinos and the Spanish Speaking (REFORMA), ALA's Serving Refugees, Immigrants, and Displaced Persons (SRIDP) committee, and various other LIS organizations.

**Candace Owens** is a woman who has achieved a lot in her career, including roles as a former educator, coach, business owner, and content creator. She earned her Master of Library Science (MLS) with a concentration in Archival Studies in August 2022 and currently works as a dedicated library clerk, collaborating with programmers and outreach coordinators. Candace is also a writer and has published books on self-love, mental health, and personal and spiritual growth. She is deeply committed to family history and volunteering in archival work. Candace has contributed to various areas of public libraries, including programming and outreach, and has even created a digital archive for a local private, two-year Historically Black College and University (HBCU). Her interest spans all aspects of public libraries, including social work and justice for those who are displaced, overlooked, under-resourced, under-served, and under-represented. At heart, Candace is motivated by the people she serves, their actions and reactions to library and archive spaces, services, and collections, as well as the staff and support staff. She is also inspired by the rich history of libraries and their ability to evolve with society's needs and desires. Most importantly, she finds her inspiration in her ancestors, who are now primarily identified as BIPOC, for their courageous efforts in fighting for equal access to literacy.

**Irene Owens**, MLS, MA, PhD, is the former dean at North Carolina Central University (2005–2016). Owens is the first African American to earn tenure at the University of Texas at the Austin School of Library and Information Science (now the I-School).

**Maletta Payne**, MLIS, is the Systems Administrator/OER Librarian at Southern University in Baton Rouge, Louisiana. She has a master's degree in library and information science. She also serves as the institutional repository administrator.

**Conrad Pegues** is a Public Services Librarian at the University of Tennessee-Martin. His work covers racial issues, Black male healing, culture, and library access for all.

**Katie Perry**, MLS, graduated from San Jose State University with her MLIS in May 2023. During her last semester she participated in an internship working as a research assistant to Tracie Hall, Executive Director of ALA and Dr. Anthony Chow, SJSU iSchool director. It was under their leadership that she started her research on the history of Black LIS education. Katie currently works as a Reference, Instruction, and Outreach Librarian at California State University, Dominguez Hills.

**Gemmicka Piper**, PhD, is the Humanities Librarian at Indiana University-Indianapolis and is versed in some digital tools, instructional design, and learning about supporting qualitative data. In addition to normal librarian duties, Piper developed a brand-new course for the Africana Studies Program, which she taught for two semesters. Piper also collaborated with the School of Urban Education to work one-on-one with coaching a small cohort of doctoral students through the writing process for their individual dissertations. The last five years Piper has concentrated on drawing upon her experiences as a humanities researcher, writing tutor, information professional, and creative thinker to redefine her role as the university's Humanities Librarian.

**Judi Belle Raines** served thirty-five years at the New York City Department of Education. In addition, Raines has served as a teacher, dean, guidance counselor, and summer camp director.

**Kelly Richards** is the president and director of the Free Library of Philadelphia and has almost three decades of library experience, having most recently served as director of the Muskegon Area District Library in Michigan and president of the Michigan Library Association. In addition, Richards served as the chairperson for Lakeshore Ethnic Diversity Alliance, an organization that trains government agencies and businesses in diversity, equity, and inclusion/belonging. Richards began his library career at the Las Vegas Clark County Library District before joining the Genesee District Library in Flint, Michigan, where he served as assistant executive director and branch operations manager overseeing nineteen branches. Richards earned an associate of arts and a bachelor of science in criminal justice at Ferris State University, and served as a police officer in Flint, Michigan, and an airport police officer at Bishop Airport, before returning to school to earn his MLS at the University of Pittsburgh. In addition, he has received certificates from the Snowbird Library Institute, the Michigan Library Association Leadership Academy, and the UCLA Anderson School of Business Executive Education program. Richards is published in two books, *In Our Own Voices: The Changing Face of Librarianship* (Scarecrow Press, 1996) and *Pioneer African American Librarians in the West* (Scarecrow Press, 2006). He is married, has three children, and is an avid angler.

**Tina Rollins**, MLS, serves as Library Director at Hampton University. She completed her MLS degree at North Carolina Central University. Her national leadership is extensive: adjunct professor at Syracuse University's School of Information Studies; advisory board member of Old Dominion University's Library and Information Studies program; executive board member of the HBCU Library Alliance; mentor and program partner with Digital Library Federation (DLF) Authenticity Project as well as the Association of Research Libraries (ARL) Leadership Fellows Programs; and principal investigator on two Institute of Museum and Library Service projects. Rollins is completing a PhD in educational management with an emphasis in higher education from Hampton University.

**Jamillah Scott-Branch** is an accomplished library professional who has worked in academic libraries in the United States and abroad. Currently, she serves as the acting director of the library at Georgetown University in Doha, Qatar. Previously, she worked as the assistant director of Library Services at North Carolina Central University (NCCU) and earned her Master of Library Science degree from NCCU's School of Library and Information Sciences. Her research interests include library leadership, emerging technology, first-year experience, and open educational resources.

**Aletta Seales**, MLS, is a retired New York City educator and administrator who went back to college after retirement to get her MLS from Queens College the City University of New York. She worked in the Queens Public Library as an assistant to the children's librarian, coordinating and implementing projects for the after-school program. She has also volunteered at the Queens Public Library sharing her love of literature with children and adults. During 2021–2022, she wrote a column, "Friends Speaking," in the NYLA digital magazine. Seales was the secretary of the Friends of the Cambria Heights Library and advocates for libraries and is a member of NYLA/NYBLC, NYLA/FLS, BCALA, NAUW L.I. Branch, and ABENY.

**Courtney Shareef** is the Strategic Initiatives Librarian and Diversity Resident for the University of Louisville Libraries. As such, she collaborates with colleagues to develop and support the university's initiatives in scholar services, innovation and entrepreneurship, and student success. Courtney joins the RAI team from The HistoryMakers, the nation's largest African American video oral history archive. A lover of archives and literature of all kinds, she is a firm believer in the transformational power of narrative and information.

**Victor E. Simmons Jr.** is a seasoned library professional with more than twenty-five years of service in public libraries. He has over twenty-eight years of experience in the library sector, having served the New York Public Library for more than eighteen years and the Fulton County Library System (previously known as the Atlanta-Fulton Public Library System) for almost ten years. He is currently the Library Administrator/Director of the Auburn Avenue Research Library on African American Culture and History, a position he has held since 2016. He played a key role in revitalizing the library after a $20 million renovation project that lasted two years. Mr. Simmons holds two master's degrees: one in library science from Queens College, New York, and another in fine arts, with a focus on film studies, from the City University of New York's City College. He currently lives in a suburb of Atlanta, Georgia, with his wife and two sons.

**Earl G. Simons** is a member of the Queens Public Library's Board of Trustees and currently serves as Chair. He has been a member of the board for the past eight years. Dr. Simons also serves as Executive Director of Government Relations and Strategic Initiatives at York College/CUNY.

**Melanie Sims**, EdD, is Associate Librarian/Head of Access Services and Government Information at Louisiana State University Law Library in Baton Rouge, Louisiana. Sims was the second African American to be elected as president of the Louisiana Library Association in 2009/2010. Sims is very active in the profession and has served on various national and state committees within the American Library Association, American Association of Law Libraries, and Louisiana Library Association. Sims's research interests include advocacy, access, diversity, and reference services.

**Genevia Chamblee-Smith**, MLIS, is an early career librarian and archivist working as the Resident Librarian at the University of Texas at Austin. Genevia is in her second year working as the Economic Liaison Resident Librarian. In her first year she worked at the LLILAS Benson and the Alexander Architecture Archives processing collections. Her research interests include peer mentoring, teaching in the archives using primary sources, and archival collection assessment.

**Jessie Carney Smith**, educator, scholar, and librarian, has written or edited over thirty books. She holds degrees from North Carolina A&T, Michigan State, and Vanderbilt universities, and a PhD in library administration from the University of Illinois. She retired from Fisk University and was named Librarian Emerita.

**Marcia Smith-Woodard** retired from the Indiana State Library, Library Development Office, September 1, 2014, after thirty-four years of library service in several public and special libraries. Her BA in journalism from Purdue University, AMLS from the University of Michigan, work, and life experiences helped to prepare her for her current adventure in genealogy!

**Lisa Soler** is a customer service specialist at the Queens Public Library.

**Ahalya Sudev**, MLIS, is a PhD student in the library and information science discipline. She received her Master of Library and Information Science from the Department of Library and Information Science at the University of Calicut, and she is a Junior Research Fellowship holder. Her areas of interest include inclusive learning, access and accessibility of information, digital literacy, and disability studies.

**Willa Liburd Tavernier**, MLIS, LLM, LEC, LLB, is the Research Impact and Open Scholarship Librarian at Indiana University Bloomington. Her research interests are in public open digital scholarship, equitable scholarly communication, and how the idea of community intersects with open access and scholarly communication resources and providers. She holds an MLIS and graduate certificate in college teaching from the University of Iowa, an LLM in international business from American University Washington College of Law, an LEC from the Norman Manley Law School, and an LLB from the University of West Indies at Cave Hill.

**Miriam Thomas**, EdD, is a lecturer of School Library and Information Science in the College of Education at the University of Houston Clear Lake in the Houston, Texas, area. Dr. Thomas instructs graduate students seeking the MS degree seeking a certification as a school librarian. Dr. Thomas has been a certified educator and teacher for over fifteen years in K-12 and higher education settings. She has also served in various training and corporate capacities for over thirty years. Her research interests include information research in secondary schools and young adult literacy through recreational reading.

**Monique Threatt**, MLS, is Head of Media Services (2001–present) and liaison to the Department of Religious Studies (2022–present) at Indiana University Bloomington, Indiana. In addition to overseeing and managing a department, she oversees the budget, collection development and selection, and participates in digitization for the preservation of rare and archival films. She introduced streaming to faculty in 2002, and over the years has witnessed many technological advances in streaming options and delivery methods. She has been an active reviewer with Educational Media Reviews Online (2003–present), served as an Executive Board Member with Video Trust (2021–2023), chaired the IFLA Audiovisual and Multimedia Section (2021–2023), and served as past chair and treasurer for ALA's Film and Media Round Table.

**Stephanie Tolson**, PhD, is retired and now residing in Maryland.

**Amina Turner** (née Elaine Jacqueline Josey) is the only child of the late E. J, Josey, PhD, and the late Rev. Dorothy J. Josey. Turner has resided in North Carolina for forty-five years having served as a library trustee, school board member, international telecommunications executive, interim director for Parents for Public Schools, and state executive director of the North Carolina NAACP.

**Janet Umenta**, MD, is from Queens, New York. With a passion for health and community health, Janet started her pediatrics residency last year.

**Kelvin Watson**, MBA, MLS, is Executive Director of the Las Vegas Clark County Library District. Regarded as one of the most highly respected thought leaders in the library industry, Kelvin is credited with expanding his customer base in multiple library management roles, through outreach efforts to underserved and diverse populations. Kelvin has deep experience in fund-raising, technology, program development, and demonstrated success in addressing the digital divide.

**Vera N. Whisenton**, spouse of fifty-three years-plus years; BA biology/chemistry, Spelman College; MSLS, Atlanta University; first Black Intern, Descriptive Cataloging, Library of Congress; established Tech Services Department, Federal City College (University of the District of Columbia, Washington, DC); director, Office of Telecommunications Policy Research Center, White House; director, United States Department of Commerce Library; administrator, Office of Administrative Services, Office of the Secretary, United States Department of Commerce.

**Binnie Tate Wilkin**, after a multifaceted career as librarian, lecturer, consultant, activist, and writer, is an award-winning storyteller. In 2021, she received the National Storytelling Network *Western Region Oracle Award*. Wilkin continues library services consultation and, in the last two years, presented symposiums for the School of Information SJSU.

**Jamia Williams**, MLS, is the Consumer Health Program Specialist with the Network of the National Library of Medicine (NNLM) Training Office. She earned her BS in history from the State University of New York (SUNY) at Brockport and earned her Master of Library Science from North Carolina Central University. Williams is the cocreator and cohost of the podcast *LibVoices*, which amplifies the voices of Black, Indigenous, and People of Color who work in archives and libraries. Jamia founded the *Diversity Fellow's* blog, a platform to document her journey as a Black librarian.

**Leslie Williams** has worked in public libraries in Ohio, Connecticut, and Colorado. She loves dogs, graphic novels, walking, and traveling.

**Joyce C. Wright** is professor emerita at the University Library of the University of Illinois-Urbana-Champaign.

**Christine Zarett** is the curator for the Black Heritage Reference Center at the Langston Hughes Community Library and Cultural Center, a branch of the Queens Public Library. To be entrusted with the care of this special collection is a responsibility she takes very seriously.

# About the Editors

**Andrew "Sekou" Jackson** is an adjunct instructor, Queens College Graduate School of Library and Information Studies (CUNY) and York College, Black Studies Program, History, Anthropology & Philosophy Department (CUNY) and a member of the Queens Public Library's board of trustees.

**Marva L. DeLoach**, PhD, retired professor/head technical services and collection development librarian, Diablo Valley College, Pleasant Hill, California, and former adjunct professor San Jose State University/SIS; coeditor with E. J. Josey of *Handbook of Black Librarianship, Second Edition*.

**Michele Fenton**, MLIS, is a monographs catalog librarian at the Indiana State Library, the secretary for the executive board of the Black Caucus of the American Library Association, Inc., and the creator/blogger for the *Little Known Black Librarian Facts Blog*.